BUSINESS
RESEARCH METHODS

Fourth Edition

BUSINESS
RESEARCH METHODS

Boris F. Blumberg

Donald R. Cooper and Pamela S. Schindler

London Boston Burr Ridge, IL Dubuque, IA Madison, WI New York San Francisco
St. Louis Bangkok Bogotá Caracas Kuala Lumpur Lisbon Madrid Mexico City Milan
Montreal New Delhi Santiago Seoul Singapore Sydney Taipei Toronto

Business Research Methods, Fourth Edition
Boris F. Blumberg, Donald R. Cooper and Pamela S. Schindler
ISBN-13 9780077157487
ISBN-10 0077157486

Published by McGraw-Hill Education
Shoppenhangers Road
Maidenhead
Berkshire
SL6 2QL
Telephone: 44 (0) 1628 502 500
Fax: 44 (0) 1628 770 224
Website: www.mcgraw-hill.co.uk

British Library Cataloguing in Publication Data
A catalogue record for this book is available from the British Library

Library of Congress Cataloguing in Publication Data
The Library of Congress data for this book has been applied for from the Library of Congress

Executive Editor: Natalie Jacobs
Commissioning Editor: Kiera Jamison
Development Editor: Alexander Krause
Senior Production Editor: James Bishop
Marketing Manager: Alexis Gibbs

Text design by Ian Youngs
Cover design by Adam Renvoize
Printed and bound in Great Britain by Ashford Colour Press Ltd

First Edition published in 2005 by McGraw-Hill Education
Second Edition published in 2008 by McGraw-Hill Education
Third Edition published in 2011 by McGraw-Hill Education

ISBN-13 9780077157487
ISBN-10 0077157486

Dedicated

To my academic teachers

Brief table of contents

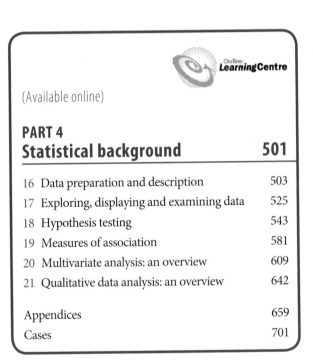

(Available online)

Detailed table of contents

Preface

The previous three European editions of this book have been well received by both lecturers and students alike; this new edition takes the successes of the preceding editions and continues to build on them. The new edition has focused on developing the book further in a number of core areas:

Balanced Approach – One of the strengths of the text has been its aim to provide a balanced approach to both qualitative and quantitative methods. This has been advanced further in the fourth edition by expanding the qualitative coverage: case study research has its own chapter; and the coverage of qualitative methods, such as content analysis, action research, ethnographic research, narrative analysis and grounded theory has been expanded. The fourth edition also contains a chapter on the primary collection of qualitative data, which covers qualitative interviews, focus groups and participant observation. Finally, a new chapter on qualitative analysis methods has been added to Part IV covering the statistical background, which is available on the Online Learning Centre for the book.

Theory vs Practice – The text has always offered students an insight into all aspects of research methods, providing them with the theoretical understanding they need, as well as the practical guidance required to effectively apply this. This continues in the new edition, through a combination of core textual content and pedagogic features.

Streamlined Pedagogy – The new edition offers a revised plethora of pedagogy for students and to aid teaching. Practical boxes focusing on real life research methods help students to understand the application of research within a day to day context. *Deeper Insights* boxes provide in-depth information on more challenging topics, for those students who want it. *Student Research* boxes help students to understand their own research and how they can get the most out of it. *Research Methods in Real Life* boxes help students to see how research methods can be applied to real life situations. Finally, the *Running Case Study* boxes at the end of each chapter show how two student projects developed – one using qualitative methods, and one using quantitative methods – helping students to understand how to apply the content of each individual chapter to a real life project.

The new edition is more wholly focused on helping the student with whatever their task may be: learning business research methods; or completing an independent research project. Simultaneously the content provides a sound and balanced introduction to business research methods to teach from.

Covering Recent Trends in Methodology – Developments in information technology and the World Wide Web offer many new opportunities. The new edition picks up those recent developments and discusses software to analyse qualitative data as well as the opportunities and problems regarding collecting data on the web.

As a lecturer I understand the increasing importance of additional supplementary material to help aid teaching and learning. In conjunction with re-developing the book content, the supplements package has also undergone further development to ensure that it is tailored to lecturer and student needs. The Online Learning Centre (OLC) for this fourth edition retains the core content from the previous edition, including all the fundamental resources like PowerPoints and an EZTest question bank. In addition to this, the new edition also includes:

- An expanded *Research Skills Centre* for students which includes links to study skills material from our successful Open University Press list, examples of good and bad proposals, template documents for research, and primers for Excel and SPSS. This should help students get the most out of research.
- The statistical chapters available on the website now have explicit linkages to the *SPSS Survival Manual* by Pallant and questions where students need to run SPSS to answer them have been added.

The reviews of the previous edition have enabled this new edition to be updated in a way that benefits both students and lecturers. The continued feedback received from users is invaluable. Thank you to all who have provided it.

Boris F. Blumberg

Acknowledgements

Publisher's acknowledgements

Our thanks go to the following reviewers for their comments at various stages in the text's development:

Dilani Jayawarna – University of Liverpool
Gerrit Rooks – Technische Universiteit Eindhoven
Malcolm Ash – University of Staffordshire
Crystal Zhang – Leeds Metropolitan University
John Dakin – University of Derby
Keith Mattacks – University of Brighton
Marijke Leliveld – University of Groningen

Bruce Mitchell – Oxford Brookes University
Ernst C. Osinga – Tilburg University
Tony Kinder – University of Edinburgh
Ashish Dwivedi – Hull University
Alexander Alexiev – VU University, Amsterdam
Chengwei Liu – University of Warwick
Karsten Bobek – Copenhagen Business School

Every effort has been made to trace and acknowledge ownership of copyright and to clear permission for material reproduced in this book. The publishers will be pleased to make suitable arrangements to clear permission with any copyright holders whom it has not been possible to contact.

Author's acknowledgements

Although what was right in research methods ten years ago is still right, the developments in research methodology are tremendous. Advances in information technology and the ubiquity of the web are the main stimuli for these developments. Software packages support researchers in all phases of the research process and have become very accessible. The web has also created many new opportunities to collect data. In the new edition I have accommodated these developments and discussed the opportunities and problems they create.

In the last years I have taught research methods courses for Master's and PhD students at Maastricht University School of Business and Economics, the Maastricht School of Governance and the Maastricht School of Management. Discussions in these courses are a continuous source of inspiration to change and improve the book. I learn so much from my students.

Moreover, for sharing their thoughts on research and teaching with me, I want to thank:

Harold Alvarez, Yannick Bammens, Pascal Beckers, Richard Blundel, Iwan Bos, Astrid Bötticher, Ulrich Braukmann, Caren Butter, Pia Camardese, Martin Carree, Christina Cataldo, Yunhyung Chung, Stewart Clegg, Maarten Cuijpers, Johannes Dick, Bas van Diepen, Stuart Dixon, Bart Dormans, Hetty van Emmerik, Tom Elfring, Ayman El Tarabishy, Hans Frankort, Wil Foppen, Brooke Foucault, Anita van Gils, Ursula Glunk, Dietmar Grichnik, Andrea Günster, Hannes Günter, Peter Groenewegen, John Hagedoorn, Ben Hardy, Mariëlle Heijltjes, Koen Heimeriks, Sarah Horn, Anna Huppertz, Kathrin Hussinger, Ad van Iterson, Ron Jacobs, Teemu Kautonen, Daniela Kirchberg, Martijn Jungst, Heinz Klandt, Lambert Koch, Tom Kuypers, Mindel van de Laar, Emmanuel Lazega, Wilko Letterie, Jia Li, Boris Lokshin, Carina Lomberg, Gabriele Marconi, Elke Messenholt, Darja Miscenko, Guido Möllering, Aad van Mourik, Chris de Neubourg, Woody van Olffen, René Olie, Sebastian Pacher, Jose Maria Peiro, Mark Peterson, Gerard Pfann, Jonathan Raelin, Anneloes Raes, Werner Raub, Robert Roe, Gerrit Rooks, Sarah Safay, Patrick Sassmannshausen, Katharina Schmitz, Bert Schreurs, Desiree Schumacher, Omar Solinger, Shuhua Sun, Sjer Uitdewilligen, Phillip Vergauwen, Christine Volkmann, Marc van Wegberg, Sonja Zaar and Ann-Kristin Zobel

The dedication of the McGraw-Hill team to the 4th edition has again been wonderful. My thanks go to Alexis Gibbs, James Bishop, Natalie Jacobs, Kiera Jamison and Alexander Krause. My thanks also extend to the copy editor Graham Gill and proofreader Elaine Bingham. Throughout the revision of the 4th edition I could count on valuable comments from different reviewers (listed at the top of this section) who read parts of, or even the whole book. Thank you very much.

Boris F. Blumberg

Wuppertal, August 2013

About the author

Boris F. Blumberg is Asssistant Professor and Academic Director of MBA programmes in the Department of Organization and Strategy at Maastricht University, the Netherlands. He obtained an MSc in business administration from Mannheim University and a PhD in sociology from Utrecht University. Boris has a broad teaching experience. In the last few years he has taught courses on research methods for Masters as well as PhD students. Furthermore, he teaches courses in strategic management, entrepreneurship and innovation.

His research focuses mainly on entrepreneurship, networks and methodology. Boris has published in refereed international journals such as *Small Business Economics*, *Organization Studies* and *Entrepreneurship & Regional Development*. He has served on the editorial boards of *International Sociology* (2004–2009), *Journal of Small Business Management* (2010–present) and *Organizational Research Methods* (2014–present).

Online resources

Visit **www.mcgraw-hill.co.uk/textbooks/blumberg** today.

Online Learning Centre (OLC)

After completing each chapter, log on to the supporting Online Learning Centre website. Take advantage of the study tools offered to reinforce the material you have read in the text, and to develop your knowledge of business research methods in a fun and effective way.

Resources for students include:

- *Statistics chapters*
- *Research Skills Centre, including chapters on study skills, examples on good and bad proposals, templates, primers and other useful content to aid studying*
- *Video Tutorials*
- *Multiple-choice questions*
- *Weblinks*
- *Glossary*
- *Case studies*
- *Dataset examples*
- *PowerPoint tutorial*
- *Appendices to the main text*

Also available for lecturers:

- *Extra tests and questions*
- *PowerPoint presentations*
- *Lecture outlines and case study teaching notes*
- *Artwork*

Test Bank available in McGraw-Hill EZ Test Online EZ TEST ONLINE

A test bank of over 1,000 questions is available to lecturers adopting this book for their module. A range of questions is provided for each chapter, including multiple-choice, true or false, and short-answer or essay questions. The questions are identified by type, difficulty and topic to help you to select questions that best suit your needs and are accessible through an easy-to-use online testing tool, McGraw-Hill EZ Test Online.

McGraw-Hill EZ Test Online is accessible to busy academics virtually anywhere – in their office, at home or while travelling – and eliminates the need for software installation. Lecturers can choose from question banks associated with their adopted textbook or easily create their own questions. They also have access to hundreds of banks and thousands of questions created for other McGraw-Hill titles. Multiple versions of tests can be saved for delivery on paper or online through WebCT, Blackboard and other course management systems. When created and delivered though EZ Test Online, students' tests can be immediately marked, saving lecturers time and providing prompt results to students.

To register for this FREE resource, visit www.eztestonline.com

Let us help make our **content** your **solution**

At McGraw-Hill Education our aim is to help lecturers to find the most suitable content for their needs delivered to their students in the most appropriate way. Our custom **publishing solutions** offer the ideal combination of content delivered in the way which best suits lecturer and students.

Our custom publishing programme offers lecturers the opportunity to select just the chapters or sections of material they wish to deliver to their students from a database called CREATE™ at

www.mcgrawhillcreate.co.uk

CREATE™ contains over two million pages of content from:
- textbooks
- professional books
- case books – Harvard Articles, Insead, Ivey, Darden, Thunderbird and BusinessWeek
- Taking Sides – debate materials

Across the following imprints:
- McGraw-Hill Education
- Open University Press
- Harvard Business Publishing
- US and European material

There is also the option to include additional material authored by lecturers in the custom product – this does not necessarily have to be in English.

We will take care of everything from start to finish in the process of developing and delivering a custom product to ensure that lecturers and students receive exactly the material needed in the most suitable way.

With a **Custom Publishing Solution**, students enjoy the best selection of material deemed to be the most suitable for learning everything they need for their courses – something of real value to support their learning. Teachers are able to use exactly the material they want, in the way they want, to support their teaching on the course.

Please contact your local **McGraw-Hill representative** with any questions or alternatively contact Warren Eels e: **warren_eels@mcgraw-hill.com.**

Study skills

Guided tour

Learning objectives

When you have read this chapter, you should understa

1 what research is, and the different types of research available

2 the difference between good and poor or unprofessi research

3 that research is embedded in different research

Learning objectives

Each chapter opens with a set of learning objectives, introducing you to the topics you should come to understand after having worked through the chapter.

Key terms

These are in **green** and bold throughout each chapter and defined in a glossary at the end of the book for your reference.

Descriptive

A **descriptive study** tries to discover answers to the questions w The researcher attempts to describe, or define, a subject, often by c or events. Such studies may involve the collection of data and an e times the researcher observes a single event or characteristic (this i involve an assessment of the interaction of two or more variables.

In the Akademiska Sjukhuset case, the researcher must present da who uses managed healthcare programmes (both doctors and p technology in diagnosing illness or the severity of injury, and the referrals and technology use patterns

Research Methods in Real L

Price fixing at the petrol sta
the invisible hand

Is there price fixing at the petrol station? This allegation runs he: regularity. Shortly before school vacations, petrol prices go up – no o differ. Oil companies argue that the price increases are a natural mark Consumers, however, suspect that oil companies take advantage of up their tank to reach their vacation destination. In February 2011,

Research Methods in Real Life

These boxes provide succinct, real-life illustrations through varied and pertinent snapshots of research methods.

Exhibits

A number of exhibits are provided in each chapter to help you visualize the various research models, and to illustrate and summarize important concepts.

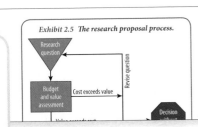

Exhibit 2.5 *The research proposal process.*

Student Research

Literature search appli

Some months ago I received an e-mail from a student. Patricia C written by a colleague and by me, and wondered whether I would project. Patricia had not only studied business, but she also had Therefore, she was interested in contracting, more specifically con later, we met in my office to discuss our ideas on the topic.

We soon came to the conclusion that it might be worthwhile to inv

Student Research

These boxes offer direct insight into real student projects. They explain some of the situations and research decisions faced and offer hints and tips for your own projects.

Deeper Insight into Research Methods

This feature offers you more in-depth insights into specialized topics of research designed to broaden your understanding.

Deeper Insight into Research

Example of a 'good' research proje

Below is an example of a good research project proposal that a stude a research project supervisor. It is a good proposal, but not a perfect project looked different from what was originally proposed, but still i

Research project proposal

Running Case Study

Sampling

In developing a sample set, Rebecca has created a couple of lists school, she has copied the names from the participant lists of c taken. She has used these name lists to create email addresses b student's name, which finally resulted in 407 unique email add According to the website of the school about 650 Master's stu programmes, thus her email lists cover more than 60 per cent o

Running Case Study

The running case study maps the progress of two real-life student research projects as they develop, helping you to put the relevant concepts into context. Questions are presented throughout to stimulate thought on your own project.

Summary, Discussion questions and Recommended further reading

Positioned at the end of each chapter, summaries and discussion questions review and reinforce your understanding of the main topics and skills covered. Reading and class discussion sessions provide pathways for taking your study further.

Summary

1 With respect to literature sources, one can distinguish primary ture includes all kinds of articles, books and reports in their compilation of primary literature. Examples of secondary liter dictionaries, encyclopaedias, handbooks and directories.

2 The process for searching bibliographic databases applies to b
   a Select a database appropriate to your topic.
   b Construct a search query (or search statement).

Discussion questions

Terms in review

1 Define the distinctions between primary and secondary literatur
2 Describe, briefly, the different steps in the literature review proc
3 Describe the objective, advantages and disadvantages of meta a
4 What is meant by 'critical' in a critical review?

Making research decisions

Discussion questions

Each chapter includes four categories of discussion questions, each of which encourages readers to review and apply the knowledge acquired from each chapter. The four categories cover the main types of learning used in the book: **Terms in review, Making research decisions, From concept to practice,** and **Class discussion.**

PART 1

Essentials of research

Part contents

CHAPTER 1

The nature of business and management research

Chapter contents

Learning objectives

When you have read this chapter, you should understand:

1 what research is, and the different types of research available

2 the difference between good and poor or unprofessional research

3 that research is embedded in different research philosophies and their basic principles, assumptions and implications

4 how to formulate a solid research hypothesis.

Why study research?

Assume for the moment that you are the new head of the South European office of a Swedish machinery manufacturer. Your appointment makes you the fourth person to hold this post in just three years. Some of the sales and service staff, who have worked for the company for more than 10 years, have packed in their jobs, and complaints from customers regarding poor after-sales service are on the increase. What will you do? How do you begin to think about how to solve this problem?

Here is another decision-making scenario. You are talking with the head of the academic department of the subject you are studying. She chairs the committee that is responsible for selecting the textbook for the research methodology course. How should she begin to evaluate the committee's options?

Finally, the production of a research project marks the end of your business studies course. A research project requires more from you than just a comprehensive overview of the current literature related to your research topic. Research projects that offer at least a small new contribution to our understanding of the issues investigated usually receive a better assessment. However, how do you set up a research project – that is, how do you come to a problem statement? And once you have a research problem and research questions, how will you arrive at answers to these research questions? Research methods provide you with ideas, instruments and models that demonstrate how to conduct sound research.

The study of research methods will provide you with the knowledge and skills you need to solve the problems and meet the challenges of a fast-paced decision-making environment. **Business research** may be defined as a systematic inquiry whose objective is to provide the information that will allow managerial problems to be solved. Business research courses recognize that students preparing to manage business, not-for-profit and public organizations – in all functional areas – need training in a disciplined process that will enable them to investigate and solve a research or **management dilemma** (i.e. any problem or opportunity that requires a management decision). Three factors have stimulated an interest in this scientific approach to decision-making:

1 the need for more and better information as decisions become more complex
2 the availability of improved techniques and tools to meet this need
3 the resulting information overload if discipline is not employed in the process.

The past two decades have seen dramatic changes in the business environment. Emerging from what is, historically, an economic role, the business organization has evolved in response to the social and political mandates of national public policy, explosive technology growth and continuing innovations in global communications. These changes have created new knowledge needs for the manager and new publics that should be considered when evaluating any decision. Other knowledge demands have arisen as a result of problems with mergers, trade policies, protected markets, technology transfers and macroeconomic savings–investment issues.

The current trend towards complexity has increased the risks associated with making business decisions, meaning that it is more important than ever to have a sound information base. Likewise, the complexity of the phenomena that scientists are investigating impedes our understanding of what is really happening. Rather than concluding that 'all depends on almost everything', we must strive for meaningful explanations. Below is a list of factors that characterize the complex business decision-making environment; each demands that managers and scientists have more and better information on which to base their decisions:

- There are more variables to consider in every decision.
- More knowledge exists in every field of management.
- Global and domestic competition is more vigorous, with many businesses downsizing in order to refocus on primary competences, reduce costs and make competitive gains.
- The quality of theories and models available to explain tactical and strategic results is improving.
- Government is continuing to show concern for all aspects of society, becoming increasingly aggressive in protecting these various publics.
- The explosive growth of company websites on the World Wide Web, e-commerce, and the availability of company publications via desktop and electronic publishing, have heralded the presence of extensive new arrays of information. Its quality, however, is not always impeccable.

- Workers, shareholders, customers and the general public are demanding to be included in company decision-making; they are better informed and more sensitive to their own interests than ever before.

To succeed in such an environment, we need to know how to identify high-quality information and how to recognize the solid, reliable research on which high-risk decisions can be based. Luckily, while the decision-making environment has become more complicated, business research tools have at the same time become more sophisticated and improvements in information technology have served to streamline the research process. Each of the factors listed below demonstrates how recent developments have affected the business research process:

- Organizations are increasingly practising data-mining – learning to extract meaningful knowledge from volumes of data contained within internal databases.
- Advances in computing technology have allowed businesses to create the architecture required for data ware-housing – electronic storehouses where vast arrays of collected, integrated data are kept, ready for mining.
- The power and user-friendliness of today's computers means that data may easily be analysed and used to deal with complex managerial problems.
- Quantitative analysis techniques take advantage of increasingly powerful computing capabilities.
- The communication and measurement techniques used in research have been enhanced.

As a researcher, you will need to know how to conduct such research. If you are to develop the skills required in this area, you will need to understand the scientific method as it applies to the managerial decision-making environment. That is why this book addresses your needs as an information processor. Throughout the text we give a slight emphasis to the perspective of an academic researcher or student, as we believe that most users of the text currently belong to these two groups. However, business decisions and research are also often conducted, or at least requested, by managers. By and large, academic researchers, students and managers encounter the same methodological problems while conducting business or management research, although the former often emphasize aspects other than the latter. As many of our users are currently students who will become managers in the near future, we will also address issues that pertain to research in a commercial rather than an academic setting.

What is research?

Having seen *why* research is a vital part of the business decision-making process, it is time to look at just what research is. We will begin with a few examples of management problems that involve decision-making based on information-gathering. When you have read through each of these, you will be able to abstract the essence of research. How is it carried out? What can it do? What should it not be expected to do? As you read the four cases below, bear in mind the possible range of situations available for conducting business research, and think about how you might answer the following questions:

1 What is the decision-making dilemma facing the researcher or manager?
2 What must the researcher accomplish?

Cases

Air Swiss

You work for Air Swiss, an aviation company that is searching for new international partners. The senior vice-president for development asks you to head a task force to investigate six companies that are potential candidates. You assemble a team composed of representatives from the relevant functional areas. Pertinent data are collected from public sources because of the sensitive nature of the project. You examine all of the following: company annual reports; articles in business journals, trade magazines and newspapers; financial analysts' assessments; and company advertisements. Your team members then develop summary profiles of the candidate firms based on the characteristics gleaned from these sources. The final report highlights the opportunities and problems that acquisition of the target firm would bring to all areas of the business.

Akademiska Sjukhuset

You are the commercial manager of Akademiska Sjukhuset, a major academic hospital in Sweden. A prominent manufacturer of medical equipment has contacted you to ask whether you would be willing to purchase a new-generation MRI scanner, which uses magnetism, radio waves and a computer to produce images of body structure.

The doctors' committee at the hospital, to which you will need to make a recommendation, will have to decide on this question. If they choose to purchase the new scanner, they will also agree to test new applications for it and report back to the manufacturer on their experiences. In exchange for this they will get access to the latest technology at a significantly reduced price, and become a member of the manufacturer's network of preferred hospital partners.

You begin your investigation by mining data from patient files to learn how your current MRI scanner is used and what kind of diagnoses it can be used for. You then consult other Swedish hospitals to find out how well equipped they are with MRI technology, and how many patients might, potentially, be treated in your hospital if you invest in the technology. You attempt to confirm your data with information from professional and association journals.

Based on this information, you develop a profile that details the number of patients that could be treated and the overheads and potential revenue that would be realized as a result of purchasing the new scanner.

ColorSplash

ColorSplash, a paint manufacturer, is having trouble maintaining profits. The owner believes inventory management is a weak area of the company's operations. In this industry, the many paint colours, types of paint and container sizes make it easy for a firm to accumulate large inventories and still be unable to fulfil customer orders.

The owner asks you to make some recommendations. You look into the company's present warehousing and shipping operations, and find excessive sales losses and delivery delays because of out-of-stock conditions. An informal poll of customers confirms your impression. You suspect that the present inventory database and reporting system do not provide the prompt, usable information that is needed to allow appropriate production decisions to be made.

Based on this supposition, you familiarize yourself with the latest inventory management techniques in a local college library. You ask the warehouse manager to take an accurate inventory and you review the incoming orders for the last year. In addition, the owner shows you the production runs for the last year and the method he uses to assess the need for a particular colour or paint type.

Modelling the last year of business using production, order and inventory management techniques, you select the method that, in theory, will provide the greatest profit. You run a pilot line using the new control methodology. After two months, the data show a much lower inventory and a higher order fulfilment rate. You recommend that the owner adopt the new method.

York College

You work for York College's alumni association. It is eager to develop closer ties with its ageing alumni in order to encourage increased donation levels and to persuade older, non-traditional students to return to education and thus supplement enrolment numbers. The president's office is considering the construction of a retirement community that is geared towards university alumni and asks your firm to assess the attractiveness of the proposal from an alumni viewpoint. Your director asks you to divide the study into four parts as follows.

Phase 1 First, you are to report on the number of alumni in the appropriate age bracket, the rate of new entries per year and the actuarial statistics for the group. This information will allow your director to assess whether the project is worth pursuing.

Phase 2 Your early results reveal that there are sufficient alumni to make the project feasible. The next step in the study is to describe the social and economic characteristics of the target alumni group. You review gift statistics, analyse job titles, and assess home locations and values. In addition, you review files from the last five years to see how alumni responded when they were asked about their income bracket. When you have finished, you are able to describe the alumni group for your director.

Phase 3 It is evident that the target alumni can easily afford to join a retirement community as proposed. The third phase of the study is to explain the characteristics of the alumni who would be interested in a university-related retirement community. For this phase, you engage the National Pensioners Convention (NPC) and a retirement community developer. In addition, you search for information on senior citizens from federal government sources.

From the developer you learn what characteristics of retirement community planning and construction are most attractive to retirees. From the NPC you learn about the main services and features that potential retirees look for in a retirement community. From government publications you become familiar with existing regulations and recommendations for operating retirement communities, and uncover a full range of descriptive information on the typical retirement community dweller.

You make an extensive report to both the alumni director and the university president. It covers the number of eligible alumni, their social and economic standing, and the characteristics of those who would be attracted by the retirement community.

Phase 4 The report excites the college president. She asks for one additional phase to be completed. She needs to predict the number of alumni who would be attracted to the project so that she can adequately plan the size of the community. At this point, you call on the college business school's research methods class for help in designing a questionnaire for the alumni. By providing telephones and funding, you arrange for the class to conduct a survey among a random sample of the eligible alumni population. In addition, you have the class devise a second questionnaire for alumni who will become eligible in the next 10 years.

Using the data collected, you can predict initial demand for the community and estimate growth in demand over the next 10 years. You submit your final report to the director and the president.

What is the dilemma facing the researcher or manager?

The researcher's/manager's predicament is fairly well defined in the four cases described above. Let us see how carefully you read and understood them.

- In the Air Swiss case, the senior vice-president for development must make a proposal to the president, or possibly the board of directors, about which is the preferred international partner with which to join forces.
- In the Akademiska Sjukhuset case, the doctors in the group must decide whether to purchase the new-generation MRI scanner.
- In the ColorSplash case, the owner of the paint manufacturer must decide whether to implement a new inventory management system.
- At York College, the president must propose to the board of directors whether to fund the development of a retirement community.

How did you do? If you did not come to the same conclusions, reread the cases before proceeding to find out what you missed. Make sure that you have a strong grasp of the process before you read on.

In real life, management dilemmas are not always so clearly defined. In the ColorSplash case, rather than pinpointing the problem as a simple one of inventory management, the paint manufacturer's owner could have faced several, possibly intertwining, problems:

- a strike by employees that had an adverse effect on inventory delivery to retail and wholesale customers
- the development of a new paint formula that offers superior coverage but requires a hard-to-source ingredient in its manufacture, thereby affecting production rates
- a fire that destroyed the primary loading dock of the main shipping warehouse in Belgium
- the simultaneous occurrence of all three of these events.

As the research process begins with the manager's decision-making task, it is of paramount importance to have an accurate definition of the dilemma; this, however, can often prove difficult. We address this issue in Chapter 2.

What must the researcher accomplish?

The different types of study represented by the four cases can be classified as reporting, descriptive, explanatory or predictive. We look at these in more detail below.

Reporting

At the most elementary level, a **reporting study** may be produced simply to provide an account or summation of some data, or to generate some statistics. The task may be quite simple and the data readily available. At other times, the information may be difficult to find. A reporting study calls for knowledge and skill in using information sources and dealing with their gatekeepers. Such a study usually calls for little in the way of inference or conclusion drawing.

In the Air Swiss case, the researcher needs to know what information should be assessed in order to value the company. In the study of management, this knowledge would primarily be acquired in courses on financial management, accounting and marketing.

Knowing the type of information needed, the researcher in the Air Swiss case identifies possible sources, like trade press articles and annual reports. Because of the possible effects of the evaluation of potential partners on the company's stock prices, only public sources are used. Other reporting studies of a less sensitive nature might have the researcher interviewing source gatekeepers. In the York College case, for example, interviewing the director of a local retirement facility might have revealed other sources that could be included in the research. Such an expert is considered a gatekeeper.

Purists claim that reporting studies do not qualify as research, although data that are gathered carefully can have great value. Others argue that at least one form, investigative reporting, has a great deal in common with widely accepted qualitative and clinical research.[1] A research design does not have to be complex, or require the use of inference, for a project to be labelled research.

Descriptive

A **descriptive study** tries to discover answers to the questions who, what, when, where and, sometimes, how. The researcher attempts to describe, or define, a subject, often by creating a profile of a group of problems, people or events. Such studies may involve the collection of data and an examination of the distribution and number of times the researcher observes a single event or characteristic (this is known as a **research variable**). They may also involve an assessment of the interaction of two or more variables.

In the Akademiska Sjukhuset case, the researcher must present data that reveal who is affiliated with the insurer, who uses managed healthcare programmes (both doctors and patients), general trends in the use of imaging technology in diagnosing illness or the severity of injury, and the relationship of patient characteristics, doctor referrals and technology use patterns.

Descriptive studies may or may not have the potential for drawing powerful inferences. Organizations that maintain databases of their employees, customers and suppliers (internal information) already have significant data that can be used to conduct descriptive studies. Yet many firms that have such data files do not mine them regularly in order to take advantage of the decision-making insight they might provide.

A major deficiency of descriptive studies based on existing data sources, however, is that they cannot explain why an event has occurred or why the variables interact in the way they do.

The descriptive study is popular in business research because of its versatility across disciplines. In not-for-profit corporations and other organizations, descriptive investigations have a broad appeal to administrators and policy analysts for planning, monitoring and evaluating. In such contexts, 'how' questions address issues such as those related to quantity, cost, efficiency, effectiveness and adequacy.[2]

Explanatory

Academics have debated the relationship between the next two types of study – explanatory and predictive – in terms of which one should precede the other. Both types of research are grounded in theory, and theory is created to answer 'why' and 'how' questions. For our purposes, an **explanatory study** goes beyond description and attempts to explain the reasons for the phenomenon that the descriptive study has only observed.

Research that studies the relationship between two or more variables is also referred to as a correlational study. In an explanatory study, the researcher uses theories, or at least hypotheses, to account for the forces that caused a certain phenomenon to occur.

In the ColorSplash case, believing that the problem with paint stock-outs is the result of poor inventory management, the owner asks the researcher to detail warehousing and shipping processes. Had it stopped there this would be a descriptive study; but if problems in the processes can be linked with sales losses due to an inability to make timely deliveries to retail or wholesale customers, then an explanatory study will emerge. The researcher tests this hypothesis by modelling the last year of business using the relationship between processes and results.

Predictive

If we can provide a plausible explanation for an event after it has occurred, it is desirable for us to be able to predict when and in what situations such an event might reoccur. A **predictive study**, the fourth type, is rooted as much in theory as in explanation.

National governments in Europe are always interested in economic predictions for the coming year, as a country's economic situation largely determines the tax revenues it will receive, as well as likely government expenditure (e.g. on unemployment benefits). Economic research institutes, such as the CPB in the Netherlands, the DIW and IFO in Germany or the CEBR and NIESR in the UK, and the research departments of banks, use complex theory-driven models to predict key economic figures (e.g. economic growth). The variables included in such models are – among many others – firms' current investments in equipment, consumer confidence, currency exchange rates and so on.

Research Methods in Real Life
Price fixing at the petrol station or the invisible hand

Is there price fixing at the petrol station? This allegation runs headlines in newspapers with surprising regularity. Shortly before school vacations, petrol prices go up – no one doubts the fact. But the explanations differ. Oil companies argue that the price increases are a natural market force reaction to increasing demand. Consumers, however, suspect that oil companies take advantage of the fact that many families need to fill up their tank to reach their vacation destination. In February 2011, the price for petrol at German stations crossed the €1.50 line again. Oil companies argued that the war in Libya and the expected shortages in supply explained the recent price increase. But how does it come that the last time the petrol price was that high, the price for a barrel of crude oil was around US$150, while it is now US$110.

In May 2011, the German cartel authority (Bundeskartellamt) closed its investigation on price fixing in the fuel market. They did not suspect the five major oil companies BP, Shell, Total, Esso (Exxon) and Jet (Conoco Phillips) to have made a handshake agreement on prices; but they investigated the market structure and found it impedes market forces to work properly as those five companies control 70 per cent of the station market and only those five have access to refineries, i.e. they control the upstream market fully. In their conclusion they stated that further mergers will not be allowed and that they will install a price monitoring system that requires all companies to report their current prices at each petrol station.

In May 2013, the London offices of BP, Shell, Statoil and the reporting platform Platts were raided by competition authority investigators, as there had been allegations that petrol prices might have been fixed

▶

for a decade. As in Germany, the correlation between the price for crude oil and the station price is surprisingly low. Moreover, whistleblowers have reported that price fixing occurred. The important question is, however, whether authorities could really prove it.

References and further reading

http://www.handelsblatt.com/politik/deutschland/tankstellenmarkt-roesler-nimmt-benzin-kartell-ins-visier/4209506.html

http://www.guardian.co.uk/business/2013/may/16/oil-price-fixing-criminal

http://www.bbc.co.uk/news/uk-politics-22540650

http://www.sueddeutsche.de/wirtschaft/die-krise-in-libyen-und-der-benzinpreis-das-machtkartell-1.1065504

http://www.bundeskartellamt.de/wEnglisch/download/pdf/11-085_Abschlussbericht_SU_Kraftstoffe_Zusammenfassung-E.pdf

This type of study often calls for a high level of inference. Why, for example, would increasing consumer confidence stimulate economic growth in one year, while in other years the effect of consumer confidence is hardly detectable? The answer to such a question would be of great value in improving the models employed as well as future predictions. In business research, prediction is found in studies conducted to evaluate specific courses of action or to forecast current and future values.

Sometimes, we want to get an idea about how the future might look like but lack solid theories allowing such predictions. Other methods to predict the future include scenario models and expert surveys. In the former, the researcher works out different scenarios based on different assumptions on the course of key factors. For example, you might want to know how the market for private insurance will develop in China in the next 20 years. Your prediction will depend on your assumption of how many Chinese have sufficient income to be interested in such insurance. Expert surveys are mostly based on qualitative interviews with experts on a given issue and distilling the most likely from these expert opinions. Although these two latter models do not rely on an explicit theoretical model, the researcher and the experts questioned certainly work with implicit theories on which they base their assessment of the future.

The researcher is asked to predict for the York College president the success of the proposed retirement facility for alumni, based on the number of applications for residency the project will attract. This prediction will be based on the explanatory hypothesis that alumni frequent programmes and projects sponsored by the institution because they feel attached to their university and alumni associations bear the images of youthfulness as well as mental and physical stimulation.

Finally, once we can explain and predict a phenomenon, we would like to be able to control it. Being able to replicate a scenario and dictate a particular outcome is the objective of **control**. In the York College case, if we assume that the college goes ahead with its retirement community and enjoys the success predicted, the president will feel encouraged to build a similar facility to serve another group of alumni and duplicate that success.

Control is a logical outcome of prediction. The complexity of the phenomenon and the adequacy of the prediction theory, however, are largely responsible for deciding success in a control study. At York College, if a control study were carried out to examine the various promotional approaches used with alumni to stimulate images of youthfulness, the promotional tactics that drew the largest number of alumni applications for residency could be identified. Once known, this knowledge could be used successfully with different groups of alumni *only if* the researcher could account for and control all other variables influencing the applications.

Is research always problem-solving based?

In the four cases detailed above, researchers were asked to respond to particular 'problems' that managers needed to solve. **Applied research** has a practical problem-solving emphasis, although the need for problem-solving is not always generated by a negative circumstance. Whether the 'problem' is negative, like rectifying an inventory system that is resulting in lost sales (as in the ColorSplash case) or, say, an opportunity to increase stockholder wealth through acquiring another firm, problem-solving plays a very important part in business research.

The problem-solving nature of applied research means that it is conducted in order to reveal answers to specific questions related to action, performance or policy needs. In this respect, all four of the case examples above appear to qualify as applied research. Pure, or basic, research is also problem-solving based, but in a different sense. It aims to solve perplexing questions (i.e. problems) of a theoretical nature that have little direct impact on action, performance or policy decisions.

As business is an applied science **pure research** or **basic research** is not often conducted, rather business research relies upon basic research in other disciplines, such as economics, psychology and sociology. Game theoretically motivated experiments on co-operation using the well-known prisoners' dilemma are an example of basic research that is relevant for business studies investigating how companies achieve co-operation. Likewise, psychological studies on how humans react to certain stimuli informs business researchers investigating consumer choices. Some authorities equate research with basic or scientific investigations and would reject all four cases. History shows, however, that science typically has its roots in the pragmatic problems of real life. Interest in basic research comes much later, following the development of knowledge in a particular field. Research that is restricted to basic or pure research is too narrowly defined.

One respected author defines scientific research as a 'systematic, controlled, empirical, and critical investigation of natural phenomena guided by theory and hypotheses about the presumed relations among such phenomena'.[3] The terms 'systematic' and 'controlled' in this definition refer to the degree to which the observations are controlled and alternative explanations of the outcome are ruled out. The terms 'empirical' and 'critical' point to requirements for the researcher to test subjective beliefs against objective reality, and to leave the findings open to further scrutiny and testing. These qualities are what the author means by 'scientific'. Whether all business research needs to be this stringent or should be 'guided by theory and hypotheses about presumed relations' is, however, debatable.

The answer to the question posed at the beginning of this section, 'Is research always problem-solving based?' is yes. Whether basic or applied, simple or complex, all research should provide an answer to a question. If managers always knew what was causing problems or offering opportunities in their realm of responsibility, there would be little need for applied research, pure research or basic research; intuition would be all that was necessary to make effective decisions.

Any of the four types of study – reporting, descriptive, explanatory or predictive – can properly be called research. We also can conclude from the various examples that we have seen that research is a systematic inquiry aimed at providing information to solve managerial problems. This defines the basic requirements that any effort must meet in order to be called research.

All four cases match this definition, but they suggest different stages of scientific development. A rough measure of the development of science in any field is the degree to which explanation and prediction have replaced reporting and description as research objectives. By this standard, the development of business research is in a comparatively formative stage.

 ## What makes good research?

Good research generates dependable data, which is derived through practices that are conducted professionally and that can be used and relied upon. In contrast, poor research is carelessly planned and conducted, resulting in data that we cannot trust; that is, we cannot be sure whether the results give an appropriate account of the reality and consequently we cannot base policy advice or any business decisions on these results. Good research follows the structure of the **scientific method**. Several defining characteristics of the scientific method are listed in Exhibit 1.1 and below, where the managerial dimensions of each are discussed.

Exhibit 1.1 What actions guarantee good research?

Characteristics of research	How can researcher achieve it?	Where to find out more
1 Purpose clearly defined	In applied research, the researcher distinguishes between the defined symptom of organization's problem, the manager's perception of the problem and the research problem; in pure research, it is also wise to clearly separate the research dilemma addressed and the research problem actually investigated	Chapter 2
2 Research process detailed	Researcher provides complete research proposal	Chapter 2
3 Research design thoroughly planned	Exploratory procedures are outlined with constructs defined Sample unit is clearly described, along with sampling methodology Data collection procedures are selected and designed	Chapters 2, 6–14
4 High ethical standards applied	Safeguards are in place to protect study participants, organizations, clients and researchers Recommendations do not exceed the scope of the study The study's methodology and limitations sections reflect researcher restraint and concern for accuracy	Chapter 4
5 Limitations frankly revealed	Desired procedure is compared with actual procedure in report Desired sample is compared with actual sample in report Impact on findings and conclusions is detailed	Chapters 6, 15
6 Adequate analysis for decision-maker's needs	Sufficiently detailed findings are tied to collection instruments	Chapters 16–21
7 Findings presented unambiguously	Findings are clearly presented in words, tables and graphs Findings are logically organized to facilitate reaching a decision about the manager's problems Executive summary of conclusions is outlined Detailed table of contents is tied to the conclusions and findings presentation	Chapters 15–21
8 Conclusions justified	Decision-based conclusions are matched with detailed findings	Chapters 15–21
9 Researcher's experience reflected	Researcher provides experience/credentials with report	Chapter 15

The nine criteria summarized in Exhibit 1.1 together make up desirable, decision-oriented research. They are especially useful guidelines for managers who are performing research themselves. This is because they create barriers that prevent the researcher from adjusting his or her findings to meet their desired ends rather than allowing them to reflect reality.

1 Purpose clearly defined

The purpose of the research – the problem involved or the decision to be made – should be clearly defined and sharply delineated in a form that is as unambiguous as possible. Getting it down in writing is valuable even in instances where the decision-maker and researcher are the same person. Any statement of the decision or problem should include its scope, its limitations, and the precise meanings of all words and terms significant to the research. Failure of the researcher to do this adequately may raise legitimate doubts in the minds of research report readers as to whether the researcher has sufficient understanding of the problem to make a sound proposal for action.

2 Research process detailed

The research procedures used should be described in sufficient detail to permit another researcher to repeat the research (it should be replicable). Except when secrecy is imposed, research reports should reveal with candour the sources of the data and the means by which they were obtained. Omission of significant procedural details makes it difficult, or even impossible, to estimate the validity and reliability of the data, and justifiably weakens the confidence of the reader in the research itself as well as any recommendations based on the research.

3 Research design thoroughly planned

The procedural design of the research should be planned carefully to yield results that are as objective as possible. When sampling of a population is involved, the report should include evidence concerning the degree of representativeness of the sample. A survey of opinions or recollections ought not to be used when more reliable evidence is available from documentary sources or by direct observation. Bibliographic searches should be as thorough and complete as possible. Experiments should have satisfactory controls. Direct observations should be recorded in writing as soon as possible after the event. Efforts should be made to minimize the influence of personal bias in selecting and recording data.

4 High ethical standards applied

Researchers often work independently and have significant latitude in designing and executing research projects. A research design that includes safeguards against causing mental or physical harm to participants and that makes data integrity a first priority should be valued highly. Ethical issues in research reflect important moral concerns about the practice of responsible behaviour in society. Ethical research issues are discussed at length in Chapter 4.

Researchers frequently find themselves precariously balancing the rights of their subjects against the scientific dictates of their chosen method. When this occurs, they have a responsibility to guard the welfare of the participants in the studies and also the organizations to which they belong, their clients, their colleagues and themselves. Careful consideration must be given to those research situations in which there is the possibility of physical or psychological harm, exploitation, invasion of privacy and/or loss of dignity. The research requirements must be weighed against the potential for adverse effects. Typically, you will be able to redesign a study, but on occasion you will not. As a researcher, you should be prepared for this dilemma.

5 Limitations frankly revealed

The researcher should report, with complete frankness, any flaws in procedural design, and estimate their effect on the research findings. There are few perfect research designs. Some of the imperfections may have little effect on the validity and reliability of the data; others may invalidate them entirely. A competent researcher should be sensitive to the effects of imperfect design, and his or her experience in analysing the data should provide a basis for estimating their influence. As a decision-maker, you should question the value of a piece of research that reports no limitations.

6 Adequate analysis for decision-maker's needs

Analysis of the data should be extensive enough to reveal its significance, and the methods of analysis used should be appropriate. The extent to which this criterion is met is frequently a good measure of the competence of the researcher. Adequate analysis of the data is the most difficult phase of research for the novice. The validity and reliability of data should be checked carefully. The data should be classified in ways that assist the researcher in reaching pertinent conclusions and that clearly reveal the findings that have led to those conclusions. When statistical methods are used, the probability of error should be estimated and the criteria of statistical significance applied.

7 Findings presented unambiguously

Some evidence of the competence and integrity of the researcher may be found in the report itself. For example, language that is restrained, clear and precise, assertions that are carefully drawn and hedged with appropriate reservations, and an apparent effort to achieve maximum objectivity tend to give the decision-maker a favourable impression of the researcher. Generalizations that outrun the evidence on which they are based, exaggerations and unnecessary verbiage, however, tend to have the opposite effect. Such reports are not valuable. The presentation of data should be comprehensive, easily understood by the decision-maker, and organized so that the decision-maker can readily locate critical findings.

Research Methods in Real Life
What are the consequences of faking data in research?

Is it more than an ethical dilemma if you falsify the description of your methodology or if you modify your sampling plan? These are ethical and procedural issues that researchers, even famous ones, face. In its December 2001 issue, *FastCompany* asked author, consultant and motivational speaker Tom Peters to revisit the writing of *In Search of Excellence*, the 1982 bestselling business title. In his confession #3, Peters is quoted as saying that he 'faked the data' that resulted in the eight underlying principles – principles that guided American business for much of the next decade.

Rather than evolving from a large study of businesses, where each was selected based on its performance metrics (a probability study), Peters switched the research design and he, along with partner and co-author Robert Waterman, asked McKinsey colleagues and other contacts to identify 'cool' companies (a non-probability, judgement sample). They conducted detailed personal interviews with contacts in those initial 62 companies, and then reduced the list to 43 by a post-interview review of performance metrics.

Peters, in confession #7, admits that he missed some of the emerging 'excellence' factors because they were 'too superficial to make an impact'. Some of the things his study missed were early signs of the growing influence of information technology and the importance that speed would come to have in business.

Do you think that his confession diminishes the importance of the results?

References and further reading

http://www.businessweek.com/stories/2001-12-02/the-real-confessions-of-tom-peters

Peters, Tom and Waterman, Robert, *Excellence: In Search of Excellence, Lessons from America's Best-Run Companies*. New York: Warner Books, 1982, pp. 13–24.

http://www.fastcompany.com/44077/tom-peterss-true-confessions

8 Conclusions justified
Conclusions should be limited to those for which the data provide an adequate basis. Novice researchers are often tempted to broaden the basis of induction by including personal experiences and their own interpretations – which are not, of course, subject to the controls under which the research data were gathered. Equally undesirable is the all-too-frequent practice of drawing conclusions from a study of a limited population and applying them universally. Some researchers may also be tempted to rely too heavily on data collected in a prior study and use it in the interpretation of a new one. This sometimes occurs among research specialists who confine their work to clients in a small industry. These actions tend to decrease the objectivity of the research and undermine readers' confidence in its findings. Good researchers always specify the conditions under which their conclusions are valid.

9 Researcher's experience reflected
Greater confidence in the research is warranted if the researcher is experienced, has a good reputation in the research field and is a person of integrity. Were it possible for the reader of a research report to obtain sufficient information about the researcher, this criterion would perhaps be one of the best bases for judging the degree of confidence a piece of research warrants and the value of any decision based upon it. For this reason, the research report should always contain information about the qualifications of the researcher.

Deeper Insight into Research Methods

Are you a good researcher?

In the previous sections, we discussed criteria for good research, but what might be more important for you is whether you are the kind of person likely to be a good researcher.

The following mock questionnaire is certainly not a reliable and valid predictive test to determine whether you are a good researcher or not (see Chapter 13 for why it is not); rather, it should sensitize you to what good researchers bring with them.

Exhibit 1.2 Mock questionnaire on researchers' qualifications.

	Yes	No
Do you open doors to see what is behind them?	☐	☐
If people act strangely, do you ask them why they do so.	☐	☐
Do you look things up in dictionaries or encyclopaedias?	☐	☐
Do you go on holiday to the same place?	☐	☐
Do you question numbers presented in newspaper articles?	☐	☐
Do you like to take the other side in a discussion just to tease the other with 'brilliant' arguments?	☐	☐
Are you easily satisfied?	☐	☐

In essence good researchers have a general critical attitude and are not easily satisfied. This also explains why research project supervisors always have suggestions for improvement although you thought that the draft presented was close to a final draft. More specifically, good researchers realize that they know very little and that there is much to learn. Once you have developed an attitude that you know a lot about a subject, you might be an expert, but you are not a researcher any more. Next to realizing that there is much more to learn, a good researcher also wants to learn. That means they are willing to put time and effort into learning new things. The desire to go far and deep is a necessary condition for producing excellent research. For a good researcher, doing research has a higher priority than personal convenience. The highest level can only be reached if you are comfortable about yourself.

Suppose there is a situation in which a lot of students find themselves, where they have to work on their research project but do not like it. They might try to avoid the work for some time, but in the end they cannot avoid it and are unhappy doing that work. True researchers look at the research project work from a different perspective. They perceive it as an opportunity to learn something new and once they have learnt something new, they look for new exploration opportunities. The desire to go far and deep comes along with a strong commitment to one research area. As research has become more specialized, it is simply not possible to become a master of all trades. Many good researchers have devoted their whole life to a particular research area. But even if you have studied a certain area for many years, good researchers avoid becoming pre-occupied with certain kinds of thinking. An open attitude towards new ideas is essential. Good researchers are not so much interested in being right; they are more interested in identifying the right ideas. In a good research environment, two researchers, A and B, start a discussion with two different viewpoints, but at the end of the discussion A is convinced that B's idea is more fruitful, while B is convinced that A's idea is better.

Finally, researchers need to be patient, as research costs time. Most students already experience that doing your research project usually takes longer than initially planned. Moreover, in social sciences the process between finishing the research and publication in a journal takes years. Given that a publication is the ultimate reward for a researcher, the time span between effort and reward is long and as a researcher you need to cope with this.

Research philosophies

We introduced the importance of thinking about what research is in a rather pragmatic way. However, how research should be conducted is embedded in the broader philosophies of science. Research is based on reasoning (theory) and observations (data or information). How observations and reasoning are related to each other is an old and still ongoing philosophical debate on the development of knowledge. Although many researchers conduct sound research without a thought for underlying philosophical considerations, some knowledge of research philosophies is beneficial for you as a researcher as it helps to clarify the research design and facilitates the choice of an appropriate one. Furthermore, understanding the basic assumptions of research philosophies can enable researchers to reach designs beyond their past experience.[7] In the following, we provide an overview of the two most distinguished research philosophies, **positivism** and **interpretivism** (also called phenomonology). Between these two positions various other research philosophies exist, relying on some principles of positivism or interpretivism, while relaxing others and incorporating principles of the opposing philosophy. The most notable of these is **realism**, which will be discussed later.

Looking at the often fierce debates between positivists and interpretivists, one might get the impression that research is either conducted on planet 'positivarium' or on planet 'interpretivarium', and research has to be embedded in one philosophy. Using the survey methodology seems to imply a deductive approach rooted in positivism, and an ethnographic observational study using inductive reasoning seems to follow interpretivism. By and large, such classifications are reasonable, but research practice shows that researchers rarely subscribe consistently to one philosophy and, in management research in particular, a more pragmatic view prevails.

Positivism

Positivism is a research philosophy adopted from the natural sciences. Its three basic principles are:

1 The social world exists externally and is viewed objectively.
2 Research is value-free.
3 The researcher is independent, taking the role of an objective analyst.

Auguste Comte, an early proponent of positivism, said that 'all good intellects have repeated, since Bacon's time, that there can be no real knowledge but that which is based on observed facts'.[8] According to positivism, knowledge develops by investigating the social reality through observing objective facts. This view has important implications for the relationship between theory and observations, as well as for how research is conducted. Theory development starts with hypothesizing fundamental laws and deducing what kind of observations support or reject the theoretical predictions of the hypotheses. Consequently, the research process starts with identifying causalities forming the base of fundamental laws. Then research is conducted to test whether observations of the world indeed fit the derived fundamental laws and to assess to what extent detected causalities can be generalized (i.e. are applicable to the whole world).

Positivism implies the following assumptions:

• The social world is observed by collecting objective facts.
• The social world consists of simple elements to which it can be reduced.

A scientist following this research tradition believes (assumes) that observable facts are objective, because they are external; that is, we cannot influence them, and research is conducted value-free. This implies that different researchers observing a social phenomenon, such as the takeover battle between two firms, arrive at the same facts describing the social world. As a consequence, concepts need to be operationalized to allow a quantitative measurement of the facts. Further, the social world can be reduced to simple elements. Distilling its elements and reducing them to fundamental laws is the best way to investigate a phenomenon. This explains why studies following the positivism approach often single out one explanation in order to understand a phenomenon and deliberately neglect other aspects, which are often investigated in separate studies.

Interpretivism

Unlike positivists, interpretivists hold the view that the social world cannot be understood by applying research principles adopted from the natural sciences and propose that social sciences require a different research philosophy. The three basic principles of interpretivism are:

1 The social world is constructed and is given meaning subjectively by people.
2 The researcher is part of what is observed.
3 Research is driven by interests.

Interpretivists argue that simple fundamental laws are insufficient to understand the whole complexity of social phenomena. More important, however, they claim that an objective observation of the social world is impossible, as the social world has a meaning for human beings and is constructed by intentional behaviour and actions. Knowledge is developed and theory built through developing ideas inducted from the observed and interpreted social constructions. The researchers' emphasis on making sense of what is happening sometimes even generates surprising findings beyond the current common scientific knowledge. Interpretivists attempt to understand subjective realities and to offer interpretative explanations, which are meaningful for the participants of the research. The involvement of the researcher in the research is most apparent in action research (see Chapter 10), where the researchers engage in active collaboration with participants to address real-life problems in a specific context, and aim to offer and implement feasible solutions to the problem.

Interpretivists also reject the notion that research is value-free. As researchers offer an interpretation of how people interpret the social world, the researchers' interpretation is also socially constructed, reflecting their motives and beliefs. As Habermas stated, human interests not only channel our thinking, but also guide how we investigate the world (i.e. which questions we ask), and how we construct our knowledge (i.e. how we formulate the answers found).[9] Thus, our approach to research social phenomena also reflects the currently common construction of our knowledge about and basic beliefs to do with the world.

Interpretivism implies the following assumptions:

- The social world is observed by seeing what meanings people give to it and interpreting these meanings from their viewpoint.
- Social phenomena can only be understood by looking at the totality.

Gathering and measuring facts will not disclose the essence of a social phenomenon; rather, researchers need to explore why people have different experiences and to understand how these differences result in the different constructions and meanings people give to the social world. Interpretivists research social phenomena by making sense of how people interpret the social world. This requires the researcher to dig into the processes of subjective interpretation, acknowledging the specific motivations and interests of the participants. Compared to natural phenomena, social phenomena are characterized by a high complexity and are often unique, as they result from multiple circumstances constructed by many individuals. This means that interpretivism does not attach a great deal of importance to the generalizability of findings. The world, and especially the business world, is constantly changing and what seemed sensible three years ago may not hold at all now. Hence, in an ever-changing world, generalization, even over short periods of time, becomes questionable.

Realism

Realism is a research philosophy sharing principles of positivism and interpretivism. Like positivism, its exponents believe that social sciences can rely on the research approach dominant in the natural sciences. More specifically, it accepts the existence of a reality independent of human beliefs and behaviour. However, it also concedes that understanding people and their behaviour requires acknowledgement of the subjectivity inherent to humans. In the realists' view, there are social processes and forces beyond the control of humans, which affect our beliefs and behaviour. These processes and forces operate at the macro level. At the micro level (i.e. at the level of individual human beings), subjective individual interpretations of reality are important for a full understanding of what is happening. Still, most realists would accept that these subjective interpretations are not unique and that people share similar interpretations, partly because the external forces at the macro level influence everyone. Thus, research requires the identification of external factors describing general forces and processes influencing humans, as well as the investigation of how people interpret and give meaning to the setting they are situated in. Critical realism, a branch of realism, recognizes the existence of a gap between the researcher's concept of reality and the 'true' but unknown reality. This implies that research is not value-free, and is conducted within a broader framework based on our current knowledge and concept of reality.

Research implications of positivism and interpretivism

The opposing stances taken by positivists and interpretivists are summarized in Exhibit 1.3. These differences in basic principles and assumptions have several implications for how researchers should conduct research. In the following, we will discuss how the two research philosophies affect research design.

Exhibit 1.3 Positivism and interpretivism compared.

	Positivism	Interpretivism
Basic principles		
View of the world	The world is external and objective	The world is socially constructed and subjective
Involvement of researcher	Researcher is independent	Researcher is part of what is observed and sometimes even actively collaborates
Researcher's influence	Research is value-free	Research is driven by human interest
Assumptions		
What is observed?	Objective, often quantitative, facts	Subjective interpretations of meanings
How is knowledge developed?	Reducing phenomena to simple elements representing general laws	Taking a broad and total view of phenomena to detect explanations beyond the current knowledge

Positivism starts from the idea that the world can be described by objective facts, which are then investigated. Therefore, one needs to assess whether observations are indeed objective facts. The constructs used are operationalized to ensure that two researchers observing the same phenomenon measure it in the same way. In practice, constructs are often operationalized in quantitative terms, as representing facts using numbers facilitates comparisons. The interpretivist is interested in subjective meanings and interpretations of phenomena to detect what is happening in a specific situation. As each observation is subjective, he or she relies ideally on multiple sources and different methods to collect information on the phenomena. An example will serve to illustrate this.

Assume company performance is an essential aspect of the phenomena investigated. A study following the positivistic philosophy will ideally use a set of quantitative indicators reflecting performance, such as profit, sales, market share, growth or a relative measure such as return on assets. Interpretivists might even use key financial indicators from annual reports, but they would put more emphasis on subjective assessments of performance by management and employees. These subjective assessments can result in a quite different picture of the performance than financial indicators suggest and can even provide hints as to why a firm is or is not doing well.

A common study structure in the positivistic tradition is that researchers investigate a research problem by testing whether theoretically derived hypotheses hold for the situations investigated. If the objective facts support the hypothesis, the underlying fundamental laws are applicable and their validity is enforced. The value of the research usually increases with the generalizability of the findings, because a detected relationship, which cannot be linked to other similar circumstances, does not qualify as a fundamental law. This calls for large sample sizes to ensure that the findings based on the sample investigated represent the whole population. Interpretivistic studies follow a different structure. They offer a thick and rich description of the investigated phenomena, which is interpreted to understand what is happening. As they claim that generalization is of minor importance, as discussed above, smaller sample sizes (often just one) are sufficient.

Some people suggest that a 'perfect' research study combines positivism and interpretivism. However, there are major practical and theoretical restrictions questioning the feasibility of such a combined approach. Practical restrictions include the immense effort required to conduct a study in both traditions. For example, positivistic studies usually rely on larger samples while interpretivistic studies emphasize the thickness of the provided descriptions. Unfortunately, thickness of description and sample size have a substitutive relationship, as shown in Exhibit 1.4. Good research not only exists in extreme forms, but is much more often an intelligent combination of the two. Good research operates on a line between the light- and the dark-shaded areas: moving too much into the dark-shaded area is, even if feasible, not efficient. Using a research design far away from the optimal line and in the white area is not sufficient to gain insight into what is happening. If your study is based on just a few cases and the information you collected on each case does not exceed what is usually obtained in large-scale surveys, your research has nothing of interest to offer. In the next section we discuss how you decide what position on the optimal line you wish to occupy.

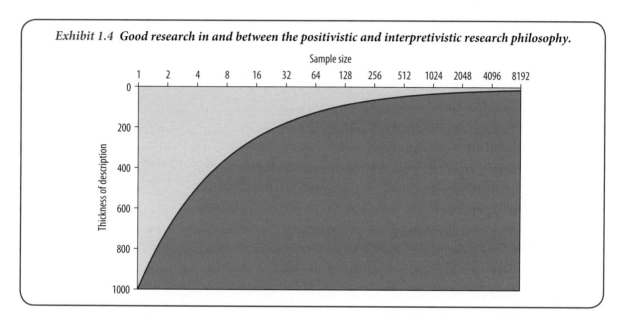

Exhibit 1.4 Good research in and between the positivistic and interpretivistic research philosophy.

A major theoretical restriction of combining different research philosophies is that the research questions asked often differ slightly between the different approaches. It is hard to design a sound interpretivistic study for a research problem framed positivistically. For example, research questions that result in testable hypotheses or that try to find out whether a single observation made holds for a broader set of situations require a positivistic approach. Finally, the different assumptions (see Exhibit 1.3) make it very difficult for researchers from different research traditions to find a common ground to start from. Interpretivists are very sceptical towards all forms of measurement and will argue that even time is not measurable, although many of us will use years to measure a person's age or hours and minutes to measure a certain activity, such as the flight time between London and Hong Kong. For positivists, measuring age in years and flight times in hours and minutes is unproblematic and they might not understand what the problem is as both measurements are applied by many people across different cultures. An interpretivist would, however, argue that also time is subject to individuals' interpretations. For example, two people aged 65 might have very different ideas about their age; one might feel young and energetic and looking forward to starting a lot of new initiatives as soon as she gets retired, while the other feels old and unneeded after his retirement.

Scientific reasoning

Characteristic of scientific research, whether it is a master's research project, a research project or a large-scale government-sponsored research programme, is the inclusion of theory. The place where you introduce theory can differ. You may start with theory in order to test it or solve a theoretical contradiction, or you may close with theoretical considerations drawn from your observations. The position, or role, of theory in your research is directly linked to two different reasoning approaches: deduction and induction.

Research Methods in Real Life
Blue isn't blue?

At a first sight, one might think that determining the colour of a car, a chair or a bottle is not that difficult and in many cases all of us agree that that Ferrari is red and the wooden chair is brown. However, once we have to sort empty bottles for the waste glass recycling container, we sometimes doubt whether a certain bottle is still green or already brown. Likewise, does a turquoise tone look more blue or green to you? One reason for our doubts at the waste glass container or quarrels with friends on whether turquoise is more blue or more green is that colour is a perceptual property; that is, our eyes and our brain derive colours when light with different wavelengths meets our eyes and is then processed in our brain.

While dyschromatopsia (colour blindness) is caused by genetic disorders or damage to the eye and brain, how we perceive colours is also culturally determined. In Russian there is no word for blue; Russians know two words for blue, one *goluboy* describing more light-blue tones and the other *siniy* describing more dark-blue tones. This difference between Russian and English allows for an interesting experiment on whether colour is subjective. If a British person would categorize a light-blue and a dark-blue shirt under the same main colour, while a Russian might categorize it under two different main colours, this would show that colour is culturally determined and therefore also depending on subjective interpretations. An experiment set up by researchers at the MIT presented 26 Russian-speaking and 24 English-speaking participants with cards, showing a blue square at the top and two blue squares at the bottom. All squares were slightly differently coloured. Then participants were asked which of the two squares at the bottom matched better with the square on the top of the card. The result was that if the two squares of the bottom belonged to the two different 'blue' categories used in Russian, the Russians were better in discriminating the colours than the British, because their language had taught them two categories of blue.

If even colour, an apparently rather objective measure, gives room for so much subjective interpretation, how about even more abstract phenomena, such as solidarity, innovation and so on?

Does it make sense to attempt to measure them despite the fact that different people have rather different understanding of them?

References and further reading

Winawer, Jonathan et al., 'Russian blues reveal effects of language on color discrimination', *Proceedings of the National Academy of Sciences of the United States of America* 104(19), 2007, pp. 7780–7785. **The original article**.

www.wellstyled.com/tools/colorscheme2/index-en.html **A website that allows you to see how people with different forms of dyschromatopsia will see your PowerPoint presentation**.

Deduction

Deduction is a form of inference that purports to be conclusive – that is, the conclusion must necessarily follow from the reasons given. These reasons are said to have led to the conclusion and therefore represent proof. This form of argument calls for a stronger link between reasons and conclusions than is found in induction. For a deduction to be correct, it must be both true and valid:

- Premises (reasons) given for the conclusion must agree with the real world (true).
- The conclusion must necessarily follow from the premises (valid).

A deduction is valid if it is impossible for the conclusion to be false if the premises are true. Logicians have established rules by which we can judge whether a deduction is valid. Conclusions are not logically justified if one or more premise is untrue or the argument form is invalid. A conclusion may still be a true statement, but for reasons other than those given. Consider, for example, the following simple deduction:

- All regular employees can be trusted not to steal. (*Premise 1*)
- John is a regular employee. (*Premise 2*)
- John can be trusted not to steal. (*Conclusion*)

The conclusion can only be accepted as a sound deduction if the argument form is valid and the premises are true. In this case, the argument form is valid if (1) the conclusion connects one element of each premise – one element is 'can be trusted not to steal' from premise 1 and the other element is 'John' from premise 2 – and (2) the remaining element (regular employees) is identical in the two premises. In the example above that is the case. Actually the element occurring in both premises reveals the mechanism why we trust John not to steal: because he is a regular employee.[10] But are the premises true? Premise 2 can easily be confirmed. However, many may challenge the sweeping premise that 'All regular employees can be trusted not to steal'.

We may still believe that John will not steal, but such a conclusion is a sound deduction only if both premises are accepted as true. If one premise fails the acceptance test, then the conclusion is not a sound deduction. This is so even if we still have great confidence in John's honesty, but probably we have other reasons to come to the conclusion that John will not steal. For example we might know that John feels very committed to his employer. In that case our deduction would be:

- Committed employees can be trusted not to steal. (*Premise 1*)
- John is a committed employee. (*Premise 2*)
- John can be trusted not to steal. (*Conclusion*)

Induction

An inductive argument is radically different from the deductive type. It does not have the same strength of relationship between reasons and conclusions. To induce something is to draw a conclusion from one or more particular facts or pieces of evidence. The conclusion explains the facts, and the facts support the conclusion.

To illustrate this point, suppose your firm spends €1 million on a regional promotional campaign and sales do not increase. This is a fact: sales did not increase during or after the promotional campaign. Under such circumstances we might ask, 'Why didn't sales increase?'

One likely answer to this question is the conclusion that the promotional campaign was poorly executed. This conclusion is an **induction** because we know from experience that regional sales should go up during a promotional event. We also know that if the promotion is poorly executed, sales will not increase. The nature of induction, however, is that the conclusion is only a hypothesis. It is one explanation, but there are others that fit the facts just as well. For example, each of the following hypotheses might explain why sales did not increase:

- Regional retailers did not have sufficient stock to fill customer requests during the promotional period.
- A strike by the employees at the haulage firm prevented stock from arriving in time for the promotion to be effective.
- A serious hurricane caused all our retail locations in the region to be closed for 10 days during the promotion.

This example illustrates the essential nature of inductive reasoning. The inductive conclusion is an inferential jump beyond the evidence presented – that is, although one conclusion explains the fact that there was no sales increase, other conclusions can also explain this fact. It may even be the case that none of the conclusions we advanced correctly explains the failure of sales to increase.

Let us look at another example. Consider the situation of Tracy Nelson, a salesperson at the Square Box Company. Tracy has one of the poorest sales records in the company. Her unsatisfactory performance prompts us to ask the question, 'Why is she performing so poorly?' From our knowledge of Tracy's sales practices, the nature of box selling and the state of the market, we might conclude (hypothesize) that her problem is that she makes too few sales calls per day to build a good sales record. Other hypotheses might also occur to us on the basis of available evidence. These hypotheses include the following:

- Tracy's territory does not have the market potential of other territories.
- Tracy's sales-generating skills are so poorly developed that she is not able to close sales effectively.

- Tracy does not have the authority to lower prices and her territory has been subject to intense price-cutting by competing manufacturers, causing her to lose many sales to competitors.
- Some people just cannot sell boxes, and Tracy is one of those people.

Each of the above hypotheses is an induction we might base on the evidence of Tracy's poor sales record, plus some assumptions or beliefs we hold about her and about the selling of boxes. All of them have some chance of being true, but we would probably have more confidence in some than in others. All require further confirmation before they gain our confidence. Confirmation comes with more evidence. The task of research is largely to:

- determine the nature of the evidence needed to confirm or reject hypotheses, and
- design methods by which to discover and measure this other evidence.

Combining induction and deduction

Induction and deduction are used in research reasoning in a sequential manner. John Dewey describes this process as the **double movement of reflective thought**.[11] Induction occurs when we observe a fact and ask, 'Why is this?' In answer to this question, we advance a tentative explanation (hypothesis). The hypothesis is plausible if it explains the event or condition (fact) that prompted the question. Deduction is the process by which we test whether the hypothesis is capable of explaining the fact:

1 You promote a product but sales don't increase. (*Fact 1*)
2 You ask the question, 'Why didn't sales increase?' (*Induction*)
3 You infer a conclusion (hypothesis) to answer the question: 'The promotion was poorly executed.' (*Hypothesis*)
4 You use this hypothesis to conclude (deduce) that the sales will not increase during a poorly executed promotion. You know from experience that ineffective promotion will not increase sales. (*Deduction 1*)

This process is illustrated in Exhibit 1.5.

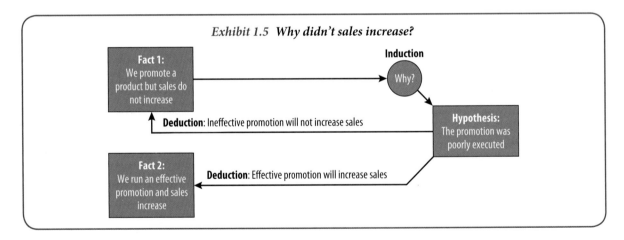

Exhibit 1.5 *Why didn't sales increase?*

This example, an exercise in circular reasoning, indicates that one must be able to deduce the initiating fact from the hypothesis advanced to explain that fact. A second critical point is also illustrated in this exhibit: to test a hypothesis, one must be able to deduce from it other facts that can then be investigated. This is what classical research is all about. We must deduce other specific facts or events from the hypothesis and then gather information to see if the deductions are true. In this example, we deduce the following:

5 A well-executed promotion will result in increased sales. (*Deduction 2*)
6 We run an effective promotion and sales increase. (*Fact 2*)

How would Dewey's 'double movement of reflective thought' work when applied to Tracy Nelson's problem? The process is illustrated in Exhibit 1.6. The initial observation (fact 1) leads to hypothesis 1: that Tracy is lazy. We deduce several other facts from the hypothesis. These are shown as fact 2 and fact 3. We use research to find out if facts 2 and 3 are true. If they are found to be true, they confirm our hypothesis. If they are not, our hypothesis is not confirmed, and we must look for another explanation.

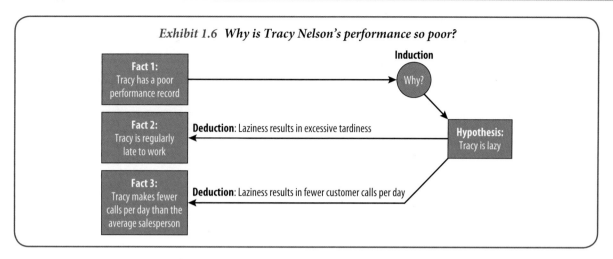

Exhibit 1.6 Why is Tracy Nelson's performance so poor?

In most research, the process is more complicated than these simple examples suggest. For instance, we often develop multiple hypotheses by which to explain the phenomenon in question. Then we design a study to test all the hypotheses at once. Not only is this more efficient, but it is also a good way to reduce the attachment (and potential bias) of the researcher to any given hypothesis.

Reflective thought and the scientific method

Induction and deduction, observation and hypothesis testing can be combined in a systematic way to illustrate the scientific method. The ideas that follow, originally suggested by Dewey and others for problem-solving analysis, represent one approach to assessing the validity of conclusions about observable events. They are particularly appropriate for researchers whose conclusions depend on empirical data.[12] The researcher:

- encounters a curiosity, doubt, barrier, suspicion or obstacle
- struggles to state the problem – asks questions, contemplates existing knowledge, gathers facts, and moves from an emotional to an intellectual confrontation of the problem
- proposes hypotheses to explain the facts that are believed to be logically related to the problem
- deduces outcomes or consequences of the hypotheses – attempts to discover what happens if the results are (i) the opposite to those predicted or (ii) support the expectations
- formulates several rival hypotheses
- devises and conducts a crucial empirical test with various possible outcomes, each of which selectively excludes one or more hypotheses
- draws a conclusion – an inductive inference – based on acceptance or rejection of the hypotheses
- feeds information back into the original problem, modifying it according to the strength of the evidence.

Eminent scientists who claim that there is no such thing as the scientific method, or do not apply it overtly in their work, caution researchers about using template-type approaches. They are right to do so, and it should be added that the ideas presented in this book are highly interdependent, not sequentially fixed and may be expanded upon or eliminated according to the nature of the problem and the perspective from which it is viewed. Nevertheless, novice researchers should understand that research, when conducted scientifically, is most definitely a process.

The research process that explores the relationship between reflective thought and scientific method is described in detail in Chapter 3.

The scientific attitude

If the tools of thinking are the 'mind' of science, then the scientific attitude is its spirit. The scientific attitude unleashes the creative drive that makes discovery possible. The stories of scientists involved in some of the most spectacular discoveries of the twentieth century – Crick, Watson, Pauling and others – are ones of imagination, intuition, curiosity, suspicion, anguish, self-doubt and the urge to know. Such predispositions are not only, however, the preserve of the natural scientist. All researchers exercise imagination in the discovery process, in capturing the most essential aspect of a problem or in selecting the technique that will reveal a phenomenon in its most natural state.

Curiosity in its many forms has long characterized persistent efforts to understand the relationship between productivity and worker satisfaction. Starting first with the Hawthorne studies, it was thought that employee satisfaction improved productivity.[13] Later research did not bear this out, and the second general conclusion was that satisfaction and productivity were not directly connected since the relationship was affected by a number of other variables. Currently, it is believed that satisfaction is sought for reasons not consistently related to work, and that productivity varies from simple to challenging tasks.

Many contextual variables are now viewed as essential to understanding the original relationship.[14] Over 30 years elapsed while this research was being sorted out. The curiosity needed to ask questions, together with the passion not to let go and an unwillingness to just accept existing answers, sustained these researchers through periods of failure and self-doubt.

Thomas Kuhn, writing in *The Structure of Scientific Revolutions*, has also addressed the question of why scientists attack their problems with such passion and devotion. Scientific inquiry, he says, attracts people for a variety of motives: 'Among them are the desire to be useful, the excitement of exploring new territory, the hope of finding order, and the drive to test established knowledge.'[15] From applied researchers addressing a manager's need to academicians fascinated with the construction of grand theories, the attitude of science is the enabling spirit of discovery.

1.7 Understanding theory: components and connections

When we do research, we seek to discover what we need to know in order to understand, explain and predict phenomena. We might want to answer the question 'What will employees' reaction be to the new flexible work schedule?' or 'Why did the stock market price surge higher when all normal indicators suggested it would go down?' When dealing with such questions, we must agree on definitions: which employees, what kind of reaction, what are the normal indicators? To do this requires the use of concepts, constructs and definitions. These components, or building blocks, of theory are reviewed in this section.

Later in this chapter we use variables and hypotheses to make statements and propose tests for the relationships expressed in our research questions.

Concepts

To understand and communicate information about objects and events, there must be some common ground on which to do it. Concepts serve this purpose. A **concept** is a generally accepted collection of meanings or characteristics associated with certain events, objects, conditions, situations and behaviours. Classifying and categorizing objects or events that have common characteristics beyond any single observation create concepts. The terms 'height', 'width' and 'depth', for example, symbolize a conception of the properties of a physical object. Similarly, the economic term 'profit' points to a property of the financial situation of an organization.

We abstract such meanings from reality and use words as labels to designate them. For example, we see a man go by and acknowledge that he is running, walking, skipping, crawling or hopping. These movements all represent concepts. We have also abstracted certain visual elements by which we identify that the moving object is an adult male, rather than an adult female or a truck or a horse. We use a host of concepts in our everyday thinking, conversing and other activities.

Sources of concepts

Concepts that are in frequent and general use have been developed over time through shared usage. We have acquired them through personal experience. If we lived in another society, we would hold many of the same concepts (though in a different language). Some concepts, however, are unique to a particular culture and are not readily translated into another language.

Ordinary concepts make up the bulk of communication even in research, but we will often run into difficulties when trying to deal with an uncommon concept or a newly advanced idea. One way to handle this problem is to borrow from other languages or areas (e.g. gestalt psychology) or from other fields (e.g. impressionism, say, from art). The concept of gravitation, for instance, has been borrowed from physics and used in marketing in an attempt to explain why people shop where they do. The concept of 'distance' is used in attitude measurement to describe the degree of variability between the attitudes of two or more people; the term 'faultlines' is used to describe heterogeneity in teams and is borrowed from geology; while 'velocity' is a term borrowed by the economist from the physicist.

Borrowing is not always practical, though, so we sometimes need to adopt new meanings for words (i.e. make a word cover a different concept) or develop new labels (words) for concepts. The recent broadening of the meaning of the term 'model' is an example of the first instance; the development of concepts such as sibling and status stress are examples of the second.

When we adopt new meanings or develop new labels, we begin to develop a specialized jargon or terminology. Researchers in medicine, the physical sciences and related fields frequently use terms that are unintelligible to outsiders. Jargon no doubt contributes to the efficiency of communication among specialists, but it tends to exclude everyone else.

The importance of concepts to research

Concepts are basic to all thought and communication, yet in everyday use we pay scant attention to the problems encountered in their use. In research, special problems grow out of the need for concept precision and inventiveness. We design hypotheses using concepts. We devise measurement concepts by which to test these hypothetical statements. We gather data using these measurement concepts. We may even invent new concepts to express ideas. The success of research hinges on:

- how clearly we conceptualize, and
- how well others understand the concepts we use.

For example, when we survey people on the question of tax equity, the questions we use need to tap faithfully the attitudes of the respondents. Attitudes are abstract, yet we must attempt to measure them using carefully selected concepts.

The challenge is to develop concepts that others will clearly understand. We might, for example, ask respondents for an estimate of their family's total income. This may seem to be a simple, unambiguous concept, but we will receive varying and confusing answers unless we restrict or narrow the concept by specifying, say:

- time period (weekly, monthly or annually)
- fixed or variable income
- before or after tax
- head of family only or all family members
- salary and wages only, or also include dividends, interest and capital gains
- income in kind, such as living rent-free and employee discounts.

Problems in concept use

The use of concepts presents difficulties that are accentuated in a research setting. First, people differ in the meanings they include under any particular label. This problem is so great in normal human communication that we often see cases where, although people use the same language, they do not understand each other. We may all agree to the meaning of concepts such as dog, table, electric light, money, employee and wife. We might encounter more difficulty, however, when we communicate concepts such as household, retail transaction, dwelling unit, regular user and debit. Still more challenging are concepts that are familiar but not well understood, such as leadership, motivation, personality, social class and fiscal policy.

Personality, for example, has been defined in the research literature in more than 400 ways.[16] Although this may seem extreme, writers are not able to express the complexity of the determinants of personality and its attributes (e.g. authoritarianism, risk-taking, locus of control, achievement orientation and dogmatism) in a fashion that leads to agreement.

The concepts described represent progressive levels of abstraction – that is, the degree to which the concept does or does not have objective referents. 'Table' is an objective concept in that we can point to a table and we can conjure up in our minds an image of a table. An abstraction like personality is much more difficult to visualize. Such abstract concepts are often called **constructs**.

Constructs

As used in research in the social sciences, the term 'construct' refers to an image or idea specifically invented for a given research and/or theory-building purpose. We build constructs by combining the simpler concepts, especially when the idea or image we intend to convey is not directly subject to observation.

Concepts and constructs are easily confused. Here is an example to clarify the differences involved. A human resource analyst at CadSoft, an architectural software company that employs technical writers to work on its product manuals, is analysing the task attributes of a job that is in need of a redesign. She knows that the job description for a technical writer consists of three components: presentation quality, language skill and job interest. Her job analysis reveals more specific characteristics.

Exhibit 1.7 illustrates some of the concepts and constructs she is dealing with. The concepts at the right of the exhibit (format accuracy, manuscript errors and keyboarding speed) are the most concrete and easily measured. We can observe keyboarding speed, for example, and even with crude measures agree on what constitutes slow and fast 'keyboarders'. Keyboarding speed is one concept in the group that defines a construct that the human resource analyst calls 'presentation quality'. Presentation quality is in itself, though, a non-existent entity, a 'constructed type'. It is used to communicate the combination of meanings presented by the three concepts. The analyst uses it as a label for the concepts she has found empirically to be related.

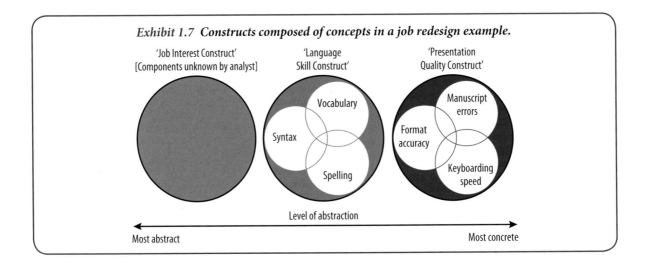

Exhibit 1.7 Constructs composed of concepts in a job redesign example.

'Job Interest Construct'
[Components unknown by analyst]

'Language Skill Construct'

'Presentation Quality Construct'

Vocabulary

Syntax

Spelling

Manuscript errors

Format accuracy

Keyboarding speed

Level of abstraction

Most abstract

Most concrete

Concepts in the middle of Exhibit 1.7 are vocabulary, syntax and spelling. The analyst also finds them to be related. They form a construct that she calls 'language skill'. She has chosen this term because these three concepts together define the language requirement in the job description. Language skill is placed at a higher level of abstraction in the exhibit because two of the concepts that comprise it – vocabulary and syntax – are difficult to observe and their measures more complex.

Looking at the left part of the exhibit, you will see that the analyst has not yet measured the last construct: 'job interest'. This is the least observable and most difficult to measure. It is likely to be composed of numerous concepts – many of which will be quite abstract. Part of job interest, for example, could be the match between activities one likes to do and activities the job consists of. Researchers sometimes refer to such entities as hypothetical constructs because they can be inferred only from data; thus, they are presumed to exist but must await confirmation from further testing.

Definitions

Confusion about the meaning of concepts can destroy a research study's value without the researcher or client realizing it. If words have different meanings for the different parties involved, then they will not be communicating on the same wavelength. Having a mutually acceptable set of definitions is one way to reduce this danger.

Researchers must struggle with two types of definition: dictionary definitions and operational definitions. In the more familiar dictionary definition, a concept is defined with a synonym. For example, a customer is defined as a patron; a patron, in turn, is defined as a customer or client of an establishment; a client is defined as one who employs the services of any professional and also, loosely, as patron of any shop.[17] These 'circular' definitions may be adequate for general communication but not for research. In research, we must measure concepts and constructs, and this requires more rigorous definitions.

Operational definitions

An **operational definition** is one stated in terms of specific testing or measurement criteria. These terms must have empirical referents (i.e. we must be able to count, measure or in some other way gather the information via our senses). Whether the object to be defined is physical (e.g. a machine tool) or highly abstract (e.g. achievement motivation), the definition must specify characteristics and how they are to be observed. The specifications and procedures must be so clear that any competent person using them would be able to classify the objects in the same way.

For example, suppose college undergraduates are to be classified by class. No one has much trouble understanding terms such as fresher (first-year student), sophomore (second-year student), and so on; but the task may not be that simple if you must determine which students fall into which class. To do this, you need operational definitions.

Operational definitions may vary, depending on your purpose and the way you choose to measure them. Here are two different situations that require different definitions of the same concepts.

1 You conduct a survey among students and wish to classify their answers by their class status. You merely ask them to report their class status and you record it. In this case, class is divided into fresher, second-year student, junior (third-year student) or senior (fourth- or final-year student), and you accept the answer each respondent gives as correct. This is a rather casual definition process but none the less an operational definition. It is probably adequate in this case even though some of the respondents may report inaccurately.

2 You wish to make a tabulation of the class status of students for the university registrar's annual report. The measurement task here is more critical, so your operational definition needs to be more precise. You decide to define class status in terms of 'hours of credit' (i.e. the number of hours of attendance completed by the end of the spring term and recorded in each student's record in the registrar's office), as indicated below:
   - Fresher: fewer than 30 hours' credit
   - Second-year student: 30–59 hours' credit
   - Junior: 60–89 hours' credit
   - Senior: more than 90 hours' credit.

The two examples given above deal with relatively concrete concepts, but operational definitions are even more critical in treating abstract ideas. Suppose you want to measure a construct called 'organizational commitment'. You may intuitively understand what this means, but it is difficult to attempt to measure it among workers. You would probably need to develop a commitment scale of your own, or you may be able to use a scale that has already been developed and validated by someone else. This scale then operationally defines the construct.

While operational definitions are needed in research, they also present some problems. One ever-present danger is thinking that a concept and its operational definition are the same thing. We forget that our definitions provide only a limited insight into what a concept or construct really is. In fact, the operational definition may be quite narrow and quite dissimilar to that someone else might use when researching the same topic. When measurements by two different definitions correlate well, this correlation supports the view that each definition measures the same concept adequately.

The problem of operational definitions is particularly difficult when dealing with constructs. Constructs have few empirical referents by which to confirm that an operational definition really measures what we hope it does. The correlation between two different definition formulations strengthens the belief that we are measuring the same thing. On the other hand, if there is little or no correlation, this may mean that we are tapping several different partial meanings of a construct. It may also mean that one or both of the operational definitions are not true labels.

Whether you use a dictionary or operational definition, its purpose in research is basically the same: to provide a way of understanding and measuring concepts. You may need to provide operational definitions for only a few critical concepts, but these will almost always be the definitions used to develop the relationships found in hypotheses and theories.

Variables

Scientists operate at both theoretical and empirical levels. At the theoretical level, there is a preoccupation with identifying constructs and their relationship to propositions and theory. At this level, constructs cannot, as we have already said, be observed. At the empirical level, where the propositions are converted to hypotheses and testing occurs, the scientist is likely to be dealing with variables. In practice, the term **variable** is used as a synonym for construct, or the property being studied. In this context, a variable is a symbol to which we assign a numeral, or value.[18]

The numerical value assigned to a variable is based on that variable's properties. For example, some variables, said to be **dichotomous variables**, have only two values, reflecting the presence or absence of a property. For example, employed/unemployed and male/female have two values, generally 0 and 1. Gender is a typical example for such a dichotomous variable. You can either be female (the value of the variable is 1) or not female, that is male (the value of the variable is 0).

Variables also take on values that represent the addition of further categories, such as the demographic variables of race or religion. All variables that produce data that fit into categories are said to be discrete, since only certain set values are possible. A car brand variable, for example, where Renault is assigned a 5 and Volkswagen a 6, provides no option for 5.5.

Income, temperature, age or a test score are examples of **continuous variables**. These variables may take on values within a given range or, in some cases, an infinite set. Your test score may range from 0 to 100, your age may be 23.5 and your present income could be €24,583.

Independent and dependent variables

Researchers are most interested in relationships among variables. For example, does a participative leadership style (independent variable) influence job satisfaction or performance (dependent variables) or can a superior staff-member's modelling of ethical behaviour influence the behaviour of her subordinates?

Exhibit 1.8 lists some terms that have become synonyms for independent variable and dependent variable. It is important to remember that there are no preordained variables waiting to be discovered 'out there' that are automatically assigned to one category or the other. As one writer notes:

"There's nothing very tricky about the notion of independence and dependence. But there is something tricky about the fact that the relationship of independence and dependence is a figment of the researcher's imagination until demonstrated convincingly. Researchers hypothesize relationships of independence and dependence: They invent them, and then they try by reality testing to see if the relationships actually work out that way."[19]

Exhibit 1.8 Defining independent and dependent variables.

Independent variable	Dependent variable
Presumed reason	Presumed effect
Stimulus	Response
Predicted from . . .	Predicted to . . .
Antecedent	Consequence
Manipulated	Measured outcome
Predictor	Criterion

In each relationship, there is at least one **independent variable** (IV) and one **dependent variable** (DV). It is normally hypothesized that, in some way, the IV 'causes' the DV to occur. It should be noted, however, that while it is easy to establish whether an IV influences a DV, it is much harder to show that the relationship between an IV and DV is a causal relationship (see also Chapter 5). In Exhibit 1.9a, this relationship is illustrated by an arrow pointing from the independent variable 'participation in training' to the dependent variable 'productivity'. For simple relationships, all other variables are considered extraneous and are ignored.

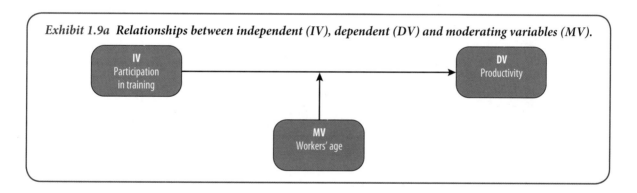

Exhibit 1.9a Relationships between independent (IV), dependent (DV) and moderating variables (MV).

Moderating or interaction variables

In many study situations, however, such a simple one-to-one relationship needs to be conditioned or revised to take other variables into account. Often, we can use another type of explanatory variable that is of value here: the **moderating variable** (MV). A moderating or interaction variable is a second independent variable that is included because it is believed to have a significant contributory or contingent effect on the original IV–DV relationship. The arrow pointing from the moderating variable to the arrow between the IV and DV in Exhibit 1.9a exemplifies the difference between an IV directly affecting the DV and an MV affecting the relationship between an IV and the DV. For example, one might hypothesize that in an office situation:

"Training (IV) will lead to higher productivity (DV), especially among younger workers (MV)."

In this case, there is a differential pattern of relationship between training and productivity that is the result of age differences among the workers. Hence, after following training the productivity gain for younger workers is higher than that for older workers. It should be noted that the effect of the moderating or interaction variable is the 'surplus' of the combined occurrence of introducing a four-day working week and being a younger worker. To illustrate this point, assume that the productivity of younger workers is 6 percentage points higher than that for older workers, and that the productivity of workers having received training is 12 percentage points higher than those of workers without training. If the productivity of a younger trained worker is only 18 percentage points higher than the productivity of an older untrained worker, there is no interaction effect, because the 18 percentage points are the sum of the main effects. There would be an interaction effect if the productivity of the younger trained worker was, for example, 25 percentage points higher than the productivity of the older untrained worker.

Whether a given variable is treated as an independent or moderating variable depends on the hypothesis under investigation. If you were interested in studying the impact of training, you would make training the IV. If you were focusing on the relationship between age of worker and productivity, you might use training as an MV.

Intervening or mediating variables

The variables mentioned with regard to causal relationships are concrete and clearly measurable – that is, they can be seen, counted or observed in some way. Sometimes, however, one may not be completely satisfied by the explanations they give. Thus, while we may recognize that training results in higher productivity, we might think that this is not the whole story – that training affects some **intervening variable** (IVV) or **mediating variable** that, in turn, results in higher productivity.

An IVV is a conceptual mechanism through which the IV and MV might affect the DV. In the case of the training hypothesis, one might view the intervening variable (IVV) to be skills, giving a hypothesis such as:

"Training (IV) will lead to higher productivity (DV) by increasing the skill level (IVV)."

Here we assume that training increases skill level. Exhibit 1.9b illustrates how 'theoretical' constructs, which are not directly observed, fit into our model.

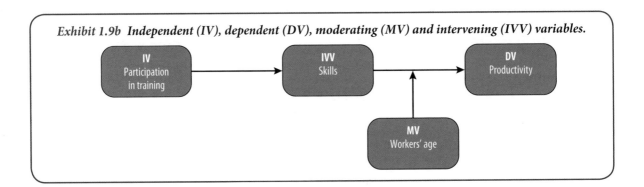

Exhibit 1.9b Independent (IV), dependent (DV), moderating (MV) and intervening (IVV) variables.

Control variables

Typical for phenomena in business research is that they are multi-causal, i.e. there are influencing factors, variables. The ones we are interested in from a theoretical perspective are treated as IVs, MVs or IVVs, but others are excluded from the study. Fortunately, an infinite number of variables has little or no effect on a given situation. Most can safely be ignored, as their impact occurs in such a random fashion as to have little effect. Others might influence the DV, but their effect is not at the core of the problem we investigate.

Still, we want to check whether our results are influenced by them. Therefore, we include them as **control variables** (CVs) in our investigation to ensure that our results are not biased by not including them. Taking the example of the effect of training on productivity again, one can easily think about other variables influencing productivity. Examples are weather conditions, the imposition of an income tax, the appointment of a new plant manager, and thousands of similar events and conditions could have some effect on productivity. In Exhibit 1.9c, sunshine is shown as a control variable; the broken line indicates that we included it in our research because it might influence the DV, but we consider the CV as irrelevant for the investigation of our research problem, as we do not believe that sunshine affects the relation between training and productivity.

Typical control variables in business research that are widely used, mainly due to their availability, are gender, age, ethnicity, place of living for individuals and size, sector, place of establishment and age for organizations.

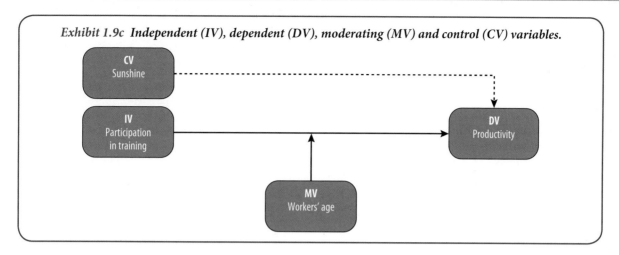

Exhibit 1.9c Independent (IV), dependent (DV), moderating (MV) and control (CV) variables.

1.8 Propositions and hypotheses

We define a **proposition** as a statement about concepts that may be judged as true or false if it refers to observable phenomena. When a proposition is formulated for empirical testing, we call it a hypothesis. As a declarative statement, a **hypothesis** is of a tentative and conjectural nature.

Hypotheses have also been described as statements in which we assign variables to cases. A case is defined in this sense as the entity, or thing, the hypothesis talks about. The variable is the characteristic, trait or attribute that, in the hypothesis, is ascribed to the case.[21]

For example, we might form the following hypothesis:

"Executive Jones (case) has a higher than average achievement motivation (variable)."

If our hypothesis were based on more than one case, it would be a generalization. For example:

"Executives in Company Z (cases) have a higher than average achievement motivation (variable)."

Descriptive hypotheses

Both of the above hypotheses are examples of **descriptive hypotheses**. These are propositions that typically state the existence, size, form or distribution of some variable. For example:

"In Denmark (case), the October seasonally adjusted unemployment rate (variable) stands at 5.8 per cent of the labour force."

"The Member States of the European Union (case) are experiencing budget difficulties (variable)."

"The majority of Company Z stockholders (case) favour increasing the company's cash dividend (variable)."

Researchers often use a research question rather than a descriptive hypothesis. Thus, in place of the above hypotheses, we might use the following questions:

- What is the unemployment rate in Denmark?
- Are European States experiencing budget difficulties?
- Do stockholders of Company Z favour an increased cash dividend?

Either format is acceptable, but the descriptive hypothesis format has several advantages as follows:

- It encourages researchers to crystallize their thinking about the likely relationships to be found.
- It further encourages them to think about the implications of a supported or rejected finding.
- It is useful for testing statistical significance.

Relational hypotheses

The research question format is less frequently used with a situation calling for **relational hypotheses**. These are statements that describe a relationship between two variables with respect to a particular case. For example:

> "Foreign (variable) cars are perceived by Italian consumers (case)
> to be of better quality (variable) than domestic cars."

In this instance, the nature of the relationship between the two variables ('country of origin' and 'perceived quality') is not specified. Is there only an implication that the variables occur in some predictable relationship, or is one variable somehow responsible for the other? The first interpretation (unspecified relationship) indicates a correlational relationship; the second (predictable relationship) indicates an explanatory, or causal, relationship. **Correlational hypotheses** state merely that the variables occur together in some specified manner without implying that one causes the other. Such weak claims are often made when we believe there are more basic causal forces that affect both variables or when we have not developed enough evidence to claim a stronger linkage. Here are three sample correlational hypotheses:

> "Young machinists (under 35 years of age) are less productive than those who are 35 years of age or older."

> "The height of women's hemlines varies directly with the level of the business cycle."

> "People in the UK give the European Commission a less favourable rating than do people in France."

By labelling these as correlational hypotheses, we make no claim that one variable causes the other to change or take on different values. Other researchers, however, may view one or more of these hypotheses as reflecting cause-and-effect relationships.

With **explanatory (causal) hypotheses**, there is an implication that the existence of, or a change in, one variable causes or leads to a change in the other. As noted earlier, the causal variable is typically called the independent variable (IV) and the other the dependent variable (DV). 'Cause' means roughly to '*help* make happen'; so the IV need not be the sole reason for the existence of, or change in, the DV.

Here are three examples of explanatory hypotheses:

> "An increase in family income (IV) leads to an increase in the percentage of income saved (DV)."

> "Exposure to the company's messages concerning industry problems (IV) leads to more favourable
> attitudes (DV) from production workers towards the company."

> "Loyalty to a particular grocery store (IV) increases the probability of purchasing the own-label goods
> (DV) sponsored by that store."

In proposing or interpreting causal hypotheses, the researcher must consider the direction of influence. In many cases, this is obvious from the nature of the variables. Thus, one would assume that family income influences savings rate rather than vice versa.

Sometimes our ability to identify the direction of influence depends on the research design. In the worker attitude hypothesis, if exposure to the message clearly precedes attitude measurement, then the direction of exposure to attitude seems clear. If sets of information about both exposure and attitude were collected at the same time, the researcher might be justified in saying that different attitudes led to selective message perception or non-perception. Store loyalty and the purchasing of store brands, for example, appear to be interdependent. Loyalty to a store may increase the probability of buying the store's own-label goods, but satisfaction with the store's own-label goods may also lead to greater store loyalty.

The role of the hypothesis

In research, a hypothesis serves several important functions:

- It guides the direction of the study.
- It identifies those facts that are relevant and those that are not.
- It suggests which form of research design is likely to be most appropriate.
- It provides a framework for organizing the conclusions.

A frequent problem in research is a proliferation of interesting information. Unless the researcher curbs their urge to include additional elements, a study can be diluted by trivial concerns that do not answer the basic questions posed by the management dilemma (i.e. the focus of the research). The virtue of a hypothesis is that, if taken seriously and adhered to, it limits what will be studied.

To consider the role of the hypothesis in determining the direction of a piece of research, suppose we take this example:

"Husbands and wives agree in their perceptions of their respective roles in purchase decisions."

The hypothesis specifies who will be studied (married couples), in what context they will be studied (their consumer decision-making), and what in particular will be studied (their individual perceptions of their roles). The nature of this hypothesis and the implications of the statement suggest that the best research design would be a communication-based study, probably a survey or interview. We have at this time no other practical means to ascertain perceptions of people except to ask about them in one way or another. In addition, we are interested only in the roles that are assumed in the purchase or consumer decision-making situation. The study should not, therefore, involve itself in seeking information about other types of role that husbands and wives might fulfil.

Reflection on this hypothesis might also reveal that husbands and wives disagree on their perceptions of their roles, but these differences may be explained in terms of additional variables, such as age, social class, background, personality differences and other factors not associated with their difference in gender.

What makes a good hypothesis?

A good hypothesis should fulfil three conditions. It should be:

- adequate for its purpose
- testable
- better than its rivals.

For a descriptive hypothesis, adequacy for its purpose means that it clearly states the condition, size or distribution of some variable in terms of values that are meaningful to the research task. If it is an explanatory hypothesis, it must explain the facts that gave rise to the need for explanation. Using the hypothesis, plus other known and accepted generalizations, one should be able to deduce the original problem condition.

A hypothesis is testable if it meets the following conditions:

- It does not require techniques that are currently unavailable.
- It does not require an explanation that defies known laws.
- There are consequences or derivatives that can be deduced for testing purposes.

Generally, a hypothesis is better than its rivals if:

- It has a greater range than its rivals.
- It explains more facts than its rivals.
- It explains a greater variety of facts than its rivals.
- It is simple, requiring few conditions or assumptions.

Research Methods in Real Life
Fairness of price discrimination

In September 2000, customers of Amazon.com discovered that they were charged different prices for the same product, such as a DVD, based on their previous buying history. The prices to be paid ranged from US$80–100 for the complete second series of *The X-files*. After discussion on online platforms and customers' complaints against this practice, Amazon announced that it did not use previous buying behaviour to set prices, but that they were rather testing customer responses to various prices. Nevertheless, Amazon refunded 6,896 customers an average of US$3 to calm the public outcry.

►

Looking at any marketing textbook, you will find that asking different prices in different markets is a well-known strategy which is often applied. Other examples are: (1) Due to the weakness of the British pound, for example, prices at UK online shops for many electronic goods were lower than in other European countries in 2010. (2) As the Dutch government charges a heavy luxury tax upon registering a car in the Netherlands, car manufacturers charge substantially lower base prices for a car in the Netherlands than, for example, in Germany.

Liu Qingling wondered what could explain whether consumers would accept differentiated prices. Her suspicion was that culture determines whether differentiated prices are perceived as fair or not. More specifically, she derived among others the following hypotheses:

- People from collectivistic cultures are more likely to perceive price discrimination as unfair than people from individualistic cultures.
- People from feminine cultures are more likely to perceive price discrimination as unfair than people from masculine cultures.
- People from collectivistic cultures are less likely to perceive price discrimination as unfair than people from individualistic cultures if price discrimination is socially motivated.
- People who perceive price discrimination as unfair are less likely to purchase the product or service.

What do you think about those hypotheses? Could you think of other determinants than culture to explain the perception of price discrimination? Would those alternative determinants form better hypotheses?

Theory

Hypotheses play an important role in the development of **theory**. While theory development has not, historically, been an important aspect of business research, it is gradually becoming more influential.

Someone who is unfamiliar with research might use the term theory to mean the opposite of fact. In this sense, theory is viewed as being speculative. You might hear, say, that Professor X is too theoretical, that managers need to be less theoretical, or that some idea will not work because it is too theoretical. For the researcher, this gives a distorted picture of the relationship between fact and theory.

When you are too theoretical, this is likely to mean that the basis of your explanation or decision is not sufficiently attuned to specific empirical conditions. Although this may be so, it does not prove that theory and fact are opposites. The truth is that fact and theory are each necessary for the other to be of value. Our ability to make rational decisions, as well as to develop scientific knowledge, is measured by the degree to which we combine fact and theory.

We all operate on the basis of the theories we hold. In one sense, theories are the generalizations we make about variables and the relationships among them. We use these generalizations to make decisions and predict outcomes. For example, it is midday and you note that, outside, the natural light is dimming; dark clouds are moving rapidly in from the west, the breeze is freshening and the air temperature is getting cooler. Would your understanding of the relationship between these variables (your weather theory) lead you to predict that something decidedly wet is likely to occur at any minute?

Consider a situation where you are called upon to interview two people for possible promotion to the position of department manager. Do you have a theory about the characteristics such a person should have?

Suppose you interview Ms A and observe that she answers your questions well, openly and apparently sincerely. She also expresses thoughtful ideas about how to improve departmental functioning and is articulate in stating her views. Ms B, on the other hand, is guarded in her comments and reluctant to advance ideas for improvement. She answers questions by saying 'what Mr General Manager wants'. She is also less articulate and seems less sincere than Ms A. You would probably choose Ms A, based on the way you combine the concepts, definitions and propositions mentioned into a theory of managerial effectiveness. Your theory of managerial effectiveness, while workable, may not necessarily be a good theory because of the variables it has ignored, but it illustrates that we all use theory to guide our decisions, predictions and explanations.

A theory is a set of systematically interrelated concepts, definitions and propositions that are advanced to explain and predict phenomena (facts). In this sense, we have many theories and use them continually to explain or predict what goes on around us. To the degree that our theories are sound and fit the situation at hand, we are successful in forming explanations and predictions. Thus, while a given theory and a set of facts may not 'fit', they are not opposites. Our challenge is to build a better theory and to be more skilful in fitting together theory and fact.

The ways in which theory differs from hypothesis may also be a source of confusion. A hypothesis is a statement relating two variables, while the theory provides the rationale why those two variables are related. A process of reversed deduction illustrates the difference. Exhibit 10.1 shows a deductive process that results in a hypothesis, namely that in heterogeneous teams conflict is more likely. The rationale for this statement is what we call theory, namely a theory that can explain why in heterogeneous teams conflict is more likely, thus we are looking for the link between heterogeneity and conflict. We need to find two premises that would result in our hypothesis. In our example the two premises could be: (1) heterogeneous teams communicate less and (2) less communication leads to more conflict. Each premise contains one of the variables represented in our hypothesis and both premises contain the missing link 'less communication'.

Exhibit 1.10 Hypothesis and theory explained through deduction.

	Example
Premise 1	People prefer to communicate with similar people, therefore heterogeneous teams communicate less.
Premise 2	Less communication increases the chance for team conflict.
Hypotheses	Team heterogeneity has a positive effect on team conflict.

In the example above, one could question whether heterogeneous teams do indeed communicate less. If that would not be the case, premise 1 would be wrong and consequently the hypothesis would not hold. Actually, premise 1 could also be a hypothesis 'the more heterogeneous a team is, the less it will communicate', the two premises would be 'heterogeneous teams consist of less similar people' and 'people prefer to communicate with similar people'. The theory link here is similar people and the preference of people for people who are similar to them, and is known as homophily theory;[22] it can be summarized by the proverb *birds of a feather flock together*. Homophily theory has a much broader application range than explaining team heterogeneity and conflict. The same theory can be used to explain why personnel managers prefer applicants that graduated at the same university as them.

Theory and research

It is important for researchers to recognize the pervasiveness and value of theory. Theory serves us in many useful ways. It:

- narrows the range of facts we need to study
- suggests which research approaches are likely to yield the greatest meaning
- suggests a system for the researcher to impose on data in order to classify them in the most meaningful way
- summarizes what is known about an object of study, and states the uniformities that lie beyond immediate observation
- can be used to predict any further facts that may be found.

Models

The term **model** is used in various fields of business and allied disciplines with little agreement as to its definition. This may be because of the numerous functions, structures and types of model that exist. Most definitions agree, however, that models represent phenomena through the use of analogy. A model may be defined for our purposes as the representation of a system that is constructed to study some aspect of that system or the system as a whole.

Models differ from theories in that a theory's role is explanation, whereas a model's role is representation:

> "A model is not an explanation; it is only the structure and/or function of a second object or process. A model is the result of taking the structure or function of one object or process and using that as a model for the second. When the substance, either physical or conceptual, of the second object or process has been projected onto the first, a model has been constructed."[23]

Many ideas about new product adoption, for example, can be traced to rural sociology models. These describe how information and innovations spread throughout communities or cultures, starting with opinion leaders. The behaviour of a respected leader is subsequently embraced by society as a whole to express homage to that leader and retain social acceptance.

Models may be used for applied or highly theoretical purposes. Almost everyone is familiar with queuing models of service: banks, post offices, telephone voice-response units and airport security units 'feed' patrons from a single queue to multiple service points. Other models, for assembly lines, transportation and inventory, also attempt to solve immediate practical needs. A model to advance a theory of quality of working life, for example, could target employee behaviour under conditions of flexitime, permanent part-time, job-sharing and compressed working week.

Description, explication and simulation are the three major functions of modelling. Each of these functions is appropriate to applied research or theory building:

- Descriptive models: describe the behaviour of elements in a system where theory is inadequate or non-existent.
- Explicative models: extend the application of well-developed theories or improve our understanding of their key concepts.
- Simulation models: clarify the structural relationships of concepts and attempt to reveal the process relationships among them.[24]

The latter can be:

- static (i.e. represent a system at one point in time)
- dynamic (i.e. represent the evolution of a system over time).

Monte Carlo simulation models are examples of static simulations. They simulate probabilistic processes using random numbers. Redistribution of market share, brand switching and prediction of future values are just some examples of areas that can benefit from dynamic modelling.

Running Case Study 1

Two student projects

In the running case study, we follow the struggles of two students, Mehmet Celik and Rebecca Nash, who are conducting their final research projects ('dissertations' as they are referred to in the UK, or final 'theses' as they are referred to in other European countries). In each chapter you will find out why this specific chapter is valuable for Mehmet and Rebecca and track their progress. You will also be asked to consider how the relevant methods and issues discussed affect their projects. As you will see, both conduct very different research projects, not only regarding the topic they investigate, but especially regarding the methods they employ. Therefore, some chapters will be more useful for Mehmet, others more useful for Rebecca, but most will be useful for both. This reflects the general attitude of this book towards research methods; namely, that there are no good or better methods. There is certainly good and better research, but not because of the methods used but because of how well they are applied.

Mehmet Celik, a future migrant entrepreneur?

Mehmet Celik is the third child out of four and his grandparents migrated from Turkey in the 1960s. His father Ahmed was the first in his family to complete a high school education, but never attended a university. Rather he became self-employed with a taxi company specializing in shuttle buses to nearby airports. He quickly diversified his business, expanding it to a travel agency that did not only offer local transport to the airport, but also specialized in selling cheap flights to Turkey. Around the same time, Turkey developed into a popular tourist destination and Ahmed Celik started to offer holiday packages not only to his Turkish fellows, but increasingly also to natives. Today, Dolphin Travel is the largest travel agency in its region, employing 52 people in eight travel shops, of which only four are located in neighbourhoods with a high concentration of migrants. In short, Ahmed Celik and his family are a model case of successful integration.

Ahmed's son Mehmet is the second in his family with a university degree, next to his sister Cecik who has just completed her Masters in fashion design. The one thing that Mehmet needs to get his degree in business is to write his final research project. He does not know what to do thereafter. He could step into his father's business but does not like that idea because, like his father, he does not like to work for others. He is thinking about starting his own business maybe just because he wants to show his father that he can do it as well, but he has also attended career weeks at his university that provided him with job opportunities at various companies. Perhaps he will become a consultant and later on found his own consultancy firm to become the McKinsey of the twenty-first century. Nevertheless, currently his main interest is entrepreneurship and more specifically he wants to write about Turkish entrepreneurs. Yesterday he emailed Dr Flowermountain to ask whether he would be willing to supervise his final research project entitled 'Success determinants of Turkish entrepreneurs'. Dr Flowermountain replied stating that Mehmet needed to focus on the topic and to be more explicit on what he would like to research, as there are millions of success determinants on which he could focus. He asked him to write one or two pages and to think about more specific questions that interested him. Moreover, Mehmet had to develop some ideas about how he would research the topic and he needed to come up with a list of articles that he had already read about it. After Mehmet had done that, they would have a meeting. Mehmet had hoped for an immediate meeting, but he realized that only a general idea for the topic of his research project was not sufficient. He had to prepare more.

What should he do? He talked to his sister Cecik. She suggested that he wrote a case study on Dolphin Travel to find out why their father has been so successful, as many other Turkish entrepreneurs could learn from his experiences. Mehmet was reluctant to do this as he had the feeling it would be too much of a descriptive study and, moreover, he was sceptical about whether what made his father successful 20 years ago would still be valuable today. Then Cecik told him about her plans to start a fashion office and asked him whether they could combine their businesses. Mehmet could help her with the start-up and use that as a case for his research project. But Mehmet was again sceptical, as this sounded like writing a business plan rather than a research project.

Mehmet started thinking about what was interesting about Turkish entrepreneurs. The success of his father was more an exception than the rule; other self-employed relatives and friends operated small businesses mostly in migrant neighbourhoods, employing family members and serving mainly Turkish migrants. In Mehmet's eyes his father was much more successful, but wasn't his uncle Ender, who runs a small grocery shop, as happy as, or maybe even happier than, his father?

Mehmet had a lot of questions but no answers. Who was he to judge who has been successful and what are the criteria for success? Shouldn't he leave this judgement to the individual? But would people be honest if he asked them about their success? Mehmet had reached a point where he felt lost. On the one hand business success can mean different things to different people but, on the other hand, €20,000 profit remains €20,000 profit.

Rebecca Nash's sense of justice

Rebecca Nash is the only daughter of a clergyman and a primary school teacher. She has always been a good student, but never a swot, at least in her own perception. At school she loved maths and numbers; she also learned to play the violin and she even won an essay competition in a local newspaper. Before she enrolled at university, she went to Israel for six months and worked in a kibbutz, an experience she found much more inspiring and valuable than her last years at school.

Once at university Rebecca continued to get good marks in her courses, even in those considered hard by fellow students. And she liked to go to classes, to read the recommended books, articles and beyond. In short, she loved to be a student. There was only one thing she got angry about and that was free-riding and cheating. Just three months ago she saw it with her own eyes. During her exam on corporate finance, the student in front of her opened his ballpoint pen and took a small piece of paper out of it. She did not want to tell on him, but she was angry, especially since she knew him well. In another course, she was in the same group as that same student and they had to write a paper as a group assignment. In the end she and another friend wrote the paper as he never kept his promises.

Maybe Rebecca had this sense of justice because her father was a clergyman but she was really angry about all that cheating and she wanted to find out more about it in her final research project. Who was more likely to cheat? Did it depend more on opportunity or did it depend on the individual's personality? How would others react; did they have better strategies to deal with free-riders in a group? Later on she discussed a research plan with her friend Tom. He reckoned that the main reason for cheating was the laissez-faire attitude of lecturers. They simply did not care. If they enforced harder sanctions, nobody would cheat or free-ride. He suggested expelling students for one year at the first attempt, and permanently if it happened again. But Rebecca was rather unsure whether harder sanctions would really help.

The more Rebecca thought about her subject, the more facets of the problem arose. It seemed that so many intertwined factors had to be considered and that it would take years to investigate all these different factors. When she later met with her project supervisor, Monica Yardman, she was told to focus on just a small set of questions. For example, she could write about how different rules and sanctions affect unethical conduct by comparing different universities or she could have a look at how students react to other students' free-riding behaviour, but she could not investigate both or even think about a third alternative.

Monica Yardman told her that it was up to her to find the right question. What was most important was that she was really interested in the question and topic. Writing a research project is a process with ups and downs. At the beginning most students are enthusiastic, but there is always a point where the process gets stuck and you get disappointed. In such moments, you should at least like the topic otherwise it can get very difficult.

1 What type of study are Mehmet and Rebecca thinking about right now?
2 Looking at this chapter's running case study, try to relate the arguments and considerations made in the case study to different research philosophies. Thus, which of Mehmet's and Rebecca's thoughts sound more positivistic and which sound more constructivistic?
3 Identify and discuss the concepts Mehmet and Rebecca will address in their research.
4 Is it already possible to distinguish between the dependent and independent variables in Mehmet's and Rebecca's research plans?

Summary

1 Research is any organized inquiry that is carried out in order to provide information that can be used to solve problems. Business research is a systematic inquiry that provides information to guide business decisions. This includes reporting, descriptive, explanatory and predictive studies. This book emphasizes the last three.

2 What characterizes good research? Generally, we expect good research to be purposeful, with a clearly defined focus and plausible goals, with defensible, ethical and replicable procedures, and with evidence of objectivity. The reporting of procedures – their strengths and weaknesses – should be complete and honest. Appropriate analytical techniques should be used; conclusions drawn should be limited to those clearly justified by the findings; and reports of findings and conclusions should be presented clearly and be professional in tone, language and appearance. Managers should always choose a researcher who

has an established reputation for good-quality work. The research objective and its benefits should be weighed against any potentially adverse effects.

3   Research in management and business is rooted in different research philosophies. The most prominent ones are positivism and interpretivism. Positivism is the research philosophy adopted from the natural sciences. Its proponents believe that the social world exists externally and can be viewed objectively. Hence, a real truth exists and it can best be understood by reducing it to the simplest possible elements. Moreover, they claim that research is value-free and that researchers should take an independent role as objective analysts. Interpretivism supposes that the social world is constructed and people give subjective meaning to it. Hence, the social world is an individual construction and, to understand it, the researcher needs to look at a total picture. Unlike positivists, interpretivists believe that research is driven by interests and that the researcher is part of what is observed.

4   The demand for information tomorrow will be much greater than it is today. Research will make a major contribution to providing this knowledge. The knowledge of research methods will be of value in many situations for managers, public policy-makers and scientific researchers. They may need to conduct research either for themselves or for others. As users and readers of research results they will need to be able to judge research quality. Finally, they may become research specialists themselves.

5   Styles of thinking are perspectives, or filters, for determining how we view and understand reality. They affect what we accept as truth and govern how rigorously we test the information we receive before endorsing it. Although the scientific method is the pre-eminent means by which we secure empirical information, it is not the only source of truth. Other styles of thinking also have an apparent, and often useful, influence on business disciplines, and give their approval to the theory-building and problem-solving approaches of those fields.

Scientific inquiry is grounded in the inference process. This process is used for the development and testing of various propositions, largely through the so-called 'double movement of reflective thinking'. Reflective thinking involves sequencing induction and deduction in order to explain inductively (by hypothesis) a puzzling condition/dilemma. In turn, the hypothesis is used in the deduction of further facts that can be sought to confirm or deny the truth of the hypothesis.

Researchers think of 'doing science' as an orderly process that combines induction, deduction, observation and hypothesis testing into a set of reflective thinking activities. Although the scientific method consists of neither sequential nor independent stages, the problem-solving process it reveals provides insight into the way that research is conducted.

6   Scientific methods and scientific thinking are based on concepts – the symbols that we attach to bundles of meaning that we hold and share with others. We invent concepts to help us to think about and communicate abstractions. We also use higher-level concepts – constructs – for specialized scientific explanatory purposes that are not directly observable. Concepts, constructs and variables may be defined descriptively or operationally. Operational definitions, which are essential in research, must specify adequately the empirical information needed and state how it will be collected. In addition, they must have the proper scope or 'fit' for the research problem at hand.

Concepts and constructs are used at the theoretical level; variables are used at the empirical level. Variables can be allocated numerals or values for the purpose of testing and measurement. They may be classified as explanatory (independent, dependent or moderating), extraneous or intervening.

7   Propositions are of great interest in research because they may be used to assess the truth or falsity of relationships among observable phenomena. When we advance a proposition for testing, we are hypothesizing. A hypothesis describes the relationships between or among variables. A good hypothesis is one that can explain what it claims to explain, is testable, and has greater range, probability and simplicity than its rivals.

Sets of interrelated concepts, definitions and propositions that are advanced to explain and predict phenomena are called theories. Models differ from theories in that models are analogies or representations of some aspect of a system or of the system as a whole. Models are used for description, explication and simulation.

Discussion questions

Terms in review

1 What is research? Why should there be any question about the definition of research?

2 What is the difference between applied and basic or pure research? Use a decision about how a salesperson is to be paid, by commission or salary, and describe the question that would guide applied research versus the question that would guide pure research.

3 Distinguish among the following sets of items, and suggest the significance of each in a research context.
   a   concept and construct
   b   deduction and induction
   c   operational definition and dictionary definition
   d   concept and variable
   e   hypothesis and proposition
   f   theory and model
   g   scientific method and scientific attitude

4 Describe the basic principles and assumptions of positivism and interpretivism.

5 Describe the characteristics of the scientific method.

6 Listed below are some terms commonly found in a management setting. Are they concepts or constructs? Give two different operational definitions for each.
   a   first-line supervisor
   b   employee morale
   c   assembly line
   d   overdue account
   e   line management
   f   leadership
   g   price–earnings ratio
   h   union democracy
   i   ethical standards

7 In your company's management development programme there was a heated discussion between some people who claimed that 'Theory is impractical and thus no good' and others who claimed that 'Good theory is the most practical approach to problems'. What position would you take and why?

8 An automobile manufacturer observes demand for its brand increasing as per capita income increases. Sales increases also follow low interest rates, which ease credit conditions. Buyer purchase behaviour is seen to be dependent on age and gender. Other factors influencing sales appear to fluctuate almost randomly (e.g. competitor advertising, competitor dealer discounts, introduction of new competitive models).
   a   If sales and per capita income are positively related, classify all variables as dependent, independent, moderating, extraneous or intervening.
   b   Comment on the utility of a model based on the hypothesis.

Making research decisions

9 A human resources manager needs information in order to help him or her decide whether to create a 'custom-built' motivation programme or purchase one offered by a human resources consulting firm. What are the dilemmas the manager faces in selecting either alternative?

10 You are manager of the European division of a major corporation, supervising five animal feed plants scattered over four counties. Corporate headquarters asks you to conduct an investigation to determine whether any of these plants should be closed, expanded, moved or downsized. Is there a possible conflict between your roles as researcher and manager? Explain.

11 Advise each of the following people on a specific research study that he or she might find useful. Classify each proposed study as reporting, descriptive, explanatory or predictive.
  a When the management decision problem is known:
    i   manager of a full-service restaurant with high employee turnover
    ii head of an academic department committee charged with selecting a research methods textbook.
  b When the management decision problem has not yet been specified:
    i   manager of a restaurant
    ii   plant manager at a shoe factory
    iii director of the TV programme *Who Wants To Be A Millionaire?* in charge of sponsor recruitment
    iv data analyst with ACNielsen (research specialist)
    v   human resources manager at a university
    vi product manager for the Mercedes A Class
    vii family services officer for your county
    viii office manager for a paediatrician.

12 The new president of an old, established company is facing a problem. The company is currently unprofitable and is, in the president's opinion, operating inefficiently. The company sells a wide range of equipment and supplies to the dairy industry. It manufactures some items and sells many wholesale to dairies, creameries and similar plants. Because the industry is changing in several ways, survival will become more difficult in the future. In particular, many equipment companies are bypassing wholesalers and selling direct to dairies. In addition, many independent dairies are being taken over by large food chains. How might research help the new president make the right decisions? In answering this question, consider the areas of marketing and finance as well as the company as a whole.

13 You have received the results of a research report carried out by a consultant on behalf of your firm, a life insurance company. The study is a survey of morale in the home office and covers the opinions of about 500 secretaries and clerks, as well as about 100 executives and actuaries. You are asked to comment on its quality. What will you look for?

14 As area sales manager for a company that manufactures and markets outboard engines, you have been assigned the responsibility of conducting a research study to estimate the sales potential of your products in the Scandinavian market. Discuss the key issues and concerns arising from the fact that you, the manager, are also the researcher.

15 You observe the following condition: 'Our female sales representatives have lower customer defections than do our male sales representatives.'
  a Propose the concepts and constructs you might use to study this phenomenon.
  b How might any of these concepts and/or constructs be related to explanatory hypotheses?

16 You are the office manager of a large firm that prides itself on its high-quality customer service. Lately, complaints have surfaced which reveal that an increasing number of incoming calls are being misrouted or dropped. Yesterday, when passing the main reception area, you noticed the receptionist fiddling with his hearing aid. In the process, a call came in and would have gone unanswered if not for your intervention. This particular receptionist had earned an unsatisfactory review three months earlier for tardiness. Your inclination is to urge this employee – who has been with the firm for 20 years – to retire, or to fire him if retirement is rejected. However, you know the individual is well liked and seen as a fixture in the company.
  a Suggest several hypotheses that might account for dropped or misrouted incoming calls.
  b Using the 'double movement of reflective thought', show how you would test these hypotheses.

From concept to practice

17 Apply the principles in Exhibit 1.1 to the research scenario in question 8.

18 Using Exhibits 1.5 and 1.6 as a guide, draw up graphs to illustrate the inductions and deductions in the following statements. (If there are gaps, supply what is needed to make them complete arguments.)
  a Repeated studies indicate that economic conditions vary with – and lag 6–12 months behind – the changes in the national money supply; therefore, we may conclude that money supply is the basic economic variable.

    b Research studies show that heavy smokers have a higher rate of lung cancer than do non-smokers; therefore, heavy smoking causes lung cancer.

    c Show me a person who goes to church regularly, and I will show you a reliable worker.

Class discussion

19 Suppose you are part of an international team of social experts asked to assess the organizational culture within a large life insurance company. All class members born in the months January–June should follow the positivistic research philosophy, while those class members born in the months July–December should take the interpretivism route. Discuss how the organizational culture of the company could be assessed.

20 Business decisions are often taken under immense time pressure. Often, there is just not enough time to collect information based on good research. Discuss which criteria of good research you would compromise on if you just did not have enough time; or would it be better to abandon the research altogether, if it cannot be conducted well, as the obtained information is likely to be invalid and unreliable?

Recommended further reading

Beardsley, Monroe, *Practical Logic*. Englewood Cliffs, NJ: Prentice Hall, 1969. A lucid discussion of deduction and induction, as well as excellent coverage of argument analysis.

Browne, M. Neil and Keeley, Stuart M., *Asking the Right Questions: A Guide to Critical Thinking* (7th edn). Upper Saddle River, NJ: Prentice Hall, 2003. Addresses question-asking skills and the techniques necessary for evaluating different types of evidence.

Bryman, Allan and Bell, Emma, *Business Research Methods*. Oxford: Oxford University Press, 2003. Chapter 1 offers a fine philosophical-based introduction to research methods.

Churchman, C.W., *The Design of Inquiring Systems*. New York: Basic Books, 1971. An essential work for understanding the connections between philosophy, science and the nature of inquiry.

Haas, Peter J. and Springer, J. Fred, *Applied Policy Research: Concepts and Cases*. New York: Garland Reference Library of Social Science, No. 1051, 1998. Chapter 2 discusses policy research strategies and contributions.

Hoover, Kenneth R. and Donovan, Todd, *The Elements of Social Scientific Thinking* (6th edn). New York: Worth Publishers, 1994. A brief but highly readable treatise on the elements of science and scientific thinking.

Kaplan, Abraham, *The Conduct of Inquiry*. San Francisco, CA: Transaction Publications, 1998. A good source of information on the philosophy of science and logical reasoning.

Kerlinger, Fred N. and Lee, Howard B., *Foundations of Behavioral Research* (4th edn). New York: HBJ College & School Division, 1999. Especially Part 1: 'Introduction to Business Research'.

Medema, Steven G. and Samuels, Warren J. (eds), *Foundations of Research in Economics: How do Economists do Economics?* Cheltenham: Edward Elgar, 1997. This edited volume offers insights from outstanding economists on how to conduct economic research. Although it focuses on economics, the insights provided are also useful for other social sciences.

Random, Matthew, *The Social Scientist in American Industry*. New Brunswick, NJ: Rutgers University Press, 1970. A research report detailing the experiences of social scientists employed in industry. Chapter 7 presents a summary of findings.

Remenyi, Dan *et al.*, *Doing Research in Business and Management: An Introduction to Process and Method*. Thousand Oaks, CA: Sage, 1998. Chapters 1 and 2 establish the business research perspective for management students.

Transfield, D. and Starkey, K., 'The nature, social organization and promotion of management research: towards policy', *British Management Journal* 9, 1998, pp. 341–53. An article emphasizing the application side of management research and the significance of cross-fertilization between science and business practice.

Get started with understanding statistical techniques!

When you have read this chapter, log on to the Online Learning Centre website at *www.mcgraw-hill.co.uk/textbooks/blumberg* to explore chapter-by-chapter test questions, additional case studies, a glossary and more online study tools for *Business Research Methods*.

Notes

1 See, for example, Murray Levine, 'Investigative reporting as a research method: analysis of Bernstein and Woodward's 'All the President's Men', *American Psychologist* 35 (1980), pp. 626–38.

2 See, for example, Elizabethann O'Sullivan and Gary R. Rassel, *Research Methods for Public Administrators*. New York: Longman, 1999.

3 Fred N. Kerlinger and Howard B. Lee, *Foundations of Behavioral Research* (4th edn). New York: HBJ College & School Division, 1999, p. 15.

4 A hypothesis is a statement that is advanced for the purpose of testing its truth or falsity.

5 An exploratory study describes an investigation when the final research problem has not yet been clearly fixed. Its aim is to provide the insights needed by the researcher to develop a more formal research design.

6 Reprinted with the permission of Macmillan Publishing Co., Inc. from Robert Dubin, *Theory Building* (rev. edn, 1978). Copyright © 1969, Free Press, a division of Macmillan Co.

7 Mark Easterby-Smith, Richard Thrope and Andy Lowe, *Management Research: An Introduction*. London: Sage, 1991, p. 20.

8 Auguste Comte, *The Positive Philosophy of Auguste Comte*. London: Trubner & Co., 1853.

9 Jürgen Habermas, 'Knowledge and interest', in D. Emmet and A. MacIntyre (eds), *Sociological Theory and Philosophical Analysis*. London: Macmillan, 1970.

10 Howard Kahane, *Logic and Philosophy* (2nd edn). Belmont, CA: Wadsworth, 1973, p. 3.

11 John Dewey, *How We Think*. Boston, MA: Heath, 1910, p. 79.

12 This section is based on Dewey, *How We Think*, and John R. Platt, 'Strong inference', *Science*, 16 October 1964, pp. 347–53.

13 F.J. Roethlisberger and W.J. Dickson, *Management and the Worker*. Cambridge, MA: Harvard University Press, 1939.

14 Paul R. Lawrence, 'Historical development of organizational behaviour', in Jay W. Lorsch (ed.), *Handbook of Organizational Behaviour*. Englewood Cliffs, NJ: Prentice Hall, 1987, p. 6.

15 Thomas S. Kuhn, *The Structure of Scientific Revolutions*. Chicago, IL: University of Chicago Press, 1970, p. 37.

16 Kenneth R. Hoover, *The Elements of Social Scientific Thinking* (5th edn). New York: St. Martin's Press, 1991, p. 21.

17 *Merriam-Webster's Collegiate Dictionary* (10th edn). Springfield, MA: Merriam-Webster, 1999, www.m-w.com/cgi-bin/dictionary.

18 Fred N. Kerlinger and Howard B. Lee, *Foundations of Behavioral Research* (4th edn). New York: HBJ College & School Division, 1999.

19 Hoover, *Elements of Social Scientific Thinking*, p. 71.

20 Bruce Tuckman, *Conducting Educational Research*. New York: Harcourt Brace Jovanovich, 1972, p. 45.

21 William N. Stephens, *Hypotheses and Evidence*. New York: Thomas Y. Crowell, 1968, p. 5.

22 M. McPherson, L. Smith-Lovin, and J.M. Cook. 'Birds of a Feather: Homophily in Social Networks'. *Annual Review of Sociology* 27 (2001), pp. 415–444.

23 Leonard C. Hawes, *Pragmatics of Analoguing: Theory and Model Construction in Communication*. Reading, MA: Addison-Wesley, 1975, p. 111.

24 Hawes, *Pragmatics of Analoguing*, pp. 116–22.

CHAPTER 2

The research process and proposal

Chapter contents

Learning objectives

When you have read this chapter, you should understand:

1 that research is decision- and dilemma-centred

2 that the research question results from careful exploration and analysis, and sets the direction for the research project

3 that planning research design demands an understanding of all stages of the research process

4 the purpose of the proposal, and how it is used

5 the two processes available for evaluating the quality of proposals, and when each is used.

2.1   The research process

The research task is usually described as a sequential process that involves several clearly defined steps. However, it does not necessarily require that each step is completed before going on to the next one: a certain amount of recycling, circumventing and skipping of steps is likely to occur often. Sometimes steps are taken out of sequence, two or more may be carried out at the same time, and some may be omitted altogether. Especially in qualitative studies the steps outlined are often taken simultaneously in a recycling pattern. Despite these real-life variations, the idea of a basic sequence is useful in developing a project and in keeping things orderly as it unfolds.

Exhibit 2.1 illustrates the sequence of the **research process**. You will be referred back to this exhibit often as we discuss each step on the subsequent pages. Our discussion of the questions that guide project planning and data-gathering is incorporated into the model (look at the elements within the down-pointing triangle in Exhibit 2.1 and compare them with what is shown in Exhibit 2.2). Exhibit 2.1 also depicts the structure of this chapter in the upper part and introduces the remainder of the book in the bottom part.

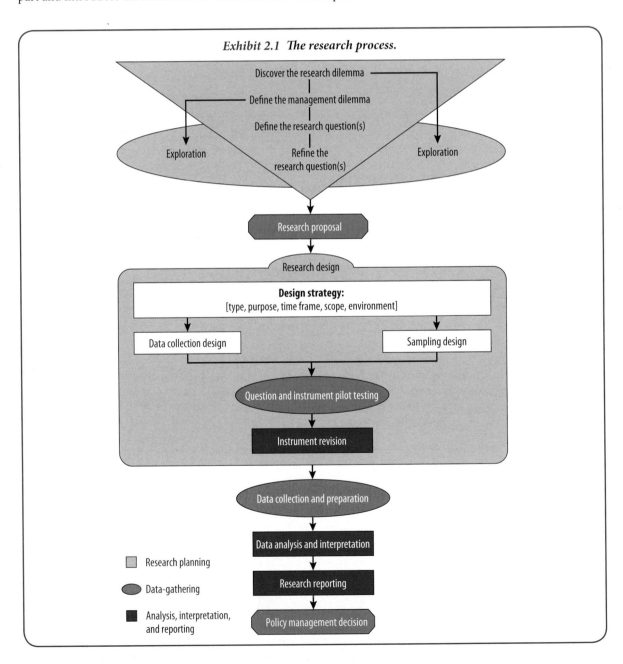

Exhibit 2.1 The research process.

The research process usually begins as follows. A **management/ research dilemma** triggers the need for investigating how the dilemma can be solved (as discussed in the previous chapter). A management dilemma refers to a current problem, such as growing number of customer complaints, poor results after an advertising campaign or increasing turnover of personnel are all examples of outcomes which signal that all is not well in a business. In other situations, a controversy might arise, a major commitment of resources is called for, or conditions in the environment might signal the need for a

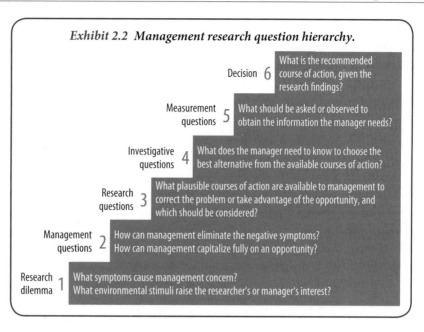

Exhibit 2.2 Management research question hierarchy.

Decision 6 — What is the recommended course of action, given the research findings?

Measurement questions 5 — What should be asked or observed to obtain the information the manager needs?

Investigative questions 4 — What does the manager need to know to choose the best alternative from the available courses of action?

Research questions 3 — What plausible courses of action are available to management to correct the problem or take advantage of the opportunity, and which should be considered?

Management questions 2 — How can management eliminate the negative symptoms? How can management capitalize fully on an opportunity?

Research dilemma 1 — What symptoms cause management concern? What environmental stimuli raise the researcher's or manager's interest?

decision. A research dilemma arises if observations made in the real world contradict common theoretical predictions. For example, how can one explain that in an industry that is characterized by a strong concentration in the number of firms, new small firms suddenly emerge and the former concentration trend is reversed.

Such events cause managers to reconsider their purpose or objectives, and researchers to question existing theories, define a problem that requires solution or develop strategies for solutions they have already identified.

For our purposes, the research question – its origin, selection, statement, exploration and refinement – is the critical activity in the research process sequence. Throughout this chapter we emphasize the problem-related steps. A well-known quote from Albert Einstein, which is no less apt today, supports this view:

"The formulation of a problem is far more often essential than its solution, which may be merely a matter of mathematical or experimental skill. To raise new questions, new possibilities, to regard old problems from a new angle requires creative imagination and marks real advance in science."[1]

Whether the researcher is involved in academic or business research, a thorough understanding of the management/ research dilemma is fundamental to success in the research enterprise. In business research the emphasis is on providing solutions to current management problems by using scientific knowledge and methods. Academic research should address questions relevant to management and business but also contribute to the academic field by adding to the base of scientific knowledge. A consequence is that business research often focuses on providing a solution for one company, while academic research has a broader scope and results should enhance our understanding of the business world in more general terms.

Academic teamwork

Although research projects are often solo projects, the majority of academic articles in business and management research are currently written by teams. Moreover, group assignments in which students need to work together on a course paper have also become common practice in most universities. While teams in companies usually have an assigned team leader, student teams as well as author teams often do not have a formal leader. As a consequence team projects often lose momentum, as no one feels responsible to manage the team process. In teams writing academic articles, team members often have the implicit assumption that the first author has the main responsibility for the project and therefore should manage the process. The first author gets most of the fame, especially regarding articles with three and more authors, because citations to those articles usually only mention the first author. However, the first author does not need to be the person with the best management capabilities. Thus, the order of the authors is not the most effective criteria to assign the team coordinator function. Some people are simply better than others in managing a team and if you have a talented team manager on board you should ask them to take over that role. This also holds for student teams and it is advisable that you talk right at the beginning about who is taking the coordinator role.

The second important issue in teamwork is the division of tasks. Division of labour in research is not as easy as in Adam Smith's pin factory, as deep intellectual discussions with colleagues are an essential part of academic work. A common task division is that one writes the theory, while the other conducts the analyses. You should be aware that despite that division the interdependencies between the researchers are large and that no one can completely specialize. Taking the example from the theorist and analyst, the former still needs to understand what the analyst does; the theorist as well needs to be able to interpret the results. Likewise, the analyst needs to understand the theoretical fundaments of the article, as otherwise they cannot make the right analysis decisions. Thus, academic teamwork knows some specialization, but there needs to be sufficient overlap between the knowledge of the team members.

2.2 Management research and measurement questions

A useful way to approach the research process is to state the basic dilemma that prompts the research and then try to develop other questions. This is done by progressively breaking down the original question into other more specific questions. Think of the outcome of this process as the **management research question hierarchy**. Exhibit 2.2 offers examples of the kinds of question asked at each level of the hierarchy, while Exhibit 2.3 further explains the

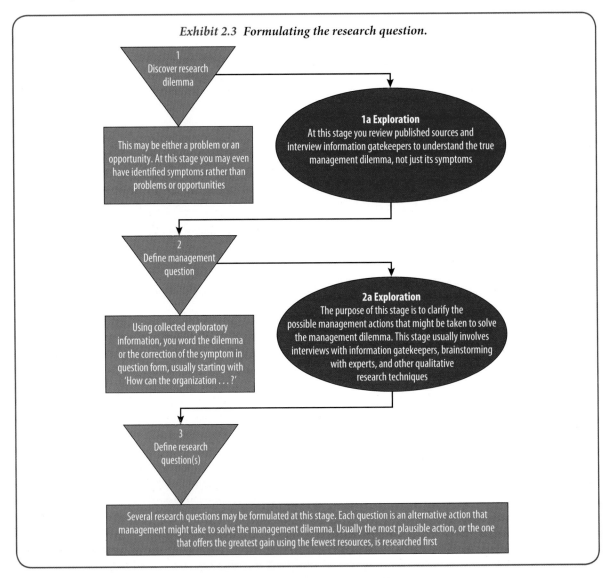

Exhibit 2.3 Formulating the research question.

1
Discover research dilemma

This may be either a problem or an opportunity. At this stage you may even have identified symptoms rather than problems or opportunities

1a Exploration
At this stage you review published sources and interview information gatekeepers to understand the true management dilemma, not just its symptoms

2
Define management question

Using collected exploratory information, you word the dilemma or the correction of the symptom in question form, usually starting with 'How can the organization . . . ?'

2a Exploration
The purpose of this stage is to clarify the possible management actions that might be taken to solve the management dilemma. This stage usually involves interviews with information gatekeepers, brainstorming with experts, and other qualitative research techniques

3
Define research question(s)

Several research questions may be formulated at this stage. Each question is an alternative action that management might take to solve the management dilemma. Usually the most plausible action, or the one that offers the greatest gain using the fewest resources, is researched first

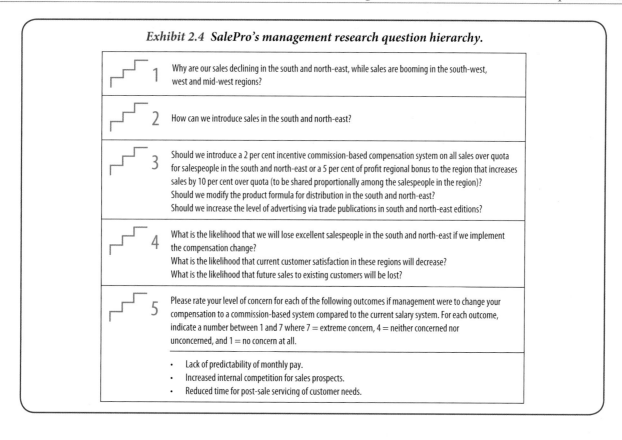

Exhibit 2.4 SalePro's management research question hierarchy.

1 Why are our sales declining in the south and north-east, while sales are booming in the south-west, west and mid-west regions?

2 How can we introduce sales in the south and north-east?

3 Should we introduce a 2 per cent incentive commission-based compensation system on all sales over quota for salespeople in the south and north-east or a 5 per cent of profit regional bonus to the region that increases sales by 10 per cent over quota (to be shared proportionally among the salespeople in the region)?
Should we modify the product formula for distribution in the south and north-east?
Should we increase the level of advertising via trade publications in south and north-east editions?

4 What is the likelihood that we will lose excellent salespeople in the south and north-east if we implement the compensation change?
What is the likelihood that current customer satisfaction in these regions will decrease?
What is the likelihood that future sales to existing customers will be lost?

5 Please rate your level of concern for each of the following outcomes if management were to change your compensation to a commission-based system compared to the current salary system. For each outcome, indicate a number between 1 and 7 where 7 = extreme concern, 4 = neither concerned nor unconcerned, and 1 = no concern at all.

- Lack of predictability of monthly pay.
- Increased internal competition for sales prospects.
- Reduced time for post-sale servicing of customer needs.

question formulation process in management terms, and Exhibit 2.4 provides example questions at each stage for SalePro, a national sales organization that is facing unexplained sales variations by territory.

Management/research dilemma

The process begins at the most general level with a management dilemma, which is usually a symptom of an actual problem. The dilemma might be:

- rising costs
- the discovery of an expensive chemical compound that would increase the efficacy of a drug
- increasing numbers of tenants vacating an apartment complex
- declining sales
- increased employee turnover
- a larger number of product defects during the manufacturing process
- an increasing number of customer complaints about post-purchase service.

It is rarely difficult to identify management dilemmas (unless the organization in question fails to track its performance factors – like sales, profits, employee turnover, manufacturing output and defects, on-time deliveries, customer satisfaction, and so on). The difficulty may lie in choosing one dilemma on which to focus. Choosing incorrectly will direct valuable resources (time, manpower, money and equipment) on a path that may not provide the required decision-making information (which is, of course, the purpose of good research).

Making this choice is like learning to balance a pencil point-down on your finger, a coin on its edge or a pyramid on its pinnacle. Only practice will make the researcher/manager proficient.

In all exhibits related to the research process model, in this and subsequent chapters, a pyramid is used to represent the management research question hierarchy and to emphasize the precarious nature of the research process's foundation decisions.

Management question

You as a researcher must move from **management/research dilemma** to **management question** in order to proceed with the research process. The management question restates the dilemma in question form, as in the following examples:

- What should be done to reduce employee turnover?
- How should the firm enter foreign markets?
- What should be done to reduce costs?

Firms' managers ask for the investigation of such management questions as a response to a current problem. One example is a student's research project conducted in cooperation with a firm, such as on human resource management, internationalization strategies or productivity issues.

Research Methods in Real Life

Research and the valuation of ethics in the textile industry

On 24 April 2013, a textile factory building collapsed in Dhaka, the capital of Bangladesh, costing 1,127 textile workers their lives and leaving more than 2,500 workers injured. This was not the first incident. In September 2012 a garment factory and a shoe factory both in Pakistan caught fire. Those fatal industry disasters are just the tip of an iceberg, the hazardous working conditions in the textile and apparel factories throughout Southeast Asia are well known. People, especially woman, work with unsafe machinery in badly lit places long hours for low wages (€50 per month), which allows them to have a roof above their head and sufficient food but not more. Are the low wages and miserable labour conditions a new form of slavery or is it just a stage in the economic development of countries?

The mean annual income in Bangladesh is €650, thus just slightly higher than the wage income of the textile workers. Responding to internal and international pressure, the Bangladeshi government increased the minimum wage after the factory collapse. Which role do retailers, like H&M, Inditex (Zara and Mango), Gap and Wal-Mart play? In their first reaction the response of these multinationals was split. While some announced they would minimize the ties to suppliers that operated facilities in the collapsed building, others promised to help the families of the victims. Two weeks later H&M and Inditex signed a legally binding agreement for stricter fire and building safety. While GAP and Wal-Mart responded that they already had implanted stricter policies in 2012. European retailers called for global agreement to improve factory safety and working conditions that would include dispute resolutions with local trade unions. Wal-Mart, GAP and JC Penney are in favour of preventing fires, but involving trade unions is one step too far for them. That leaves PVH, producing the Hilfiger and Calvin Klein brand, the only US company joining this global initiative. Other companies like Disney solve the problem by delisting Bangladesh from their preferred source country list.

The tragedy in Dhaka raised many questions relevant for management. One important question is, 'Which standards of corporate social responsibility should we apply?' How could research help to find an answer to this question? The companies have shown different responses. What are the effects of these responses for the workers in Bangladesh, the consumers and the companies themselves? Which effects would one need to take into account?

References and further reading

http://www.nytimes.com/2013/05/01/world/asia/retailers-split-on-bangladesh-factory-collapse.html

http://www.businessweek.com/articles/2013-05-13/h-and-m-pledges-to-make-bangladeshi-factories-safer

http://www.businessweek.com/articles/2013-05-15/bangladesh-safety-accord-is-too-binding-for-american-retailers

Management question categories

Management questions are too numerous to list, but we can categorize them as follows:

- choice of purpose or objectives
- generation and evaluation of solutions
- troubleshooting or control situation.

The first type of question concerns the choice of purpose or objectives. The general question is, 'What do we want to achieve?' At company level the question might be, 'Should we at Metal-Works Corporation reconsider our basic corporate objectives as they concern our public image?' More narrowly, a management question on objectives might ask, 'What goals should MetalWorks Corporation try to achieve in its next round of labour negotiations?' In academic research, possible objectives are attempts to explain current inconsistencies within or between theoretical considerations, testing new theoretical ideas or giving a well-reasoned account, which is theoretically backed, of an observed phenomena.

A second category of management questions concerns the generation and evaluation of solutions. The general question is, 'How can we achieve the ends we seek?' Research projects in this group usually deal with concrete problems. Projects can involve questions such as the following:

- How can we achieve our five-year goal of doubled sales and net profits?
- How can we reduce employee turnover and increase the organizational commitment of our workers?
- What should be done to reduce post-purchase service complaints?
- How can we explain new firms' successful entrance into a mature and concentrated industry?
- How can we explain that the stock price of highly diversified firms is lower than the stock price of less diversified firms, even if we consider differences in returns?

A third class of management questions concerns the troubleshooting, or control, situation. The problem usually involves monitoring or diagnosing various ways in which an organization is failing to achieve its established goals. This class includes questions such as, 'Why does our department incur the highest costs?' and 'How well is our programme meeting its goals?'.

No matter how the management question is defined, research can take many directions. A specific question can, for example, give rise to many studies. So, concern for MetalWorks' company image might lead to:

- a survey among various groups to discover their attitude towards the company
- secondary research into what other companies are doing to enhance their image
- a study to forecast expected changes in social attitudes.

The question concerning MetalWorks' labour negotiation objectives might prompt research into recent settlements in the industry or a survey among workers to find out how well management has met its concerns about the quality of their working life. It is the joint responsibility of the researcher and the manager to choose the most productive project.

The nature of the management question

Assume that a researcher is asked to help the new management of a bank. The president is concerned about erosion of the bank's profitability (the management dilemma) and wants to turn this situation around. BankChoice is the oldest and largest of three banks in a region with a population of about 500,000. Profits have stagnated in recent years. The president and the researcher discuss the problem facing the organization and settle on this management question: 'How can we improve our profit picture?'

This question does not specify what kind of research is to be done. It is strictly managerial in thrust. It implies that the bank's management faces the task of developing a strategy for increasing profits. The question is broad. Notice that it doesn't indicate whether management should increase profits via encouraging a larger number of deposits, by downsizing personnel, outsourcing the payroll function, or by some other means.

Further discussion between the bank president and the researcher reveals that there are really two questions to be answered. The problem of low deposit growth is linked to concerns of a competitive nature. While lowered deposits directly affect profits, another part of the profit weakness is associated with negative factors within the organization that are increasing operation costs. The experienced researcher knows that the management question as stated is too broad to guide a definitive research project. Such a broadly worded question is fine as a starting point, but BankChoice will want to refine its management question into more specific sub-questions as follows:

- How can we increase the number of deposits?
- How can we reduce costs?

This separation of the management question into two sub-questions may not have occurred had there not been a discussion between the researcher and the manager.

BankChoice has done no formal research in the past. It has little specific information about competitors or customers, and has not analysed its internal operations. To move forward in the management research question hierarchy and define the research question, the client needs to collect some exploratory information on:

- what factors are contributing to the bank's failure to achieve a stronger growth rate in deposits
- how well the bank is doing in terms of work climate, efficiency of operations compared to industry norms, and financial condition compared to industry norms and competitors.

To do this, a small focus-group exercise is conducted among employees, and trade association data are acquired to facilitate a comparison of financial and operating statistics from company annual reports and end-of-year division reports. From the results of these two exploratory activities, it is obvious that BankChoice's operations are not as progressive as its competitors, but that it has its costs well in line. So the revised management question becomes: 'What should be done to make the bank more competitive?'

The area of **exploration** may surface within the research process in several locations (see Exhibit 2.3). An exploration typically begins with a search of published **data**. In addition, researchers often seek out people who are well informed on the topic in question, especially those who have clearly stated positions on controversial aspects of the problem.

Take the case of TechByte, a company interested in enhancing its position in a given technology that appears to have potential for future growth. This interest or need might quickly elicit a number of questions:

- How fast might this technology develop?
- What are the likely applications of this technology?
- Which companies now possess it, and which are likely to make a major effort to get it?
- How much will it take in resources?
- What are the likely payoffs?

In the above investigation of opportunities, researchers would probably start off by looking at specific books and periodicals. They would be looking only for certain aspects in this literature, such as recent developments, predictions by informed figures about the prospects of the technology, identification of those involved in the area, and accounts of successful ventures or failures by others in the field.

Having familiarized themselves with the literature, researchers might seek interviews with scientists, engineers and product developers who are well known in the field. They would pay special attention to those who represent the two extremes of opinion with regard to the prospects of the technology. If possible, they would talk with persons having information on particularly thorny problems in development and application. Although much of the information will be confidential and competitive, skilful investigation can uncover many useful indicators.

An unstructured exploration allows the researcher to develop and revise the management question and determine what is needed to secure answers to the proposed question.

Research questions

Once the researcher has a clear statement of the management question, she must work with the manager to translate it into a **research question**. This step is often a rather large one, especially if you conduct research sponsored by an organization, as practitioners formulate questions in terms of the problem to be solved and not in terms of the research it is necessary to conduct. Consider the research question to be a fact-oriented, information-gathering question. There are many different ways to address most management dilemmas. It is at this point in formulating research questions that the insight and expertise of the manager come into play. Only reasonable alternatives should be considered. If the researcher is not part of the manager's decision-making environment, then she may be of minimal help in this translation; the direction that the manager gives the researcher is most important. If, however, the researcher is an integral part of the decision-making environment, she may assist the manager in evaluating which courses of action should and can be researched.

Let us go back to our earlier example: MetalWorks Corporation. Currently, MetalWorks has lower productivity than comparable companies in the industry and it pays wages according to the latest contract between unions and the industry association, plus additional benefits related to tenure. A year ago MetalWorks closed an unprofitable plant in northern England. Recently, the media have published stories about disrupted relations between management and labour representatives resulting in a worrisome public image. The more specific management question reads, 'What should MetalWorks Corporation achieve in the next round of labour negotiations?' In a brainstorming session, MetalWorks' management hypothesized several problems that may have resulted in the lower productivity and the disturbed relations with workers. Some of these problems are not as easy to correct as others (e.g. demand for MetalWorks' products is only partly within the firm's immediate control – it is also determined by the current economic situation). If MetalWorks does not survey its employees about job satisfaction and their organizational commitment on a regular basis, an exploratory study might have to be undertaken to determine employees' major concerns.

Defining the research question incorrectly is a fundamental weakness in the research process. Time and money can be wasted studying an alternative that will not help the manager rectify the dilemma.

The researcher's task is to assist the manager in formulating a research question that fits the need to resolve the management dilemma. A research question is the hypothesis of choice that best states the objective of the research study. It is a more specific management question that must be answered. It may be just one question, or more than one. A research process that answers this more specific question will provide the manager with the information necessary to make the decision he or she is facing.

After consulting with a labour expert, MetalWorks' management identifies several credible options to be achieved in the labour negotiations:

- more flexible working hours, which will allow the company to adjust hours worked to suit current demand
- relate additional benefits for workers not to their length of tenure but to the company's profit
- establish 'round tables' of workers, management and local (labour) representatives in each plant to discuss current problems at the plant level
- start a public relations campaign to improve MetalWorks' image and secure more positive media coverage.

These choices lead to several research questions, as follows:

- What are the effects of different flexible working time systems on productivity?
- What are the effects of payment schemes for additional benefits on MetalWorks' profitability, and how should such schemes be designed?
- What are the effects of 'round tables' on MetalWorks' productivity?
- What are the effects of public relations campaigns on the perceived image of MetalWorks?

Meanwhile at BankChoice, the president has agreed that the research should be guided by the following research question: 'How does the image of BankChoice affect its number of customers and cost structure?'

Fine-tuning the research question

The term 'fine-tuning' might seem to be an odd usage for research, but it creates an image that most researchers come to recognize. Fine-tuning the question is precisely what a skilful practitioner must do once the initial exploration is complete. At this point, a clearer picture of the management and research questions begins to emerge. After a preliminary review of the literature, a brief exploratory study, or both, the project begins to crystallize in one of two ways:

1 It is apparent that the question has been answered and the process is finished
2 A different question from that originally addressed has become apparent.

The research question does not have to be materially different, but it will have evolved in some fashion. This is no cause for discouragement, however. The refined research question (or questions) will have a better focus and will help to move the research forward with more clarity than the initial question (or questions) that were formulated.

In addition to fine-tuning the original question, other research question-related activities should be addressed in this phase in order to enhance the progress of the project. These are as follows:

1 Examine the concepts and constructs to be used in the study. Are they defined satisfactorily? Have operational definitions been employed where appropriate?
2 Review the research questions with the intent of breaking them down into specific second- and third-level questions.
3 If hypotheses are used, ensure that they meet the quality criteria mentioned in the preceding chapter.
4 Determine what evidence must be collected to answer the various questions and hypotheses.
5 Set the scope of the study by stating what is *not* part of the research question. This will establish a boundary that will help to separate contiguous problems from the primary objective.

When the characteristics or plausible causes of the problem have been defined accurately and the research question clearly stated, it is possible to develop the essential sub-questions that will guide planning of the project at this stage of the research process. However, if the research question is at all poorly defined, the researcher will need further exploration and question revision to refine the original question and generate the material necessary to construct suitable investigative questions.

Student Research

Broken Santa Claus – learning from bad practice

Julia Becker, a student in the master programme 'management of learning', wrote a research project about complaint management. Previous research has shown that a bad response to a customer's complaint damages the relationship, while a good response even strengthens it. She got the idea for this research project during an internship for a medium-sized mail order company operating in Germany, the Netherlands and the UK. Most research on complaint management focuses on it as an element in the management of customer relations. But Julia's interest was different. During her internship, she often talked to the manager of the service division about how one could improve the company's complaint management. Out of these discussions it became obvious that reducing complaints is more efficient than handling them to the satisfaction of the customer.

An example illustrates this point. One of the company's very successful products is a 1 kg chocolate Santa Claus that sold like crazy. Soon after the first were sent out, the company faced a growing number of complaints, requests and returns addressed to different contact points within the company, as many Santa Clauses were broken upon arrival. Finally, the aggregated large amount of complaints was noticed by the service department who initiated tests to improve the wrapping of the Santa Claus. The wrapping was improved and subsequently was carefully kept track of. They had to change it two more times until it was so improved that almost every Santa Claus reached the customer in good shape. A few months later the same wrapping was used for the 1 kg chocolate Easter bunny.

Julia's discussion with the service department management resulted in the management question, 'How can complaint management reduce complaints?' The key to answering the question was how the information collected in the complaint management department finds its way back into the other departments and how these other departments use that information. In other words, how can the mail order company learn from customer complaints? These questions mark the research question.

The investigative questions were: What are the different customer contact points? What are large or repetitive service failures? How are customer problems resolved? How are solutions communicated to the customer? How are service failures classified? How are service failures and solutions integrated in internal databases and how are the databases used?

As Julia's research project was an in-depth case study based on unstructured interviews and document research, she did not develop a questionnaire, but rather relied on an interview guideline that ensured that the topics addressed in the investigative questions were covered.

Investigative questions

Once the research question(s) has been selected, the researcher's thinking needs to move to a more specific level – that of **investigative questions** (see Exhibit 2.4). These questions reveal the specific pieces of information that one needs to know in order to answer the research question. With this and the following step in the management question hierarchy, we enter also a different phase in the research design. In qualitative research those investigative questions are the core of your interview guide (see also Chapter 7), while in quantitative research they identify the concepts that need to be measured in the following step.

Investigative questions are questions that the researcher must answer to arrive at a satisfactory conclusion about the research question. To formulate them, the researcher takes a general research question and breaks it into more specific questions about which to gather data. This 'fractionating' process can continue down through several levels of increasing specificity. Investigative questions should be included in the research proposal because they guide the development of the research design – they are the foundation on which the research data-collection instrument is based.

The researcher working on the BankChoice project develops two major investigative questions for studying the market, with several sub-questions under each, as presented below. The questions provide insight into the lack of deposit growth:

1 What is the public's position regarding financial services and their use?
  a What specific financial services are used?
  b How attractive are various services?
  c What bank-specific and environmental factors influence a person's use of a particular service?
2 What is the bank's competitive position?
  a What are the geographic patterns of our customers and our competitors' customers?
  b What demographic differences are revealed among our customers and those of our competitors?
  c What words or phrases does the public (both customers and non-customers) associate with BankChoice? With BankChoice's competitors?
  d How aware is the public of the bank's promotional efforts?
  e What opinion does the public hold of the bank and its competitors?
  f How does growth in services compare among competing institutions?

Measurement questions

Measurement questions should be outlined by completion of the project-planning activities, but usually await pilot testing for refinement. There are two types of measurement question (see also Chapters 13 and 14):

1 pre-designed or pre-tested questions
2 custom-designed questions.

Pre-designed measurement questions are those that have been formulated and tested by previous researchers, are recorded in the literature, and may be applied literally or adapted to the project at hand. Some studies lend themselves to the use of these readily available measurement devices. This provides enhanced validity and can reduce the cost of the project. More often, however, the measurement questions need to be tailored to the investigative questions. The resources required for this task will be the collective insights from all the activities in the research process completed to this point, particularly insights arising from exploration. Later, during pilot testing of the data-collection instrument(s), these custom-designed questions will be refined.

Measurement questions constitute the fifth level of the hierarchy (see Exhibit 2.2). In surveys, measurement questions are the questions we actually ask the respondents. They appear on our questionnaire. In an observation study, measurement questions are the observations researchers must record about each subject studied.

BankChoice decides to conduct a survey of local residents. Its questionnaire contains many measurement questions, seeking information that will provide answers to the bank's investigative questions. A total of 200 residents complete questionnaires and the information collected is used to guide a reorientation of the bank's image.

The assumptions and facts used to structure the management research question hierarchy set the direction of the project. Using the hierarchy for guidance is a good way to think methodically about the various issues. Think of the hierarchy as six sequential levels moving from the general to the specific. While our approach suggests six discrete levels – concluding with the management decision – the hierarchy is actually more of a continuum. The investigative question stage, in particular, may involve several levels of questioning before it is possible to develop satisfactory measurement questions.

2.3 Research process

Above we discussed the importance of good questions in all phases of the research process. But what distinguishes a good research question from a mediocre one? In the following we elaborate on this issue.

Formulation research dilemma

Any excellent research starts with a good research problem. How do you know that your idea for a research problem is a good one? The list below raises a couple of issue that help you in this assessment:

- Scientific research always involves theory and therefore you need to ensure that some theoretical considerations are available addressing your research problem. If you cannot think of a theory clearly related to your problem, your problem is most likely not scientific enough.
- Scientific research should address non-trivial problems. A good test to check whether your problem is not trivial is to ask three ordinary people, for example friends not studying business or your parents, whether they would have a good answer to your problem. If all three have a good and similar answer, your problem is probably rather trivial. A promising strategy to avoid trivial problems is to ask why a certain relation exists; that is, what are the mechanisms behind it? For example, it is trivial to investigate the relationship between gender and promotion chances. Despite equal opportunity laws, women still are less likely to get a promotion. The problem becomes, however, more interesting if you think about the underlying reasons. Is the gender difference rooted in characteristics of female employees, do supervisors perceive the work of women different from that of men, and does it depend on the company culture, and so on.
- Good research problems are narrowly defined. Do not try to explain the whole world but remain focused. Above, we suggested looking at mechanisms rather than relationships. It is advisable to select just one or two mechanisms that you are interested in. Likewise, your research problem should not build on more than one or two theories, as the scope of a research project or article usually does not allow reflecting on many theories in sufficient depth.
- Good research problems are relevant; that is, the problem provides a meaningful contribution to the field (see also Chapter 15). Thinking about who would be interested in reading the study, what others can learn and how they could benefit from your study helps you assess its relevance.

Issues in the research problem formulation

Although it is desirable for research to be thoroughly grounded in management decision priorities, studies can wander off-target or be less effective than they should be. Some of the reasons for this are described below.

Politically motivated research

It is important to remember that a manager's motives for seeking research are not always obvious. Managers might express a genuine need for specific information on which to base a decision. This is the ideal scenario for quality research. Sometimes, however, a research study may not really be desirable but is authorized anyway, chiefly because its presence may win approval for a certain manager's pet idea. At other times, research may be authorized as a measure of 'personal protection' for a decision-maker in the event that he or she is criticized later. In these less than ideal cases, the researcher may find it more difficult to win the manager's support for an appropriate research design.

Ill-defined management problems

Some categories of problem are so complex, value-laden and bound by constraints that they prove to be intractable to traditional forms of analysis. These questions have characteristics that are virtually the opposite of those of well-defined problems. One author describes the differences like this:

> "To the extent that a problem situation evokes a high level of agreement over a specified community of problem solvers regarding the referents of the attributes in which it is given, the operations that are permitted, and the consequences of those operations, it may be termed unambiguous or well defined with respect to that community. On the other hand, to the extent that a problem evokes a highly variable set of responses concerning referents of attributes, permissible operations, and their consequences, it may be considered ill-defined or ambiguous with respect to that community."[2]

Another author points out that ill-defined research questions are least susceptible to attack from quantitative research methods because such problems have too many interrelated facets for measurement to handle with accuracy.[3] Yet another authority suggests that there are some research questions of this type for which methods do not presently exist or, if the methods were to be invented, they still might not provide the data necessary to solve them.[4] Inexperienced researchers should avoid ill-defined problems. Even seasoned researchers will want to conduct a thorough exploratory study before proceeding with the latest approaches.

Unresearchable questions

Not all management questions are researchable and not all research questions answerable. To be researchable, a question must be one for which observation or other data collection can provide the answer. Many questions cannot be answered on the basis of information alone.

Questions of value and policy must often be weighed in management decisions. In our MetalWorks example, management may be asking, 'Should we hold out for a liberalization of the seniority rules in our new labour negotiations?' While information can be brought to bear on this question, additional considerations such as 'fairness to the workers' or 'management's right to manage' may be important to the decision.

It may be possible for many of these questions of value to be transformed into questions of fact. With regard to 'fairness to the workers', one might first gather information from which to estimate the extent and degree to which workers will be affected by a rule change; then one could gather opinion statements from the workers about the fairness of seniority rules. Even so, substantial value elements remain. Questions left unanswered include, 'Should we argue for a policy that will adversely affect the security and well-being of older workers who are least equipped to cope with this adversity?'

Even if a question can be answered by facts alone, it might not be researchable because currently accepted and tested procedures or techniques are inadequate.

Research design

The **research design** is the blueprint for fulfilling objectives and answering questions. Selecting a design may be complicated by the availability of a large variety of methods, techniques, procedures, protocols and sampling plans. For example, you may decide on a secondary data study, case study, survey, experiment or simulation. If a survey is selected, should it be administered by mail, computer, telephone, the Internet or personal interview? Should all relevant data be collected at one time or at regular intervals? What kind of structure will the questionnaire or interview guide possess? What question wording should be employed? Should the responses be scaled or open-ended? How will reliability and validity be achieved? Will characteristics of the interviewer influence responses to the measurement questions? What kind of training should the data collectors receive? Is a sample or a census to be taken? What types of sampling should be considered?

These questions represent only a few of the decisions that have to be made when just one method is chosen. The creative researcher can, however, actually benefit from this confusing array of options. The numerous combinations spawned by the abundance of tools available may be used to construct alternative perspectives on the same problem.

By creating a design using diverse methodologies, researchers are able to achieve greater insight than if they followed the most frequent method encountered in the literature or suggested by a disciplinary bias. Although it must be conceded that students (and managers) rarely have the resources to pursue a single problem from a multi-method, multi-study strategy, the advantages of several competing designs should be considered before settling on one.

The favoured technique syndrome

Some researchers are method-bound. They recast the management question so that it is amenable to their favourite methodology – a survey, for example. Others might prefer to emphasize the case study, while others still would not consider either approach. Not all researchers are comfortable with experimental designs. The past reluctance of most social scientists to use experimental designs is believed to have inhibited the development of scientific research in the social science arena.

The availability of a technique is an important factor in determining how research will be done or whether a given study can be carried out. People who are knowledgeable about and skilled in some techniques but not in others are too often blinded by their special competences. Their concern for technique dominates the decisions concerning what will be studied (both investigative and measurement questions) and how (research design).

Sampling design

Another step in planning the design is to identify the target population and select the sample if a census is not desired. The researcher must determine who and how many people to interview, what and how many events to observe, or what and how many records to inspect.

A **sample** is part of the target population, carefully selected to represent that population. When researchers under-take sampling studies, they are interested in estimating one or more population values and/or testing one or more statistical hypotheses.

If a study's objective is to examine the attitudes of British automobile assemblers about quality improvement, the population may be defined as the entire adult population of auto assemblers employed by the auto industry in the UK. Definition of the terms 'adult' and 'assembler', and the relevant job descriptions included under 'assembly' and 'auto industry', may further limit the population under investigation. The investigator may also want to restrict the research to readily identifiable companies in the market, vehicle types or assembly processes. The sampling process must then give every person within the target population a known non-zero chance of selection if probability sampling is used.

Pilot testing

The data-gathering phase of the research process typically begins with **pilot testing**. Pilot testing may be skipped if the researcher wishes to condense the project time frame. A pilot test is conducted to detect weaknesses in design and instrumentation, and to provide proxy data for selection of a probability sample. It should, therefore, draw subjects from the target population and simulate the procedures and protocols that have been designated for data collection. If the study is a survey to be executed by mail, the pilot questionnaire should be mailed. If the design calls for observation by an unobtrusive researcher, this behaviour should be practised. The size of the pilot group may range from 5 to 100 subjects, depending on the method to be tested, but the respondents do not have to be statistically selected. In very small populations or special applications, pilot testing runs the risk of exhausting the supply of respondents and sensitizing them to the purpose of the study. This risk is generally over-shadowed by the improvements made to the design by a trial run.

There are a number of variations on pilot testing. Some of them are restricted, intentionally, to data-collection activities. One form, pre-testing, may rely on colleagues, respondent surrogates or actual respondents to refine a measuring instrument. This important activity has saved countless survey studies from disaster by using the suggestions of the respondents to identify and change confusing, awkward or offensive questions and techniques. One interview study was designed by a group of college professors for EducTV, an educational television consortium. In the pilot test, they discovered that the wording of nearly two-thirds of the questions was unintelligible to the target group, later found to have a median eighth-grade education. The revised instrument used the respondents' language and was successful. Pre-testing may be repeated several times to refine questions, instruments or procedures.

Data collection

The gathering of data may range from a simple observation at one location to a grandiose survey of multinational corporations at sites in different parts of the world. The method selected will largely determine how the data are collected. Questionnaires, standardized tests, observational forms, laboratory notes and instrument calibration logs are among the devices used to record raw data.

But what are data? One writer defines data as the facts presented to the researcher from the study's environment. Data may be characterized further by their abstractness, verifiability, elusiveness and closeness to the phenomenon.[5] As abstractions, data are more metaphorical than real. For example, a growth in gross national product (GNP) cannot be observed directly; only the effects of it may be recorded.

Second, data are processed by our senses, which are often limited in comparison to the senses of other living organisms. When sensory experiences consistently produce the same result, our data are said to be trustworthy because they may be verified.

Third, capturing data is elusive, complicated by the speed at which events occur and the time-bound nature of observation. Opinions, preferences and attitudes vary from one milieu to another and with the passage of time. For example, attitudes about spending during the late 1980s differed dramatically one decade later within the same population, due to sustained prosperity within the final four years of the millennium.

Finally, data reflect their truthfulness by proximity (closeness) to the phenomena. Secondary data have had at least one level of interpretation inserted between the event and its recording. Primary data are sought for their proximity to the truth and control over error. These cautions remind us to exercise caution in designing data-collection procedures and generalizing from results.

Data are edited to ensure consistency across respondents and to locate omissions. In the case of survey methods, editing reduces errors in the recording, improves legibility, and clarifies unclear and inappropriate responses. Edited data are then put into a form that makes analysis possible. Because it is impractical to place raw data into a report, alphanumeric codes are used to reduce the responses to a more manageable system for storage and future processing. The codes follow various decision rules that the researcher has devised to assist with sorting, tabulating and analysing. Personal computers have made it possible to merge editing, coding and data entry into fewer steps even when the final analysis may be run on a larger system.

Company database strip-mining

The existence of a pool of information, or a database, can distract a manager, seemingly reducing the need for other research. As evidence of the research-as-expense-not-investment mentality mentioned in Chapter 1, managers frequently hear this sort of thing from their superiors: 'We should use the information we already have before collecting more.' Modern management information systems are capable of providing massive volumes of data. However, this is not the same as saying modern management information systems provide substantial *knowledge*.

Each field in a database was originally created for a specific reason, a reason that may or may not be compatible with the management question facing the organization. In the Netherlands, many supermarket chains have introduced customer cards, which entitle the owner to specific special offers. Each time a customer pays at the cash register their card is scanned along with all the products purchased. The scanned information is at the root of a large database, which can be used for various market research purposes, such as customer segmentation, the identification of high-volume customers, and so on. For example, the supermarket can investigate whether specific groups of customers purchase fresh products, such as meat. However, this system does not allow one to investigate why certain customers do not purchase meat. Is a customer dissatisfied with the meat quality offered and prefers to go to a local butcher or is the customer a vegetarian?

Mining management information databases is fashionable and all types of organization increasingly value the ability to extract meaningful information from the data. While such data-mining is often the starting point in decision-based research, rarely will such activity answer all management questions related to a particular management dilemma.

Analysis and interpretation

Readers of a study, such as managers, need information, not raw data. Researchers generate information by analysing data after its collection. **Data analysis** usually involves reducing accumulated data to a manageable amount, developing summaries, looking for patterns and applying statistical techniques. Scaled responses on questionnaires and experimental instruments often require the analyst to derive various functions, as well as to explore relationships among variables. Further, researchers must interpret these findings in light of the client's research question or determine if the results are consistent with their hypotheses and theories. Increasingly, managers are asking research specialists to make recommendations based on their interpretation of the data.

The larger the amount of data gets, the more researchers have to rely on statistical techniques to summarize them and to detect patterns. Here is an example to illustrate this point.

A telecommunications firm is interested in the question, 'How well will a new mobile telephone – with colour display and other features such as Internet access and email – be received by (potential) customers?' The management board of the firm appoints a project team of three people to investigate this question. The project team could, for example, invite a couple of customers to a focus group meeting to reflect on the new phone. The team could also ask a market research company to interview 500 people by telephone. The focus group discussion will provide mainly qualitative data, and the analysis and interpretation is likely to be a qualitative account based on the project team's observations in the focus group discussion. Even if just 10 questions are asked in the telephone survey, this would result in a data matrix with 5,000 data points. Such an amount of data points exceeds human cognitive capabilities. It is just impossible to look through the telephone interviews or at the data matrix and get a general idea of what the 500 respondents think about the new mobile telephone. Standard statistical techniques allow the researcher to summarize the data (e.g. by calculating means for each question) and to detect patterns (e.g. by calculating the correlation between a respondent's age and the importance of a colour display in the buying decision).

Reporting the results

Finally, it is necessary to prepare a report and transmit the findings and recommendations to the manager for the intended purpose of decision-making. The researcher adjusts the style and organization of the report according to the target audience, the occasion and the purpose of the research. The results of applied research may be communicated via conference call, letter, written report, oral presentation, or some combination of any or all of these methods.

Reports should be developed from the manager's or information user's perspective. The sophistication of the design and sampling plan, or the software used to analyse the data may help to establish the researcher's credibility, but in the end the manager's foremost concern is solving the management dilemma. Thus, the researcher must assess the manager's needs accurately throughout the research process and incorporate this understanding into the final product: the research report.

The management decision-maker occasionally shelves a research report without taking action. Inferior communication of results is one reason for this outcome. With this possibility in mind, a research specialist should strive for:

- insightful adaptation of the information to the client's needs
- careful choice of words in crafting interpretations, conclusions and recommendations.

Sometimes, organizational and environmental forces beyond the researcher's control argue against the implementation of results.

At a minimum, a research report should contain the following:

- an executive summary consisting of a synopsis of the problem, findings and recommendations
- an overview of the research – the problem's background, literature summary, methods and procedures, and conclusions
- a section on implementation strategies for the recommendations
- a technical appendix with all the materials necessary to replicate the project.

Resource allocation and budgets

General notions about research budgets have a tendency to single out data collection as the most costly activity. Data collection requires substantial resources but perhaps less of the budget than clients might expect. Employees must be paid, training and transport must be provided, and other expenses incurred must be paid; but this phase of the project often accounts for no more than one-third of the total research budget. The geographic scope and the number of observations required do affect the cost, but much of the cost is relatively independent of the size of the data-gathering effort. Thus, a guide might be that (i) project planning, (ii) data-gathering and (iii) analysis, interpretation and reporting each share about equally in the budget.

Without budgetary approval, many research efforts are terminated due to lack of resources. A budget may require significant development and documentation as in grant and contract research, or it may require less attention as in some in-house projects or investigations funded out of the researcher's own resources. The researcher who seeks funding must not only be able to persuasively justify the costs of the project, but also to identify the sources and methods of funding. One author identifies three types of budget in organizations where research is purchased and cost containment crucial:

1 Rule-of-thumb budgeting involves taking a fixed percentage of some criterion. For example, a percentage of the prior year's sales revenues may be the basis for determining the marketing research budget for a manufacturer.
2 Departmental or functional area budgeting allocates a portion of total expenditures in the unit to research activities. Government agencies, not-for-profits and the private sector alike will frequently manage research activities out of functional budgets. Units such as human resources, marketing or engineering then have the authority to approve their own projects.
3 Task budgeting selects specific research projects to support on an ad hoc basis. This type is the least proactive but does permit definitive cost–benefit analysis.[6]

Research evaluation

There is a great deal of interplay between budgeting and value assessment in any decision to conduct research. An appropriate research study should help managers avoid losses and increase sales or profits, otherwise research can be wasteful. The decision-maker wants a firm cost estimate for a project and an equally precise assurance that useful information will result from the study. Even if the researcher can give good cost and information estimates, the managers still must judge whether the benefits outweigh the costs. Such costs/benefits considerations are equally important in assessing the value of more academic research, as resources are limited in terms of research time and available financial means to conduct the research.

Conceptually, the value of applied research is not difficult to determine. In a business situation, the research should produce added revenues or reduce expenses in much the same way as any other investment of resources. One source suggests that the value of research information may be judged in terms of 'the difference between the result of decisions made with the information and the result that would be made without it'.[7] While such a criterion is simple to state, its actual application presents difficult measurement problems.

Evaluation methods

If there is any measurement of the value of research, this is usually done as an after-the-fact (*ex-post facto*) event; that is, ***ex-post facto* evaluation**. Twedt reports on one such effort, an evaluation of marketing research done at a major corporation.[8] He secured 'an objective estimate of the contribution of each project to corporate profitability'.

He reports that most studies were intended to help management determine which one of two (or more) alternatives was preferable. He guesses that in 60 per cent of the decision situations, the correct decision would have been made without the benefit of the research information. In the remaining 40 per cent of the cases, the research led to the correct decision. Using these data, he estimates that the return on investment in marketing research in this company was 351 per cent for the year studied. However, he acknowledges that the return-on-investment figure was inflated because only the direct research costs were included.

This effort at cost–benefit analysis is commendable even though the results come too late to guide a current research decision. However, such analysis may sharpen the manager's ability to make judgements about future research proposals. The critical problem remains, though, that of project evaluation before the study is done.

Another evaluation option is **prior or interim evaluations**. A proposal to conduct a thorough management audit of operations in a company may be a worthy one, but neither its costs nor its benefits are easily estimated in advance. Such projects are sufficiently unique that managerial experience seldom provides much aid in evaluating such a proposal. Even in these situations, however, managers can make some useful judgements. They may determine that a management audit is needed because the company is in dire straits and management does not understand the scope of its problems. The management information need may be so great as to ensure that the research is approved. In such cases, managers may decide to control the research expenditure risk by doing a study in stages. They can then review costs and benefits at the end of each stage and give or withhold further authorization. If the research design can be stated clearly, one can estimate an approximate cost. The critical task is to quantify the benefits from the research. At best, estimates of benefits are crude and largely reflect an orderly way to estimate outcomes under uncertain conditions.

2.4 The research proposal

Exhibit 2.1 depicts the research **proposal** as an activity that incorporates decisions made during the early project planning phases of the study, including the management research question hierarchy and exploration.

The proposal thus incorporates the choices that the investigator makes in the preliminary steps, as depicted in Exhibit 2.5.

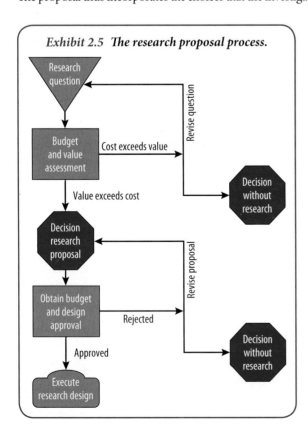

Exhibit 2.5 *The research proposal process.*

A written proposal is often required when a study is being suggested. This ensures that all the parties involved concur on the project's purpose and on the proposed methods of investigation, and each party's obligations and responsibilities are apparent. A blueprint for the construction of a house, for instance, is the proposal for conducting a research project. Proposals soliciting financial means, such as a funding request put to governmental science foundations, or tenders for commercial research, have to spell out time schedules and budgets. Depending on the needs and desires of the manager, substantial background detail and elaboration of proposed techniques may be included.

The length and complexity of research proposals differ widely. Business research proposals normally range from one to ten pages. Applicants for foundation or government research grants typically file a proposal request of a few pages, often in a standardized format specified by the granting agency. A research proposal may also be oral, where all aspects of the research are discussed but not codified in writing. Proposals for student papers are sometimes presented orally to a research project tutor, although it is also common for supervisors to ask students to prepare a written document.

Proposal content

Every proposal, regardless of length, should include two basic sections:

1 statement of the research question
2 brief description of the research methodology.

In a brief memo-type proposal, the research question may be incorporated into a paragraph that also sets out the management dilemma, management question and categories of investigative question. The following statements present the management question facing the respective managers and indicate the nature of the research that will be undertaken:

1 BankChoice, currently the leading bank in the city, has not been growing as fast as its major competitors. Before developing a long-range plan to enhance the bank's competitive position, it is important to determine the bank's present competitive status, its advantages and opportunities, and its major deficiencies. The primary objective of this proposed research is to develop a body of benchmark information about BankChoice, its major competitors and the market for banking services.
2 ArtDeco Appliances must choose a location for a new plant to serve eastern markets. Before this location decision is made, a feasibility study should be conducted to determine, for each of five sites, the estimated:
    a costs of serving existing customers
    b building, relocation, tax and operating costs
    c availability of local labour in the six major crafts used in production
    d attractiveness of the living environment for professional and management personnel.

A second section includes a statement of what will be done: the bare bones of the research design. For BankChoice, the researcher might propose the following:

> "Personal interviews will be conducted with a minimum of 200 residents to determine their knowledge of, use of and attitudes toward local banks. In addition, information will be gathered about their banking and financing practices and preferences. Other information of an economic or demographic nature will also be gathered from published sources and public agencies."

Often, research proposals are much more detailed and describe specific measurement devices that will be used, time and cost budgets, sampling plans and many other details. Still, even the very brief proposals above reveal that the formulation of the research question needs to be rather specific. From the beginning of a project, it is only helpful if one has a clear understanding of what will be researched and what not.

We look at the research proposal in much greater detail below.

The purpose of the research proposal

As noted earlier in this chapter, the research proposal is an individual's or company's offer to produce a product or render a service to a potential buyer or sponsor. To reiterate, the purpose of the research proposal is to:

- present the management or research question to be researched and relate its importance
- discuss the research efforts of others who have worked on related management questions
- suggest the data necessary for solving the question and how the data will be gathered, treated and interpreted.

In addition, a research proposal must present the researcher's plan, services and credentials in the best possible way to encourage the proposal's selection over competitors. In contract research, the survival of companies depends on their ability to develop winning proposals.[9] A proposal is also known as a work plan, prospectus, outline, statement of intent or draft plan.[10] The proposal tells us what, why, how and where the research will be done, and whom it will approach. It must also show the benefit of doing the research.[11]

Many students and inexperienced researchers view the proposal as unnecessary work. The research proposal is essentially a road map, showing clearly the location from which a journey begins, the destination to be reached, and the method of getting there. Well-prepared proposals include potential problems that may be encountered along the way, and methods for avoiding or working around them, much as a road map indicates alternate routes for a detour. Thus, the proposal is an essential planning tool for researchers themselves. Once you know exactly what question you want to research, it is much easier to decide which books and articles should be included in a literature review and which books and articles are beyond the scope of your research. Having thought about what and how you would like to collect the data enables you to plan the data-collection process. It clarifies, for example, whether you already need to obtain a larger sample that you will approach with a questionnaire or whether you need to make appointments with key informants on a specific issue or event.

Sponsor uses

All research has a sponsor in one form or another. The student researcher, for example, is responsible to their class instructor. In a corporate setting, whether the research is being done in-house by a research department or under contract to an external research firm, management sponsors the research. University-, government- or corporate-sponsored (grant) research uses grant committees to evaluate the work.

A research proposal allows the sponsor to assess the sincerity of the researcher's purpose, the clarity of their design, the extent of their relevant background material, and their suitability for undertaking the project. Depending on the type of research and the sponsor, various aspects of a standard proposal design are emphasized. The proposal displays the researcher's discipline, organization and logic. It thus allows the research sponsor to assess both the researcher and the proposed design, to compare them against competing proposals on current organizational, scholastic or scientific needs, and to make the best selection for the project.

A poorly planned, poorly written or poorly organized proposal damages the researcher's reputation more than the decision not to submit a proposal.

Comparison of the research project results with the proposal is also the first step in the process of evaluating the overall research. By comparing the final product with the stated objectives, it is easy for the sponsor to decide if the research goal – a better decision on the management question – has been achieved.

Another benefit of the proposal is the discipline it brings to the sponsor. Many managers requesting research from an in-house, departmental research project do not adequately define the problem they are addressing. The research proposal acts as a catalyst for discussion between the person conducting the research and the manager. The researcher translates the management question, as described by the manager, into the research question and outlines the objectives of the study.

On review, the sponsor may discover that the interpretation of the problem does not encompass all the original symptoms. The proposal, then, serves as the basis for additional discussion between the sponsor and the researcher until all aspects of the management question are understood. Parts of the management question may not be researchable, or at least not subject to empirical study. An alternate design, such as a qualitative or policy analysis study, may need to be proposed.

On completion of the discussions, the sponsor and researcher should agree on a carefully worded research question. As Exhibit 2.6 reveals, proposal development can work in an iterative fashion until the sponsor authorizes the research to proceed.

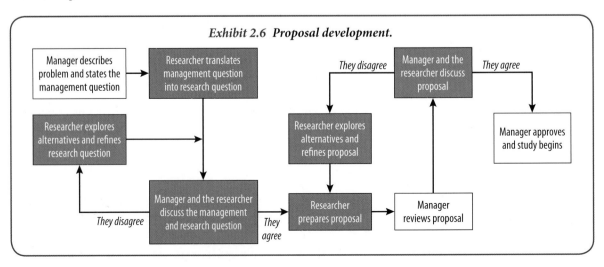

Exhibit 2.6 Proposal development.

For an outside research contract, the process is different. Proposals are usually submitted in response to a request for bid, or **request for proposal (RFP)**. The researchers may wish to convince the sponsor that their approach to the research question differs from that indicated by the management question specified in the initial RFP. In this way, the researcher can show superior understanding of the management dilemma compared to researchers submitting competing proposals.

Researcher benefits

A proposal is as beneficial for the researcher as for the sponsor. The process of writing a proposal encourages the researcher to plan and review the project's logical steps. Related management and research literature should be examined in developing the proposal. This review prompts the researcher to assess previous approaches to similar management questions and revise the research plan accordingly. Additionally, developing the proposal offers the opportunity to spot flaws in the logic, errors in assumptions, or even management questions that are not addressed adequately by the objectives and design.

The in-house or contract researcher uses the approved research proposal as a guide throughout the investigation. Progress can be monitored and milestones noted. On completion, the proposal provides an outline for the final research report.[12]

As in any other business, a contract researcher makes their profit from estimating costs correctly and pricing the research project appropriately. A thorough proposal process is likely to reveal all possible cost-related activities, thus making cost estimation more accurate. As many of these cost-associated activities are related to time, a proposal benefits a researcher by forcing a time estimate for the project. These time and cost estimates encourage researchers to plan the project so that work progresses steadily towards the deadline. Since many people are inclined to procrastinate, having a schedule helps them work methodically towards the completion of the project.

Types of research proposal

In general, research proposals can be divided into those generated for internal and external audiences. An internal proposal is produced by staff-specialists or by the research department within the firm. External proposals sponsored by university grant committees, government agencies, government contractors, not-for-profit organizations or corporations can be classified further as either **solicited** or **unsolicited**. With few exceptions, the larger the project, the more complex the proposal. In public-sector work, the complexity is generally greater than in a comparable private-sector proposal.

There are three general levels of complexity: exploratory studies, small-scale studies and large-scale studies (these levels are illustrated in Exhibit 2.7). The exploratory study generates the most simple research proposal. More complex and common in business is the small-scale study – either an internal study or an external contract research project. The large-scale professional study is the most complex proposal we deal with here (and can be worth millions of pounds). Government agency large-scale project RFPs usually generate proposals that run to several hundred pages and use the modules that we discuss next. However, each agency has unique requirements, making generalized coverage beyond the scope of this text.

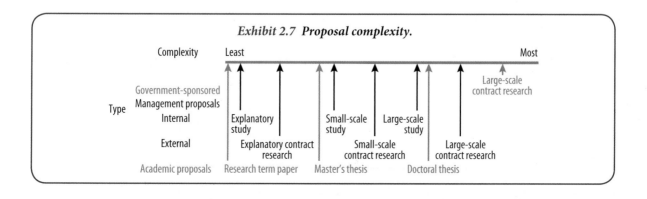

Exhibit 2.7 Proposal complexity.

Exhibit 2.8 displays a set of modules for building a proposal. Their order can represent an outline for a proposal. Based on the type of proposal you are writing you may choose the appropriate modules for inclusion. This is a general guide, but deviations are often appropriate if they serve a specific purpose. For example, most small-scale studies do not require a glossary of terms. Terms are defined within the body of the proposal. However, if the proposal deals with a subject that is not familiar to management, it is appropriate to add a glossary. For a solicited study, the RFP will indicate both the content headings and their order.

Exhibit 2.8 Modules to include in proposals: a comparison of management-oriented proposals and student proposals.

Proposal modules	Management Internal — Exploratory study	Management Internal — Small-scale study	Management Internal — Large-scale study	Management External — Exploratory contract	Management External — Small-scale contract	Management External — Large-scale contract	Government — Large-scale contract	Student — Term paper	Student — Master's thesis	Student — Doctor's thesis
Executive summary		✔	✔	✔	✔	✔	✔		(✔)	(✔)
Problem statement	✔	✔	✔	✔	✔	✔	✔	✔	✔	✔
Research objectives	✔	✔	✔	✔	✔	✔	✔	✔	✔	✔
Literature review			✔			✔	✔		✔	✔
Importance/benefits of study			✔	✔	✔	✔	✔			✔
Research design	✔	✔	✔	✔	✔	✔	✔		✔	✔
Data analysis						✔	✔			✔
Nature and form of results		✔	✔		✔	✔	✔		✔	✔
Qualifications of researchers				✔	✔	✔	✔			
Budget		✔	✔	✔	✔	✔	✔			
Schedule	✔	✔	✔	✔	✔	✔	✔		(✔)	✔
Facilities and special resources			✔	✔	✔	✔	✔		✔	✔
Project management			✔			✔	✔			
Bibliography			✔			✔	✔	✔	✔	✔
Appendices/glossary of terms			✔			✔	✔		✔	✔
Measurement instrument			✔			✔	✔			✔

Take some time to review Exhibit 2.8. Compare the proposal modules suggested for each type of study. This will increase your understanding of proposals.

Internal proposals

Internal proposals are more succinct than external ones. At the least complex end of the continuum shown in Exhibit 2.7, a one- to three-page memo from the researcher to management outlining the problem statement, study objectives, research design and schedule is enough to start an exploratory study. Privately and publicly held businesses are concerned with how to solve a particular problem, make a decision or improve an aspect of their business. Seldom do businesses start research studies for other reasons.

Regardless of the intended audience, in the small-scale proposal, the literature review and bibliography are consequently not emphasized and can often be stated briefly in the research design. Since management insists on brevity, an executive summary is mandatory for all but the most simple of proposals (projects that can be proposed in a two-page memo do not need an executive summary). Schedules and budgets are necessary for funds to be committed. For the smaller-scale projects, descriptions are not required for facilities and special resources, nor is there a need for a glossary. Since managers familiar with the problem sponsor small projects, the associated jargon, requirement and definitions should be included directly in the text. The measuring instrument and project management modules are not required; managers will typically leave this detail for researchers.

External proposals

An external proposal is either solicited or unsolicited. A solicited proposal is often in response to an RFP. The proposal is likely to be competing against several others for a contract or grant. An unsolicited proposal represents a suggestion by a contract researcher for research that might be done. An example of such a proposal might be a consulting firm proposing a research project to a client that has retained the consultancy for other purposes. Another example of an unsolicited proposal might be a research firm that proposes an omnibus study to a trade association to address problems arising from a change in the cultural or political–legal environments. The unsolicited proposal has the advantage of not competing against others but the disadvantage of having to speculate on the ramifications of a management dilemma facing the firm's management. In addition to being an outsider assessing an internal problem, the writer of an unsolicited proposal must decide to whom the document should be sent. Such proposals are often time-sensitive, so the window of opportunity might close before a redirected proposal finds its appropriate recipient.

The most important sections of the external proposal deal with the objectives, design, qualifications, schedule and budget. In contract research, the results and objectives sections are the standards against which the completed project is measured. The executive summary of an external proposal may be included within the letter of transmittal. As the complexity of the project increases, more information is required about project management and the facilities and special resources. As we move towards government-sponsored research, particular attention must be paid to each specification in the RFP. To ignore or not meet any specification is to automatically disqualify your proposal as 'non-responsive'.[13]

Structuring the research proposal

Look again at Exhibit 2.8. Using it for reference, you can put together a set of modules that tailors your proposal to the intended audience. Each of the following modules is flexible, so its content and length may be adapted to specific needs.

Executive summary

You might find it valuable to revisit the management research question hierarchy and the research process model (see above) prior to reading this section.

The **executive summary** allows a busy manager or sponsor to understand quickly the thrust of a proposal. It is essentially an informative abstract, giving executives the chance to grasp the essentials of the proposal without having to read the details.[14] The goal of the summary is to secure a positive evaluation by the executive who will pass the proposal on to the staff for a full evaluation. As such, the executive summary should include brief statements of the management dilemma and management question, the research objectives/research question(s), and the benefits of your approach. If the proposal is unsolicited, a brief description of your qualifications is also appropriate.

Problem statement

This section needs to convince the sponsor to continue reading the proposal. You should capture the reader's attention by stating the management dilemma, its background, its consequences and the resulting management question. The importance of answering the management question should be emphasized here if a separate module on the importance/benefits of study is not included later in the proposal. In addition, this section should include any restrictions or areas of the management question that will not be addressed.

Problem statements that are too broadly defined cannot be addressed adequately in one study. It is important for the management question to clearly distinguish the primary problem from related problems. Be sure your problem statement is clear, and does not use idiom or clichés. After reading this section, the potential sponsor should know the management dilemma and the question, its significance, and why something should be done to change the status quo.[15]

Research objectives

This module addresses the purpose of the investigation. It is here that you lay out exactly what is being planned by the proposed research. In a descriptive study, the objectives can be stated as the research question. Recall that the research question can be broken down further into investigative questions. If the proposal is for a causal study, then the objectives can be restated as a hypothesis.

The objectives module flows naturally from the problem statement, giving the sponsor specific, concrete and achievable goals. It is best to list the objectives either in order of importance or in general terms first, moving to specific terms (i.e. research question followed by underlying investigative questions). The research question(s) (or hypotheses, if appropriate) should be separated from the flow of the text for quick identification.

The research objectives section is the basis for judging the remainder of the proposal and, ultimately, the final report. Verify the consistency of the proposal by checking to see that each objective is discussed in the research design, data analysis and results sections.

Literature review

The **literature review** section examines recent (or historically significant) research studies, company data or industry reports that act as a basis for the proposed study. Begin your discussion of the related literature and relevant secondary data from a comprehensive perspective, moving to more specific studies that are associated with your problem. If the problem has a historical background, begin with the earliest references.

Avoid the extraneous details of the literature; do a brief review of the information, not a comprehensive report. Always refer to the original source. If you find something of interest in a quotation, find the original publication and ensure you understand it. In this way, you will avoid any errors of interpretation or transcription. Emphasize the important results and conclusions of other studies, the relevant data and trends from previous research, and particular methods or designs that could be duplicated or should be avoided. Discuss how the literature applies to the study you are proposing; show the weaknesses or faults in the design, discussing how you would avoid similar problems. If your proposal deals solely with secondary data, discuss the relevance of the data and the bias or lack of bias inherent in it.

A literature review might reveal that the sponsor can answer the management question with a secondary data search rather than the collection of primary data. We discuss this more fully in Chapter 9.

The literature review may also explain the need for the proposed work to appraise the shortcomings and/or informational gaps in secondary data sources. This analysis may go beyond scrutinizing the availability or conclusions of past studies and their data, to examining the accuracy of secondary sources, the credibility of these sources, and the appropriateness of earlier studies.

Close the literature review section by summarizing the important aspects of the literature and interpreting them in terms of your problem. Refine the problem as necessary in light of your findings.

Importance/benefits of the study

In this section you describe explicit benefits that will accrue from your study. The importance of 'doing the study now' should be emphasized. Usually, this section runs to no more than a few paragraphs. If you find it difficult to write, then you have probably not clarified the research dilemma adequately. Return to the analysis of the problem and ensure – through additional discussions with your sponsor or your research team, or by a re-examination of the literature – that you have captured the essence of the problem.

This section also requires you to understand what is most troubling to your sponsor. If it is potential trade union activity, you cannot promise that an employee survey will prevent unionization. You can, however, show the importance of this information and its implications. This benefit may allow management to respond to employee concerns and forge a link between those concerns and unionization.

The importance/benefits section is particularly important to the unsolicited external proposal. You must convince the sponsoring organization that your plan will meet its needs.

Research design

Up to now, you have told the sponsor what the problem is, what your study goals are, and why it is important for you to do the study. The proposal has presented the study's value and benefits. The design module describes what you are going to do in technical terms. This section should include as many sub-sections as needed to show the phases of the project. Provide information on your proposed design for tasks such as sample selection and size, data-collection method, instrumentation, procedures and ethical requirements. When more than one way exists to approach the design, discuss the methods you have rejected and why the approach you have selected is superior.

We discuss design strategies in Chapter 6.

Data analysis

A brief section on the methods used for analysing the data is appropriate for large-scale contract research projects and doctoral research projects. With smaller projects, the proposed data analysis would be included within the research design section. It is in this section that you describe your proposed handling of the data and the theoretical basis for using the selected techniques. The object of this section is to assure the sponsor that you are following correct assumptions and using theoretically sound data analysis procedures.

This module is often an arduous section to write. You can make it easier to write, read and understand your data analysis by using sample charts and tables featuring 'dummy' data.

When there is no statistical or analytical expertise in the company, sponsors are more likely to hire professional help to interpret the soundness of this section.

The data analysis section is so important in evaluating contract research proposals that the researcher should contact an expert to review the latest techniques available for use in the particular research study and compare these to the proposed techniques.

Nature and form of results

On completion of this section, the sponsor should be able to go back to the statement of the management question and research objectives, and discover that each goal of the study has been covered. You should also specify the types of data to be obtained and the interpretations that will be made in the analysis. If the data are to be turned over to the sponsor for proprietary reasons, make sure that this is reflected. Alternatively, if the report will go to more than one sponsor, that should be noted.

This section also contains the contractual statement telling the sponsor exactly what types of information will be received. Statistical conclusions, applied findings, recommendations, action plans, models, strategic plans, and so on, are examples of forms of results.

Qualifications of researchers

You should look for this element in a proposal when hiring a contract researcher. This section should begin with the principal investigator, and then provide similar information on all individuals involved with the project. Two elements are critical:

1 professional research competence (relevant research experience, the highest academic degree held, and memberships of business and technical societies)
2 relevant management experience.[16]

With so many individuals, research speciality firms and general consultancies providing research services, the sponsor needs assurance that the researcher selected is professionally competent. Past research experience is the best barometer of competence, followed by the highest academic degree earned. To document relevant research experience, the researcher provides concise descriptions of similar projects. Highest degree usually follows the person's name (e.g. S. Researcher, Ph.D. in Statistics). Society memberships provide some evidence that the researcher is cognizant of the latest methodologies and techniques. These follow the relevant research experience as a string or bullet list, with organization name followed by term of membership and any relevant leadership positions.

Research Methods in Real Life

Gourmet Olympics

Going out for dinner is no longer merely an activity that involves taking in the necessary nutrition for physical survival, or enjoying the companionship of friends and thus satisfying the desire for social interaction. More and more people also enjoy the pleasures of eating for its own sake. The *Michelin* and *Gault Millau* Guides are a well-known and respected resource for people looking for an exceptional dining experience. Three Michelin stars or four Gault Millau chef's hats promise an exceptional experience for the senses. A chef de cuisine restaurant getting one, two or three Michelin stars, or the equivalent of one to four Gault Millau chef's hats, attracts more guests.

On 24 February 2003, Bernard Loiseau, owner and chef de cuisine of La Cote d'Or in Saulieu, France, killed himself after Gault Millau downgraded his restaurant from 19 out of the maximum of 20 points to 17. Paul Bocuse, the 80-year-old legend of chefs de cuisine, commented, 'Bravo Gault Millau, you have won, your verdict has cost a man's life.'

On what is this verdict based? Pascal Remy, for 16 years a restaurant inspector for the *Michelin Guide*, revealed in an interview with the French newspaper *Le Figaro* that just five inspectors evaluate, dine out about 200 times a year and check about 10 per cent of the restaurants. Despite these questionable assessment procedures, gaining a Michelin star or Gault Millau hat can make restaurants and chefs de cuisine, while losing one can break them.

How would you proceed to assess the quality of restaurants in your country or town? As a chef de cuisine, how would you act to earn a star or chef's hat, and how would you respond if you lost one?

References and further reading

Habets, Joep, 'De vier mutsen van Gault Millau' [The four chef's hats of Gault Millau], NRC Handelsblad, 17 February 2004, p. 15.

Henley, Jon, 'Top chef kills himself after losing points in food guide' (www.guardian.co.uk/world/2003/feb/26/france.jonhenley).

www.michelin.com

www.gaultmillau.com

Researchers are increasingly in the business of providing advice, not just research services. Businesses are looking for high-quality advice. In addition, the researcher who demonstrates relevant management or industry experience will be more likely to receive a favourable nod to their proposal. The format of this information should follow that used for relevant research experience. The entire curriculum vitae of each researcher need not be included unless required by the RFP. However, researchers often place complete CV information in an appendix for review by interested sponsors.

Research companies often subcontract specific research activities to firms or individuals that specialize in or offer specific resources or facilities. This is especially true for studies involving qualitative research techniques such as in-depth personal interviews and focus groups. Brief profiles of these companies are usually provided in this section only if their inclusion enhances the credibility of the researcher. Otherwise, profiles of such subcontractors are included in an appendix of the final report, rather than in the proposal.

Budget

The budget should be presented in the form the sponsor requests. For example, some organizations require secretarial assistance to be individually budgeted, whereas others insist it should be included in the research director's fees or the overheads of the operation. In addition, limitations on travel, per diem rates and capital equipment purchases can change the way in which you prepare a budget. Typically, the budget should run to no more than one to two pages. Exhibit 2.9 shows one format that can be used for small contract research projects. Additional information, back-up details, quotes from vendors, and hourly time and payment calculations should be put into an appendix if required, or kept in the researcher's file for future reference.

The budget statement in an internal research proposal is based on employee and overhead costs. The budget presented by an external research organization is not just the wages or salaries of its employees but the person/hour price the contracting firm charges.

The detail the researcher presents may vary depending on both the sponsor's requirements and the contracting research company's policy. Some research companies, particularly in database and computerized analysis areas, quote on the basis of 'man/machine hours' involved in a project. The man/machine hour is the hourly fee charged for a person with computer hardware and organizational resources. Here, rather than separating the 'other costs' of Exhibit 2.9, these costs are embedded in a combined rate. One reason why external research agencies avoid giving detailed budgets is the possibility that disclosures of their costing practices will make their calculations public knowledge, reducing their negotiating flexibility.

Some costs are more elusive than others. Do not forget to build the cost of proposal writing into your fee. Publication and delivery of final reports can be a last-minute expense that may easily be overlooked in preliminary budgets.

Proposals for student research projects do not usually have an explicit budget section, as the student does not usually request any financial support. However, even for a small-scale student project, it is worth spending a little time considering the costs involved in a project, because most students' projects are self-financed from a rather low monthly budget.

Exhibit 2.9 Sample proposal budget for a research programme.

Budget items	Rate	Total days	Charge
A. Salaries			
1. Research director, Jason Henry	€200/hr	20 hours	€4,000
2. Associate	100/hr	10 hours	1,000
3. Research assistants (2)	20/hr	300 hours	6,000
4. Secretarial (1)	12/hr	100 hours	1,200
Sub-total			€12,200
B. Other costs			
5. Employee services and benefits			
6. Travel			€2,500
7. Office supplies			100
8. Telephone			800
9. Rent			
10. Other equipment			
11. Publication and storage costs			100
Sub-total			€3,500
C. Total of direct costs			€15,700
D. Overhead support			5,480
E. Total funding requested			€21,180

Schedule

Your schedule should include the major phases of the project, their timetables and the milestones that signify completion of a phase. For example, major phases may be:

- exploratory interviews
- final research proposal
- questionnaire revision
- field interviews
- editing and coding
- data analysis
- report generation.

Each of these phases should have an estimated time span. Planning the schedule of your research is very important to ensure time efficiency. Even small-scale student projects are often so complex, involving the simultaneous and sequential execution of different tasks and activities, that one can easily lose track of the final objective, which results in a considerable delay finishing the project. In research, you need to handle time efficiently, because time passes quickly and deadlines loom into sight faster than originally expected. This is an experience shared by both students preparing a term paper and researchers working on sponsored research.

It may be helpful to you and your sponsor if you draw up a schedule. If the project is large and complex, a **critical path method (CPM)** of scheduling may be included.[17] In a CPM chart, the nodes represent major milestones, and the arrows suggest the work needed to get to each milestone. More than one arrow pointing to a node indicates that all those tasks must be completed before the milestone has been met. A number is usually placed on the arrow 'shaft' showing the number of days or weeks required for that task to be completed (see Exhibit 2.10).

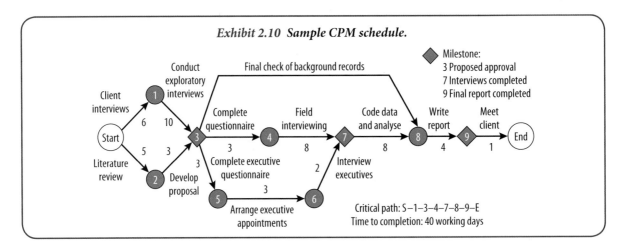

Exhibit 2.10 Sample CPM schedule.

Drawing a CPM chart, like the one shown in Exhibit 2.10, draws your attention to two points. First, it allows you to see which tasks can be conducted simultaneously. For example, the process of collecting data often has 'dead' periods, because you have to wait until mailed questionnaires are returned or because of the time lag between making an appointment for an interview and administering the interview. The CPM method visualizes which other tasks you could conduct in such periods (e.g. refine your literature review). Second, once you have drawn the CPM chart, the pathway from start to end that takes the longest time to complete is called the 'critical path' because any delay in an activity along that path will delay the end of the entire project. Software programs designed for project management simplify scheduling and charting the schedule; most are available for personal computers.

Facilities and special resources

Often, projects will require special facilities or resources that should be described in detail. For example, a contract exploratory study may need specialist facilities for focus group sessions.

Computer-assisted telephone or other interviewing facilities may be required. Alternatively, your proposed data analysis may require sophisticated computer algorithms and, therefore, you will need access to an adequate system. These requirements will vary from study to study. The proposal should specify in list form the relevant facilities and resources that will be used. The costs for such facility use should be detailed in your budget.

Project management

The purpose of the **project management** section is to show the sponsor that the research team is organized in a way that will enable it to do the project efficiently. A master plan is required for complex projects to show how all the phases will be brought together. The plan should include:

- the research team's organization
- management procedures and controls for executing the research plan
- examples of management and technical reports
- the research team's relationship with the sponsor
- financial and legal responsibility
- management competence.

Tables and charts are very helpful in the presentation of the master plan. The relationships between researchers and assistants need to be shown when several researchers are part of the team. Sponsors must know that the director is an individual capable of leading the team and acting as a useful liaison point for the sponsor. In addition, procedures for information processing, record control and expense control are critical to large operations and should be shown as part of the management procedure.

The type and frequency of progress reports should be recorded so that the sponsor can expect to be kept up to date and the researchers can expect to be left alone to do the research. The sponsor's limits on control during the process should be delineated.

This section also discusses any details such as printing facilities, clerical help or information processing capabilities to be provided by the sponsor rather than the researcher. In addition, rights to the data, the results, and authority to speak for the researcher and for the sponsor are included.

Payment frequency and timing are also covered in the master plan. Finally, proof of financial responsibility and overall management competence is provided.

Bibliography

For all projects that require a literature review, a bibliography is necessary. Use the bibliographic format required by the sponsor. If none is specified, a standard style manual will provide the details necessary to prepare the bibliography.[18] Many of these sources also offer suggestions for successful proposal writing.

Appendices

The researcher should include a **glossary** of terms whenever there are many words unique to the research topic and not understood by the general management community. This is a simple section consisting of terms and definitions, similar in format to the glossary in this book. Also, the researcher should define any acronyms used, even if they are defined within the text; for example, 'CATI (computer-assisted telephone interviewing)'.

Measurement instrument

For large projects, it is appropriate to include samples of the measurement instruments if they are available when you assemble the proposal. This allows the sponsor to discuss particular changes in one or more of the instruments. If the proposal includes the development of a custom-designed measurement instrument, omit this appendix section.

Other

Any detail that reinforces the body of the proposal can be included in an appendix. This includes researcher CVs, profiles of firms or individuals to which work will be subcontracted, budget details, and lengthy descriptions of special facilities or resources.

Evaluating the research proposal

Proposals are subject to either formal or informal reviews. Formal reviews are carried out regularly for solicited proposals. The formal review process varies, but typically includes:

- development of review criteria, using RFP guidelines
- assignment of points to each criterion, using a universal scale
- assignment of a weight for each criterion, based on importance of each criterion
- generation of a score for each proposal, representing the sum of all weighted criterion scores.

The sponsor should assign the criteria, the weights and the scale to be used for scoring each criterion before the proposals are received. The proposal should then be evaluated with this checklist of criteria to hand. Points are recorded for each criterion, reflecting the sponsor's assessment of how well the proposal meets the company's needs relative to that criterion (e.g. on a scale of 1–10, where 10 is the largest number of points assigned to the best proposal for a particular criterion). After the review, the weighted criterion scores are added to provide a cumulative total. The proposal with the highest number of points wins the contract.

Several people, each of whom may be assigned to a particular section, typically review long and complex proposals. The formal method is most likely to be used for competitive government, university or public-sector grants, and also for large-scale contracts.

Small-scale contracts and student proposals are more likely to be submitted to informal evaluation.

In an informal review, the project needs, and thus the criteria, are well understood but are not usually well documented. In contrast to the formal method, a system of points is not used and the criteria are not ranked.

In practice, many factors contribute to a proposal's acceptance and funding. Primarily, the content discussed above must be included to the level of detail required by the sponsor's RFP.

Beyond the required modules, other factors can quickly eliminate a proposal from consideration or improve the sponsor's reception of the proposal, among them:

- neatness
- organization, in terms of being both logical and easily understood
- completeness in fulfilling the RFP's specifications, including budget and schedule
- appropriateness of writing style
- submission within the RFP's timeline.

Although a proposal produced with a word-processing application and bound with an expensive cover will not overcome design or analysis deficiencies, a poorly presented, unclear or disorganized proposal will not receive serious attention from the reviewing sponsor. Given that multiple reviewers may be evaluating only a given section, the reviewer should easily be able to skim through the proposal to any section of interest.

In terms of the technical writing style of the proposal, the sponsor must be able to understand the problem statement, the research design and the methodology. The sponsor should clearly understand why the proposed research should be funded, and the exact goals and concrete results that will come from the study.

Finally, a late proposal will not be reviewed. While current project disqualification due to lateness may appear to be the worse result here, there is a possible longer-term effect of this. Lateness communicates a level of disrespect for the sponsor – that the researcher's schedule is more important than the sponsor's. A late proposal also communicates a weakness in project management, which raises an issue of professional competence. This concern about competence may continue to plague the researcher during future project proposal reviews.

Deeper Insight into Research Methods

Example of a 'good' research project proposal

Below is an example of a good research project proposal that a student prepared for the first meeting with a research project supervisor. It is a good proposal, but not a perfect one and, of course, the final research project looked different from what was originally proposed, but still investigated the problem proposed.

Research project proposal

Social Capital and Entrepreneurship

I Introduction and problem statement

In recent years, the role of social capital and networking is no longer limited to sociology (Granovetter, 1985) as a resource for social action (Baker, 1990; Burt, 1992; Coleman, 1988, 1990), but has gradually emerged as a medium for understanding entrepreneurial behaviour (Liao and Welsch, 2003). Empirical research found that social capital is positively related to firm performance (Baker, 1990), product innovation and value creation (Tsai and Ghoshal, 1998), and industry-wide network formation (Walker et al., 1997). According to Westlund and Bolton (2003), social capital is even as important to enterprises as financial, real and human capital. Therefore, it appears as if entrepreneurs would be well advised to develop and promote networks of all sorts (Davidsson and Honig, 2003).

> *Gives a general overview of the problem and begins to name some important references, which allow the reader to immediately place the study.*

However, most studies investigating the relation between social capital and entrepreneurship have focused on social capital as an individual resource and neglect another prominent perspective on social capital, namely, a resource that is nested within communities (Putnam, 2000). Henceforth, the research problem will be referred to as *social capital differences in the Netherlands*. Examining the nature of social capital across different regions in the Netherlands may help to clarify how to promote regional dynamism resulting from venture creation and entrepreneurship, which is a key concept for understanding future socio-economic changes (Yamada, 2002).

> *Gives a clear motivation of the problem statement in terms of a theoretical gap.*

What is the influence of regional differences in social capital on entrepreneurship?

Furthermore, the general research question has been divided into two sub-questions with the aim of developing a comprehensive idea about social capital dynamics and regional economic development:

> *Provides sub-questions to the research problem that facilitate the readers' understanding about what the proposal really is.*

1 What are the necessary conditions that facilitate the creation of social capital networks and subsequently enhance entrepreneurial activity?
2 How do social capital networks interact with different business sectors?

II Research objectives – contributions of the study

In sum, the contributions of this paper are: (1) to add an analysis of the effects of social capital at the community level on entrepreneurship, (2) to investigate the social capital at the community level, (3) to examine the interplay of regional differences in social capital networks and entrepreneurship at the same time in the analysis, (4) to identify the underlying processes that determine the contributions of

> *This part briefly summarizes the motives for the study, so the reader is informed of the questions that will be addressed.*

entrepreneurial gestation activities, (5) to provide an integrative framework of entrepreneurship activities based on social capital, and (6) to test it empirically by means of a country-wide secondary data set. Hence, this paper will explore social capital within the context of Dutch entrepreneurship and it will be centred on the two research questions mentioned above.

▶

III Literature review

As Granovetter (1985) points out, economic action is not at all independent of the social relationships surrounding an economic actor. Strategically engaging in social activities and wisely managing social relations save significant transaction costs in the search for critical information and provide unique economic opportunities (Chung *et al.*, 2000). Abbel *et al.* (2001) also confirm that social networks provide information and contacts on how to raise capital or whom to sell goods and services to. Informal social relations and tacit social arrangements are hence a critical aspect for businesses (Spence *et al.*, 2003).

Social capital is formally defined as *'the sum of actual and potential resources embedded within, available through, and derived from the network of relationships possessed by individual or social units'* (Nahapiet and Ghoshal, 1998, p. 243), that is simply speaking, a set of social resources rooted in relationships (Burt, 1992; Loury, 1977).

Granovetter (2000) highlights the importance of informal relationships, trust and solidarity for [. . .] business development. In view of the fact that the accumulation of knowledge, information, and other resources through social ties opens new *'productive opportunities'* (Penrose, 1959) that constitute a driving force in the growth of new ventures (Penrose, 1959), social ties raise the attention of both academics and practitioners.

Another key feature of social capital emerging from the literature is that it is crucial for effective collective action. Pingle (2001) even goes as far as maintaining that *'at the very least, its presence appears to enable collective action needed for economic development, it is held to strengthen democracy, and promote good governance'*. However, mutual networks of trust that characterize a community might also inhibit entrepreneurship rather than facilitate it. For example, tight bonds between individuals may strangle the temptation to *'march to a different pipe'* or *'colouring outside the lines'* rather than encourage entrepreneurship (Westlund and Bolton, 2003). Heavily saturated social capital networks may result in closed recruitment opportunities or even unfair pricing agreements, representing the dark side of social capital (Putnam, 2000, pp. 350–63). By creating relationships with customers and suppliers, a firm may exploit its established network to shut out potentially more productive capital from the market.

> *Previous paragraphs also highlight important references related to the topic. Here, the student clearly shows that he has a good command of the literature in this field.*

Despite the recognition of social capital networks' significance on entrepreneurship, other scholars have addressed the effects of social capital on firm dissolution (Pennings *et al.*, 1998), knowledge and competence development (Zahra *et al.*, 1999), alliance formation (Chung *et al.*, 2000), or even its impact on political alliance patterns and national policy outcomes (Broadbent, 2000). Although there has been much theorizing about social capital, only scant systematic attention has been paid to the development of a dynamic rather than a static concept of social capital. Among the exceptions to this are Cooke and Wills (1999), and Lyons (2002), who both examined how businesses respond to attempts by policy-makers to *create* rather than simply make use of *existing* social capital in an effort to achieve economic development goals. In addition, apart from Onyx and Bullen (2000), who measured differences in social capital across five Australian communities, and Putnam (1993), who concludes in his work on Italian regions that variation in prosperity between regional economies was associated with variation in the degree to which social capital was present or absent, few contributions have explicitly discussed the link between regional differences in social capital networks. Yet, although Onyx and Bullen's as well as Putnam's study serves as a foundation for the paper at hand with regard to the creation of meaningful categories for the explanatory variables of social capital, it fails to reflect its impact on entrepreneurial activities. Consequently, the author seeks to make a contribution to filling the gap and argues that gaining a more complete view of how social capital affects new business development starts by examining entrepreneurial activities as a function of social capital across different regions.

> *Here the student introduces entrepreneurship as a further specification of the problem. This is the least convincing part of the proposal, as it remains unclear why the researcher investigates the theoretical gap identified before in this area. Here it becomes apparent that the student has read much more about social capital than about entrepreneurship.*

IV Research design and nature of results

The unit of analysis of this study is the community, as I am interested in the relation between community social capital and entrepreneurial activities within the community. Given this unit of analysis, the information (data) required should inform about the key concepts employed at the same level, that is the community. Such information is fortunately available from secondary data sources that provide aggregated information for communities and regions.

The topical scope of the study will be the Netherlands. The following publicly accessible databases contain information that could be used to investigate the research problem proposed:

- Regional statistics of Statistics Netherlands (CBS)
- European Social Survey
- Economic statistics from EUROSTAT

It is really important for the proposal that you mention what information you are going to use and how you will get it. The reason is that there are many very interesting research problems, which have not yet been investigated because it might be very hard, costly or even unfeasible to obtain the information. This part is essential to assess the feasibility of the study.

Data obtained from these three sources will be combined to build up a data set suitable for quantitative analysis, such as multiple regression analysis.

V Schedule

The table below shows a rough schedule of tasks to complete within six months.

Reasonable standard time schedule.

Time	Tasks
November 2009	Discuss proposal with supervisor and obtain approval.
December 2009	Write introduction chapter, examine databases, and prepare theory chapter. Hand in introduction chapter before Christmas.
January 2010	Revise introduction chapter and write theory chapter(s).
February 2010	Complete theory chapter by mid-February. Start building database.
March 2010	Discuss theory chapter with supervisor, then go skiing in Austria (one week)☺, then revise theory chapter and start analysis.
April 2010	Analysis and hand in first draft of research project (without conclusions) to discuss it in mid-April.
May 2010	Revise all chapters based on discussion of first draft and write conclusions. Revise second draft by mid-May. Hand in research project end of May.
June 2010	Oral defence of research project.

References

Abbel, P., Crouchley, R. and Mills, C., 'Social capital and entrepreneurship in Great Britain', *Enterprise and Innovation Management Studies* 2, 2001, 119–44.

Baker, Wayne, 'Market networks and corporate behavior', *American Journal of Sociology* 96, 1990, 589–625.

Baker, George P., 'Incentive contracts and performance measurement', *Journal of Political Economy* 100, 1992, 598–614.

Broadbent, J., 'Social capital and labor politics in Japan: cooperation or cooptation?' *Policy Science* 33, 2000, 307–21.

Burt, R.S., *Structural Holes: The Social Structure of Competition*. Cambridge: Harvard University Press, 1992.

Chung, S.A., Singh, H. and Lee, K., 'Complementarity, status similarity and social capital as drivers of alliance formation', *Strategic Management Journal* 21, 2000, 1–20.

▶

Coleman, J.S., 'Social capital in the creation of human capital', *American Journal of Sociology* 94, 1988, S95–S120.

Coleman, James S., *Foundations of Social Theory*. Cambridge MA: Harvard University Press, 1990.

Cooke, P. and Wills, D., 'Small firms, social capital and the enhancement of business performance through innovation programmes', *Small Business Economics* 13, 1999, 219–34.

Davidsson, P. and Honing, B., 'The role of social and human capital among nascent entrepreneurs', *Journal of Business Venturing* 18, 2003, 301–31.

Granovetter, M., 'Economic action and social structure: the problem of embeddedness', *American Journal of Sociology* 91, 1985, 481–510.

Granovetter, M., 'The economic sociology of firms and entrepreneurs', in Swedberg, R. (ed.) *Entrepreneurship: The Social Science View*. Oxford: Oxford University Press, 2000, pp. 244–75.

Liao, J. and Welsch, H., 'Social capital and entrepreneurial growth aspiration: a comparison of technology – and non-technology-based nascent entrepreneurs', *Journal of High Technology Management Research* 14, 2003, 149–70.

Loury, G.C., 'A dynamic theory of racial income differences', in Wallace, P.A. and Lamond, A. (eds). *Women, Minorities and Employment Discrimination*. Lexington, MA: Lexington Books, 1977.

Lyons, T.S., 'Building social capital for rural enterprise development: three case studies', *Journal of Developmental Entrepreneurship* 7, 2002, 193–216.

Nahapiet, J. and Ghoshal, S., 'Social capital, intellectual capital, and the organizational advantage', *Academy of Management Review* 23, 1998, 242–66.

Onyx, J. and Bullen, P., 'Measuring social capital in five communities', *Journal of Applied Behavioural Science* 36, 2000, 23–42.

Pennings, L., Lee, K. and van Witteloostuijn, A., 'Human capital, social capital, and firm dissolution', *Academy of Management Journal*, 1998, 425–40.

Penrose, E.T., *The theory of the growth of the firm*. Oxford: Oxford University Press, 1959.

Pingle, V., *Identity Landscapes, Social Capital and Entrepreneurship: Small Business in South Africa*. Doornfontein: Centre for Policy Studies, 2001.

Putnam, R.D., *Making Democracy Work: Civic Traditions in Modern Italy*. Princeton, NJ: Princeton University Press, 1993.

Putnam, R.D., *Bowling Alone*. New York: Simon & Schuster, 2000.

Spence, L.J., Schmidpeter, R. and Habisch, A., 'Assessing social capital: small and medium sized enterprises in the UK and Germany', *Journal of Business Ethics* 47, 2003, 17–29.

Tsai, W. and Ghoshal, S., 'Social capital and value creation: the role of intra-firm networks', *Academy of Management Journal* 41, 1998, 464–76.

Walker, G., Kogut, B. and Shan, W., 'Social capital, structural holes and the formation of an industry network', *Organization Science* 8, 1997, 109–25.

Westlund, H. and Bolton, R., 'Local social capital and entrepreneurship', *Small Business Economics* 21, 2003, 77–113.

Yamada, J., *Entrepreneurship as Knowledge and Social Capital Creation: Theoretical Analysis of the Startup Stage of Firms*. Kagawa University: The Institute of Economic Research. Working Paper Series, No. 50, 2002.

Zahra, S.A., Nielsen, A.P. and Bogner, W.C., 'Corporate entrepreneurship, knowledge, and competence development', *Entrepreneurship Theory & Practice* 23, 1999, 169–90.

Running Case Study 2
To start with: Write a proposal

Rebecca and Mehmet alike decided to contact their research project supervisors for a first appointment by sending them an email.

From: **Mehmet Celik** <mehmet.celik@dolphin-travel.co.uk>
Date: Fri, Jul 05, 2013 at 00:38 AM
Subject: Appointment
To: "Flowermountain" <b.flowermountain@maastrichtuniversity.nl>

Dear Mr. Flowermountain,

As you might recall, I approached you a couple of weeks back asking you whether you would be willing to supervise my final master thesis on success determinants of migrant entrepreneurs. In your response you asked me to become a bit more specific on the topic. Although I have thought a lot about the topic and I know that a thesis research needs to be well focused, I find it hard to come up with a well-defined project. Nevertheless, I attached a small proposal and would like to ask you for an appointment to discuss the proposal and the steps to be taken.

Kind regards,

Mehmet Celik

RESEARCH PROPOSAL

MEHMET CELIK (ID: 096009)

MIGRANT ENTREPRENEURSHIP, INTEGRATION AND SUCCESS

Introduction

Immigrant businesses illustrate the ever more visible footprint migrants are leaving in Western societies over the last years. Over the past decades most Western countries including the Netherlands have seen a notable increase of immigrant business ownership, especially for migrants originating from non-Western countries (ITS 2007, CBS Statline 2009). While immigrant entrepreneurship can be a promising alley enabling individuals to gain economic mobility and social recognition (Van den Tillaart 2001, Choenni 1997), it is commonly discredited on the grounds of being low value-added, little innovative, and marginally profitable (Light & Rosenstein 1995, Waldinger 1996, Kloosterman, Rath & Van der Leun 1997).

Explorative studies by Van den Tillaart (2001), EIM (2004) and Rusinovic (2006), however, suggest that the traditionally gloomy image of migrant entrepreneurship needs to be reassessed as a "new" group of migrant entrepreneurs – namely the children of migrants or the so-called second generation – has started businesses in more promising sectors of the economy.

From a theoretical perspective the thesis contributes to the field by broadening our understanding of migrant entrepreneurship. Most of the current literature on migrant entrepreneurship has emphasized human and social capital as important drivers for becoming an entrepreneur (see, e.g., Fairlie 1999, Clark

& Drinkwater 2000, Ram et al. 2000, Levent et al. 2003, Arenius & De Clercq 2005, Wilson et al. 2007, Andersson & Hammarstedt 2010), while I attempt to address the outcomes of migrant ventures and want to focus more on firm and firms' strategy characteristics.

Research Problem

Exploring migrant entrepreneurship has become an interesting and import research field covering many issues (Kloosterman & Rath, 2003). Therefore, this thesis takes a broad approach that allows to take the whole context of migrant entrepreneurship into account. More specifically, migrant entrepreneurship in Dutch cities encompasses many important issues, for example:

- To what extent does entrepreneurship contribute to happiness, success and upward social mobility?
- What is their contribution to the local economies?
- How does migrant entrepreneurship affects integration?

Theoretical Background

One cannot research migrants in Western European societies without discussing integration. And not surprisingly migrant entrepreneurship is closely related to migrant integration trajectories in their host societies. Integration trajectories have been intensively studied to date (Portes and Zhou 1993, Alba and Nee 2004, Portes, Fernandez-Kelly & Haller 2008, Pels 1991, Vermeulen and Penninx 1994, 2000, Lindo 1996, Crul 2000, Dagevos 2001), but surprisingly, the literature turns a blind eye at self-employment, although labour market positions are portrayed as an important outcome of integration. Alike in the labour market, it is expected that integration into the host society increases the chance to enter self-employment and raises the developmental prospects of the founded firms, because integration enhances migrants' abilities to access vital business information and to mobilise necessary resources (see also Constant & Zimmermann 2006, Evans 1989, Le 2000).

I employ the integration definition of Vermeulen and Penninx (1994, 2000) who distinguish between two dimensions of integration: the socio-cultural and the structural dimension. The socio-cultural dimension reflects interpersonal relations with the native Dutch population and the extent of cultural, attitudinal, and behavioural changes towards the host society (i.e. Dagevos, Gijsberts and Van Praag, 2003; Dagevos, 2001; Vermeulen and Penninx, 2000; Veenman, 1995; Rusinovic, 2006). Structural integration refers to the participation of immigrants in core institutions of society and is usually measured by educational attainment, position in the labour market, and residential integration (Dagevos, 2001; Rusinovic, 2006). Using Vermeulen & Penninx (1994, 2000) integration terminology, the socio-cultural and structural integration of the five major migrant groups in the Netherlands will be assessed.

The mixed embeddedness framework developed by Kloosterman, van der Leun and Rath (1999) offers a useful theoretical approach. The framework builds upon interaction theory (Aldrich & Waldinger 1990; Light & Rosenstein 1995) and considerations regarding social embeddedness (Granovetter 1985). It departs from the notion that immigrant entrepreneurship depends on a multitude of contingencies determining the interplay of individual characteristics of the entrepreneur on the one side and characteristics of the wider social, economic and politico-institutional environment on the other side. The latter context, which Kloosterman et al. (1999) coined opportunity structures, describes the setting creating business opportunities for prospective and established entrepreneurs. Opportunity structures are shaped by economic factors both on the supply side, such as entrepreneurs' individual and cultural characteristics, as well as on the demand side, e.g. the presence of an accessible customer base. At the same time politico-institutional factors, namely existing national rules and legislations, institutions and laws enable or hamper businesses start-ups and development.

Socio-cultural and structural integration affect opportunity structures of prospective and established migrant entrepreneurs as they foster the main-stream market match between the supply side (products/services offerings) and the demand side (products/services demanded by customers). In other words, integration determines to what extent migrant entrepreneurs are able to identify and seize business opportunities in main-stream markets. In terms of the mixed embeddedness framework, the integration differences observed for first and second generation migrant entrepreneurs result in a divergence of opportunity structures relating to the socio-cultural and economic (and possible also politico-institutional) dimensions. Generally, we expect that integration in society fosters entrepreneurial prospects of migrants, because they have better opportunities to address a broader range of potential markets.

Research Design

I propose a two stage research design. In the first stage I want to sketch the situation of migrants and especially migrant entrepreneurs in the Netherlands using secondary public data. In the second stage I want to address the research questions above by conducting in depth interviews with migrant entrepreneurs using an interview guide to be developed. As I know a many migrant entrepreneurs personally, I will start to approach potential participants in the study through these contacts and later will extend my sample through snowball sampling.

Time Schedule

January 2010	Fine tuning of research problem and draft of theory chapters.
February 2010	Secondary data analysis for chapter "Sketch of migrant entrepreneurs in the Netherlands", Developing interview guideline.
March 2010	Fieldwork (interviews with migrant entrepreneurs)
April 2010	Analysis of qualitative data
May 2010	Writing it up and finished by end of May.

From: **Rebecca Nash** <r.m.nash@gmail.com>
Date: Tue, Jul 2, 2011 at 10:10 AM
Subject: Final Thesis
To: "Monica Yardman" <m.yardman@maastrichtuniversity.nl>

Dear Professor Yardman,

In our short talk a couple of weeks ago, you advised me to concentrate my research project proposal on one question. After reading some more literature, I decided to focus my project on the issue of unethical behaviour and institutions. Please, find attached a more detailed proposal, which I would like to discuss with you next week. I would be available any day except Wednesday and Friday afternoon.

Best wishes,

Rebecca

RESEARCH PROPOSAL

Rebecca Nash

Version: May 2011

Introduction

Over the last decades ethics has become a major issue in the business community. Numerous scandals about the behavior of managers in companies such as AIG, Tyco, Enron or BP have sensitized the public

▶

and started discussion on the ethical responsibilities of decision makers. It is of public interest whether Ralph Cioffi and Matthew Tannin, prior hedge fund managers at Bear Stearns, are held responsible for criminal charges. Likewise, the behavior of bank executives that lead to the financial crisis starting in the autumn 2008, is considered as highly unethical (Cohan, 2009). Despite the continuously refreshed interest in this topic, there still exists no clarity about the reasons for ethical misconduct.

Although lessons have been learnt from the recent financial crisis, it is crucial to avoid unethical behaviour and not only to limit its consequences. In particular business students will become the managers of tomorrow and previous research shows that business students are more open to unethical practices than students from other disciplines (Nill et al. 2004). For example 88% of business students have admitted to having engaged in serious cheating incidents in the past year (Davis et al., 1992). Recently, there has been a huge debate on the appropriateness of expelling 17 students from Teeside University, which have been caught plagiarizing coursework. These examples demonstrate that already business students engage in unethical behavior.

Discussions on ethical behavior are, however, rather difficult, as there is often no general consensus what is ethically acceptable and what not (Evening Gazette, 2010). In this line of argumentation Lowery & Beadles (2009) state that there seems to be a difference between work-related behaviour and non-work-related behaviour; unethical behaviour is apparently more acceptable in work surrounding than in private life. Thus, perceptions of ethics do not only differ between persons, but also within a person depending on the context it is in. Therefore, it is necessary to consider person and context when analyzing ethics.

Problem statement

From the discussion above it becomes evident that unethical behaviour in universities is a topic that needs to be paid attention to not at least because business students will be future business managers. There exists a lot of ambiguity regarding a clear and sound definition of what unethical behaviour among business student means. While some students might regard copying another student's words as acceptable, other students or professors judge this behaviour as unethical. Furthermore, prior research failed to specifically address context factors, although we know that context matters.

This leads to the following problem statement:

How do student-specific situational and individual factors impact the degree of unethical behaviour of business students in university?

To answer this research question, the following sub-questions are addressed:

- How to differentiate between ethical and unethical behaviour?
- How to define unethical behaviour in business faculties?
- Which situational and individual factors exist that are unique in university and are likely to influence business students' ethicality?

The contribution of the research is threefold.

1. This research is meant to define the concept of unethical behaviour and causes for why business students behave unethically. The research at hand aims to provide further insights in business students' ethicality.
2. Developing a better understanding of what business students define as unethical behaviour as well as which factors are most likely to increase students' openness to unethical actions. This understanding is a premise for counteracting this behaviour. It is of great importance to understand which situational and individual factors exist in business schools and how these factors impact students' likelihood to behave unethically.
3. As the research approach is quantitative it will be possible to draw inferences about what students perceive as unethical and which factors are most likely to induce unethical behaviour.

Research design

In this study the interrelation between context, personal characteristics and ethical behavior forms the core. To capture different contexts, I want to study students from different universities in the Netherlands, but want to focus on universities that have a business program, as I want to restrict my sample to business students.

To survey the students, I will make use of an online survey. Another point of concern is certainly, how to measure ethical behaviour. I suggest to use a couple of different questions, some asking about whether students behaved unethical in the past and others will ask them how they would react in a hypothetical situation.

Timeline

June 10	July 10	August 10	September 10	October 10	November 10
Introduction and first draft literature review	Polishing literature review and designing questionnaires	Vacation and finalizing questionnaires	Set-out questionnaires at the beginning of the academic year September 1st.	Analysis	Write-up

1 Taking the information provided in the case try to fill in the question hierarchy.
2 Discuss Mehmet's and Rebecca's short proposals.
3 How realistic would Mehmet's and Rebecca's time lines be at your university?

Summary

1 Research originates in the decision process. A manager needs specific information for setting objectives, defining tasks, finding the best strategy by which to carry out the tasks or judging how well the strategy is being implemented.

   A dilemma-centred emphasis – the problem's origin, selection, statement, exploration and refinement – dominates the sequence of the research process. A management dilemma can originate in any aspect of an organization. A decision to do research can be inappropriately driven by the availability of coveted tools and databases. To be researchable, a problem must be subject to observation or other forms of empirical data collection.

2 How one structures the research question sets the direction for the project. A management problem or opportunity can be formulated as a hierarchical sequence of questions. At the most general level is the management dilemma. This is translated into a management question and then into a research question – the major objective of the study. In turn, the research question is further expanded into investigative questions. These questions represent the various facets of the problem to be solved, and they influence research design, including design strategy, data-collection planning and sampling. At the most specific level are measurement questions that are answered by respondents in a survey or answered about each subject in an observational study.

3 Exploration of the problem is accomplished through familiarization with the available literature, interviews with experts, focus groups, or some combination of these. Revision of the management or research question(s) is a desirable outcome of exploration and enhances the researcher's understanding of the options available for developing a successful design.

   Decisions concerning the type of study, the means of data collection, measurement and sampling plans must be made when planning the design. Most researchers undertake sampling studies because of an interest in estimating population values or testing a statistical hypothesis. Carefully constructed delimitations are essential for specifying an appropriate probability sample. Non-probability samples are also used.

4   Budgets and value assessments determine whether most projects receive the necessary funding. Their thorough documentation is an integral part of the research proposal. Proposals are required for many research projects and should, at a minimum, describe the research question and the specific task the research will undertake.

Pilot tests are conducted to detect weaknesses in the study's design, data-collection instruments and procedures. Once the researcher is satisfied that the plan is sound, data collection begins. Data are collected, edited, coded and prepared for analysis.

Data analysis involves reduction, summarization, pattern examination and the statistical evaluation of research projects. A written report describing the study's findings is used to transmit the results and recommendations to the intended decision-maker. By cycling the conclusions back into the original problem, a new research iteration may begin, and findings may be applied.

5   A proposal is an offer to produce a research product or render a service to the potential buyer or sponsor. The research proposal presents a problem, discusses related research efforts, outlines the data needed for solving the problem, and shows the design used to gather and analyse the data.

Proposals are valuable to both the research sponsor and the researcher. The sponsor uses the proposal to evaluate a research idea. The proposal is also a useful tool to ensure that the sponsor and investigator agree on the research question. For the inexperienced researcher, the proposal enables learning from other researchers. In addition, the completed proposal provides a logical guide for the investigation.

6   We discussed two types of proposal: internal and external. Internal and external proposals have a problem-solving orientation. The staff of a company generates internal proposals. External proposals are prepared by an outside firm to obtain contract research. External proposals emphasize the qualifications of the researcher, special facilities and resources, and project management aspects such as budgets and schedules. Within each type of proposal there are varying degrees of complexity; a proposal can vary in length from a 2-page memo to more than 100 pages, from a telephone conversation to a multimedia presentation.

Proposals can be written with a set of sections or modules. The difference in type of proposal and level of project complexity determines what modules should be included.

7   Proposals can be evaluated formally or informally. The formal process uses a list of criteria and an associated point scale. The informal process is more qualitative. Important aspects beyond content include presentation style, timeliness and credibility.

Discussion questions

Terms in review

1 Some questions are answerable by research and others are not. Using some management problems of your choosing, distinguish between them.

2 A company is experiencing a poor inventory management situation and receives alternative research proposals. Proposal 1 is to use an audit of last year's transactions as a basis for recommendations. Proposal 2 is to study and recommend changes to the procedures and systems used by the materials department. Discuss issues of evaluation in terms of:
   a *ex-post facto* versus prior evaluation
   b evaluation using option analysis and decision theory.

Making research decisions

3 Confronted by low productivity, the president of Oaks Ltd asks a research company to study job satisfaction in the corporation. What are some of the important reasons for which this research project may fail to make an adequate contribution to the solution of management problems?

4 You have been approached by the editor of *Gentlemen's Magazine* to carry out a research study. The magazine has been unsuccessful in attracting shoe manufacturers as advertisers. When members of the sales force tried to secure advertising from shoe manufacturers, they were told men's clothing stores are a small and dying segment of their business. Since *Gentlemen's Magazine* goes chiefly to men's clothing stores, the manufacturers reasoned that it was, therefore, not a good vehicle for their advertising. The editor believes that a survey (via mail questionnaire) of men's clothing stores in the UK will probably show that these stores are important outlets for men's shoes and are not declining in importance as shoe outlets. He asks you to develop a proposal for the study and submit it to him. Develop the management research question hierarchy that will help you to develop a specific proposal.

5 Based on an analysis of the last six months' sales, your boss notices that sales of beef products are declining in your chain's restaurants. As beef entrée sales decline, so do profits. Fearing beef sales have declined due to several newspaper stories reporting *E. coli* contamination discovered at area grocery stores, he suggests a survey of area restaurants to see if the situation is pervasive.
   a   What do you think of this research suggestion?
   b   How, if at all, could you improve on your boss's formulation of the research question?

6 You are the new manager of market intelligence in a rapidly expanding software firm. Many product managers and corporate officers have requested market surveys from you on various products. Design a form for a research proposal that can be completed easily by your research staff and the sponsoring manager. Discuss how your form improves communication of the research objectives between the manager and the researcher.

7 Consider the new trends in desktop publishing, multimedia computer authoring and display capabilities, and inexpensive videotaping and playback possibilities. How might these be used to enhance research proposals? Give several examples of appropriate use.

8 You are manager of research in a large department store chain. Develop a list of criteria for evaluating the types of research activities listed below. Include a point scale and weighting algorithm.
   a   Market research
   b   Advertising effectiveness
   c   Employee opinion surveys
   d   Credit card operations
   e   Computer service effectiveness at individual store level

From concept to practice

9 Develop the management research question hierarchy (see Exhibits 2.2, 2.3 and 2.4), citing management dilemma, management question and research question(s) for each of the following:
   a   the production manager of a shoe factory
   b   the president of a home healthcare services firm
   c   the vice-president of labour relations for an auto manufacturer
   d   the retail advertising manager of a major metropolitan newspaper
   e   the chief of police in a major city.

10 Develop the management research question hierarchy for a management dilemma you face at work or with an organization for which you volunteer.

11 Develop a memo proposal for a research study in which 300 interviews are conducted to address the management question you defined in question 9.

12 Select an article from a scientific management journal. Outline a proposal for the research as if it had not yet been performed. Make estimates of time and costs. Generate a CPM schedule for the project following the format in Exhibit 2.10.

13 Compare the example of a good proposal with a bad proposal, which is available at the Online Resource Centre (ORC).

14 Using Exhibit 2.3 as your guide, what modules would you suggest be included in a proposal for each of the following cases?
  a   A bank interested in evaluating the effectiveness of its community contributions in dollars and loaned executive time.
  b   A manufacturer of leather custom-designed teacher development portfolios evaluating the market potential among teachers, who are now legally required to execute a professional development plan every three years.
  c   A university studying the possible calendar change from three 11-week quarters to two 16-week semesters.
  d   A dotcom that monitors clicks on banner ads interested in developing a different pricing structure for its service.

Class discussion

15 Discuss the problems of trading off exploration and pilot testing under tight budgetary constraints. What are the immediate and long-term effects?

16 The educational board of your faculty is considering changing the rules for writing a research project. One suggestion is that students have to write a research proposal (about five pages), which is formally assessed before a research project supervisor is assigned. Discuss the pros and cons of writing a full proposal for a research project and the formal assessment of it.

Recommended further reading

Baker, Michael J., 'Writing up and getting published', *Marketing Review* 1(4), 2001, pp. 441–72. The last part of a series by Michael Baker on how to plan and conduct research, appearing in the first volume of *Marketing Review*.

Fox, David J., *The Research Process in Education*. New York: Holt, Rinehart & Winston, 1969. Chapter 2 includes a research process model to compare with the one in this chapter.

Krathwohl, David R., *How to Prepare a Research Proposal* (3rd edn). Syracuse, NY: Syracuse University Press, 1988. A practical guide and framework for student projects.

Leedy, Paul D., *Practical Research: Planning and Design* (9th edn). Englewood Cliffs, NJ: Prentice Hall, 2009. Practical and readable sections guide students through the research process.

Locke, Lawrence F., Spiduso, Waneen Wyrick and Silverman, Steven J., *Proposals That Work: A Guide to Planning Dissertations and Grant Proposals* (5th edn). Thousand Oaks, CA: Sage, 2007. An excellent guide for students and faculty advisers covering all aspects of the proposal process.

Molfese, Victoria, Karp, Karen S. and Siegel, Linda S., 'Recommendations for writing a successful proposal from the reviewer's perspective', *Journal of Research Administration* 33(3), 2002, pp. 21–5. A case study reflecting the experience of three individuals in obtaining research funding in Canada.

Punch, Keith F., *Developing Effective Research Proposals* (2nd edn). Thousand Oaks, CA: Sage, 2006. A guide to how to prepare a well-constructed research proposal.

Raimond, P., *Management Projects*. London: Chapman & Hall, 1993. Chapter 4 offers a good overview of creative techniques that can be used to identify research ideas.

Get started with understanding statistical techniques!

When you have read this chapter, log on to the Online Learning Centre website at *www.mcgraw-hill.co.uk/textbooks/blumberg* to explore chapter-by-chapter test questions, additional case studies, a glossary and more online study tools for *Business Research Methods*.

Notes

1 Albert Einstein and L. Infeld, *The Evolution of Physics*. New York: Simon & Schuster, 1938, p. 95.

2 Walter B. Reitman, 'Heuristic decision procedures, open constraints, and the structure of ill defined problems', in W. Maynard Shelly, II and Glenn L. Bryan (eds), *Human Judgments and Optimality*. New York: Wiley, 1964, p. 285.

3 Carl M. Moore, *Group Techniques for Idea Building* (2nd edn). Thousand Oaks, CA: Sage, 1994.

4 Fred N. Kerlinger, *Foundations of Behavioral Research* (3rd edn). New York: Holt, Rinehart & Winston, 1986, pp. 436–7.

5 Paul D. Leedy, *How to Read Research and Understand It*. New York: Macmillan, 1981, pp. 67–70.

6 Walter B. Wentz, *Marketing Research: Management, Method, and Cases*. New York: Harper & Row, 1979, p. 35.

7 Robert D. Buzzell, Donald F. Cox and Rex V. Brown, *Marketing Research and Information Systems*. New York: McGraw-Hill, 1969, p. 595.

8 Dik Warren Twedt, 'What is the "return on investment" in marketing research?', *Journal of Marketing* 30 (January 1966), pp. 62–3.

9 Charles T. Brusaw, Gerald J. Alred and Walter E. Oliu, *Handbook of Technical Writing* (4th edn). New York: St. Martin's Press, 1992, p. 375.

10 Paul D. Leedy, *Practical Research: Planning and Design* (2nd edn). New York: Macmillan, 1980, p. 9.

11 R. Lesikar and John Pettit, *Report Writing for Business* (9th edn). Burr Ridge, IL: Irwin, 1995.

12 Ibid., p. 51.

13 William J. Roetzheim, *Proposal Writing for the Data Processing Consultant*. Englewood Cliffs, NJ: Prentice Hall, 1986, p. 106.

14 Brusaw, Alred and Oliu, *Handbook*, p. 11.

15 Philip V. Lewis and William H. Baker, *Business Report Writing*. Columbus, OH: Grid, 1978, p. 58.

16 Robert G. Murdick and Donald R. Cooper, *Business Research: Concepts and Guides*. Columbus, OH: Grid, 1982, p. 112.

17 Many texts cover project management and include details of scheduling and charting techniques such as CPM charts, which are beyond the scope of this text. See, for example, Chapter 3, 'Network analysis', in Don T. Philips, A. Ravindran and James J. Solberg, *Operations Research: Principles and Practice*. New York: Wiley, 1976; or Chapter 6, 'Network models', in K. Roscoe Davis and Patrick G. McKeon (eds), *Quantitative Models for Management*. Boston: Kent, 1981.

18 See, for example, Kate L. Turabian, *A Manual for Writers of Term Papers, Research Projects, and Dissertations*. Chicago: University of Chicago Press, 1996; Joseph Gibaldi and Walter S. Achtert, *MLA Handbook for Writers of Research Papers*. New York: Modern Language Association of America, 1999; and the *Publication Manual of the American Psychological Association*. Washington, DC: APA, 1994.

CHAPTER 3

Literature review

Chapter contents

Learning objectives

When you have read this chapter, you should understand:

1 what a scientific literature review is and the purposes it serves

2 how to select sources and search them for information

3 the structure of a good review.

Aims and objectives of a review

This chapter addresses an essential part of every research project: the review of the current literature. Scientific reviews of literature are rather different from the review of, say, a writer's novel, which you might find in national newspapers such as *Frankfurter Allgemeine, Le Monde, The Times* or *de Volkskrant*. Such reviews serve mainly to draw the attention of a potential audience to a new book and to contribute to contemporary literary debate. A scientific literature review, however, serves other purposes, namely to:

- establish the context of the problem or topic by reference to previous work
- understand the structure of the problem
- relate theories and ideas to the problem
- identify the relevant variables and relations
- show the reader what has been done previously
- show which theories have been applied to the problems
- show which research designs and methods have been chosen
- rationalize the significance of the problem and the study presented
- synthesize and gain a new perspective on the problem
- show what needs to be done in light of the existing knowledge.

Establishing the context of the problem by reference to previous work

Progress in science is made by the continuous accumulation of knowledge. Hence, you need to embed in your study the context of the problem, by reference to previous work of others. We will use the metaphor of knowledge as a cathedral to illustrate the process. Each study and article is just another brick added to the construction of the cathedral of knowledge. Some studies just reconfirm previous knowledge, often in slightly different settings. For example, the first empirical tests of transaction cost economics were carried out in the automotive industry.[1] Later on, other scholars applied transaction cost arguments to other industries – for example, relations in the utility sector and in the rail freight sector.[2] These studies in other industries added a new brick to the chapel of transaction cost economics and demonstrated the broader applicability of the theory. Sometimes new studies lay the foundations for a new chapel and if these prove to be solid enough to build a chapel on then the contributions involved are likely to attract the highest academic merit, perhaps in the form of a Nobel Prize. Ronald Coase's article on the boundaries of a firm is one of the foundations of transaction cost economics and appeared in 1937 in *Economica*. It earned Coase the Nobel Prize in 1990, because it inspired many other scholars, who contributed to the building of the chapel of transaction cost economics.[3] Oliver Williamson provided essential bricks for the further development of the theory, earning him the Nobel Prize in 2009.[4] Finally, Monteverde and Teece as well as Palay and Joskow (cited in notes 1 and 2 above) provided bricks of empirical testing.

So, using the metaphor of knowledge as a cathedral, the first function of a literature review is to embed the current study (the new brick) in the existing structure of knowledge (the cathedral). It allows the reader to understand much better which particular issue (chapel of the cathedral) the study addresses, where it contributes to the knowledge (foundations, walls or roof) and how it relates to the other bricks. In a complex world, isolated knowledge has no value; the value of your contribution increases if you relate it to the existing knowledge. The single brick is of limited beauty, but being part of the cathedral it contributes significantly to its overall beauty.

Understanding the structure of the problem

Although management science is a discipline or field of its own, it is clearly embedded in the broader area of the social sciences, which includes many other disciplines, such as communication and media studies, community studies, cultural studies, economics, gender studies, economic geography, economic and social history, political studies, psychology, religious studies, social and political theory, social anthropology and sociology. This list is by no means exhaustive and could be extended by the addition of many other research fields (e.g. environmental studies). This embeddedness of management science and business studies within other disciplines creates inter-dependencies between these fields, which means that, to research a problem in management, it is often necessary to acquaint oneself with existing knowledge in related disciplines. In addition, seeking to familiarize oneself with these different knowledge areas offers a fruitful approach to finding new (and often better) answers to current problems.

The literature review allows you to show the reader your understanding of the problem and its structure. Taking once again the metaphor of the cathedral, you can show the reader in which chapels you are going to work and which specific aspects you will investigate. Assume that you wish to investigate the question, 'Why do people become self-employed?' Plausible factors to explain the choice of self-employment include: general economic conditions, higher income than in paid labour, social background or personality traits. Each of these factors relates to a different chapel, that is theory or perspective. The first refers to macroeconomics, the second to micro-economic consideration of utility maximizing, the third to sociology and the fourth to psychology. Clearly, a single study cannot cover every perspective in the same depth and a researcher needs to choose between the possible perspectives. In a study, the literature review is a good place to argue why you selected a specific perspective, and what relationships and aspects you want to investigate within the chosen perspective.

Showing the reader what has been done previously

The two previous objectives of a literature review positioned your study in the cathedral of science. However, the literature review is also an instrument with which you can describe the chapel to which your study (brick) contributes. It offers a brief summary of the previous work that is clearly related to the problem of your study. This is an important function of the review, because you cannot assume that every reader is as knowledgeable about the field as you are. In such a summary and discussion of the previous literature, you show which theoretical concepts others have applied to the problems, what research designs and methods they have chosen to investigate the problem, and the results that others have found. Hence, you use the literature review to present the reader with a rich description of the current state of the chapel, by pointing out the beautiful parts, but also addressing its current shortcomings.

Even for a well-informed reader (one who has read and knows most of the literature you discuss), your review is an important piece of information. The literature review allows the well-informed reader, an expert in the field, to assess at a glance how knowledgeable the writer is. For example, if a friend of yours purported to be an expert in the history of world soccer, but did not once refer to the Brazilian team, you would have good reason to question his expertise. Similarly, a research paper that aims to investigate the 'make or buy' decisions of firms but does not mention transaction cost economics is less than convincing.

Deeper Insight into Research Methods
Meta analysis

Recently, **meta analysis**[5] has become increasingly popular to review and summarize studies addressing the same topic. It dates back to the work of Glass and Smith on psychotherapy in the 1970s.[6] Science is a cumulative activity and one research problem is explored and investigated by a large number of studies. For example, studies on who is likely to become self-employed, firms' choices of internationalization strategies, and so on, are countless. Meta analysis allows you to investigate quantitatively which outcomes are supported by most studies and which outcomes are more ambiguous. Further, you can identify whether differences in the research set-up, such as differences in sample size, different types of population, and so on, explain differences in the outcome. To some extent, a meta analysis is a very quantitative approach to a literature review.

Advantages and disadvantages of meta analysis

Meta analysis is a particularly powerful tool for reviewing an already well-investigated research field (i.e. a field in which quantitative empirical studies have been published). It offers a very structured approach to summarize the cumulated knowledge of all the studies included and is often able to detect relationships that narrative summaries of a research field have been unable to uncover. The structured approach of meta analysis (i.e. the tracking and recording of many characteristics of the studies, such as sample size, included variables, sample population, correlations between included variables, etc.) provides a way of organizing and handling such a large amount of information, which is usually less efficient and comprehensive if you use only notes and index cards to summarize the literature. This structured approach, however, is also a disadvantage of meta analysis, as it can only take account of the quantifiable characteristics of a study. It misses other important evaluation criteria, such as the methodological quality of a study or its social context, which can be accounted for in a narrative summary.

A major criticism of meta analysis is that it compares apples and oranges, and misses. For example, a meta analysis of studies on internationalization strategies can include studies that follow distinct theoretical ideas and therefore use different sets of independent variables. This problem, however, is only substantial if you attempt to average all studies to obtain an overall mean effect size. It is less of a problem if your main objective is to compare different (groups of) studies. A final disadvantage of meta analysis is the tremendous effort involved in conducting such an analysis.

Conducting a meta analysis

Meta analysis starts, like any research project, with the formulation of a problem statement. What is the research objective or, in other words, along what lines (criteria) do you want to compare or summarize the selected studies? A quantitative comparison and summary of studies requires that we obtain quantitative information for each study. In meta analysis this information is called the **effect size statistic**. Exhibit 3.1 provides an overview of common effect size statistics, but as a researcher you are free to develop other meaningful statistics that might serve the purpose of your meta analysis better than the common ones. Depending on the information available for each study, you can of course investigate multiple effect size statistics.

Exhibit 3.1 Common effect size statistics in meta analysis.

Effect size statistic	Objective and example of an application
Central tendency description	Compares descriptive statistics of variables, such as mean, mode or proportion, describing a central tendency across various samples
	Suppose you analyse various studies investigating the proportion of women reaching top management positions. This statistic provides you with the distribution of the proportions in the various studies and could be analysed by relating it to other characteristics of the study and sample
Pre-post contrast	Compares a central tendency at two points of time to examine changes and requires that all studies included provide information for both points of time
	Related to the example above, the proportion of women in top management positions in the 1990s and in the 2000s is compared and is used to examine changes
Group contrast	Comparison is not between two points of time but between two groups, which can be distinguished
	Related to the example above, the proportion of women in top management positions in business firms and in public institutions, such as hospitals, ministries, and so on
Association between variables	Comparing of the covariation between two variables, for example the correlation coefficient
	Related to the example above, the correlation between having a working mother and achieving a top management position

Once you have formulated your research problem and decided which effect size statistics are relevant to answering it, you need to develop a coding scheme to record the relevant information from the studies included in your meta analysis. Exhibit 3.2 provides you with an overview of possible information that

▶

> ### Exhibit 3.2 Useful information to collect and code for each study.
>
> - Variables and their definition
> - Sample size
> - Time and place of data-collection (study)
> - Descriptive statistics of each variable (mean, mode, standard deviation, variances)
> - Reliability scores for measurements
> - Correlation coefficients between two variables
> - Regression coefficients and their confidence intervals
> - Statistical methodology used

could usefully be coded for each study. This and other information is then coded in a spreadsheet or data file (such as Microsoft Excel) and statistical application software, with the studies in the rows and the different information items in the columns. Once you have organized all the information in one data file you can use statistical software to perform standard and sophisticated statistical analyses.

Exhibit 3.3 The systematic review process.

Stage I: Planning

Phase 1: Identification for review need

Phase 2: Review proposal

Phase 3: Development review protocol

Stage II: Conducting review

Phase 4: Identification of research

Phase 5: Study selection

Phase 6: Study quality assessment

Phase 7: Data extraction and monitoring

Phase 8: Data synthesis

Stage III: Reporting and dissemination

Phase 9: Report and recommendations

Phase 10: Getting evidence into practice

There is one major concern regarding narrative literature reviews and that is whether the literature reviewed is exhaustive and unbiased. Obviously it is impossible to include all articles and book chapters that had been written on alliance, work life balance or whatever topic you are interested in given the vast amount of scientific literature that is published every year. An additional problem is that the evidence often points in different directions, which probably is caused through different research design strategies and different analysis techniques. Meta analysis discussed above has rather strict requirements to include studies, e.g. all studies must contain the same concepts. Moreover, it is usually limited to an analysis of bivariate correlations, although we know that in the social and business sciences considering control variables is of utmost importance. Between a potentially subjective narrative literature review and the highly statistical meta analysis, there is a third form: the systematic review.

Originally systematic reviews were developed in the medical sciences, but Denyer and Tranfield[7] brought it to management sciences. Exhibit 3.3 shows the three stages with sub-phases of a systematic review. In the planning stage it is advisable not only to rely on the expertise of academics but also of practitioners that form a review panel. The task of the review panel is to determine the scope of the study and subject, considering different disciplinary perspectives, and to put the conclusion of those discussions into a review proposal. As management reviews are often a more exploratory exercise, it might be necessary to change the proposal in the process. This is possible but needs to be documented in the review protocol.

Conducting the review happens in stage II. In the first phases, efforts are made to ensure that the search for literature is unbiased. Defining key terms and appropriate search strings before one selects specific studies is essential to reduce bias. The search process needs to be documented well and results in a first list of studies. All these studies need to be evaluated whether their investigation matches with the subject. As defining the key terms and deciding which studies to include suffers from subjectivity, it is advisable that multiple researchers conduct this task independently. In the next phases, the methodological rigour of the remaining studies is evaluated according to specific quality criteria. All studies passing this hurdle are included and all relevant information regarding the research design, the analysis techniques and the results is extracted. The extracted information is summarized and integrated in the final phase 8. In stage III the researchers need to ensure that their findings are reported in a way that are also understood by the broader interested community, including practitioners.

Rationalizing the significance of the problem and the study presented

A literature review is, however, more than a summary of previous work. The summary of the status quo merely lays the foundations for a discussion of what needs to be done in the light of existing knowledge. Taking the metaphor of the cathedral once again, you use the picture of the current chapel (summary of the previous literature) to convince others that your idea for the next brick would make a valuable contribution in improving the chapel. Such improvements are usually refinements or reinforcements of current perspectives, where you fill an existing gap by adding a new brick or replacing an old brick. In the same way as a fifteenth-century master builder was likely to change the appearance of a cathedral from Roman to Gothic, by replacing Roman (round) arches with Gothic (pointed) ones, synthesizing current perspectives in a summary of the literature often gives rise to convincing ideas that will help readers gain a new perspective.

General problems of literature review

Pulling together all the ideas that stem from different disciplines is often difficult, as authors can be rooted in certain styles of thinking and writing that are specific to certain disciplines. For example: psychological studies often place a strong emphasis on measurement issues, and are rather rigid when it comes to discussions of validity and reliability; economists are less concerned with measurement issues, but rigid in terms of model building and the usage of statistical methods; management scholars place a strong emphasis on the applicability of theories to real-world management problems, but are less bothered about theory development and rigorous methodology. There is no perfect review. Each is written from a particular perspective, often rooted in a certain discipline or school of thought. Reviews are usually written with a particular reader in mind and, consequently, the literature review of an economic study on entrepreneurs will differ a great deal from that of a sociological study on the same topic.

Assessment of a 'good' literature review

There is no single best structure for a review. Sometimes the literature is reviewed throughout a whole book or article; other studies review the relevant literature in a specific chapter or section. Exhibit 3.4 provides a list of the ingredients a good literature review should contain. This list falls into two parts. Adding the first three ingredients to your review ensures that it will give a decent account of the literature and inform the reader about what has been done so far in the field. The last three ingredients serve as 'seasoning'. Without this seasoning your literature review is only a description of the field, a summary of previous studies. Through the addition of seasoning it becomes your own work as it reflects your thoughts and assessment of the current literature. Further, the last three ingredients are a necessity if you plan to use the literature review to point out why your current study makes an important contribution to the field.

Exhibit 3.4 The ingredients of a good literature review.

Basic ingredients

1 Literature mentioned and discussed relates to the problem statement of the study
2 Mentions (different) theoretical ideas contributing to the further exploration or explanation of the study's problem statement
3 Summarizes previous studies addressing and investigating the current study's problem statement

'Seasoning'

4 Discusses the theoretical ideas mentioned against the background of the results of previous studies
5 Analyses and compares previous studies in the light of their research design and methodology
6 Demonstrates how the current study fits in with previous studies, and shows its specific new contribution(s)

Exhibit 3.5 shows a short literature review, which is part of an empirical study to investigate the interplay between corporate social responsibility and stakeholder theory. Certainly, this review is by no means complete. It is written from a management perspective, hence neglecting studies that address those issues from a philosophical perspective.

Exhibit 3.5 Example of a literature review from a student's study on corporate social responsibility and stakeholder theory.

LITERATURE REVIEW

What are the moral duties of corporations? In the following I will discuss different approaches of 'Corporate Social Responsibility' (CSR) and stakeholder theory. It is relevant to address the progression in CSR as it overlaps with stakeholder theory (Crane and Matten, 2004) and investigates as well the concept of Fair Trade (Alvarez et al., 2010; Andorfer and Liebe, 2012; Castaldo, et al., 2009; De Pelsmacker et al., 2003; Fukukawa, 2003; Jaffee et al., 2009).

Corporate social responsibility

The academic disciplines of organization theory and business ethics, led to the concept of stakeholder theory (Crane and Matten, 2004), a different business approach, to consider a larger group of relevant actors, that are affected by and conversely affect the organization as well (Crane and Matten, 2004; Dervitsiotis, 2003; Freeman, 2001; Greenwood, 2007; Greenwood and Van Buren, 2010; Hosmer and Kiewitz, 2005). Within organizational literature, from the strategic perspective of the firm, originated the concept of CSR (Crane and Matten, 2004) a theoretical stance and practical development, that brought merit to corporations in terms of aligning business's strategic goals with social initiatives undertaken (Du et al., 2011; Greenwood, 2007; Lamberti and Lettieri, 2009; Luo and Bhattacharya, 2006; Porter and Kramer, 2006). On the next level CSR can be dissected in to three different types of strategies being: legally, ethically or economically oriented, of course in practice pure forms are found less and one can identify combinations of strategies (Schwartz and Carroll, 2003). In these three types of strategies, businesses have trust generating mechanisms, each with different impact on the consumer. Zooming in on the consumer level, a new type of consumer emerged, defined as the ethical consumer, which can be subdivided according to ethical interest being; animal rights, pollution and toxics and human rights (Barnett et al., 2005; Bird and Hughes, 1997; Carrington et al., 2010; Crane and Matten, 2004). As businesses come to understand their main consumer better, and also identify which ethical considerations their main target group hold, they can pose relevant strategic questions that feed into the logic design of CSR policies (Porter and Kramer, 2006). By balancing the interest of their relevant stakeholders and excelling in performance, businesses act responsibly, have logical CSR practices and can be perceived as more trustworthy by their main stakeholders (Corbett, 2004). Before reflecting on trust, the next section will first describe developments in stakeholder theory.

Stakeholder theory

Originating in business ethics and termed most popular and also most influential theory on business's role and responsibilities in society (Crane and Matten, 2004), stakeholder theory deserves to be treated here, to better explain the context in which organizations and consumers relate to each other. The book written by Freeman, that propelled the concept of the stakeholder into management and academic literature: *Strategic Management: A Stakeholder Approach* (1984) lay the foundation for the investigation of the stakeholder concept (Crane and Matten, 2004; Donaldson and Preston, 1995). The key proposition of stakeholder theory is that it focuses on the various groups to which corporations have a responsibility, recognizing that beyond shareholders, there are other groups in society that have an interest in the organization beyond stock returns (Crane and Matten, 2004). Stakeholder theory posits that fiduciary duties be extended beyond stockholders to any other party affected by the firm's actions, implying that managers act on behalf of the interest of all stakeholders, not just shareholders, and can be held legally responsible, towards the other actors affected by its business (Greenwood and Van Buren, 2010). From the traditional management model, customers were also considered relevant to the organization, but it was interpreted as one-directional – consumers passively depended on that what companies had to offer. The Stakeholder model considers many more groups in society and identifies all relations, including customers to be two-directional (Crane and Matten, 2004). A stakeholder is defined as "*Any group or individual who can affect or is affected by the achievement of the organization's objectives*" (Freeman, 2001; Mitchell et al., 1997). To understand stakeholder theory three approaches need to be considered: the normative, the instrumental, and the descriptive perspective (Crane and Matten, 2004; Donaldson and Preston, 1995; Mitchell et al., 1997).

Normative perspective

This perspective on stakeholder theory analyzes why corporations *should* consider other stakeholder interests (Crane and Matten, 2004; Donaldson and Preston, 1995). Based on Freeman's and Evan's principles (1993), Crane and Matten (2004) adapt Freeman's (1984) initial definition as follows: '*A stakeholder of a corporation is an individual or group which either is harmed by, or benefits from, the corporation or, whose rights can be violated, or have to be respected, by the corporation.*' By this definition they also underline that corporation's responsibilities are extended to other stakeholders, beyond shareholders, that are as well identified by law and social groups as relevant actors to consider. This definition at the same time also addresses Friedman's (1970) main argument against the social responsibilities of organizations. According to Friedman (1970, p. 122)

> "There is one and only one social responsibility of business – to use its resources and engage in activities designed to increase its profits so long as it stays within the rules of the game, which is to say engages in open and free competition without deception or fraud."

The main issue according to Friedman, is that corporations, unlike individuals cannot assume a moral position (Crane and Matten, 2004). Moore (1999), however, concludes, that organizations can be held morally responsible. This argument is developed on the legal status of corporations. Making corporations a legal person, does not imply that individuals and corporations hold the same moral position, however, as the legal status assigns them duties and responsibilities, a moral attitude naturally follows, where corporations are termed moral agents (Moore, 1999). Friedman further argues that laws and legislation should be left to governmental institutions. However, considering the size and reach of multinational corporations (MNCs) it seems reasonable to question the relevance of national laws, and to which national laws the organization should abide. Moreover if MNCs operate in countries where governments and lawful activity are difficult to control and corruption prevails, determining legal obligations becomes questionable (Bales, 1999; Prasad et al., 2004). Regulation through consumer demand, has most likely a larger impact than any law ever could establish (Hendriks, 2003).

Instrumental perspective

The stakeholders that matter most for an organization's survival and which needs have to be satisfied at all times are those that also have the most influence on the organization, according to the instrumental perspective (Hill and Jones, 2007). Mitchell et al. (1997) argue that the most influential, hence perceived important stakeholders carry the following three relationship attributes: (1) power; the impact of stakeholders actions, (2) legitimacy; the degree of desirable actions by stakeholders (3) urgency; the need for attention to stakeholder claims. The stakeholders that possess all these attributes are also termed definitive stakeholders, and require active engagement (Crane and Matten, 2004; Mitchell et al., 1997). The instrumental *or strategic* perspective thus looks into whether it is beneficial for an organization to consider stakeholder interests (Crane and Matten, 2004; Donaldson and Preston, 1995). However, it is not the only one to consider, as it would strip stakeholder theory from its key proposition – addressing the impact on all stakeholders, not just those that have the largest impact on financial returns. According to Friedman, this part of stakeholder theory is equivalent to maximizing profits under the traditional model (Crane and Matten, 2004). His argument seems just; however, the perspective of stakeholder theory is broader, and incorporates the interests of stakeholders and their role in strategic considerations, to a much larger extent, than the traditional model does.

Descriptive perspective

The stakeholder model is descriptive as it depicts all relations that constitute the organization, and its accuracy of doing so can be tested, by comparing it to other models (Donaldson and Preston, 1995). It thus investigates, if and in what way corporations actually consider the interests of stakeholders (Crane and Matten, 2004; Donaldson and Preston, 1995) as such it overlaps with the CSR literature. One of the arguments that Friedman (1970) makes against corporations social involvements seems to have become obsolete judged by current reality, namely that corporations cannot take up social responsibility and this should be assigned to governments. In today's society, corporations have started to assume political roles, due to two developments: governmental failure and increasing power and influences of corporations (Crane and Matten, 2004).

Stakeholder paradigm as the new management model?

Moore (1999) argues that the assumption of corporate moral responsibility has far-stretching implications for stakeholder theory. In that sense, it requires stakeholder models to become more defined, and better explain the reciprocal responsibilities of each stakeholder involved, including the corporation, but also the supplier, the customer and the shareholder. Caldwell and Karri (2005) argue that even the stakeholder model falls short on generating trust, as its main objective is balancing different stakeholder interests instead of seeking synergies in stakeholders' differing objectives. The Stewardship theory is what they propose and which coincides with Moore's (1999) critiques, as it considers reciprocal duties and rights.

A comparison of the dominant theories, illustrates the progression made in academic research, and the differences between these models. The table below captures some of these elements, which are adapted from the table provided by Caldwell and Karri (2005). The ethical focus progressed substantially, where consumers were considered a means to an end – making profit – they became the focal point of operations throughout the past decades. The zero-sum game which was the managerial focus of the traditional model, built on agency theory, in which Friedman also embedded his argumentation, seems to have been traded for models that have an objective that strives for greater utility for all, without sacrificing that of a few. Greenwood (2007) in line with the above criticism, argues that stakeholder engagement does not imply the same as corporate social behaviour; it could even imply immoral behaviour or very simply an act detached from any moral stance. The argument Greenwood makes, however, focuses on the obligations of the organizations, and lesser on the reciprocal rights and needs that Moore mentions, or synergistic objectives as the Stewardship model proposes.

	Agency Theory (1930s)	Stakeholder Theory (1980s)	Stewardship Theory (1990s)
Ethical focus	Goal oriented	Utilitarian needs of all stakeholders	Virtue ethics based upon a commitment to society
Managerial focus	Maximize short-term wealth for the principal	Balancer of demands and advocate of collective interests	Integrator of shared interests
Manager motivation	Serving principals and preserving self-interest	Equalizing benefits to all parties	Virtues and values and society
Use of information	Maximizes profitability	Creates understanding about interests and needs and identifies trade-offs	Achieve synergies
Basis of trust	Competence	Equity	Integrity
Organizational goal	Create highest possible short-term wealth	Create wealth and preserve relationships. Serve all parties fairly	Create long-term wealth and achieve best interests of all
Vision	Protection of self-interest	Integrating shareholder and organizational interests	Increasing organizational wealth to serve all interests
Assumptions about people	People seek rewards in an exchange relationship and are individualistic utility maximizers	People are concerned with equity and fairness and want to be dealt with justly. Utility is measured on distributive basis.	People are collective self-actualizers who achieve utility through organizational achievement

Stakeholder theory is therefore justifiably questioned as being able to model and require the trust needed in nowadays society, or framing it differently, 'Is equity enough for today's consumers'? Would consumers accept trade-offs, especially when it comes to fair trade items? Depicting these models also clearly demonstrates which responsibilities society expects from organizations. In the classical agency model, society is either not considered or positioned in an interest conflict with organizations. In recent years, societies' interests have, however, become an integrated part of firms' goal functions.

References

Alvarez, G., Pilbeam, C. and Wilding, R. (2010). Nestle Nespresso AAA sustainable quality program: an investigation into the governance dynamics in a multi-stakeholder supply chain network. *Supply Chain Management – an International Journal, 15*(2), 165–82.

Andorfer, V. and Liebe, U. (2012). Research on Fair Trade Consumption – A Review. *Journal of Business Ethics, 106*(4), 415–35.

Bales, K. (1999). *Disposable people. New slavery in the global economy*: University of California Press.

Barnett, C., Cloke, P., Clarke, N. and Malpass, A. (2005). Consuming ethics: articulating the subjects and spaces of ethical consumption. *Antipode, 37*(1), 23–45.

Barney, J.B. and Hansen, M.H. (1994). Trustworthiness as a source of competitive advantage. *Strategic Management Journal, 15*(S1), 175–90.

Bird, K. and Hughes, D.R. (1997). Ethical consumerism: The case of "Fairly-Traded" coffee. *Business Ethics: A European Review, 6*(3), 159–67.

Caldwell, C. and Karri, R. (2005). Organizational governance and ethical systems: A covenantal approach to building trust. *Journal of Business Ethics, 58*(1–3), 249–59.

Carrington, M., Neville, B. and Whitwell, G. (2010). Why Ethical Consumers Don't Walk Their Talk: Towards a Framework for Understanding the Gap Between the Ethical Purchase Intentions and Actual Buying Behaviour of Ethically Minded Consumers. *Journal of Business Ethics, 97*(1), 139–58.

Castaldo, S., Perrini, F., Misani, N. and Tencati, A. (2009). The missing link between corporate social responsibility and consumer trust: the case of fair trade products. *Journal of Business Ethics, 84*(1), 1–15.

Corbett, D. (2004). Excellence in Canada: Healthy organizations – Achieve results by acting responsibly. *Journal of Business Ethics, 55*(2), 125–33.

Crane, A. and Matten, D. (2004). *Business ethics: a European perspective: managing corporate citizenship and sustainability in the age of globalization*: Oxford University Press.

De Pelsmacker, P., Driesen, L. and Rayp, G. (2003). *Are fair trade labels good business? Ethics and coffee buying intentions*: Ghent University, Faculty of Economics and Business Administration.

Dervitsiotis, K.N. (2003). Beyond stakeholder satisfaction: aiming for a new frontier of sustainable stakeholder trust. *Total Quality Management & Business Excellence, 14*(5), 511–524.

Donaldson, T. and Preston, L.E. (1995). The stakeholder theory of the corporation: Concepts, evidence, and implications. *Academy of Management Review*, 65–91.

Du, S., Bhattacharya, C.B. and Sen, S. (2011). Corporate Social Responsibility and Competitive Advantage: Overcoming the Trust Barrier. *Management Science, 57*(9), 1528–45.

Evan, W. and Freeman, E. (1993). A stakeholder theory of the modern corporation. In G.D. Chryssides and J.H. Kaler (eds), *An Introduction to Business Ethics*. London: Chapman and Hall, 254–66.

Freeman, R.E. (1984). *Strategic management: A stakeholder approach*. Cambridge, Mass.: Ballinger.

Freeman, R.E. (2001). A Stakeholder Theory of the Modern Corporation. In T. Beauchamp, L. and N.E. Bowie (eds), *Ethical theory and business* (Vol. 6, pp. 56–65). Baskerville: Prentice-Hall.

Friedman, M. (1970). The social responsibility of business is to increase its profits. *New York Times Magazine*, September 13: 32–3, 122–4.

Fukukawa, K. (2003). A theoretical review of business and consumer ethics research: Normative and descriptive approaches. *The Marketing Review, 3*(4), 381–401.

Greenwood, M. (2007). Stakeholder engagement: Beyond the myth of corporate responsibility. *Journal of Business Ethics, 74*(4), 315–27.

Greenwood, M. and Van Buren, H.J. (2010). Trust and Stakeholder Theory: Trustworthiness in the Organisation-Stakeholder Relationship. *Journal of Business Ethics, 95*(3), 425–38.

Hendriks, M.R. (2003). Modern Slavery and the Production of Consumer Goods in a Global Economy: Consumer Choice-Not Law-Will Trigger the Next Diaspora. *Thomas M Cooley Law Review, 20*, 431.

Hill, C.W.L. and Jones, G.R. (2007). *Strategic management: An integrated approach*: South-Western Pub.

Hosmer, L.R.T. and Kiewitz, C. (2005). Organizational justice: A behavioral science concept with critical implications for business ethics and stakeholder theory. *Business Ethics Quarterly, 15*(1), 67–91.

Jaffee, D., Kloppenburg, J.R. and Monroy, M.B. (2009). Bringing the "Moral Charge" Home: Fair Trade within the North and within the South*. *Rural Sociology, 69*(2), 169–96.

Lamberti, L. and Lettieri, E. (2009). CSR Practices and Corporate Strategy: Evidence from a Longitudinal Case Study. *Journal of Business Ethics, 87*(2), 153–68.

Limoncelli, S.A. (2010). The Slave Next Door: Human Trafficking and Slavery in America Today. *Contemporary Sociology-a Journal of Reviews, 39*(3), 277–79.

Luo, X. and Bhattacharya, C.B. (2006). Corporate social responsibility, customer satisfaction, and market value. *Journal of marketing*, 1–18.

Mitchell, R.K., Agle, B.R. and Wood, D.J. (1997). Toward a theory of stakeholder identification and salience: Defining the principle of who and what really counts. *Academy of management Review*, 853–86.

Moore, G. (1999). Corporate moral agency: review and implications. *Journal of Business Ethics, 21*(4), 329–43.

Porter, M.E. and Kramer, M.R. (2006). Strategy & Society: The Link Between Competitive Advantage and Corporate Social Responsibility. *Harvard Business Review, 84*(12), 78–92.

Prasad, M., Kimeldorf, H., Meyer, R. and Robinson, I. (2004). Consumers of the World Unite: A Market-based Response to Sweatshops. *Labor Studies Journal, 29*(3), 57–79.

Schwartz, M.S. and Carroll, A.B. (2003). Corporate social responsibility: A three-domain approach. *Business Ethics Quarterly*, 503–30.

Looking at Exhibit 3.5 you will see that, first, the literature mentioned refers to the problem statement. The objective of the study is to advance the understanding of corporate social responsibility (CSR) by employing stakeholder theory. As new research often bridges fields that are as yet unconnected, or extends the applicability of a theory to a new field, it is not surprising that reviews often discuss literature that does not completely tie in with the objective of the current study. Were you to read the literature cited, you would soon see that most of the studies mentioned do not cover both corporate social responsibility and stakeholder theory, but all studies cited do address at least one part of the problem statement.

Second, the review in Exhibit 3.5 mentions different approaches of stakeholder theory, namely the normative, instrumental and descriptive approach.

Third, it summarizes the literature by providing very brief accounts of previous studies. In this particular review, the author runs through three approaches of stakeholder theory and briefly reports considerations made in previous studies concerning these different approaches. Although a literature review cannot encompass all previous literature, the selection of literature to be cited should never be based on the correspondence of previous studies' results with one's own expectations or even one's own views. Neglecting counter-evidence in other studies, of which the informed reader is often aware, leads to the conclusion that the author is not very knowledgeable about the field, and can often raise the suspicion that the paper as a whole is as incomplete and poorly put together as the literature review.

Fourth, in a literature review it is important to discuss new theories alongside the results of previous studies. In the literature review example in Exhibit 3.5, the author concludes that incorporating considerations from corporate social responsibility into stakeholder theory leads to a new theory, namely stewardship theory.

Fifth, in management, economics and social science, studies are often based on different theoretical assumptions, which produce conflicting conclusions. The reasons for such contradictions are numerous and include differences in philosophies, methodological approaches and so on. Hence, a good literature review should also analyse and compare previous studies in the light of different approaches used. In the example in Exhibit 3.5, the author discusses, for example, the position of Friedman (1970) who claims that social corporate responsibility is contraproductive to companies and the economic system. Moreover, the table compares three related, different approaches to deal with the problem.

Sixth, and finally, the literature review should be used to demonstrate how well the current study fits in with previous studies and to highlight the new contributions it makes. In the example, the review concludes with a historic timeline of theoretical developments ranging from agency theory over stakeholder theory to stewardship theory.

Critical review

In the first two sections we discussed how researchers document and reflect on the scientific literature that forms the base of their study. This kind of literature review usually follows the introduction of an article and is often also labelled 'theory'. There is, however, another kind of review very common in the academic field, the critical review. Some academic journals have a feature called 'book reviews', in which colleague scientists write an assessment about a certain book. These reviews are usually published once the book is on the market. Another kind of critical review is an essential part of the whole publishing process; they are solicited before the book is published. For example chapters of this book were sent out to other lecturers who are involved in teaching research methods. Some of the reviewers used the previous edition of this book in their courses, while other reviewers used a different textbook on research methods.

Similarly, most academic journals use a system called 'peer review' to decide which manuscripts they publish. The editor of the journal will ask two to three other scientists who have published on related topics to read a submitted manuscript and then write a review which will be between one and ten pages long. This whole process is anonymous: i.e. the reviewer does not know who the authors are and the authors do not know who the reviewers are. Based on the reviewers' reports the editor decides whether to reject the manuscript or whether they invite the authors to revise and resubmit. The authors have then the chance to improve their manuscript and respond to the comments of the reviewers. Afterwards, the revised manuscript is again sent to the reviewers and they will assess whether the changes made did improve the paper sufficiently. In good journals, two and even three rounds of reviews and revisions are rather common.

As author, one is of course often not really delighted by those reviews as the reviews are often critical to one's own work, and most people do not like to be criticized. If such reviews are solicited before publication, they offer, however, a tremendous source of inspiration on how the book could be improved, as they help the authors to understand how the book is read. The changes and improvements we have made for each new edition of this book are often initiated by reviewer comments. Often, reviewers are also very constructive, i.e. they do not only criticize a certain aspect but also suggest solutions. To express our gratitude to these reviewers we thank them on page xii. Likewise, articles in scientific journal often include a footnote to the title in which the authors thank people they have discussed their study with, but also the editor and the anonymous reviewers.

As already mentioned, the objective of a review is to assess the quality of a text and to provide a short summary. The latter is especially important if you write a review about a book that is already published and from which other people will decide whether it is worth reading the book. In the academic field, critics are not just negative, a critical review also mentions what the reviewer liked, i.e. a fair evaluation lists both weak and strong points.

The typical structure of critical review is:

1 Introduction
2 Summary
3 Critique
4 Conclusion

The introduction is usually just one paragraph. It begins by naming the authors (if known) and the title of the book or article. Then the main objectives and results of the text are summarized and a concise evaluation closes the review. After having read the introduction, the reader should know whether the book or article was liked or disliked.

The summary gives a brief overview of the book by listing the key points and the authors' purposes. The summary should not be more than 30 per cent of the text. The reader should get an idea of what the book is about; but the summary is not a substitute for reading the book. The summary is usually not included in reviews that are solicited in the publication process, as the main receivers of such reviews are the authors, who do not need a summary of their own work.

The main part of any review is the **critique**. In the critique you mention the weak and strong points and discuss these using specific criteria (see Exhibit 3.6 below for examples). There are several ways to structure the critique. One way is to write the critique alongside the structure of the reviewed text; another way is to identify a couple of issues around which you assess the text. The sequence of these issues can be from most important to least important issue or to mention first the weak points and then strong points or vice versa. One advice is to start with strong points, if overall the critique is negative; start with weak points, if overall the critique is positive. The critique can also make suggestions how the problems raised could be tackled. Especially in reviews written before the text has been published, it is common that reviewers will share their ideas on how a text could be improved.

Finally, the conclusion is a very short paragraph containing the overall verdict on the text plus some explanations for it.

Exhibit 3.6 Criteria used in critical reviews.

Criteria	Question to be raised
Contribution to the field	What is the author's aim and has it been achieved?
	What does the text add to the scientific knowledge base?
	Is the problem addressed relevant?
Argumentation	Is the problem statement clear?
	Are hypotheses clearly formulated?
	Is the argumentation based on theoretical logical reasoning?
	Is the reasoning consistent?
	Are arguments supported by evidence and how valid and reliable is the evidence?
	Are conclusions drawn backed up by the results?
	Is there a red thread throughout the text?
Methods and analysis	Are the methods and analysis techniques used appropriate for the purpose of the study?
	Are there any biases in the methods and analysis techniques?
	Have the method and analysis techniques been applied well?
	Are the results reliable and valid?
Writing	Is the language used adequate for the audience (scientists or informed public)?
	Is the text well structured?
	Is the text easy to read and to follow?

3.4 Process and organization

Writing a literature review is an iterative process of three tasks:

1 searching information (literature)
2 assessing the information obtained
3 synthesizing the assessment of information.

Literature search and sources

Literature search

It is likely that the preparation of a literature review will start with a **literature search**. A literature search calls for the use of a library's online catalogue, and one or more **bibliographic databases** or **indexes**. For some topics, it may be useful to consult a handbook or specialist encyclopaedia first to establish a list of key terms, people or events that have influenced the topic under investigation, and also to determine the major publications and the foremost authors in the field. Other reference materials will be incorporated into the search strategy as needed. In general, this literature search has five steps:

1 Define your management dilemma or management question.
2 Consult encyclopaedias, dictionaries, handbooks and textbooks to identify key terms, people or events relevant to your management dilemma or management question.
3 Apply these key terms, people or events in searching indexes, bibliographies and the web to identify specific secondary sources.
4 Locate and review specific secondary sources for relevance.
5 Evaluate the value of each source and its content.

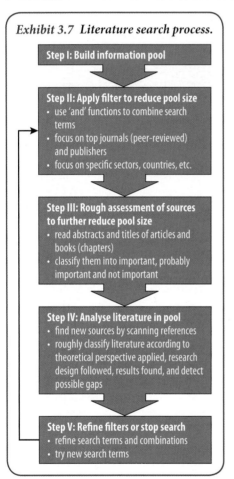

Exhibit 3.7 Literature search process.

In economic and business studies, the main problem is not finding literature that is related to a certain topic, but filtering the really relevant and good literature, and distinguishing it from irrelevant literature and dubious sources. The Internet has without doubt facilitated access to a wide range of different information, and students are now less dependent on the quality and thematic focus of their local university libraries. Using academic databases, such as ABI Inform, ECONLIT or EBSCO, it has become much easier to find a wide range of literature related to a certain topic. Furthermore, many libraries now subscribe to services that permit electronic access to the full text of many academic journals. The amount of information available has, however, become so vast that it is impossible to read all the information to assess its quality and relevance to one's own research. Hence, researchers need some guidelines to help them decide on the relevance of available information resources. The application of such guidelines and 'filters' has the drawback that some relevant information might not be discovered and may slip through the net. That is why an iterative search-refining process is useful in ensuring search efficiency, and helps to minimize the chances of relevant information being missed. The steps to be followed are listed in Exhibit 3.7.

Before one can start the research process, one needs at least an idea of the problem involved or, better, a problem statement to give the search some direction. In this phase the search process has a broad orientation and one tries to find out what others have written on this and related topics. The primary aim is to build up a pool of potential information. One can usually distinguish two departure points for creating such a pool and you should use both. The first is your pre-knowledge. Such pre-knowledge can be based on earlier similar research you have done or simply on a course with a related topic that you have followed. You can add the literature you used in previous related research or during a related course to your pool of potential information.

Another important point of departure is the aforementioned databases of academic books and articles, such as EBSCO. You should start your search by generating a list of search terms. Words that appear in the working title of your study and the names of the theoretical concepts you propose to use form important search terms that should be on your list. One common problem with databases is that they are often designed with a particular discipline in mind. For example, EBSCO covers mainly economic- and business-related sources, PSYCHLIT covers psychological sources and SOCIOFILE covers sociological sources. If your problem, or the perspective you want to take on the problem, bridges several disciplines you will also need to carry out the search in each of these databases or use a mega search engine that allows you to select various databases, which will be searched simultaneously. To fully utilize the potential of a database you have to learn how to use it. By using it you will learn automatically which search strategies and terms achieve the best results, as well as the limitations of a database in terms of coverage.

Depending on the search terms used, a search can retrieve thousands of hits. Such a high number of sources can by no means be examined thoroughly. Therefore, you need to apply filters to reduce the pool size (i.e. the number of hits). Particularly for academic studies, it is often useful to restrict your search to academic peer-reviewed publications. **Peer-reviewed** publications only publish articles after other scholars – peers – have evaluated and approved the scientific quality of the work. Hence, peer review is a kind of quality mark, which ensures that the work published in such journals fulfils the quality standards of sound scientific research (see Chapter 2 to recap on these standards). More detailed information on the scientific quality of the work can be obtained from various rankings, which are often based on the Social Science Citation Index. This counts how often articles from a specific journal have been cited in other articles. Another effective method for reducing the number of hits is to combine your search terms with the logical operator 'and', and then the search system will retrieve only those sources that contain both search terms. This method is especially useful in combining search terms that are rather generic, such as utility, management, innovation, leadership and the like. Finally, it is often also wise to limit the search to a specific application field, such as, say, an industrial sector or country. You should continue using a filter to refine this until the number of hits has reached a manageable number.

In the third step of the process you take a first look at the sources. The main objective of this step is to make a rough assessment of all the sources in terms of their usefulness for your study. If the number of sources is still rather high, you might just scan the titles to decide whether the book or article could be relevant for your own study. If the number of information sources is moderate, or once you have scanned the titles, you can use the abstracts (short summaries of the articles cited) of the articles and books to assess whether they are related to your study. At the end of this step, you will have compiled a list of articles and books that are clearly related to some aspect of your own research; then you must obtain the full text of these sources.

In step four, you read and begin to analyse your sources. To start with, it is often sufficient to skim through the text. The aim of this is to decide whether the source makes an important contribution in terms of theoretical background, research design and methods used, and qualitative or quantitative findings. Placing each article in one or more of these categories also allows you to check which part of your study still might lack literature. Although there is no golden rule as to how many articles you need overall and in each category for a comprehensive review, such a structured overview can reveal substantial imbalances in your literature coverage.

You should also check the reference section of each source to see whether it contains titles that sound promising but are not yet on your list. Such a process tends to lead to a snowball effect: references in one source point you to a new source, and that source's references in turn point you to another source, and so on. This is a very useful way to discover the (theoretical) origins of a field and to broaden your literature search across more disciplines. The main disadvantage of this system is that it is past-oriented – that is, each source will only point you to articles and books that have been published before the source itself was published. Hence, it is useful to start such a 'snowball search' with very recent articles or books. Another way to make sure your search is up to date is to identify through the snowball system prominent authors and journals. You can then search for articles that these authors have published recently and also check the latest volumes of the journals that frequently publish articles in the field in which you are interested.

Some journals, such as the *Journal of Economic Literature* or *Academy of Management Review*, publish review articles, which usually offer a good overview of the current state of affairs in a particular field. Other journals sometimes publish 'special issues' devoted to one specific theme. Guest editors, who summarize the articles and place them in the field's current scientific discussion, often introduce such special issues. Thus, review articles and special issues of journals are an extremely useful information source for determining the relevant literature for your study and literature review.

The fifth step involves either the decision to refine your search arguments with the information obtained during step four, or the decision to stop the search. A useful hint on whether to call a halt to your search is to take a close look at the reference sections of the core articles of your literature review. When your list of literature resembles the references of the core articles and also contains some additional, more recent, articles, you know that your coverage of the relevant literature in the field is good.

Deeper Insight into Research Methods
Advanced searching

In advanced searches, you use your knowledge of the database to make the search more productive.

Construct the search query

Use the keywords from your management question to prepare a query for the database. Bibliographic data-bases, including libraries' online catalogues, all have similar search options, such as a basic keyword search, an advanced search and a way to choose a subject from a browse list. In most bibliographic databases, all searches are keyword searches, but it is possible to search for a specific author, title or series (a known-item search) by limiting your results to a specific field of the bibliographic record.

The most important thing to remember about search engines for the web or for databases is that they do not all work in the same way. In fact, they have widely varying search protocols. What you do not know can act against you. So, if finding good information is important to you, take a couple of minutes to determine what special features and search options are used. For instance, if you enter a multiword term, what happens? Does the database search your term as a phrase? Or does it insert a connector such as 'and' or 'or' between each word? How does it handle stop-words ('the', 'in' and other similar small words)? The results will vary considerably in these three scenarios (see Exhibit 3.8).

Exhibit 3.8 Review of advanced search options.

Expanding your search	Narrowing your search	
[OR] Use OR to search for plurals, synonyms, or spelling variations. Either or both terms will be present in results: • woman OR women • business OR corporation • international OR foreign	**[AND]** Use AND to require that all terms you specify be present in the results: • child AND advertising	**[Phrases]** Use a term consisting of two or more words. Some phrases require double quotes to enclose the phrase, while others do not: • human resource management • "human resource management"
Truncation Symbols (?, *, !) that replace one or more characters or letters in a word or at the end of a word: • electr* (retrieves electricity, electric, electrical) • child? (retrieves children, childish, child's)	**[NOT]** Use NOT to eliminate terms from your search. But use NOT with care. It is easy to eliminate the good with the unwanted: • medicine NOT nursing • Caribbean NOT Cuba	**[ADJ]** ADJ requires the first term specified to immediately precede the last term specified: • six ADJ sigma
	Limiters Conditions (date, publication, type, language) for limiting your search. Most databases also offer *field limiting*, limiting the occurrences of your search to a specific database field, such as the author field, title, and so on. Some bibliographic databases offer the convenience of limiting the search results to peer-reviewed articles or to articles only available in full text. Use the latter with care as some significant articles may be overlooked even though they are in the library.	

Search strategy options

Basic searching

If you have a unique term, try a basic search using that term. Most bibliographic databases will present the results list in reverse date order – that is, those items published most recently will appear first. Review the list of items your search has retrieved. Are there too many? Not enough? Are they very relevant or not very relevant? If they meet the 'Goldilocks test' of 'just right', then you can move on to the next step (saving results).

Advanced searching

If you have retrieved too few or no relevant items, or if you have retrieved hundreds of items, you should consider modifying your search query. Start with the most relevant items in the results list. Then do one of the following:

- search for the cited works (the bibliography) of the full-text articles
- search for other works by the author or authors of the relevant citations
- check the subject headings assigned to the articles (Are there any more precise terms or synonyms that would improve your search results? More importantly, are there pairs of terms that appear in all the most relevant items? Is there a thesaurus with the database that defines or expands the terminology used in the subject headings?).

As a result of your examination of the relevant citations and any background preparation you have done in other sources such as encyclopaedias, you should now have one or more keywords and synonyms for each concept. You can now use Boolean operators or connectors (see Exhibit 3.8) to combine terms or sets of terms to expand or narrow your search. There are four basic Boolean operators or connectors: OR, AND, NOT and ADJ.

Think of your management question as a series of keywords. For example, your management question might be, 'How can I design an appropriate training or awareness programme to prevent sexual harassment lawsuits in my company?' In this example, concept A would be training, concept B would be harassment, and concept C would be lawsuits. In the most basic of keyword searches, you could use a keyword search with the operator AND to combine them:

[training AND harassment AND lawsuits]

If your search results are inadequate, you might need to expand your search statement with synonyms connected with the operator OR. If your search results are too numerous, you will need to limit your search.

Student Research
Literature search applied

Some months ago I received an e-mail from a student. Patricia Carvalho wrote that she had read articles written by a colleague and by me, and wondered whether I would be interested in supervising her research project. Patricia had not only studied business, but she also had followed courses at the school of law. Therefore, she was interested in contracting, more specifically contracting between business firms. A week later, we met in my office to discuss our ideas on the topic.

We soon came to the conclusion that it might be worthwhile to investigate what different purposes business contracts serve. The economic literature assumes that firms sign contracts as safeguards against potential opportunism by the other party. However, other studies suggest that contracts may also serve other purposes than opportunism mitigation, namely coordination and signalling. Having access to a data set that assesses the contracts of exchange transactions between business firms quite extensively, Patricia attempted to investigate the topic of 'contractual functions' more deeply. Exhibit 3.9 shows how she used the EBSCO database to get a comprehensive overview of the literature; this also formed the basis of her literature review.

►

Exhibit 3.9　Hits for a keyword search in EBSCO.

Search entries used	Result
Contract* and opportunism	63 articles in peer-reviewed sources
Contract* and mitigation	32 articles in peer-reviewed sources
Contract* and signal*	182 articles in peer-reviewed sources

Note: an asterisk (*) at the end of the search term indicates that the search engine should look not only at the specific term (e.g. contract), but also other words starting with the letters 'contract', such as contracts, contracting, and so on.

She quickly screened the abstracts of all these articles online to determine the relevance of each of the references for our study. She ended up with a list of about 33 articles, some of which she already knew from classes followed. The articles she did not yet know were printed out and the whole text was scanned through. In this way she was able to compile a list of about 13 core articles. Then she looked at the reference lists of these core articles to see whether she had missed any important articles that were cited frequently. While checking the reference lists of the core articles she looked in particular for articles that had been published in legal journals, as our research topic deals with the interface of legal and business studies, and the database she consulted did not list legal journals. She identified another five articles that had been published in legal journals.

Exhibit 3.10　List of important databases.

Databases covering disciplines

ABI/INFORM Database: a database covering more than 1,000 leading business and management publications from 1971 on; from 1987 it provides full text.

EBSCO: a database covering nearly 3,800 leading business and management journals; it provides abstracts of the articles and even full text of some articles from more than 1,100 peer-reviewed journals.

ECONLIT: a database covering more than 1,000 leading economic publications; it contains more than 610,000 records from 1969 to the present.

SOCIOFILE: a database covering about 2,000 leading sociological journals; it provides abstracts of the articles, and full text for some articles dating back to 1974.

psycArticles: a database covering respected sources from 1987 to the present, including 33,000 full-text articles from publications of the American Psychological Association.

Google Scholar is not really a database but a search engine that is specialized in finding academic sources. It is very useful in finding articles and also books, but the sources found are often not full-text accessible.

Working papers databases

In business science it often takes years until a research paper is finally published in a respectable journal. However, before that, many papers are available as working papers, also called discussion papers. These working papers are often available at the websites of the schools the authors are affiliated to or on the researchers' home pages. Besides that, a couple of institutions bundle working papers that appear at the different schools.

www.cepr.org

www.nber.org/papers/

papers.ssrn.com/

Publishers' databases

Major publishers of academic journals currently allow you to search all articles that have appeared in their journals. Access to full text is mostly limited to those schools that also have a subscription to a specific journal. In business science, the most prominent journal and book publishers are Chicago University Press, Edward Elgar, Elsevier, Emerald, Harvard Business, McGraw-Hill, Oxford University Press, Palgrave Macmillan, Routledge, Sage, Springer and Wiley.

Literature sources

Literature can be found in both primary and secondary sources. **Primary sources** are full-text publications of theoretical and empirical studies, and represent the original work. **Secondary sources** are compilations of information, either in printed or digital form.

Secondary sources

There are several bibliographic databases available to business researchers. Some of the more popular and comprehensive business bibliographic databases are listed in Exhibit 3.10 (see also Appendix A and the accompanying website).

Most of the databases listed in Exhibit 3.10 offer numerous purchase options, both in terms of the amount and type of coverage. Some include abstracts. Nearly all the databases include the contents of around two-thirds of the indexed journals in full-text form, although the amount and the specific titles may vary widely from database to database. Search options also vary considerably from database to database. It is for these reasons that most libraries that support business programmes offer more than one business periodical database.

Search process

The process of searching bibliographic databases and retrieving results applies to all databases:

1 Select a database appropriate to your topic.
2 Construct a **search query** (also called a **search statement**).
    a Review and evaluate search results.
    b Modify the search query, if necessary.
3 Save the valuable results of your search.
4 Retrieve articles not available in the database.
5 Supplement your results with information from web sources.

1 Select a database

Most of us select the most convenient database with little regard for its scope, but considering the database contents and its limitations and criteria for inclusion at the beginning of your search will probably save you time in the long run. Remember that a library's online catalogue is a bibliographic database that will help identify books and perhaps other media on a topic. While journal or periodical titles are listed in a library's online catalogue, periodical or journal articles are rarely included. Use books for older, more comprehensive information. Use periodical articles for more current information or for information on very specific topics. A librarian can suggest one or more appropriate databases for the topic you are researching.

2 Construct search query

For tips on how to construct search queries, see the Deeper Insight box on page 102.

3 Save the results of the search

While the temptation to print may be overwhelming, remember that if you download your results, you can cut and paste quotations, tables and other information into your proposal without any need for rekeying. In either case, make sure you keep a note of the bibliographic information for your footnotes and bibliography. Most databases offer the choice of marking the records and printing or downloading them all at once or printing them one by one.

4 Retrieve articles

For articles not available in full-text form online, retrieval will normally require the additional step of searching the library's online catalogue (unless there is a link from the database to the catalogue) to determine whether the desired issue is available and where it is located. Many libraries offer a document delivery service for any articles that are not available online. Some current articles may be available on the web or via a fee-based service.

There are dozens of types of information sources, each with a special function. In this section we describe five of the information types used most by business researchers. Later in this chapter we provide a more in-depth examination of three information types: bibliographic databases, government information and the World Wide Web.

Indexes and bibliographies

Indexes and bibliographies are the mainstay of any library because they help the researcher to identify and locate a single book or journal article from among the millions published. The single most important **bibliography** in any library is its online catalogue. As with all other information types, there are many specialized indexes and bibliographies unique to business topics. These can be very useful in a literature search to find authors and titles of prior works on the topic of interest. (A list of key business resources is provided in Appendix A and on the accompanying website.)

Directories

Directories are used for finding names and addresses, as well as other data. Directories in digitized format, which can be searched by certain characteristics or sorted and then downloaded, are far more useful. Many are available free via the web, but the most comprehensive directories are proprietary (i.e. they must be purchased).

Primary sources

In science, a specific study is often pre-published in the form of a research project, report, unpublished manuscript or conference proceeding, before it is published as an article in a scientific journal or as a chapter in a book. Such pre-publications serve two functions. First, authors circulate an unpublished manuscript among colleagues or present it at a conference to receive comments, which helps them to improve the study. Second, as the date of the pre-publication appears, the author can claim that he or she had a particular theoretical thought or empirical finding at this specific time and not later on.

Just a brief glance at the reference list of any academic article reveals that by far the greatest number of references stem from academic books or journals. Hence, these two forms of publication are the most important and relevant sources for any academic research. However, other publications, such as professional and trade journals, newspapers, and working papers or conference proceedings, often also form a rich source of information. Exhibit 3.11 offers an overview of the different literature sources and characterizes their usefulness for scientific work, their coverage in databases and their availability.

The Internet as literature source

The World Wide Web is such a vast information, business and entertainment resource that it would be difficult, if not foolish, to overlook. Millions of pages of data are publicly available, and the size of the web doubles every few months.[8] But searching and retrieving reliable information on the web is a great deal more problematic than searching a bibliographic database. There are no standard database fields, no carefully defined subject hierarchies (known as controlled vocabulary), no cross-references, no synonyms, no selection criteria and, in general, no rules. There are dozens of search engines and they all work differently, but how they work is not always easy to determine. Nonetheless, the convenience of the web and the extraordinary amount of information to be found on it are compelling reasons for using it as an information source.

As you can see in Exhibit 3.12, the basic steps to searching the web are similar to those outlined for searching a bibliographic database. As you approach the web, you start at the same point: focusing on your management question. Are you looking for a known item (e.g. the personal website of a famous scholar)? Are you looking for information on a specific topic?

If you are looking for a specific topic, what are its parameters? For example, if your topic is managed healthcare, are you hoping to find general statistics, public policy issues, accounting standards or evidence of its impact on small businesses?

There are perfectly legitimate reasons to browse for information, and with its hypertext linking system, the web is the ultimate resource for browsing. The trick is to browse but to stay focused on the topic at hand. In the browse mode you do not have any particular target. You follow hypertext links from site to site for the sheer joy of discovery. This is somewhat analogous to window shopping at the mall or browsing the bookshelves in a library. It may or may not be fruitful. Neither is browsing likely to be efficient: researchers often work to tight deadlines, as managers often cannot delay critical decisions; therefore, researchers rarely have the luxury of undirected browsing.

Below are detailed those steps in the web search process that call for altered behaviour to that used in bibliographic searches.

Search engines

A search for specific information or for a specific site that will help you solve your management question requires a great deal more skill and knowledge than browsing. Start by selecting one or more Internet search engines. Web search engines vary considerably in the following ways:

- the types of Internet sources they cover (http, telnet, Usenet, ftp, etc.)
- the way they search web pages (every word? titles or headers only?)
- the number of pages they include in their indexes
- the search and presentation options they offer
- the frequency with which they are updated.

Exhibit 3.11 Overview of primary literature.

Source	Usefulness for scientific work	Coverage in databases, abstracts and indexes	Likely availability
(Refereed) academic journals	Form the basis of any scientific work as they contain articles reflecting the current scientific discussion, show recent theoretical developments, and provide empirical assessments of problems and theoretical ideas. Peer-reviewed academic journals in particular are a very useful source as their articles meet the high-quality standards of science	Usually very well covered. However, investigations of problems that cross different scientific disciplines call for the scanning of various databases, as most databases specialize in a particular discipline (e.g. EBSCO in management studies, ECONLIT in economics, SOCFILE in sociology and PSYLIT in psychology); these comprehensive databases are available on CD-ROM for journal abstracts	University libraries usually have the most important journals in stock. Further, access to electronic databases containing the full text of journals has become more and more common recently
Professional and trade journals	Professional and trade journals are a useful source of information concerning the practical relevance of a problem. In addition, they often publish studies or provide data that can be useful in illustrating the background of the research or even the arguments made	Such journals are not as well covered in academic databases, although EBSCO contains a large number of these journals	Some of these journals may be included in the collections of university libraries. Furthermore, public libraries often hold some of these journals
Books	Books are as important as academic journal articles as sources of recent discussions, developments, theories and empirical investigations concerning a certain research topic. It often depends on the specific research field whether the relevant authors publish more in books or in journals. Edited volumes (i.e. books containing contributions from several authors) often provide a comprehensive overview of the topic. In particular a book's Introduction can often offer an assessment of the different contributions and how they fit into the bigger picture of the topic. Books written by one author are often a reflection of their own work in the last decade or so and can offer a richer and deeper description of the theoretical ideas and the empirical investigations. For example, books describing an empirical study often contain the complete questionnaire used and detailed information on the sample	Usually well covered in electronic databases, and in abstract and index sources. In addition, recent books are often reviewed and discussed in academic journals, such as the *Journal of Economic Literature*, *Administrative Science Quarterly* or *Organization Studies*. These reviews usually offer a comprehensive summary of the book, and a critical assessment of the strengths and weaknesses of the book. They are very helpful when deciding whether it is worth reading the whole book	University libraries have a large stock collection of academic books. If one is not available in the local university library, a copy can be sourced through inter-university lending. A common problem is that recently published books will be popular with other users and it may take some time before one can recall or reserve them. Hence, it is useful to identify as soon as possible books that are relevant to your research to ensure that you can stick to the time project
Newspapers and public opinion journals	Newspapers and public opinion journals are useful sources of real-world examples (stylized facts), which will make your work much more lively. This holds especially for well-known newspapers and journals, such as the *Financial Times*, *BusinessWeek*, *The Economist*, and so on	These days, the larger national and international newspapers in particular offer databases that will allow you to search their back issues and download specific articles at reasonable cost. However, these databases are newspaper-specific and will often require you to take out a subscription to the newspaper	National and some international newspapers are usually available in university and public libraries. In addition, some newspapers offer articles from their back issues via the Internet. However, the costs of such services can be considerable, as you may need to take out a subscription for a longer period

Exhibit 3.11 Continued

Source	Usefulness for scientific work	Coverage in databases, abstracts and indexes	Likely availability
Conference proceedings/ unpublished manuscripts	Similar to refereed journals, as most articles published in academic journals have been presented before at conferences or circulated as manuscripts in the scientific community. However, not every manuscript or conference contribution will finally be published in an academic journal. Hence, the quality does not always meet the high academic standards for good research and you will have to check for yourself whether these standards really are met. The big advantage of conference proceedings and unpublished manuscripts is that the information is much more recent as the time lag between writing down the ideas and results, and publishing is much shorter. Hence, this source becomes much more important if you are working on a problem that is rather new (e.g. research about the Internet) or fast-developing (e.g. research on AIDS)	Usually, electronic databases, abstracts and index sources do not cover this source. Information on conference contributions is, however, often available on the websites of the conferences themselves. Unpublished manuscripts are often available at the websites of university research institutes, university departments or the homepage of the researcher	University libraries will often possess printed conference proceedings from major conferences, and the unpublished manuscripts of faculty staff. Further, some well-established working paper series, such as *NBER and CPER*, are available via the Internet. Another alternative to sourcing unpublished manuscripts is to email the author(s) directly and ask for an electronic copy of the paper or to check if they are available on the personal homepage(s) of the author(s)
Reports	Reports are a useful source of specific information, which you might want to use during your own research. Further, they often offer descriptive data, which are useful in illustrating the importance or relevance of a statement or argument you have made	The number of reports is indefinite, but unfortunately there is no one database that holds information on all existing reports. In academic reference databases the coverage of reports is usually quite poor. Often, you can find information on the reports themselves by looking at the websites of the institutions that published them (e.g. government agencies, industrial and professional associations, and also companies)	Many reports have been written to find answers to the very specific real-world problems of a company or state institution. Reports often contain interesting but also proprietary information and, as a consequence, are not in the public domain
Research projects	Ph.D. research projects share a number of characteristics with other unpublished manuscripts, and parts of some of the better ones are likely to be published in scientific journals at some point. What distinguishes Ph.D. research projects from other unpublished working papers is that they are much more exhaustive and usually contain a very comprehensive literature review as well as an extensive description of the theories and methodologies used. Master's research projects, except for the very good ones, often do not meet the high standards of sound academic work. However, like reports, they often offer interesting background information and descriptive data. Further, their literature review section and reference list can be used as a departure point for your own literature search	Usually very bad. There are some specialized research projects databases; however, these are usually restricted to Ph.D. research projects, and to a specific country or even university	The physical circulation of Ph.D. research projects is very limited and often only the Ph.D.-granting university holds a copy of the research project in its library. The availability of Master's research projects depends very much on the policy of the university involved, and many universities are rather restrictive with respect to public access to research projects

Exhibit 3.12 *The web search process compared to the bibliographic search process.*

Bibliographic search process	Web search process
1 Select a database appropriate to your topic	1 Select a search engine or directory
2 Construct a search query	2 Determine your search options
• review and evaluate search results	3 Construct a search query
• modify the search query	• review and evaluate search results
3 Save valuable results of your search	• modify the search query
4 Retrieve articles not available in the bibliographic database	4 Determine your search options
5 Supplement your results with information from web sources	5 Supplement your results with information from non-web sources

Furthermore, some publicly indexable pages via the web are not retrievable at all using current web search engines. Among the material open to the public, but not indexed by search engines, is the following:[9]

- pages that are proprietary (that is, fee-based) and/or password-protected, including the contents of bibliographic and other databases
- pages accessible only through a search form (databases), including such highly popular web resources as library catalogues, e-commerce catalogues (such as Amazon.com and similar offerings), and the Security and Exchange Commission's EDGAR catalogue of SEC filings
- poorly designed framed pages
- some non-HTML or non-plain-text pages, especially PDF graphics files, for which no text alternative is offered. These pages cannot be retrieved using any current search engine.

The search engine, portal or directory you select may well be determined by how comprehensive you want your results to be.[10] If you want to use some major sites only, then start with a directory such as Yahoo! or Google. At least within the publicly indexable pages, one approach emphasizes selectivity, and the other comprehensiveness. If you are interested in comprehensiveness, use more than one search engine.

Determine your search options
Nearly all search services have a 'Help' button that will lead you to information about the search protocols and options of that particular search engine. How does the search engine work? Can you combine terms using Boolean operators (AND, OR, NOT) or other connectors? How do you enter phrases? Truncate terms? Determine output display? Limit by date or other characteristic? Some search engines provide a basic and an advanced search option. How do they differ?

Construct a search query and enter your search term(s)
The web is not a database, nor does it have a controlled vocabulary. Therefore, you must be as specific as possible, using the keywords in your management question and any variations you can think of. It is up to you to determine synonyms, variant spellings, and broader or narrower terms that will help you retrieve the information you need. This may involve some trial and error. For instance, a general term (such as 'business') would be useless in a search engine that purports to index every word in every document.

Save the results of your search
If you have found good information, you will want to keep it for future reference so that you can cite it in your proposal or refer to it later in the development of your investigative questions. If you do not keep documents, you may have to reconstruct your search. At a future time, given that some portion of the web is revised and updated daily, those same documents may no longer be available.

A cautious note on using Internet sources

Clearly the Internet offers much useful information, especially if you know how to find it. Nevertheless, a great deal of valuable information in books, journals and other print sources is not available on the web or only available if you have an often costly subscription. While many novice researchers start and end here, the more sophisticated researcher knows that a web search is just one of many important options.

Another issue is the credibility of Internet sources. Currently, there are thousands of sites offering descriptions, explanations and articles on scientific theories and concepts. Many of these sites are, however, not moderated or it is not clear who moderates the content. You need to be careful even with well-known sites such as Wikipedia. Test this for yourself by looking up a theory or construct that you know really well and check how sites such as Wikipedia explain it. Chances are high that as an expert you are not really satisfied with the information provided. This also explains why many lecturers advise students only to use moderated sites in their references.

Reading and evaluating research

Reading for review differs from reading for pleasure, as it requires the reader to distil the relevant information and to unravel the reasoning. Furthermore, as the number of potentially interesting books and articles is uncountable, one needs to read efficiently. Start by reading the title and then try to get an idea of the general structure of the text. In the case of a book you will study the table of contents and in the case of an article you will read the abstract. Try to identify what is the main point the book or article wants to make.

The whole reading process is guided by two questions. First, is the reading relevant for my study; that is, does the article at least touch on the issues and question I wish to address? Second, if it is relevant, does it add to the arguments or information I offer? (The latter question also includes information and articles opposing your own thinking.) If you are convinced that either of these two questions will be answered with a 'no' you can skip the article.

For example, if you intend to investigate the internationalization strategies of Dutch family firms, not all articles dealing either with internationalization strategies OR family businesses will be relevant for your study. However, an AND criterion could be too strict, as a study investigating growth strategies in family firms might offer useful insights. The second selection question refers to the fact that, often, the information presented in one literature source is hardly different from the information presented in another. For example, there are certainly hundreds of studies addressing the difficulties of medium-sized or family firms in following an internationalization strategy. Even a comprehensive literature review does not need to deal with all such studies. If a certain theoretical argument or empirical finding is documented in many studies, it is usually sufficient to refer to just a few of them. But, to which should you refer? There are no strict guidelines as to which studies should be taken into account and which should not. However, the following are some useful criteria:

- Time of publication. One mentions the study that was published first to give credit to the author(s) who made a certain argument or presented a specific finding first. This rule explains that some classical works, written more than 100 years ago, are still often mentioned. Sometimes, it is also advisable to mention quite recent studies, especially with respect to empirical results, as effects may change over time. For example, a study from the 1930s investigating who took over a family business is likely to find that the eldest son has a higher chance of becoming the successor. With the start of the new millennium, the effects of children's gender and birth rank are likely to be much smaller.
- Most scholars will usually include articles from (top) sources in their own academic field. Thus, a sociologist is more likely to include articles published in the *American Journal of Sociology*, an economist articles published in the *Journal of Political Economy* and a business scientist articles published in the *Academy of Management Journal* or the *Strategic Management Journal*.
- The scope of the study. Particularly in the case of empirical studies, studies with a broader scope (i.e. a higher external validity) are more likely to be included in a review than studies with a rather narrow scope.

Exhibit 3.13 provides a list of criteria to help assess the relevance and value of an article, chapter or book to be included in a literature review. With the steadily increasing number of books, journals and articles available, hardly anyone can claim to write a complete literature review. It is inevitable that some literature will have to be omitted, and, often, the choice of which literature should be omitted informs us of the perspective the author has on the field. However, a good literature review needs to include references to the classical and most prominent studies. For this reason articles or (book) chapters that are frequently cited by other scholars working in the field need to be mentioned. For example, if you write a literature review on studies related to transaction cost

---

Exhibit 3.13 Criteria for the relevance and value of articles and (book) chapters.

Criteria	Relevance or value increasing
Prominence of article or (book) chapter documented by citations or the source	The more an article or (book) chapter has been cited, the more it has been appreciated by other scholars
Recency of the article or (book) chapter	The world is changing, and so is our view of it and knowledge of it. Hence, more recent articles usually offer a better idea than older ones of the current state of knowledge
Methodological quality of the article or (book) chapter	Any article or (book) chapter referred to should meet the criteria of good research (see Chapter 1)
Comparability of your arguments with the arguments put forward in the article or (book) chapter	The criterion refers to whether or not the article or (book) chapter relates to the arguments you make, either by supporting them or by contradicting them
Uniqueness of the articles or (book) chapter	How original (unique) is the contribution of the article? Is it a repetition of a previous study in a slightly different context or is it a fundamentally new study?

---

theory, you need to include references to the work of the Nobel Prize winners Coase (1937) and Williamson (1975, 1985).[11]

Another indicator of the prominence of an article or book is the relative importance of the journal or publisher. Articles that appear in one of the top management journals or in books issued by a well-known publisher usually have a greater impact (i.e. are more prominent) than articles from 'smaller' journals or publishers. In general, the more recent literature is more important, as it is built on a larger knowledge base. When writing a review of the literature, you must bear in mind that older or even outdated articles might state thoughts or ideas that were considered reasonable at the time the article was published, but are not acceptable today, as later evidence has clarified matters. This is not, however, the case for classical studies or books that form the foundations of the knowledge base and still hold true. The reputation of the publisher, journal and the authors is an indication of the scientific quality of a piece of work, but it is only an indicator and in the end you have to use your own judgement; many well-known authors have published less convincing pieces and many really important articles have been published by people who were little known at the time their work was published. Hence, whether you want to include a study in your review of the literature depends on your quality of judgement along the lines of the criteria for good research presented in Chapter 1.

Without a doubt, many interesting and excellent studies have been published, but that does not mean you have to include them all in your literature review. Any other study is relevant for your study if it relates clearly to the arguments you make, either by supporting them or by contradicting them. Any articles or (book) chapters that do not relate to your study sufficiently distract the reader of your study from the points you want to make and may even disappoint the reader (as every reference to a specific piece of work creates expectations, which you will be unable to fulfil if your study does not address the problem and arguments of the study referred to). Similarly, many studies in the literature largely address the same research problem. For example, there are hundreds of studies investigating why people choose to become self-employed. To decide which of these studies you want to include in your literature review, you have to assess what is the unique contribution of a study to this field of research. Who put forward a new argument, who looked at the issue from a (slightly) different angle, and so on?

How to read

Once you have chosen to read an article or book for review, never start by attempting to read every sentence, but try to get the gist of the research. The following steps offer a useful strategy for quickly grasping the main issues in a piece of literature:

1 Skim through the book to discover its structure, topic, style, general reasoning, data and references.
   a Read the title.
   b Read the chapter titles or section headings.

   c Check whether empirical evidence is presented and, if so, what kind of evidence (purely theoretical work or qualitative research or quantitative research).

   d Check the references to see whether you already know some of the literature or authors cited. (Checking references becomes more important the more literature you have seen on an issue. If you are not a complete novice to an issue and read through the references of an article or book without recognizing one of the cited articles or at least authors, this should arouse your suspicions. In such a case it is likely that the article does not really address what you are interested in.)

2 Survey each chapter of the book/each section of the article.

   a Read the sub-headings and try to determine the main structure of the book/article.

   b Take a closer look at the figures and tables provided, as they often summarize (parts of) the text.

3 Skim over and read the Preface and Introduction to identify the main ideas.

4 Read the parts and chapters that are important to your own area of interest.

Once you have embarked upon a more thorough reading of a book or article, it is important to distil the essentials of the text. Exhibit 3.14 lists the important elements of many texts.

Exhibit 3.14 *The important elements of a text.*

Introduction, problem statement	Theoretical sections/chapters	Sections/chapters covering methodology, analysis and conclusions
Definitions	Arguments	Techniques
Events	Concepts	Design
Evidence	Hypotheses	Results
Motives	Interpretations	Conclusions
Perspective	Justification	Summary
Problem	Theory	Recommendations
Questions	Styles of thinking	
Standpoints		

The questions you should be able to answer after reading a book or article are as follows:

1 What is the problem addressed?
2 What are the proposed theories or ideas?
3 How has it been investigated? What methods were used?
4 What are the results in terms of the problem stated?

Writing down the answers to these questions will often take you some way towards compiling your own review.

The writing process

This section cannot provide a detailed account of how to write a review, article or book. There are many books on general writing techniques that might be worth a look at (also Chapter 15 and the Recommended Further Reading at the end of Chapter 15). However, we will still give you a broad outline of the writing process and how you can improve your writing. As with most other tasks, doing something well requires you to make a plan, and it is a good idea to write down such a plan. Your plan should contain at least the following elements:

1 the aims and objectives of the review
2 the audience for the review
3 a brief summary of your main points
4 a draft outline
5 a list of the main material you have selected (in the case of a review, note down the main pieces of literature you will discuss in your review).

Right from the start it should be clear to you why you are writing the review. Do you just want to give a summary of the existing literature on a specific topic? Do you want to critically assess the current literature on a topic and use the conclusions of your review as a point of departure for motivating your own research?

It is clear that a review for a scientific journal, which aims to illustrate the current state of the art with regard to a specific topic, differs from a review that is part of an article investigating a particular question, and where the review is used to place the research conducted into a specific context.

The audience for your review is a crucial consideration when deciding on many aspects during the review process. The more knowledgeable your audience, the less time you need to spend planning the review. If you are writing an article for a scientific journal, where you can expect that most of the readers will know the literature as well as you do, you do not need to give a short summary of each piece of literature you include. If you are reviewing the literature for a scientific audience that does not know the specific literature involved, then you should give your readers more information on the content of the literature under review. Finally, if you are writing a review for an educational audience, which is not (yet) acquainted at all with the field, you need to provide much more information on each piece of literature included. To sum up, the better informed your audience, the more your review can be your own reasoned interpretation of the current state of affairs in the field and the less need there is to present an overview of existing studies.

Reviewing the literature usually means more than providing a brief summary of it. Every literature review should also try to make a point with regard to what the author thinks about the field. Some possible themes for points to make are as follows:

- What are the remaining unsolved puzzles in the field?
- On which aspects do most authors agree, and on which aspects do you find much disagreement?
- Given the current state of affairs, what are promising and fruitful future research directions?
- What are the current lacunae in the field?

Synthesizing the literature

A literature review is a piece of academic writing and it must be logically structured and clear. This chapter has already talked about the aims and objectives of a review and the purposes it should serve. Any review of the literature requires you to deliver an appropriate summary of prior work. In the sections above, we have indicated how you can scan the enormous amount of literature available efficiently, and how to select the pieces of literature most relevant to your review.

A common students' mistake is that their review is a sequential summary of the most relevant articles. A review, however, is more than a well-structured summary of the literature; a good review also contains considerable insight from the writer, as it is not only a précis, but a well-reasoned piece of criticism too. Before you start writing the review you need to be clear what is the purpose of your literature review, that is, what do you want to achieve with it? Roughly, we can distinguish between two different purposes, namely:

1 The review provides an account of the development of a field or broader topic.
2 The literature review is just a part of a study.

In the first case, the literature reviews often form a scientific contribution on its own. Review articles often written by authors established in the field are a typical example for this type of a literature review (see Section 3.5). If the literature review is just part of the study, the literature review should serve and support the objective of the study. Before you come to write down your review, you need to clarify which points you want to make, how you will use the review to support your points, and how you can structure the review to make your points. In quantitative empirical studies an often-used structure for the review is along either the independent or dependent variables. In more qualitative-oriented studies, the literature review is often structured along a couple of key themes. In both cases, you should be aware that synthesizing starts with comparisons to identify differences and congruencies, but does not stop there. In a second step it is important to explain or interpret the differences and congruencies found.

Effective criticism

Whenever you write an academic literature review or participate in a scientific discussion, it is worth considering the main points of effective criticism:

- You should base your criticism on an assessment of weaknesses and strengths.
- You should criticize theories, arguments, ideas and the methodology, but not the authors or their motives.
- You should reflect on your own critique, providing reasons for the choices you have made, and recognizing and pointing out any weaknesses in your criticism.
- You should treat the work of others with due respect; that is, give a fair account of the views and arguments of others when summarizing.

Further, you must always provide reasons for your disagreement with a certain view or argument; just stating that you disagree is wrong and insufficient. Finally, you should focus on the major parts of an argument. If you base your criticism on minor details or construct hypothetical examples to show that under very specific circumstances the argument might not hold, your criticism is not usually a strong one.

Literature review as independent scientific contribution

Motivation and objectives

Up to now, we emphasized the literature review as part of a larger empirical study. However, reviews have also a long-lasting tradition in the evaluation of business research. In these cases the systematic review itself forms a scientific contribution to the field. The primary objective of a systematic review is the evaluation of a research field through assessing a complete set of the relevant studies covering the field.

As you will learn throughout the book, it is impossible to conduct a perfect empirical study. Even the best studies have their limitations, as you can easily see if you read the limitation section of an article published in a top scientific journal. Therefore, we hesitate to rely on just one study and prefer to see replications of a study in slightly different contexts. Once a couple of studies have been conducted, it becomes important to obtain an overall picture and to learn which explanations are probably true and which are ambiguous. Systematic reviews provide these insights.

Types of reviews

Systematic reviews can take different forms; they can be qualitative or quantitative evaluations. The literature review shown above is an example of a qualitative review and these reviews are also most common if the review is part of an empirical study. A typical example of a quantitative research is meta analysis (see Deeper Insight into Research Methods (p. 90) for more details on meta analysis).

Review structures

Literature reviews as evaluations of a field differ from literature reviews as part of an empirical study in their objectives and therefore they often have a different structure. An often-used option is the chronological structure. You start with the earlier studies and then you explain how later studies have built upon them and how they differed. The advantage of the chronological structure is that you can easily show how the field changed over time and how it improved. The chronological structure is only advisable if there are just a few development paths. If, however, a field is characterized by many parallel developments, merging paths and splitting paths, the chronological order easily becomes chaotic. Sometimes fields are characterized by different schools or perspectives. In such a case a structure along the schools is a logical choice. But you should be aware that a pitfall of a structure along the schools is that you just provide rather independent summaries for each school and that you are inclined to overemphasize differences between the schools. Moreover, some studies, for example those which address both perspectives, cannot be assigned to one of the schools. Finally, it is always an option to structure the review along the outcome variables or antecedents, as we discussed earlier.

Running Case Study 3
Visiting the library

Mehmet

Mehmet has always loved to talk to people much more than reading. If he was planning a weekend trip to Barcelona, he would rather talk to a friend who had been there than buy a pocket travel guide. At university he preferred to read textbooks and applied articles rather than the often dull articles in so called 'A-journals'. When he started with his thesis, he heard via a friend, that a friend of friend called Hassan studying sociology had just finished a dissertation on migrant entrepreneurship. He had called Hassan and Hassan had emailed him his thesis. Hassan's thesis was about what municipality could do to encourage entrepreneurship among migrant minorities. To Mehmet's surprise, it did not have any empirical part except for two interviews with a deputy mayor of Utrecht and a local entrepreneur. Nevertheless, it had an impressive reference list and Mehmet used the introduction chapter to write his proposal. Mehmet did not copy a single sentence of Hassan's thesis; he just used parts of the structure and then wrote his own text. Moreover, rather than reading all the articles, he trusted the summaries in Hassan's dissertation. That saved a lot of reading time.

Later on, the literature discussed in Hassan's dissertation became the backbone of Mehmet's theory chapter. But Mehmet did more. In his many talks with people he collected a lot a written documentation including PR material, newspaper clippings and official reports. Mehmet thought that this literature was much more informative than the articles in academic journals. First, many articles in the journals referred to studies in the USA and Mehmet was convinced that the situation in the Netherlands was completely different. You could simply not compare Afro-Americans in Chicago with Turks in Amsterdam, they had nothing in common. Second, in his view the scientific studies seemed to forget the migrant entrepreneur. Just a few qualitative academic studies included citations of entrepreneurs, while other researchers had apparently not even talked to a migrant entrepreneur. One study in a prestigious journal was based on data collected from the Dutch statistical office – the three authors were a native Dutch and two Americans, one with an English name and the other with a Chinese name. How could they write about migrant entrepreneurship in the Netherlands? Mehmet had a strong feeling that in the prestigious journals, missing knowledge of the field was camouflaged with complicated statistics that only a few enlightened people could understand.

Rebecca

Rebecca's approach was very different from Mehmet's. Her first step was a visit to the library and she spent days walking through the stacks and browsing electronic databases. Even at night at home she browsed through these databases.

Rebecca started her search on Google scholar (http://scholar.google.com) with the words "students' ethics" which resulted in 1,210 hits. Although Rebecca loves reading, that seemed too much even for her. Thus she combined "students' ethics" with other search terms. The table below shows how many hits were generated for the combination of "students' ethics" with each other term.

Number of hits for "students' ethics" combined with . . .			
Response*	449	Reaction	98
Sanction*	104	Consequence*	337
Coping	50	Plagiarism	120
Factor*	482	Cheating	181
Determinant*	42	"empirical study"	74
Explain*	377	Survey	461

Looking at the results, she was surprised to see that many references were useless, as those studies did not look at how ethical students behave, but rather looked at which students were more likely to choose an ethics course or how one should design an ethics course.

Nevertheless, she printed out the result lists and started to highlight those articles that seemed interesting to her. Later on, she identified the articles that came up on multiple lists. In the end, she had a list of 37 articles, which she started to retrieve from the databank. After reading the abstract, she decided whether she would print it or disregard it; she printed 31 articles and started reading. While reading them, Rebecca discovered more and more articles through the references provided. Rebecca started to understand why good references are so helpful for a reader. It did not take long for Rebecca to develop some idea which scientists were most interested in the topic. Out of curiosity she searched for the home pages of these people. What would they be like? On the authors' homepages, she learnt that one was an amateur photographer, while another had won an Olympic silver medal in archery. Rebecca did not even know that archery was an Olympic discipline. Next to this more popular information, Rebecca also discovered that some scholars offered downloads of their articles and working papers on their websites. The working papers were especially interesting, as they were much more recent than the articles and therefore also contained more recent references.

In the meantime, Rebecca had studied about 70 articles. She had not read all of these articles from the first to the last letter, but she had at least read some paragraphs of each. Slowly she had the feeling that additional articles did not offer new insights and that the same articles were always cited. Of course, now and then she would discover a new reference, but mostly these 'new' articles were very similar to those she had already read. But how could she be sure that she had read all the relevant literature? And there was another concern Rebecca had. The previous weekend she had visited her parents and discussed her research project with them; her mother especially had been very interested in it. She had given her a stack of books on ethics. Up to now she had not really looked at those books, but looking through her list of literature, she realised that the scientific literature hardly referred to the classic works her mother had lent her. How could that be?

1 Discuss how Mehmet and Rebecca conducted their search for literature.
2 Think about the search queries used. How could one improve them?
3 Discuss the Internet as an information source.

Summary

1 With respect to literature sources, one can distinguish primary and secondary literature. Primary literature includes all kinds of articles, books and reports in their original form. Secondary literature is a compilation of primary literature. Examples of secondary literature include indexes and bibliographies, dictionaries, encyclopaedias, handbooks and directories.

2 The process for searching bibliographic databases applies to both print and online sources:
   a Select a database appropriate to your topic.
   b Construct a search query (or search statement).
      • Review and evaluate search results.
      • Modify the search query, if necessary.
   c Save the valuable results of your search.
   d Retrieve articles not available in the database.
   e Supplement your results with information from web sources.

Many online and web-based sources use Boolean logic to construct search queries, but protocols do differ. One reason to review the results of your original search is to modify it with newly discovered information. The researcher should check the bibliographies of cited works, check the subject headings assigned to the extracted articles, and search for works by referenced authors.

3 The basic steps for searching web-based sources include a critical last step that novice researchers often skip:

a Select a search engine or directory.

b Determine your search options.

c Construct a search query and enter your search term(s).
- Review and evaluate the search results.
- Modify your search query, if necessary.

d Save the valuable results of your search.

e Supplement your results with information from non-web sources.

When doing a web-based search, several options are available: known-item searches, 'who' searches, 'where' searches and 'what' searches. Due to the special characteristics of each type of search, each starts with a different search strategy. Several special sites have evolved to offer the researcher assistance for each type of search. These can be found in Appendix A.

4 Meta analysis allows the summarization of various empirical studies that investigate the same research problem. It is a very structured approach, which summarizes, compares and analyses the differences between studies along many characteristics of the studies including employing statistical methodology. On the one hand, the rigorous structure and quantification approach often results in the detection of patterns and relations that are unnoticed by more narrative summaries of a research field. On the other hand, the rigorous approach can often not account for important issues, such as differences in the methodological soundness of the studies included.

Discussion questions

Terms in review

1 Define the distinctions between primary and secondary literature.

2 Describe, briefly, the different steps in the literature review process.

3 Describe the objective, advantages and disadvantages of meta analysis.

4 What is meant by 'critical' in a critical review?

Making research decisions

5 How can you structure your critique in a critical review?

6 What are promising search strategies?

7 How do you decide which literature should be included in a review?

8 If you have written your own literature review for a research problem in which you have an interest, do you think conducting a meta analysis on the literature covered in your narrative review would be useful? If not, why not? If so, what would you like to investigate by applying meta analysis?

From concept to practice

9 Using Exhibits 3.8, 3.9 and 3.10, state a research question and then plan a bibliographic and web search.

10 Choose a field that you would like to review and:

a draft the outline of the review

b select the literature that, according to you, must be included.

11 Write a critical review:

a on a published book ar article

b on a paper of a fellow student

c on an unpublished manuscript (ask your lecturer or look for working paper series at your university).

Classroom discussion

12 Brainstorm within your class or sub-groups useful search terms that could be employed to start a literature search for the following problem statements:

   a   Who becomes an entrepreneur and what does it take to be a successful one?

   b   What explains the differences in internationalization strategies chosen by financial institutions in Europe?

   c   How effective is impression management in the consultancy industry?

13 A common problem for students starting off on a Master's research project is that they cannot track down the relevant literature. Given the thousands of studies published every year in the field of management science, it is highly unlikely that there are no, or very few, related studies. Discuss in the class why many students, despite the vast amount of studies published, still have serious problems finding relevant literature, and what can be done to solve this problem.

Recommended further reading

Bedeian, Arthur C., 'The manuscript review process: the proper roles of authors, reviewers and editors', *Journal of Management Inquiry* 12(4), 2003, pp. 331–8. A paper investigating the experiences of authors that have published in the *Academy of Management Journal*, one of the leading journals in management science.

Bell, Judith, *Doing your Research Project* (3rd edn). Buckingham: Open University Press, 1999. Chapter 6 offers an excellent guide on how to organize a literature review.

Hard, Chris, *Doing a Literature Review*. Thousand Oaks, CA: Sage, 1998. This book addresses issues such as searching for existing knowledge, analysing arguments and ideas, and writing a literature review.

Katz, William A., *Introduction to Reference Work, Volume I and Volume II*. New York: McGraw-Hill, 2001. An excellent text on how to work with references.

Saunders, Mark et al., *Research Methods for Business Students* (4th edn). Harlow: Pearson Education, 2006. Chapter 3 is an excellent guide for students and lecturers alike on literature review.

Woy, James (ed.), *Encyclopedia of Business Information Sources* (14th edn). Gale Group, 2000. An excellent database on sources containing useful information for business and management research.

 **Get started with understanding statistical techniques!**

When you have read this chapter, log on to the Online Learning Centre website at *www.mcgraw-hill.co.uk/textbooks/blumberg* to explore chapter-by-chapter test questions, additional case studies, a glossary and more online study tools for *Business Research Methods*.

Notes

1 Kirk Monteverde and David J. Teece, 'Supplier switching costs and vertical integration in the automotive industry', *Bell Journal of Economics* 13 (1982), pp. 206–313.

2 Thomas M. Palay, 'Comparative institutional economics: the governance of rail freight contracting', *Journal of Legal Studies* 13 (1984), pp. 263–87; and Paul J. Joskow, 'Contract duration and relation-specific investments: empirical evidence from coal markets', *American Economic Review* 77 (1987), pp. 168–83.

3 Ronald Coase, 'The nature of the firm', *Economica* 4 (1937), pp. 386–403.

4 Oliver E. Williamson, *Markets and Hierarchies: Analysis and Antitrust Implications*. New York: Free Press, 1973; and Oliver E. Williamson, *The Economic Institutions of Capitalism*. New York: Free Press, 1985.

5 This section on meta analysis builds on Mark W. Lipsey and David B. Wilson, *Practical Meta Analysis*. Thousand Oaks, CA: Sage, 2000.

6 G.V. Glass, 'Primary, secondary and meta-analysis of research', *Educational Researcher* 3 (3–8) (1976); M.L. Smith and G.V. Glass, 'Meta analysis of psychotherapy outcome studies', *American Psychologist* 32 (1977), pp. 732–60.

7 D. Denyer and D. Tranfield, 'Producing a systematic review'. In D. A. Buchanan and A. Bryman (Eds.), *The SAGE Handbook of Organizational Research Methods*, pp. 671–89. London: SAGE, 2009.

8 Good sources for web size estimates are the studies by Steve R. Lawrence and C. Lee Giles, 'Searching the World Wide Web', *Science* 280 (April 1998), pp. 98–100, and 'Accessibility of information on the web', *Nature* 400 (8 July 1999), pp. 107–9, with updated summary data at www.wwwmetrics.com.

9 Michael Dahm, 'Counting angels on a pinhead: critically interpreting web size estimates', *Online* 24 (January/February 2000), pp. 33–44. This article further interprets the pioneering research by authors Steve R. Lawrence and C. Lee Giles (op. cit.).

10 The May/June 1999 issue of *Online* focuses on search engine technology. See, for example, Danny Sullivan, 'Crawling under the hood: an update on search engine technology', *Online* 23 (May/June 1999), pp. 30–8. See also Danny Sullivan's 'Search engine watch' (www.searchenginewatch.com/) and Greg Notess's 'Search engine showdown' (www.notess.com/search/) for current information about search engines and their features.

11 Ronald Coase, 'The nature of the firm', *Economica* 4 (1937), pp. 386–403; Oliver E. Williamson, *Markets and Hierarchies: Analysis and Antitrust Implications*. New York: Free Press, 1973; and Oliver E. Williamson, *The Economic Institutions of Capitalism*. New York: Free Press, 1985.

CHAPTER 4

Ethics in business research

Chapter contents

Learning objectives

When you have read this chapter, you should understand:

1   what issues are covered in research ethics

2   the goal of 'no harm' for all research activities and what constitutes 'no harm'

3   the differing ethical dilemmas and responsibilities of researchers and sponsors

4   the role of ethical codes of conduct in professional associations.

What are research ethics?

As in other aspects of business, all parties in research should exhibit ethical behaviour. **Ethics** is the study of the 'right behaviour' and addresses the question of how to conduct research in a moral and responsible way. Thus, ethics not only addresses the question of how to use methodology in a proper way to conduct sound research, but also addresses the question of how the available methodology may be used in the 'right' way. Conducting empirical research, either quantitative or qualitative, often requires that you as a researcher have to compromise between what methodological theory recommends and what is feasible from a practical viewpoint. Likewise, you have to resolve whether the way you conduct your research is morally defensible towards all parties involved in the research.

Ethics, then, are moral principles, norms or standards of behaviour that guide moral choices about our behaviour and our relationships with others. In business research, ethical issues come to the fore whenever a conflict arises between the desire to conduct research that meets the highest quality standards or the requests of the sponsor on the one hand, and rights of participants or, in general, societal values – like, say, privacy, freedom and honesty – on the other.

There is no single approach to ethics. There are two dominant philosophical standpoints on research ethics: deontology and teleology. In the deontological view, the ends never justify the use of the means that are questionable on ethical grounds. For example, even if fully informing a respondent about the purpose and procedures of a study is likely to affect the (response) behaviour of this respondent in such a way that the obtained information is barely usable to answer the research question, any deception of the respondent would be unethical.

Business researchers often ascribe to the teleological principle, which posits that the morality of the means has to be judged by the ends served. Hence, the benefits of a study are weighed against the costs of harming the people involved. There are two major problems with this position. First, the benefits of a study, that is the ends served, may be morally questionable. Second, a simple comparison of the total costs and benefits cannot, however, offer a straightforward answer to an ethical dilemma. If the costs are borne by some, for example, the respondents, while others, for example, the researchers, reap the benefits, conducting the research becomes problematic from an ethical perspective. Thus, any deviation from ethical standards, such as deceiving respondents, must be based on thorough reasoning.

As a researcher, you have the responsibility to find the middle ground between being completely code-governed and ethical relativism. The foundation for that middle ground is an emerging consensus on ethical standards for researchers. Codes and regulations guide researchers and sponsors. Review boards and peer groups help researchers examine their research proposals for ethical dilemmas. Many design-based ethical problems can be eliminated by careful planning and constant vigilance. In the end, responsible research anticipates ethical dilemmas and attempts to adjust research design, procedures and protocols during the planning process rather than treating them as an afterthought. Ethical research requires personal integrity from the researcher, the project manager and the research sponsor.

Because integrity in research is vital, we are discussing its components early in this book. This chapter is organized around the theme of ethical treatment of respondents, fellow researchers, and clients or research sponsors. Also highlighted are appropriate laws and codes, resources for ethical awareness and cases for application. Exhibit 4.1 relates each ethical issue under discussion to the research process introduced in Chapter 2.

 ## Ethical treatment of participants

When ethics are discussed in research design, we often think first about protecting the rights of the participant, respondent or subject. Whether data are gathered in an experiment, interview, observation or survey, the respondent has many rights to be safeguarded. In general, research must be designed so a respondent does not suffer physical harm, discomfort, pain, embarrassment or loss of privacy. To safeguard against these things, the researcher should follow three guidelines:[1]

1 explain the benefits of the study
2 explain the participant's rights and protection
3 obtain informed consent.

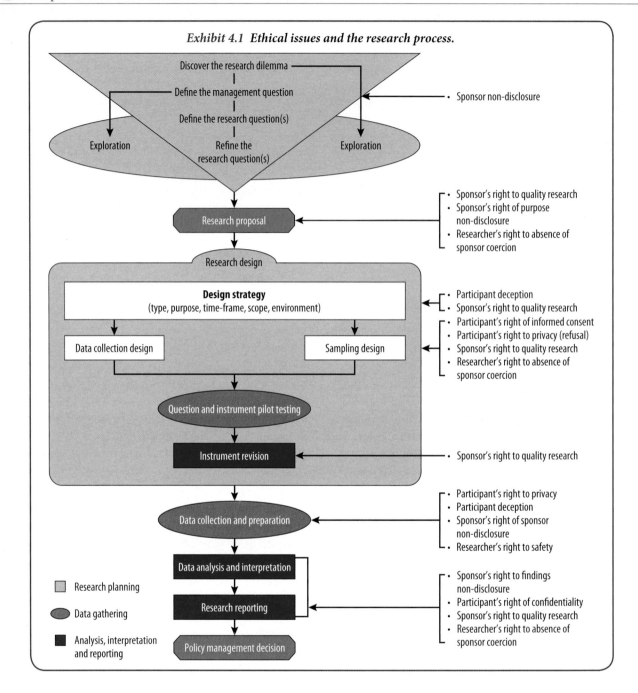

Exhibit 4.1 Ethical issues and the research process.

Benefits

Whenever direct contact is made with a participant, the researcher should explain the purpose of the study and discuss its benefits, being careful to neither overstate nor understate the benefits. An interviewer should begin an introduction with their name, the name of the research organization, and a brief description of the purpose and benefit(s) of the research. This puts participants at ease, lets them know to whom they are speaking, and motivates them to answer questions truthfully. In short, knowing why one is being asked questions improves cooperation through honest disclosure of purpose. Furthermore, you should provide the respondent with the contact details of the person responsible for the research. Inducements to participate, financial or otherwise, should not be disproportionate to the task or presented in a fashion that results in coercion.

Sometimes the actual purpose and benefits of your study or experiment must be concealed from respondents to avoid introducing bias. The need to conceal objectives leads directly to the problem of deception.

Deception

Deception occurs when participants are told only part of the truth or when the truth is fully compromised. Some believe that this should never occur. Others suggest two reasons for deception:

1 to prevent biasing participants before the survey or experiment
2 to protect the confidentiality of a third party (e.g. the sponsor).

The benefits to be gained by deception should be balanced against the risks to participants. When possible, an experiment or interview should be redesigned to reduce reliance on deception. In addition, participants' rights and well-being must be protected adequately. In instances where deception in an experiment could produce anxiety, a subject's medical condition should be checked to ensure that no adverse physical harm ensues. The American Psychological Association's Ethics Code states that the use of deception is inappropriate unless deceptive techniques are justified by the study's expected scientific, educational or applied value, and equally effective alternatives that do not use deception are not feasible.[2] Finally, participants must have given their informed consent before participating in the research.

Informed consent

Securing **informed consent** from participants is a matter of fully disclosing the procedures of the proposed survey or other research design before requesting permission to proceed with the study. Having obtained the consent of the respondent, the researcher is obliged to stick to the procedures outlined previously. You should, for example, not prolong the interview or observation beyond the time agreed or suddenly expand the scope of the research.

For most business research, oral consent is sufficient and the willingness of a respondent to participate in the research after you informed them that participation is voluntary is often interpreted as consent.[3]

There are exceptions that argue for a signed consent form. When dealing with children, it is wise to have a parent or other person with legal standing sign a consent form. When doing research with medical or psychological ramifications, it is also wise to have a consent form. If there is a chance the data could harm the participant or if the researchers offer only limited protection of confidentiality, a signed form detailing the types of limit should be obtained. An example of how informed consent procedures are implemented is shown in Exhibit 4.2.

Exhibit 4.2 *Informed consent procedures for surveys.*

Content

Surveys conducted by the Lakeside University Centre for Survey Research contain the following informed consent components in their introductions:

1 Introduce ourselves – interviewer's name and Lakeside University Centre for Survey Research
2 Briefly describe the survey topic (e.g. barriers to early retirement plans)
3 Describe the geographic area we are interviewing (e.g. people in Wales) or target sample (e.g. employees above 55 in a management position)
4 Tell who the sponsor is (e.g. Ministry of Welfare)
5 Describe the purpose(s) of the research (e.g. satisfaction with services received/provided by a local agency)
6 Give a 'good-faith' estimate of the time required to complete the interview
7 Promise anonymity and confidentiality (when appropriate)
8 Tell the respondent the participation is voluntary
9 Tell the respondent that item non-response is acceptable
10 Ask permission to begin

Sample introduction

Hello, I'm [fill in NAME] from the Centre for Survey Research at Lakeside University. We're surveying residents in Wales to ask their opinions about early retirement plans. This study is sponsored by the Ministry of Welfare and its results will be used to research the effect of community ties on attitudes towards early retirement. The survey takes about 40 minutes. Your participation is anonymous and voluntary, and all your answers will be kept completely confidential. If there is any question that you don't feel you can answer, please let me know and we'll move to the next one. So, if I have your permission, I'll continue.

Sample conclusion

The respondent is given information on how to contact the principal investigator. For example: Hirkani Gupta is the principal investigator for this study. Would you like Dr Gupta's address or phone number in case you want to contact him about the study at any time?

In this example, a university research centre demonstrates how it adheres to the highest ethical standards for survey procedures.[4]

In situations where participants are intentionally or accidentally deceived, they should be debriefed once the research is complete.

Debriefing participants

Debriefing involves several activities that follow the collection of data:

- explanation of any deception
- description of the research project, goal or purpose of the study
- post-study sharing of results
- post-study follow-up medical or psychological attention.

First, the researcher shares the truth of any deception with the participants, as well as the reasons for using deception in the context of the study's goals. In cases where severe reactions occur, follow-up medical or psychological attention should be provided to continue to ensure that participants remain unharmed by the research.

Even when research does not deceive participants, it is good practice to offer them follow-up information as a matter of course. This retains the goodwill of the participant, providing an incentive to participate in future research projects. For surveys and interviews, participants can be offered a brief report on the findings. They will not usually request additional information; occasionally, though, the research will be of particular interest to a participant. A simple set of descriptive charts or data tables can be generated for such an individual.

For experiments, all participants should be debriefed in order to put the experiment into context. Debriefing usually includes a description of the research project being tested and the purpose of the study. Participants who were not deceived will still benefit from a debriefing session; they will be able to understand why the experiment was created. The researchers will also gain important insight into what the participants thought about during and after the experiment. This may lead to modifications in future research designs. Like survey and interview respondents, participants taking part in experiments and observational studies should be offered a report of the findings.

To what extent do debriefing and informed consent reduce the effects of deception?

Research suggests that the majority of participants do not resent temporary deception and may have more positive feelings about the value of the research after debriefing than those who did not participate in the study. Nevertheless, deception is an ethically thorny issue and should be addressed with sensitivity and concern for research participants.

Rights to privacy

Privacy laws in Europe, as well as in the USA and other countries, are taken seriously. In 2002, at a summit in Nice, the member states of the European Union (EU) signed a charter of fundamental rights. Article 8, on the protection of personal data, reads:

> "1. Everyone has the right to the protection of personal data concerning him or her.
>
> 2. Such data must be processed fairly and on the basis of consent of the person concerned or some other legitimate basis laid down by the law. Everyone has the right of access to data which have been collected concerning him or her and the right to have it rectified."

By 1995, the EU had already passed a directive and required member states to incorporate it into national laws by 1998; however, it allowed each member state to extend the directive and alter its detailed meanings.

The importance of the **right to privacy** may be illustrated with an example.

An employee of MonsterVideo, a large video company, is also a student at the local university. For a research project, this student and his team members decide to compare the video-viewing habits of a sample of customers. Using telephone interviews, the students begin their research. After enquiring about people's viewing habits and the frequency of rentals versus purchases, the students move on to the types of film people watch. They find that most respondents answer questions about their preferences for children's shows, classics, bestsellers, mysteries and science fiction. However, cooperation ceases when the students question the viewing frequency of pornographic movies. Without the guarantee of privacy, most people will not answer this kind of question truthfully, if at all. The study then loses key data.

The privacy guarantee is important not only in retaining the validity of research but also in protecting respondents. In the example above, imagine the harm that could be caused by releasing information on the viewing habits of particular citizens. Clearly, the confidentiality of survey answers is an important aspect of respondents' right to privacy.

Once the guarantee of confidentiality has been given, it is essential to protect that confidentiality. The researcher protects respondent confidentiality in several ways:

- obtaining signed non-disclosure documents
- restricting access to participant identification
- revealing participant information only with written consent
- restricting access to data instruments where the participant is identified
- non-disclosure of data sub-sets.

Researchers should restrict access to information that reveals names, telephone numbers, addresses or other identifying features. Only researchers who have signed **non-disclosure** confidentiality forms should be allowed access to the data. Links between the data or database and the identifying information file should be weakened. Individual interview response sheets should be inaccessible to everyone except the editors and data-entry personnel. Occasionally, data-collection instruments should be destroyed once the data are in a data file. Data files that make it easy to reconstruct the profiles or identification of individual participants should be carefully controlled. For very small groups, data should not be made available because it is often easy to pinpoint a person within the group. Employee satisfaction survey feedback in small units can easily be used to identify an individual through descriptive statistics alone. These last two protections are particularly important in human resources research.[5]

Privacy is more than confidentiality, however. A right to privacy means that one has the right to refuse to be interviewed or to refuse to answer any question in an interview. Potential participants have a right to privacy in their own homes, including not admitting researchers and not answering telephones. Samples of household surveys are often taken from telephone directories, which are sold by telecommunications providers. These lists of telephone numbers are often incomplete, because people can request that their number is not listed. As more and more people are choosing to go ex-directory, direct marketing and research agencies are now employing random dialling – where a computer generates at random a telephone number to be dialled – to approach respondents for telephone interviews. Random dialling is, however, forbidden in certain countries (such as the Netherlands). People also have the right to engage in private behaviour in private places without fear of observation. In some countries, even in public places, people have to be informed that the area is under surveillance (e.g. by erecting signs which state that a property is monitored by video cameras).

The right to privacy is also an important issue regarding the linking of databases. Privacy laws restrict to what extent different databases can be combined to get a more complete picture of a respondent. In the MonsterVideo example, above, it would be undesirable if it was possible to link the information obtained through the telephone interviews with the record of video rentals and purchases of a specific customer.

To address these rights to privacy, ethical researchers:

- inform participants of their right to refuse to answer any questions or participate in the study
- obtain permission to interview participants
- schedule field and telephone interviews.

Research Methods in Real Life

Business intelligence and espionage? Where to draw the thin line?

In any course on strategic management, students learn that analysing a firm's competitors is a crucial step in strategic analysis. But how do you obtain information about your competitors? Thomas Steinberg, chief executive officer (CEO) of the office supply retailer Staples, got his wife Dola to apply for a job at Office Depot's order delivery centre to learn more about their competitor's logistics.

Adrian Kirby, no. 1348 on the *Sunday Times* 2009 rich list, was sentenced to six months' jail for paying a private detective agency £47,000 (then €69,000) to spy on environmental activists. Martin Witherington noticed a stranger opening an underground telephone junction box in Thornhaugh. He informed British Telecom (BT), but they had not sent a technician to Thornhaugh. When they checked the junction box, BT detected several bugs. The man placing the bugs could be traced back to a private investigator in London and their biggest customer was Atlantic Waste Services Ltd., a company operating a landfill next to Thornhaugh. At that time Atlantic Waste Services faced serious opposition from activists in Thornhaugh and local regulatory bodies. Adrian Kirby, who partly owned Atlantic Waste Services, had ordered the telephone bugging, as he considered selling the business at that time.

Also in 2007, McLaren Mercedes was fined US$50 million as it had copied technical documents from Ferrari, a main competitor in Formula 1. The espionage came to light accidentally in the small English village of Cranleigh. A manager of a documenting centre became suspicious when a woman brought an 800-page Ferrari manual for scanning. He telephoned Ferrari and then it became known that the woman was the wife of a McLaren engineer.

These examples might be pretty obvious cases of espionage, but what about hiring a former employee of a competitor? What about a consulting firm that interviews industry experts and pretends to work on an industry study, while also working for a competitor of the interview partners? A report on competitive intelligence draws a line between unethical and appropriate behaviour with two examples: (1) It is unethical and illegal to steal the briefcase of a competitor during an exhibition or trade fair, but it is acceptable to wait until the end of trade fair and then walk around to look for documents others have accidently left at their booth. (2) A competitor's employee has difficulties holding his tongue. You can use this information in a report but you should only identify the type of source and not the full name.

References and further reading

news.bbc.co.uk/2/hi/business/7220063.stm

http://wiki.telfer.uottawa.ca/ci-wiki/index.php/Ethics_in_Competitive_Intelligence#.22The_Bible_of_BI_Ethics.22

Stemberg, Thomas (1996) *Staples for Success*. Santa Monica, CA: Knowledge Exchange.

 ## 4.3 Data collection in cyberspace

Some ethicists argue that the very conduct that results in resistance from participants – interference, invasiveness in their lives, and denial of privacy rights – has encouraged researchers to investigate topics online that have long been the principal commodity of offline investigation. The novelty and convenience of communicating by computer has led researchers into cyberspace in search of abundant sources of data.

In a special ethics issue of *Information Society*, scholars involved in cyberspace research concluded:

> "All participants agree that research in cyberspace provides no special dispensation to ignore ethical precepts. Researchers are obligated to protect human subjects and 'do right' in electronic venues as in more conventional ones. Second, each participant recognizes that cyberspace poses complex ethical issues that may lack exact analogy in other types of inquiry. The ease of covert observation, the occasional blurry distinction between public and private venues, and the difficulty of obtaining the informed consent of subjects make cyber-research particularly vulnerable to ethical breaches by even the most scrupulous scholars. Third, all recognize that because research procedures or activities may be permissible or not precluded by law or policy, it does not follow that they are necessarily ethical or allowable. Fourth, all agree that the individual researcher has the ultimate responsibility for assuring that inquiry is not only done honestly, but done with ethical integrity."[6]

Issues relating to cyberspace in research also relate to data-mining. The information collection devices available today were once the tools of the spy, the science-fiction protagonist or the superhero. Smart cards, biometrics (finger printing, retinal scans, facial recognition), electronic monitoring (closed-circuit television, digital camera monitoring), global surveillance and genetic identification (DNA) are just some of the technological tools being used by today's organizations to track and understand employees, customers and suppliers. Every time you surf on the web, the hosts of the websites you visit, intentionally or even unintentionally, can make contact with your computer and monitor your activity by storing small programs, such as cookies, on it. Technically, it is possible for them to obtain a great deal of information about you in this way, such as the location of your computer, the websites you have visited in the past and even the information stored on your computer. However, despite the fact that you may have visited a certain website deliberately, this does not imply that you are willing to give personal information to the host of that website. The data-mining of all this information, collected from advanced and not necessarily obvious sources, offers infinite possibilities for research abuse.

Social media sites, such as Facebook or LinkedIn, create new ethical dilemmas. To what extent is it ethical to extract the information from thousands of Facebook sites for research purposes? The ethical dilemma boils down to two questions: (1) is a Facebook page public or private; and (2) could it do harm to aggregate the data of 1,000 Facebook pages? Currently, there is no clear answer to these questions. Some might argue their pages are private; others will argue that as you were willing to share them, they are not private. Similarly, some will argue that aggregation cannot do harm; others will argue that through aggregation third parties can draw conclusions about the individual, which the individual wouldn't like to be public. Given the unclear situation in this regard, the only advice one can give a researcher is probably: 'Would you mind if a newspaper reports about your scraping of social media sites and what you did?' If your answer is yes, you have crossed an ethical boundary.

The primary ethical data-mining issues are privacy and consent. Smart cards – those ubiquitous credit-card-sized devices that imbed personal information on a computer chip, which is then matched to purchase, employment or other behavioural data – offer the researcher implied consent to participant surveillance. The surface benefits of card use, however, may be enough to obscure from an unsuspecting user the data-mining purpose of the card (see Research Methods in Real Life, p. 128).

Retailers, wholesalers, medical and legal service providers, schools, government agencies and resorts, to name but a few, use smart cards or their equivalent. In most instances, participants provide, sometimes grudgingly, the personal information requested by enrolment procedures. In others – for instance, when smart technology is used to monitor those convicted of crimes and sentenced to municipal or state correction facilities, or those attending specific schools – enrolment is mandatory. In some instances, mandatory sharing of information is initially for personal welfare and safety, such as when you admit yourself for a medical procedure and provide detailed information about medication or prior surgery. In others, enrolment is for less critical, but potentially attractive, monetary benefits – for example, free car-care services when a smart card is included with the keys to a new vehicle. The bottom line is that, whatever perceived benefit is gained by the cardholder, the organization collecting the information gains a major benefit: the potential for better understanding and competitive advantage.

Research Methods in Real Life
Customer privacy

In 1998, Albert Heijn, the Dutch branch of the multinational Ahold (a retail company operating in more than 20 countries and serving 30 million customers), introduced its 'bonuscard' entitling holders to special discounts on certain products, which changed weekly. Households could obtain this card by filling in an application form, which included a short questionnaire. Then, every time the cardholder shops at Albert Heijn the card is scanned with the purchases made. Through scanning the bonuscard, information about purchasing habits can be linked to the individual profile of the customer acquired through the application form questionnaire, as well as to other information sources. For example, the company can link address information to an existing database on neighbourhood demographics.

Civil rights organizations have been harsh critics of the bonuscard and have warned that, one day, Albert Heijn and other firms might know more about their customers than even their best friends do. They even suggested strategies that would undermine the value of the information collected, such as swapping bonuscards with friends. As a consequence of this public turmoil, Albert Heijn eventually agreed to issue an anonymous bonuscard.

Supermarkets have increasingly introduced loyalty cards to bind customers by offering price reductions or added-value rewards. However, a recent survey by IGD, a research firm specializing in the food and grocery industry, reveals that 38 per cent of British shoppers do not have any loyalty card and 40 per cent of cardholders get fed up with these cards (partly because they have serious privacy concerns). In the USA an increasing awareness of customer associations concerning loyalty cards and the associated privacy protection can be observed.

Supermarkets collect your shopping lists and some demographic information – very limited compared with what Twitter, Facebook and Google know about you. Eben Haben, a scientist at IBM's Almaden research centre, posts that linking consumer behaviour to their demographics is very ineffective; a better way is to understand the psychological profiles of consumers. His group developed software that measures the five big personality traits (extraversion, neuroticism, consciousness, openness and agreeableness) by looking what words people use in their Twitter messages or blogs. The software is based on a paper of Tal Yarkoni, who scanned through 694 blogs and related the usage of specific words to personality measurement. Extroversion, for example, correlates with crowd and bar, while neuroticism is related to awful and depressing.

What are the ethical limits of combining and exploring databases?

References and further reading

Albert Heijn bonuscard (www.ah.nl/bonuskaart)

www.nocards.org

www.economist.com/news/science-and-technology/21578357-plan-assess-peoples-personal-characteristics-their-twitter-streams-no

www.sciencedirect.com/science/article/pii/S0092656610000541

General privacy laws may not be sufficient to protect the unsuspecting in the cyberspace realm of data collection. Fifteen EU countries started the new millennium by passing the European Commission's Data Protection Directive. Under this directive, commissioners can prosecute companies and block websites that fail to live up to its strict privacy standards. Specifically, the directive prohibits the transmission of names, addresses, ethnicity and other personal information to any country that fails to provide adequate data protection. This includes direct mail lists, hotel and travel reservations, medical and work records and orders for products, among a host of other examples.

US industry and government agencies have resisted regulation of data flow, but the EU insists that it is the right of every citizen to find out what information about them is in a database and to correct any mistakes. Few US companies would willingly offer such access due to the high costs incurred; a perfect example of this reluctance is the difficulty individuals experience in correcting erroneous credit reports, even when such information is based on transactions using stolen personal identity or credit cards.

Yet questions remain regarding the definition of specific ethical behaviours for cyber research, the sufficiency of existing professional guidelines and the issue of ultimate responsibility for respondents. If researchers are responsible for the ethical conduct of their research, are they then solely responsible for the burden of protecting participants from every conceivable harm?

4.4 Ethics and the sponsor

There are also ethical considerations to bear in mind when dealing with the research client or sponsor. Whether undertaking product, market, personnel, financial or other research, a sponsor has the right to receive research that has been conducted ethically.

Confidentiality

Some sponsors wish to undertake research without revealing their identity. They have a right to several types of confidentiality, including sponsor non-disclosure, purpose non-disclosure and findings non-disclosure.

Companies have a right to dissociate themselves from the sponsorship of a research project. This type of confidentiality is called **sponsor non-disclosure**. Due to the sensitive nature of the management dilemma or the research question, sponsors may hire an outside consulting or research firm to complete research projects. This is often done when a company is testing a new product idea, to avoid potential consumers being influenced by the company's current image or industry standing. Alternatively, if a company is contemplating entering a new market, it may not wish to reveal its plans to competitors. In such cases, it is the responsibility of the researcher to respect this desire and devise a plan that safeguards the identity of the research sponsor and the rights of the respondent. The sponsor's right to conceal their identity can come into conflict with the respondent's right to be fully informed about the objectives of the study. Sometimes, respondents even ask for whom the study is being conducted. The ethically correct way to deal with such a situation requires the respondent to be told that you cannot reveal the name of the sponsor, thus risking that the respondent may refuse to answer.

Purpose non-disclosure involves protecting the purpose of the study or its details. A research sponsor may be testing a new idea that is not yet patented and may not want the competition to know of its plans. It may be investigating employee complaints and may not want to spark union activity. Perhaps the sponsor might be contemplating a new public stock offering, where advance disclosure would spark the interest of the authorities or cost the firm thousands or even millions of euros. Finally, even if a sponsor feels no need to conceal its identity or the study's purpose, most sponsors want the research data and findings to remain confidential, at least until the management decision has been made. Thus, sponsors usually demand and receive **findings non-disclosure** between themselves or their researchers and any interested but unapproved parties.

Right to quality research

An important ethical consideration for the researcher and the sponsor is the sponsor's **right to quality** research. This right entails:

- providing a research design appropriate for the research question
- maximizing the sponsor's value for the resources expended
- providing data-handling and reporting techniques appropriate for the data collected.

From the proposal through the design to data analysis and final reporting, the researcher guides the sponsor on the proper techniques and interpretations. Often sponsors will have heard about a sophisticated data-handling technique and will want it used even when it is inappropriate for the problem in hand. The researcher should guide the sponsor so that this does not occur. The researcher should propose the design most suitable for the problem, and should not propose activities designed to maximize researcher revenue or minimize researcher effort at the sponsor's expense.

Finally, we have all heard the saying that there are 'lies – damn lies – and statistics'; it is the researcher's responsibility to make sure that any statistics produced are truthful. The ethical researcher always follows the analytical rules and conditions for results to be valid, and reports findings in a way that minimizes the drawing of false conclusions. The ethical researcher also uses charts, graphs and tables to show the data objectively, whatever the sponsor's preferred outcome.

Sponsor's ethics

Occasionally, research specialists may be asked by sponsors to participate in unethical behaviour. Compliance by the researcher would be a breach of ethical standards. Some examples to be avoided are:

- violating participant confidentiality
- changing data or creating false data to meet a desired objective
- changing data presentations or interpretations
- interpreting data from a biased perspective
- omitting sections of data analysis and conclusions
- making recommendations beyond the scope of the data collected.

We now examine the effects of complying with these types of coercion. A sponsor may offer a promotion, future contracts or a larger payment for the existing research contract; or the sponsor may threaten to fire the researcher or tarnish the researcher's reputation. For some researchers, the request may seem trivial and the reward high – but of what value are distorted results?

Suppose you investigate what employees of a medium-sized service company think about the plan for a large restructuring of the company. Your research reveals that most employees understand that a major restructuring of the firm is necessary, but they have doubts that the suggested new structure will result in the predicted productivity gains, as it requires much more coordination across the different locations of the firm. Imagine now that the firm's management has asked you to focus in your research report on the first result, namely that the majority of employees understand the need for restructuring, and neglect the doubts of the employees. Maybe the management will be pleased with your report and you will be more likely to be asked to conduct future research. But how will such behaviour affect your reputation as a researcher? What will happen if others get to know that your report contains only half the truth? Finally, is it wise to confirm management's view that the employees support their restructuring plans, although you know that many employees do not agree with the management? What is the value to management of such distorted information?

What is the ethical course?

Often, this calls for a confrontation of the sponsor's demands and for the researcher to take the following action:

- educate the sponsor in the purpose of research
- explain the researcher's role in fact-finding versus the sponsor's role in decision-making
- explain how distorting the truth or breaking faith with participants leads to future problems
- failing moral persuasion, terminate the relationship with the sponsor.

Researchers and team members

Another ethical responsibility of researchers is their team's safety, as well as their own. In addition, responsibility for ethical behaviour rests with the researcher who, along with their assistants, is charged with protecting the anonymity of both the sponsor and the participant.

Safety

It is the researcher's responsibility to design a project so that the safety of all interviewers, surveyors, experimenters or observers is protected. It may be important to consider several factors in ensuring a researcher's **right to safety**. Some urban areas and undeveloped rural areas may be unsafe for research assistants. If, for example, the researcher must personally interview people in a high-crime district, it is reasonable to provide a second team member to protect the researcher. Alternatively, if an assistant feels unsafe after visiting a neighbourhood by car, a different researcher should be assigned to the destination.[7] It is unethical to require staff members to enter an environment where they feel threatened. Researchers who are insensitive to these concerns face both research and legal risks – the least of which involves having interviewers falsify instruments.

Ethical behaviour of assistants

Researchers should require ethical compliance from team members just as sponsors expect ethical behaviour from the researcher. Assistants are expected to carry out the sampling plan, to interview or observe respondents without bias, and to record all necessary data accurately. Unethical behaviour, such as filling in an interview sheet without having asked the participant the questions, cannot be tolerated. The behaviour of the assistants is under the direct control of the responsible researcher or field supervisor. If an assistant behaves improperly in an interview or shares a participant's interview sheet with an unauthorized person, it is the researcher's responsibility. Consequently, all assistants should be well trained and supervised.

Protection of anonymity

As discussed previously, researchers and assistants protect the confidentiality of the sponsor's information and the anonymity of the respondents. Each researcher handling data should be required to sign a confidentiality and non-disclosure statement.

 ## 4.6 Ethical obligations to the research community

As a researcher you not only have an ethical obligation towards your research fellows, who cooperate with you in specific projects, but also to the (research) community as a whole. Every piece of research is a serious attempt to shed some light on what is true. In Chapter 2, we discussed which requirements good research has to fulfil in order to claim that the research's findings are a truthful reflection of reality. While less than two centuries ago the truthfulness of an argument was proved by referring to God, these days references to scientific studies are used to prove a claim. In public debates the introductory phrase, 'God said . . .' has been replaced by phrases such as, 'Research by the University of Hull reveals that . . .', 'An article just published in the *European Economic Review* shows that . . .' or 'Various independent scientific studies give clear evidence that . . .'. This increasing reference to the findings of scientific research in order to demonstrate the truth of an argument shows that the general public place great confidence in the accuracy of research.

The research community has earned this confidence in the accuracy of its findings by repeatedly showing that the public can trust the results of sound research. Despite this, however, the accuracy of research findings is often questioned. This scepticism towards the findings of research studies is fuelled by improperly conducted research.

Exhibit 4.3 gives examples of what kind of behaviour leads to poor research. Producing poor research also has an ethical element. Whenever researchers – intentionally or merely because they can't do any better – conduct a research study without complying with the standards of good research, they find themselves on ethically questionable grounds. If research is irrelevant and inconsequential, then no one will base their decisions upon it; at the very least, poor research damages the trust people have in the reliability of research in general.

As a researcher, you need to be aware that others will use the results you produce to make decisions or to convince others in a debate. Therefore, you have to ensure that people are not misled by your results and conclusions. This also requires you to be open and honest about the limitations of your research. Everybody who has ever conducted empirical research knows that it is impossible to do research that is 100 per cent perfect. Time and budget constraints, respondents' capacities and motivations, information researchers cannot access, and so on, often limit

---

Exhibit 4.3 *Examples of unethical behaviour on a sliding scale.*

Speculative interpretation of the results
- Expand the answers provided beyond the original research question

Neglecting the limitations of the research
- Measurement problems
- Sample biases (e.g. experiments with student participants are generalized to the whole population)
- Design deficiencies (e.g. missing control groups in experiments)

Capitalizing on chance (reporting the best)
- Not analysing or reporting insignificant effects
- Selecting the 'best' model out of the thousands estimated

Fabrication of data
- Deleting observations (to alter results)
- Modifying the answers of respondents
- Faking the results of analyses

---

research. Ethical standards do not require the researcher to refrain from any research that cannot be conducted perfectly, but they do require the researcher to be honest and open about methodological limitations, as the revealing of limitations allows others to assess the quality and reliability of the results more efficiently.

With modern computer techniques it has become very quick and easy to estimate thousands of models. Despite the many benefits of this, the ease with which one can analyse data also has a pitfall. As it is so easy to analyse data, the researcher might be tempted to estimate many slightly different models, change the scaling of a variable that is close to significance, use only the significant effects, and so on. Repeated analysis of data is fine as long as you use this to assess the robustness of your results (i.e. to check whether you obtain the same results if you estimate the model slightly differently). However, as soon as you re-estimate your model to search for a better one, you begin to capitalize on chance. The thinking behind the problem of chance capitalization is that, in quantitative analyses, we use the 5 per cent (or sometimes even 10 per cent) significance level to establish whether or not a variable makes a difference (i.e. whether the effect of an independent on the dependent variable or the difference in the means of two variables really differs from zero). If we find that the means of two variables are different at the 5 per cent level, in 5 per cent of the cases there is no real difference in the mean. In other words, 1 in 20 mean comparisons report a difference although there is no difference. Thus, we check whether the means of two variables are different and we compare the two means 20 times, and every time they are a little bit different, it is likely that we will get one comparison suggesting a significant difference at the 5 per cent level, because once in 20 cases the laws of probability misled us.

To put it simply: you will always find a significant result if you search long enough for it. If you search long enough you will certainly, for instance, find a Portuguese person who speaks Finnish fluently. However, having found a fluent Finnish-speaking Portuguese person would not allow you to conclude that Portuguese people speak Finnish.

Sometimes, researchers restrict their analyses to the significant results, especially when their sample size is small. You should note, however, that there is a difference between excluding something from the analysis and not reporting that you excluded something for certain reasons. Often researchers have an inclination to value significant results more than non-significant ones. However, insignificant results are also very important and can be fruitful. For example, many studies including gender as an influencing factor indeed find significant differences between women and men. Suppose you investigate the motivation of employees in a firm and the results of your study show that there are no differences between men and women. Such an outcome contradicts the results of previous studies and is exciting, especially if you are able to explain why in your study you do not find differences between women and men.

Student Research
Strategies for achieving good marks with little effort

The curriculum of the school of business and economics at Maastricht University is organized in four seven-week-long blocks each year. In a typical course, students are not only assessed by an exam at the end, but also for their participation during classes and for a course assignment that is often done in teams of 3–4 students. The work in student teams is often problematic as each team member receives the same grade regardless of individual efforts, which creates an incentive to free-ride or socially loaf.

Till Prinz was interested in this topic and his principal idea was that social loafing needs two parties – the social loafer and the other team member. Social loafing is like a door; personality characteristics of the team determine whether the door is closed (social loafing is not accepted) or open. The personality characteristics of each student describe whether one goes through the open door (i.e. rides free) or not.

Till conducted his research in a course on entrepreneurship that was taken by 140 students that formed 37 teams that have to write a paper on how one could turn an existing invention into an innovation.

The teams were randomly selected to reduce the chance that friends who knew each other well formed teams. Each team member had to fill in three questionnaires: the first, two weeks after the course started that also included a personality trait questionnaire; a second, five weeks after the course starts; and a third, when the project was finished. In each questionnaire respondents were asked to rate the contribution of themselves and the other team members. To ensure that all students participate in the course, Till visited the course meetings and asked students to fill out the questionnaire during the meeting, which usually took about 15 minutes.

A central problem of studying social loafing is that as soon as you announce that you will investigate it, people are likely to watch out and refrain from it. Till employed the following strategies to reduce that problem. First, the objective of the study was masked. In the first meeting, he told the student that he was writing a research project on teamwork, but did not mention the terms 'social loafing' or 'free-riding'. Right after the data collection all participants were debriefed. They received an email in which it was stated that the real objective of the study was 'social loafing'. Moreover, the participants were offered the opportunity to withdraw from the research, that is, Till would destroy their details if they thought they would not have participated if they had known the true objective. Second, in all questionnaires people were asked to rate the contributions of the others, but only the last questionnaire contained questions on a social loafing scale.

In the end, out of the 140 students, 38 could be characterized as social loafers. It also turned out that most social loafers behave strategically. Just three students did contribute considerably less than the other group members during the whole project. The vast majority (35 students) contributed as everybody else in the beginning, but reduced their contributions towards the end of the project, when most work had to be done.

Insignificant results are an important part of our knowledge; it is not only useful to know what are influencing factors, but also what factors are not influencing, especially if others believe they have an impact. You need to be very careful if you suppress insignificant results. All types of behaviour described so far can be justified if you assess the consequences thoroughly. It starts to become unethical as soon as you perform such activities to arrive at the results you would like to have or to suppress results that do not fit with your own perspective on the issue. Methodology and statistics are powerful tools for getting to grips with what is going on; however, they can also be misused to conceal the truth.

In recent years, major newspapers have frequently published stories on researchers who have falsified research results or indulged in **plagiarism**. Such stories mostly refer to researchers in the so-called 'hard sciences', such as physics and medicine. However, a group of US researchers argues that falsifying results might be even more common in economics and other social sciences, as the cost of falsifying results might be lower. **Falsification** of results in drug research could harm patients and even result in deaths; populations may be harmed by falsified or exaggerated reports on poverty in British cities.

A group of US researchers carried out a survey among the participants of the American Economic Association's annual meeting in Chicago in 1998. Their survey revealed that about 4 per cent of the participating economists confessed to having falsified research data.[8] Falsification or fabrication of data is unethical whatever the means. Although 4 per cent is not that great a figure, and might include research that has never been published, it is still much too high. Research falsification is a serious threat to the reputation and integrity of the research community as a whole.

In the third issue of the 1999 volume, the editors of *Kyklos*, a European economic journal, informed their readers that one reader had told them that an article published by Hans W. Gottinger in *Kyklos* in 1996 was identical to an article published by G.J. Watts in *Economics of Innovations and New Technology* in 1992. As Gottinger was unable to give a convincing explanation for the similarity of his work to the previously published work, the editor viewed it as a clear case of plagiarism. Plagiarism is a serious offence and is a form of unethical behaviour, because it involves stealing the intellectual property of someone else. Even if you copy just a single paragraph from the work of someone else without mentioning your source, you have crossed the line of plagiarism.

As explained in Chapter 2, new research usually builds on previous research and, consequently, you will be required to mention the ideas and results of others in your own reporting. You must identify any parts of your own work that are based on or mention ideas, arguments or results from the work of others, and acknowledge their previous work using a system of references. This makes it quite obvious to readers which parts of the study originate from you and which parts do not.

Plagiarism is a hot issue in university communities; students may copy each other's assignments if they know different lecturers will grade them. Copying from other sources (plagiarism) has existed for a long time, but with the birth of the Internet, it has become far easier. From your own desk at home you can easily access thousands of sources, and search engines can assist you in finding appropriate sites where you will be able to locate suitable texts or even whole papers. In addition, as this information is provided digitally, you do not even have to retype the text – just using a basic copy-and-paste function will allow you to insert text from other sources into your own work in the blink of an eye.

Currently, however, the advantages offered by information technology are turning against the plagiarist. Software such as that found at turnitin.com or plagiarism.com[9] allows tutors to check very easily whether text submitted by a student contains elements from uncredited sources or is very similar to something submitted by another student. Many universities are becoming better equipped to detect plagiarism and, once it has been uncovered, the consequences for plagiarists can be severe.

The most important argument against plagiarism at college and university is that students who merely copy the work of others do not learn anything, despite the fact that they go to school to advance their knowledge and to learn skills. Thus, those people who use plagiarism as an easy way of getting marks fail to achieve what they set out to do.

Ethical approval procedures

Above we outlined the ethical issues often present in business and management studies. In medical studies, ethical issues are usually more severe and therefore the decision of what is ethically acceptable is not left to the researcher. Rather, researchers must seek prior approval for their research projects from special ethical committees. Currently, almost all medical schools have established ethical approval committees and some schools related to the social sciences, especially psychology departments, have already followed. In the future, it is likely that ethic approvals become more and more common, especially regarding the privacy rights of respondents. A checklist of questions pointing you at potential ethical issues in your project are as follows:

- Will you describe the main procedures to participants in advance?
- Will you tell participants that their participation is voluntary?
- Will you obtain written consent for participation?
- If the research is observational, will you ask participants for their consent to being observed?
- Will you tell participants that they may withdraw from the research at any time and for any reason?
- With questionnaires and interviews will you give participants the option of omitting questions they do not want to answer?
- Will you tell participants that their data will be treated with full confidentiality and that, if published, it will not be identifiable as theirs?
- Will you give participants the opportunity to be debriefed, that is, to find out more about the study and its results?
- Will your project deliberately mislead participants in any way?

- Is there any realistic risk of any participants experiencing either physical or psychological distress or discomfort?
- Do participants fall into any of the following groups: children under 18 years of age, people with communication or learning difficulties, patients, people in custody, people who could be regarded as vulnerable and people engaged in illegal activities?

Exhibit 4.4 depicts a flow chart of an ethical approval process for a student's project. The starting point is a check whether the project touches upon ethical issues. If there are no ethical issues, student and supervisor sign a research disclaimer and submit it to the faculty and the project proceeds. If there are ethical issues, the student needs to complete an approval form. The supervisor sends this form to the faculty ethics committee for approval. If the faculty committee believes that the project requires approval at the university level, it informs the university ethics committee. Either the faculty or the university committee approves the project and informs the applicants accordingly. After approval the project can proceed. In cases where the committee does not approve the project, the student applicant and supervisor are notified of the issues that need to be addressed and asked to revise the project. The revised project is then reconsidered by the responsible ethics committee.

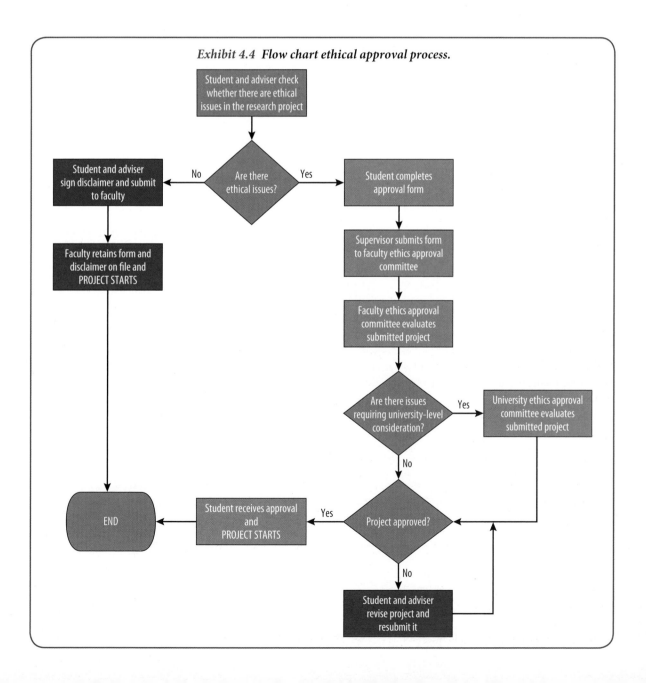

Exhibit 4.4 Flow chart ethical approval process.

Professional standards

Deeper Insight into Research Methods
Professional standards

As is the case with many other professions (accountants, estate agents and the like) the various bodies to which professional researchers belong have developed their own standards.

Many professional associations' codes have detailed research sections; one such code is the code of ethical conduct of the European Science Foundation (see Exhibit 4.5); other examples are the European Federation of Psychologist Associations and the International Sociologist Association (ISA). Such bodies update their codes frequently.

Exhibit 4.5 Example of a professional standard.

Executive Summary of the Code of Conduct European Science Foundation

1.1 The Code
Researchers, public and private research organisations, universities and funding organisations must observe and promote the principles of integrity in scientific and scholarly research.

These principles include:

- honesty in communication
- reliability in performing research
- objectivity
- impartiality and independence
- openness and accessibility
- duty of care
- fairness in providing references and giving credit
- responsibility for the scientists and researchers of the future.

Universities, institutes and all others who employ researchers, as well as agencies and organisations funding their scientific work, have a duty to ensure a prevailing culture of research integrity. This involves clear policies and procedures, training and mentoring of researchers, and robust management methods that ensure awareness and application of high standards as well as early identification and, wherever possible, prevention of any transgression.

Fabrication, falsification and the deliberate omission of unwelcome data are all serious violations of the ethos of research. Plagiarism is a violation of the rules of responsible conduct vis-à-vis other researchers and, indirectly, harmful for science as well. Institutions that fail to deal properly with such wrongdoing are also guilty. Credible allegations should always be investigated. Minor misdemeanours should always be reprimanded and corrected. Investigation of allegations should be consistent with national law and natural justice. It should be fair, and speedy, and lead to proper outcomes and sanctions. Confidentiality should be observed where possible, and proportionate action taken where necessary. Investigations should be carried through to a conclusion, even when the alleged defaulter has left the institution.

Partners (both individual and institutional) in international collaborations should agree beforehand to cooperate to investigate suspected deviation from research integrity, while respecting the laws and sovereignty of the states of participants. In a world of increasing transnational, cross-sectional and interdisciplinary science, the work of OECD's Global Science Forum on *Best Practices for Ensuring Scientific Integrity and Preventing Misconduct* can provide useful guidance in this respect.

1.2 The Principles of Research Integrity
These require *honesty* in presenting goals and intentions, in reporting methods and procedures and in conveying interpretations. Research must be *reliable* and its communication fair and full. *Objectivity* requires facts capable of proof, and transparency in the handling of data. Researchers should be *independent* and *impartial* and communication with other researchers and with the public should be *open* and honest. All researchers have a *duty of care* for the humans, animals, the environment or the objects that they study. They must show *fairness* in providing references and giving credit for the work of others and must show *responsibility for future generations* in their supervision of young scientists and scholars.

1.3 Misconduct
Research *misconduct* is harmful for knowledge. It could mislead other researchers, it may threaten individuals or society — for instance if it becomes the basis for unsafe drugs or unwise legislation — and, by subverting the public's *trust*, it could lead to a disregard for or undesirable restrictions being imposed on research.

Research misconduct can appear in many guises:

- *Fabrication* involves making up results and recording them as if they were real.
- *Falsification* involves manipulating research processes or changing or omitting data.
- *Plagiarism* is the appropriation of other people's material without giving proper credit.
- Other forms of misconduct include *failure to meet clear ethical and legal requirements* such as misrepresentation of interests, breach of confidentiality, lack of informed consent and abuse of research subjects or materials. Misconduct also includes *improper dealing* with infringements, such as attempts to cover up misconduct and reprisals on whistleblowers.
- *Minor misdemeanours* may not lead to formal investigations, but are just as damaging given their probable frequency, and should be corrected by teachers and mentors.

The response must be proportionate to the seriousness of the misconduct: as a rule it must be demonstrated that the misconduct was committed intentionally, knowingly or recklessly. Proof must be based on the preponderance of evidence. Research misconduct should not include honest errors or differences of opinion. Misbehaviour such as intimidation of students, misuse of funds and other behaviour that is already subject to universal legal and social penalties is unacceptable as well, but is not 'research misconduct' since it does not affect the integrity of the research record itself.

1.4 Good Research Practices

There are other failures to adhere to good practices – incorrect procedures, faulty data management, etc. – that may affect the public's trust in science. These should be taken seriously by the research community as well. Accordingly, *data practices* should preserve original data and make it accessible to colleagues. Deviations from *research procedures* include insufficient care for human subjects, animals or cultural objects; violation of protocols; failure to obtain informed consent; breach of confidentiality, etc. It is unacceptable to claim or grant undeserved authorship or deny deserved authorship. Other *publication-related* lapses could include repeated publication, salami-slicing or insufficient acknowledgement of contributors or sponsors. Reviewers and editors too should maintain their independence, declare any conflicts of interest, and be wary of personal bias and rivalry. Unjustified claims of authorship and ghost authorship are forms of falsification. An editor or reviewer who purloins ideas commits plagiarism. It is ethically unacceptable to cause pain or stress to those who take part in research, or to expose them to hazards without informed consent.

While principles of integrity, and the violation thereof, have a universal character, some rules for good practice may be subject to cultural differences, and should be part of a set of national or institutional guidelines. These cannot easily be incorporated into a universal code of conduct. National guidelines for good research practice should, however, consider the following:

1. Data: All primary and secondary data should be stored in secure and accessible form, documented and archived for a substantial period. It should be placed at the disposal of colleagues. The freedom of researchers to work with and talk to others should be guaranteed.
2. Procedures: All research should be designed and conducted in ways that avoid negligence, haste, carelessness and inattention. Researchers should try to fulfil the promises made when they applied for funding. They should minimize impact on the environment and use resources efficiently. Clients or sponsors should be made aware of the legal and ethical obligations of the researcher, and of the importance of publication. Where legitimately required, researchers should respect the confidentiality of data. Researchers should properly account for grants or funding received.
3. Responsibility: All research subjects – human, animal or nonliving – should be handled with respect and care. The health, safety or welfare of a community or collaborators should not be compromised. Researchers should be sensitive to their research subjects. Protocols that govern research into human subjects must not be violated. Animals should be used in research only after alternative approaches have proved inadequate. The expected benefits of such research must outweigh the harm or distress inflicted on an animal.
4. Publication: Results should be published in an open, transparent and accurate manner, at the earliest possible time, unless intellectual property considerations justify delay. All authors, unless otherwise specified, should be fully responsible for the content of publication. Guest authorship and ghost authorship are not acceptable. The criteria for establishing the sequence of authors should be agreed by all, ideally at the start of the project. Contributions by collaborators and assistants should be acknowledged, with their permission. All authors should declare any conflict of interest. Intellectual contributions of others should be acknowledged and correctly cited. Honesty and accuracy should be maintained in communication with the public and the popular media. Financial and other support for research should be acknowledged.
5. Editorial responsibility: An editor or reviewer with a potential conflict of interest should withdraw from involvement with a given publication or disclose the conflict to the readership. Reviewers should provide accurate, objective, substantiated and justifiable assessments, and maintain confidentiality. Reviewers should not, without permission, make use of material in submitted manuscripts. Reviewers, who consider applications for funding, or applications by individuals for appointment or promotion or other recognition, should observe the same guidelines. The primary responsibility for handling research misconduct is in the hands of those who employ the researchers. Such institutions should have a standing or *ad hoc* committee(s) to deal with allegations of misconduct. Academies of Sciences and other such bodies should adopt a code of conduct, with rules for handling alleged cases of misconduct, and expect members to abide by it. Researchers involved in international collaboration should agree to standards of research integrity as developed in this document and, where appropriate, adopt a formal collaboration protocol either *ab initio* or by using one drafted by the OECD Global Science Forum.

Exhibit 4.5 shows the executive summary of the code of ethical conduct of the European Science Foundation, a professional organization serving scholars and practitioners in management (a full version of the code is available online at www.esf.org/fileadmin/Public_documents/Publications/Code_Conduct_ResearchIntegrity.pdf). Professional associations in specific social science disciplines use similar codes: for example, the Academy of Management code can be viewed at http://aom.org/uploadedFiles/About_AOM/Governance/AOM_Code_of_Ethics.pdf; the European Federation of Psychologist Associations code can be viewed at www.efpa.be; and the ISA at www.ucm.es/info/isa/servers.htm.

Ethical codes are not only imposed by professional organizations, but funding organizations also ask that research conducted with their funds fulfils certain ethical standards. Exhibit 4.6 depicts the minimum requirements of the Economic and Social Research Council (ESRC), a major funding organization in the UK.

Exhibit 4.6 Summary of the ESRC's minimum requirements.

The ESRC does not seek to impose a detailed model for ethics evaluation and conduct, but the following requirements will constitute the minimum standard for a research proposal to be eligible for ESRC funding, including studentships.

1. Ethics issues must always be addressed in the proposal.

Research Ethics Committees (RECs) must consider all proposals that have been recommended for award by the ESRC before the research starts.

2. All ESRC-funded research must be subject to at least a light-touch review.

Where the potential risk of 'substantive' harm to participants and others affected by the proposed research is minimal, this may be all that is necessary (for a list of possible risk groups see 'Types of Review' below). Light-touch reviews can be handled by a REC sub-committee who monitor all proposals including those of students. They may use an initial check list for this purpose (see Appendix A). The use of approved research ethics protocols for commonly occurring situations may limit the number of research proposals that need to go to a full ethics review.

3. On-going review.

As research progresses, further ethics issues may arise. In these cases, Principal Investigators should go back to their RECs and have any changes approved both by the REC and ESRC. Monitoring should be proportionate to the nature and degree of risk entailed in the research. If an ethics review is required at a later stage in the project, this should be discussed and funding arrangements agreed in advance with the ESRC.

4. Expedited review.

In exceptional circumstances, it may be necessary for a proposal involving possible risk of harm to receive a full review at short notice. An expedited review is carried out by one or more members of a REC, commonly its Chair, but not by a member of the department due to carry out the research.

5. Requests for Research Ethics Committee approval.

Where a light-touch review has confirmed that a research proposal requires full ethics review and approval, this should be carried out by a REC. This needs to be constituted and operate in accordance with standards and guidelines given in Section 1.

6. Procedures for institutional monitoring should be in place.

Universities and other research organisations should establish appropriate procedures to monitor the conduct of research which has received ethics approval until it is completed, and to ensure appropriate continuing review where the research design anticipates possible changes over time that may need to be addressed.

7. Complaints procedures should be in place.

Research organisations must have mechanisms for receiving and addressing complaints or expressions of concern about the conduct of research carried out under their auspices.

8. Arrangements should be made for training.

The ESRC expects social scientists to be able to engage with ethics issues from the start of their research careers. Research organisations must ensure that social science postgraduate training programmes incorporate the range of issues addressed in this Framework.

The full document is available here: www.esrc.ac.uk/_images/Framework-for-Research-Ethics_tcm8-4586.pdf

---

While this book commends professional societies and business organizations for developing standards, without enforcement these will be ineffectual. Effective codes:

- are regulative
- protect the public interest and the interests of the profession served by the code
- are behaviour-specific
- are enforceable.

A study that assessed the effects of personal and professional values on ethical consulting behaviour concluded:

> "The findings of this study cast some doubt on the effectiveness of professional *codes of ethics* and corporate policies that attempt to deal with ethical dilemmas faced by business consultants. A mere codification of ethical values of the profession or organization may not counteract ethical ambivalence created and maintained through reward systems. The results suggest that unless ethical codes and policies are consistently reinforced with a significant reward and punishment structure and truly integrated into the business culture, these mechanisms would be of limited value in actually regulating unethical conduct."[10]

Running Case Study 4
How to get respondents

In the last few weeks, Rebecca has spent hours in the library and behind the computer to get a more theoretical grip on her topic. She has almost finished her theoretical chapter and derived a couple of hypotheses. She has also developed a draft version of a questionnaire she will discuss with her supervisor in the next few days. She realized that the real research was about to start; although she was delighted that up to now she was on schedule, she was also worried.

A couple of days ago she met Alexander, a fellow student she knows from other courses they have taken together. Alexander told her that he started with his research project five months ago and now he was getting frustrated, as nobody filled in his questionnaire. His supervisor told him that some meaningful statistical analyses would require a sample of about 100, but although he has posted requests to participate in his online survey at the school's website, he still had just 46 responses. He had planned to complete his data collection two months ago and he feared that it would take months until he has 100 filled-in questionnaires. Rebecca tried to cheer Alexander up and bought a coffee and a chocolate muffin. But Alexander was desperate. He told her that he has even placed his survey on www.surveymonkey.com: just three respondents filled in the complete survey, while more than 20 respondents had either returned an incomplete questionnaire or filled in answers that were inconsistent, and most probably the people answering the questions filled it in at random or faked answers. Rebecca looked concerned. 'How do you decide whether an answered questionnaire is serious or should be deleted?' she asked.

'That is the point', Alexander replied, 'you never know whether people fill it in seriously or whether they are careless or even want to make fun of you. You know – I already thought to fill in a couple of questionnaire myself. I will simply put myself in the role of certain types of students and then answer the questionnaire on their behalf.'

'That is against the rules – it's unethical,' Rebecca interrupted him.

'There are no written rules in the study regulations. But, the point is that I can produce more reliable answers playing the role of some students than real student respondents, because I know what the research is about and it will save me time.'

'Oh, Alexander, why would you collect data at all, if you already know it? You can't do it. Although it is not mentioned in the regulation, you know it is wrong. You will feel bad, because this is cheating.' Alexander promised not to fake questionnaires and wait for another two weeks. Maybe if he obtained 70 respondents that would be sufficient.

The conversation with Alexander worried Rebecca, as she wanted to collect her data online as well. The problem was how to get the attention of other students and to convince them to fill in an online questionnaire. You could post such requests on a special school website, but Alexander's experiences were not encouraging. Rebecca could imagine why. From time to time she looked at that site because on the same site students could sell their used study books, offer and ask for lifts to other cities, sublease their rooms etc.

▶

She had also seen requests to fill in questionnaires for students' research projects, but had never completed one. You must be completely bored if you click on such a link, she thought. But what could she do. The university did not allow you to send emails to all students of the school or university. If they discovered that you did, they would block your email account for at least a week. Not that she was using her university account; she usually used her Gmail account. But it would be embarrassing if they did block her account.

A day later she had a brilliant idea of how she could approach students. She would open another email account at a free mail provider. Then she would look up names from the university student address book. As the structure of the student email addresses was firstinitial.name@student.maastrichtuniversity.nl, she could easily create a list of student email addresses once she knew the students' names. She would not violate the university rules and she could also ask friends at other universities whether they could provide her with name lists, as she needed answers from different universities. In the evening she phoned her school class mate Brenda, who just had finished her psychology Master's at the University of Amsterdam. Rebecca asked Brenda whether it would be possible to get her a list with a lot of student names.

Brenda has always been pragmatic and said: 'You know what, I will simply send your link to the online questionnaire to the student lists from my university account. I do not know whether it is allowed or not at our university, but in case it is not allowed who cares. I do not use that account anymore since I started working in London and they will not take away my degree I suppose. Just send me the link and the text for the email and the whole University of Amsterdam will know about your research project.'

Rebecca was delighted and was sure she would get many respondents from most Dutch universities.

1 Discuss how Rebecca obtained the (email) addresses of her respondents from an ethical perspective.
2 Discuss how Rebecca could have ensured the anonymity of her respondents.
3 Take the ethical code/code of conduct of your university and investigate whether the code covers the ethical conduct of students in their research projects.

Summary

1 Ethics are norms or standards of behaviour that guide moral choices about our behaviour and our relationships with others. Ethics differ from legal constraints, in which generally accepted standards have defined penalties that are universally enforced. The goal of ethics in research is to ensure that no one is harmed or suffers adverse consequences from research activities.

As research is designed, several ethical considerations must be balanced:
- protect the rights of the participant or subject
- ensure the sponsor receives ethically conducted and reported research
- follow ethical standards when designing research
- protect the safety of the researcher and team
- ensure the research team follows the design.

2 In general, research must be designed so that a participant does not suffer physical harm, discomfort, pain, embarrassment or loss of privacy. Begin data collection by explaining to respondents the benefits expected from the research. Explain that their rights and well-being will be adequately protected and say how this will be done. Be sure that interviewers obtain the informed consent of the respondent.

The use of deception is questionable; when it is used, debrief any participant who has been deceived.

3 Many sponsors wish to undertake research without revealing themselves. Sponsors have the right to demand and receive confidentiality between themselves and the researchers. Ethical researchers provide sponsors with the research design needed to solve the managerial question. The ethical researcher shows the data objectively, regardless of the sponsor's preferred outcome(s).

The research team's safety is the responsibility of the researcher. Researchers should require ethical compliance from team members in following the research design, just as sponsors expect ethical behaviour from the researcher.

4 Many corporations and research firms have adopted a code of ethics. Several professional associations have detailed research provisions. Of particular interest are those of the professional associations in the field you are working in. Federal, state and local governments have laws, policies and procedures in place to regulate research on human beings.

Discussion questions

Terms in review

1 Name the basic ethical considerations when conducting research and whom (you as researcher, research community, research sponsors or research participants) they affect.

Making research decisions

2 When the manager for market intelligence of AutoCorp, a major automotive manufacturer, boarded a plane in Stuttgart, her mind was on shrinking market share and late product announcements. As she settled back to enjoy what was left of a hectic day, she reached for the in-flight magazine, which was jammed into the seat pocket in front of her.

Crammed into this already tiny space was a report with a competitor's logo, marked 'Confidential – Restricted Circulation'. It contained a description of new product announcements for the next two years. Not only was it intended for a small circle of senior executives, it also answered the questions she had recently proposed to an external research firm.

The proposal for the solicited research could be cancelled. Her research budget, already savaged, could be saved and it could boost her career.

She foresaw only one problem. In the last few months, AutoCorp's newly hired ethicist had revised the firm's Business Conduct Guidelines. They now required company employees in possession of a competitor's report to return it or face dismissal. But it was still a draft and not formally approved. She had the rest of the flight to decide whether to return the document to the airline or slip it into her briefcase.

a What are the most prudent decisions that she can make about her responsibilities to herself and others?
b What are the implications of those decisions even if there is no violation of law or regulation?

3 The city commissioners of Miro Beach proposed limits on boaters who anchor offshore in waterfront areas of the St. Lucinda River adjoining the city. Residents had complained of pollution from live-aboard boaters. This 'car park' for boats created an unsightly view.

The city commissioners based its proposed ordinance on research done by staff. The staff did not hold graduate degrees in either public or business administration, and it was not known if staff members were competent to conduct research. The staff requested a proposal from a team of local university professors who had conducted similar work in the past. The research cost was $10,000. After receiving the proposal, the staff chose to do the work themselves and not expend resources on the project. Through an unidentified source, the professors later learned that their proposal had contained enough information to guide the city's staff and suggested data-collection areas that might provide information that could justify the boaters' claims.

Based on the staff's one-time survey of waterfront litter, 'pump-out' samples and a weekly frequency count of boats, an ordinance was drafted and a public workshop held. Shortly afterwards, a group of concerned boat owners formed Boaters Inc., an association to promote boating, raise funds and lobby the commission. The group's claims were that the boaters (i) spent thousands of dollars on community goods and services, (ii) did not create the litter, and (iii) were being unjustly penalized because the commission's fact-finding was flawed.

With the last claim in mind, the boaters flooded the city with public record requests. The clerks reported that in some weeks the requests were one per day. Under continued pressure, the city attorney hired a private investigator (PI) to infiltrate Boaters Inc. to collect information. He rationalized this on the grounds that the boaters had challenged the city's grant applications in order to 'blackmail the city into dropping plans to regulate the boaters'.

The PI posed as a college student and worked for a time in the home of the boater organization's sponsor while helping with mailings. Despite the PI's inability to corroborate the city attorney's theory, he recommended conducting a background investigation on the organization's principal, an employee of a tabloid newspaper. The PI was not a boating enthusiast and soon aroused suspicion. Simultaneously, the organization turned up the heat on the city by requesting what amounted to 5,000 pages of information: 'studies and all related documents containing the word "boat" '. Failing to get a response from Miro Beach, the boaters filed a suit under the Florida Public Records Act. By this time, the city had spent $20,000.

The case stalled, went to appeal, and was settled in favour of the boaters. A year later, the organization's principal filed an invasion of privacy and slander suit against the city attorney, the PI and the PI's firm. After six months, the suit was amended to include the city itself and sought $1 million in punitive damages.
a   What are the most prudent decisions the city can make about its responsibilities to itself and others?
b   What are the implications of these decisions even if there is no violation of law or regulation?

4   It was John's first year of college teaching, and there were no summer teaching assignments available to new employees. However, the university was kind enough to steer him towards an aviation firm, Avionics, which needed help creating an organizational assessment survey. The assignment was to last five weeks, but it paid about the same as teaching all summer. The work was just about as perfect as it gets for an organizational behaviour specialist. Avionics' vice-president (VP), who John met on his first day, was cordial and smooth. John would report to a senior manager who was coordinating the project with the human resources and legal departments.

It was soon apparent that in the 25-year history of Avionics, there had never been an employee survey. This was understandable given management's lack of concern for employee complaints. Working conditions had deteriorated without management intervention, and government inspectors counted the number of heads down at desks as an index of performance. A serious organizing effort was planned before the VP could approve the survey.

Headquarters dispatched nervous staffers to monitor the situation and generally involve themselves with every aspect of the questionnaire. Shadowed, the young researcher began to feel apprehension turn to paranoia. He consoled himself, however, with the goodwill of 500 enthusiastic, cooperative employees, who had pinned their hopes of a better working environment on the results of this project.

John's data collection was textbook perfect. No one had asked to preview his findings or indeed shown any particular interest. In the fifth week, he travelled with the VP and senior manager to make a presentation at headquarters. Respondents at the headquarters location were invited to attend. Management was intent on showing its confidence in the isolated nature of 'a few engineers' complaints'. They had also promised to engage the participants in action planning over the next few days.

An hour into the journey, the Avionics VP turned from his reading to the young researcher and said, 'We have seen your results, you know. And we would like you to change two key findings. They are not all that critical to this round of fixing the "bone orchard" and you'll have another crack at it as a real consultant in the autumn.'

'But that would mean breaking faith with your employees,' replied John, 'people who trusted me to present the results objectively. It's what I thought you wanted.'

'Yes, well, look at it this way,' responded the VP. 'All of your findings we can live with except these two. They're an embarrassment to senior management. Let me put it plainly. We have government contracts into the foreseeable future. You could retire early with consulting income from this place. Someone will meet us with new slides just before the meeting.'

How do you respond to this message from the VP?
a   What are the most prudent decisions Avionics can make about its responsibilities to itself and others?
b   What are the implications of those decisions even if there is no violation of law or regulation?

5 SupplyCo is a supplier to a number of firms in an industry. This industry has a structure that includes suppliers, manufacturers, distributors and consumers. Several companies are involved in the manufacturing process – from processed parts to the creation of the final product – with each firm adding some value to the product.

By carefully mining its customer data warehouse, SupplyCo reveals a plausible new model for manufacturing and distributing industry products that would increase the overall efficiency of the industry system, reduce the costs of production (leading to greater industry profits and more sales for SupplyCo), and result in greater sales and profits for some of the industry's manufacturers (SupplyCo's customers).

On the other hand, implementing the model would damage the sales and profits of other firms that are also SupplyCo's customers but that are not in a position (due to manpower, plant or equipment limitations) to benefit from the new manufacturing/distribution model. These firms would lose sales, profits and market share, and potentially go out of business.

Does SupplyCo have an obligation to protect the interests of all its customers and to take no action that would harm any of them, since it had the data within its warehouse only because of its relationship with its customers? (It would betray some of its customers if it were to use the data in a manner that would cause these customers harm.) Or does it have a more powerful obligation to its stockholders and employees to aggressively pursue the new model that research reveals would substantially increase its sales, profits and market share against competitors?

a   What are the most prudent decisions SupplyCo can make about its responsibilities to itself and others?

b   What are the implications of those decisions even if there is no violation of law or regulation?

Class discussion

Split the class into two groups, for example, according to the half of the year in which they have their birthday. One group has a more lenient opinion regarding ethics while the other advocates that behaviour needs to follow strict ethical rules. Discuss the following issues, or one of three questions in the section on 'Making research decisions', above.

6 Several websites on the Internet provide broad catalogues of Master's research projects at reasonable prices and others even offer Master's research projects on demand. Is there something wrong with seeking such assistance when you have to write your own research project? In the end, your career goal is to become a manager, and you will then seek such services from professionals. Moreover, what you need to know about research you have already learned in this course.

7 'With statistics you can prove everything' and 'I only trust statistics that I faked myself' are well-known sayings. The rules of good research are often bent to produce evidence in support of a point one wants to make, or to serve one's own purpose. What is the value of applying such research rules strictly if others apply them more leniently?

Recommended further reading

Carrigan, Marylyn and Kirkup, Malcolm, 'The ethical responsibilities of marketers in retail observational research: protecting stakeholders through the ethical "research covenant"', *International Review of Retail, Distribution and Consumer Research* 11(4), 2001, pp. 415–36. This article discusses how new technologies can raise ethical issues in consumer research.

Huws, U., Dench, S. and Iphofen, R., *An EU Code of Ethics for Socio-Economic Research*. Brighton: Institute of Employment Studies, 2004. A report on the development of ethical guidelines for socio-economic research.

Mauthner, Melanie, Birch, Maxine, Jessop, Julie and Miller, Tina (eds), *Ethics in Qualitative Research*. Thousand Oaks, CA: Sage, 2002. Examines the practical and theoretical aspects of ethical dilemmas in qualitative research, addressing also the issue of the implications if private information becomes public.

Miles, Matthew B. and Huberman, A. Michael, *Qualitative Data Analysis*. Thousand Oaks, CA: Sage, 1994. Chapter 11 discusses several ethical issues from the perspective of the consequences for data analysis.

National Academy of Sciences, *On Being a Scientist: Responsible Conduct in Research* **(2nd edn). Washington, DC: National Academy Press, 1995.** Written for beginning researchers, this source describes the ethical foundations of scientific practices, personal and professional issues, and research applications for industrial, governmental and academic settings.

Oliver, Paul, *The Student's Guide to Research Ethics.* **Buckingham: Open University Press, 2003.** A comprehensive book examining ethical issues in academic and professional research.

Rosnow, Ralph L. and Rosenthal, Robert, *People Studying People: Artifacts and Ethics in Behavioral Research.* **New York: Freeman, 1997.** A potent source of analysis and advice; particularly appropriate for the chapters that include content on observation and Chapter 12 on experimentation.

Get started with understanding statistical techniques!

When you have read this chapter, log on to the Online Learning Centre website at *www.mcgraw-hill.co.uk/textbooks/blumberg* to explore chapter-by-chapter test questions, additional case studies, a glossary and more online study tools for *Business Research Methods.*

Notes

1 Elizabethann O'Sullivan and Gary R. Rassel, *Research Methods for Public Administrators.* New York: Longman, 1999.

2 American Psychological Association, *Ethical Principles of Psychologists and Code of Conduct.* Washington, DC: APA, 1997.

3 According to the EU Directive on Data Protection 1994, agreeing to participate in an interview is an adequate consent. However, collecting sensitive data on, say, medical records, criminal records, ethnicity, religion, trade union membership, sexual orientation, and so on, requires an 'explicit' consent. The directive does not offer a definition of 'explicit' consent.

4 Exhibit 4.2 shows the standard procedures used for informed consent in surveys conducted by the Indiana University Center for Survey Research. Wording and protocol by CSR IU.

5 Robert A. Baron and Donn Byrne, *Social Psychology: Understanding Human Interaction.* Boston: Allyn & Bacon, 1991, p. 36.

6 Floyd J. Fowler, Jr., *Survey Research Methods* (rev. edn). Beverly Hills, CA: Sage, 1988, p. 138.

7 Robert O'Harrow, 'Privacy rules send US firms scrambling', *Washington Post*, 20 October 1998.

8 List, John A., Charles D. Bailey, Patricia J. Euzent and Thomas L. Martin, 'Academic economists behaving badly? A survey on three areas of ethical behavior', *Economic Inquiry* Vol. 39, January 2001, pp. 162–70.

9 An overview of the features of plagiarism-detection software and links to the suppliers of such software is available at www.fdewb.unimaas.nl/eleum/plagiarism/plagiarism.html.

10 Jeff Allen and Duane Davis, 'Assessing some determinant effects of ethical consulting behavior: the case of personal and professional values', *Journal of Business Ethics* (1993), p. 449.

PART 2
Research methods

Part contents

CHAPTER 5

Quantitative and qualitative research

Chapter contents

Learning objectives

When you have read this chapter, you should understand:

1 the basic stages of research design

2 the major descriptors classifying research design

3 the major types of research design

4 the relationships that exist between variables in research design and the steps for evaluating those relationships.

5.1 Qualitative and quantitative studies

Before we look deeper into different aspects of the research design we will discuss a widely used distinction for research study, namely the one between qualitative and quantitative studies. This distinction is based mainly on the kind of information used to study a phenomenon. As their names suggest, quantitative studies rely on quantitative information (i.e. numbers and figures), while qualitative studies base their accounts on qualitative information (i.e. words, sentences and narratives). One textbook creates a verbal picture to help differentiate between the two:

> "Quality is the essential character or nature of something; quantity is the amount. Quality is the what; quantity the how much. Qualitative refers to the meaning, the definition or analogy or model or metaphor characterizing something, while quantitative assumes the meaning and refers to a measure of it . . . The difference lies in Steinbeck's [1941] description of the Mexican Sierra, a fish from the Sea of Cortez. One can count the spines on the dorsal fin of a pickled Sierra, 17 plus 15 plus 9. 'But,' says Steinbeck, 'if the Sierra strikes hard on the line so that our hands are burned, if the fish sounds and nearly escapes and finally comes in over the rail, his colors pulsing and his tail beating the air, a whole new relational externality has come into being.' Qualitative research would define the being of fishing, the ambience of a city, the mood of a citizen, or the unifying tradition of a group."[1]

It must be emphasized that one cannot decide whether qualitative or quantitative studies are better or more useful. It is important to note that there are no pre-determinates for the appropriateness of either a qualitative or a quantitative study. Although quantitative studies seem to be more common in economics and qualitative studies in anthropology, there are plenty of examples of very insightful qualitative studies in economics and good quantitative studies in anthropology. Further, in many social sciences, such as management studies, sociology, psychology, and so on, there is no such clear predominance of qualitative or quantitative studies. Similarly, a new investigation often starts with qualitative studies exploring new phenomena and, later on, quantitative studies follow to test the validity of propositions formulated in previous qualitative studies. Although this process is often observed in chronologically ordered studies on one phenomenon, this should not give the idea that quantitative studies are never explorative, or that it is ridiculous to combine qualitative study and tests of propositions or validity assessments.

From the above, it is obvious that many research problems can be investigated qualitatively as well as quantitatively. Nevertheless, most scholars show a strong preference for either type of study. However, these preferences usually reflect scholars' view on science and knowledge, that is the research philosophy (see Chapter 1) they adhere to. Thus, the choice for either a qualitative or quantitative method is an epistemological issue. Epistemology theory of knowledge is concerned with the question of how one acquires knowledge. For positivistic researchers the knowledge acquisition process consists of deducting hypotheses (explanations) and testing those by measuring the reality. Researchers following an interpretivistic approach acquire knowledge more by developing an understanding of phenomena through a deep-level investigation and analysis of those phenomena. Consequently, quantitative methods are more common in the positivist tradition, while qualitative methods are more common in interpretivism. It should, however, be noted that the line between positivism and interpretivism is not completely identical to the line between quantitative and qualitative research.

Many problems in business and management research can be researched both ways, qualitative and quantitative, although the answers obtained may have a different nature as the research questions asked depend often on the perspective. Chapter 2 gives the example of the project team of a telecommunications provider, which is tasked with investigating the likely market acceptance of a newly designed mobile telephone with many new features. In this example the project team could either form consumer focus groups and discuss within these groups how well the new mobile telephone is likely to be received, or it could telephone-interview about 500 consumers about which features of a mobile telephone they would appreciate. Focus-group-based research is a typical example of a qualitative study, while telephone surveys qualify as a quantitative study. Which study is more appropriate depends very much on what the project team seeks, as the focus-group study will provide different answers to the telephone survey.

Let us take another example. Assume that you want to investigate how the rich and the poor live in your country. A typical quantitative version of such a study would start with a numeric definition of who is considered rich and who is considered poor – for example, the rich are those people who earn at least three times the mean income and the poor are those who can spend half or less of the mean income. Your description of the rich and the poor would depend on information included in a general survey. For example, the questions in such a survey could address: demographic information on the respondent and their household (age, married or unmarried, number of children, etc.), the respondent's educational background and occupation, their ownership of durable consumer goods (fridge, piano, car), the respondent's norms and values, the respondent's scores on personality traits, and so on. The list of possible questions you could ask is endless and your selection among all the possible questions will be driven by the specificities of your research problem. Are you interested in how the rich and poor generate income or how they spend it, or are you more interested in their lifestyles?

A more qualitative account of such an investigation could also emphasize the generation of income, its spending, or respondents' lifestyles. However, such a qualitative investigation would not use a large-scale survey to learn something about the life of rich and poor people; rather, it would be based on observations or deeper and less-structured interviews. Within an observational study, researchers could, for example, follow an average week in the life of some wealthy and some poor people. They could accompany the respondents to their workplace or to any social welfare institutions, participate in how they spend their evenings and the weekend, go shopping with them, and so on. Likewise, they could talk with a number of poor and a number of rich people, holding intensive interviews to cover the life story of each of them. In such a qualitative research setting the researchers would still, to a large extent, control the kind of information gathered. They would do this in two ways. First, they would exercise control by selecting the (leading) questions asked, or by deciding how and when the observation will be conducted. Second, qualitative research is usually much less rigorously structured than quantitative research and, consequently, the researcher is more likely to miss some information. Even by taking the utmost care, researchers will not be able to note down all the information available; rather, they will choose – subconsciously and deliberately – some of the information provided and neglect other parts of it. However, compared to a quantitative study, a qualitative study is more likely to obtain unexpected information, as the more structured approach of quantitative studies directs the researcher more, leaving less leeway to explore other avenues. That is why explorative studies often have a more qualitative character, although quantitative research, for example data-mining (see Chapter 9), is also used for explorations.

You should be aware that there are no general guidelines as to when a qualitative or quantitative method is more appropriate. When making the choice as to whether to conduct a qualitative or quantitative study you need to consider the following questions:

- What is your research problem?
- Are you attempting to conduct an explorative, descriptive, causal or predictive study?
- What is the objective (i.e. what kind of outcomes are you looking for)?
- What kind of information do you want to obtain and what do you already have access to?

Nevertheless, two researchers with similar, or even the same, answers to these questions may still come to different conclusions regarding the choice between qualitative and quantitative study. It is often impossible to determine whether a qualitative or quantitative study would be best able to answer a research problem, as a cost–benefit calculation of the trade-off between the two options does not always provide an unambiguous answer. The quality of any research study does not so much depend on whether it is qualitative or quantitative, but rather it depends on the quality of its design and how well it is conducted. In scientific and business research, there are plenty of examples of excellent qualitative and quantitative studies; unfortunately, however, there are also many examples of poorly conducted studies.

Comparing articles in scientific management journals from today with those from 30 years ago will show you especially that the methods used have become much more advanced. There are several reasons for this development. First, information technology has facilitated not only the use of statistics but also the development of new statistical analysis techniques, which spread rather easily as soon as they become a feature in standard statistical software packages. Information technology has also advanced qualitative research as text analysis software (see

Chapter 10 for an overview) allows researchers to analyse larger chunks of text data efficiently and to detect more complex patterns. Second, scientists have become much more critical of the work of others. Decades ago, scientists formed rather closed circles in which people would know each other well and one trusted each other's intellectual capacity and virtue. The number of scientists has grown tremendously; the Academy of Management, the largest professional organization for scientists in management, had 1,200 members in 1970, but counts more than 19,000 members in 2011. In such large communities, control cannot anymore be based on trust alone and, therefore, other criteria have been developed to ensure the soundness of academic work.

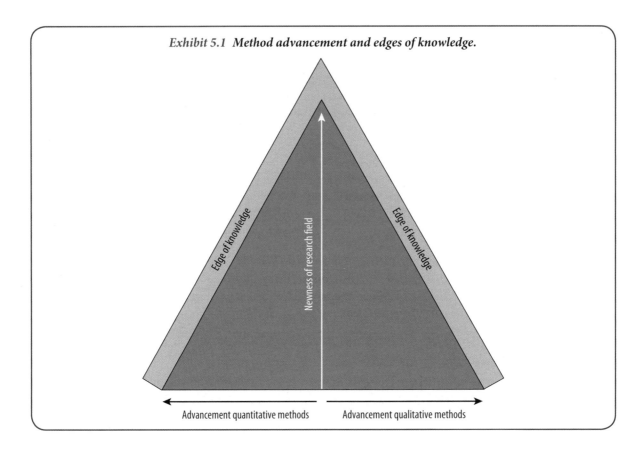

Exhibit 5.1 Method advancement and edges of knowledge.

Methods used in a field of research usually become more advanced over time. Still, differences can be observed within that field. Exhibit 5.1 illustrates this further. The main objective of scientific research is gaining new knowledge, and top research that is published in leading academic journals needs to be at the very edge of knowledge. Where that edge is also depends largely on the amount of previous research. Thus, if the field of research is fairly new, you can get published in the top journals although the methods used are not very advanced, while in fields building upon a large body of literature, new research needs to be methodologically very rigorous to get attention. Two examples might illustrate. In established fields, previous researchers often have developed validated scales to measure abstract constructs, such as motivation. Thus, if you want to work on motivation, you will use such validated scales or you must develop a new scale and provide sufficient reliability and validity checks to convince others that your scale is indeed better than the previous one. In a new field, you are often the first who attempts to measure a new construct, e.g. effectuation is a rather new construct in entrepreneurship research. So while a motivation researcher would be close to the bottom of the triangle, the effectuation researcher is closer to the top of the triangle. Another example refers to the application field. There are currently thousands of studies that have investigated different aspects of R&D cooperation between firms. Consequently, if you start a study on R&D cooperation, you are closer to the bottom of the triangle and you would either need very large datasets, a new method or a very specific and enlightening case to reach that edge of knowledge. However, if you research crowd sourcing, you are closer to the top of the triangle and you will succeed even with rather limited methods, because only a few studies have been published on crowd sourcing (at least in 2012).

Student Research

The super rich

Sampada Mulagapati was always fascinated by the glamour stories in popular business and management magazines. She really admired those who made a fortune out of nothing and belonged to the wealthiest people, the super rich. In her research project Sampada asked the question, 'What distinguishes those extremely successful from the usual successful?' Is it pure luck or do they have something in common that makes them so successful?

In the Netherlands, *Quote* magazine publishes a list ranking the 500 wealthiest people in the Netherlands each year, similar to the Forbes list at an international scale. Sampada took the lists of 2004, 2005 and 2006 as point of departure for her project. An obvious problem was that many persons included on the list did not earn their wealth but rather inherited it. Those people were excluded, resulting in a list of 210 persons who made it on their own, not necessarily from nothing as some inherited, for example, a (small) family business but still increased the business value substantially by at least €100 million.

The *Quote* list included next to the person's name and the accumulated wealth some additional information, such as age, gender and place of residence. Moreover, Sampada consulted newspaper archives and the Internet to systematically collect information about the person's education and family background as well as characteristics of the wealth sources. These data allowed Sampada to write a descriptive account that gave her some general insights into the world of the extremely successful. This descriptive quantitative study, however, only scratched the surface of the phenomena and Sampada wanted to go deeper.

The only possibility to obtain deeper insights was to conduct personal interviews. Therefore, Sampada approached people from the list to ask whether they would be willing to talk to her about their careers. At first sight, her plan seemed ridiculous; would any super rich waste time for an interview for a student research project? Surprisingly, Sampada was able to secure 11 personal interviews with people from that list. Her richest respondent was no. 27 on the list with an accumulated wealth of €796 million and her 'poorest' respondent was no. 177 who was still worth €147 million. She met her respondents at their homes, their companies or in hotel lounges and the interviews took between one and two hours. The qualitative data obtained in those interviews allowed Sampada to get an idea of what made them so successful. According to their accounts, luck hardly played a role; what mattered was devotion to their ideas and businesses and working long hours. Many of her interviewees mentioned that they do not have any spare time and that all their friends are business partners; even at a private dinner the main topic of conversation is business.

What do you think about Sampada's idea to combine qualitative analysis of basic secondary data with qualitative research?

Research Methods in Real Life

We do not need market research and consumer surveys

Aldi is one of the largest discount retail chains in Europe, with over 7,500 shops worldwide, and also has outlets in the USA. Every day millions of consumers visit one of its shops to buy groceries, but increasingly also non-food articles such as textiles, stationery, toys, and so on. Regularly, the organization opens new shops, adds new products to its regular or incidental portfolio of products sold. In 2005, the word 'Aldisierung' [Aldization] was announced as word of the year in Switzerland. The word describes a recent trend that more and more people, including those with rather high incomes, have become very price-sensitive for almost all consumer goods and they buy frozen pizza, coffee beans, DVD players and suncream where they can pay the lowest price and Aldi is often their final choice.

Surprisingly, Aldi has never spent a cent on external market research. They also do not track what individual customers buy through registering their purchases and combine it with information stored on a customer card. They cannot because they do not have customer cards. But what do they do? The Aldi management decides on common sense. Even top-level executives visit stores and talk to store managers and employees on a weekly basis. According to Dieter Brandes, a former Aldi manager, the best market research is to shop in your own stores and keep your eyes open. Then you will understand immediately why some articles sell well and others do not and you will learn much more than any figures that market research can tell you.

How does the management decide whether a new product should be added, which is a very strategic decision, as a typical Aldi holds just about 1,000 products compared to 20,000 in their competitors' stores? The management board of Aldi, consisting of the general managers of its regional subsidiaries, each overseeing about 70 stores, will decide by discussing the proposal and trying the product, but no extensive market research is involved.

References and further reading

Brandes, D. (2004) *Bare Essentials: The ALDI Way of Retailing.* London: Cyan/Campus.

BusinessWeek, 26 April 2004, 'The next Wal-Mart?'

5.2 Research design classifications

What is research design?

There are many definitions of **research design**, but no single definition imparts the full range of important aspects. Several examples from leading authors can be cited:

> "The research design constitutes the blueprint for the collection, measurement, and analysis of data. It aids the scientist in the allocation of his limited resources by posing crucial choices: Is the blueprint to include experiments, interviews, observation, the analysis of records, simulation, or some combination of these? Are the methods of data collection and the research situation to be highly structured? Is an intensive study of a small sample more effective than a less intensive study of a large sample? Should the analysis be primarily quantitative or qualitative?"[2]

> "Research design is the plan and structure of investigation so conceived as to obtain answers to research questions. The plan is the overall scheme or program of the research. It includes an outline of what the investigator will do from writing hypotheses and their operational implications to the final analysis of data. A structure is the framework, organization, or configuration of . . . the relations among variables of a study. A research design expresses both the structure of the research problem and the plan of investigation used to obtain empirical evidence on relations of the problem."[3]

These definitions differ in detail, but together they give the essentials of research design:

- the design is an activity- and time-based plan
- the design is always based on the research question
- the design guides the selection of sources and types of information
- the design is a framework for specifying the relationships among the study's variables
- the design outlines procedures for every research activity.

Thus, the design provides answers for questions such as these:

- What kind of answers is the study looking for and which methods will be applied to find them?
- What techniques will be used to gather data?
- What kind of sampling will be used?
- How will time and cost constraints be dealt with?

Classification of designs

Early in any research study, one faces the task of selecting the specific design to use. A number of design choices exists but, unfortunately, no simple classification system defines all the variations that must be considered. Exhibit 5.2 classifies research design using eight different descriptors.[4] Following on from this, a brief discussion of these descriptors serves to illustrate their nature and contribution to research.

The purpose of the study

The essential difference between a **descriptive study** and a **causal study** lies in their objectives. If the research is concerned with finding out who, what, where, when or how much, then the study is descriptive. If it is concerned with learning why – that is, how one variable produces changes in another – it is causal. Research on crime is descriptive when it measures the types of crime committed,

Exhibit 5.2 Descriptors of research designs.

The purpose of the study	Descriptive Causal Predictive
The degree to which the research question has been crystallized	Exploratory study Formal study
The method of data collection	Monitoring Interrogation/communication Archival sources
The power of the researcher to influence the variables under study	Experimental *Ex-post facto*
The time dimension	Cross-sectional Longitudinal
The research environment	Field setting Laboratory research Simulation

how often, when, where and by whom. A causal study tries to explain relationships among variables – for instance, why the crime rate is higher in Paris than in Oslo. Descriptive and causal studies can be both quantitative and qualitative. For example, the reports published by governments' statistical agencies are often quantitative descriptive studies, as they only provide a sketch of the current situation. Qualitative case studies can be descriptive if the emphasis is on reporting what has been observed, as in many anthropological studies, or causal if the case study explores a case to present new theoretical explanations.

Predictive studies ask what will happen in the future. A sound predictive study must be based on a very solid body of theory, as prediction requires that we have very good understanding of the causal factors that explain a phenomenon. Think about how many people work in government agencies, commercial banks, central banks and financial consultancies to predict the Sterling Euro Exchange Rate movement in the next year or to give estimates on how the share price of Unilever and many other companies will develop – and think about how often they get it wrong despite the manpower invested in such predictions.

Degree of research question crystallization

A study may be viewed as exploratory or formal. The essential distinctions between these two options are the degree of structure and the immediate objective of the study. **Exploratory studies** tend towards loose structures with the objective of discovering future research tasks. The immediate purpose of exploration is usually to develop hypotheses or questions for further research. The **formal study** begins where the exploration leaves off – it begins with a descriptive account of the current situation followed by the hypotheses or research question, and involves precise procedures and data source specifications. The goal of a formal research design is to provide a valid representation of the current state and to test the hypotheses or answer the research questions posed.

The exploratory–formal study dichotomy is less precise than some other classifications. All studies have elements of exploration in them, and few are completely uncharted. The results of quantitative studies often raise new research questions and contain therefore an explorative element. Likewise, qualitative studies very often provide convincing evidence for theoretical explanations. The sequence discussed in Chapter 2 (see Exhibit 2.1) suggests that more formalized studies contain at least an element of exploration before the final choice of design. More detailed consideration of exploratory research is discussed later in this chapter.

Method of data collection

This classification distinguishes between the monitoring and interrogation/communication processes. **Monitoring** includes studies in which the researcher inspects the activities of a subject or the nature of some material without attempting to elicit responses from anyone. Traffic counts at an intersection, licence plates recorded in a restaurant car park, a search of the library collection, an observation of the actions of a group of decision-makers – all are examples of monitoring. In each case the researcher notes and records the information available from observations.

In the **interrogation/communication study**, the researcher questions the subjects and collects their responses by personal or impersonal means. The collected data may result from (i) interview or telephone conversations, (ii) self-administered or self-reported instruments sent through the mail, left in convenient locations, or transmitted electronically or by other means, or (iii) instruments presented before and/or after a treatment or stimulus condition in an experiment. As discussed in Chapter 8, the researcher is not always required to collect data. Often, the information required to answer a research problem is already available and the researcher can rely on these secondary data.

Qualitative and quantitative studies can rely on both methods of data collection. A quantitative study does not need to rely on communication; observational studies (see Chapters 7 and 8) can for example be also quantitative. Likewise, a good qualitative study should be based on monitoring and communication (see Chapter 8).

Researcher control of variables

In terms of the researcher's ability to manipulate variables, we must differentiate between experimental and *ex-post facto* designs. In an **experiment**, the researcher attempts to **control** and/or manipulate the variables in the study. It is enough that we can cause variables to be changed or held constant in keeping with our research objectives. Experimental design is appropriate when one wishes to discover whether certain variables produce effects in other variables. Experimentation provides the most powerful support possible for a hypothesis of causation.

With an *ex-post facto* design, investigators have no control over the variables in the sense of being able to manipulate them. They can only report what has happened or what is happening. It is important that the researchers using this design do not influence the variables, as to do so introduces bias. The researcher is limited to holding factors constant by judicious selection of subjects according to strict sampling procedures and by the statistical manipulation of findings.

The time dimension

Cross-sectional studies are carried out once and represent a snapshot of one point in time. **Longitudinal studies** are repeated over an extended period. The advantage of a longitudinal study is that it can track changes over time. Further, longitudinal studies are also more powerful regarding tests of causality, as a causal relationship between A and B requires that A happened before B. Having measurements of A at time t = 0 and B at time t = 1 ensures that A indeed happened before B. The distinction between cross-sectional and longitudinal studies is again not related to the distinction between qualitative and quantitative studies. Both time dimensions are possible for both studies. However, good case studies, as an example for a qualitative study, are usually longitudinal, that is the investigated phenomenon is observed over a certain time span.

In longitudinal studies of the **panel** variety, the researcher may study the same people over time. In marketing, panels are set up to report consumption data on a variety of products. These data, collected from national samples, provide a major databank on relative market share, consumer response to new products, and new promotional methods. Other longitudinal studies, such as **cohort** groups, use different subjects for each sequenced measurement.

The service industry might have looked at the needs of ageing baby-boomers by sampling 40–45-year-olds in 1990 and 50–55-year-olds in 2000. Although each sample would be different, the population of 1945–1950 cohort survivors would remain the same.

Some types of information, once collected, cannot be collected a second time from the same person without the risk of bias. The study of public awareness of an advertising campaign over a six-month period, for example, would require different samples for each measurement.

While longitudinal research is important, the constraints of budget and time impose the need for cross-sectional analysis. Some benefits of a longitudinal study can be revealed in a cross-sectional study by adroit questioning about past attitudes, history and future expectations. Responses to these kinds of question should be interpreted with care, however.

The research environment

Designs also differ as to whether they occur under actual environmental conditions (**field conditions**) or under staged or manipulated conditions (**laboratory conditions**) or even artificially (**simulations**).

In the field condition, we observe or interrogate people in the usual environment, such as their homes, their workplaces or the shops they visit. In the laboratory condition, we are able to manipulate the environment although the laboratory might be designed as the usual environment; for example the laboratory might look like a shopping aisle in a supermarket. To simulate is to replicate the essence of a system or process. Simulations are used increasingly in research, especially in operations research. The major characteristics of various conditions and relationships in actual situations are often represented in mathematical models. Role-playing and other behavioural activities may also be viewed as simulations.

5.3 Exploratory, descriptive and causal studies

Exploratory studies

The **exploratory study (exploration)** is particularly useful when researchers lack a clear idea of the problems they will meet during the study. Through exploration, researchers develop concepts more clearly, establish priorities, develop operational definitions and improve the final research design. Exploration may also save time and money: if the problem is found not to be as important as it was first thought, subsequent more formal studies can be cancelled.

Exploration serves other purposes as well. The area of investigation may be so new or so vague that a researcher needs to do an exploration just to learn something about the research or management dilemma. Important variables may not be known or may not be defined thoroughly. Hypotheses for the research may be needed. Also, the researcher may explore to be sure that it is practical to do a formal study in the area. A federal government agency, the Office of Industry Analysis, proposed that research be done on how executives in a given industry made decisions about raw material purchases. Questions were planned asking how (and at what price spreads) one raw material was substituted for another in certain manufactured products. An exploration to discover if industry executives would divulge adequate information about their decision-making on this topic was essential for the study's success.

Despite its obvious value, researchers and managers alike pay exploration less attention than it deserves. There are strong pressures for quick answers. Moreover, exploration is sometimes linked to old biases about qualitative research: accusations of subjectiveness, non-representativeness and non-systematic design. More realistically, exploration saves time and money, and should not be slighted.

Qualitative techniques

The objectives of exploration may be accomplished with different techniques. Both qualitative and quantitative techniques are applicable, although exploration relies more heavily on **qualitative techniques**.

When we consider the scope of qualitative research, several methods are adaptable for exploratory investigations of management questions:

- in-depth interviewing (usually conversational rather than structured)
- participant observation (to perceive at first hand what participants in the setting experience)
- films, photographs and videotape (to capture the life of the group under study)
- projective techniques and psychological testing (such as a thematic apperception test, projective measures, games or role-playing)
- case studies (for an in-depth contextual analysis of a few events or conditions)
- street ethnography (to discover how a cultural sub-group describes and structures its world at street level)
- elite or expert interviewing (for information from influential or well-informed people in an organization or community)
- document analysis (to evaluate historical or contemporary confidential or public records, reports, government documents and opinions)
- proxemics and kinesics (to study the use of space and body-motion communication respectively).[8]

When these methods are combined, four exploratory techniques emerge with wide applicability for the management researcher:

1 secondary data analysis
2 experience surveys
3 focus groups
4 two-stage designs.

Secondary data analysis

The first step in an exploratory study is a search of the secondary literature. Studies made by others for their own purposes represent **secondary data**. It is inefficient to discover anew through the collection of **primary data** or original research what has already been done and reported at a level sufficient to solve the research question.

Within secondary data exploration, a researcher should start with an organization's own data archives. Reports of prior research studies often reveal an extensive amount of historical data or decision-making patterns. By reviewing prior studies, you can identify methodologies that proved successful and unsuccessful.

Another source of secondary data is published documents prepared by authors outside the sponsor organization. There are tens of thousands of periodicals and hundreds of thousands of books on all aspects of business. Data from secondary sources help us decide what needs to be done and can be a rich source of hypotheses.

If one is creative, a search of secondary sources will supply excellent background information as well as many good leads. Yet if we confine the investigation to obvious subjects in bibliographic sources we will often miss much of the best information. Suppose the Copper Industry Association is interested in estimating the outlook for the copper industry over the next 10 years. We could search through the literature under the headings 'copper production' and 'copper consumption'. However, a search restricted to these two topics would miss more than it finds. When a creative search of the copper industry is undertaken, useful information turns up under the following reference headings: mines and minerals; non-ferrous metals; forecasting; planning; econometrics; consuming industries such as automotive and communications; countries where copper is produced, such as Chile; and companies prominent in the industry, such as Anaconda and Kennecott.

Experience survey

While published data are a valuable resource, it is seldom the case that more than a fraction of the existing knowledge in a field is put into writing. A significant portion of what is known on a topic, while in writing, may be proprietary to a given organization and thus unavailable to an outside searcher. Also, internal data archives are rarely well organized, making secondary sources, even when known, difficult to locate. Thus, we will profit by seeking information from persons experienced in the area of study, tapping into their collective memories and experiences.

When we interview persons in an **experience survey**, we should seek their ideas about important issues or aspects of the subject, and discover what is important across the subject's range of knowledge. The investigative format we use should be flexible enough to allow us to explore various avenues that emerge during the interview:

- What is being done?
- What has been tried in the past without success? With success?
- How have things changed?
- What are the change-producing elements of the situation?
- Who is involved in decisions and what role does each person play?
- What problem areas and barriers can be seen?
- What are the costs of the processes under study?
- On whom can we count to assist and/or participate in the research?
- What are the priority areas?

The product of such questioning may be a new hypothesis, the discarding of an old one, or information about the practicality of doing the study. Probing may show whether certain facilities are available, what factors need to be controlled and how, and who will cooperate in the study.

Discovery is more easily carried out if the researcher can analyse cases that provide special insight. Typical of exploration, we are less interested in getting a representative cross-section than in getting information from sources that might be insightful. Assume we study Star-Auto's automobile assembly plant. It has a history of declining productivity, increasing costs and a growing number of quality defects. People who might provide insightful information include:

- newcomers to the scene – employees or personnel who may recently have been transferred to this plant from similar plants
- marginal or peripheral individuals – persons whose jobs place them on the margin between contending groups (first-line supervisors and lead workers are often neither management nor worker but something in between)
- individuals in transition – recently promoted employees who have been transferred to new departments
- deviants and isolates – those in a given group who hold a different position from the majority, as well as workers who are happy with the present situation, highly productive departments and workers, and loners of one sort or another
- 'pure' cases or cases that show extreme examples of the conditions under study – the most unproductive departments, the most antagonistic workers, and so on
- those who fit well and those who do not – the workers who are well established in their organizations versus those who are not, those executives who fully reflect management views and those who do not
- those who represent different positions in the system – unskilled workers, assemblers, superintendents, and so on.[9]

Focus groups

Originating in sociology, **focus groups** became widely used in marketing research during the 1980s and are used for increasingly diverse research applications today.[10] The most common application of focus-group research continues to be in the consumer arena. However, many corporations are using focus-group results for diverse exploratory applications.

The topical objective of a focus group is often a new product or product concept. The output of the session is a list of ideas and behavioural observations, with recommendations by the moderator. These are often used for later quantitative testing. As a group interview tool, focus groups have applied research potential for other functional areas of business, particularly where the generation and evaluation of ideas or the assessment of needs is indispensable. In exploratory research, the qualitative data that focus groups produce may be used for enriching all levels of research questions and hypotheses, and for comparing the effectiveness of design options.

Focus groups are also a useful method in the research process regarding pre-testing questionnaires, experiments, and so on. A prior focus-group discussion of the research design and the instruments used in the research can improve the research considerably, as sources of error and misunderstanding are handled before the study is conducted. Using a focus group to assess the research design and instruments before they are put into a pilot test is advantageous because pilot groups usually only contain people who could be respondents. For example, one of the authors of this book conducted a survey among business starters. Before the questionnaire was tested in pilot interviews with entrepreneurs, it was also discussed in focus groups. These focus groups included entrepreneurs (the potential respondents), but also people close to business starters, such as bankers, accountants and people from the Chamber of Commerce.

Deep Insight into Research Methods
Two-stage design

A useful way to design a research study is as a two-stage design. With this process, exploration becomes a separate first stage with limited objectives: (i) clearly defining the research question and (ii) developing the research design.

In arguing for a two-stage process, we recognize that much about the problem is not known but should be known before effort and resources are committed. In these circumstances, one is operating in unknown areas, where it is difficult to predict the problems and costs of the study. Proposals that acknowledge the practicality of this process are particularly useful when the research budget is inflexible. A limited exploration for a specific modest cost carries little risk for both sponsor and researcher, and often uncovers information that reduces the total research cost.

An exploratory study is finished when the researchers have achieved the following:

- established the major dimensions of the research task
- defined a set of subsidiary investigative questions that can be used as guides to a detailed research design
- developed several hypotheses about possible causes of a management dilemma
- learned that certain other hypotheses are such remote possibilities that they can be safely ignored in any subsequent study
- concluded that additional research is not needed or is not feasible.

Descriptive studies

In contrast to exploratory studies more formalized studies are typically structured with clearly stated hypotheses or investigative questions. Formal studies serve a variety of research objectives:

- descriptions of phenomena or characteristics associated with a subject population (the who, what, when, where and how of a topic)
- estimates of the proportions of a population that have these characteristics
- discovery of associations among different variables.

The third study objective is sometimes labelled a correlational study, a sub-set of descriptive studies. A descriptive study may be simple or complex; it may be done in many settings. Whatever the form, a descriptive study can be just as demanding of research skills as the causal study, and we should insist on the same high standards for design and execution.

The simplest descriptive study concerns a univariate question or hypothesis in which we ask about, or state something about, the size, form, distribution or existence of a variable. For example, in an account analysis at BankChoice, we might be interested in developing a profile of savers. We may first want to locate them in relation to the main office. The question might be, 'What percentage of the savers live within a two-mile radius of the office?' Using the hypothesis format, we might predict, 'Sixty per cent or more of the savers live within a two-mile radius of the office.'

We may also be interested in securing information about other variables, such as the relative size of accounts, the number of accounts for minors, the number of accounts opened within the last six months, and the amount of activity (number of deposits and withdrawals per year) in accounts. Data on each of these variables, by themselves, may have value for management decisions. Bivariate relationships between these or other variables may be of even greater interest. Cross-tabulations between the distance from the account owner's residence or employment to the branch and account activity may suggest that differential rates of activity are related to account owner location. A cross-tabulation of account size and gender of account owner may also show interrelation. Such findings do not imply a causal relationship. In fact, our task is to determine if the variables are independent (or unrelated) and if they are not, then to determine the strength or magnitude of the relationship. Neither procedure tells us which variable is the cause. For example, we might be able to conclude that gender and account size are related but not that gender is a causal factor in account size.

Descriptive studies are often, however, much more complex than this example suggests. One study of savers began as described and then went into much greater depth. Part of the study included an observation of account records that revealed a concentration of nearby savers. Their accounts were typically larger and more active than those whose owners lived at a distance. A sample survey of savers provided information on stages in the family life cycle, attitudes towards savings, family income levels and other matters. Correlation of this information with known savings data showed that women owned larger accounts. Further investigation suggested that women with larger accounts were often widowed or working single women who were older than the average account holder. Information about their attitudes and savings practices led to new business strategies at the bank.

Some evidence collected led to causal questions. The correlation between proximity to the branch and the probability of having an account at the branch suggested the question 'Why would people who live far from the branch have an account there?' In this type of question a hypothesis makes its greatest contribution by pointing out directions that the research might follow. It might be hypothesized that:

1 Distant savers (operationally defined as those with addresses more than two miles from the branch) have accounts at the branch because they once lived near the branch; they were 'near' when the account decision was made.
2 Distant savers actually live near the branch, but the address on the account is outside the two-mile radius; they are 'near', but the records do not show this.
3 Distant savers work near the branch; they are 'near' by virtue of their work location.
4 Distant savers are not normally near the branch but responded to a promotion that encouraged savers to bank via a computer; this is another form of 'nearness' in which this concept is transformed into one of 'convenience'.

When these hypotheses were tested, it was learned that a substantial portion of the distant savers could be accounted for by hypotheses 1 and 3. The conclusion: location was closely related to saving at a given association. The determination of cause is not so simple, however, and these findings still fall within the definition of a descriptive study.

Causal studies

The correlation between location and probability of account holding at BankChoice looks like strong evidence to many, but the researcher with scientific training will argue that correlation is not causation. Who is right? The essence of the disagreement seems to lie in the concept of cause.

The concept of cause

One writer asserts that:

> "There appears to be an inherent gap between the language of theory and research which can never be bridged in a completely satisfactory way. One thinks in terms of theoretical language that contains notions such as causes, forces, systems, and properties. But one's tests are made in terms of covariations, operations, and pointer readings."[11]

The essential element of causation is that A 'produces' B or A 'forces' B to occur. But that is an artefact of language, not what happens. Empirically, we can never demonstrate an A–B causality with certainty. This is because we do not 'demonstrate' such causal linkages deductively or use the form or validation of premises that deduction requires for conclusiveness. Unlike deductive syllogisms, empirical conclusions are inferences – inductive conclusions. As such, they are probabilistic statements based on what we observe and measure. But we cannot observe and measure all the processes that may account for the A–B relationship.

In Chapter 1 we discussed the example of sales failing to increase following a promotion. Having ruled out other causes for the flat sales, we were left with one inference that was probably, but not definitely, the cause: a poorly executed promotion.

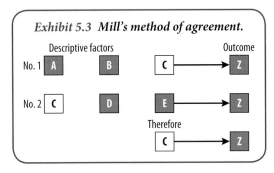

Exhibit 5.3 Mill's method of agreement.

Meeting the ideal standard of causation requires that one variable always causes another and no other variable has the same causal effect. The method of agreement, proposed by John Stuart Mill in the nineteenth century, states: 'When two or more cases of a given phenomenon have one and only one condition in common, then that condition may be regarded as the cause (or effect) of the phenomenon.'[12] Thus, if we can find Z and only Z in every case where we find C, and no others (A, B, D or E) are found with Z, then we can conclude that C and Z are causally related. Exhibit 5.3 illustrates this method.

An example of the method of agreement might be the problem of occasional high absenteeism on Mondays in a factory. A study of two groups with high absenteeism (No. 1 and No. 2 in Exhibit 5.3) shows no common job, department, demographic or personal characteristics (A, B, D and E). However, membership in a camping club (C) is common across both groups. The conclusion is that club membership is associated with high absenteeism (Z). (We return to this example in the following section.)

The method of agreement helps rule out some variables as irrelevant. In Exhibit 5.3, A, B and E are unlikely to be causes of Z, because we find the occurrence of Z in both groups, but A, B, D and E only in one of the two groups. However, there is an implicit assumption that there are no variables to consider other than A, B, C, D and E. One can never accept this supposition with certainty because the number of potential variables is infinite. In addition, while C may be the cause, it may instead function only in the presence of some other variable not included.

The negative canon of agreement states that where the absence of C is associated with the absence of Z, there is evidence of a causal relationship between C and Z. Together with the method of agreement, this forms the basis for the method of difference:

> "If there are two or more cases, and in one of them observation Z can be made, while in the other it cannot; and if variable C occurs when observation Z is made, and does not occur when observation Z is not made; then it can be asserted that there is a causal relationship between C and Z."[13]

The method of difference is illustrated in Exhibit 5.4. Although these methods neither ensure discovery of all relevant variables nor provide certain proof of causation, they help advance our understanding of causality by eliminating inadequate causal arguments.[14]

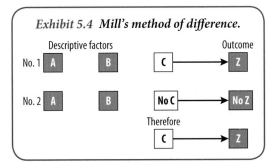

Exhibit 5.4 Mill's method of difference.

A more refined cause-and-effect model proposes that individual variables are not the cause of specific effects but that processes are the cause of processes.[15] Evidence for this position is illustrated in Exhibit 5.5. Here various cause-and-effect relationships between sales performance and feedback clarify the differences between simple and more complex notions of causality.[16]

In model A, we contend that feedback causes an increase in sales performance. An equally plausible explanation is shown in model B: improvement in sales performance causes the salesperson to behave in a proactive way, seeking more feedback to apply to the next experience.

Model C suggests the reinforcement history of the salesperson is the cause of both initiation of self-administered feedback and working harder to improve performance. In model D, we suggest that complex processes contribute to changes in feedback and performance. They are in the salesperson's environment and are unique to the person. Other examples could show how positive versus negative reinforcement could create

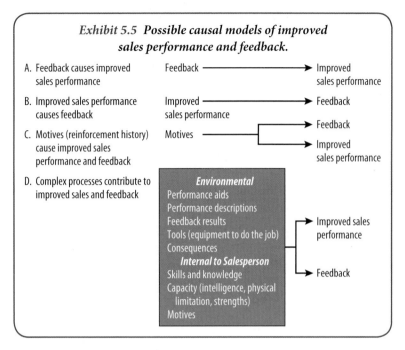

Exhibit 5.5 Possible causal models of improved sales performance and feedback.

A. Feedback causes improved sales performance

B. Improved sales performance causes feedback

C. Motives (reinforcement history) cause improved sales performance and feedback

D. Complex processes contribute to improved sales and feedback

Feedback ⟶ Improved sales performance

Improved sales performance ⟶ Feedback

Motives ⟶ Feedback / Improved sales performance

Environmental
Performance aids
Performance descriptions
Feedback results
Tools (equipment to do the job)
Consequences
Internal to Salesperson
Skills and knowledge
Capacity (intelligence, physical limitation, strengths)
Motives

⟶ Improved sales performance
⟶ Feedback

upward or downward sequences that would affect both feedback and performance. Yet all of them make predictions about presumed causal relationships among the variables.

Contemporary authors describe the way researchers substitute 'prediction' for '**causation**'. When scientists speak of causation, they are often referring to a kind of prediction. Predictions can be considered to reflect cause only when all the relevant information is considered. Of course, we can never know all the relevant information, so our predictions are, consequently, presumptive. Hence, the disillusionment in science with the concept of cause. Scientists do use the word 'cause' from time to time, but do not be misled into thinking that they mean cause in the absolute sense.[17]

Causal inferences are going to be made. Although they are neither permanent nor universal, they allow us to build knowledge of presumed causes over time. Such empirical conclusions provide us with successive approximations to the truth. Recognizing this caveat, let us look further at the types of causal relationship of interest to business researchers.

Causal relationships

Our concern in causal analysis is with how one variable effects, or is 'responsible for', changes in another. The stricter interpretation of causation, found in experimentation, is that some external factor 'produces' a change in the dependent variable. To repeat from Chapter 2, the dependent variables represent what we want to explain and the independent variables are the explaining factors. In business research, we often find that the cause-and-effect relationship is less explicit. We are more interested in understanding, explaining, predicting and controlling relationships between variables than we are in discerning causes.

If we consider the possible relationships that can occur between two variables, we can conclude that there are three possibilities:

1 symmetrical
2 reciprocal
3 asymmetrical.[18]

A **symmetrical relationship** is one in which two variables fluctuate together but we assume the changes in neither variable are due to changes in the other. Symmetrical conditions are most often found when two variables are alternate indicators of another cause or independent variable. We might conclude that a correlation between low work attendance and active participation in a company camping club is the result of (dependent on) another factor, such as a lifestyle preference.

A **reciprocal relationship** exists when two variables mutually influence or reinforce each other. This could occur if the reading of an advertisement leads to the use of a brand of product. The usage, in turn, sensitizes the person to notice and read more of the advertising of that particular brand.

Most research analysts look for **asymmetrical relationships**. With these we postulate that changes in one variable (the independent variable, or IV) are responsible for changes in another variable (the dependent variable, or DV). The identification of the IV and DV is often obvious, but sometimes the choice is not clear. In these latter cases we evaluate independence and dependence on the basis of:

1 the degree to which each variable may be altered – the relatively unalterable variable is the independent variable (IV) (e.g. age, social status, present manufacturing technology)
2 the time order between the variables – the independent variable (IV) precedes the dependent variable (DV).

Exhibit 5.6 describes the four types of asymmetrical relationship: stimulus–response, property–disposition, disposition–behaviour and property–behaviour. Experiments usually involve stimulus–response relationships. Property–disposition relationships are often studied in business and social science research. Much of *ex-post facto* research involves relationships between properties, dispositions and behaviours.

Exhibit 5.6 Four types of asymmetrical causal relationship.

Relationship type	Nature of relationship	Examples
Stimulus–response	An event or change results in a response from some object	• A change in work rules leads to a higher level of worker output • A change in government economic policy restricts corporate financial decisions • A price increase results in fewer unit sales
Property–disposition	An existing property causes a disposition	• Age and attitudes about saving • Gender and attitudes towards social issues • Social class and opinions about taxation
Disposition–behaviour	A disposition causes a specific behaviour	• Opinions about a brand and its purchase • Job satisfaction and work output • Moral values and tax cheating
Property–behaviour	An existing property causes a specific behaviour	• Stage of the family life cycle and purchases of furniture • Social class and family savings patterns • Age and sports participation

---

Testing causal hypothesis

While no one can ever be certain that variable A causes variable B to occur, one can gather some evidence that increases the belief that A leads to B. In testing causal hypothesis projects, we seek three types of evidence.

1 Covariation between A and B.
   • Do we find that A and B occur together in the way hypothesized?
   • When A does not occur, is there also an absence of B?
   • When there is more or less of A, does one also find more or less of B?
2 Time order of events moving in the hypothesized direction.
   • Does A occur before B?
3 No other possible causes of B.
   • Can one determine that C, D and E do not co-vary with B in a way that suggests possible causal connections?

Causation and experimental design

In addition to these three conditions, successful inference-making from experimental designs must meet two other requirements. The first is referred to as control. All factors, with the exception of the independent variable, must be held constant and not confounded with another variable that is not part of the study. Second, each person in the study must have an equal chance of exposure to each level of the independent variable. This is **random assignment** of subjects to groups.

Here is a demonstration of how these factors are used to detect causation. Assume you wish to conduct a survey of Utrecht College's alumni to enlist their support for a new programme. There are two different appeals, one largely emotional and the other much more logical in its perspective. Before mailing out appeal letters to 50,000 alumni, you decide to conduct an experiment to see whether the emotional or the rational appeal will draw the greater response. You choose a sample of 300 names from the alumni list and divide them into three groups of 100 each. Two of these groups are designated as experimental groups. One gets the emotional appeal and the other gets the logical appeal. The third group is the **control group** and receives no appeal.

Co-variation in this case is expressed by the percentage of alumni who respond in relation to the appeal used. Suppose 50 per cent of those who receive the emotional appeal respond, while only 35 per cent of those receiving the logical appeal respond. Control group members, unaware of the experiment, respond at a 5 per cent rate. We would conclude that using the emotional appeal enhances response probability.

The time sequence of events does not pose a problem to the causality between sending the letter, which was done first, and receiving alumni support, which followed the letter. There is no chance that the alumni support prompted the sending of letters requesting that support. However, have other variables confounded the results? Could some factor other than the appeal have produced the same results? One can anticipate that certain factors are particularly likely to confound the results. One can control some of these to ensure that they do not have this confounding effect. If the question studied is of concern only to alumni who attended the university as undergraduates, those who only attended graduate school are not involved. Thus, you would want to be sure the answers from the latter group did not distort the results. Control would be achieved by excluding graduate students.

Randomization is the basic method by which equivalence between experimental and control groups is determined. Experimental and control groups must be established so that they are equal. Matching and controlling are useful, but they do not account for all unknowns. It is best to assign subjects to either experimental or control groups at random (this is not to say haphazardly – randomness must be secured in a carefully controlled fashion according to strict rules of assignment). If the assignments are made randomly, each group should receive its fair share of different factors. The only deviation from this fair share would be that which results from random variation (the 'luck of the draw'). The possible impact of these unknown extraneous variables on the dependent variables should also vary at random. The researcher, using tests of statistical significance, can estimate the probable effect of these chance variations on the DV and can then compare this estimated effect of extraneous variation to the actual differences found in the DV in the experimental and control groups.

A second method to control uses **matching**. There might be a reason to believe that different ratios of alumni support will come from various age groups. To control by matching, we need to be sure that the age distribution of alumni is the same in all groups. In a similar way, control could be achieved by matching alumni from engineering, liberal arts, business and other schools. Even after using such controls, however, one cannot match or exclude other possible confounding variables. These are dealt with through random assignment.

We emphasize that random assignment of subjects to experimental and control groups is the basic technique by which the two groups can be made equivalent. Matching and other control forms are supplemental ways of improving the quality of measurement. In a sense, matching and controls reduce the extraneous 'noise' in the measurement system and in this way improve the sensitivity of measurement of the hypothesized relationship.

Causation and ex-post facto design

Most research studies cannot be carried out experimentally by manipulating variables. Yet we still are interested in the question of causation. Instead of manipulating and/or controlling exposure to an experimental variable, we study subjects who have been exposed to the independent factor and those who have not.

Consider the following question: Are innovative firms more profitable? A lot of anecdotic evidence suggests that innovation stimulates profits, such as Apple's recent success story of the iPad® introduction. But the question is whether the statement that innovation drives profits holds in general. Obviously, it is not practical to set up an experiment in which we would randomly determine which firms are innovative and which not.

Exhibit 5.7 **Data on profitability and innovativeness.**

Profitability	Innovativeness	
	Yes	No
High	20	35
Low	10	140

The better method would be to get a list of firms and measure their innovativeness and profitability. The results might look something like those found in Exhibit 5.7. The data suggest that a firm's innovativeness could be a cause for higher profitability. The co-variation evidence is consistent with this conclusion. But what other evidence will give us an even greater confidence in our conclusion?

We would like some evidence of the time order of events. It is logical to expect that if innovation causes profitability, there will be a temporal relationship. If we could establish that profitable firms had been innovative before profits rose, it would be good evidence in support of our hypothesis. Also, if high profitability occurs before a company has been innovative, the time order does not support our hypothesis anymore and would suggest that profitability may cause innovation, perhaps because more profitable firms have more resources to invest in innovation.

Of course, many other factors could be causing the high profitability of innovative firms. Here again, the use of control techniques will improve our ability to draw firm conclusions. First, in drawing a sample of innovative as well as non-innovative firms, we can build a random sample. In this way, we can be more confident of a fair representation of average firms' profitability.

Exhibit 5.8 **Cross-tabulated data on profitability and innovativeness controlled for firm size.**

Profitability	Less innovative		More innovative	
	Low	High	Low	High
Small firm	85	10	6	3
Medium-sized firm	45	10	3	5
Large firm	10	15	1	12

We cannot use assignment of subjects in *ex-post facto* research as we did in experimentation. However, we can gather information about potentially confounding factors and use these data to make cross-classification comparisons; in this way we can determine whether there is a relationship between innovation, profitability and other factors. Assume we also gather data on firm size and introduce it as a cross-classification variable; the results might look like those in Exhibit 5.8. These data suggest firms' size is also a factor. Larger firms are more likely to be profitable. Part of the high profitability among more innovative firms seems to be associated with the fact that most innovative firms are larger. Within size groups, it is also apparent that innovative firms have a higher incidence of higher profits than less innovative firms of the same size.

The post hoc fallacy

While researchers must necessarily use *ex-post facto* research designs to address causal questions, a word of warning is in order. High innovation rates among firms with high profitability is weak evidence for claiming a causal relationship. Similarly, the co-variation found between variables must be interpreted carefully when the relationship is based on *ex-post facto* analysis. The term **post hoc fallacy** has been used to describe these frequently unwarranted conclusions.

The *ex-post facto* design is widely used in business research and is often the only method feasible. In particular, one seeks causal explanations between variables that are impossible to manipulate. The variables cannot be manipulated, but also the subjects usually cannot be assigned to treatment and control groups in advance. We often find that there are multiple causes rather than one. Be careful using the *ex-post facto* design with causal reasoning. Thorough testing, validating of multiple hypotheses and controlling for confounding variables are essential.

Running Case Study 5
Choosing between numbers and letters

Last weekend Rebecca visited her parents and while they were sitting around the fireplace Rebecca told her parents about her thesis. Not surprisingly her father, a clergyman, and her mother, a teacher, had a lot to say about her topic. Her father referred to Philipp Melchanthon, whose reasoning was still based on Aristotelean philosophy and heavily opposed by Martin Luther. He also advised her to read Descartes and Dietrich Bonhoeffer; her mother added that you cannot talk about ethics without knowing the work of Immanuel Kant. Rebecca replied that she was studying businesses and she was not in humanities, as both her parents were. It was not her aim to discuss different views on ethics or even develop a new ethics. Her interest was more to find out why some people behave more ethically than others. Therefore, she would not need to read all these classics. To be honest, she had tried to read some of those philosophers and although she discovered some interesting thoughts, she often could not follow what they were writing about. You cannot understand the philosophers by reading their works, you need to study them. Her parents couldn't believe that you could study something without having a good idea what it is. But she told them that one professor at her school studies the effects of patents on competitiveness and she doubts that he knows a lot about patent law, application procedures or the technologies involved.

When she took the train back from her parents' place to Maastricht, she was thinking about the discussion with her parents the evening before. One thing she knew for sure: she would not engage in a qualitative study. It seemed to her that such a study would require a lot of background knowledge. She did not have that background knowledge and it would require her to take at least some introductory classes in philosophy. Without that she wouldn't be able to conduct open interviews. Next to her theoretical deficits, she also did not have any field experience. She had never cheated in an exam and had never engaged in plagiarism. Thus, a quantitative study in which she could rely on a structured questionnaire and pre-defined answer categories seemed to her the perfect approach to match her research interest and her own capabilities. She already started to design an online survey.

Mehmet was in doubt how he could investigate what he was interested in. The only certainty was that he wanted to write his thesis on migrant entrepreneurs. But how should he proceed. In the meantime, he had read a lot of articles. Those in the more prestigious journals, at least according to the journal list that circulated at his university, were quantitative, but he enjoyed reading the qualitative studies much more. His impression was that the quantitative studies just proved what everybody knew anyway. Is it necessary to interview thousands of people to show that people with self-employed parents are more likely to start a business and that people better embedded in networks are more successful, as well as people who start businesses in growing sectors? His grandmother could have told him that and she had just three years of school. Young entrepreneurs would not learn how to start a business successfully from numbers and regressions, but rather from good examples. These examples would serve as role models, documenting that even people with unfavourable characteristics, such as low education, could become successful entrepreneurs if they have the right ideas, the persistence in believing in them, good contacts and the willingness to work hard. These were the ingredients for success and maybe sometimes a bit of luck would also be helpful.

The more he thought about success stories of migrant entrepreneurs, the more he doubted whether collecting such stories would be the right approach. Not every business starter was successful; he had even read somewhere that half of them fail within the first two years, but you never heard their stories. Just a week ago, Mehmet had seen the closure sign at a fashion shop a few blocks down from his home. The idea of the shop was really nice. The two sisters sold modern fashion from Turkish designers at prices comparable to those of major fashion labels, such as Mexx or Oasis. He was also sure that they were hard-working; he had often seen light in the back room of the shop late at night. Thus, why did they fail? He could not imagine that the personal characteristics of the two sisters were responsible for their failure. It must have been external factors. Maybe it was not wise to open the shop in this neighbourhood; many of the Turks living here had rather traditional values and the fashion offered was rather stylish. Another reason could have been that the two sisters had studied in Amsterdam – actually in the same programme as his sister – but they grew up in Ede, a provincial town in the east. On the other hand they were well connected to fashion ateliers in Turkey. Suppose Mehmet could find out why the fashion store failed, would that enable him to explain migrant business failures? Could he transfer what he learnt from one case to another case? Maybe a mixed approach was most useful: use some quantitative information to give a good description of migrant businesses in Amsterdam and then enrich this information with in-depth interviews. That was the way to go.

1 Discuss whether it was wise that Mehmet opted for a mainly qualitative research, while Rebecca opted for a mainly quantitative research. Could you imagine making a different choice than the two?
2 Classify Rebecca's and Mehmet's research along the dimensions of research.
3 How could Mehmet and Rebecca show that suggested relations are really causal?

Summary

1 A frequently used and important distinction of research studies is quantitative versus qualitative. Which method you choose will have consequences for your research in terms of the research problems you can investigate and the kind of answers you expect. However, in business research, quantitative as well as qualitative research methods are appropriate for investigating business research problems. What matters is not the choice between quantitative and qualitative, but the quality of the research design and how well the study is conducted.

2 If the direction of a research project is not clear, it is often wise to follow a two-step research procedure. The first stage is exploratory, aimed at formulating hypotheses and developing the specific research design. The general research process contains three major stages: (i) exploration of the situation, (ii) collection of data, and (iii) analysis and interpretation of results.

3 A research design is the strategy for a study and the plan by which the strategy is to be carried out. It specifies the methods and procedures for the collection, measurement and analysis of data. Unfortunately, there is no simple classification of research designs that covers the variations found in practice. Some major descriptors of designs are:
   • exploratory versus formalized
   • observational versus interrogation–communication
   • experimental versus *ex-post facto*
   • descriptive versus causal
   • cross-sectional versus longitudinal
   • case versus statistical
   • field versus laboratory versus simulation
   • subjects perceive no deviations, some deviations or researcher-induced deviations.

4 Exploratory research is appropriate for the total study in topic areas where the developed data are limited. In most other studies, exploration is the first stage of a project, and is used to orient the researcher and the study. The objective of exploration is the development of hypotheses, not testing.

   Formalized studies, including descriptive and causal, are those with substantial structure, specific hypotheses to be tested or research questions to be answered. Descriptive studies are those used to describe phenomena associated with a subject population or to estimate proportions of the population that have certain characteristics.

Causal studies seek to discover the effect that a variable(s) has on another (or others) or why certain outcomes are obtained. The concept of causality is grounded in the logic of hypothesis testing, which, in turn, produces inductive conclusions. Such conclusions are probabilistic and thus can never be demonstrated with certainty. Current ideas about causality as complex processes improve our understanding of Mill's canons, though we can never know all the relevant information necessary to prove causal linkages beyond doubt.

5   The relationships that occur between two variables may be symmetrical, reciprocal or asymmetrical. Of greatest interest to the research analyst are asymmetrical relationships, which may be classified as any of the following types:
  • stimulus–response
  • property–disposition
  • disposition–behaviour
  • property–behaviour.

We test causal hypotheses by seeking to do three things: (i) measure the covariation among variables, (ii) determine the time-order relationships among variables, and (iii) ensure that other factors do not confound the explanatory relationships.

The problems of achieving these aims differ somewhat in experimental and *ex-post facto* studies. Where possible, we try to achieve the ideal of the experimental design with random assignment of subjects, matching of subject characteristics, and manipulation and control of variables. Using these methods and techniques, we measure relationships as accurately and objectively as possible.

Discussion questions

Terms in review

1 Distinguish between the following:
  a   exploratory and formal studies
  b   experimental and *ex-post facto* research designs
  c   descriptive and causal studies.

2 Establishing causality is difficult, whether conclusions have been derived inductively or deductively.
  a   Explain and elaborate on the implications of this statement.
  b   Why is ascribing causality more difficult when conclusions have been reached through induction?
  c   Correlation does not imply causation. Illustrate this point with examples from business.

3 Using yourself as the subject, give an example of each of the following asymmetrical relationships:
  a   stimulus–response
  b   property–disposition
  c   disposition–behaviour
  d   property–behaviour.

4 Why not use more control variables rather than depend on randomization as the means of controlling extraneous variables?

5 Researchers seek causal relationships by either experimental or *ex-post facto* research designs.
  a   In what ways are these two methods similar?
  b   In what ways are they different?

6 Discuss why the random assignment to an experimental and control group excludes alternative explanations.

7 Discuss the caveats of matching.

Making research decisions

8 You have been asked to determine how hospitals prepare and train volunteers. Since you know relatively little about this subject, how will you find out? Be as specific as possible.

9 You are the administrative assistant for a division chief in a large holding company that owns several hotels and theme parks. You and the division chief have just come from the chief executive's officer's (CEO's) office, where you were informed that guest complaints related to housekeeping and employee attitude are increasing. Your on-site managers have mentioned some tension among the workers but have not considered it unusual. The CEO and your division chief instruct you to investigate. Suggest at least three different types of research that might be appropriate in this situation.

10 Propose one or more hypotheses for each of the following variable pairs, specifying which is the IV and which is the DV. Then develop the basic hypothesis to include at least one moderating variable or intervening variable.
   a The Index of Consumer Confidence and the business cycle.
   b Level of worker output and closeness of worker supervision.
   c Student grade point average (GPA) and level of effort in a class required by student's major.

11 Is it wise to combine qualitative and quantitative research within a student's research project?

From concept to practice

12 Use the eight design descriptors in Exhibit 5.2 to profile the research described in the Research Methods in Real Life in this chapter.

Class discussion

13 Discuss the following provocative statements:
   a Qualitative research is very much like telling stories in the local pub.
   b Quantitative research is a sub-branch of higher mathematics – nice for some whizzkids, but irrelevant in practice.
   c Explorative research explores phenomena about which we already know a lot.
   d The predictive power of causal studies in the management sciences is so low that their value is close to zero.

Recommended further reading

Babbie, Earl R., *The Practice of Social Research* **(13th edn). Belmont, CA: Wadsworth, 2011.** Contains a clear and thorough synopsis of design.

Bartunek, Jean M. and Myeong-Gu, Seo, 'Qualitative research can add new meaning to quantitative research', *Journal of Organizational Behaviour* **23(2), 2002, pp. 237–42.** The authors explore how a study might have differed if a quantitative instead of a qualitative method had been used.

Bryman, Alan and Bell, Emma, *Business Research Methods* **(3rd edn). Oxford: Oxford University Press, 2011.** A good textbook on research methods, with a clear emphasis on qualitative methods.

Creswell, John W., *Qualitative Inquiry and Research Design* **(3rd edn). Thousand Oaks, CA: Sage Publishing, 2010.** A creative and comprehensive work on qualitative research methods.

Gill, J. and Johnson P., *Research Methods for Managers* **(4th edn). Thousand Oaks, CA: Sage, 2010.** Chapter 8 discusses different research methods by assessing the philosophical and theoretical assumptions of each method.

Mason, Emanuel J. and Bramble, William J., *Understanding and Conducting Research* **(2nd edn). New York: McGraw-Hill, 1989.** Chapter 1 has an excellent section on causation; Chapter 2 provides an alternative classification of the types of research.

Morgan, David L. and Kruger, Richard A. (eds), *The Focus Group Kit.* **Thousand Oaks, CA: Sage, 1997.** A six-volume set including an overview guidebook, planning, developing questions, moderating, involving community members and analysing results.

Oakshott, Lee, *Essential Quantitative Methods for Business, Management and Finance* (5th edn). London: Palgrave Macmillan, 2012. One of the best-selling books on quantitative methods in the UK.

Silverman, David, *Qualitative Research* (3rd edn). Thousand Oaks, CA: Sage, 2010. Another of the best-selling books on qualitative research in the UK.

Strauss, Anselm and Corbin, Juliet, *Basics of Qualitative Research* (3rd edn). Thousand Oaks, CA: Sage, 2008. A step-by-step guide with particularly useful sections on coding procedures.

Get started with understanding statistical techniques!

When you have read this chapter, log on to the Online Learning Centre website at *www.mcgraw-hill.co.uk/textbooks/blumberg* to explore chapter-by-chapter test questions, additional case studies, a glossary and more online study tools for *Business Research Methods*.

Notes

1 John Van Maanen, James M. Dabbs Jr. and Robert R. Faulkner, *Varieties of Qualitative Research*. Beverly Hills, CA: Sage, 1982, p. 32.

2 Reprinted with permission of Macmillan Publishing from *Social Research Strategy and Tactics* (2nd edn), by Bernard S. Phillips, p. 93. Copyright ©1971 by Bernard S. Phillips.

3 Fred N. Kerlinger, *Foundations of Behavioral Research* (3rd edn). New York: Holt, Rinehart & Winston, 1986, p. 279.

4 The complexity of research design tends to confuse students as well as writers. The latter respond by forcing order on the vast array of design types through the use of classification schemes or taxonomies. Generally, this is helpful, but because the world defies neat categorization, this scheme, like others, may either include or exclude too much.

5 Kerlinger, *Foundations of Behavioral Research*, p. 295.

6 Abraham Kaplan, *Conduct of Inquiry*. San Francisco: Chandler, 1964, p. 37.

7 W. Charles Redding, 'Research setting: field studies', in *Methods of Research in Communication*, eds. Philip Emmert and William D. Brooks. Boston, MA: Houghton Mifflin, 1970, pp. 140–2.

8 Catherine Marshall and Gretchen B. Rossman, *Designing Qualitative Research*. Newbury Park, CA: Sage, 1989, pp. 78–108.

9 This classification is suggested in Claire Selltiz, Lawrence S. Wrightsman and Stuart W. Cook, *Research Methods in Social Relations* (3rd edn). New York: Holt, Rinehart & Winston, 1976, pp. 99–101.

10 David W. Stewart, Prem N. Shamdasani and Dennis W. Rock, *Focus Groups: Theory and Practice* (2nd edn). Thousand Oaks, CA: Sage.

11 Hubert M. Blalock Jr., *Causal Inferences in Non-experimental Research*. Chapel Hill, NC: University of North Carolina Press, 1964, p. 5.

12 As quoted in William J. Goode and Paul K. Hatt, *Methods in Social Research*. New York: McGraw-Hill, 1952, p. 75.

13 From *Methods in Social Research* by William J. Goode and Paul K. Hatt. Copyright ©1952, McGraw-Hill Book Company. Used with the permission of McGraw-Hill Book Company.

14 Morris R. Cohen and Ernest Nagel, *An Introduction to Logic and Scientific Method*. New York: Harcourt Brace, 1934, Chapter 13; and Blalock, *Causal Inferences*, p. 14.

15 R. Carnap, *An Introduction to the Philosophy of Science*. New York: Basic Books, 1966.

16 Content adapted from Thomas F. Gilbert, *Human Competence*. New York: McGraw-Hill, 1978. Tabular concept based on Emanuel J. Mason and William J. Bramble, *Understanding and Conducting Research* (2nd edn). New York: McGraw-Hill, 1989, p. 13.

17 Mason and Bramble, *Understanding and Conducting Research*, p. 14.

18 Morris Rosenberg, *The Logic of Survey Analysis*. New York: Basic Books, 1968, p. 3.

CHAPTER 6

Sampling strategies

Chapter contents

Learning objectives

When you have read this chapter, you should understand:

1 the importance of the unit of analysis

2 why case studies are a very useful research approach and how they are conducted

3 the two premises on which sampling theory is based

4 the characteristics of accuracy and precision for measuring sample validity

5 the two main categories of sampling techniques and their varieties

6 the six questions that must be answered to develop a sampling plan

7 the critical issues and formulas that determine the appropriate sample size.

In this chapter sampling is discussed, which describes the idea that to find out what people are thinking, one does not need to ask the whole world, but can limit oneself to a selection of people. Before, we deal with sampling, you are introduced to the methods term 'unit of analysis', which describe what you are actually researching – this is not always the individual you obtain the information from. In section 6.2, we address the logic of sampling and the general principles, before we compare sampling to census-taking in section 6.3. In section 6.4, we introduce different sampling designs. Section 6.5 is a step-by-step guide for drawing a sample. Sections 6.6 and 6.7 give an overview over the most common probability designs and non-probability designs. The former are also known as random samples. In section 6.8, we finally discuss how we can obtain samples on the Internet.

6.1   Unit of analysis

An important step in designing research is the decision on the **unit of analysis**. The unit of analysis describes the level at which the research is performed and which objects are researched. People or individuals are a common unit of analysis. However, in business research we often apply other units of analysis than people, individuals or employees. Frequently occurring examples of other units of analysis at a 'higher' level than people are organizations, divisions, departments or more general groups. At a 'lower' level, we can think of management decisions, transactions or contracts as units of analysis.

It is important to note, however, that the unit of analysis and the kind of respondent the researcher questions to obtain information are not the same thing. For example, in a study of the internationalization strategies of medium-sized companies we might interview the general managers of such companies, but the unit of analysis is the company and not the general manager. Similarly, we might question heads of purchasing departments about a firm's contracts with its suppliers. Although we question heads of purchasing departments, the unit of analysis is the contract governing the relationship between the firms and the supplier.

Thinking carefully about a study's unit of analysis is an important way of avoiding the difficulties and errors that may occur later in problem definition and research design; this is because the unit of analysis is closely linked to all parts of the research process. When researchers define the research problem, they already need to be thinking about the unit of analysis. Is it the entire organization, or specific departments, work groups, employees or decisions? The unit of analysis is derived from the research question. However, one research question often allows for more than one unit of analysis, so the researcher has to choose.

Read through the two examples of research questions provided below.

1   Why do the self-employment rates differ so much in the countries of the EU?

At first sight the appropriate unit of analysis for this research question seems obvious. It should be countries, as we want to compare the self-employment rate of different countries. Choosing countries is not a bad idea, but whether it is really a good choice depends largely on which possible reasons we would like to investigate as explanations for the differing self-employment rates. Are the explanations we advance also at the unit level of countries? If we want to investigate whether differences in the legal system, the national culture or the industry structure of the economy do affect the self-employment rate, countries is a good choice as unit of analysis. If our explanation of the differing rates in self-employment is more rooted in individuals (e.g. differences in risk attitude or how entrepreneurs cope with difficulties in the start-up phase), it is better to use individuals or the firms they have started as the unit of analysis.

2   What are the effects of pay systems on an employee's job satisfaction?

One can derive two units of analysis from this question. First, the pay system, which might apply to the whole company or to certain work groups within the company, although it is unlikely that the company has a different pay system for every employee. Second, the question mentions the job satisfaction of the employee, which is at the level of the employee. Which unit of analysis would you choose? The entire organization, work groups or employees? There is no straightforward answer to this question – the choice of unit of analysis depends very much on the research objectives and has serious implications for further elements of the research design.

Choosing the entire organization would require that the data are collected in many organizations. Furthermore, we would need to ensure that all other variables (e.g. job satisfaction) are also measured at the organizational level, that is we would need a kind of mean job satisfaction for every organization. To obtain such a mean job satisfaction we would either have to measure the job satisfaction of a representative group of employees in each organization ourselves or we would need to have secondary information, say from previous surveys on job satisfaction among employees in the selected organizations. Further, we would have to ensure that employees within one organization are paid according to the same pay systems. Thus, the choice of entire organizations as unit of analysis entails a more complex and more costly research design. However, entire organizations as unit of analysis would also allow us to expand our research problem. For example, we could investigate whether other organizational characteristics, such as, say, centralization of decision-making, have a more significant effect on job satisfaction than pay systems. We could also research whether differences in pay systems and resulting differences in job satisfaction also lead to differences in organizational performance.

Alternatively, we could use work groups as unit of analysis. Again we would have to ensure that just one pay system applies to a work group. We would also need information on the job satisfaction of each work group. Choosing work groups as unit of analysis is likely to have the following implications for the research design:

- Depending on the number of work groups and applied pay systems in a firm, we may still need to investigate more than one organization to achieve a sufficient number of work groups (sample size).
- To obtain a sound measurement of job satisfaction, it may be necessary to question individual employees in each work group selected.

Finally, we could also use employee as unit of analysis. For example, we could survey people who are currently employed in paid labour and ask them about their job satisfaction and which system their employer uses to determine their pay. In such a design, people employed at very different organizations will be interviewed. In this design we need to ensure that differences in job satisfaction are indeed caused by differences in the payment system and not by other differences between these organizations, in areas such as labour conditions, type of company, level of payments, and so on. Furthermore, as we only ask the employees and not the firms, our assessment of the payment systems is purely based on the respondent's answers to our questions about the system. However, what happens if respondents do not know the ins and outs of the payment system used in their company?

The examples above demonstrate that the choice of unit of analysis is strongly related to the following three questions.

1 What is our research problem and what do we really want to answer?
Taking the second example, on the relationship between payment systems and job satisfaction, we need to decide whether we are more interested in job satisfaction and how a firm can improve the satisfaction of its employees, or whether we are more interested in finding out about the effects of different payment systems and which factors a firm needs to take into account when designing an optimal payment system.

2 What do we need to measure to answer our research problem?
Answering this question also allows us to define the unit of analysis. First, we identify the information needed to answer the research problem; that is, what variables do we need? Then, we have to determine which objects (decisions, individuals, organizations, etc.) are described by the variables we want to measure.

3 What do we want to do with the results of the study? To whom do we address it in our conclusions?
In the first example, it makes a difference whether our study is part of policy advice for a government or whether its results should help entrepreneurs. In the former case, the unit of analysis is countries and in the latter entrepreneurs.

6.2 The nature of sampling

Most people intuitively understand the idea of sampling. One taste of a drink tells us whether it is sweet or sour. If we select a few employment records out of a complete set, we usually assume our selection reflects the characteristics of the full set. If some of our staff members favour a flexible work schedule, we infer that others will too. These examples vary in their representativeness, but each is a sample.

The basic idea of sampling is that by selecting some of the elements in a population, we may draw conclusions about the entire population. A **population element** is the subject on which the measurement is being taken. It is the unit of study, as explained above. A **population** is the total collection of elements about which we wish to make some inferences. All office workers in the firm comprise a 'population of interest'; all 4,000 files define a population of interest. A **census** is a count of all the elements in a population. If 4,000 files define the population, a census would obtain information from every one of them.

You should note that representative samples are only a concern in quantitative studies rooted in a positivistic research approach. Qualitative studies rooted in interpretivism usually do not attempt to generalize their findings to a population, for example all British companies. Therefore sampling in qualitative research follows a replication logic in which one looks for either rather similar cases or very different cases (see Chapter 8 for more details).

Why sample?

There are several compelling reasons for sampling, including:

- lower cost
- greater accuracy of results
- greater speed of data collection
- availability of population elements.

We now look at each of these in turn.

Lower cost

The economic advantages of taking a sample rather than conducting a census are massive. Consider the cost of conducting a census. For example, the cost of the British census in 2001 was about £255 million (€387 million).[1] Is it any wonder that researchers in all types of organization ask, 'Why should we spend thousands of euros interviewing all 4,000 employees in our company if we can find out what we need to know by asking only a few hundred?'

Greater accuracy of results

Deming argues that the quality of a study is often better with sampling than with a census. He suggests: 'Sampling possesses the possibility of better interviewing [testing], more thorough investigation of missing, wrong or suspicious information, better supervision, and better processing than is possible with complete coverage.'[2] Research findings substantiate this opinion. More than 90 per cent of the total survey error in one study was from non-sampling sources and only 10 per cent or less was from random sampling error.[3] The US Bureau of the Census shows its confidence in sampling by taking sample surveys to check the accuracy of its census. However, while it is politically correct to take a census of the population, we know that segments of the population are seriously undercounted.

Greater speed of data collection

Sampling's speed of execution reduces the time between the recognition of a need for information and the availability of that information. If it takes a clothing company until the autumn to receive the first results of a survey among retailers about how they perceived the company's latest spring collection, it will be too late for any adjustments and the information from the survey will be useless. Furthermore, the larger the sample size, the longer the data collection itself will take. Long collection periods can cause biases as, within the period, events might occur that influence respondents' answer behaviour (see Chapters 7 and 14). Political opinion polls are a good example of the latter problem. In particular, in the last few months before an election voters are very sensitive.

Research Methods in Real Life
How complete is a census?

In the UK, the first official census was held on 10 March 1801, and revealed that its population was then nine million. This was a much more precise estimate than previous ones, which had ranged between eight and eleven million. But, how sure can the census takers be that they have really counted every inhabitant once? Hence, are census data really the perfect reflection of the population? For example, overall form-returning rates for England and Wales in the 2001 (1991) census were 94 per cent (96 per cent), and the figure was even worse in inner London with a response rate of 78 per cent in 2001 and 88 per cent in 1991.

This non-response is a serious threat to the representativity of the census, which is of utmost importance as census data are used in many areas of public policy: for example, they are used to determine the funding local authorities are entitled to receive from government. As the census takers expected an increase in non-responses in 2001, they developed a new strategy known as 'One Number Census' (ONC) to obtain a representation of the whole population. The central idea of this strategy is to complement the census with a follow-up survey, the 'Census Coverage Survey' (CCS), which consisted of a sample of 320,000 households who were questioned in face-to-face interviews. The Census Coverage Survey was conducted independently of the census; that is, the CCS interviewers had no access to census data, in 16,000 postcode areas, achieving an overall response rate of 91 per cent.

Combining the results of the census and the CCS results in a very high precision ±0.2 per cent (i.e. the error margin for the whole population is 104,000 people). For local authority areas, this error margin varies from 6.1 per cent in Luton to 0.6 per cent in Dudley, East Dorset, Redcar and Cleveland. More importantly, the idea of checking the census data with large-scale survey data allowed an estimate of the census's precision to be made for the first time.

The issues of non-response and coverage are still at the heart of census researchers' concerns. In 2011, when the last census was taken, a completely new methodology for collecting data was applied. Instead of using a large field force to deliver and collect forms, the forms were posted after several measures had been taken to obtain a complete database of current addresses.

References and further reading

Office for National Statistics, *The 2011 Census: A Proposed Design for England and Wales*. Discussion paper, 2003.

Office for National Statistics (www.statistics.gov.uk/census2001).

Teague, Andy, 'New methodologies for the 2001 Census in England and Wales', *International Journal of Social Research Methodology* 3, 2000, pp. 245–55.

Research Methods in Real Life
Opinions about opinions

The most popular opinion polls are those reflecting the voting intentions and expected voting behaviour in general elections. In every country, these polls are held on a regular basis and their results are published in headlines and broadcast in the news. Journalists frequently ask politicians to comment on the results. Thus, the polls have become part of the political discussion.

In election polls particularly, history has shown famous examples of successes and failures to predict the outcome of elections. One of the most famous is the 1948 US presidential race between Harry S. Truman (Democrat) and Thomas E. Dewey (Republican). Almost all opinion polls predicted that Dewey would win the election. The confidence in Dewey's victory was so strong that the *Chicago Tribune* even printed 'Dewey defeats Truman' as a headline before the official result was known. Truman became the 33rd president of the USA when he gained over two million votes more than Dewey. Later it turned out that many opinion polls were based on telephone surveys and in 1948 Republican voters were much more likely to own a telephone.

From 1948 in the USA we move to 2013 in the UK. Now close to 10 agencies poll the voting intentions of the British on a regular basis. What has become interesting is that the approaches have become different. Despite its bias, phone interviewing has been the dominant method for such polls, but that is currently changing. In the UK, for example, IPSOS and ICM still interview representative samples of around 1,000 respondents entitled to vote. Each month, both agencies phone a different sample of 1,000 people and ask them about their voting intentions. YouGov has a different approach: it uses an Internet panel that anybody can subscribe to if they want. Currently more than 33,000 people have become voluntary members of this panel. Out of these volunteers, YouGov draws a sample that is a representative match to the UK population with respect to gender, age and other demographics. The members of the panel are asked regularly about their voting intentions. Thus, while IPSOS and ICM publish monthly reports, YouGov provides figures on each weekday.

Exhibit 6.1 Voting intentions between September 2012 and May 2013 for Conservatives, Labour, Liberals and UKIP according to the polls of IPSOS Mori, ICM Guardian and YouGov.

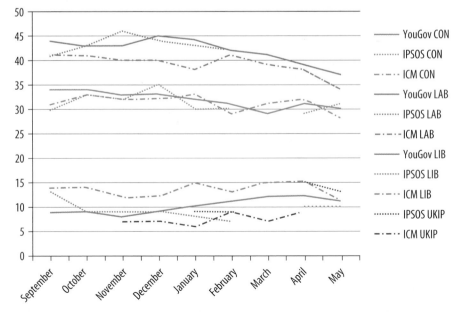

Note: New political parties are treated differently by the polling agencies; YouGiov did not ask about UKIP, and IPSOS only included UKIP at certain points in time.

We should not be so naïve as to believe that the percentage of votes for each party reported by polling organizations is based on the frequency of the answers to the question, 'Which party would you vote for if we had a general election now?' Thus, if opinion polls report that the Liberal party will get 22 per cent of the vote that does not mean that 22 per cent of the respondents answered 'Liberal party' to the above question. The process from the raw data to the actual reported figure is much more complex. IPSOS, a British polling organization, is well known for their strategy to consider only those respondents who answer that they are likely to vote. Other polling organizations use complex weighting schemes to correct for differences in actual voting among different parties, because Conservative voters are more likely to actually vote than Labour voters. In Germany, for example, it is said that sunshine on election day is good for the Social Democrats because fewer of their voters stay home if the sun shines, while Conservative voters walk to the voting booth regardless of the weather. Another important factor is that voters who intend to vote for an extreme party on the left or right are less likely to disclose their choice to interviewers, creating a systematic underestimation of more extreme parties.

Still what you see in Exhibit 6.1 is surprising, as the objective of all polling organizations is to give a correct prediction of how many people vote for a specific party. How do you explain why the polling organizations differ so much in their monthly predictions?

References and further reading

www.math.uah.edu/stat/data/1948Election.html

www.ipsos-mori.com/researchpublications/researcharchive/103/Voting-Intention-in-Great-Britain-1976present.aspx

www.guardian.co.uk/news/datablog/2009/oct/21/icm-poll-data-labour-conservatives

http://yougov.co.uk/news/categories/politics/

Availability of population elements

Some situations require sampling. When we test the breaking strength of materials, we must destroy them; a census of this type would, therefore, mean complete destruction of all materials. Sampling is also the only process possible if a population is infinite.

6.3 Sample versus census

The advantages of sampling over census studies are less compelling when the population is small and the variability within the population high. Two conditions are appropriate for a census study:

1 feasible when the population is small
2 necessary when the elements are quite different from each other.[4]

When the population is small and variable, any sample we draw may not be representative of the population from which it is drawn. The resulting values we calculate from the sample are incorrect as estimates of the population values.

Consider European manufacturers of stereo components. Fewer than 50 companies design, develop and manufacture amplifier and loudspeaker products at the high end of the price range. The size of this population suggests that a census is feasible. The diversity of their product offerings makes it difficult to sample accurately from this group. Some companies specialize in speakers, some in amplifier technology, and others in compact disc transports. In this case, then, it would be appropriate to choose a census.

What makes a good sample?

The ultimate test of a sample design is how well it represents the characteristics of the population it purports to represent. In measurement terms, the sample must be valid. Representativity of a sample depends on two considerations: accuracy and precision.

Accuracy

Accuracy is the degree to which bias is absent from the sample. When the sample is drawn properly, some sample elements underestimate the population values being studied and others overestimate them. Variations in these values offset each other; this counteraction results in a sample value that is generally close to the population value. For these offsetting effects to occur, however, there must be sufficient elements in the sample, and they must be drawn in a way that favours neither overestimation nor underestimation.

An accurate (unbiased) sample is one in which the underestimators and the overestimators are balanced among the members of the sample. There is no **systematic variance** with an accurate sample. Systematic variance has been defined as 'the variation in measures due to some known or unknown influences that "cause" the scores to lean in one direction more than another'.[5] Homes on the corner of a block, for example, are often larger and more valuable than those within a block. Thus, a sample that selects corner homes only will cause us to overestimate house values in an area. The time that respondents are questioned can also produce systematic error. For example, characteristics of travellers to the Alps will differ across seasons and younger single persons are more difficult to reach by telephone in the evening.

Another important issue in sampling is that non-response can be systematic; that is, those who respond to a survey request differ from those who refuse to participate. Assume you are interested in the role of social web communities, such as XING or LinkedIn, in job search among graduates. Chances are high that active users of such communities are more likely to respond than those who rarely or never use those communities. As a consequence it is likely that the usage of such communities is overestimated.

Precision

A second criterion of a good sample design is precision of estimate. No sample will fully represent its population in all respects. The numerical descriptors that describe samples may be expected to differ from those that describe populations because of random fluctuations inherent in the sampling process. This is called sampling error and reflects the influence of chance in drawing sample members. Sampling error is what is left after all known sources of systematic variance have been accounted for. In theory, sampling error consists of random fluctuations only, although some unknown systematic variance may be included when too many or too few sample elements possess a particular characteristic.

Precision is measured by the standard error of estimate, a type of standard deviation measurement; the smaller the standard error of estimate, the greater the precision of the sample. The ideal sample design produces a small standard error of estimate. However, not all types of sample design provide estimates of precision, and samples of the same size can produce different amounts of error variance.

Types of sample design

The researcher makes several decisions when designing a sample. These are represented in Exhibit 6.2. The sampling decisions flow from two decisions made in the formation of the management research question hierarchy: the nature of the management question and the specific investigative questions that evolve from the research question.

A variety of sampling techniques is available. The one the researcher should select depends on the requirements of the project, its objectives and the funds available. In the discussion that follows, we will use two examples:

1 a study of the feasibility of starting a dining club near the campus of Lake University
2 the study on high-technology firms featured in the Student Research box below.

The researchers at Lake University are exploring the feasibility of creating a dining club, whose facilities would be available on a membership basis. To launch this venture, they will need to make a substantial investment. Research will allow them to reduce many risks. Thus, the research question is: 'Would a membership dining club be a viable enterprise?' Some investigative questions that flow from the research question include the following:

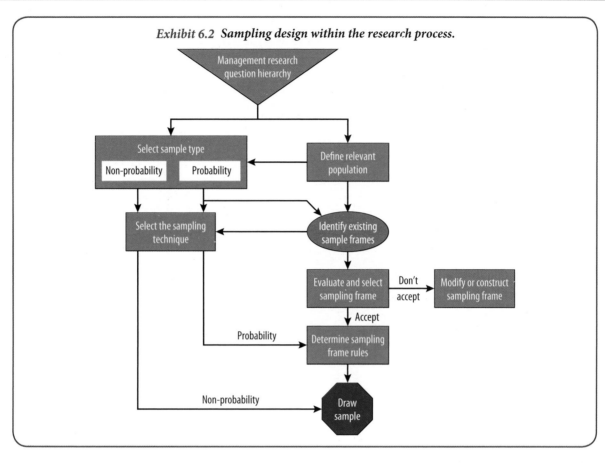

Exhibit 6.2 *Sampling design within the research process.*

1 Who would patronize the club and on what basis?
2 How many would join the club under various membership and fee arrangements?
3 How much would the average member spend per month?
4 What days would be most popular?
5 What menu and service formats would be most desirable?
6 What lunch times would be most popular?
7 Given the proposed price levels, how often per month would each member have lunch or dinner?
8 What percentage of the people in the population say that they would join the club, based on the projected rates and services?

We will use the last three investigative questions as examples, and focus specifically on questions 7 and 8 in assessing the project's risks. First, we will digress a little to look at other information and examples of sample design, coming back to Lake University in the next section.

Student Research
Characteristics of science parks

In management and business, students often focus on a particular industry or on a sub-set of firms in their research projects, such as high-technology firms. One problem they face is that comprehensive lists of population members are often not available and populations are not well defined. Taking the information technology (IT) sector as an example, complete lists of all IT firms are not available and you might question whether you should include IT consulting firms. ▶

Floris Pols faced a similar situation when he embarked on a research project investigating which characteristics of science parks are beneficial for which firms located there. Answering this research question required that Floris investigated firms in a larger number of science parks, as otherwise he would not have any variation in the characteristics describing the science parks. As the number of science parks is rather small, Floris decided to conduct his research in the whole of Europe.

His starting point was the international association of science parks who provided a directory of its members, which also included lists of the firms vested in the member science parks and their addresses. In total, Floris obtained the addresses of 2,406 firms located in 56 science parks in nine countries (Austria, Denmark, Finland, Germany, Ireland, Netherlands, Norway, Sweden and the UK). Although the population base is impressive it is not complete. There are certainly science parks in France, Spain and Italy and even in the countries covered there are more science parks than on the list. For example, for the UK he had information on just five science parks.

In a second step, Floris designed an online questionnaire and its link was emailed to 2,406 firms of which 185 (7.7 per cent) responded, but response rates differed greatly between countries, ranging from 2 per cent in Ireland to 19 per cent in Denmark. Moreover, the response rates also differed across science parks. From many science parks, just one or two firms responded while 23 firms from the Ideon Science Park in Sweden answered.

For a research project, a sample of 185 firms is impressive and it provides sufficient statistical power to conduct analyses. However, despite the relatively large sample size, one needs to be cautious, as the sample certainly suffers from systematic biases.

Exhibit 6.3 Types of sampling designs.

Element selection	Representation basis	
	Probability	Non-probability
Unrestricted	Simple random	Convenience
Restricted	Complex random	Purposive
	Systematic	Judgement
	Cluster	Quota
	Stratified	Snowball
	Double	

In decisions to do with sample design, the representation basis and the element-selection techniques, as shown in Exhibit 6.3, classify the different approaches.

Representation

The members of a sample are selected on a probability basis or by another means. **Probability sampling** is based on the concept of random selection – a controlled procedure that ensures that each population element is given a known non-zero chance of selection.

In contrast, **non-probability sampling** is arbitrary (non-random) and subjective. Each member does not have a known non-zero chance of being included. Allowing interviewers to choose sample elements 'at random' (meaning 'as they wish' or 'wherever they find them') is not random sampling. Only probability samples provide estimates of precision.

Element selection

Whether the elements are selected individually and directly from the population – viewed as a single pool – or when additional controls are imposed, element selection may also classify samples. If each sample element is drawn individually from the population at large, it is an unrestricted sample. Restricted sampling covers all other forms of sampling.

Probability sampling

The unrestricted, **simple random sample** is the simplest form of probability sampling. Since all probability samples must provide a known non-zero chance of selection for each population element, the simple random sample is considered a special case in which each population element has a known and equal chance of selection. In this section, we use the simple random sample to build a foundation for understanding sampling procedures and choosing probability samples. Exhibit 6.4 provides an overview of the steps involved in choosing a random sample.

Exhibit 6.4 *How to choose a random sample.*

Selecting a random sample is accomplished with the aid of computer software, a table of random numbers or a calculator with a random number generator. Drawing slips out of a hat or ping-pong balls from a drum serves as an alternative if every element in the **sampling frame** has an equal chance of selection. Mixing the slips (or balls) and returning them between every selection ensures that every element is just as likely to be selected as any other.

A table of random numbers (such as Appendix E, Exhibit E.10) is a practical solution when no software program is available. Random number tables contain digits that have no systematic organization. Whether you look at rows, columns or diagonals, you will find neither sequence nor order. Exhibit E.10 in Appendix E is arranged into 10 columns of five-digit strings, but this is solely for readability.

Assume the researchers want a special sample from a population of 95 elements. How will the researcher begin?

1   Assign each element within the sampling frame a unique number from 01 to 95.
2   Identify a random start from the random number table (drop a pencil point first on to the table with closed eyes. Let us say the pencil dot lands on the eighth column from the left and 10 numbers down from the top of Exhibit E.10, marking the five digits 05067).
3   Determine how the digits in the random number table will be assigned to the sampling frame to choose the specified sample size (researchers agree to read the first two digits in this column downwards until 10 are selected).
4   Select the sample elements from the sampling frame (05, 27, 69, 94, 18, 61, 36, 85, 71 and 83) using the above process. The digit 94 appeared twice and the second instance was omitted; 00 was omitted because the sampling frame started with 01.

Other approaches to selecting digits are endless: horizontally right to left, bottom to top, diagonally across columns, and so on. Computer selection of a simple random sample will be more efficient for larger projects.

6.5 Steps in sampling design

There are several decisions to be made in securing a sample. Each requires unique information. While the questions presented here are sequential, an answer to one question often forces a revision to an earlier one. In this section we consider the following questions:

1   What is the relevant population?
2   What are the parameters of interest?
3   What is the sampling frame?
4   What is the type of sample?
5   What size sample is needed?
6   How much will it cost?

What is the relevant population?

The definition of the population may be apparent from the management problem or the research question(s), but often it is not. Is the population for the dining club study at Lake University defined as 'full-time day students on the main campus of Lake University'? Or should the population include 'all persons employed at Lake University'? Or should townspeople who live in the neighbourhood be included? Without knowing the target market chosen for the new venture, it is not obvious which of these is the appropriate sampling population.

There may also be confusion about whether the population consists of individuals, households or families, or a combination of these. If a communication study needs to measure income, then the definition of the population element as individual or household can make quite a difference. In an observation study, a sample population might be non-personal: displays within a store or any ATM a bank owns or all single-family residential properties in a community. Good operational definitions are crucial in choosing the relevant population.

Assume the Lake University dining club is to be solely for the students and employees on the main campus. The researchers might define the population as 'all currently enrolled students and employees on the main campus of Lake University'. However, this does not include family members. They may want to revise the definition to make it 'current students and employees of Lake University, main campus, and their families'. In the non-probability sample, Floris Pols defined the list of the science park association as his relevant population and neglected science parks not members of that association.

What are the parameters of interest?

Population parameters are summary descriptors (e.g. incidence proportion, mean, variance) of variables of interest in the population. **Sample statistics** are descriptors of the relevant variables computed from sample data. Sample statistics are used as estimators of population parameters. The sample statistics are the basis of our inferences about the population. Depending on how measurement questions are phrased, each may collect a different type of data (see Exhibit 6.5). Each different type of data also generates different sample statistics. Data types are discussed in greater detail in Chapter 14.

Exhibit 6.5 *Parameters of interest and type of data.*

Parameter of interest	Type of data	Example scale
Attendance at a special event	Nominal	Participation in a promotion (yes, no)
Percentage of patrons who order their steak cooked rare	Ordinal	How meat is cooked (well done, medium, rare)
Mean temperature of ideal vacation destination	Interval	Temperature in degrees
Average number of store visits per month	Ratio	Actual number of store visits

When the variables of interest in the study are measured on interval or ratio scales, we use the sample mean to estimate the population mean and the sample standard deviation to estimate the population standard deviation. Asking Lake University affiliates to reveal their frequency of eating on or near campus (less than five times per week, greater than five but less than ten times per week or greater than ten times per week) would provide an interval data estimator.

When the variables of interest are measured on nominal or ordinal scales, we use the sample proportion of incidence to estimate the population proportion and the pq to estimate the population variance (pq is the product term of the population proportion p and q, which equals $1 - p$; if the population proportion p is 0.5, q is also $0.5 = 1 - 0.5$ and pq equals $0.25 = 0.5 \times 0.5$; if p is below or above 0.5, pq is smaller than 0.25. The **population proportion of incidence** 'is equal to the number of elements in the population belonging to the category of interest, divided by the total number of elements in the population'.[6]

Proportion measures are necessary for nominal data and are widely used for other measures too. The most frequent proportion measure is the percentage. In the Lake University study, examples of nominal data are the proportion of a population that expresses interest in joining the club (e.g. 30 per cent; therefore p is equal to .3 and q, those not interested, equals .7) or the proportion of married students who report that they now eat in restaurants at least five times a month. The Belgian Tourist Authority tries to examine which proportion of holidaymakers has visited the Belgian coast already in the two previous years and which proportion plans to return in the next year. These measures would result in nominal data. Exhibit 6.6 indicates population parameters of interest for our two example studies. We discuss proportion estimators in more detail later in this chapter.

There may also be important sub-groups in the population about whom we would like to make estimates. For example, we might want to draw conclusions about the extent of dining club use that could be expected from married students versus single students, residential students versus commuter students, and so on. Such questions have a strong impact on the nature of the sampling frame we accept, the design of the sample, and its size.

Exhibit 6.6 Sample population parameters.

Example	Population parameter of interest (type data)	Scale
Belgian coast	Frequency of previous holidays at the Belgian coast (interval)	More than 5 times, 3 to 5 times, once or twice, none
	Proportion of French, German and British tourists (nominal)	Actual percentage
Lake University	Frequency of eating on or near the campus within seven days (ratio data)	Actual eating experience
	Proportion of students/employees expressing interest (nominal data)	Actual percentage interest

What is the sampling frame?

The sampling frame is closely related to the population. It is the list of elements from which the sample is actually drawn. Ideally, it is a complete and correct list of population members only. As a practical matter, however, the sampling frame often differs from the theoretical population.

For the dining club study, the Lake University directory would be the logical first choice as a sampling frame. Directories are usually accurate when published in the autumn, but suppose the study is being done in the spring. The directory will contain errors and omissions because some people will have withdrawn or left since the directory was published, while others will have enrolled or been hired. Usually university directories do not mention the families of students or employees.

Just how much inaccuracy one can tolerate in choosing a sampling frame is a matter of judgement. You might use the directory anyway, ignoring the fact that it is not a fully accurate list. However, if the directory is a year old, the amount of error might be unacceptable. One way to make the sampling frame for the Lake University study more representative of the population would be to secure a supplemental list of the new students and employees, as well as a list of the withdrawals and terminations from Lake University's registrar and human resources databases. You could then add and delete information from the original directory. Or, if privacy policies permit, you might just request a current listing from each of these offices and use these lists as your sampling frame.

A greater distortion would be introduced if a branch campus population were included in the Lake University directory. This would be an example of a too inclusive frame – that is, a frame that includes many elements other than the ones in which we are interested. A university directory that includes faculty and staff retirees is another example of a too inclusive sampling frame.

Often you have to accept a sampling frame that includes people or cases beyond those in whom you are interested. You may have to use a telephone directory to draw a sample of business telephone numbers. Fortunately, this is easily resolved. You draw a sample from the larger population and then use a screening procedure to eliminate those who are not members of the group you wish to study.

The Lake University dining club survey is an example of a sampling frame problem that is readily solved. Often one finds this task much more of a challenge. Suppose you need to sample the members of an ethnic group – say, Asians residing in St. Andrews, Scotland. There is probably no directory of this population. While you may use the general city directory, sampling from this too inclusive frame would be costly and inefficient as Asians represent only a small fraction of the St. Andrews population. The screening task would be monumental. Since ethnic groups frequently cluster in certain neighbourhoods, you might identify these areas of concentration and then use a reverse area telephone or city directory, which is organized by street address, to draw the sample.

Floris Pols had a definite problem as no sample frame for science parks exists. He relied on the membership director of the European Science Park Association, but the association does not cover all science parks. A costly alternative would have been to sample firms from registration data and then in a second step ask them whether they are located in a science park. Given the few firms in science parks, Floris would have needed to contact hundreds of firms to identify one science park.

What is the type of sample?

The researcher faces a basic choice: a probability or non-probability sample. With a probability sample, the researcher can make probability-based confidence estimates of various parameters that cannot be made with non-probability samples. Choosing a probability sampling technique has several consequences. A researcher must follow appropriate procedures, so that:

- interviewers or others cannot modify the selections made
- only those selected elements from the original sampling frame are included
- substitutions are excluded except as clearly specified and controlled according to predetermined decision rules.

Despite all due care, the actual sample achieved will not match perfectly the sample that is originally drawn. Some people will refuse to participate and others will be difficult, if not impossible, to find. The latter represent the well-known 'not-at-home' problem and require that enough call-backs be made to ensure that they are adequately represented in the sample.

With personnel records available at a university and a population that is geographically concentrated, a probability sampling method is possible in the dining club study. University directories are generally available, and the costs of using a simple random sample would not be great here. Since the researchers are thinking of a major investment in the dining club, they would of course like to be confident that they have a representative sample.

What sample size is needed?

Much folklore surrounds this question. The most pervasive myths may be summarized as follows:

- A sample must be large or it is not representative.
- A sample should bear some proportional relationship to the size of the population from which it is drawn.

In reality, how large a sample should be is a function of the variation in the population parameters under study and the estimating precision needed by the researcher. A sample of 400 may sometimes be appropriate, while a sample of more than 2,000 may be required in other circumstances; in another case, perhaps a sample of only 40 is needed.

Some principles that influence sample size include:

- The greater the dispersion or variance within the population, the larger the sample must be to provide estimation precision.
- The greater the desired precision of the estimate, the larger the sample must be.
- The greater the number of sub-groups of interest within a sample, the greater the sample size must be, as each sub-group must meet minimum sample size requirements.
- If the calculated sample size exceeds 5 per cent of the population, sample size may be reduced without sacrificing precision.

Since researchers can never be 100 per cent certain that a sample reflects its population, they must decide how much precision they need. Precision is measured by:

- the interval range in which they would expect to find the parameter estimate
- the degree of confidence they wish to have in that estimate.

The size of the probability sample needed can be affected by the size of the population, but only when the sample size is large compared with the population. This so-called finite adjustment factor enters the calculation when the calculated sample is 5 per cent or more of the population. The net effect of the adjustment is to reduce the size of the sample needed to achieve a given level of precision.[7]

Other considerations often weigh heavily on the sample size decision. The conditions under which the sample is being conducted may suggest that only certain sampling techniques are feasible. One type of sample may be inappropriate because we have no list of population elements and must therefore sample geographic units. Since various designs have differing statistical and economic efficiencies, the choice of design will also affect the size of the sample.

The researcher may also be interested in making estimates concerning various sub-groups of the population; in such cases the sample must be large enough for each of these sub-groups to meet the desired level of precision. One achieves this in simple random sampling by making the total sample large enough to ensure that each critical sub-group meets the minimum size criterion. In more complex sampling procedures, the smaller sub-groups are sampled more heavily, and then the parameter estimates drawn from these sub-groups are weighted.

The larger the sample size, the greater the statistical power and the greater the chance that even small effects or differences become significant. The relation between sample size and significance level is quadratic, i.e. if you quadruple your sample size, α indicating the significance level halves. Thus, an effect with $\alpha = 0.08$ (not significant at 5%) in a sample of 200 respondents would be significant $\alpha = 0.04$, if we had a sample with 800 respondents. Very large datasets with a couple of thousand observations become more and more available and in such large datasets very tiny effects are statistically significant. This raises the question, however, whether such tiny effects are relevant. An alternative to significance levels are effect sizes that measure the strength of an effect, i.e. how much does this effect explain.[8]

How much will it cost?

Cost considerations influence decisions about the size and type of sample, and also the data-collection methods. Almost all studies have some budgetary constraints, and this may encourage a researcher to use a non-probability sample. Probability sample surveys incur list costs for sample frames, call-back costs, and a variety of other costs that are not necessary when more haphazard or arbitrary methods are used. But when the data-collection method is changed, the amount and type of data that can be obtained also change. Note the effect of a €2,000 budget on sampling considerations:

- Simple random sampling: €25 per interview; 80 completed interviews.
- Geographic cluster sampling: €20 per interview; 100 completed interviews.
- Self-administered questionnaire: €12 per respondent; 167 completed instruments.
- Telephone interviews: €10 per respondent; 200 completed interviews.[9]

Opening a dining club at Lake University is a major investment and hence a more careful but also more costly sampling design is justified.

 ## Complex probability sampling

Simple random sampling is often impractical. Reasons for this include the following:

- It requires a population list (sampling frame) that is often not available.
- It fails to use all the information about a population, thus resulting in a design that may be wasteful.
- It may be expensive to implement in terms of both time and money.

These problems have led to the development of alternative designs that are superior to the simple random design in their statistical and/or economic efficiency.

A more efficient sample in a statistical sense is one that provides a given precision (**standard error of the mean** or proportion) with a smaller sample size. A sample that is economically more efficient is one that provides a desired precision at a lower monetary cost. We achieve this with designs that enable us to lower the costs of data collection, usually through reduced travel expenses and interviewer time.

In the discussion that follows, four alternative probability sampling approaches are considered:

1 systematic sampling
2 stratified sampling
3 cluster sampling
4 double sampling.

Systematic sampling

A versatile form of probability sampling is **systematic sampling**. In this approach, every k^{th} element in the population is sampled, beginning with a random start of an element in the range of 1 to k. The kth element is determined by dividing the sample size into the population size to obtain the skip pattern applied to the sampling frame. The major advantage of systematic sampling is its simplicity and flexibility. It is easier to instruct fieldworkers to choose the dwelling unit listed on every k^{th} line of a listing sheet than it is to use a random number table. With systematic sampling, there is no need to number the entries in a large personnel file before drawing a sample.

To draw a systematic sample you merely need to follow the steps listed below:

- Identify the total number of elements in the population.
- Identify the sampling ratio (k = total population size divided by size of the desired sample).
- Identify the random start.
- Draw a sample by choosing every k^{th} entry.

Invoices or customer accounts can be sampled by using the last digit or a combination of digits of an invoice or customer account number. Time sampling is also easily accomplished.

While systematic sampling has some theoretical problems, from a practical point of view it is usually treated as a simple random sample. When similar population elements are grouped within the sampling frame, systematic sampling is statistically more efficient than a simple random sample. This might occur if the listed elements are ordered chronologically, by size, by class, and so on. Under these conditions, the sample approaches a proportional stratified sample. The effect of this ordering is more pronounced on the results of cluster samples than for element samples and may call for a proportional stratified sampling formula.[10]

One concern with systematic sampling is the possible periodicity in the population that parallels the sampling ratio. In sampling days of the week, a 1-in-7 sampling ratio would give biased results. A less obvious case might involve a survey in an area of apartment-type houses where the typical pattern is eight apartments per building. Many systematic sampling fractions, such as 1 in 8, could easily over-sample some types of apartment and under-sample others. The only protection against this is constant vigilance on the part of the researcher.

Another difficulty may arise when there is a monotonic trend in the population elements. That is, the population list varies from the smallest to the largest element, or vice versa. Even a chronological list may have this effect if a measure has trended in one direction over time. Whether a systematic sample drawn under these conditions provides a biased estimate of the population mean or proportion depends on the initial random draw. Assume that a list of 2,000 commercial banks is created, arrayed from the largest to the smallest, from which a sample of 50 must be drawn for analysis. A sampling ratio of 1 to 40 (begun with a random start at 16) drawing every fortieth bank would exclude the 15 largest banks and give a small-size bias to the findings. Ways to deal with this concern include:

- randomize the population before sampling
- change the random start several times in the sampling process
- replicate a selection of different samples.

Stratified sampling

Most populations can be segregated into several mutually exclusive sub-populations or strata. The process by which the sample is constrained to include elements from each of the segments is called **stratified random sampling**. University students, for example, can be divided by class level, school or specialism, gender, and so on. Once a population has been divided into the appropriate strata, a simple random sample can be taken within each stratum. The sampling results can then be weighted and combined into appropriate population estimates.

There are three reasons why a researcher chooses a stratified random sample:

1 to increase a sample's statistical efficiency
2 to provide adequate data for analysing the various sub-populations
3 to enable different research methods and procedures to be used in different strata.[11]

Stratification is usually more efficient statistically than simple random sampling and, at worst, equal to it. With the ideal stratification, each stratum is homogeneous internally and heterogeneous with other strata. This might occur in a sample that includes members of several distinct ethnic groups. In this instance, stratification makes for a pronounced improvement in statistical efficiency, especially if the population sizes of the sub-groups differ largely. Assume for example you are interest in female top managers. In most Western countries, the proportion of women among top managers is around 10 per cent or less. Now assume that your budget allows you to have sample size of 300. In a simple random sample that would result in a group of 30 female managers and 270 male managers. All scores of the group of female managers would have a much larger standard error due to the smaller size of the group. So, if you were to stratify the sample along gender, you could for example sample 150 female and 150 male managers. Of course, that would mean that the standard errors in the male group would increase, but the gain in the female group would compensate this loss by far.

It is also useful when the researcher wants to study the characteristics of certain population sub-groups. Thus, if one wishes to draw some conclusions about activities in the different classes of a student body, stratified sampling would be used. Stratification is also called for when different methods of data collection are applied in different parts of the population. This might occur when we survey company employees at their home office with one method but must use a different approach with employees scattered over the country.

If data are available on which to base a stratification decision, how should we go about it?[12] The ideal stratification would be based on the primary variable under investigation. If the major concern is to learn how often per month patrons would use the dining club in our example, then one would like to stratify on this expected number of use occasions. The only difficulty with this idea is that if we knew this information, we would not need to conduct the study. We must, therefore, pick a variable for stratifying that we believe will correlate with the frequency of club use per month, something like work or class schedule as an indication of when a sample element might be near campus at lunch times.

Researchers often have several important variables about which they want to draw conclusions. A reasonable approach is to seek some basis for stratification that correlates well with the major variables. It might be a single variable (class level) or it might be a compound variable (class by gender). In any event, we will have done a good stratifying job if the stratification base maximizes the difference among strata means and minimizes the within-stratum variances for the variables of major concern.

The more strata used, the closer you come to maximizing interstrata differences (differences between strata) and minimizing intrastratum variances (differences within a given stratum). You must base the decision partially on the number of sub-population groups about which you wish to draw separate conclusions. Costs of stratification also enter the decision. There is little to be gained in estimating population values when the number of strata exceeds six.[13]

The size of the strata samples is calculated with two pieces of information:

1 how large the total sample should be
2 how the total sample should be allocated among strata.

In deciding how to allocate a total sample among various strata, there are proportionate and disproportionate options.

Proportionate versus disproportionate sampling

In **proportionate stratified sampling**, each stratum is properly represented so that the sample drawn from it is proportionate to the stratum's share of the total population. This approach is more popular than any of the other stratified sampling procedures. Some reasons for this include:

- It has higher statistical efficiency than a simple random sample.
- It is much easier to carry out than other stratifying methods.
- It provides a self-weighting sample; the population mean or proportion can be estimated simply by calculating the mean or proportion of all sample cases, eliminating the weighting of responses.

On the other hand, proportionate stratified samples often gain little in statistical efficiency if the strata measures and their variances are similar for the major variables under study.

Any stratification that departs from the proportionate relationship is disproportionate. There are several disproportionate allocation schemes. One type is a judgementally determined disproportion based on the idea that each stratum is large enough to secure adequate confidence levels and interval range estimates for individual strata.

A researcher makes decisions regarding **disproportionate stratified sampling**, however, by considering how a sample will be allocated among strata. One author states, 'In a given stratum, take a larger sample if the stratum is larger than other strata; the stratum is more variable internally; and sampling is cheaper in the stratum.'[14]

If one uses these suggestions as a guide, it is possible to develop an optimal stratification scheme. When there is no difference in intrastratum variances and when the costs of sampling among strata are equal, the optimal design is a proportionate sample.

While disproportionate sampling is theoretically superior, there is some question as to whether it has wide applicability in a practical sense. If the differences in sampling costs or variances among strata are large, then disproportionate sampling is desirable. It has been suggested that 'differences of several-fold are required to make disproportionate sampling worthwhile'.[15]

The process for drawing a stratified sample is as follows:

- Determine the variables to use for stratification.
- Determine the proportions of the stratification variables in the population.
- Select proportionate or disproportionate stratification based on project information needs and risks.
- Divide the sampling frame into separate frames for each stratum.
- Randomize the elements within each stratum's sampling frame.
- Follow random or systematic procedures to draw the sample.

Cluster sampling

In a simple random sample, each population element is selected individually. The population can also be divided into groups of elements with some groups randomly selected for study. This is known as **cluster sampling**. Cluster sampling differs from stratified sampling in several ways (for a comparison of these, see Exhibit 6.7).

Exhibit 6.7 Stratified sampling versus cluster sampling.

Stratified sampling	Cluster sampling
1 We divide the population into a few sub-groups, each with many elements in it. The sub-groups are selected according to some criterion that is related to the variables under study	1 We divide the population into many sub-groups, each with a few elements in it. The sub-groups are selected according to some criterion of ease or availability in data collection
2 We try to secure homogeneity within sub-groups, heterogeneity between sub-groups	2 We try to secure heterogeneity within sub-groups and homogeneity between sub-groups
3 We randomly choose elements from within each sub-group	3 We randomly choose a number of the sub-groups, which we then typically study in depth

When done properly, cluster sampling also provides an unbiased estimate of population parameters. Two conditions foster the use of cluster sampling:

1 the need for more economic efficiency than can be provided by simple random sampling, and
2 the frequent unavailability of a practical sampling frame for individual elements.

Statistical efficiency for cluster samples is usually lower than for simple random samples chiefly because clusters are usually homogeneous. Families in the same block (a typical cluster) are often similar in social class, income level, ethnic origin, and so on.

While statistical efficiency in most cluster sampling may be low, economic efficiency is often great enough to overcome this weakness. The criterion, then, is the net relative efficiency resulting from the trade-off between economic and statistical factors. It may take 690 interviews with a cluster design to give the same precision as 424 simple random interviews, but if it costs only €5 per interview in the cluster situation and €10 in the simple random case, the cluster sample is more attractive (€3,450 versus €4,240).

Area sampling

Much research involves populations that can be identified with some geographic area. When this occurs, it is possible to use **area sampling**, the most important form of cluster sampling. This method overcomes both the problems of high sampling cost and the unavailability of a practical sampling frame for individual elements. Area sampling methods have been applied to national populations, county populations, and even smaller areas where there are well-defined political or natural boundaries.

Suppose you want to survey the adult residents of a city. You would seldom be able to secure a listing of such individuals. It would be simple, however, to get a detailed city map that shows the blocks of the city. If you take a sample of these blocks, you are also taking a sample of the adult residents of the city.

Design

In designing cluster samples, including area samples, we must answer several questions:

1 How homogeneous are the clusters?
2 Shall we seek equal or unequal clusters?
3 How large a cluster shall we take?
4 Shall we use a single-stage or multi-stage cluster?
5 How large a sample is needed?

We now look briefly at the answers to each of these questions.

1 How homogeneous are the clusters?

Clusters are homogeneous. This contributes to low statistical efficiency. Sometimes one can improve this efficiency by constructing clusters to increase intracluster variance. In our dining club study, the students might have constructed clusters that included members from all classes. In area sampling, they could combine adjoining blocks that contain different income groups or social classes. Area cluster sections do not have to be contiguous, but the cost saving is lost if they are not near each other.

2 Shall we seek equal or unequal clusters?

A cluster sample may be composed of clusters of equal or unequal size. The theory of clustering is that the means of sample clusters are unbiased estimates of the population mean. This is more likely to be true when clusters are equal. It is often possible to construct artificial clusters that are approximately equal, but natural clusters, such as households in city blocks, often vary substantially. While one can deal with clusters of unequal size, it may be desirable to reduce or counteract the effects of unequal size. There are several approaches to this, as outlined below:

- Combine small clusters and split large clusters until each approximates to an average size.
- Stratify clusters by size and choose clusters from each stratum.
- Stratify clusters by size and then sub-sample using varying sampling fractions to secure an overall sampling ratio.

In the latter case, we may seek an overall sampling fraction of 1/60 and desire that sub-samples contain five elements each. One group of clusters might average about 10 elements per cluster. In the '10 elements per cluster' stratum, we might choose 1 in 30 of the clusters and then sub-sample each chosen cluster at a 1/2 rate to secure the overall 1/60 sampling fraction. Among clusters of 120 elements, we might select clusters at a 1/3 rate and then sub-sample at a 1/20 rate to secure the 1/60 sampling fraction.[16]

3 How large a cluster shall we take?

There is no a priori answer to this question. Even with single-stage clusters, say of 5, 20 or 50, it is not clear which size is superior. Some have found that in studies using single-stage clusters, the optimal cluster size is no larger than the typical city block.[17] Comparing the efficiency of the above three cluster sizes requires that we discover the different costs for each size and estimate the different variances of the cluster means.

4 Shall we use a single-stage or multi-stage cluster?

For most area sampling, especially large-scale studies, the tendency is to use multi-stage methods.

There are four reasons that justify sub-sampling in preference to the direct creation of smaller clusters and their selection in one-stage cluster sampling:

1 Natural clusters may exist as convenient sampling units, yet may be larger than the desired economic size.
2 We can avoid the cost of creating smaller clusters in the entire population and confine it to the selected sampling units.
3 The effect of clustering is often less in larger clusters. For example, a compact cluster of four dwellings from a city block may bring into the sample similar dwellings, perhaps from one building; but four dwellings selected separately can be spread around the dissimilar sides of the block.
4 The sampling of compact clusters may present practical difficulties. For example, independent interviewing of all members of a household may seem impractical.[18]

5 How large a sample is needed?

Answering this question involves deciding how many subjects must be interviewed or observed, and depends heavily on the specific cluster design. These details can be complicated. Unequal clusters and multi-stage samples are the chief complications, and their statistical treatment is beyond the scope of this book.[19] Here we will treat only single-stage samples with equal-size clusters (known as **simple cluster sampling**). This is analogous to simple random sampling. The simple random sample is really a special case of simple cluster sampling. We can think of a population as consisting of 20,000 clusters of one student each or 2,000 clusters of 10 students each, and so on. The only difference between a simple random sample and a simple cluster sample is the size of cluster. Since this is so, we should expect that the calculation of a probability sample size would be the same for both types.

Double sampling

It may be more convenient or economical to collect some information by sample and then use this information as the basis for selecting a sub-sample for further study. This procedure is called **double sampling, sequential sampling** or **multi-phase sampling**. It is usually found with stratified and/or cluster designs. The calculation procedures are described in more advanced texts.

Double sampling can be illustrated by our dining club example. You might use a telephone survey or another inexpensive survey method to discover who would be interested in joining such a club and the degree of their interest. You might then stratify the interested respondents by degree of interest and sub-sample among them for intensive interviewing on expected consumption patterns, reactions to various services, and so on. Whether it is more desirable to gather such information by one- or two-stage sampling depends largely on the relative costs of the two methods.

Because of the wide range of sampling designs available, it is often difficult to select an approach that meets the needs of the research question and helps to contain the costs of the project. To help with these choices, Exhibit 6.8 may be used to compare the various advantages and disadvantages of probability sampling.

Non-probability sampling techniques are covered in the next section. They are used frequently and offer the researcher the benefit of low cost. However, they are not based on a theoretical framework and do not operate from statistical theory; consequently, they produce selection bias and non-representative samples. Despite these weaknesses, their widespread use demands their mention here.

Exhibit 6.8 Comparison of probability sampling designs.

Type	Description	Advantages	Disadvantages
Simple random	Each population element has an equal chance of being selected into the sample. Sample drawn using random number table/generator	Easy to implement with automatic dialling (random digit dialling) and with computerized voice response systems	Requires a listing of population elements. Takes more time to implement. Uses larger sample sizes. Produces larger errors. Expensive
Systematic	Selects an element of the population at a beginning with a random start and following the sampling fraction selects every kth element	Simple to design. Easier to use than the simple random. Easy to determine sampling distribution of mean or proportion. Less expensive than simple random	Periodicity within the population may skew the sample and results. If the population list has a monotonic trend, a biased estimate will result based on the start point
Stratified	Divides population into sub-populations or strata and uses simple random on each strata. Results may be weighted and combined	Researcher controls sample size in strata. Increased statistical efficiency. Provides data to represent and analyse sub-groups. Enables use of different methods in strata	Increased error will result if sub-groups are selected at different rates. Expensive. Especially expensive if strata on the population have to be created
Cluster	Population is divided into internally heterogeneous sub-groups. Some are randomly selected for further study	Provides an unbiased estimate of population parameters if properly done. Economically more efficient than simple random. Lowest cost per sample, especially with geographic clusters. Easy to do without a population list	Often lower statistical efficiency (more error) due to sub-groups being homogeneous rather than heterogeneous
Double (sequential or multiphase)	Process includes collecting data from a sample using a previously defined technique. Based on the information found, a sub-sample is selected for further study	May reduce costs if first stage results in enough data to stratify or cluster the population	Increased costs if used indiscriminately

Non-probability sampling

Any discussion of the relative merits of probability versus non-probability sampling clearly shows the technical superiority of the former. In probability sampling, researchers use a random selection of elements to reduce or eliminate sampling bias. Under such conditions, we can have substantial confidence that the sample is representative of the population from which it is drawn. In addition, with probability sample designs, we can estimate an interval range within which the population parameter is expected to fall. Thus, we can not only reduce the chance of sampling error but also estimate the range of probable sampling error present.

With a subjective approach like non-probability sampling, the probability of selecting population elements is unknown. There are several ways that can be used to choose persons or cases to include in the sample. Often we allow the choice of subjects to be made by fieldworkers on the scene. When this occurs, there is greater opportunity for bias to enter the sample selection procedure and to distort the findings of the study. Also, we cannot estimate any range within which to expect the population parameter. Given the technical advantages of probability sampling over non-probability sampling, why would anyone choose the latter?

Some researchers suggest that the bias of non-probability samples can be reduced by post-stratification and propensity scoring. The first method, post-stratification, requires that we have some information (usually personal (age, gender) or firm (size, industry)) demographics that are available for the whole population. If the distribution on these demographic characteristics differs between the sample and the population you can calculate weights correcting for the over- or under-representation of these characteristics. There are some practical reasons for using these less precise methods. Propensity scoring, the second method, does not require information on the whole population but a second sample from a previous research is believed to be more representative for the population than the sample you use. Comparing your sample with the second sample allows calculating propensity scores reflecting the chance that a subject of the second, more representative sample, would also be included in your sample. It should, however, be noted that both methods rely on the heavy assumption that the weights or propensity scores are really related to the variables of interest in your research. Even if you are able to apply one of these two measures you will never eliminate the bias of the non-probability sample.

Usefulness of non-probability samples

Do you really need a probability sample? The answer to this question depends crucially on the objective of your research and more specifically on the kind of conclusion you want to draw. If you want to generalize, that is you attempt to find out what percentage of students think about starting their own company, or if you are interested in the accurate size of an effect, for example how many fewer cigarettes would be sold if tobacco taxes were to be increased by €1, you need to draw a probability sample.

Often, however, you are not so much interested in the accurate size of an effect, but rather in whether there is a positive or negative effect. This holds especially for research that employs concepts (variables) that do not know a common scale. Demand in cigarettes and price can be measured in commonly accepted numbers (packages sold and price in euros), but many concepts in business research do not have a common scale, such as motivation, competitiveness, and so on. What you want to know is, for example, whether more motivated employees or more competitive firms really perform better. To investigate such a hypothesis, we do not need probability samples. All we need is a sample that contains well- and less-motivated employees (competitive firms). Thus, we just need a sample whose subjects vary sufficiently on the variables under investigation.

Let us take the example of tobacco usage and cigarettes prices. With a non-probability sample among smoking students you could investigate which factors (e.g. friends, information on the long-term effects of smoking, price) would encourage smoking students to stop. A possible result of such a study could be that the price effect is relatively small compared to the effects of friends and information. With a probability sample you could show how many students quit smoking if taxes are increased. The non-probability study would be useful for organizations attempting to find out how they could convince students to stop smoking. The probability study would help the minister of finance to calculate the effects of a tobacco tax increase. Next to these considerations regarding the objectives of the study, non-probability samples also offer practical advantages.

Practical considerations for non-probability samples

We may use non-probability sampling procedures because they meet the sampling objectives satisfactorily. While a random sample will give us a true cross-section of the population, this may not be the objective of the research. If there is no desire or need to generalize to a population parameter, then there is much less concern about whether the sample fully reflects the population. Often researchers have more limited objectives. They may be looking only for the range of conditions or for examples of dramatic variations. This is especially true in exploratory research where one may wish to contact only certain persons or cases that are clearly atypical.

Additional reasons for choosing non-probability over probability sampling are cost and time. Probability sampling clearly calls for more planning and repeated call-backs to ensure that each selected sample member is contacted. These activities are expensive. Carefully controlled non-probability sampling often seems to give acceptable results, so the investigator may not even consider probability sampling. Erik's results from his fieldwork in the restaurants would generate questionable data, but he seemed to realize the fallacy of many of his assumptions once he had spoken with a couple of local experts in the tourism industry.

While, in theory, probability sampling may be superior, there can be breakdowns in its application. Even carefully stated random sampling procedures may be subject to careless application by the people involved. Thus, the ideal probability sampling may be only partially achieved because of the human element.

It is also possible that non-probability sampling may be the only feasible alternative. In particular, if the relevant population remains vague and difficult to define, it may be unfeasible even to attempt to construct a probability sample. Erik wants to approach potential holidaymakers by inviting visitors to his website to fill in an online questionnaire. Obviously, this method will miss all those potential visitors who have not used the Internet to obtain information on the Belgian coast. As participants of online surveys are often offered a small reward or the chance to win a larger reward, these surveys may attract respondents who are not remotely interested in the Belgian coast, but only in the chance of winning a prize. In addition, the total population may not be available for study in certain cases. At the scene of a major event, it may be impractical to even attempt to construct a probability sample. A study of past correspondence between two companies, for instance, must use an arbitrary sample because the full correspondence is not usually available.

In another sense, those who are included in a sample may select themselves. In mail surveys, those who respond may not represent a true cross-section of those who receive the questionnaire. The receivers of the questionnaire decide for themselves whether they will participate. There is some element of self-selection in almost all surveys because every respondent chooses whether or not to be interviewed.

Convenience sampling

Non-probability samples that are unrestricted are called **convenience samples**. They are the least reliable design but normally the cheapest and easiest to conduct. Researchers or fieldworkers have the freedom to choose whoever they can find, hence the word 'convenience'. Examples include informal pools of friends and neighbours, people responding to a newspaper's invitation for readers to state their positions on some public issue, a TV reporter's 'man-in-the-street' intercept interviews, and using employees to evaluate the taste of a new snack food.

While a convenience sample has no controls to ensure precision, it may still be a useful procedure. Often you will take such a sample to test ideas or even to gain ideas about a subject of interest. In the early stages of exploratory research, when you are seeking guidance, you might use this approach. The results may present evidence that is so overwhelming that a more sophisticated sampling procedure is unnecessary. In an interview with students concerning some issue of campus concern, you might talk to 25 students selected sequentially. You might discover that the responses are so overwhelmingly one-sided that there is no incentive to interview further.

Purposive sampling

A non-probability sample that conforms to certain criteria is called purposive sampling. There are two major types – judgement sampling and quota sampling.

Judgement sampling occurs when a researcher selects sample members to conform to some criterion. In a study of labour problems, for example, you may want to talk only with those who have experienced on-the-job discrimination. Another example of judgement sampling occurs when election results are predicted from only a few selected precincts that have been chosen because of their predictive record in past elections.

When used in the early stages of an exploratory study, a judgement sample is appropriate. When one wishes to select a biased group for screening purposes, this sampling method is also a good choice. Companies often try out new product ideas on their employees. The rationale is that one would expect the firm's employees to be more favourably disposed towards a new product idea than the public. If the product does not pass this group, it does not have any prospect of success in the general market.

Quota sampling is the second type of purposive sampling. We use it to improve representativeness. The logic behind quota sampling is that certain relevant characteristics describe the dimensions of the population. If a sample has the same distribution on these characteristics, then it is likely to be representative of the population regarding other variables over which we have no control. Suppose the student body of Lake University is 55 per cent female and 45 per cent male. The sampling quota would call for sampling students at a ratio of 55 to 45 per cent. This would eliminate distortions due to a non-representative gender ratio. Erik van de Duivel could use quota sampling to ensure that the distribution over different nationalities of his sample reflects the current nationality distribution of visitors. For example, he might know from previous studies or tourist registration data that 35 per cent of the visitors are Dutch, 30 per cent are German, 20 per cent are British and 15 per cent are French.

In most quota samples, researchers specify more than one control dimension. Each should meet two tests. It should:

1 have a distribution in the population that we can estimate
2 be pertinent to the topic studied.

We may believe that responses to a question should vary, depending on the gender of the respondent. If so, we should seek proportional responses from both men and women. We may also feel that undergraduates differ from graduate students, so this would be a dimension. Other dimensions – such as a student's academic discipline, ethnic group, religious affiliation and social group affiliation – may also be chosen. Only a few of these controls can be used. To illustrate, suppose we consider the following example.

Gender: two categories – male, female
Class level: two categories – graduate, undergraduate
College: six categories – arts and science, agriculture, architecture, business, engineering, other
Religion: four categories – Protestant, Catholic, Jewish, other
Fraternal affiliation: two categories – member, non-member
Family socio-economic class: three categories – upper, middle, lower

In an extreme case, we might ask an interviewer to find a male undergraduate business student who is Catholic, a fraternity member and from an upper-class home. All combinations of these six factors would call for 576 ($2 \times 2 \times 6 \times 4 \times 2 \times 3 = 576$) such cells to consider. This type of control is known as precision control. It gives greater assurance that a sample will be representative of the population. However, it is costly and too difficult to carry out with more than three variables.

When we wish to use more than three control dimensions, we should depend on frequency control. With this form of control, the overall percentage of those with each characteristic in the sample should match the percentage holding the same characteristic in the population. No attempt is made to find a combination of specific characteristics in a single person. In frequency control, we would probably find that the accompanying sample array (see Exhibit 6.9) is an adequate reflection of the population, although the population may contain a considerable yet small number of married female students who are campus residents, while in our sample not a single person meets these combined characteristics.

Exhibit 6.9 Distributions of characteristics in the sample and the population.

	Population (%)	Sample (%)
Male	65	67
Married	15	14
Undergraduate	70	72
Campus resident	30	28
Independent	75	73
Protestant	39	42

Quota sampling has several weaknesses. First, the idea that quotas on some variables assume a representativeness on others is argument by analogy. It gives no assurance that the sample is representative of the variables being studied. Often, the data used to provide controls may also be outdated or inaccurate. There is also a practical limit on the number of simultaneous controls that can be applied to ensure precision. Finally, the choice of subjects is left to fieldworkers to make on a judgemental basis. They may choose only friendly looking people, people who are convenient to them, and the like.

Despite the problems with quota sampling, it is widely used by opinion pollsters, and marketing and other researchers. Probability sampling is usually much more costly and time-consuming. Advocates of quota sampling argue that while there is some danger of systematic bias, the risks are usually not that great. Where predictive validity has been checked (e.g. in election polls), quota sampling has generally been satisfactory.

Snowball sampling

This design has found a niche in recent years in applications where respondents are difficult to identify and are best located through referral networks. In the initial stage of **snowball sampling**, individuals are discovered, and may or may not be selected through probability methods. This group is then used to locate others who possess similar characteristics and who, in turn, identify others. Similar to a reverse search for bibliographic sources, the 'snowball' gathers subjects as it rolls along. Various techniques are available for selecting a non-probability snowball with provisions for error identification and statistical testing.

Snowball sampling is especially useful if you want to sample subjects that are difficult to identify, because they are nowhere registered as a population. Two examples of master research projects illustrate the power of this sampling strategy. (1) A student wanted to investigate how informal investors select the companies they invest in. Through personal relations with a few start-up companies, he was able to obtain the contact information of six informal investors, but six informal investors are certainly too few for an appropriate sample. However, in the first inter-views he conducted it appeared that those six informal investors knew many other informal investors. He asked his initial contacts whether they would be willing to provide the contact information of the investors they knew and finally succeeded in interviewing 59 informal investors. (2) A student was interested in how people who recently joined a company build up their network within the company. He started by contacting graduates that he already knew and asked them whether they would forward his questionnaire to colleagues who also joined the company recently. Using snowball sampling, he was able to build a sample that was not restricted to graduates from his own university and also included non-graduates, who moved from another company to the current company. Both examples point at another advantage of snowball sampling, namely the referral effect. The chance that a targeted person would be willing to cooperate with you as a respondent would be, of course, much higher if there was some kind of (in)direct relation. In the study of informal investors, the initial contacts often did not only provide the contact information but also telephoned and informed them about the research or agreed to be named when the researcher contacted them.

Sampling on the Internet

The popularity of the Internet has increased significantly in the past decade and almost every firm and more and more households have direct access to it. As a result, researchers have also explored the possibility of using the Internet for research. To assess the advantages and disadvantages of using the Internet for sampling issues, it is useful to distinguish between building up a population list and sampling (selecting) respondents through the Internet.

Internet populations

Definitions of the Internet population are still unclear. A wide definition includes all individuals and organizations who have access to it, while narrower definitions restrict the population to those that maintain a website, are members of a mailing list, and so on. Regardless of which definition a researcher chooses, one needs to be aware that the Internet population differs considerably from the general population, just like a city's telephone directory does not fully reflect the general population of that city. Although access to and usage of the Internet has increased enormously in recent years, the general opinion is that Internet users are still considered by the general population to be younger, better educated and wealthier.

As discussed earlier, researchers often have a population in mind, but it is difficult to obtain a complete list of all members of the population that can be used to draw a sample. The Internet can be a source of such lists, as many websites offer listings and directories, sometimes even with contact information. Furthermore, the Internet plays host to many databases that offer such information, sometimes free of charge and often at a reasonable cost.

Suppose you want to survey business-consulting companies on their codes of ethics and how they have implemented these codes in their daily work. How could you use the Internet to build up a list of consulting firms to draw a sample?

First, the Internet can direct you to the professional associations of consulting firms, which can then be asked for their membership directories if these are not available online. Furthermore, it can be used to identify those firms that are not members of any association, by searching for the websites of consulting firms.

In terms of building up a population list the Internet is a very useful tool. It can be used as a departure point, but it can also be used to supplement a list you already have. The main advantage of the Internet is that it provides information independent of your location. Suppose you study at Leeds University and you want to conduct the survey mentioned above among consulting firms in the UK. In this case you are very likely to find information and directories for this population in your local university library. However, how could you easily obtain information on consulting firms in the Czech Republic if you are located in Leeds? The Internet is one solution to this problem.

Whether using the Internet to build up a population list is a good idea depends crucially on how well the intended population is represented on the Internet. As mentioned above, the Internet does not offer a good representation of the general population of a country or a city. But it is often useful for more specific populations, such as the population of consulting firms as in the example above or the student population of your faculty based on the faculty's email list.

Internet sampling

With respect to the issue of sampling or selecting respondents by using the Internet, one has to distinguish probabilistic and non-probabilistic samples. Regarding probabilistic samples, it is of utmost importance to ensure that the Internet population reflects the targeted population. If the target population has members who are not part of the Internet population, those members have a zero chance of being included, which violates the basic principles of probability samples.

Second, you can use the Internet for drawing a non-probability sample. Take the example of dairy company, Countrylove, which invited Miranda Appels to participate in an online survey. The specific problem with this sampling approach is that you do not have any control over which people participate in the survey. Such non-probability samples may contain respondents who do not belong to your population. Countrylove assumes that mainly buyers of its products visit its website, but it does not know for sure. Visitors to its website could also be people who are interested in finding a job at Countrylove or students writing a term paper on the dairy industry. Filter questions such as 'Why did you come to our website?' are a possible measure that will help to identify types of respondent in your sample. Another problem is that it is difficult to ascertain whether a group of people voluntarily responding to online questionnaires is representative of the population as a whole, or even the population of Internet users. For example, elderly people are, in general, under-represented in Internet samples, while younger males are over-represented (see also the section on response error in Chapter 7, p. 216).

Conducting data collection through the Internet has a considerable cost advantage as the sending and returning of questionnaires is virtually without cost. One problem that needs to be considered, however, is whether the response rates are comparable to the expected response to mail or telephone surveys, which we discuss in Chapter 7.

Running Case Study 6
Sampling

In developing a sample set, Rebecca has created a couple of lists of student email addresses. For her own school, she has copied the names from the participant lists of courses she and some friends of hers have taken. She has used these name lists to create email addresses by simply adding the domain name to the student's name, which finally resulted in 407 unique email addresses of Master's students in her school. According to the website of the school about 650 Master's students are currently enrolled in different programmes, thus her email lists cover more than 60 per cent of the total population. Her friend Brenda (see Running Case Study 4) has sent her request to all (821) psychology students at her school. Moreover, Rebecca has used her Facebook account to track other people she knows at other universities. She has approached them and asked them to fill in the questionnaire and to forward it to other friends at their university. As she did not know how well the last group of her friends had spread her questionnaire, she could not calculate exactly how many students were invited to participate in her questionnaire. Nevertheless, she knew for sure that at least 1,252 people were approached (821 in Amsterdam, 407 at her school and at least 24 Facebook friends she has approached directly). Rebecca thought that 1,252 was quite an impressive number and she was rather confident at receiving at least 100 responses.

Although Rebecca used an identical questionnaire for each of the three groups, she used three different links, which allowed her to trace back whether a respondent received the mail through Brenda, through the list she compiled for her school or through her Facebook friends. After two weeks she sent a reminder to the students of her own school and to her direct Facebook contacts. She could not send a reminder to the psychology students in Amsterdam, as Brenda received a warning from the system administrator regarding her inappropriate use of the email services. Brenda apologized saying that she was not aware of the conditions for using the university email system, as she thought that for research purposes it would have been acceptable, but she promised to fully comply with the rules in the future. After six weeks, Rebecca had the responses depicted in the table for each group.

Group	Emails sent	Valid questionnaires filled in	Response rate
Through Brenda	821	43	5%
Rebecca's school	407	76	19%
Facebook friends	24	38	158%

Although Rebecca was delighted to have so many responses, exactly 161, she was also a little disappointed that most of the people she approached did not respond and she was especially worried about the large differences in the response rate. Although, the second and third group received a reminder, it could still not account for the large difference: Rebecca had received 63 questionnaires from her school before she sent out the first reminder; after the first reminder this number rose to 75; the second reminder yielded just one extra respondent.

In a meeting with her supervisor, they discussed how Rebecca could take into account differences between the universities. Of her respondents, 76 studied in Maastricht, 43 in Amsterdam, but the 38 respondents approached through her Facebook friends were scattered across 11 universities, with 5 respondents even studying outside the Netherlands. In the end she had the strong feeling that she could not use the 38 respondents acquired through her Facebook contacts, as she did not have sufficient respondents for each university they studied at. Would the distribution of the respondents across different universities allow her to investigate differences between universities? Rebecca wanted to ask her supervisor about how to handle this problem.

Mehmet had progress as well. He had talked to self-employed friends and also asked them whether they could direct him to other self-employed people they knew. Moreover, he has become active in local business networks and even visited two small conferences: a regional business plan competition for business founders planning to start businesses with high growth expectations, mainly smaller high-tech companies; and a conference on migrant entrepreneurs organized by a national think tank that brings together entrepreneurs, policy makers and scientists from various fields. In a short time, Mehmet collected a huge stack of business cards, too many to enable each to be approached for an extensive interview. But how should he proceed? Which contacts should he approach with the request for a longer interview? Should he first approach those he knew best, i.e. friends? Or should he approach those who seem most important to him, as they owned sizable businesses or held senior positions in the municipality, banks and other organizations?

1 Try to identify the sampling types Rebecca is thinking about.
2 What is the main sampling problem of the population Mehmet is interested in?
3 Discuss how many respondents Rebecca needs to have a sufficiently large sample.

Summary

1   The unit of analysis is a key concept in research and its choice determines what kind of problems and questions the research can answer and how the results of the research can be applied. Sound research requires that either the unit of analysis is kept the same or that differences in the unit of analysis are controlled.

2   Case study research is an important, and in business science also widely used, research approach. Unlike survey research it does not follow the sampling logic but the replication logic, and case study results are therefore not generalizable to a population but to a theoretical proposition. The main advantage of the case study approach compared to other approaches is that it relies on multiple sources of evidence, such as interviews, observations and documents.

3   Sampling is based on two premises. One is that there is enough similarity among the elements in a population that a few of these elements will adequately represent the characteristics of the total population. The second premise is that while some elements in a sample underestimate a population value, others overestimate this value. The result of these tendencies is that a sample statistic such as the arithmetic mean is generally a good estimate of a population mean.

4   A good sample has both accuracy and precision. An accurate sample is one in which there is little or no bias or systematic variance. A sample with adequate precision is one that has a sampling error that is within acceptable limits for the study's purpose.

5   A variety of sampling techniques is available. They may be classified by their representation basis and element selection techniques, as shown in the table.

Probability sampling is based on random selection – a controlled procedure that ensures that each population element is given a known non-zero chance of selection. In contrast, non-probability selection is 'not random'. When each sample element is drawn individually from the population at large, it is unrestricted sampling. Restricted sampling covers those forms of sampling in which the selection process follows more complex rules.

Element selection	Representation basis	
	Probability	Non-probability
Unrestricted	Simple random	Convenience
Restricted	Complex random	Purposive
	Systematic	Judgement
	Cluster	Quota
	Stratified	Snowball
	Double	

6   The simplest type of probability approach is simple random sampling. In this design, each member of the population has an equal chance of being included in a sample. In developing a probability sample, six procedural questions need to be answered:
   a   What is the relevant population?
   b   What are the parameters of interest?
   c   What is the sampling frame?
   d   What is the type of sample?
   e   What size sample is needed?
   f   How much will it cost?

Two kinds of estimate of a population parameter are made in probability sampling. First, we make a point estimate that is the single best estimate of the population value. Then we make an interval estimate that covers the range of values within which we expect the population value to occur, with a given degree of confidence. All sample-based estimates of population parameters should be stated in terms of a confidence interval.

7 The specifications of the researcher and the nature of the population determine the size of a probability sample. These requirements are largely expressed in the following questions:
   a What is the degree of confidence we want in our parameter estimate?
   b How large an interval range will we accept?
   c What is the degree of variance in the population?
   d Is the population small enough that the sample should be adjusted for finite population?

   Cost considerations are also often incorporated into the sample size decision.

8 Complex sampling is used when conditions make simple random samples impractical or uneconomical. The four major types of complex random sampling discussed in this chapter are systematic, stratified, cluster and double sampling. Systematic sampling involves the selection of every k^{th} element in the population, beginning with a random start between elements from 1 to k. Its simplicity in certain cases is its greatest value.

   Stratified sampling is based on dividing a population into sub-populations and then randomly sampling from each of these strata. This method usually results in a smaller total sample size than would a simple random design. Stratified samples may be proportionate or disproportionate.

   In cluster sampling, we divide the population into convenient groups and then randomly choose the groups to study. It is typically less efficient from a statistical viewpoint than the simple random because of the high degree of homogeneity within the clusters. Its great advantage is its savings in cost – if the population is dispersed geographically – or in time. The most widely used form of clustering is area sampling, in which geographic areas are the selection elements.

   At times it may be more convenient or economical to collect some information by sample and then use it as a basis for selecting a sub-sample for further study. This procedure is called double sampling.

   Non-probability sampling also has some compelling practical advantages that account for its widespread use. Often probability sampling is not feasible because the population is not available.

   Then, too, frequent breakdowns in the application of probability sampling discount its technical advantages. You will also find that a true cross-section is often not the aim of the researcher. Here the goal may be the discovery of the range or extent of conditions. Finally, non-probability sampling is usually less expensive to conduct than probability sampling.

   Convenience samples are the simplest and least reliable forms of non-probability sampling. Their primary virtue is low cost. One purposive sample is the judgemental sample in which one is interested in studying only selected types of subject. The other purposive sample is the quota sample. Subjects are selected to conform to certain predesignated control measures that secure a representative cross-section of the population. Snowball sampling uses a referral approach to reach particularly hard-to-find respondents.

Discussion questions

Terms in review

1 Explain the concept of unit of analysis. What is it? What problems do you encounter when you have to define it?

2 Indicate the unit of analysis (individual, group, organization, etc.) suggested by the following statements:
   a Over the last 30 years, the average size of companies in the UK has declined.
   b Company scandals, which are widely covered by the media, cause significant drops in the share price of the involved companies.
   c Economic growth is lower in Germany than in other EU member states.

d Among the unemployed, the chance of finding a new job is associated with the frequency of contact with friends and former colleagues.

e Students enrolled at the business faculty have a stronger intention to vote for a liberal party than students from any other faculty.

3 Distinguish between:
a statistic and parameter
b sample frame and population
c restricted and unrestricted sampling
d simple random and complex random sampling
e convenience and purposive sampling
f sample precision and sample accuracy
g systematic and error variance
h variable and attribute parameters
i point estimate and interval estimate
j proportionate and disproportionate samples.

4 Under what kind of conditions would you recommend the following:
a A probability sample? A non-probability sample?
b A simple random sample? A cluster sample? A stratified sample?
c Using the finite population adjustment factor?
d A disproportionate stratified probability sample?

5 You plan to conduct a survey using unrestricted sampling. What subjective decisions must you make?

6 You draw a random sample of 300 employee records from the personnel file and find that the average length of service per employee is 6.3.
a Can you derive from this information how reliable the mean estimate is?
b What further information would you need to assess how reliable the mean estimate of 6.3 years is?

Making research decisions

7 You are working for Kiddybooks, a small publisher of children books. Although Kiddybooks children's books have won many awards, the exposure of your books in book shops is shoddy. Book shops claim that despite the awards you have won parents are not demanding your books. Apparently the relationship between awards for good books and sales of good books does not work in your case.

How could you investigate why the relationship between awards and book sales does not work for Kiddybooks? Formulate different research questions and identify the unit of analysis.

8 Your task is to interview a representative sample of attendees for the large concert venue where you work. The new-season schedule includes 200 live concerts featuring all types of musicians and musical groups. Since neither the number of attendees nor their descriptive characteristics are known in advance, you decide on non-probability sampling. Based on past seating configurations, you can calculate the number of tickets that will be available for each of the 200 concerts. Thus, collectively, you will know the number of possible attendees for each type of music. From attendance research conducted at concerts held during the previous two years, you can obtain gender data on attendees by type of music.

How would you conduct a reasonably reliable non-probability sample?

9 A Vietnamese sports shoemaker produces shoes in two grades for the European and Russian markets. European retailers require the size labelling to be precise, while for the Russian market it does not matter. Up to now the firm has mainly produced shoes for the Russian market, but it has the chance to contract with a large shoe discounter in Europe if it is able to comply with the specified quality requirement (i.e. the labelled shoe size is the actual shoe size).

Explain how these facts affect decisions regarding quality control in sample design, confidence intervals and sample size.

10 You wish to take an unrestricted random sample of undergraduate students at Lake University to ascertain their levels of spending per month on food purchased off-campus and eaten on the premises where purchased. You ask a test sample of nine students about their food expenditure and find that on average they report spending €20, with two-thirds of them reporting spending from €10 to €30.

What size sample do you think you should take? (Assume your universe is infinite.)

11 You wish to adjust your sample calculations to reflect the fact that there are only 2,500 students in your population. How does this additional information affect your estimated sample size in question 10?

12 Your large firm is facing its first union negotiation. Your superior wants an accurate evaluation of the morale of its large number of computer technicians. What size sample would you draw if it was to be an unrestricted sample?

From concept to practice

13 Design a non-probability sample of students at your university that is representative.

14 How would you draw a cluster sample among students at your university?

15 Using Exhibit 6.7 as your guide, for each sampling technique describe the sampling frame for a study of employers' skill requirements of new employees using the industry in which you are currently working or wish to work.

Classroom discussion

16 Discuss how the problem of non-response can affect the results of analyses based on randomly selected samples, and how these problems can eventually be eased.

Recommended further reading

Barnett, Vic, *Sample Survey* (3rd edn). London: Hodder & Stoughton, 2002. A text offering a good overview of classic sampling techniques as well as recent developments, such as sampling on the Internet.

Best, Samuel J. and Krueger, Brian S. *Internet Data Collection*. Thousand Oaks, CA: Sage, 2004. Chapter 3 offers a concise overview on Internet sampling.

Deming, W. Edwards, *Sample Design in Business Research*. New York: Wiley, 1990. A classic by the late author, an authority on sampling.

Diamantopolous, Adamantios and Schlegelmilch, Bodo B., *Taking the Fear out of Data Analysis*. Thomson Learning, 1997. Chapter 2 discusses sampling issues in an entertaining manner.

Ellis, Paul. *The Essential Guide to Effect Sizes: Statistical Power, Meta-Analysis, and the Interpretation of Research Results*. Cambridge University Press, 2010. A very accessible statistics book that introduces students and researchers to the dependencies between effect size, statistical power and sample sizes.

Kish, Leslie, *Survey Sampling*. New York: Wiley, 1995. A widely read reference on survey sampling, recently updated.

Simsek, Zeki and Veiga, John F., 'A primer on internet organizational surveys', *Organizational Research Methods* 4(3), 2001, pp. 218–35. This paper presents and discusses strategies for using Internet samples.

Yates, Frank, *Sampling Methods for Censuses and Surveys* (4th edn). New York: Oxford University Press, 1987. A readable text with an emphasis on sampling practices.

Get started with understanding statistical techniques!

When you have read this chapter, log on to the Online Learning Centre website at *www.mcgraw-hill.co.uk/textbooks/blumberg* to explore chapter-by-chapter test questions, additional case studies, a glossary and more online study tools for *Business Research Methods*.

Notes

1   Office for National Statistics, 3 August 2004 (at www.statistics.gov.uk/census2001/cb_2.asp).

2   W.E. Deming, *Sample Design in Business Research*. New York: Wiley, 1960, p. 26.

3   Henry Assael and John Keon, 'Nonsampling versus sampling errors in survey research', *Journal of Marketing Research*, Spring 1982, pp. 114–23.

4   A. Parasuraman, *Marketing Research* (2nd edn). Reading, MA: Addison-Wesley, 1991, p. 477.

5   Fred N. Kerlinger, *Foundations of Behavioral Research* (3rd edn). New York: Holt, Rinehart & Winston, 1986, p. 72.

6   Amir D. Aczel, *Complete Business Statistics*. Burr Ridge, IL: Irwin, 1996, p. 180.

7   The correction for a finite population is shown in the example below.

     If a finite population of 20,000 is considered, the sample size is 256 for an interval of $\pm.5$ meals and 95 per cent confidence.

$$\sigma_{\bar{x}} = \frac{S}{\sqrt{n-1}} \times \sqrt{\frac{N-n}{N-1}} = 0.255 = \frac{4}{\sqrt{n-1}} \times \frac{20{,}000-n}{20{,}000-1} \quad \text{or}$$

$$n = \frac{s^2 N + \sigma_{\bar{x}}^2 (N-1)}{s^2 N + \sigma_{\bar{x}}^2 (N-1)}$$

     where

     N = size of the population

     n = size of the sample

8   Aguinis, H. and Harden, E.E. (2009). 'Sample size rules of thumb'. In Charles E. Lance and Robert J. Vandenberg (eds), *Statistical and Methodological Myths and Urban Legends*, pp. 267–86.

9   All estimates of costs are hypothetical.

10   Leslie Kish, *Survey Sampling*. New York: Wiley, 1965, p. 188.

11   Ibid., pp. 76–7.

12   Typically, stratification is carried out before the actual sampling, but when this is not possible, it is still possible to stratify after the fact. Ibid., p. 90.

13   W.G. Cochran, *Sampling Techniques* (2nd edn). New York: Wiley, 1963, p. 134.

14   Ibid., p. 96.

15   Kish, *Survey Sampling*, p. 94.

16   For detailed treatment of these and other cluster sampling methods and problems, see Kish, *Survey Sampling*, pp. 148–247.

17   J.H. Lorie and H.V. Roberts, *Basic Methods of Marketing Research*. New York: McGraw-Hill, 1951, p. 120.

18   Kish, *Survey Sampling*, p. 156.

19   For specifics on these problems and how to solve them, the reader is referred to the many good sampling texts available. Two that have been mentioned already are Kish, *Survey Sampling*, Chapters 5, 6 and 7; and Cochran, *Sampling Techniques*, Chapters 9, 10 and 11.

CHAPTER 7

Primary data collection with surveys

Chapter contents

Learning objectives

When you have read this chapter, you should understand:

1 the process for selecting the appropriate and optimal communication approach

2 what factors affect participation in survey studies

3 the major sources of error in survey studies, and how to minimize them

4 the major advantages and disadvantages of the three communication approaches

5 the major advantages and disadvantages of structured observations.

Characteristics of data collection

Conducting empirical research in business requires data. In the following chapters, we will discuss different approaches how researchers can acquire data (see also Exhibit 7.1). The different approaches to acquiring data can be classified along three dimensions. The first dimension distinguishes between whether researchers collect data specifically for a current study or whether they make use of already existing data, so-called secondary data, such as official or administrative databases. Specifically collected data for a current study are called primary data, while data collected for a purpose other than the current study are called secondary data. In Chapters 7, 8, 10, 11 and 12, we address different approaches to primary data collection. Chapter 9 covers the use of secondary data, which are, however, often the outcome of previous primary data collection efforts by other researchers. The second dimension describes what kind of data are collected and, as we discussed in Chapter 5, we distinguish between quantitative and qualitative data. The third dimension refers to the method of data collection and distinguishes between the communication and the observation approach. In the communication approach the researcher asks questions either personally, as in face-to-face interviews and phone surveys, or indirectly through (web) surveys. In the observation approach, researchers observe certain phenomena or events and record what they see.

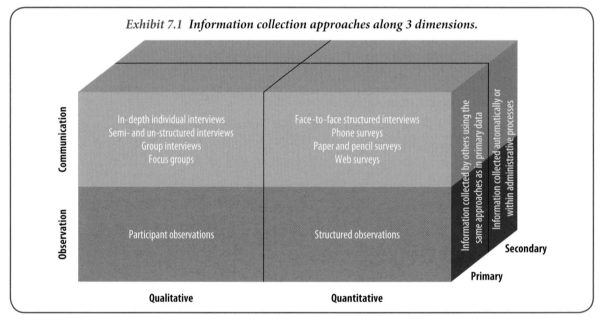

Exhibit 7.1 Information collection approaches along 3 dimensions.

Observation is often associated with qualitative research, but is also suitable for quantitative research, although how the method is applied differs between qualitative and quantitative research. Qualitative studies often use the term **participant observation** (discussed in Chapter 8), while quantitative studies refer to **structured observation** (discussed in this chapter at the end). Similarly, the tools used in the communication approach differ according to the kind of data to be collected. In this chapter, we address survey research that aims for the collection of quantitative data by questioning the respondent face to face, by phone or by using self-administered questionnaires either in paper and pencil or in online formats. Independent of the delivery approach, common to survey approaches is that the communication with the respondent is highly structured, i.e. questions and often answer choices as well are given. In Chapter 8, we address unstructured or qualitative interviews in which the respondent is free to answer in any way they want and questions often change from respondent to respondent. Qualitative interviews with a single respondent or group of respondents (focus groups) are at the base of different qualitative research methods, such as case studies (discussed in Chapter 11), content analysis, narrative method, action research, ethnographic studies and grounded theory (all discussed in Chapter 10).

When collecting quantitative data, the researcher determines the data-collection approach largely by identifying the types of information needed – investigative questions the researcher must answer – and the desired data type (nominal, ordinal, interval or ratio) for each of these questions. The characteristics of the sample unit – specifically, whether a participant can articulate their ideas, thoughts and experiences – also play a role in the decision. Part A of Exhibit 7.2 shows the relationship of these decisions to the research process detailed in Chapter 2. Part B of Exhibit 7.2 indicates how the researcher's choice of a communication (versus observation) approach affects the following:

- the creation and selection of the measurement questions
- sampling issues (explored in Chapter 6), which drive contact and call-back procedures
- instrument design (discussed in Chapter 13), which incorporates attempts to reduce error and create participant-screening procedures
- data-collection processes, which create the need for follow-up procedures (when self-administered instruments are used) and possible interviewer training (when personal or telephone interviewing methods are used).

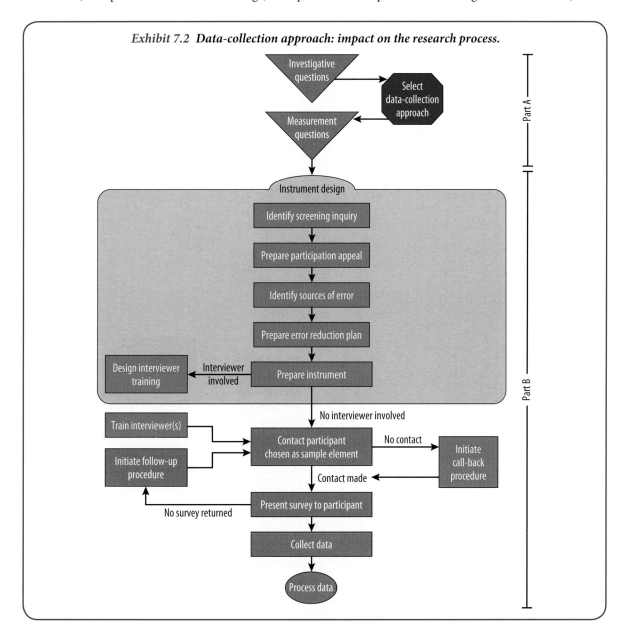

Exhibit 7.2 Data-collection approach: impact on the research process.

Research designs can be classified by the approach used to gather primary data. There are really only two alternatives: we can observe conditions, behaviour, events, people or processes; or we can communicate with people about various topics, including participants' attitudes, motivations, intentions and expectations. This chapter focuses on the collection of quantitative data. Predominantly we discuss the **communication approach**, but at the end we also address the **observation** approach.

7.2 Characteristics of the communication approach

The communication approach involves surveying people and recording their responses for analysis. The great strength of the communication approach as a primary data-collecting approach is its versatility. It does not require there to be a visual or other objective perception of the information sought by the researcher. Abstract information of all types can be gathered by questioning others. We seldom learn much about opinions and attitudes except by asking respondents directly. This is also true of intentions and expectations. Information about past events is often available only through surveying people who remember the events. Thus, the choice of a communication versus an observation approach may seem an obvious one, given the directions in which investigative questions may lead, as illustrated in Exhibit 7.3.

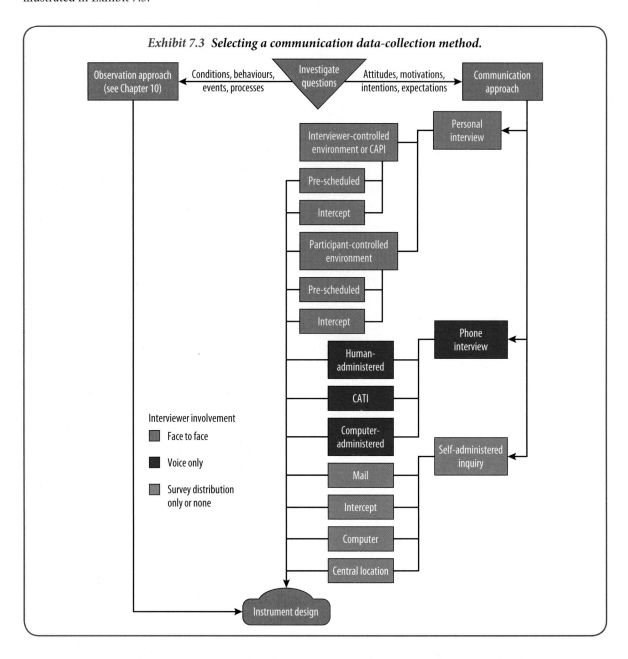

Exhibit 7.3 Selecting a communication data-collection method.

However, sometimes the investigative questions leave the option of choosing either approach. Surveying is more efficient and economical than observation. A few well-chosen questions can yield information that would take much more time and effort to gather by observation. Using the telephone, mail or the Internet as the medium of communication can expand geographic coverage at a fraction of the cost and time required by observation.

The most appropriate applications for surveying are those where participants are uniquely qualified to provide the desired information. We expect such facts as age, income and immediate family situation to be appropriate survey topics.

Questions can be used to inquire about subjects that are exclusively internal to the participant. Included here are items such as attitudes, opinions, expectations and intentions. Such information can be made available to the researcher if the right questions are asked of participants. It becomes, finally, a matter of whether to ask direct or indirect questions in order to collect the most meaningful data.

The communication approach has its shortcomings, however. Its major weakness, as depicted in Exhibit 7.4, is that the quality and quantity of information secured depends heavily on the ability and willingness of participants to cooperate. Often, people refuse an interview or fail to reply to a mail- or computer-delivered survey. There may be many reasons for this unwillingness to cooperate. Certain people at certain times fail to see any value in participation; they may be suspicious of or fear the interview experience for some reason; or they may view the topic as too sensitive and thus the interview as potentially embarrassing or intrusive. Previous encounters with marketers who have attempted to disguise their sales pitch as a research survey can also erode participants' willingness to cooperate.

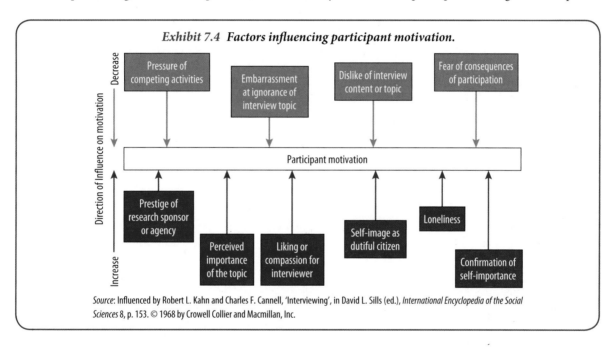

Exhibit 7.4 Factors influencing participant motivation.

Source: Influenced by Robert L. Kahn and Charles F. Cannell, 'Interviewing', in David L. Sills (ed.), *International Encyclopedia of the Social Sciences* 8, p. 153. © 1968 by Crowell Collier and Macmillan, Inc.

Even if individuals agree to participate, they may not possess the knowledge that is being sought. If we ask participants to report on events that they have not experienced personally, we need to assess their replies carefully. If our purpose is to learn what the participant understands to be the case, it is legitimate to accept the answers given, but if our intent is to learn what the event or situation actually was, we must recognize that the participant is reporting second-hand data and the accuracy of the information declines. We should not depend on these second-hand sources if a more direct source can be found. A family or group member should be asked about another member's experience only when there is no other way to get the information directly.

Sometimes a participant may not have an opinion on the topic of concern. Under such circumstances, their proper response should be 'don't know' or 'have no opinion'. Too often, though, participants feel obliged to express some opinion even if they do not have one. In such cases, it is difficult for researchers to know how true or reliable the answers are.

Participants may also interpret a question or concept in a way that differs from the researcher's intention. This occurs when the individual answers a question that differs from the one being asked. Also, a participant may intentionally mislead the researcher by giving false information. It is difficult for a researcher to identify these occasions. Thus, survey responses should be accepted for what they are: statements by individuals that reflect varying degrees of truth. Despite these weaknesses, communicating with research participants is a principal method of management research.

7.3 Choosing a communication method

What has been said in section 7.2 applies to the communication approach in general, independent of whether the researcher wants to collect quantitative information through survey techniques or qualitative information through unstructured interviews. In the remaining sections of this chapter, we will focus on survey research, i.e. collecting quantitative information through structured questioning. Thus, when we use the term 'interview' in the following sections, we refer to a highly structured interview in which the researcher reads out questions from a questionnaire and often even offers all the answer choices. Once the researcher has determined that surveying is the appropriate data-collection approach, various means may be used to secure information from individuals. A researcher can conduct a survey by face-to-face interview, telephone, mail, computer or a combination of these. Before we discuss personal interviews, telephone interviews, self-administered surveys and web surveys in detail, we discuss their commonalities.

General requirements for success

Three broad conditions must be met in order to have a successful survey:

1 The participant must possess the information being targeted by the investigative questions.
2 The participant must understand his or her role in the interview as the provider of accurate information.
3 The participant must perceive adequate motivation to cooperate.

Information

The interviewer can do little about the participant's information level. Screening questions can qualify participants when there is doubt about their ability to answer. This is the study designer's responsibility. Furthermore, the researcher can ask prospective respondents, in a letter announcing the study and confirming the interview date, to have certain information to hand. In a study on the contracting behaviour of business firms in alliances, for example, one of the authors asked the respondents to have the contract at hand during the interview.

Motivation to participate[1]

In personal and telephone interviews, participant motivation is a responsibility of the interviewer; in self-administered and web-based surveys, accompanying text written by the researchers has to fulfil that role.

Interviewers can motivate participants in many ways. An interviewer can explain what kind of answer is sought, how complete it should be, and in what terms it should be expressed. Interviewers can even do some coaching in the interview, although this can be a biasing factor. Studies of reactions to many surveys show that participants can be motivated to participate in personal interviews and, in fact, can even enjoy the experience. In one study, more than 90 per cent of participants said the interview experience was interesting, and three-quarters reported that they were willing to be interviewed again.[2] In self-administered and web-based surveys, the researcher's primary objective is to increase response and to encourage participants to complete the survey. In both cases an introduction as well as intermediate statements in the questioning process are helpful. Moreover, a skilfully designed questionnaire (see Chapter 13) increases response as well as completion rates.

Increasing participants' receptiveness

As depicted in Exhibit 7.4, a variety of forces can affect participant motivation in an interview. In personal and telephone interviews, many of these involve the interviewer. At first, it may seem easy to question another person about various topics, but research interviewing is not so simple. What we do or say as interviewers can make or break a study. Participants often react more to their feelings about the interviewer than to the content of the questions. It is also important for the interviewer to ask the questions properly, record the responses accurately, and probe meaningfully. To achieve these aims, he or she must be trained to carry out those procedures that foster a good interviewing relationship. These issues also play a role in self-administered and web-based surveys, although those approaches lack direct personal contact. Nevertheless, such survey question and answer alternatives must also be carefully formulated.

The first goal is to establish a friendly relationship with the participant. Three factors will help with participant receptiveness:

1 The participant must believe that the participation experience will be pleasant and satisfying.
2 The participant must believe that answering the survey is an important and worthwhile use of his or her time.
3 The participant must dismiss any mental reservations that he or she might have about participation.

Whether the experience will be pleasant and satisfying depends heavily on how a survey is introduced, how questions are asked and whether participants have the feeling that the interviewer or researcher is really interested in their answers. For the participant to think that answering the survey is important and worthwhile, some explanation of the study's purpose is necessary, although the extent of this will vary. Usually, the purpose of the study should be stated, as well as how the information will be used and what is expected of the participant. Participants should feel that their cooperation would be meaningful to themselves and to the survey results. When this is achieved, more participants will express their views willingly. Participants often have reservations about being interviewed that must be overcome. They may suspect that the sponsor of the research has different objectives, such as selling certain products or services or even has an illegitimate purpose. In addition, they may also feel inadequate or fear the questioning will embarrass them.

Especially in personal but also in telephone interviews, interviewers themselves affect crucially the motivation to participate. Typically, participants will cooperate with an interviewer whose behaviour reveals confidence and who engages people on a personal level. Effective interviewers are differentiated not by demographic characteristics but by these interpersonal skills. By confidence, we mean that most participants are immediately convinced that they will want to participate in the study and cooperate fully with the interviewer. An engaging personal style is one where the interviewer instantly establishes credibility by adapting to the individual needs of the participant.

Successful interviews and surveys require that the participant is kept receptive throughout the different phases of the interview.

Introduction

The participant's first reaction to the request for an interview or survey is at best a guarded one. Appearance and action are critical in forming a good first impression. In personal and telephone interviews, interviewers should immediately identify themselves by name and organization, and provide any special identification necessary (introductory letters or other information to confirm the study's legitimacy). In this brief but critical period, the interviewer must display friendly intentions and stimulate the participant's interest. Similarly, self-administered and web surveys should start with an introduction section revealing the purpose of the study, the identity of the sponsor and who is conducting it, including an address participants can turn to in case they have questions or even complaints.

Introductory explanations should be no more detailed than necessary. Too much information can introduce a bias. Usually, the introduction section should explain the objective of the study, its background, how the participant was selected, the confidential nature of the interview (if it is confidential), and the benefits of the research findings. Typical questions that might be asked when they are invited to participate in research are: 'How did you happen to pick me?' 'Who gave you my name?' 'Why don't you go next door?' 'Why are you doing this study?' or a comment such as 'I don't know enough about this.'[3] As a researcher, you should prepare convincing standardized answers to those questions.

In personal and telephone interviews, it can happen that the interviewer gets the impression that the participant is busy. Then it may be a good idea to give a general introduction and try to stimulate enough interest to arrange an interview at another time. If the designated participant is not at home, the interviewer should briefly explain the proposed visit to the person who is contacted. It is desirable to establish good relations with intermediaries since their attitudes can help in contacting the desired participant. Interviewers contacting participants door to door often leave calling or business cards, which have details of their affiliation and a number where they can be reached to reschedule the interview.

During the interview: establishing a good relationship

The successful interview is based on rapport – meaning a relationship of confidence and understanding between researcher/interviewer and participant. Interview situations are often new to participants, and they need help in defining their roles. The interviewer can help by conveying that the interview is confidential (if it is) and important, and that the participant can discuss the topics with freedom from censure, coercion or pressure. In self-administered and web surveys, procedural rules can help to establish trust between the participant and the researcher. Companies often hold job-satisfaction surveys among employees guaranteeing anonymity. But how anonymous can a survey be if it contains information on gender, age, education, tenure and department? Such general information is sufficient to easily identify individuals. A common measure to guarantee anonymity is to ask a neutral agency to administer the questionnaires and analyse the data. Under these conditions, the participant can obtain much satisfaction from 'opening up' without pressure being exerted.

Dealing with non-response error

In communication studies, **non-response error** occurs when the responses of participants differ in some systematic way from the responses of non-participants. This occurs when the researcher (i) cannot locate the person (the predesignated sample element) to be studied or (ii) is unsuccessful in encouraging that person to participate. This is an especially difficult problem when you are using a probability sample of subjects. If the researcher must interview predesignated persons, the task is to find them. Failure to locate a predesignated participant can be due to inaccessibility. In central cities, getting access to the participant can be a problem, as apartment security and locations that produce safety problems for night-time follow-up may complicate household access.[4] One study of non-response found that only 31 per cent of all first calls (and 20 per cent of all first calls in major metropolitan areas) were completed.

Solutions to reduce errors of non-response include:

- establishing and implementing call-back procedures
- creating a non-response sample and weighting results from this sample
- substituting another individual for the missing participant.

Call-backs

The most reliable solution to non-response problems is to make call-backs. If enough attempts are made, it is usually possible to contact most target participants, although unlimited call-backs are expensive.[5] An original contact plus three call-backs should usually secure about 85 per cent of the target participants. Yet in one study, 36 per cent of central city residents had still not been contacted after three call-backs.[6] One way to improve the productivity of call-backs is to vary them by time of day and day of week. Sometimes neighbours can suggest the best time to call.

Weighting

Another approach that has been used successfully is to treat all remaining non-participants as a new subpopulation after a few call-backs. A random sample is then drawn from this group, and every effort is made to complete this sample with a 100 per cent response rate. Findings from this non-participant sample can then be weighted into the total population estimate.[7] In a survey in which central city residents are under-represented, we can weight the results of interviews that are completed with such residents to give them full representation in the results. The weakness of this approach is that weighted returns often differ from those that would be secured if successful call-backs were made. Thus, an unknown – but possibly substantial – bias is introduced. Weighting for non-response after only one contact attempt will probably not overcome non-response bias, but participant characteristics converge on their population values after two to three call-backs.[8]

Substitution

A third way to deal with the non-response problem is to substitute someone else for the missing participant. This is, however, dangerous. 'At home' participants are likely to differ from 'not at home' persons in systematic ways.

One study suggested that 'not at home' persons are younger, better educated, more urban and have a higher income than the average.[9]

If it is absolutely necessary to substitute, it is better for the interviewer to ask others in the household about the designated participant. This approach has worked well 'when questions are objective, when informants have a high degree of observability with respect to participants, when the population is homogeneous, and when the setting of the interview provides no clear-cut motivation to distort responses in one direction or another'.[10]

Research Methods in Real Life
Counting eggs

The living conditions that egg-laying hens are forced to endure are cruel. Most hens are held in cages that offer less space per hen than the size of a page of this book. Photos showing how hens produce our breakfast eggs have appeared in the media and animal activists have used them to draw consumers' attention to this issue. Although poultry associations argue that the current usage of cages for hens does not violate animal rights, the European Commission decided that, from 2006, egg producers must provide more space for their hens. The EU directive distinguishes three egg production conditions offering increasing levels of space for hens – (1) cage, (2) barn and (3) free-range – and egg producers have to mark each egg according to the production conditions. In this way, consumers can have a say in the hens' living conditions by revealing their preference at the supermarket checkout.

Exhibit 7.5 shows which eggs German consumers say they prefer (inner circle) and which eggs they actually buy (outer circle). The difference between the two circles (derived from different data sources, namely a consumer survey and secondary statistics) is astonishing. Only 1 out of 20 consumers concedes preferring cage eggs, yet 12 out of 20 eggs sold come from caged hens. How can these differences be

explained? Is social desirability of answering behaviour the only explanation? What do you think about the explanation that the 5 per cent of consumers confessing that they buy eggs from caged hens are heavy egg consumers, while those that buy free-range eggs consume fewer eggs? What do you think about the comment that the population between the two statistics differs – the one on buying preferences consists only of households, while the purchase statistic also includes small businesses, such as restaurants, who buy their eggs from retailers?

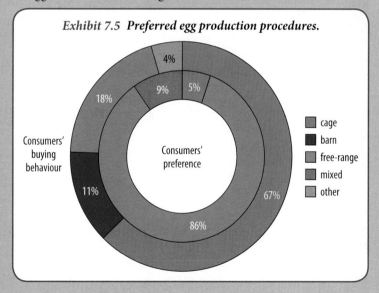

Exhibit 7.5 Preferred egg production procedures.

7.4 Communication methods compared

While there are commonalities among these approaches, several considerations are unique to each. Exhibit 7.6 provides an overview and the following sections will explain in detail.

The choice of a communication method is not as complicated as it might first appear. By comparing your research objectives with the strengths and weaknesses of each method, you will be able to choose one that is suited

Exhibit 7.6 Comparison of communication approaches.

	Personal interviews	Telephone interviews	Self-administered surveys	Web-based surveys
Description	People selected to be part of the sample are interviewed in person by trained interviewer	People selected to be part of the sample are interviewed on the telephone by a trained interviewer	Questionnaires are: a mailed, faxed or couriered to be self-administered – with return mechanism generally included b people intercepted/studied via paper in central location – without interviewer assistance	Questionnaires are: a emailed or accessible on a website, web server to be self-administered – with return mechanism generally included b surveys appear as a pop-up window on the computer screen
Advantages	• Good cooperation from respondents • Interviewer can answer questions about survey, probe for answers, use follow-up questions, and gather information by observation • Special visual aids and scoring devices can be used • Illiterate and functionally illiterate respondents can be reached • Interviewer can pre-screen respondent to ensure he or she fits the population profile • CAPI – computer-assisted personal interviewing: responses can be entered into a laptop to reduce error and cost	• Lower costs than personal interview • Expanded geographic coverage without dramatic increase in costs • Uses fewer, more highly skilled interviewers • Reduced interviewer bias • Fastest completion time • Better access to hard-to-reach respondents through repeated call-backs • Can use computerized random-digit dialling • CATI – computer-assisted telephone interviewing: responses can be entered directly into a computer file to reduce error and cost	• Allows contact with otherwise inaccessible respondents (e.g. CEOs) • Expanded geographic coverage without increase in costs • Requires minimal staff(a) • Perceived as more anonymous • Allows respondents time to think about questions (a) • More complex instruments can be used (a) • Rapid data collection (b) • Sample frame lists viable locations rather than prospective respondents (b) • Visuals may be used	• Allows contact with otherwise inaccessible respondents (e.g. CEOs) • Very low-cost option • Expanded geographic coverage without increase in costs • Requires minimal staff • Perceived as more anonymous • Allows respondents time to think about questions (a) • More complex instruments can be used (a) • Fast access to the computer-literate • Rapid data collection (b) • Respondent who cannot be reached by phone (voice) may be accessible • Sample frame lists viable locations rather than prospective respondents (a) • Visuals and movies may be used • Easy and inexpensive use of colours
Disadvantages	• High costs • Need for highly trained interviewers • Longer period needed in the field collecting data • May be wide geographic dispersion • Follow-up is labour-intensive • Not all respondents are available or accessible • Some respondents are unwilling to talk to strangers in their homes • Some neighbourhoods are difficult to visit • Questions may be altered or respondent coached by interviewers	• Response rate is lower than for personal interview • Interview length must be limited • Many phone numbers are unlisted or not working, making directory listings unreliable • Some target groups are not available by telephone • Responses may be less complete • Illustrations cannot be used	• Printing and postage costs • Low response rate in some modes • No interviewer intervention available for probing or explanation (a) • Cannot be too long or complex • Accurate mailing lists needed (a) • Often respondents returning survey represent extremes of the population – skewed responses (a) • Anxiety among some respondents (b) • Need for low-distraction environment for survey completion (b)	• Low response rate in some modes • No interviewer intervention available for probing or explanation • Cannot be long or complex • Accurate email addresses needed (a) • Often respondents returning survey represent extremes of the population – skewed responses • Anxiety among some respondents • Computer security • Need for low-distraction environment for survey completion (b)

to your needs. The summary of advantages and disadvantages of personal interviews, telephone interviews and self-administered questionnaires presented in Exhibit 7.6 should be useful in making such a comparison.

When your investigative questions call for information from hard-to-reach or inaccessible participants, the telephone interview, mail- or computer-delivered survey should be considered. However, if data must be collected very quickly, the mail survey is likely to be ruled out because of lack of control over the returns. Alternatively, you may decide that your objective requires extensive questioning and probing – then the personal interview should be considered.

If none of the choices turns out to be a particularly good fit, it is possible to combine the best characteristics of two or more alternatives into a mixed mode. Although this decision will incur the costs of the combined modes, the flexibility of tailoring a method to your unique needs is often an acceptable trade-off.

Ultimately, all researchers are confronted by the practical realities of cost and deadlines. As Exhibit 7.6 suggests, on average, personal interviews are the most expensive communication method and take the most field time unless a large field team is used. Telephone interviews are moderate in cost and offer the quickest option, especially when **computer-assisted telephone interviewing (CATI)** is used. Questionnaires administered by mail are the least expensive, although these traditionally require a longer data-collection period. When your desired sample is available via the Internet, emerging Internet surveying may prove to be the least expensive communication method with the most rapid (simultaneous) data availability. The use of the computer to select participants, and reduce coding and processing time will continue to improve the cost-to-performance profiles of these methods in the future.

Most of the time, an optimal method will be apparent. However, managers' needs for information often exceed their internal resources. Factors such as specialized expertise, a large field team, unique facilities or a rapid turnaround prompt organizations to seek assistance from research vendors of survey-related services.

7.5 Personal interviews

A **personal interview** (i.e. face-to-face communication) is a two-way conversation initiated by an interviewer to obtain information from a participant. The differences in the roles of interviewer and participant are pronounced. They are typically strangers, and the interviewer generally controls the topics and patterns of discussion. The consequences of the event are usually insignificant for the participant, who is asked to provide information but has little hope of receiving any immediate or direct benefit from this cooperation.

Evaluation of the personal interview

There are real advantages as well as clear limitations to personal interviewing. The greatest value lies in the depth of information and detail that can be secured. It far exceeds the information secured from telephone and self-administered studies, such as **mail surveys** or web surveys. The interviewer can also do more things to improve the quality of the information received than with another method.

The absence of assistance in interpreting questions is a clear weakness that can be improved by the presence of an interviewer. Interviewers can note conditions of the interview, probe with additional questions and gather supplemental information through observation.

Interviewers also have more control than is the case when using other kinds of interrogation. They can pre-screen to ensure the correct participant is replying, and they can set up and control interviewing conditions. They can use special scoring devices and visual materials, as is done with **computer-assisted personal interviewing (CAPI)**. Interviewers can also adjust the language of the interview as they observe any problems and the effects the interview is having on the participant.

With such advantages, why would anyone want to use any other survey method? Probably the greatest reason is that personal interviewing is costly, in terms of both money and time. A personal interview may cost anything from a few euros to several hundred for an interview with a hard-to-reach person. Costs are particularly high if the study covers a wide geographic area or has stringent sampling requirements.

An exception to this is the **intercept interview** that targets participants in centralized locations, such as shoppers in retail malls. Intercept interviews reduce the costs associated with travel. Product and service demonstrations can also be coordinated, further reducing costs. Their cost-effectiveness, however, is offset as samples for intercept interviews are usually not representative. Moreover, the surprise nature of intercept interviews limits the length and possible complexity of the interview considerably. Exhibit 7.7 offers some helpful tips when intercept interviews are an appropriate research design.

Exhibit 7.7 *Tips on intercept survey design.*

1 When screening for multiple studies at the same time, make your questionnaire distinctive:
   a use coloured paper
   b use paper with a distinctive coloured or patterned edge
2 Make surveys clipboard-friendly:
   a never print questions on both sides of the paper
   b keep font style and point size legible in inconsistent and dim light
   c confine your questionnaire to four pages or fewer
3 Write the 'respondent approach' section to include answers to the following often-asked questions:
   a What's the study about?
   b What's in it for me if I participate?
   c How long will it take?
4 Limit the number of screening questions (also known as 'screeners') to avoid participant termination:
   a keep screening question(s) to the point – ask only for critical data
   b build screening questions on facts, not assumptions or generalities
   c if you need to speak with the primary purchaser, don't specify gender, family status or age in the screeners
5 Keep screening question(s) safe from respondents' eyes:
   a choose normal, not bold, type style
   b put these in parenthesis or use another separation device
6 Don't overuse skip patterns: the more cumbersome the patterns, the more likely they won't be followed consistently or effectively.
7 Don't force the interviewer to remember responses to questions on previous pages in order to ask questions on the current page.
8 Tally where respondents terminate the screening process or survey:
   a include a horizontal string of question numbers at the bottom of each page so that the interviewer can circle the number of the next question after termination.

Source: www.quirks.com; E.B. Feltser, 'Pain-free mall intercepts', *Quirk's Marketing Research Review*, November 1996.

Costs

While professional interviewers' wage scales are typically not high, interviewing is still costly, and these costs continue to rise. Much of the cost results from the substantial interviewer time taken up with administrative and travel tasks. Participants are often geographically scattered, and this adds to the cost. Repeated contacts (recommended at six to nine per household) are expensive. In recent years, some professional research organizations have attempted to gain control of these spiralling costs. Interviewers have typically been paid an hourly rate, but this method rewards inefficient interviewers and often results in field costs exceeding budgets.[11] The alternative – to pay interviewers for each completed interview – is, however, also problematic, as this creates incentives to cut down interviewing time and even to falsify interviews.

Other bad news is that costs have risen rapidly in recent years for most communication methods because changes in the social climate have made personal interviewing more difficult. Many people today are reluctant to talk with strangers or to permit visits to their homes. Interviewers are reluctant to visit unfamiliar neighbourhoods alone, especially for evening interviewing. Finally, results of personal interviews can be affected adversely by interviewers who alter the questions asked or in other ways bias the results. (Interviewer bias is discussed in more depth later in this chapter.) If we are to overcome these deficiencies, we must appreciate the conditions necessary for interview success.

An approach for reducing field costs has been to pre-schedule personal interviews. Telephone calls to set up appointments for interviews are reported to reduce personal calls by 25 per cent without reducing cooperation rates.[12] Telephone screening is also valuable when a study is concerned with a rare population. In one such case, where blind persons were sought, it was found that telephone screening of households was one-third of the cost of screening on a face-to-face basis.[13]

A third means of reducing high field costs is to use self-administered questionnaires. In one study, a personal interview was conducted in the household with a self-administered questionnaire left for one or more other members of the household to complete. In this study, the cost per completed case was reduced by half when compared to conducting individual personal interviews. A comparison between a personal interview and a self-administered questionnaire seeking the same data showed that there was generally sufficient similarity of answers to enable them to be combined.[14]

Interviewing techniques

As mentioned before, interviewers have a crucial role in personal and telephone interviews. The success of a study depends on the interpersonal and communication skills of the interviewers. Having explained the purpose of the study, and so on in the introductory section and having established an initial rapport, the interviewer can turn to the technical task of gathering information. The interview centres on a prearranged question sequence. The technical task is well defined in studies with a structured survey procedure (in contrast to an exploratory interview situation). The interviewer should follow the exact wording of the questions, ask them in the order presented and ask every question that is specified. If any questions are misunderstood or misinterpreted, they should be repeated.

A difficult task in interviewing is to make certain the answers satisfy the question's objectives adequately. To do this, the interviewer must learn the objectives of each question from a study of the survey instructions or by asking the research project director. It is important to bear this information in mind because many first responses are inadequate even in the best-planned studies.

The technique of stimulating participants to answer more fully and relevantly is termed **probing**. Since it presents a great potential for bias, a probe should be neutral and appear as a natural part of the conversation. Appropriate probes (those that, when used, will elicit the desired information while injecting a limited amount of bias) should be specified by the designer of the data-collection instrument. There are several different probing styles, as outlined below:

- A brief assertion of understanding and interest: with comments such as 'I see', 'yes' or 'uh' or 'aha', the interviewer can let the participant know that she or he is listening and is interested in hearing more.
- An expectant pause: the simplest way to encourage the participant to say more is to pause, along with an expectant look or a nod of the head. This approach must be used with caution: some participants have nothing more to say, and frequent pausing could create some embarrassing silences and make them feel uncomfortable, reducing their willingness to participate further.
- Repeating the question: this is particularly useful when the participant appears not to understand the question or has strayed from the subject.
- Repeating the participant's reply: the interviewer can do this while writing it down. Such repetition often serves as a good probe. Hearing thoughts restated often promotes revision or further comment.
- A neutral question or comment: such comments make a direct bid for more information; for example, 'How do you mean?' 'Can you tell me more about your thinking on that?' 'Why do you think that is so?' and 'Anything else?'.[15]
- Question clarification: when the answer is unclear or is inconsistent with something already said, the interviewer may suggest that the participant failed to understand fully. Typical of such probes is, 'I'm not quite sure I know what you mean by that – could you tell me a little more?' or 'I'm sorry, but I'm not sure I understand. Did you say previously that . . . ?' It is important that the interviewer take the blame for this failure to understand so as not to appear to be cross-examining the participant.

A specific type of response that requires persistent probing is the 'I don't know' answer. This is a satisfactory response if the participant really does not know. Too often, however, 'I don't know' means the participant does not understand, wants time to think or is trying to evade the question. The interviewer can best probe this type of reply by using the expectant pause or by making a reassuring remark such as 'We are interested in your ideas about this.'[16]

Recording the interview

While the methods used in recording will vary, the interviewer usually writes down the participant's answers. The following guidelines show how to make this task more efficient. First, record responses as they occur. If the interviewer waits until later, they will lose much of what is said. If there is a time constraint, the interviewer should use some sort of shorthand system that will preserve the essence of the participant's replies without converting them into the interviewer's paraphrases. Abbreviating words, leaving out articles and prepositions, and using only keywords are good ways to do this.

Another technique is for the interviewer to repeat the response while writing it down. This helps to hold the participant's interest during the writing and checks the interviewer's understanding of what the participant said. Normally the interviewer should start the writing when the participant begins to reply. The interviewer should also record all probes and other comments on the questionnaire in parenthesis to separate them from the responses.

Study designers sometimes create a special interview instrument for recording participant answers. This may be integrated with the interview questions or may be a separate document. In such instances the likely answers are anticipated, allowing the interviewer to check participant answers or to record ranks or ratings. However, all interview instruments must permit the entry of unexpected responses.

Response error

When the data reported differ from the actual data, **response error** occurs. Response error can occur during the interview (created by either the interviewer or participant) or during the preparation of data for analysis.

Participant-initiated error occurs when the participant fails to answer fully and accurately – either by choice, or because of inaccurate or incomplete knowledge. One study found that participants typically underestimated cash and other liquid assets by as much as 25–50 per cent. Other data, such as income and purchases of consumer durables, are more accurately reported. Participants also have difficulty in reporting fully and accurately on topics that are sensitive or involve ego matters. Consistent control or elimination of this bias is a problem that has yet to be solved. The best advice is to use trained interviewers who are knowledgeable about such problems.

Interviewer error is also a major source of response bias. From the introduction to the conclusion of the interview, there are many points where the interviewer's control of the process can affect the quality of the data. Study designers should strive to eliminate several different kinds of error, as outlined below, evolving from the interview techniques discussed above:

- Failure to secure full participant cooperation: the sample loses credibility and is likely to be biased if interviewers do not do a good job of enlisting participant cooperation.
- Failure to consistently execute interview procedures: the precision of survey estimates will be reduced and there will be more error around estimates to the extent that interviewers are inconsistent in ways that influence the data. Interview procedures are especially important if the interviews are conducted by different interviewers, as is common in larger surveys.
- Failure to establish appropriate interview environment: answers may be systematically inaccurate or biased when interviewers fail to 'train' and motivate participants appropriately or fail to establish a suitable interpersonal setting.[17]
- Falsification of individual answers or whole interviews: perhaps the most insidious form of interviewer error is cheating. Surveying is difficult work, often done by part-time employees, usually with only limited training and

under little direct supervision. At times, falsification of an answer to an overlooked question is perceived as an easy solution to counterbalance the incomplete data. This easy, seemingly harmless first step can be followed by more pervasive forgery. It is not known how much of this occurs, but it should be of constant concern to research directors as they develop their data-collection design, and to those organizations that outsource survey projects. Falsifications of the interview also include the skipping of questions, either because they are difficult to ask or because they take a lot of time. One of the authors of this book recalls being interviewed for a market research survey on travel. One of the questions asked him was to list all the foreign countries he had visited in the past two years. When he had named five countries, the interviewer stopped him saying that for each named country he now wished to ask a couple of additional questions.

- Inappropriate influencing behaviour: it is obvious that an interviewer can distort the results of any survey by inappropriate suggestions, word emphasis, tone of voice, body language and question rephrasing. These activities, whether premeditated or merely due to carelessness, are widespread. This problem was investigated using a simple structured questionnaire and 'planted' participants, who then reported on the interviewers. The conclusion was that 'the high frequency of deviations from instructed behaviour is alarming'.[18] In the travel survey mentioned above, the interviewer also suggested that the author answer a question on the total costs of a trip to a specific country with the option 'don't know', as – according to him – nobody knows exactly the total costs of such a trip. He was right: most people will have difficulty in recollecting the exact cost of a trip. However, a good interviewer will never suggest the 'don't know' option, but will instead ask for a reasonable estimate if the respondent does not know the exact answer.
- Failure to record answers accurately and completely: error may result from an interview recording procedure that forces the interviewer to summarize or interpret participant answers, or that provides insufficient space to record answers as provided by the participant.
- Physical presence bias: interviewers can influence participants in unperceived ways. Older interviewers are often seen as authority figures by young participants, who modify their responses accordingly. Some research indicates that perceived social distance between interviewer and participant has a distorting effect, although the studies do not fully agree on just what this relationship is.[19]

In light of the numerous studies on the various aspects of interview bias, the safest course for researchers is to recognize that there is constant potential for response error.

 ## 7.6 Telephone interviews

The telephone can be helpful in arranging personal interviews and screening large populations for unusual types of participants. Studies have also shown that making prior notification calls can improve the response rates of mail surveys. However, the telephone interview makes its greatest contribution in survey work as a unique mode of communication to collect information from participants.

Evaluation of the telephone interview

Of the advantages that telephone interviewing offers, probably none ranks higher than its moderate cost. One study reports that sampling and data-collection costs for telephone surveys can run from 45 to 64 per cent lower than comparable personal interviews.[20] Much of this saving comes from cuts in travel costs and administrative savings from training and supervision. When calls are made from a single location, the researcher may use fewer yet more skilled interviewers. Telephones are especially economical when call-backs to maintain probability sampling are involved and participants are widely scattered. Long-distance service options make it possible to interview nationally, and even internationally, at a reasonable cost.

With the widespread use of computers, telephone interviewing can be combined with immediate entry of responses into a data file by means of terminals, PCs or voice data entry. This brings added savings in time and money. Computer-assisted telephone interviewing (CATI) is used in research organizations throughout the world. A CATI facility consists of acoustically isolated interviewing carrels organized around supervisory stations. The telephone interviewer in each carrel has a PC or terminal that is networked to the telephone system and to the central data-processing unit. A software program that prompts the interviewers with introductory statements, qualifying questions and pre-coded questionnaire items drives surveying. These materials appear on the interviewers' monitors. CATI works with a telephone number management system to select numbers, dial the sample and enter responses.

Another means of securing immediate response data is the **computer-administered telephone survey**. Unlike CATI, there is no interviewer. A computer calls the telephone number, conducts the interview, places data into a file for later tabulation and terminates the contact. The questions are voice-synthesized, and the participant's answer and computer timing trigger continuation or disconnect. Advancements in IT technology including voice recognition have improved such systems tremendously and specialized firms, e.g. SurveyMonkeys, offer such services for a moderate cost (about 10 cents per call). This mode is often compared to the self-administered questionnaire (discussed later in this chapter) and offers the advantage of participant privacy. One study showed that the **non-contact rate** for the electronic survey mode is similar to other telephone interviews when a random telephone list is used. It also found that rejection of this mode of data collection affects the **refusal rate** (and thus non-response bias) because people will hang up more readily on a computer than on a human.[21] The non-contact rate is a ratio of potential but unreached contacts (no answer, busy, answering machine, and disconnects but not refusals) to all potential contacts. The refusal rate refers to the ratio of participants who decline the interview to all potential contacts.

When compared to either personal interviews or mail surveys, the use of telephones brings faster completion of a study, sometimes taking only a day or so for the fieldwork. When compared to personal interviewing, it is also likely that interviewer bias – especially bias caused by the physical appearance, body language and actions of the interviewer – is reduced by using the telephone.

There are also disadvantages to using the telephone for research. A skilled researcher will evaluate the use of a telephone survey to minimize the effect of the following disadvantages:

- inaccessible households (no telephone service)
- inaccurate or non-functioning numbers
- limitation on interview length (fewer measurement questions)
- limitations on use of visual or complex questions
- ease of interview termination
- less participant involvement
- distracting physical environment.

We will now look at each of these in turn.

Inaccessible households

Many households move each year, generating many obsolete numbers and new households for which numbers have not yet been published. Also, individuals increasingly opt to have unlisted numbers. Another recent problem encountered in telephone surveys is the increasing number of people who only have a mobile telephone, but no fixed-line subscription. In some European countries (e.g. in the UK, Belgium and Portugal) the number of main fixed telephone lines is actually declining, while subscriptions to mobile telephone services are rising every year. In 2000, subscription to mobile telephones (235 million) exceeded the number of fixed telephone lines (204 million) for the first time in the EU member states.[22] Ten years later, there were almost three times more mobile subscriptions than fixed lines in Europe (726 million mobile and 263 million fixed lines). In 2012, Finland, the front runner in mobile phone penetration, had 173 subscriptions per 100 inhabitants followed by Austria with 161. In Germany and the UK, each inhabitant had 1.31 mobile subscriptions and France is the only EU country that has fewer mobile subscriptions than inhabitants – its penetration rate is 98 per cent.[23] Although people carry their mobile telephones with them most of the time and are therefore easily contactable, most research agencies have been reluctant to contact people on their mobile telephones, as it is impossible to know what they are doing and where they are when called. Such variations in participant availability by telephone is a source of bias, as for example, more and more younger people only have a mobile subscription.

Research Methods in Real Life

Mobile phone technology – opportunity or threat?

The mobile phone already celebrates its 40th birthday. The first mobile phones were the size of a large briefcase and could only be used as a phone. Today the majority of mobile phones are smartphones that combine a phone, video camera and a small computer. For a long time, the increasing penetration of mobile phones had been worrying for researchers, especially those who relied heavily on phone surveys. Ten years ago almost every household in Western countries had a fixed-line phone and consequently the phone directory was a pretty good representation of the population in a country. This has changed as more and more people do not own a fixed line anymore. One large group of only-mobile-phone users are students. Thus, fixed-line phone directories are not anymore representative and up to now there is no alternative directory. You might think that almost everybody has an email account, but this does still not apply to the elderly, and reliable email directories do not exist. Mobile telecommunication has changed the world and also how research needs to be done.

What is often neglected are the opportunities that mobile phones and especially smartphones offer. The distinctive feature of a smartphone is the so-called 'app', an executable application. Currently, for all operating systems, thousands of useful and less useful apps exist. Many of these apps are free or available for just a few euros. Data collection and the selling of the collected data is part of the business model of some apps. Supermarkets offer free apps that show the user weekly special offers and help them to find the next shop. In return, the supermarkets get detailed information which special offers the user looked at, and whether the user visited a shop or even a competitor's shop. These kind of apps produce 'big data' (see also Chapter 9 on big data) and offer detailed information on consumer behaviour.

While smartphone users often do not realize that they reveal a lot of information about themselves by using an app, other apps have been developed to conduct surveys. Internet surveys have existed for a long time and, thus, it is not a surprise that this idea has shifted to the smartphone environment. The biggest limitation for app-based surveys is often the screen size of the mobile devices. Nielsen, one of the biggest market research companies, has conducted a couple of experiments to investigate which features app-based surveys should have and how mobile surveys perform compared to classical web-based surveys. Their conclusions were:

- mobile surveys need to be accustomed to the size of the screen, that means short questions
- not too many answer categories (avoid the respondent having to scroll)
- short questionnaires
- avoid grid items.

These suggestions seem to be common sense given the screen limitations. The shorter answer lists also prevented the occurrence of primacy effects (see Chapter 13). What was surprising, however, was that mobile survey respondents are equally likely to respond to open questions as respondents using a computer. And more surprising was that response rates were higher and break-off rates lower compared to other delivery modes. Thus mobile technology indeed offers new opportunities for researchers, but we need to adapt to them.

References and further reading

www.nielsen.com

Inaccurate or non-functioning numbers

Several methods have been developed to overcome the deficiencies of directories; among them are techniques for choosing telephone numbers by using random-digit dialling or combinations of directories and random-digit dialling.[24] **Random dialling** procedures normally require choosing telephone exchanges or exchange blocks and then generating random numbers within these blocks for calling.[25] However, increasing demand for multiple telephone lines by both households and individuals has generated new telephone area codes and local exchanges. This too increases the inaccuracy rate. It should also be noted that using random dialling procedures is forbidden by law in some countries, such as the Netherlands.

Limitation on interview length

A limit on interview length is another disadvantage of the telephone, but the degree of this limitation depends on the participant's interest in the topic. Ten minutes has generally been thought of as ideal, but interviews of 20 minutes or more are not uncommon. Interviews ran for one and a half hours in one long-distance survey.[26]

Limitations on use of visual or complex questions

In telephone interviewing, it is difficult to use maps, illustrations, visual aids, complex scales or measurement techniques (however, in some instances, these might be supplied via email prior to the pre-scheduled interview). The medium also limits the complexity of the survey and the use of visualization techniques possible with personal interviewing. For example, in personal interviews, participants are sometimes asked to sort or rank an array of cards containing different responses to a question. For participants who cannot visualize a scale or other measurement device that the interview is attempting to describe, one solution has been to employ a nine-point scaling approach and to ask the participant to visualize it by using the telephone dial or keypad.[27] In the future and with the spreading of video phoning these limitations will be overcome.

Ease of interview termination

Some studies suggest that the response rate in telephone studies is lower than for comparable face-to-face interviews. One reason is that participants find it easier to terminate a telephone interview. Telemarketing practices may also contribute. Public reaction to investigative reports of wrongdoing and unethical behaviour within telemarketing activities places an added burden on the researcher, who must try to convince a participant that the telephone interview is not a pretext for soliciting contributions or selling products.

Less participant involvement

Telephone surveys can result in less-thorough responses, and those interviewed by telephone find the experience to be less rewarding than a personal interview. Participants report less rapport with telephone interviewers than with personal interviewers. Given the growing costs and difficulties of personal interviews, it is likely that an even higher share of surveys will be by telephone in the future. Thus, it is the responsibility of management researchers using telephone surveys to attempt to improve the enjoyment of the interview. One authority suggests that:

> "We need to experiment with techniques to improve the enjoyment of the interview by the participant, maximize the overall completion rate, and minimize response error on specific measures. This work might fruitfully begin with efforts at translating into verbal messages the visual cues that fill the interaction in a face-to-face interview: the smiles, frowns, raising of eyebrows, eye contact, etc. All of these cues have informational content and are important parts of the personal interview setting. We can perhaps purposefully choose those cues that are most important to data quality and participant trust and discard the many that are extraneous to the survey interaction."[28]

Distracting physical environment

Speculation has also surfaced with regard to the increasing practice of substituting one's home or office telephone with mobile telephones. In terms of telephone surveys, this raises concerns about the changing environment in which such surveys might be conducted. With a fixed line, you reach respondents always at their homes. If you use a mobile number, you do not know where you reach your respondent and concerns arise regarding the quality of data collected under possibly distracting circumstances, and the possible increase in refusal rates.

7.7 Self-administered surveys

The **self-administered questionnaire** has become ubiquitous in modern living. Service evaluations of hotels, restaurants, car dealerships and transportation providers furnish ready examples. Often, a short questionnaire is left to be completed by the participant in a convenient location or is packaged with a product. Self-administered mail surveys are delivered not only by national mail firms, such as Royal Mail and Deutsche Post, but also via fax and courier service. Other methods of distribution include intercept studies, in which the researcher hands short questionnaires to passers-by, for example, in a shopping mall (see section 7.5) and web-based surveys (see section 7.8).

Evaluation of self-administered surveys

Much of what researchers know about self-administered surveys has been learned from experiments conducted with mail surveys and personal experience. So as we explore the strengths and weaknesses of the various self-administered methods, we will start with this body of knowledge.

Costs

Self-administered surveys of all types typically cost less than personal interviews. Telephone and mail costs are in the same general range, although in specific cases either may be lower. It should be noted, however, that the time involved in collecting the information is much greater for telephone surveys, which increases the costs substantially if the interviewers have to be paid. A mail survey costs less because it is often a one-person job.

Sample accessibility

Another advantage of using mail is that researchers can contact participants who might otherwise be inaccessible. Some people – such as major corporate executives or doctors – are difficult to reach in person or by telephone, as gatekeepers (secretaries, office managers and assistants) limit access. Researchers can, however, often access these special participants by mail. When the researcher has no specific person to contact – say, in a study of corporations – the mail or computer-delivered survey may be routed to the appropriate participant. Questionnaires sent to a corporation without a personal name will often not be returned as the general mail office of the corporation might not know to whom the questionnaire should be forwarded. Furthermore, the researcher cannot control whether the appropriate person answered the questionnaire. If you do not have personal names, the second-best solution is to address the questionnaire to a certain job function, such as 'head of the sales department'. This is more effective if the corporation is not too large, because large corporations may have hundreds of heads of sales departments. In general, it is advisable to put considerable effort into finding out the personal names of the people you want to contact.

Response time

While telephone surveys pressure participants to answer immediately, mail survey participants can postpone their response. This is a double-edged sword. The possibility to postpone a response improves survey quality if respondents interrupt their answering to collect facts, talk with others or consider replies at length. It reduces survey quality, however, if a postponed response turns into a non-response or people answer a questionnaire in chunked parts.

Anonymity

Mail surveys are typically perceived as more impersonal, providing greater anonymity than the other communication modes, including other methods for distributing self-administered questionnaires. For example, in the Dutch Family Survey, researchers interviewed the head of the household and his or her spouse with a combination of personal interview and self-administered questionnaire. The self-administered questionnaire included questions on satisfaction with their relationship and their partner, which respondents might understandably have been reluctant to answer honestly if the partner were present!

Topic coverage

A major limitation of self-administered surveys concerns the type and amount of information that can be secured. Researchers normally do not expect to obtain large amounts of information and cannot probe too deeply into topics. Participants will generally refuse to cooperate with a long and/or complex mail, computer-delivered or intercept questionnaire unless they perceive a personal benefit. Returned mail questionnaires with many questions left unanswered testify to this problem, but there are also many exceptions. One general rule of thumb is that the participant should be able to answer the questionnaire in no more than 10 minutes (similar to the guidelines proposed for telephone studies). On the other hand, one study of the general population found more than a 70 per cent response to a questionnaire calling for 158 answers.[29]

Non-response error in mail and web-based surveys

Another major weakness of the self-administered and web-based study is non-response error. Many studies have shown that better-educated participants and those more interested in the topic answer mail surveys. A high percentage of those who reply to a given survey have usually replied to others, while a large share of those who do not respond are habitual non-participants.[30] Response rates of business firms also differ considerably between countries: in general they are higher in Japan than in Europe, and higher in Europe than in the US.[31] In either case, there are many non-respondents, and we usually know nothing about how those who answer differ from those who do not.

Reducing non-response error

The research literature is filled with ways to improve mail survey returns, and much of this knowledge may be applied to other modes of delivering self-administered surveys. Seemingly every possible variable has been studied. Over 200 methodological articles have been published on efforts to improve mail response rates. Three review articles concluded that few variables consistently showed positive response rates.[32] Several practical suggestions emerge from the conclusions.[33]

Follow-ups

Follow-ups, or reminders, are very successful in increasing response rates. Since each successive follow-up produces more returns, the very persistent (and well-financed) researcher can potentially achieve an extremely high total response rate. However, the value of additional information thus obtained must be weighed against the costs required for successive contacts.

Preliminary notification

There is evidence that advance notification, particularly by telephone, is effective in increasing response rates; it also serves to accelerate the rate of return. However, follow-ups are a better investment than preliminary notification.

Concurrent techniques

1 Questionnaire length: although common sense suggests that short questionnaires should obtain higher response rates than longer questionnaires, research evidence does not support this view.
2 Survey sponsorship: there is little experimental evidence concerning the influence of survey sponsorship on response rates; however, the sparse evidence that does exist suggests that official or 'respected' sponsorship increases response rates.
3 Return envelopes and postage for mail-surveys: the inclusion of a stamped addressed envelope encourages response because it simplifies questionnaire return. Many tests regarding postage are reported in the literature, but few studies have tested the same variables. The existing evidence shows that expedited delivery is very effective in increasing response rates. Findings do not show a significant advantage for first class over third class, for commemorative stamps over ordinary postage, for stamped mail over metered mail or for multiple small denomination stamps over single larger denomination stamps.
4 Personalization: personalization of the mailing has no clear-cut advantage in terms of improved response rates. Neither personal inside addresses nor individually signed cover letters significantly increased response rates; personally typed cover letters proved to be somewhat effective in most but not all cases cited. The one study that tested the use of a titled signature versus one without a title did show a significant advantage in favour of the title.

5 Cover letters: the influence of the cover letter on response rates has received almost no experimental attention, although the cover letter is considered an integral part of the mail survey package. It is the most logical vehicle for persuading individuals to respond, yet the few studies that are reported offer no insights as to its formulation.

6 Anonymity: experimental evidence shows that the promise of anonymity to participants, either explicit or implied, has no significant effect on response rates.

7 Size, reproduction and colour: the few studies that examined the effects of questionnaire size, method of reproduction and colour found no significant difference in response rates.

8 Money incentives: a monetary incentive sent with the questionnaire is very effective in increasing response rates. Larger sums bring in added response, but at a cost that may exceed the value of the added information. In studies among organizations in particular, an interesting incentive is to promise the respondent a report highlighting the findings of the research. You might even choose to offer a customized report, which compares the respondent's answers with the average of the sample or a specified sub-sample.

9 Deadline dates: the few studies that tested the impact of deadline dates found that they did not increase the response rate; however, they did serve to accelerate the rate of questionnaire return.

Deeper Insight into Research Methods
Total design method (TDM)

Researchers are equivocal about the above suggestions and conclusions because 'the manipulation of one or two techniques independently of all others may do little to stimulate response'.[34] Efforts should be directed towards the more important question of maximizing the overall probability of response. The total design method (TDM), consisting of two parts, is proposed to meet this need.[35] First, the researcher must identify the aspects of the survey process that affect the response rate, either qualitatively or quantitatively. Each aspect must be shaped to obtain the best response. Second, the researcher must organize the survey effort so the design intentions are carried out in detail. The results achieved in 48 surveys using TDM showed response rates of 50–94 per cent, with a median response rate of 74 per cent.[36] TDM procedures suggest minimizing the burden on participants by designing surveys that:

- are easy to read
- offer clear response directions
- include personalized communication
- provide information about the survey in a cover letter (or via advance notification)
- are followed by researcher contacts to encourage response.[37]

Maximizing response

To maximize the overall probability of response, attention must be given to each point of the survey process where the response may break down.[38] For example:

- the wrong (email) address and wrong postage can result in non-delivery or non-return
- the envelope or fax cover sheet may look like junk mail and be discarded without being opened
- lack of proper instructions for completion may lead to non-response
- the wrong person may receive the envelope or email and fail to call it to the attention of the right person
- a participant may find no convincing explanation for completing the survey and thus discard it
- a participant may temporarily set the questionnaire aside and fail to complete it.
- the return address may be lost so the questionnaire cannot be returned.

Efforts to overcome these problems will vary according to the circumstances, but some general suggestions can be made for mail surveys and, by extension, for self-administered questionnaires using different delivery modes. With a questionnaire, a cover letter and return mechanism should be sent. Incentives, such as euro notes, gift coupons or prepaid phone cards, are often attached to the letter in commercial studies. Follow-ups are usually needed to get the maximum response. Opinions differ about the number and timing of follow-ups – in general, the timing of follow-ups should be adapted for different delivery modes. TDM uses the follow-ups described below.

▶

1 One week later: a pre-printed postcard or email is sent to all recipients thanking them for returns and reminding others to complete and mail the questionnaire.
2 Three weeks after the original mailing: a new questionnaire is sent, along with a letter telling nonparticipants that the questionnaire has not been received and repeating the basic appeal of the original letter.
3 Seven weeks after the original mailing: a third cover letter and questionnaire are sent by certified mail to the remaining non-participants of mail surveys and by regular mail to the non-participants of web-based surveys.

An appeal for cooperation is essential and may be altruistic or more expedient. The former is often found when the questionnaire is short, easy to complete and does not require much effort from a participant. Anonymity may or may not be mentioned. A brief letter emphasizes the 'Would you do me a favour?' approach. Often a token is sent to symbolize the researcher's appreciation. Sometimes this is not powerful enough. Then an appeal must stress how important the problem is to a group with which the participant identifies.

The cover letter should also convey that the participant's help is needed to solve a problem. Researchers are portrayed as reasonable people making a reasonable appeal for help. They are intermediaries between the person asked for help and an important issue. The total effect must be personalized to convey to participants that they are important to the study. The standard is to make the appeal comparable in appearance and content to what one would expect in a business or professional letter.

Finally, a mixed model can be used to improve response. One study compared the use of 'drop-off' delivery of a questionnaire to a mail survey.[39] Under the drop-off system, a lightly trained survey-taker personally delivered the questionnaires to target households and returned in a couple of days for the completed instrument. Response rates for the drop-off system were typically above 70 per cent – much higher than for comparable mail surveys. In addition, the cost per completed questionnaire was from 18 to 40 per cent lower than for mail surveys.

Student Research
Mixed methods and business angels

Before preparing for his final study year, Samuel Buckley engaged in a three-month internship in the private banking department of a large national bank. During that internship, Samuel learned that banks do not only provide finance to start-up companies from their own sources, but also often only advise wealthy clients on such investment opportunities. These experiences triggered Samuel to investigate informal investors more closely, as not much is known about these investors, also called business angels, especially outside the USA.

While the bank would not give Samuel a list of their clients that were business angels, the bank was willing to send a questionnaire to the 72 clients that had invested informally in start-ups on the advice of the bank. Although response rates for mailed questionnaires are usually rather low, 24 per cent of the contacted clients responded. Still 17 responses were too little to conduct any meaningful quantitative analysis.

Along with his contacts through his internship, Samuel attended the final ceremony of a local business plan competition to find additional informal investors. During that event he was able to schedule four personal interviews with business angels. In those personal interviews Samuel asked the same questions as in the questionnaire mailed to the bank clients. However, at the end of each interview he asked the business angel, whether she or he would know another business angel that would be interested in participating in his research. Through this snowball sampling, Samuel could contact an additional 41 business angels. Six of them he spoke to in a personal interview, while the remaining 35 were interviewed on phone. Again he asked the same questions as in the mailed questionnaire to the bank clients.

What do you think about using different approaches for the same study? Does Samuel accumulate the disadvantages or the advantages of the three approaches? Can Samuel compare the data collected by different means? Given the problems of using different approaches, what are the potential benefits?

Beyond a higher response rate and lower cost per response, the drop-off delivery gives greater control over sample design, permits thorough identification of the participants' geographic location and allows the researcher to eliminate those who fall outside a predefined sample frame (persons of the wrong age, income or other characteristics). Additional information can be gathered by observation on the visits. However, the cost advantage is probably restricted to studies where participants can be reached with little travel.

Drop-off delivery has much in common with intercept studies that employ self-administered completion of a questionnaire. The researcher can encourage the selected participant to complete the questionnaire, stressing the importance of his or her participation and the ease of completion, and then indicate the procedure for returning it. These activities are likely to increase response rates and reduce non-response error.

In business research, the respondents are often organizations – for example individuals representing a company – and not private persons. As the respondents are representatives of an organization their willingness to respond does not only depend on their motivation, but also on their capacity and authority to respond (in large organizations in particular, the required knowledge is often spread over different persons and departments). Authority to respond is another problem when approaching organizations (e.g. subsidiaries are less likely to respond). Surveying organizations require that specificities of organizational research are considered in the survey design. In particular, researchers should take into account the following points:[40]

- Is asking for financial information really necessary for the purpose of the study? Asking for such information can trigger non-response and you might be able to obtain basic financial information through secondary sources.
- If you approach a subsidiary, you need to clarify that you are interested in the specific subsidiary and not the company as a whole. Otherwise such organizations might not respond as they feel that they are not authorized to respond or think that they do not have the information.
- As with all other surveys, people might be reluctant to answer as filling in the survey takes time. A very useful strategy in this context is to ask the top management for cooperation in the study. They can help to identify respondents in the organization but, more importantly, if they support a survey in their organization people feel obliged to answer.

7.8 Web-based surveys

In 2011, 74 per cent of the population in Europe had Internet access at home. However, the percentage of Internet use differs considerably between countries: while in Scandinavian countries more than 90 per cent of the population uses the Internet, in Greece, Hungary and Romenia, just 56, 58 and 50 per cent, respectively, of the people use the Internet in 2012.[41] Is it any wonder that computer-delivered self-administered surveys have caught the imagination of business (see Exhibit 7.8)?

Computer surveying is surfacing at trade shows, where participants complete surveys while making a visit to a company's stand. Continuous tabulation of results provides a stimulus for attendees to visit a particular exhibit as well as giving the exhibitor detailed information for evaluating the productivity of the show. This same technology transfers easily to other situations where large groups of people congregate.

Companies are now using intranet capabilities to evaluate employee policies and behaviour. Ease of access to electronic mail systems makes it possible for both large and small organizations to use computer questioning with both internal and external participant groups. Many techniques of traditional mail surveys can easily be adapted to computer-delivered questionnaires (e.g. follow-ups to non-participants are more easily executed and are less expensive).

It is not unusual to find registration procedures and full-scale surveying being done on the World Wide Web. University sites are asking prospective students about their interests, and university departments are evaluating current students' use of online materials. A short surf on the Internet reveals organizations using their sites to evaluate customer service processes, build sales-lead lists, evaluate planned promotions and product changes, determine supplier and customer needs, discover interest in job openings, evaluate employee attitudes, and more. Advanced and easier-to-use software for designing web surveys can also be found.

Web-based surveys are a special form of self-administered surveys and their advantages and disadvantages are rather similar to those of mail surveys. However, some important differences will be discussed in this section. More specifically, one can distinguish the following types of web-based surveys.

1 Target web survey: here the researcher retains control over who is allowed to participate in the survey. The researcher sends invitations to specified and selected persons to participate in the survey, either by sending a survey in an email or by sending a web link to a survey server. Although not suited for student projects, it should be noted that many research agencies have access to so-called 'web panels', i.e. they have a large group of people who regularly answer survey requests from them, usually for a small amount of money or for the chance to win a prize, such as an iPad.

2 Self-selected surveys: here the researcher has no or very limited control on who is responding to the survey. The classical example is a window that pops up on your computer screen when you visit some websites inviting you to participate in an online survey. If self-selected surveys are used, it is important to use a couple of questions to ensure that one can ex-post identify whether the respondent belonged to the target group. Moreover, one should include quality checks on the reliability of the answers; for example, asking reversed questions or identifying strange answer patterns, such as filling in '3' on all Likert scales in a questionnaire. A further issue is that one needs to ensure that nobody can answer the questionnaire more than once. Storing the IP address of the respondent is one option to avoid a double answer or at least to identify them ex-post.

3 Social-media-based surveys: in between target and self-selected surveys are surveys that use social media sites, such as Facebook, LinkedIn, Xing, Twitter, to reach potential respondents. The researcher posts a note in their social media account and asks people to participate in the survey and to spread it among their friends and followers. What develops then is a kind of a snowball sampling system (see Chapter 6) where you do not only approach friends, but also friends of friends of friends. Such snowball samples increase the dissemination of your survey considerably at the cost of having less control over who enters the sample. However, you can regain some control by defining well the kind of respondents required and who to approach in the first step. In a recent student research, Olga was interested how consultants cope with the immense work pressure. She designed a web survey and sent the link to her brother, who worked as a consultant, and to classmates who just had taken jobs in the consultancy sectors and asked her first contacts to spread the link with other colleagues. To ensure that only consultants would enter the survey, Olga included a filter question in which she asked what kind of job the person was doing. Olga started with contacts to five consultants she knew and in the end she had responses from 147 people and 139 of those responses were valid, i.e. came from people working as consultants.

Evaluation of web-based surveys

Web-based surveys offer many features that are attractive from a survey quality perspective, but sometimes they are also unattractive. As web-based surveys use the telecommunication infrastructure that connects the world, their reach and speed are similar to telephone interviews, but they offer even more design features than self-administered questionnaires. Once a questionnaire is designed, market agencies promise to have responses from a couple of hundred people within a few days. Although this speed can also be reached by phone interviews, the required effort is much greater as you need a large interviewer pool to phone hundreds of respondents. Given the speed and the low cost, web-based surveys allow you also to contact people more frequently. Given the call for more longitudinal research in academia, this possibility makes web-based surveys also very attractive for more scientific research. Moreover, web-based surveys allow you to approach populations that are geographically widely spread or far away. Next to speed and range, the tremendous amount of design possibilities are an additional bonus for web-based surveys. For example, other media elements, such as photographs, small video and audio clips, can be easily embedded. It is also easy and almost costless to produce questionnaires using different colours, which gives web-based surveys a more professional appearance and makes them more appealing to respondents.

The biggest challenge of web-based questionnaires from a methodological view point is whether you draw the right sample. All other approaches discussed here draw a sample of well-defined directories, such as phone directories or address databanks. Even if you use a target web survey, the quality of email address databanks is often questionable. Assume you want to send a questionnaire to a sales director of a medium-sized company. Usually it is easy to find databases with the name of the sales director and the company's address and once you send a letter, you can at least be sure that the letter reaches the director's secretary. But those address databases rarely contain personal email accounts, but just general email accounts, such as info@company.com. The chances that a questionnaire or link sent to such an account is replied are close to zero. Web-based surveys are built on information technology and despite the many advantages discussed above, technology also creates challenges. First, as a researcher you need to acquire some basic knowledge on web survey technology. Although software packages and websites discussed below have made the technology accessible for many, it will always take some time until you are accustomed to such programs. Second, the compatibility of the software with the IT devices a respondent uses is often not 100 per cent. For example whether a respondent opens a web survey on a tablet or standard PC makes a large difference and you often need to design different questionnaires that are compatible with different operating systems. But even within one operating system, the appearance of a questionnaire will differ depending on the respondents' screen size and width, whether they use an English keyboard or a keyboard designed for a different language. Special characters, like currency symbols, such as € and £, or special letters such as ä, å, æ, ç, ê, ï, ø, ÿ and many more which are uncommon in English but very common in other languages, might not appear correctly on the respondent's screen. Many of these technological issues can be overcome, but it requires more effort and often specialized computer expertise, which does not come cheap. Exhibit 7.8 summarizes the mentioned advantages and disadvantages and links them to examples from real life.

Exhibit 7.8 The web as a research venue.[42]

Web attractions	Example
Short turnaround of results; results are tallied as respondents complete surveys	A soft-drink manufacturer got results from a web survey in just five days
Ability to use visual stimuli	Florida's tourism office used eye-movement tracking to enhance its website and improve its billboard and print ads
Ability to do numerous surveys over time	A printer manufacturer did seven surveys in six months during the development of one of its latest products
Ability to attract participants who wouldn't participate in another research project, including international respondents	An agricultural equipment manufacturer did a study using two-way pagers provided free to farmers to query users about its equipment – respondents usually unavailable by telephone or PC
Respondents feel anonymous	Anonymity was the necessary ingredient for a study on impotence conducted by a drug manufacturer
Shortened turnaround from survey draft to execution of survey	A Hewlett-Packard survey using Greenfield *Quick Take* took two weeks to write, launch, and field – not the standard three months using non-web venues
Experiences unavailable by other means	One major advertising agency is conducting web research using virtual supermarket aisles that respondents wander through, reacting to client products and promotions. LiveWorld has developed a packaging study showing more than 75 images of labels and bottle designs
Web drawbacks	**Example**
Recruiting the right sample is costly and time-consuming; unlike telephone and mail sample frames, no lists exist	TalkCity, working for Whitton Associates and Fusion5, set up a panel of 3,700 teens for a survey to test new packaging for a soft drink using telephone calls, referrals, email lists, banner ads and website visits. It drew a sample of 600 for the research. It cost more than $50,000 to set up the list
Converting surveys to the web can be expensive	LiveWorld's teen study cost $50,000–100,000 to set up, with additional fees with each focus group or survey. The total price tag was several hundred thousand dollars
It takes technical as well as research skill to field a web survey	A 10–15 minute survey can take up to five days of technical expertise to field and test
While research is more compatible with numerous browsers, the technology isn't perfect	A well-known business magazine did a study among a recruited sample only to have the survey abort on question 20 of a larger study

Costs

The web survey, however, has made the collective execution of many design suggestions more attractive. Once the web survey is crafted, the costs of data collections are really low. Thus, web-based surveys require some initial investments either in terms of time or money to learn the software and to design a first questionnaire template that is also error-proofed. But once this money is invested, operating costs are very low. Reminding and redelivery, preliminary notification via email, personalization of the cover letter or the whole survey, are less costly and often easier than for mail surveys. Even the delivery of monetary and other incentives has been simplified with the use of e-currencies.

Non-response

However, employing all the stimulants for participation that have been researched cannot overcome a participant's inability to complete an Internet survey due to technological problems. Such glitches are likely to continue to plague participation as long as researchers and participants use different computer platforms, operating systems and software.

Another major problem is spam email. As emailing has been such a cheap process to address even millions of users, many serious and even more less-serious firms use email to approach others. As a consequence, all email providers filter incoming emails, mark unknown emails as spam and even return very suspicious emails to the sender without delivering them. The spam problem and the related problem that many people delete emails without reading them results in high non-response levels of web surveys. Moreover, some people, such as company directors, currently receive several requests to participate in surveys a week in their email box and therefore disregard all requests. As an alternative one might currently reconsider using the old-fashioned mail survey approach, as it might positively surprise the prospective respondent.

Tools to build web-based questionnaires

The **web-based questionnaire** has the power of CATI systems, but without the expense of network administrators, specialized software or additional hardware. As a solution for Internet or intranet websites, you need only a personal computer and web access. Most products are browser-driven with design features that allow custom survey creation and modification.

Two primary options are proprietary solutions offered through research firms and software packages designed for researchers who possess the knowledge and skills described here and in Chapter 13. The latter is increasingly offered through cloud services. With fee-based services, you are guided (often online) through problem formulation, questionnaire design, question content, response strategy, and wording and sequence of questions. Staff then generate the questionnaire code, host the survey at their server, and provide data consolidation and reports. The proprietary option is most costly and useful for those who have a very limited knowledge of research methodology.

Designing the questionnaire yourself is a strong alternative. Many schools own licences for online survey tools, such as Qualtric, that students can use for their research projects. In addition, several web companies, such as SurveyMonkeys, offer survey tool platforms on the web (see also Exhibit 7.9 for a comparison of different survey-tool platforms).

General advantages of web-based surveys include:

- question and scale libraries
- automated publishing to a web server
- real-time viewing of incoming data
- rapid transmission of results
- flexible analysis and reporting mechanisms.

Ease of use is not the only influence pushing the popularity of web-based instruments – cost is a major factor and web-based research is much less expensive than conventional survey research. Although fees are based on the number of completions, a sample of 100 might cost one-sixth of a conventional telephone interview. Bulk mailing and email data collection have also become more cost-effective because any instrument may be configured as an email questionnaire. For students most platforms offer either limited free versions or standard versions for a modest monthly fee. Designing surveys via Google Forms and Google Docs is even free and unlimited, but misses some of the other features. The differences between the systems are small: all offer advanced question-builder tools, advanced logical skipping and branching of questions, various possibilities to embed elements, such as videos, website links, links to social media platforms, the possibility to down- and upload files, tools to import and export data files, and respondent management and notifications systems, as well as some reporting and analysis tools. Regarding the latter for more academic work, it will still be required to export the data to statistical software packages like SPSS, R or Stata to conduct more advanced analysis. Each of the programs described below offers some special things, such as the payment option in Wufoo or the design of mobile surveys in Survey Gizmo. The best way to find out which survey tool suits you best is to visit the companies' websites where you can find examples, demos and trial versions.

Exhibit 7.9 Overview of online survey platforms.

Package	Wufoo	Google Docs	Survey Monkey	Survey Gizmo	Qualtric
Price (as of 2 July 2013)	Free: 10 questions, 100 respondents/month €11.00/month: account that includes all features useful in most student research	Free and no limits	Free: 10 questions, 100 respondents/month €25.00/month: account that includes all features useful in most student research	Student account for €6.00/month includes all features useful in most student researches	Not disclosed, but many business schools hold a licence
General features	Tools to build questionnaires with different question formats including advanced survey logic and branching, different templates and free design options, embedding of other elements (links, Facebook pages, videos, other documents), respondents can upload files, respondent management and notifications systems, data import and export, reporting and analysis tools				
Special features	Possibility to include payment options to collect donations		Offers access to respondents starting from €1.00 per completed response	Questionnaires for mobile applications	Most advanced package

In the end, the question whether web surveys are useful boils down to the question of quality of data obtained. Data quality suffers from selection biases, response biases and measurement errors. Selection bias has diminished over recent years but can still not be neglected. Selection bias is closely related to the penetration and usage rate of the web. Since the beginning of the century, both have increased substantially and in many industrialized countries these rates have reached a plateau. In industrialized countries, almost everybody has an email account and access to the Internet. However, people still differ largely in their usage: while, for example, younger people are connected and reachable all day, older people check their email accounts much more irregularly. Moreover, the perception of messages and information differs between people. Thus, even if the Internet penetration is close to 100 per cent web surveys will still have a selection bias in favour of young people with above-average education.

Response error is a growing concern in survey research independent from the communication approach used; response rates are declining and it takes more effort to achieve reasonable response rates. Web surveys are not an exception to this trend and nor do they show higher response rates than other approaches. One of the reasons is the abundance of web surveys itself. Through the Internet, the collection of survey data has become more democratic as web surveys cost much less (no printing and postage costs), but this has led to a flood of surveys that respondents are invited to participate in every day. Just think about how often you close pop-up windows inviting you to assess a website or to reflect on your shopping experience in an online shop. In section 7.3 we discussed several factors that influence the response rates. For example, we know that advanced letters, enclosed incentives, personalized signatures, etc. increase response rates in classical mail surveys. These tools are, however, not always transferable to web surveys and right now we know little about how one should design web surveys to increase response, as current studies on this issue often lack methodological rigour.

It is easy to imagine that the wording of a question can influence the answer given, but it is even worse as not only the wording, but also the position of the question, the ranking of answer alternatives and the layout of the page influences answers. These errors are called measurement errors. The problem is exaggerated in web surveys as, depending on the used browser, hardware and settings, the appearance of a survey will differ between users. For example, while some users might see a question with many answer alternatives on one screen, others might need to scroll down to see the answer alternatives at the bottom. Thus, different browsers will probably increase measurement errors. On the other hand, web surveys allow features that will reduce measurement errors. From mail survey research we know that the position of an answer alternative affects how often it is ticked: the first being ticked more often. In web surveys, one can easily randomize the position of the answer alternatives and thereby reduce the systematic error caused by the first alternative being ticked more often. Likewise, the availability of graphic features that are costly in printed surveys (colour, high-resolution photography) do not cost more in web surveys and might enhance the clarity of a question.

7.9 Structured observations

Next to asking people, observing them is another way to obtain information. Observation qualifies as scientific inquiry when it is conducted specifically to answer a research question, is systematically planned and executed, uses proper controls, and provides a reliable and valid account of what happened. The versatility of observation makes it an indispensable primary source method and a supplement for other methods.

Despite its broad applicability, many academics have a limited view of observation, relegating it to a minor technique of field data collection. This ignores its potential for forging business decisions and denies its historic stature as a creative means of obtaining primary data. Similar to Exhibit 7.2, Exhibit 7.10 illustrates the use of observation in the research process.

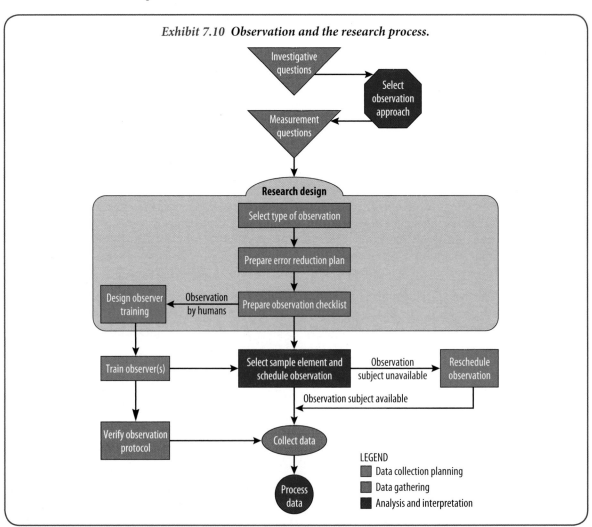

Exhibit 7.10 Observation and the research process.

Research Methods in Real Life
Shopping together ends in quarrels

Tim Denison conducted an extensive observational study on the shopping behaviour of women and men, looking at about 2,000 people who shopped alone or in company with someone else. Overall, he observed that men stop their shopping after 72 minutes, while women still have the energy or pleasure to continue for another half an hour. Denison also observed other gender differences. Men are hunters, who know what they want, target their object, buy it and leave. Women are collectors; they look around, inspect this product and that product, and compare them. They take their time. This difference in observable behaviour is also supported by the physical state of the shoppers. The blood pressure of men rises at the start of the shopping process, reaches rather high levels, but drops considerably as soon as the product is bought. Women's blood pressure rises less quickly, does not reach as high a level as that of men, but continues to be high even 15 minutes after the purchase. These different patterns in shopping behaviour explain the friction that emerges if men and women shop together. On average, it is less than half an hour before they begin to argue.

The description of behavioural differences provided above supports common wisdom (and experience) on shopping. But is this study any more than a rich description? What can we infer from the observed differences in physical condition (blood pressure) between women and men?

References and further reading

Intermediair, 'Samen winkelen: niet te lang [Shopping together: not for too long]', Intermediair (2 October 2003), p. 11.

General advantages of observational method

Observation poses a number of unique and relative advantages compared to other methods, such as interviews or archival and secondary data research:

1 Observation is the only method capable of obtaining information from subjects that cannot adequately articulate themselves, such as young children or people with severe mental disabilities. Moreover, it is possible to gather information on the status or condition of objects.
2 Observation allows us to collect the original data at the time it occurs and thereby reduce retrospective biases.
3 We need not depend on reports by others and thereby reduce the respondent bias which is an issue with all other approaches no matter how well intended respondents are. Forgetting occurs, and there are reasons why the respondent may not want to report fully and fairly. Although observation does suffer less from respondents' biases, it still involves **method reactivity biases**, which occur if respondents change their behaviour because they know they are observed.
4 We can secure information that most participants would ignore either because it is so common and expected, or because it is not seen as relevant. For example, applicants will not know how often they avoided eye contact in a job interview or if you are observing buying activity in a store, there may be conditions important to the research study that the shopper does not notice or consider important, such as: 'What is the weather like?' 'What is the day of the week or the time of the day?' 'How heavy is customer traffic?' 'What is the level of promotional activity in competing stores?' We can expect to learn only a few of the answers to these questions from most participants.
5 Observation alone can capture the whole event as it occurs in its natural environment. Whereas the environment of an experiment may seem contrived to participants, and the number and types of question limit the range of responses gathered from respondents, observation is less restrictive than most primary collection methods. Also, the limitations on the length of data-collection activities imposed by surveys or experiments are relaxed for observation. You may be interested in all the conditions surrounding a confrontation at a bargaining

session between union and management representatives. These sessions may extend over time, and any effort to study the unfolding of the negotiation is facilitated by observation. Questioning could seldom provide the insight of observation for many aspects of the negotiation process.

6 Participants seem to accept an observational intrusion better than they respond to questioning. Observation is less demanding of them and normally has a less biasing effect on their behaviour than does questioning. In addition, it is also possible to conduct disguised and unobtrusive observation studies much more easily than disguised questioning.

Limitations of observational method

The observational method has some research limitations:

1 The observer must normally be at the scene of the event when it takes place, yet it is often impossible to predict where and when the event will occur. One way to guard against missing an event is to observe for prolonged periods until it does occur, but this strategy brings up a second disadvantage.

2 Observation is a slow and expensive process that requires either human observers or costly surveillance equipment.

3 Observation is restricted to information that can be learned by overt action or surface indicators. For example, attitudes, values and opinions are hard to detect through observations. To go below the surface, the observer must make inferences. Two observers will probably agree on the nature of various surface events, but the inferences they draw from such data are much more variable. Combining observations with interviews is a remedy for this limitation.

4 The research environment is probably more suited to subjective assessment and recording of data than to controls and quantification of events. When control is exercised through active intervention by researchers, their participation may threaten the validity of what is being assessed. Even when sample sizes are small, observation records can be disproportionately large and difficult to analyse.

5 Observation is limited as a way to learn about the past. It is similarly limited as a method by which to learn what is going on in the present at some distant place. It is also difficult to gather information on such topics as intentions, attitudes, opinions or preferences. Nevertheless, any consideration of the merits of observation confirms its value when used with care and understanding.

Conducting structured observation

Structured observation attempts to systemically record behaviour along predefined aspects. It resembles survey research, but rather than asking respondents what they are doing, you observe what they are doing. One of the major advantages of structured observations is that it largely eliminates the respondent bias, at least as long as a respondent does not change his or her behaviour while being observed. It also allows observing unintended or automatic behaviour. For example, it does not make sense to ask people how often they say 'eeh' while answering a question, but you can easily count the number of 'eehs'.

Unlike the participant, the observer never gets involved in the activities in structured observation. We can classify structured observations along two dimensions: direct versus indirect observation and concealed versus not concealed.

Direct observation occurs when the observer is physically present and personally monitors what takes place. This approach is very flexible because it allows the observer to react to and report subtle aspects of events and behaviours as they occur. He or she is also free to shift places, change the focus of the observation, or concentrate on unexpected events if they occur. A weakness of this approach is that observers' 'perception circuits' may become overloaded as events move quickly, and observers must later try to reconstruct what they were not able to record. Also, observer fatigue, boredom and distracting events can reduce the accuracy and completeness of observation.

Indirect observation occurs when the recording is done by mechanical, photographic or electronic means. For example, a special camera that takes one frame every second may be mounted in a department of a large store to study customer and employee movement. Indirect observation is less flexible than direct observation but is also much less biasing and may be less erratic in terms of accuracy. Another advantage of indirect observation is that the permanent record can be reanalysed to include many different aspects of an event. Electronic recording devices, which have improved in quality and declined in cost, are being used more frequently in observation research. Tracking the surf behaviour of web users has recently become very popular to learn more about consumer preferences and interests.

The second dimension concerns whether the participant should know of the observer's presence. When the observer is known, there is a risk of atypical activity by the participant. The initial entry of an observer into a situation often upsets the activity patterns of the participants, but this influence usually dissipates quickly, especially when participants are engaged in some absorbing activity or the presence of observers offers no potential threat to the participants' self-interest. The potential bias from participant awareness of observers is always a matter of concern, however.

Observers use **concealment** to shield themselves from the object of their observation. Often technical means such as one-way mirrors, hidden cameras or microphones are used. These methods reduce the risk of observer bias but bring up the question of ethics. Hidden observation is a form of spying, and the propriety of this action must be reviewed carefully. A modified approach involves partial concealment. The presence of the observer is not concealed, but the objectives and participant of interest are.

Behavioural and non-behavioural observation

Observations can be directed at behavioural and non-behavioural activities and conditions, which, as shown in Exhibit 7.11, can be classified roughly as follows.

Exhibit 7.11 *Behavioural and non-behavioural observation.*

Behavioural observations	Non-behavioural observations
Non-verbal analysis	Record analysis
Linguistic analysis	Physical condition analysis
Extra-linguistic analysis	Physical process analysis
Spatial analysis	

Non-behavioural observation

A prevalent form of structured observation is **record analysis**. This may involve historical or current records, and public or private records. They may be written, printed, sound-recorded, photographed, videotaped or may be any records generated by information and communication technology devices. Historical statistical data are often the only sources used for a study. Other examples of this type of observation are the content analysis (described in this chapter) of competitive advertising and the analysis of personnel records.

Physical condition analysis is typified by store audits of merchandise availability, studies of plant safety compliance, analysis of inventory conditions and analysis of financial statements. **Process (activity) analysis** includes time/motion studies of manufacturing processes and analysis of traffic flows in a distribution system, paperwork flows in an office and financial flows in the banking system. It should be noted that non-behavioural observations sometimes allow inferences on behaviour. For example, the cookies stored temporarily on a personal computer reflect the web-surfing behaviour of the user. Similarly, counting the oil spots on the ground in a public car park tells us something about which car parks are used most often.

Research Methods in Real Life
'Best before end' – how do you know?

Marks & Spencer Mint Sauce – best before end 10 December 2013. How can the producer determine such precise dates? How do they know? Surprisingly, governments demand that producers give a 'best before end' date for all prepacked food (with a few exceptions of sugar, salt, vinegar and wine), but how the date is determined is up to the producers. The 'best before end' date does not of course mark the day when a product is spoiled and likely to turn green and sprout hairs. Most food can be consumed without any danger to one's health days and weeks after the date specified.

The 'best before end' date is not determined by keeping the food and checking when the first samples are spoiled. The dates are established by tasting teams that observe and assess the physical conditions of the product. Rob van Dongen, manager of the dairy company Friesland Coberco, explains that his company uses tasting teams to determine the 'best before end' date. For example, during the development of new fruit juice drinks, the team members tasted the drinks every day and assessed whether taste, smell, colour and 'mouth feel' were still good. In these tests of the physical conditions of the juice they discovered that orange juice loses some of its properties after 9 weeks, while tomato juice lasts for at least 31 weeks. Of course, they also used microbiological tests, such as counting the numbers of specific bacteria, but the results arrived at by the taste teams are just as important. Food should have a consistent quality between the date of purchase and the 'best before end' date.

References and further reading

www.frieslandcampina.com

Behavioural observation

The observational study of persons can be classified into four major categories.[43] **Non-verbal behaviour** is the most prevalent of these and includes body movement, motor expressions and even exchanged glances. At the level of gross body movement, one might study how a salesperson travels a particular area. At a fine level, one can study the body movements of a worker assembling a product, or time-sample the activity of a department's work force to discover the share of time each worker spends in various ways. More abstractly, one can study body movement as an indicator of interest or boredom, anger or pleasure in a certain environment. Motor expressions such as facial movements can be observed as a sign of emotional states. Eye-blink rates are studied as indicators of interest in advertising messages. Exchanged glances are of interest in studies of interpersonal behaviour.

Linguistic behaviour is a second frequently used form of behaviour observation. One simple type familiar to most students is the tally of 'ahs' or other annoying sounds or words a professor makes or uses during a class. More serious applications are the study of a sales presentation's content or the study of what, how and how much information is conveyed in a training situation. A third form of linguistic behaviour involves interaction processes that occur between two people or in small groups. Bales has proposed one widely used system for classifying such linguistic interactions.[44]

Behaviour may also be analysed on an extra-linguistic level. Sometimes **extra-linguistic behaviour** is as important a means of communication as linguistic behaviour. Bales has suggested that there are four dimensions of extra-linguistic activity.[45] These are: (i) vocal, including pitch, loudness and timbre, (ii) temporal, including the rate of speaking, duration of utterance and rhythm, (iii) interaction, including the tendency to interrupt, dominate or inhibit, and (iv) verbal stylistic, including vocabulary and pronunciation peculiarities, dialect and characteristic expressions. These dimensions could add substantial insight into the linguistic content of the interactions between supervisors and subordinates, or salespeople and customers.

A fourth type of behaviour study involves **spatial relationships**, especially how a person relates physically to others. One form of this study, proxemics, concerns how people organize the territory around them and how they maintain a discreet distance between themselves and others. A study of how salespeople physically approach customers and a study of the effects of crowding in a workplace are examples of this type of observation.

Measurement in structured observation

Specific conditions, events or activities that we want to observe determine the observational reporting system (and correspond to measurement questions). To specify the observation content, we should include both the major variables of interest and any other variables that may affect them. From this cataloguing, we then select those items we plan to observe. For each variable chosen, we must provide an operational definition if there is any question of concept ambiguity or special meanings. Even if the concept is a common one, we must make certain that all observers agree on the measurement terms by which to record results. For example, we may agree that variable X will be reported by count, while variable Y will be counted and the effectiveness of its use judged qualitatively.

Factual and inferential observations

Observation may be at either a **factual** or an **inferential** level. Observations at the factual level are direct descriptions of what is happening and what can be seen, while an observation at the inferential level translates what is seen to a concept that cannot be observed. For example, in 2009 the swine flu epidemic was spreading across the world and at many airports health officials observed the arriving travellers for symptoms, such as sweat on the forehead. Sweat on the forehead was observed and one inferred from it that the traveller was a potential bearer of the virus. Exhibit 7.12. shows how we could separate the factual and inferential components of a salesperson's presentation. This table is suggestive only. It does not include many other variables that might be of interest, including data on customer purchase history; company, industry and general economic conditions; the order in which sales arguments are presented; and specific words used to describe certain product characteristics. The particular content of observation will also be affected by the nature of the observation setting.

Exhibit 7.12 Content of observation: factual versus inferential.

Factual	Inferential
Introduction/identification of salesperson and customer	Credibility of salesperson/qualified status of customer
Time and day of the week	Convenience for the customer; welcoming attitude of the customer
Product presented	Customer interest in product
Selling point presented per product	Customer acceptance of selling points per product
Number of customer objections raised per product	Customer concerns about features and benefits
Salesperson's rebuttal of objection	Effectiveness of salesperson's rebuttal attempts
Salesperson's attempts to restore control	Effectiveness of salesperson's control attempt; consequences for customers who prefer interactions
Length of interview	Customer's/salesperson's degree of enthusiasm for the interview
Environmental factors interfering with the interview	Level of distraction for customer
Customer purchase decision	General evaluation of sales presentation skill

Observations of physical traces

Webb and his colleagues have given us an insight into some very innovative observational procedures that can be both non-reactive and inconspicuously applied. Called **unobtrusive measures**, these approaches encourage creative and imaginative forms of indirect observation, archival searches, and variations on simple and contrived observation.[46] Of particular interest are measures involving indirect observation based on **physical traces** that include erosion (measures of wear) and accretion (measures of deposit).

Natural erosion measures may be illustrated by the frequency of replacement of vinyl floor tiles in front of museum exhibits as an indicator of exhibit popularity. The study of wear and tear on book pages is a measure of library book use. Counting the remaining brochures in a car dealer's display rack after a favourable magazine review suggests levels of consumer interest.

Physical traces also include natural accretion such as discovering the listenership of radio stations by observing car radio settings as vehicles are brought in for service. Another type of unobtrusive study involves estimating alcohol and magazine consumption by collecting and analysing domestic rubbish. An interesting application compared beer consumption reports acquired through interviews with findings from sampled rubbish. If the interview data was valid, the consumption figure for the area was 15 per cent. However, the validity was questioned when counting the number of beer cans in the domestic rubbish suggested a 77 per cent consumption rate.[47]

William Rathje is a professor of archaeology at the University of Arizona, and founder of the Garbage Project in Tucson. His study of trash, refuse, rubbish and litter resulted in the sub-discipline that the *Oxford English Dictionary* has dubbed 'garbology'. By excavating landfills, he has gained insight into human behaviour and cultural patterns – sometimes sorting the contents of up to 150 coded categories. His previous studies have shown that 'people will describe their behaviour to satisfy cultural expectations, like the mothers in Tucson who unanimously claimed that they made their baby food from scratch, but whose garbage told a very different tale'.[48]

Physical trace methods present a strong argument for use based on their ability to provide low-cost access to frequency, attendance and incidence data without contamination from other methods or reactivity from participants. They are excellent 'triangulation' devices for cross-validation. Thus, they work well as supplements to other methods. Designing an unobtrusive study can test a researcher's creativity, and one must be especially careful about inferences made from the findings. Erosion results may have occurred because of wear factors not considered, and accretion material may be the result of selective deposit or survival.

Conducting structured observations

Suppose you are working for ProSec Electronics and its management is concerned about a deterioration in the quality in its assembled product – security cameras – towards the end of each day. The management question is: 'Why are products failing quality assurance in the afternoon?' The following research question might state: 'What factors affect the quality of assembled cameras?' Although we presume that management is correct about the time, we will allow the data to confirm this. The investigative questions could then include: 'What is the variability due to changes in parts vendors?' 'Inventory?' 'Does the manufacturing procedure change during the day?' 'Is it shift-dependent?' 'To what extent is the failure rate contingent on time of day?' 'What is the role of workplace conditions?' 'Is it linked to assembler performance?'

Designing

Designing the observational study requires us to answer the Who, What, When, How and Where questions.

Who? Assume that, through interviewing, we isolate the content of the study to assembler behaviour in the natural environment.

What? Reading the assembler's job descriptions we operationalize major variables of interest from it. Moreover, we need to measure environmental variables.

When? The problem we are interested in occurs in the afternoons. Therefore, we choose to sample during the late afternoon, initially, and we will use time sampling on a continuous basis.

How? The observation will be indirect, and we will operate from concealment using video cameras covering the assembly area. Our observations on the assemblers' behaviour and the contextual situation are recorded on checklists that will be revised after pre-testing.

Where? The assembly hall is the setting we are observing.

Data collection with checklists

Using the company's cameras, we will run one on wide angle for context and the other zoomed in to capture individual assembler behaviour on a time-interval sampling. The observation will be videotaped so a consistent stimulus may be used to train observers, pre-test and refine the checklists, and obtain a benchmark for later comparison. The behavioural checklist will be devised after studying the job descriptions and viewing the preliminary videotape.

For structured observation, checklists are a common method to record the data, usually while you observe to limit memory-induced biases. Developing a checklist is similar to designing a questionnaire and requires that we formulate questions reflecting the variables of interest and corresponding answer categories allowing quantifying what is observed. In our example above, the variables to be measured (measurement questions) were derived from the investigative questions on workplace conditions and assembler performance. Notes taken on the tour improved our understanding of contextual variables. By examining the workplace first, we can assess and begin to rule out environmental variables (lighting, temperature, noise and other variables controlled by the production facility) before moving on to behavioural characteristics. The observational checklist for the assembly environment features a range of measures from graphic rating scales to category scales. It is shown in Exhibit 7.13.

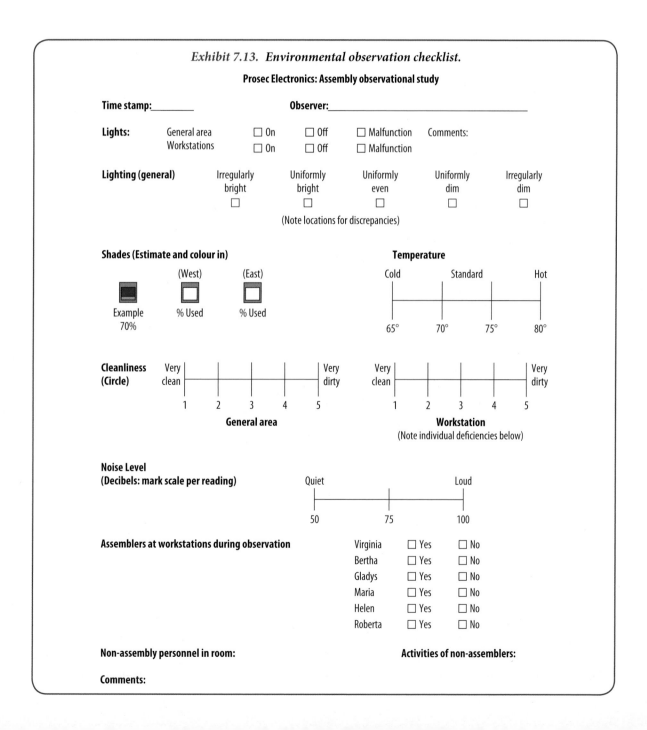

Exhibit 7.13. Environmental observation checklist.

Running Case Study 7
Surveys

In the last chapter, we learnt that Rebecca had designed a web-based questionnaire to collect her responses. But was it a wise decision to use the web? Looking at her response rate, it compares well with similar studies and compared to her friend Alexander (see Chapter 4) her response rates were impressive. Except for the Facebook approach (for which she could not really calculate a response rate, as she did not know how many people were approached through the snowball system), in her two other samples the vast majority did not respond. In the past, Rebecca has also received requests to fill in questionnaires online. In the last few months, she honoured all these requests just to see how other people designed their questionnaires, but previously she would usually only fill out those that came from other students she knew or if she was interested in the topic. She suspected that her topic 'student ethics' was also the major reason for her rather high response rates, as student ethics is a hot topic among students.

Thus, despite the fact that Rebecca had collected 161 responses, she worried about the quality of her data. One issue was whether her sample would suffer from a systematic non-response bias. It seemed obvious to her that people who knew her well were more likely to respond and she also thought that the respondents from her Amsterdam sample probably knew Brenda better than the non-respondents. But would that matter? Another worry she had was whether the respondents were really honest in answering her questions (see also the Running Case Study Chapter 13). Her final concern was the uneven distribution of respondents across university – she had just four or less respondents for universities other than Amsterdam and Maastricht. Were all her concerns justified? Her supervisor told her that she could probably compare Amsterdam and Maastricht respondents with each other, but not with the respondents from the other universities.

Next week, she has been invited to the 25th birthday of her high school friend Esther, who studied accounting in Rotterdam. Esther was one of the Facebook friends she approached and currently she has four responses from Rotterdam. Now she is considering whether to take some of the questionnaires with her to conduct a few face-to-face interviews in Rotterdam. She could either ask some of Esther's friends directly to answer the questionnaire or could even walk into the university canteen or library and ask students there whether they could spare a couple of minutes to fill out a paper and pencil questionnaire. If she could get about 20 more responses from Rotterdam, she could at least compare three universities and not just two. Would it also make sense to approach her brother Leon, who studied in Tilburg to collect 20 more responses from students in Tilburg? She could even offer to pay him €2 for each completed questionnaire. Of course she could not mention to Esther that she would be paying her brother while she did it for free.

1 Should Rebecca use the web to collect data?
2 What do you think about her measures to increase the response rate?
3 What response errors are likely to occur in Rebecca's research and what could be done to reduce, if not eliminate, them?

Summary

1 The communication approach involves questioning or surveying people and recording their responses for analysis. Communication is accomplished via personal interviews, telephone interviews or self-administered surveys, with each method having its specific strengths and weaknesses. The optimal communication method is the one that is instrumental in answering your research question, and dealing with the constraints imposed by time, budget and human resources. The opportunity to combine several survey methodologies makes the use of the mixed mode desirable in many projects.

2 Successful communication requires that we seek information the participant can provide, and that the participant understands his or her role and is motivated to play that role. Motivation, in particular, is

a task for the interviewer. Good rapport with the participant should be established quickly, and then the technical process of collecting data should begin. The latter often calls for skilful probing to supplement the answers volunteered by the participant. Simplicity of directions and instrument appearance are additional factors to consider in encouraging response in self-administered communication studies.

3   Two factors can cause bias in interviewing. One is non-response. It is a concern with all types of survey. Some studies show that first calls often secure less than 20 per cent of the designated participants. Various methods are useful for increasing this representation, the most effective being making call-backs until an adequate number of completed interviews have been secured. The second factor is response error, which occurs when the participant fails to give a correct or complete answer. The interviewer can also contribute to response error. However, the interviewer can provide the main solution to both types of error.

4   The major advantages of personal interviewing are the ability to explore topics in great depth, achieve a high degree of interviewer control and provide maximum interviewer flexibility for meeting unique situations. However, this method is costly and time-consuming, and its flexibility can result in excessive interviewer bias.

Telephone interviewing has become much more popular in recent years because of the diffusion of the telephone service in households and the low cost of this method compared with personal interviewing. Long-distance telephone interviewing has grown. There are also disadvantages in telephone interviewing: many telephone numbers are unlisted, and directory listings become obsolete quickly; there is also a limit on the length and depth of interviews conducted using the telephone.

The self-administered questionnaire can be delivered by the national postal service, facsimile, a courier service, a computer or intercept. Web-based surveys use organizational intranets, the Internet or online services to reach their participants. Participants may be targeted or self-selecting. Intercept studies may use a traditional questionnaire or a computerized instrument in environments where interviewer assistance is minimal. Web-based surveys offer many advantages, such as inexpensive delivery to respondents and the use of features, like videos, that cannot be implemented in printed surveys. They have, however, disadvantages as well, mainly in terms of often ill-defined populations and the more limited control the researcher has over the sample itself.

5   Observational methods can be divided into participant observation and structured observation. This chapter deals with structured observations producing data suitable for quantitative analysis. The strengths of observation as a data-collection method include:
- securing information about people or activities that cannot be derived from experiments or surveys
- avoiding participant filtering and forgetting
- securing environmental context information
- optimizing the naturalness of the research setting
- reducing obtrusiveness.

Structured observation may be limited by:
- the expense of observer costs and equipment
- the reliability of inferences from surface indicators
- the problems of quantification and disproportionately large records
- limitations presenting activities and inferences about cognitive processes.

The design of an observational study follows the same general pattern as other research. The researcher must define the content of the study; develop a data-collection plan that identifies participants, sampling strategy and 'acts' (often operationalized as a checklist or coding scheme); secure and train observers; and launch the study. We can classify structured observation on two dimensions: (i) Is the observation direct or indirect? (ii) Is the observer's presence known or unknown? Checklists are the primary data-gathering tool in structured observations. To ensure validity of the collected data, researchers should follow the principles of direct note-making, immediate full notes, limited observation time and rich full notes to obtain sound field notes.

Discussion questions

Terms in review

1 Distinguish among response error, interviewer error and non-response error.

2 How do environmental factors affect response rates in personal interviews? How can we overcome these environmental problems?

3 Compare the advantages and disadvantages of the survey to those of observation. Under which circumstances could you make a case for using observation?

4 Distinguish between the following:
   a   the relative value of communication and observation
   b   non-verbal, linguistic and extra-linguistic analysis
   c   factual and inferential observation.

5 Compare the advantages and disadvantages of the survey to those of observation. Under which circumstances could you make a case for using observation?

6 What ethical risks are involved in observation? In the use of unobtrusive measures?

7 Based on your present or past work experience, suggest problems that could be resolved by using observation-based data.

Making research decisions

8 Assume you are planning to interview shoppers in a shopping centre about their views on increased food prices and what the government should do about them. In what different ways might you try to motivate shoppers to cooperate in your survey?

9 In recent years, in-home personal interviews have grown more costly and more difficult to complete. Suppose, however, you have a project in which you need to talk with people in their homes. What might you do to hold down costs and increase the response rate?

10 In the following situations, decide whether you would use a personal interview, telephone survey or self-administered questionnaire. Give your reasons.
   a   A survey of the residents of a new suburb on why they happened to select that area in which to live. (You also wish to secure some information about what they like and do not like about life in the suburb.)
   b   A poll of students at Metro University on their preferences among three candidates who are running for presidency of the Student Union.
   c   A survey of 58 wholesale grocery companies in Sweden on their personnel management policies for warehouse personnel.
   d   A survey of financial officers of the Fortune 500 corporations to learn their predictions for the economic outlook in their industries in the next year.
   e   A study of applicant requirements, job tasks and performance expectations as part of a job analysis of student work-study jobs on a college campus of 2,000 students, where 1,500 are involved in the work-study programme.

11 You decide to take a telephone survey of 100 families with children in Manchester to learn how community services facilitate the combination of work and childcare. You want a good representation of all families with children in Manchester. Explain how you will carry out the sampling for such a study.

12 You plan to conduct a mail survey of the traffic managers of 1,000 major manufacturing companies across the country. The study concerns their company policies regarding the payment of moving expenses for employees who are transferred. What might you do to improve the response rate of such a survey?

13 A major corporation agrees to sponsor an internal study on sexual harassment in the workplace. This is in response to concerns expressed by its female employees. How would you handle the following issues?

a   Sample selection

b   The communication approach (self-administered, telephone, personal interview and/or mixed)

c   The purpose: fact-finding, awareness, relationship building and/or change

d   Minimization of response and non-response error.

14 Assume you are a manufacturer of modular office systems and furniture, as well as office-organization elements (desktop and wall organizers, filing systems, etc.). Your company has been asked to propose an observational study to examine the use of office space by white-collar and managerial workers for a large insurance company. This study will be part of a project to improve office efficiency and paperwork flow. It is expected to involve the redesign of office space, and the purchase of new office furniture and organization elements.

a   What are the varieties of information that might be observed?

b   Select a limited number of content areas for study, and operationally define the observation acts that should be measured.

15 Develop a checklist to be used by observers in the previous study.

a   Determine how many observers you need and assign two or three to a specific observation task.

b   Compare the results of your group members' checklists for stability of recorded perceptions.

16 You wish to analyse the pedestrian traffic that passes a given store in a major shopping centre. You are interested in determining how many shoppers pass by this store, and you would like to classify these shoppers on various relevant dimensions. Any information you secure should be obtainable from observation alone.

a   What other information might you find useful to observe?

b   How would you decide what information to collect?

c   Devise the operational definitions you would need.

d   What would you say in your instructions to the observers you plan to use?

e   How might you sample among the people passing through the shopping centre

17 Assume you are a manufacturer of modular office systems and furniture, as well as office-organization elements (desktop and wall organizers, filing systems, etc.). Your company has been asked to propose an observational study to examine the use of office space by white-collar and managerial workers for a large insurance company. This study will be part of a project to improve office efficiency and paperwork flow. It is expected to involve the redesign of office space, and the purchase of new office furniture and organization elements.

a   What are the varieties of information that might be observed?

b   Select a limited number of content areas for study, and operationally define the observation acts that should be measured.

18 Develop a checklist to be used by observers in the previous study.

a   Determine how many observers you need and assign two or three to a specific observation task.

b   Compare the results of your group members' checklists for stability of recorded perceptions.

19 You wish to analyse the pedestrian traffic that passes a given store in a major shopping centre. You are interested in determining how many shoppers pass by this store, and you would like to classify these shoppers on various relevant dimensions. Any information you secure should be obtainable from observation alone.

a   What other information might you find useful to observe?

b   How would you decide what information to collect?

c   Devise the operational definitions you would need.

d   What would you say in your instructions to the observers you plan to use?

e   How might you sample this shopper traffic?

Classroom discussion

20 Divide the class into sub-groups of up to four people. Each sub-group has the task of developing a questionnaire on the learning behaviour of students. The first group develops a mail questionnaire, the second group a phone questionnaire, the third group a questionnaire to be used in a personal interview, the fourth group a web-based questionnaire, and so on. Ask each group to use their communication approach in such a way that they will obtain answers that groups using other communication approaches are less likely to obtain.

21 Non-response can create serious biases in samples. Brainstorm the following questions in your class group:
   a When does non-response create larger biases and when smaller biases?
   b How can you design a study in a way that reduces non-response?
   c How can you assess the effects of non-response once the study has been conducted?

22 Discuss in class how students' and teachers' behaviour would change if it were being recorded on video.

Recommended further reading

Arksey, Hilary and Knight, Peter T., *Interviewing for Social Scientists: An Introductory Resource with Examples.* **Thousand Oaks, CA: Sage, 1999.** Covers design, improvisation, success rates, specialized contexts and transforming findings into results.

Dillman, Don A., *Mail and Internet Surveys: The Tailored Design Method.* **New York: Wiley, 1999.** The tailored design method, which expands on the total design concept of Dillman's classic work, takes advantage of computers, electronic mail and the Internet to better our understanding of survey requirements.

Fowler, Floyd J., Jr., *Survey Research Methods* **(2nd edn). Thousand Oaks, CA: Sage, 1993.** An excellent overview of all aspects of the survey process.

Groves, Robert M. et al., *Telephone Survey Methodology.* **New York: Wiley, 2001.** Distinguished survey experts present developments in phone surveys from different national contexts.

Harzing, Anne-Will, 'Response rates in international mail surveys: results of a 22 country study', *International Business Review* **6(6), 1997, pp. 641–62.** An investigation into response effects in different countries, including the USA and the UK.

Jobber, David, Saunders, John and Mitchell, Vince-Wayne, 'Prepaid monetary incentive effects on mail survey response', *Journal of Business Research* **57(4), 2004, pp. 347–50.** A study investigating the trade-off between increased costs for offering incentives and the marginal benefits of a higher response rate.

Lavrakas, Paul J., *Telephone Survey Methods: Sampling, Selection, and Supervision* **(2nd edn). Thousand Oaks, CA: Sage, 1993.** This specialized work takes an applied perspective of interest to students and managers. Chapters 3, 5 and 6 on supervision are particularly useful.

Nesbary, Dale, K., *Survey Research and the World Wide Web.* **Needham Heights, MA: Allyn & Bacon, 1999.** Screen shots from Windows and FrontPage, email survey construction and Internet orientation for survey research.

Webb, Eugene J., Campbell, Donald T., Schwartz, Richard D. and Sechrest, Lee B., *Unobtrusive Measures.* **Thousand Oaks, CA: Sage, 1999.** The revised edition of the classic source of information on all aspects of unobtrusive measures. Excellent examples and ideas for project planning.

Welch, Catherine, Marschan-Piekkari, Rebecca, Penttine, Heli and Tahvanainen, Marja, 'Corporate elites as informants in qualitative international business research', *International Business Review* **11(5), 2002, pp. 661–78.** An article discussing methodologies on how interviews with elite informants during the fieldwork can be incorporated into the research.

Get started with understanding statistical techniques!

When you have read this chapter, log on to the Online Learning Centre website at *www.mcgraw-hill.co.uk/textbooks/blumberg* to explore chapter-by-chapter test questions, additional case studies, a glossary and more online study tools for *Business Research Methods.*

Notes

1 One of the top research organizations in the world is the Survey Research Center of the University of Michigan. The material in this section draws heavily on the *Interviewer's Manual* (rev. edn.). Ann Arbor, Survey Research Center, University of Michigan, 1976; and Floyd J. Fowler, Jr., *Survey Research Methods*. Beverly Hills, CA: Sage, 1988, Chapter 7.

2 Robert L. Kahn and Charles F. Cannell, *The Dynamics of Interviewing*. New York: Wiley, 1957, pp. 45–51.

3 Survey Research Center, *Interviewer's Manual*, p. 8.

4 In one study, 5.5 per cent of white participants and 11 per cent of non-white respondents were still not contacted after six calls. See W.C. Dunkleberg and G.S. Day, 'Nonresponse bias and callbacks in sample surveys', *Journal of Marketing Research*, May 1974, Table 3.

5 Ibid.

6 Fowler, *Survey Research Methods*, p. 50.

7 C.H. Fuller, 'Weighting to adjust for survey nonresponse', *Public Opinion Quarterly*, Summer 1974, pp. 239–46.

8 Dunkleberg and Day, 'Nonresponse bias', Table 3.

9 Ibid., pp. 160–8.

10 Eleanore Singer, 'Agreement between inaccessible respondents and informants', *Public Opinion Quarterly*, Winter 1972/73, pp. 603–11.

11 Seymour Sudman, *Reducing the Costs of Surveys*. Chicago: Aldine, 1967, p. 67.

12 Ibid., p. 59.

13 Ibid., p. 63.

14 Ibid., p. 53.

15 Survey Research Center, *Interviewer's Manual*, pp. 15–16.

16 Ibid., p. 17.

17 Fowler, *Survey Research Methods*, p. 111.

18 B.W. Schyberger, 'A study of interviewer behavior', *Journal of Marketing Research*, February 1967, p. 35.

19 B.S. Dohrenwend, J.A. Williams, Jr. and C.H. Weiss, 'Interviewer biasing effects: toward a reconciliation of findings', *Public Opinion Quarterly*, Spring 1969, pp. 121–9.

20 Robert M. Groves and Robert L. Kahn, *Surveys by Telephone*. New York: Academic Press, 1979, p. 223.

21 Michael J. Havice, 'Measuring nonresponse and refusals to an electronic telephone survey', *Journalism Quarterly*, Fall 1990, pp. 521–30.

22 Statistical Office of the European Communities, 'Statistics on the information society in Europe: data 1996–2002', 2003, pp. 42–4.

23 Data taken from the World Telecommunications/ICT Indicators Database (www.itu.int/en/ITU-D/Statistics/Pages/stat/default.aspx).

24 G.J. Glasser and G.D. Metzger, 'Random digit dialing as a method of telephone sampling', *Journal of Marketing Research*, February 1972, pp. 59–64; Seymour Sudman, 'The uses of telephone directories for survey sampling', *Journal of Marketing Research*, May 1973, pp. 204–7.

25 A block is defined as an exchange group composed of the first four or more digits of a seven-digit number, such as 721-0, 721-1, and so on.

26 Sudman, *Reducing the Costs of Surveys*, p. 65.

27 J.J. Wheatley, 'Self-administered written questionnaires or telephone interviews', *Journal of Marketing Research*, February 1973, pp. 94–5.

28 Groves and Kahn, *Surveys by Telephone*, p. 223.

29 Don A. Dillman, *Mail and Telephone Surveys*. New York: Wiley, 1978, p. 6.

30 D. Wallace, 'A case for and against mail questionnaires', *Public Opinion Quarterly*, Spring 1954, pp. 40–52.

31 Harzing, Anne-Will, 'Response rates in international mail surveys: results of a 22 country study', *International Business Review* 6 (1997), pp. 641–65.

32 Leslie Kanuk and Conrad Berenson, 'Mail surveys and response rates: a literature review', *Journal of Marketing Research*, November 1975, pp. 440–53; Arnold S. Linsky, 'Stimulating responses to mailed questionnaires: a review', *Public Opinion Quarterly* 39 (1975), pp. 82–101; Julie Yu and Harris Cooper, 'A quantitative review of research design effects on response rates to questionnaires', *Journal of Marketing Research* 20 (1983), pp. 36–44.

33 Kanuk and Berenson, 'Mail surveys', p. 450. Reprinted from the *Journal of Marketing Research*, published by the American Marketing Association.

34 Dillman, *Mail and Telephone Surveys*, p. 8.

35 Ibid., p. 12.

36 Ibid., pp. 22–4.

37 Total Design Method (http://survey.sesrc.wsu.edu/tdm.htm), 4 February 2000. Don Dillman is Professor of Sociology and Rural Sociology and Deputy Director of Research and Development of the Social and Economic Sciences Research Center at Washington State University.

38 Dillman, *Mail and Telephone Surveys,* pp. 160–1.

39 C.H. Lovelock, Ronald Still, David Cullwick and Ira M. Kaufman, 'An evaluation of the effectiveness of drop-off questionnaire delivery', *Journal of Marketing Research,* November 1976, pp. 358–64.

40 Donald Tomaskovic-Devey, Jeffrey Leiter and Shealy Thompson, 'Organizational survey nonresponse', *Administrative Science Quarterly*, 1994, pp. 439–57.

41 Data taken from the World Telecommunications/ICT Indicators Database (www.itu.int/en/ITU-D/Statistics/Pages/stat/default.aspx).

42 These examples are drawn from the personal experience of the authors, as well as from Noah Shachtman, 'Why the web works as a market research tool', *AdAge.com*, Summer 2001 (http://adage.com/tools2001).

43 K.E. Weick, 'Systematic observational methods', in *The Handbook of Social Psychology*, Vol. 2, eds. G. Lindzey and E. Aronson, Reading, MA: Addison-Wesley, 1968, p. 360.

44 R. Bales, *Interaction Process Analysis*. Reading, MA: Addison-Wesley, 1950.

45 Weick, 'Systematic observational methods', p. 381.

46 E.J. Webb, D.T. Campbell, R.D. Schwartz, L. Sechrest and J.B. Grove, *Non-reactive Measures in the Social Sciences* (2nd edn.). Boston: Houghton Mifflin, 1981.

47 W.L. Rathje and W.W. Hughes, 'The garbage project as a non-reactive approach: garbage in . . . garbage out?' in *Perspectives on Attitude Assessment: Surveys and their Alternatives*, eds. H.W. Sinaiko and L.A. Broedling, Washington, DC: Smithsonian Institution, 1975.

48 William Grimes, 'If it's scientific, it's "garbology"', *International Herald Tribune* (15–16 August), 1992, p. 17.

CHAPTER 8

Primary data collection: qualitative data

Chapter contents

Learning objectives

When you have read this chapter, you should understand:

1 what distinguishes unstructured from structured interviews

2 how to conduct unstructured interviews

3 the purpose of focus groups and how to use them

4 when and how to conduct participant observations

In this chapter, we address the three main approaches to collecting qualitative information. We start with qualitative, unstructured interviews which are central to most qualitative research. In section 8.2, we discuss focus groups, a widely used special form of group interview and in section 8.3 we discuss observation as a way to collect qualitative information.

Qualitative interviews

Unstructured versus structured interviews

In Chapter 7 we discussed the different communication approaches used in survey research and structured observations. Common to all these communication approaches is that the survey, either face to face, by telephone or self-administered, is highly structured. In qualitative research, the interviews are usually much less structured and therefore called semi-structured or unstructured. **Semi-structured interviews** usually start with rather specific questions but allow the interviewee to follow his or her own thoughts later on. Probing techniques are widely used to evoke additional information from the respondents. A well-known example for a semi-structured interview is the TV interview of a journalist with a political decision-maker in a newscast. **Unstructured interviews** mostly start with a respondent's narrative and may not have any specific question or topic list to be covered. Semi-structured or unstructured interviews are very common in qualitative research and are therefore also often called **qualitative interviews**.

Exhibit 8.1 lists the main differences between structured and semi-structured or unstructured interviews. Structured interviews are useful if the goal of your study is to describe or explain, but they do not allow you to explore a topic, as the questions and answer choices for the respondents are predefined by the researcher. Exploring a topic needs at least a semi-unstructured approach that gives the respondent the option to turn the interview in different directions and to come up with new sub-topics that the researcher often has not thought about beforehand. The differences between structured and unstructured interviews are partly connected with the aforementioned methodological polarizations concerning the underlying research philosophy (positivism versus interpretivism), the data-collection strategy (quantitative versus qualitative) and the sampling strategy (sample versus case study).[1]

Exhibit 8.1 Structured and unstructured interviews.

	Structured	Semi-structured or unstructured
Type of study	Explanatory or descriptive	Exploratory and explanatory (semi-structured)
Purpose	Providing valid and reliable measurements of theoretical concepts	Learning the respondent's viewpoint regarding situations relevant to the broader research problem
Instrument	Questionnaire (i.e. specified set of predefined questions)	Memory list interview guide
Format	Fixed to the initial questionnaire	Flexible depending on the course of the conversation, follow-up and new questions raised

This chapter is similarly structured as Chapter 7 but focuses on the collection of qualitative data. We start with communication as a data collection approach. While surveys are always answered by one specific person, communication approaches for qualitative data are much more flexible. This does not only apply to the way respondents are questioned as discussed above, but also to whether one approaches just one respondent or a group of respondents at the same time. We start with the unstructured, qualitative interview assuming that it is conducted with one interviewee. Then we proceed with focus groups, a qualitative interview technique that addresses simultaneously a group of respondents and builds upon the group dynamics that will occur in such interviews. Having discussed qualitative communication approaches, we turn to observational studies again, but focus on participant observation, which again produces qualitative data.

Semi-structured or unstructured interviews are particularly useful if the research problem refers to a wide-ranging problem area and you as a researcher need to detect and identify the issues relevant to understanding the situation. The central idea of unstructured interviews is that you as a researcher want to gain insight into what the respondents consider relevant and how they interpret the situation. Possible explanations or causes of the situation are not predefined and hence the course of the interview itself is left open. In fully unstructured interviews, the interviewer usually has a mental list of relevant topics or themes to be addressed and this will be especially useful if the interview peters out. In semi-structured interviews, researchers use an interview guide containing a list of rather more specific questions to ensure that the interviewer covers the necessary areas and asks the questions in a similar, if not identical, way in all interviews. An interview guide is especially useful if interviews are conducted by different interviewers, the interviews are conducted in different settings (e.g. at two different companies), and the researchers already have an idea about which aspects are important to an understanding of the situation under investigation. In both cases, the researcher is, however, free to ask additional questions and to change the order of the questions.

Suppose you want to investigate the working climate in a call centre. In a structured interview, you would, for example, ask respondents to rate their level of agreement with statements such as, 'I enjoy coming to work' on a Likert scale; you would ask how many calls a respondent handles per hour, and so on. An unstructured interview would start with a question such as, 'Tell me something about your job; please describe to me what a typical day is like and whatever else is important.' Depending on the answers, you would ask follow-up questions such as, 'You just mentioned that at certain times of the day the call centre is very busy and callers have to wait for a long time and get annoyed. How do you deal with such stressful moments?'

A major criticism of structured interviews is that they stifle communication, as the interviewer has little opportunity to resolve any communication problems.[2] For example, even the rather simple survey question, 'Have you worked in the last month?' can lead to responses such as, 'What do you mean by work?' among participants who do not have a paid job, but might have worked as a volunteer or followed a programme to reintegrate the long-term unemployed. Unclear terms pose a more serious threat in structured interviews, as some respondents will not report that terms are unclear and as interviewers often clarify terms in a way that differs from the researcher's intention. In unstructured interviews the problem of unclear questions is alleviated because how a question is interpreted is part of the answer.

The response opportunities of unstructured interviews are often very much appreciated by respondents, because they allow them to frame a story the way they want it and they are not pressed into the corset of a structured questionnaire. Moreover, unstructured interviews are often more rewarding for the respondent than a structured interview, as it often takes elements of a discussion between the respondent and interviewer/researcher, that is, the interview itself can become interesting for the respondent, because he or she learns through comments and points made by the interviewer.

Purpose: when are qualitative interviews appropriate?

We have already discussed that qualitative interviews are much better suited for any kind of qualitative research, especially for explorative studies in which the researcher does not have expectations regarding the explanations of phenomena, but rather searches for yet unknown explanations.

Qualitative interviews are, as well, very useful if the objective of your study is to detect the meanings respondents attach to a phenomenon, which is typical for the phenomenological approach. In such studies you would use the qualitative interview to obtain a solid account of what a respondent thinks about a specific phenomenon. Qualitative interviews are appropriate here as such studies require that researchers cross-check their interpretations of the data (obtained information) with the respondents. As it is not known up front what the answers will be and which interpretations will be cross-checked, unstructured interviews are the only way to gain such insights.

Instruments: questions in semi-structured and unstructured interviews

Writing an interview guide is an important part of qualitative interviewing. An objective of qualitative interviews is to learn more about the respondents' viewpoints regarding phenomena relevant to the broader research problem. The main functions of an interview guide are:

- It serves as a memory list to the interviewer to ensure that the same issues are addressed in every interview and not forgotten in some interviews.
- It increases the comparability of multiple qualitative interviews by ensuring that the questions are asked similarly.

Obviously, a semi-structured interview builds upon a more specific and structured guide than unstructured interviews. Designing an interview guide, however, involves a trade-off. The more specific the interview guide gets – that is the more structured the interview becomes – the less flexible the interviewer is in responding to the suggestions of the respondents. Thus, more structured guides improve the comparability of the answers, but reduce the explorative character of the interview.

A good starting point for an interview guide is to ask yourself the question, 'What do I want to know or why does the phenomenon interest me?' The basic principles of writing an interview guide are not very different from the principles of good questionnaire design (see Chapter 13) and you should ensure:

- Your guide contains questions that deal with all topics that could be important and order them so that they flow well, but be prepared to deviate from this path of questioning in the interview.
- You formulate your questions in a language that is easily understood by the interviewees.
- The questions you ask are not too specific and the interviewee has ample opportunity to reflect on the issue at hand.
- You reduce your influence as an interviewer as much as possible by avoiding leading or suggestive questions.
- You also record some general and some specific demographics or facts about the respondent (such as age, gender, department they are working in, years with the company, etc.).

Question types

In unstructured interviews, several different question types (as outlined below) can be distinguished, each serving a different purpose, and it should be emphasized that a researcher's primary task in interviewing is *listening*:[3]

- *Introductory questions* – usually rather general questions that get the interview started and help to establish a relationship with the interviewee, such as: 'Thank you very much for your willingness to talk to me about your company. I have looked at the company's website and have some idea about your company. But still, could you tell me something more about the company and your role in it?'
- *Follow-up* questions are used to ask the respondent to elaborate further on a given question or to clarify whether you have understood them correctly. Examples are: 'That is interesting. Please could you say a little bit more on this?' 'Can you illustrate this with an example?' and 'What exactly do you mean by . . . ?'
- *Probing questions* are similar to follow-up questions, but refer more specifically to a part of the answer. For example, if the respondent has just mentioned that the firm entered the Hungarian market recently: 'How was the decision to enter the Hungarian market made?' 'Why did you choose to enter the Hungarian market?'
- *Specifying questions* ask the interviewee to elaborate on the answer and to offer more information. Examples include: 'What happened after the decision was taken?' 'How did the trade unions react to this announcement?'
- *Direct questions* provide information on how interviewees assess a situation from their viewpoint and often ask them to describe an opinion or feeling. For example: 'What was your point of view regarding entering the Hungarian market?' 'Do you consider yourself an influential person in the organization?'
- *Indirect questions* are not directed at the interviewee personally, but ask for a general assessment sometimes followed up by a similar direct question. For example: 'What do people around here think about the entry into the Hungarian market?'
- *Structuring questions* are used when you have the feeling that the topic talked about has been covered sufficiently. One way of avoiding moving on too early is to ask: 'If we have not missed any important aspects of this subject, I would like to move on to [next topic].'
- *Silence* (i.e. pausing) is an important way of letting the interviewee know that you would like to hear more.
- *Interpreting questions* are asked in order to confirm that you have interpreted the information provided correctly. For example: 'Do you mean that without your efforts the decision to enter the Hungarian market would have been made much later or not at all?'

Practical considerations

Information recording

Unstructured interviews provide such an immense amount of information that it is hard to make a note of it all during the interview. This is why unstructured interviews are usually recorded. The main advantages of recording the interview are that as an interviewer you can focus on the course of the conversation rather than on taking notes. In addition, you (and others who did not take part in the actual interview) can listen to it again and make an accurate transcript of the interview. Moreover, direct quotes from interviewees, which often provide the 'spice' in a qualitative report, may be more easily collected.

The disadvantage with tape-recording interviews is that many people feel uncomfortable when their responses are recorded and, consequently, this may influence their answering behaviour. For example, their answers might be less controversial. Technical problems with equipment can also disturb the course of the interview. Moreover you should ensure that the recording device you use offers a good sound. Built-in microphones are often of poor quality, especially if more than two people participate in the interview and if the distance between the device and the interviewer(s) and interviewees becomes larger. External microphones are a common technical solution to this problem. Finally, transcribing the information recorded is very time-consuming, especially if the interviews are fairly long. The process of transcribing can, however, be shortened by only transcribing the relevant parts of interviews and leaving out answers that cannot be related to the research problem.

If you are unable to record the interview, you might think about conducting the interview with two interviewers. This has the additional advantage that four ears hear more than two and two brains create better follow-up questions than one. You need, however, to coordinate who is responsible for taking the notes at any point of the interview. You can switch the role of asking questions and note-taking during the interview, but you need to ensure that one of you takes the notes. Chances are high that both of you are absorbed by the course of the interview and forget to take notes.

Interviewer qualifications

The demands on the interviewer are much higher in an unstructured than in a structured interview. In a structured interview, the interviewer's main task is to convince the respondent to participate, to read clearly the questions and answer possibilities and to keep the respondent motivated and perfectly willing to continue. Of course, it is better if the interviewer has some background knowledge on the study and the topic, but he or she does not need to be an expert. The situation in the unstructured interview is completely different. Here the interviewer should be an expert in the field and therefore unstructured interviews are mostly done by the researchers involved in the study, while structured interviews are often outsourced to research agencies.

The interviewer for an unstructured interview needs to be well informed if not an expert for the following reasons:

1 One of the interviewer's tasks is to direct the interview, which is crucial if a respondent deviates from the interview topic. Then you have to decide whether to let the respondent continue, because the new route chosen might bring up some interesting novel ideas or to stop the respondent and redirect the interview. You cannot make such a decision if you have no knowledge on the topic.
2 In unstructured interviews, it is often necessary to probe respondents, that is, to ask them to continue on a topic by asking the same or a similar question again. Thus, here you need to decide whether what you have heard so far is sufficient or whether it would be better to get more, and again you cannot make this decision without knowing the topic well.
3 In unstructured interviews, respondents often expect you to be an expert. People do not like to waste their time talking with people who do not know anything about the topic.

Additional interviewer characteristics that are beneficial in unstructured interviews are that interviewers should be good at active listening. Active listening is more than listening, because it requires making short comments and clarifying questions. Doing so signals to the respondent that you are interested in him or her and what is said. Moreover, the ability to establish trust and a good atmosphere is an important asset, because respondents will simply tell you more if they trust you.

Student Research

Coordinating public works

Large public infrastructure projects, such as building a new motorway, usually end in a mess, delivery is postponed by months if not years and the final costs often exceed the initial budget by multiples. The A2 motorway, one of the main connections between the Netherlands and Belgium, runs right through Maastricht and interrupts the traffic flow as the motorway becomes a simple road with stop lights and pedestrian crossings. In 1999, the Dutch Ministry of Transport, Public Works and Water Management decided to replace the current motorway with a 2.3 km-long tunnel to be completed in 2016 and costing more than €500 million. Given the experiences with former infrastructure projects, it was decided to use a new tendering procedure. Rather than writing specifications and granting the project to the lowest bidder, the tender embarked with a fixed available budget and a list of compulsory requirements and additional wishes. All bidders had to present plans on how to realize the tunnel. Each plan had to remain within the budget and fulfil all compulsory requirements and selection was based on which additional requirements were realized.

Obviously, such a large project involves many public actors. In this case the main actors are the Ministry of Transport, the Directorate General for Public Work responsible for executing public works, the province of Limburg and the municipalities of Maastricht and Meersen. The parties established the project office A2, which had to prepare the tendering. Jos Eussen, a student in the executive MBA programme at Maastricht University, had been involved in that project as an independent consultant and was interested in the question of how one can achieve cooperation in a complex project with a new innovative tendering procedure.

Jos opted for a single case study as a research approach, because such large infrastructure projects are rare and one cannot isolate them from their specific contexts. To obtain the information, Jos relied on the one hand on an immense amount of documentation consisting of project plans, contracts between the public actors and public announcements and on the other hand on unstructured interviews with executives from the project office, senior officials from the Ministry, the Directorate General and the municipality as well as an alderman of Maastricht. In each interview, Jos went through the last years with the informants and asked them about their interests and positions, what they thought about the other parties and how that had changed over time. The information obtained allowed Jos to document the dynamics of the relationships among the involved parties and how they developed and maintained trust to achieve fruitful cooperation.

 ## 8.2 Focus groups

Qualitative interviews can be held with an individual or with a group of people. The first is often referred to as an in-depth or depth interview, while the latter is called a group interview, often conducted in a special way: the focus group interview. Individual in-depth interviews take the form of an unstructured one-to-one discussion with a well-chosen respondent, who has a deep insight into the relevant topic. In group interviews, a panel of experts is asked to discuss some open questions and topics. The difference between a group interview and a focus group interview is that group interviews are mostly organized for efficiency reasons, i.e. to get quickly responses of various respondents. In focus groups, however, next to the individual contributions of the participants, the interaction and dynamics between the participants are important.

Focus group characteristics

A focus group is a panel of people, led by a moderator, who meet for one to two hours. The facilitator or moderator uses group dynamics principles to focus or guide the group in an exchange of ideas, feelings and experiences on a specific topic. Typically the focus group panel is made up of 6–10 respondents. Too small or too large a group results in less effective participation. Focus groups are very similar to unstructured or semi-structured interviews, but as more people participate, you will also initiate interactions among the respondents (Exhibit 8.2).

Exhibit 8.2 *Advantages and disadvantages of focus groups.*

Advantages	Disadvantages
• Enables researcher to observe interaction between respondents • Helps in detecting different views on a topic • Cost- and time-effective approach to obtain information from a group of people	• Requires a well-trained moderator • Individuals might dominate the group • Respondents might be reluctant to speak up or remain in their role

The main advantage of focus group interviews is that it allows observing the interaction between different respondents. This is often helpful in detecting different views on a topic, as other focus group participants can openly disagree, while a researcher has to remain neutral. In addition, different contributions of participants can be combined to new insights, which encourage further contributions and often offer insights into a topic that would have remained hidden in a one-by-one conversation. Focus group interviews are also cost- and time-effective as they allow a researcher to collect the ideas, opinions and knowledge of a larger group of people within two hours. Nevertheless conducting a focus group requires resources and a budget, e.g. to give participants a small present.

Holding focus group interviews requires, however, a well-trained and experienced moderator with good social and communication skills. Good moderators stimulate and structure discussions but also bring an issue to an end if the group is going in circles. Moreover, they need to encourage inhibited participants and curb dominant ones. The latter issue points at a general problem – group dynamics can have a negative impact if one or two people dominate the discussion or are reluctant to speak up freely due to social pressure.

Conducting focus groups

Participant selection

As qualitative research does not attempt to make inferences to the whole population, we do not need to strive for a representative composition of our focus groups. However, we need to ensure that we include the whole range of perspectives on an issue in our research. Thus, it is wise to think about who are the main stakeholders in an issue and invite all perspectives to participate. As mentioned before, 6–10 people is a good size for a focus group, but smaller groups can be useful if sensitive issues, for example sexual harassment, are discussed. Selected participants should receive an invitation stating session time, date and location as well as the purpose of the session. In some cases the discussion points are included as well. You should also select and invite more people as some will decline to participate or not show up. Small incentives, a few euros for student groups and small gifts, will increase the willingness to participate.

A crucial issue in participant selection is whether one forms homogeneous or heterogeneous focus groups. Homogeneous grouping is more common and tends to promote more intense discussion and freer interaction. If group members are too similar, discussions might not emerge and assumptions shared by the group members remain unsaid. In groups of people who work closely together, existing social patterns will be reflected in the focus group and open discussions suppressed. Heterogeneous groups lead to more argumentative interactions and syntheses might develop out of the contributions. If the differences in the assumptions and perspectives of the participants are very large and if participants hold dominant positions, the interactions often reduce to a repeated exchange of rhetoric arguments. Thus, heterogeneous focus groups work best if participants are still open to each other and can find some common ground. If you hold several focus group interviews, it is often wise to maximize the differences across the groups, rather than mix them. For example, if you are interested in the perspectives of middle and top managers on an issue, you would organize one focus group with top management and another one with middle managers.

Running the sessions

The success of focus group interviews depends on well-functioning logistics. The room should have a pleasant atmosphere, comfortable chairs and, very importantly, a good acoustic. Ensure that participants can get light refreshments. Additional space in the room where people can informally gather until everybody has arrived is convenient. You also need to check beforehand that the electronic equipment, audio or video recorders, is working properly and batteries are fully charged. Make test recordings to make sure the equipment captures the voices from all places in the room well.

Exhibit 8.3 Online resources for focus groups

Resources	URL
Small video clips explaining focus groups	• http://www.youtube.com/watch?v=mwaYzapf7nQ • http://www.youtube.com/watch?v=T5EASWcuOXI
Focus group examples on video	• http://www.youtube.com/watch?v=bKujUdCRKoQ • http://www.youtube.com/watch?v=BQMEDGgraKl
Commercial providers of online focus groups	• http://www.onlinefocusgroups.co.uk • http://www.focusgroupsonline.ie • http://www.dvj-insights.com • http://www.earsandeyes.com/de/marktforschung/methoden/qualitative-forschung/online-fokusgruppe/

Before the session, you need to develop a script that guides the moderator. Such a script contains the introduction to open the session, directions for participants, an opening question, questions to ask if the discussion falls dead or takes a direction the researcher is not interested in, and closing words. In the introduction, the moderator should introduce the participants to each other, explain the purpose and objective of the discussion and introduce the discussion house rules, such as only one person should speak at a time and that all viewpoints are important and should be respected by others.

During the session, the moderator has the most demanding job as outlined above. In addition the moderator needs to manage the time well. To ease the later interpretation of the discussion, one can ask participants for their key points of the discussion at the end of the session. As with all unstructured interviews, audio or video recording the session is useful, obviously with the consent of the participants. If that is not possible, a second person should be a note-taker so that the moderator can focus on the discussion process. When taking notes or transcribing audio recording, it is important not only to write down what has been said, but also who said it. Especially if discussions are vibrant and participants speak at the same time, it can become difficult to capture exactly who said what. Video recordings offer better possibilities to re-listen to the discussion and to match voices to faces and names.

Online focus groups

As we have seen earlier, information technology and especially the web has created new opportunities for conducting research. While traditional focus groups required that people would meet physically in a room, it is also possible to organize such meetings virtually. Online focus groups are organized either synchronously or asynchronously. Synchronous meetings refer to sessions where participants meet at the same time. Live chats or online conferencing and seminar tools, such as Webex, are widely used technologies here. Asynchronous focus groups use discussion boards, listservers and email. Participants read and respond to others' comments at any time, not necessarily at the same time others are contributing.

The advantages of online focus groups are decreased costs and the ease of bringing together geographically separated people. Moreover, online focus groups automatically generate recordings and, in the case of written interaction, even transcripts of the communication. In asynchronous focus groups, people can schedule their participation according to their own agenda. Another advantage often mentioned is that the virtual environment provides a perceived anonymity, which creates a larger openness. However, recent discussion around web privacy puts a question mark over the assumption that the web is anonymous.

Disadvantages of online focus groups include that participants need to have access to the web, a concern that is still valid, but becomes less relevant with increasing web access penetration rates. Online focus groups also reduce communication to content only, leaving out facial expressions and differences in vocal intonation. Moreover, the more formal the appearance will reduce the incidence of spontaneous comments and the willingness to engage in playful discussion to explore a topic. Audio or even video online conferences reduce these concerns, but the virtual focus group still occurs in a different setting and atmosphere than a physical one.

8.3 Participant observation

In the previous chapter, we discussed structured observations, whose checklist resembles a survey. Participant observation is a different approach originating from sociology and anthropology. The central idea of participant observation is that researchers attempt to fully dive into the world they research to understand it. Participant observation is rather popular among constructivists, as one of their main assumptions is that there is no objective world but only subjective worlds constructed differently by (groups of) human beings. Given this assumption, unravelling how an individual sees the world requires a research approach that digs deep into that constructed world. Participant observation offers this: the researcher becomes a part, participates in the participant's world and, thereby, can develop a feeling how they understand and give meaning to it.

> "At one end of the continuum are methods that are unstructured and open-ended. The observer tries to provide as complete and non-selective a description as possible. On the other end of the continuum are more structured and predefined methods that itemize, count, and categorize behaviour. Here the investigator decides beforehand which behaviour will be recorded and how frequently observations will be made. The investigator using structured observation is much more discriminating in choosing which behaviour will be recorded and precisely how [it is] to be coded."[4]

Bailey classifies observational studies by the degree of structure in the environmental setting and the amount of structure imposed on the environment by the researcher,[5] as reflected in Exhibit 8.4. The researcher conducting a class 1, completely unstructured, study would be in a natural or field setting endeavouring to adapt to the culture. A typical example would be an ethnographic study in which the researcher,

Exhibit 8.4 Classification of observation studies.

Research class		Purpose	Research tool
1	Completely unstructured	Generate hypotheses	
2	Unstructured		
3	Structured		Observation checklist
4	Completely structured	Test hypotheses	Observation checklist

as a participant-observer, becomes a part of the culture and describes in great detail everything surrounding the event or activity of interest. Donald Roy, in the widely used case on organizational behaviour, 'Banana Time', took a punchpress job in a factory to describe the rituals that a small work group relied on to make their highly repetitive, monotonous work bearable.[6] With other purposes in mind, business researchers may use this type of study for hypothesis generation.

Class 4 studies – completely structured research – are at the opposite end of the continuum from completely unstructured field investigations. The research purpose of class 4 studies is to test hypotheses; therefore, a definitive plan for observing specific, operationalized behaviour is known in advance. The classic example of a class 4 study was Bales' investigation into group interaction.[7] Many team-building, decision-making and assessment centre studies follow this structural pattern.

The two middle classes (2 and 3) of observation studies emphasize the best characteristics of either researcher-imposed controls or the natural setting. In class 2, the researcher uses the facilities of a laboratory – videotape recording, two-way mirrors, props and stage sets – to introduce more control into the environment while simultaneously reducing the time needed for observation. In contrast, a class 3 study takes advantage of a structured observational instrument in a natural setting. An example for a case 3 study is Mary Waller's research on crew interactions in crisis situations, in which a video taped pilots in flight simulators and analysed the pilot and co-pilot's communication in critical moments.[8]

Conducting observational studies

The design of an observational study follows the same pattern as other research. Once the researcher has specified the investigative questions, it is often apparent that the best way to conduct the study is through observation. Guidance for conducting an observation and translating the investigative question(s) into an observational checklist is the subject of this section. We first review the procedural steps and then explain how to create a checklist. Most studies that use the observational method follow a general sequence of steps that parallel the research process. Here we adapt these steps to the terminology of the observational method:

- Prepare an observational study (define the content and identify the observational targets, sampling strategy and acts).
- Secure and train observers.
- Collect the data.
- Analyse the data.

Define the content of the study and observation plan

The content of your study and your observation plan depends crucially on your research questions, but all observational studies investigate specific conditions, events or activities. And even if your research question has a very explorative nature, you do not start without any idea in your head. Much more likely you are interested in a not well-understood specific phenomenon or you have heard a story about a company that caught your scientific interest.

Suppose you are a researcher in leadership and you hear the story about a chamber orchestra working without a conductor. This is an interesting case and you might want to understand how a group of around 20 musicians can play well together without someone coordinating and leading the group, as is common in most other orchestras, but also in other groups of people working together. Now, you have the opportunity to accompany an orchestra for a couple of months, observing them during rehearsals and also live performances. Most likely before you start accompanying the orchestra, you will read a lot about conductor-less orchestras but also about leadership in teams, and so on.

Preparing for an observational study is essential for its success. You need to be well informed about the context and your observation target and you need also a broad background knowledge regarding the existing scientific insights into the phenomena you are interested in. If you observe the conductor-less orchestra to understand leadership then you need to be up to date on that topic; if you are more interested in the culture of such an orchestra, you need to be knowledgeable on theories about organizational culture.

Access

An essential key of observational studies is gaining access to an organization or group that is appropriate for your research questions. In companies, you will usually need the consent of higher management before you can observe activities within that company. Like convincing respondents to answer a survey, gaining access for an observational study is about motivating a third party to support you in your research. For observational studies it holds as well, that getting cooperation from an organization for your research project is not a yes/no decision, but often a negotiation process. Rather than not getting access, it is often wiser to pour some water into the wine and adapt the original research design to what is possible in that specific company. In addition, companies often expect something back if they allow you such broad access to their inner circle. Exhibit 8.5 summarizes some tools increasing your chances.

Observer training

If you are working in a team on the observation – for example, if a fellow student and you make a joint data-collection effort and write related research projects – it becomes important to train the observers (often including you) to reduce observer biases so it does not matter whether you observe a specific situation or another person does. You both would recognize the same.

Exhibit 8.5 Access tools.

Utilize your personal network

Ask family members, friends, and so on whether they can bring you into contact with an organization that would be suitable for you.

Get an inside mentor

Having a person within the organization you are investigating who is fully supporting you and helps you to find your way through the organization is of immense value. Often such persons are those of your personal network or someone who has been contacted through your network.

Reciprocity

It is also helpful if you can do something in return for the company. Researchers often promise to present their findings or write a report. However, you should be careful not to become a consultant; your primary objective is conducting valuable scientific research.

Approach companies prepared and step by step

When you approach a company you should also be well prepared and appear as an expert on that subject. The function of a first meeting is to get to know each other and its objective is to arrange a second meeting. In the first meeting, you will explain your project and provide a rough outline of what you expect from the company and get some references to other relevant persons in the organization. In the second meeting the company and you will talk in more detail about the project and they and you will determine how the study will be conducted within the company.

There are a few general guidelines for the qualification and selection of observers:

- Concentration: ability to function in a setting full of distractions.
- Detail-oriented: ability to remember details of an experience.
- Unobtrusive: ability to blend with the setting and not be distinctive.
- Experience level: ability to extract the most from an observation study.

An obviously attractive observer may be a distraction in some settings but ideal in others. The same can be said for the characteristics of age or ethnic background.

If observation is at the surface level and involves a simple checklist or coding system, then experience is less important. Inexperience may even be an advantage if there is a risk that experienced observers may have preset convictions about the topic. Regardless, most observers are subject to fatigue, halo effects and observer drift , which refers to a decay in reliability or validity over time that affects the coding of categories.[9] Only intensive videoed training relieves these problems.

The observers should be thoroughly versed in the requirements of the specific study. Each observer should be informed of the precise content elements to be studied. Observer trials with the instrument and sample videos should be used until a high degree of reliability is apparent in their observations. When there are interpretative differences between observers, they should be reconciled.

Data collection

The data-collection plan specifies the details of the task. In essence, it answers the questions: who, what, when, how and where.

Who?   What qualifies a participant to be observed? Must each participant meet a given criterion – those who initiate a specific action? Who has responsibility for the various aspects of the study? Who fulfils the ethical responsibilities to the participants?

What?   The characteristics of the observation must be set as sampling elements and units of analysis. This is achieved when event–time dimension and 'act' terms are defined. In **event sampling**, the researcher records selected behaviour (events), and in **time sampling** the researcher must choose among a time-point sample, continuous real-time measurement or a time-interval sample. For a time-point sample, recording occurs at fixed points for a specified length. With continuous measurement, behaviour or the elapsed time of the behaviour is recorded. Like continuous measurement, time-interval sampling records every behaviour in real time but counts the behaviour only once during the interval.[10]

Assume the observer is instructed to observe a quality-control inspection for 10 minutes out of each hour (a duration of two minutes each, five times). Over a prolonged period, if the samples are drawn randomly, time sampling can give a good estimate of the pattern of activities. In a time-interval sampling of workers in a department, the outcome may be a judgement of how well the department is being supervised. In a study of sales presentations using continuous real-time sampling, the research outcome may be an assessment of a given salesperson's effectiveness or the effectiveness of different types of persuasive message.

Other important dimensions are defined by *acts*. What constitutes an act is established by the needs of the study. It is the basic unit of observation. Any of the following could be defined as an act for an observation study: a single expressed thought, a physical movement, a facial expression or a motor skill.

Although acts may be well defined, they often present difficulties for the observer. A single statement from a sales presentation may include several thoughts about product advantages, a rebuttal to an objection about a feature or some remark about a competitor. The observer is hard pressed to sort out each thought, decide whether it represents a separate unit of observation and then record it quickly enough to follow continued statements.

When?   Is the time of the study important, or can any time be used? If you observe employees in a supermarket it matters whether you observe them in peak times (on Friday night and Saturday) or on a calmer Wednesday morning.

How?   Will the data be directly observed? If there are two or more observers, how will they divide the task? How will the results be recorded for later analysis? How will the observers deal with various situations that may occur – when expected actions do not take place, say, or when someone challenges the observer in the setting?

In observational studies the two most common collection formats are field notes and checklists. In both formats the researcher needs to record the information as systematically as possible to reduce biases due to selective perception and memory restrictions.

Where?   Within a spatial confine, where does the act take place? In a retail traffic pattern study, the proximity of a customer's pause space to a display or directional sign might be recorded. Must the observation take place in a particular location within a larger venue? The location of the observation, such as a sales approach observation within a chain of retail stores, can significantly influence the acts recorded.

Observers face unlimited variations in conditions. Fortunately, most problems do not occur simultaneously. When the plans are thorough and the observers well trained, observational research is quite successful.

Up to this point, our discussion has focused on direct observation as a traditional approach to data collection. Like surveys and experiments, some observational studies – particularly participant observation – require the observer to be physically present in the research situation. This contributes to a **reactivity response**, a phenomenon where participants alter their behaviour in response to the researcher. (You are familiar with the historic research at Western Electric and the so-called Hawthorne effect – introduced in Chapter 5 – and the reactions interviewers produce in participants that bias the findings of a study.)

Data analysis

A systematic analysis of the collected data is essential, even if the research objective is more exploratory. As the amount of information collected is often immense, data reduction and categorization is a major concern in the analysis of observational data. Techniques discussed in the section on content analysis (see Chapter 10.1) are especially useful in this respect. In addition, interpretations of the obtained data should be subject to cross checks. As discussed, triangulation is one approach to increase the validity of the findings. A second approach is to discuss the outcomes of the analysis with experts and participants. This allows you to find out whether your perspective on the phenomena is shared by those involved and makes sense to them.

Research Methods in Real Life
Being a waitress, tabloid journalist or a Turk in Germany

Barbara Ehrenreich, an activist, writer and journalist, went under cover to find an answer to the puzzling question of 'how can one live on $6 per hour'. Rather than interviewing unskilled workers, she left her life as writer and journalist and took various low-paid jobs throughout the USA for 18 months. She started as a waitress in Florida, became a house-cleaning maid in Maine and finished her journey working for Wal-Mart in Minnesota. In each place she tried to find a low-paid job. Of course, she concealed the fact that she holds a Ph.D. in biology and is a successful writer; rather she presented herself as a divorced homemaker re-entering the workforce after many years with three years of college education using the real name of the true school she went to.

Her book *Nickel and Dimed* gives a full account of her experiences as a low-paid waitress and how she managed to live from her earnings. She reveals, for example, that it had been impossible to find a safe and clean apartment to rent in metropolitan areas for the money she was earning. Thus, she often was coerced into living in a cheap motel or trailer park with only a microwave for cooking. Without a kitchen, however, she had to dine out which was only possible in fast-food restaurants given the budget constraint.

In Germany, Günter Wallraff is widely known for his under-cover investigations. His first remarkable story occurred while he was a reporter for the German tabloid *Bild*. For three months he became Hans Eser working as a reporter for the tabloid revealing how the daily paper made news by twisting facts and even employing illegal investigation methods. In later projects he masqueraded as a Turkish immigrant, a rough sleeper and an African asylum-seeker and gained experience on how people on the street, authorities and companies treated him. These roles allowed him to give a full account of the problems people at the bottom of society faced. Moreover, he documented that discrimination is the rule rather than the exception in German society.

Do you believe that Ehrenreich's and Wallraff's observations provide a good account of the real world? How would a scientific study differ from their approach?

References and further reading

Ehrenreich, Barbara, *Nickel and Dimed*. New York: Metropolitan Books, 2001.

www.guenter-wallraff.com

www.barbaraehrenreich.com

Observer – participant relationship

As the researcher dives deep into the participants' world, issues concerning the relationship between observer and participant become important. The relationship between the two can be classified along two dimensions. The first dimension reflects whether the observer takes an active part in the life of the participant; that is, does the researcher observe the participants' actions distantly from an umpire's chair or is the researcher actively involved? The second dimension refers to whether the observer is concealed or not, that is, whether the participants know/realize that they are being observed.

The issue of becoming actively involved in the participants' world allows a researcher to get a better understanding of what the situation is and how the participants feel. The Research Methods in Real Life 'Being a waitress, tabloid journalist or a Turk in Germany' above provides two examples of journalists taking another identity to experience and understand people often at the bottom of society. A distant observer is more likely to perceive the research object and its environment through his or her own filter that dissolves if the researcher becomes actively involved.

Taking the role of observer and participant simultaneously makes a dual demand on the observer. Recording can interfere with participation, and participation can interfere with observation. The observer's role may influence the way others act. Balancing these two roles and ensuring that on the one hand one's own involvement does not drive the action of others and on the other hand that the researcher's view and interpretation is not manipulated by the interests of the observed, is a crucial issue in participant observation.

The second dimension is concealment. Sometimes, the researcher is known as an observer to some or all of the participants; at other times the true role is concealed. While reducing the potential for bias, this again raises an ethical issue. Often participants will not have given their consent and will not have knowledge of or access to the findings. After being deceived and having their privacy invaded, what further damage could come to the participants if the results became public? This issue needs to be addressed when concealment and covert participation are used (see also Chapter 4 on ethical issues in research).

Conducting participant observation

A key issue in participant observation is the question who and what you should observe. Participant observation usually relies on convenience and snowball sampling (see Chapter 6). For example, assume your research interest is understanding how an open innovation strategy can be successfully implemented and specifically how a company can achieve competitive advantages and at the same time offer others (almost) free access to its knowledge. First, you need to find a company that follows an open innovation strategy and through personal contacts, for example a good friend, you can obtain access to a medium-sized computer game development company. Then you would start observing one project, for example the development of a new car race game, because your friend is working mainly on that project. Your choice of this specific company as well as the choice of the car race game project would qualify as a convenience sample. In the course of your fieldwork, you hear about other interesting projects for your research and you also get into contact with external parties that are related to the car race game project. You decide to include another project in your fieldwork and you also attend meetings with external parties, which can be described as a snowball sampling strategy.

The more distant you are as an observer the more descriptive are your observations. More actively involved, that is, participating, observers often complement their observations with qualitative and informal interviews. Descriptive observation usually starts by taking note of the physical setting. You walk around and try to get to know the people and the processes. In the example above, you would find out who is involved in the project, which task each project team member has, how the project is organized and who are the key players. While walking around, you also start observing the behaviour and interactions of the people and start listening to their conversations. If you are a more participating observer, you will get more involved in the conversations and ask questions that will help you to obtain important information to answer your research question. This will often include asking people what their perspective on a specific issue is or asking them to explain their behaviour and activities.

Field notes are the primary tool for collecting data in participant observations. Four principles help to ensure that selective memory and failing recalls reduce the threats to validity:

1 *Direct note*: record key words while you are on the setting either on a small notepad or use a voice recorder.
2 *Immediate full notes*: write your full notes immediately after you leave the setting and before you share them with others.
3 *Limit observation moment*: limit the time you are at the setting, because writing full field notes is laborious; noting down your observations of one hour is likely to take four hours.
4 *Rich full notes*: the full field notes should be very complete and include everything that you noticed. You need to ensure that you can understand the field notes even months later.

Running Case Study 8
Rebecca's focus groups

Being very conscientious and dutiful, Rebecca had difficulties understanding why fellow students would free-ride and cheat. She just couldn't imagine how anyone would do that. If she ever free-rode, she would crawl under a rock rather than return to university where she would meet her fellow students that she had let down. She knew that her friend Claire was easier about those things. Usually Claire would work hard, but sometimes opportunities presented themselves that were more enjoyable than studying. Just last week-end, Claire went off to Brussels to a movie festival, although on Tuesday a group assignment was due and the group hadn't done much work on it. Claire came to the group with her broad smile and said: 'You will not believe it, but Leo a school friend of mine has two premium passes for the Brussels movie festival and asked me to join him. This is the chance of my lifetime; I always wanted to go there.' Although she promised to do her share of work, her contribution was less in the end. The group worked hard on the weekend and everybody was commenting on Claire's absence. On Monday when Claire returned, those comments were, however, not repeated and all listened to Claire as she joyfully presented stories of glamour and inspiration. That she did not contribute as much as the others did not matter anymore.

Rebecca wanted to understand this better. Surely every student has experienced free-riding, many have engaged in it, but how should you respond? Report it to the professor? No, that is joining the enemy. What are strategies to prevent it? Rebecca decided to ask Claire's group if they would participate in a focus group on this issue in exchange for her famous home-made cake and coffee. She invited two groups and in both groups she raised that issue. Below you find a couple of citations from these focus groups:

Participant A: 'You know, they are asking so much from us, you have to work together – giving and taking is necessary to survive.'

Participant B: 'I really want to get good marks, but in a group you cannot expect that everybody has the same aspiration – if I want to get better marks I have to put more effort than others in it.'

Participant C: 'But then others profit from you, somehow that is not fair.'

Participant B: 'If the others do something, it is hard to tell them to do more.'

Participant A: 'As said it is give and take, next time the other will do more or he buys you a beer.'

Participant C: 'If I buy you are beer, I can become lazy and do nothing.'

Participant A: 'Not that directly. You know my English is not the best, so I have often asked Brenda to read through and correct my individual papers and then I invite her for a pizza. Is that cheating?'

Participant D: 'That is different. Brenda just helps you a bit, but she does not write the paper for you.'

Mehmet interviews everybody

Since Mehmet has started with his research project, he has talked to many people: entrepreneurs, business angels, policy makers, scientists and so on. He only talks about entrepreneurship. If he buys his groceries in the Turkish shop down the street and chats with the owner, he asks how business is going or how everything started. He tells them that he is conducting some research on this topic for his research project at the university. In the evening he joins the party, tells others about his research project and as soon as people tell him about some own experiences related to entrepreneurship he starts asking them more and more. Although all this talk has made Mehmet more knowledgeable, he had no idea how to analyse all the information he had obtained. What made matters even worse was that he did not really have notes on the interviews, what he had was an incomplete collection of business cards and a collection of all kinds of folders. As a first step, Mehmet sat down and tried to recollect the talks he had had so far and put them in some notes.

1 What can Rebecca gain out of her focus groups, given that her main research is based on a survey?
2 Do you have any suggestions how Mehmet could integrate the information he has obtained in all these informal talks?
3 What should be Mehmet's next steps?

Summary

1 Most qualitative research is based on primary data collection and unstructured interviews and are the main approach to obtain information and data. Unstructured interviews are flexible and depending on the answers of the respondent might take another course than originally expected. Different types of questions are used to stimulate the respondent to provide deeper or deeper coverage and to ensure that you, as researcher, have really understood what the respondent meant. Researchers should prepare an interview guide to ensure that all aspects they wanted to talk about are covered. In an unstructured interview the interviewer is much more involved in the interaction and therefore needs a good background knowledge on the issues discussed. It is very useful to record those interviews, as simultaneously taking notes, listening to the respondent and preparing the next question can be too demanding. Focus groups are a special form of unstructured group interviews. Next to obtaining information from a couple of participants sometimes with different perspectives, focus group interviews attempt to detect more by creating an atmosphere of active interaction that stimulates respondents to think further.

2 Observation is another method of qualitative data collection. While in structured observation, researchers attempt to observe pre-defined events or occurrences, participant observation will capture the whole. Although in most cases the researchers have some idea for what kind of behaviour and actions they are looking, they need to be prepared to notice behaviours and actions that they did not expect, but that could be key in explaining the phenomena under investigation.

Discussion questions

Terms in review

1 What are the question types in unstructured interviews?

2 Describe the potential advantages and disadvantages of focus group interviews.

3 Based on your present or past work experience, suggest problems that could be resolved by using observation-based data.

4 What is important for taking field notes?

Making research decisions

5 Take a published interview from a newspaper or magazine or even a video interview and look at all or some of the following issues:
- To what extent is it structured?
- Classify the types of questions asked.
- Where did the interviewer miss an opportunity to obtain even better information?

6 Assume you are interested in understanding how an organizational culture changes if two companies merge.
  a What are the research decisions you need to take?
  b How would you decide on the issues mentioned under a?

Classroom discussion

7 Discuss in the classroom or in sub-groups what would be needed to write a good case study on the following topics. Discuss explorative research questions for each topic, what information you would need and which sources you could approach.
  a The emergence of standards and their consequences in the telecommunications industry.

b   The effects of developments in information and communication technologies on the music recording industry.

c   The basis of Ryanair's success as a low-cost airline.

8   Discuss the following statement in class:

Unstructured interviews are like talking with a friend in a pub.

Depending on the size of the class, you could split the class into two groups; the first group runs a focus group interview, while the second group observes the discussion. After about 20 minutes both groups are asked about their experiences and observations.

9   Discuss the difference in scientific contributions between the following pairs of observational and survey research:

a   Observe the living patterns of long-term unemployed by spending a whole week with the person, compared to a large-scale mail survey among 1,000 long-term unemployed people.

b   Observe how a development team in a high-technology company works by meeting the team members several times, taking part in team discussions and even joining the team members for a beer after work, compared to personal interviews with 150 leaders of different development teams.

Recommended further reading

Bailey, Kenneth D., *Methods of Social Research* **(4th edn). New York: Free Press, 1995.** Includes a thorough discussion of observational strategies.

Denzin, Norman K. and Lincoln, Yvonna S., *The SAGE Handbook of Qualitative Research* **(3rd edn). Thousand Oaks, CA: Sage, 2005.** Of particular interest is Part 3 on strategies of inquiry, and Part 4 on methods of collecting and analysing empirical materials.

DeWalt, Katherine M. and DeWalt, Billie R., *Participant Observation: A Guide to Fieldworkers.* **Walnut Creek: Alta Mira, 2001.** An introductory text on ethnographic research, emphasizing the technique of participant observation.

Eisenhardt, Kathleen M., 'Building theory from case study research', *Academy of Management Review* **14(4), 1989, pp. 532–50.** This article describes the process of inducting theory, from case studies to writing conclusions, and discusses when case study is particularly useful.

Hammersley, Martyn and Atkinson, Paul, *Ethnography: Principles in Practice* **(3rd edn). London: Routledge, 2007.** A popular text book devoted entirely to ethnographic research methods.

Krueger, Richard A. and Casey, Mary Ann, *Focus Groups: A Practical Approach to Applied Research* **(4th edn). Thousand Oaks, CA: Sage, 2008.** A good book for those who want to conduct focus group interviews.

Kvale, Steinar and Brinkmann, Svend, *InterViews: Learning the Craft of Qualitative Research Interviewing* **(2nd edn). Thousand Oaks, CA: Sage, 2008.** A complete guide to interviews in qualitative research.

Yin, Robert K., *Case Study Research: Design and Methods* **(4th edn). Newbury Park, CA: Sage, 2008.** An excellent guide and one of the standard references for case study research. Designing and conducting a case study along the lines suggested in this text almost guarantees a good case study.

Get started with understanding statistical techniques!

When you have read this chapter, log on to the Online Learning Centre website at *www.mcgraw-hill.co.uk/textbooks/blumberg* to explore chapter-by-chapter test questions, additional case studies, a glossary and more online study tools for *Business Research Methods*.

Notes

1 Ray Pawson, 'Theorizing the interview', *British Journal of Sociology* 47, 1996, pp. 295–314.

2 Paul Beatty, 'Understanding the standardized/non-standardized interviewing controversy', *Journal of Official Statistics* 11(2), 1995, pp. 147–60.

3 Steinar Kvale, *Interview: An Introduction to Qualitative Research Interviewing* (2nd edn.). Thousand Oaks: Sage, 2008.

4 Louise H. Kidder and Charles M. Judd, *Research Methods in Social Relations* (5th edn.). New York: Holt, Rinehart & Winston, 1986, p. 292.

5 Kenneth D. Bailey, *Methods of Social Science* (2nd edn.). New York: Free Press, 1982, pp. 252–4.

6 Donald F. Roy, '"Banana time", job satisfaction, and informal interaction', *Human Organization* 18(4) (Winter 1959–60), pp. 151–68.

7 Robert F. Bales, *Personality and Interpersonal Behavior*. New York: Holt, Rinehart & Winston, 1970.

8 Mary J. Waller, 'The timing of adaptive group responses to nonroutine events', *Academy of Management Journal* 42(2), pp. 127–137.

9 Kidder and Judd, *Research Methods in Social Relations*, pp. 298–9.

10 Ibid., p. 291.

CHAPTER 9

Secondary data and archival sources

Chapter contents

Learning objectives

When you have read this chapter, you should understand:

1   the difference between primary and secondary data

2   the typical sources of secondary data, and how to select them

3   how secondary data can be used

4   what data-mining is and how it works.

Secondary data

In all the other chapters of Part 2, the different aspects and issues involved in conducting research by collecting primary information or data are discussed (i.e. how you, the researcher, can gather the information necessary to answer your research problem). An alternative to gathering information oneself is to use secondary data. Secondary data is information or data that has already been collected and recorded by someone else, usually for other purposes. A lot of information gathered by the government, for instance, is publicly available and accessible either at no or low cost.[1] Information pertaining to financial markets, such as stock prices and trading volumes, is widely available in financial newspapers or online at various financial portals. The annual reports of public companies are another source that is often used for secondary data.

Sometimes, the information you seek is not all available from one source but can be compiled from several sources, as the following example illustrates. Kwasi Bohahene works in the marketing department of a large publishing company. He would like to know whether the sales volumes of political books are related to the political orientation and participation of customers. Of course, Kwasi could hold a survey among potential customers, but it would take time to set up such a survey and Kwasi is not sure whether his boss would be willing to give him the budget required. So, he thinks about which of the data that are already available he could use to investigate his question. He can obtain the weekly sales data for each title and each bookstore from internal sources. Further, he knows that the results of the last national and regional elections for every constituency are available from government sources. Thus, by combining these two data sources he can build up a data file that contains, per constituency, the number of books sold and the party preferences and participation of the population in the last regional and national elections. Instead of using the election results from the government source, he might also choose to buy existing data on voting intentions from commercial research agencies that conduct opinion polls.

This strategy of supplementing existing data from internal sources, as in the example above, or obtained through primary data collection with secondary data can produce interesting datasets. For example, many primary surveys among business firms record the sector the firm belongs to. Secondary data containing information on different sectors can then be used to enrich the information regarding the external environment in which a firm operates.

Identifying and accessing secondary data

As a researcher, you will need to identify potential sources of secondary data. You need to know whether the information you require to answer your research problem is available, where you can find it, and whether and how you can access it. Identifying sources of secondary data can become time-consuming, especially if obtaining the desired data calls for the consultation of multiple sources, the data needs to be reorganized to be suitable for analysis and if the data are not available in electronic form. Often, you might find secondary data that contain only part of the information you need to answer your research problem, because either information (variables) is missing or the information is only available in aggregated form (e.g. the firm rather than the employee is the observation unit). If the deficiencies are not too large you might choose to reformulate your research problem by focusing on aspects that can be investigated with the available data or by addressing the problem with a different unit of analysis. A common problem in the usage of multiple sources is merging the different sources involved into one data file.

The accessibility of secondary data is often problematic too, as access to the data may be restricted. Business firms, like commercial research agencies, are unlikely to share data they have generated, because this information is a valuable asset that creates a competitive advantage. Even researchers at universities are reluctant to grant access to 'their' data, as they have invested time and effort in their collection, and want to milk them for their own studies and publications. However, if you have a good idea how existing data can be used to investigate a specific research problem, suggest collaboration, such as writing a joint paper or setting up a project. A benefit to the data owner can open doors.

Governments and other international institutions (see Exhibit 9.3 for a list of such information sources) often offer access to data free of charge, especially if the collection of the data has been financed with public funds. Other information sources are accessible at a fee that is substantially lower than the costs that would be involved if you were to collect the data for yourself. Sometimes a reduced fee will be charged if the data are to be used for academic purposes, such as a Masters or Ph.D. research project. Whenever you need to pay for access to secondary data, you need to calculate – provided that you have the funds to pay for the access – whether the benefits of the data are worth the investment.

The advantages of secondary data

The main advantages of using secondary data are that this approach saves time and money and you can obtain high quality data. As secondary data are usually already available, the researcher can rather quickly start to analyse the data and try to find an answer to his or her research problem. The often time-consuming activities of setting up the research, approaching the respondents, collecting information from respondents and recording any information obtained in a way suitable for analysis is not necessary. However, depending on the format, it might take some time until you find the opportunities the secondary database offers. This links to the second advantage of secondary data. Depending on the source of the data, such data are often of fairly high quality. This holds in particular for data offered by well-respected institutions such as local, national and international governmental institutions, or well-known research agencies. This high-quality data stems from the facts that (i) such institutions often have better access to information providers, (ii) those institutions often have rather huge budgets for data collection and (iii) many experts were involved in the research and data-collection process.

The disadvantages of secondary data

The main problem with using secondary data is that they were not collected with your specific research problem in mind. Thus, they might not fit perfectly with the requirements of your research problem. In assessing the usefulness of secondary data you need to address the following questions:

1 Is the information provided in the secondary data sufficient to answer your research problem?
   a Do the secondary data cover all the information you need?
   b Is the information available detailed enough?
   c Do the data follow the definitions you apply in your research problem?
   d Are the data accurate enough?
2 Do the secondary data address the same population you want to investigate?
   a Do the secondary data refer to the unit of analysis you want to investigate?
   b Is the sample on which the secondary data are based a good representation of the population you wish to address?
3 Were the secondary data collected in the relevant time period?

Information quality

If you cannot answer yes to all of the questions above, the usefulness of the secondary data is questionable. Question 1 and its sub-questions refer to the most common problem with secondary data. As secondary data have usually been collected for another purpose, they often do not cover all the information you need. For example, secondary data sources on the financial information of public companies often contain only the information published in annual reports. But if you are interested in how the strategic choices of firms affect their financial performance, these secondary data are insufficient, as the source contains detailed information on the latter but no information on strategic choices.

Similarly, information in secondary data is often not detailed enough. For example, company statistics often provide financial information on the corporate level, but that information is not broken down to different business units or different countries the companies are operating in. Hence, if you want to investigate the market for non-prescriptive drugs, company information is quite useless as the information provided mingles prescriptive with non-prescriptive drugs. A related problem is that the definitions used in the secondary data do not match with the definitions you wish to apply. Suppose, for example, you are interested in the position of Moroccan employees in France, but what counts as a Moroccan employee? The secondary data might only contain information on the nationality, which would exclude those of Moroccan origin but hold a French passport. The more people of Moroccan origin hold a French passport the more severe that problem becomes, as you might for example argue that holders of a French passport are better integrated into French society than non-holders.

Accuracy can be a serious problem when using secondary data if the source of the data is unknown. Earlier, we noted that secondary data can often be of a high quality if they come from official sources or well-known research agencies. Secondary data might also come from other sources, however, so before using the data you need to evaluate their source.

Sample quality

Another common problem with secondary data sources is that they often provide information on an aggregate level. For example, there are many **secondary sources** that provide a wide range of information on the level of the industrial sector, but fewer secondary sources that have the same information at company or even establishment level. The quality of the sample is another problem associated with secondary data. In particular, if the intention of your research is to predict or to generalize to a larger population, the data need to be representative. Finally, the timeliness of the data is important, as secondary data are often out of date.

Librarians evaluate and select information sources based on five factors that can be applied to any type of source, whether printed or electronic. These are:

1 purpose
2 scope
3 authority
4 audience
5 format.

Exhibit 9.1 summarizes the critical questions a researcher asks when applying these factors during information **source evaluation**.

Exhibit 9.1 Evaluating information sources.

Evaluation factor	Questions to answer
Purpose	• Why does the information exist? • How evident is the purpose it is trying to convey? • Does it achieve its purpose? • How does its purpose affect the type and bias of information presented?
Scope	• How old is the information? • How often is it updated? • How much information is available? • Is it selective or comprehensive? • What are the criteria for inclusion? • If applicable, what geographic area, time period or language does it cover? • How does the information presented compare with similar information sources? • What information did you expect to find that was missing? • Is there additional documentation on the data, such as detailed descriptions of the variables, information on the data-collection process (e.g. sampling), information on the definitions applied, and so on?
Authority	• What are the credentials of the author, institution or organization sponsoring the information? • Does the information source give you a means of contacting anyone for further information? • If facts are supplied, where do they come from?
Audience	• To whom does the information source cater? • What level of knowledge or experience is assumed? • How does this intended audience affect the type and bias of the information?
Format	• How quickly can you find the required information? • How easy to use is the information source? • Is there an index? • Is the information downloadable into a spreadsheet or word-processing program if desired?

The **purpose** of the source is what the author or institution is trying to accomplish. In general, the purpose may be to enlighten or to entertain. Among purposes in the enlighten sub-set, authors may be attempting to establish credibility, broaden knowledge within a field or discipline, or establish a company image. Once you have determined the purpose of the source, you will also want to determine whether or how it provides a bias to the information presented. Bias is the absence of a balanced presentation of information. Most researchers expect company websites to be biased in favour of the company; however, we expect sources offered by independent organizations to be more balanced, presenting both positive and negative information about relevant organizations without favouring one or the other.

Tied closely to the purpose of the source is its **scope**. What is the date of publication? What time period does this source cover? How much of the topic is covered and in what depth? Is the material covered local, regional, national or international? If the source is bibliographic, how comprehensive is it? If it is a biographical source, a directory or bibliography, what are the criteria for inclusion? If you do not know the scope of your information sources, you may miss essential information by relying on an incomplete source.

Of major concern to any information user is the **authority** of the source. We have already noted that **primary sources** are the most authoritative. In any source, both the author and the publisher are indicators of the authority. Authority also applies to web resources where anyone can post anything. In this environment it is always important to check the credentials of the site. For instance, data and statements about economic indicators on Thailand are much more likely to be authoritative if they come from a Thai government source or an international institution, such as the World Bank, than from a personal page with no information about the author or producer.

Audience is also an important factor in evaluating an information source and it too is tied to the purpose of the source. The audience for this textbook is college students – more specifically, college students who are studying or majoring in business or public administration, some of whom are practising managers. While others – for example, educators – may benefit from the information, the authors have taken great care to select appropriate examples and to write in terms that management students will easily relate to. Brokerage firm Charles Schwab has no confusion in terms of purpose or audience. In one of its ads, Charles Schwab is quoted as follows: 'I see the Internet as the single most empowering force for the individual investor.'[2] The Schwab.com website is designed to empower every single Charles Schwab customer, with rapid market summary updates, and research on companies and funds. The numerous awards Schwab has won for its website indicate that it is doing well in achieving its aims. It also uses an intranet to provide key information to its employees.[3]

Format factors may vary from source to source but, in general, relate to how the information is presented and how easy it is to find a specific piece of information. In a printed source, the arrangement of the information – alphabetical? hierarchical? chronological? – nearly always has an impact on the retrieval of information. Indexes are usually essential. Do cross-references link one term to related terms? How are acronyms handled? Is the reference to an item? Table number? Page? How do type fonts or colour help you find information? Furthermore, it is often important whether and how the information can be downloaded. In particular, if you are looking for quantitative information, whether the information is available in an electronic format and can be stored in a data matrix (preferably in the format readable by the software you use for analysis) is important, because otherwise you will have to record the information manually, which can be very time-consuming and boring.

Sources of secondary data

Exhibit 9.2 provides an overview of the different types of source of secondary data. One important distinction is whether each is an internal or external source. The data format, written or electronic, is another useful distinction criterion. These two dimensions create a 2 × 2 matrix. The two cells covering external sources can be subdivided further by the nature of the data publisher.

The distinction between written and electronic data sources has become vaguer with the increasing use of information technology (IT), as information that had formerly been stored on paper is increasingly stored electronically. Emails and written documents that have been scanned and stored in an electronic file are examples of this sort of

Exhibit 9.2 Sources of secondary data.

	Internal	External
Written	• Memos • Contracts • Invoices	Publishers of books and periodicals: • indexes • yearbooks Government and supranational institutions: • white books • reports Professional and trade associations: • (annual) reports Media sources: • newspapers and magazines • special reports (supplements) Commercial sources: • (annual) reports
Electronic	• Management information systems • Accounting records	Publishers of books and periodicals: • bibliographic databases Government and supranational institutions: • websites (of statistical offices) • CD-ROMs Professional and trade associations: • websites Media sources: • websites • CD-ROMs of complete volumes Commercial sources: • websites • datasets of previous studies

development. How information is stored electronically, however, still makes a difference to the researcher. Therefore, deciding on which data sources to use on the basis of how easily the stored information can be processed further might be a better idea.

Secondary information that is organized in a database or stored in a data-matrix format can be processed much more easily than a collection of tables containing the same information but only available as PDF files. Similarly, it makes a difference if financial information on the 50 EUROSTOXX companies is stored in one data file, such as a Microsoft Excel spreadsheet or SPSS data file, or in 50 different files (one for each company). In the latter case you would need to check whether the organization of all the files is identical, that is do they use the same labels for different items in the financial statements and do they all report in the same currency? Only after such a check and a probable reorganization of the files can you merge them.

Secondary data sources can either be internal or external. Internal sources are built up and maintained by the organization or institution for which the researcher is working. They are available only to members of this organization. All the information stored in management information systems, such as personnel records or accounting records, is clearly internal secondary data. It is mostly recorded for other purposes than research, but often provides sufficient information to investigate certain research problems. For example, the information stored in a customer relationship management (CRM) system is stored, among other reasons, to control the sales force and to register customer orders. Such a CRM database, however, is also likely to contain information that will be useful in investigating research questions, such as 'How do the efforts of the sales force relate to the volume of orders customers placed?' or 'What characterizes our high-volume customers?' In larger organizations in particular, a vast amount of information is stored for different purposes and researchers often fail to spot the potential value of such sources to their research. What complicates the usage of such data sources is that information is often stored in separate places, and the different departments of a company are often unaware of what information is available in other departments.

The term 'external secondary data source' refers to all data sources outside an organization or institution. As Exhibit 9.2 shows, external sources can be further distinguished by who provides the data. Publishers of books and journals are an important source of secondary data. The idea that books and journals mostly contain merely the analysis and interpretation of existing data is a misconception. For those studies that seek to investigate a longer time period, these are a vital source of information. Suppose you are interested in finding out how top managers and boards have changed in the last century. For such a study it would be a good idea to dig out information from books on the history of certain companies, or the biographies of (former) top managers. Periodicals and **indexes** such as yearbooks are an even more commonly used source of secondary data. Suppose you want to investigate what determines the level of transfer payments for European football players. Football yearbooks provide plenty of information on who sold and bought what player in the last season, and on characteristics of the players (such as age, position, number of internationals played and goals scored). Increasingly, such information is also available in electronic form, which often helps to ease the process of working with and processing the information.

Making up one of the most important sources of secondary data are governments and supranational institutions, such as the European Union (EU), Organization for Economic Co-operation and Development (OECD), International Monetary Fund (IMF), World Bank and the United Nations (UN). As mentioned earlier, the main advantage of such sources is that they provide data that is of a distinct high quality and accuracy. This information is available in the form of books and reports, but increasingly online and often at no cost. As well as national government and supranational institutions, regional governmental institutions also provide secondary information. For example, in Europe, many sub-national governmental bodies (e.g. the provinces in the Netherlands or the *Länder* in Germany) as well as cities collect regional information.

Trade and professional associations can also be a valuable source of secondary data if you are interested in specific industries or professions. Compared to secondary data from government sources, information obtained through trade and professional associations should be assessed carefully, however. Many trade and professional associations serve a lobbying function and hence may only publish favourable and biased information. This problem also applies to political interest groups and parties. Suppose you want to investigate whether and how oil companies, such as British Petroleum, Statoil or Shell, consider environmental issues in their strategy. Certainly, the information you might obtain from these oil companies would differ considerably from information obtained from environmental groups such as Greenpeace.

Every day, print media, radio and TV stations publish a vast amount of information. The *Financial Times* and *BusinessWeek* are two examples of a daily and a weekly print source of information on a wide array of business and economic issues. This information is based partly on press announcements from firms, governments, and so on, but also on the publications' own analyses via their journalists. In addition, many media commission research studies from commercial research agencies to learn about various aspects of a country's economic, political and social life. 'Top 100' lists are usually the outcome of such media studies commissioned from commercial research agencies (see Research Methods in Real Life below for an example). As almost all media have a website, a great deal of information is available online. Some media even maintain online archives with supplementary data and back issues, which can be very useful for research purposes, although to access them you sometimes need to subscribe to the service and pay a fee. Furthermore, most media have useful information on their readers, listeners or viewers, as this is essential for attracting advertisers. Although the information contained in such media kits may be less complete than one might wish, it can still be useful for research purposes, and is mostly available free of charge.

The final category of external sources of secondary data is the commercial source. Although every commercial firm is a potential source of secondary data – at least of data about the firm itself – we usually refer to companies that sell and publish information for a fee as commercial sources. With respect to business research in particular, the number of firms providing such services is huge and the differences between them also vast. Many companies in this field are mainly vendors of addresses and contact information that other companies need for direct marketing. For research purposes, such information is only useful for sampling purposes, especially if the address database covers (almost) the full population. Other commercial sources provide much more information than just addresses. Research firms such as Gallup and Infratest specialize in public opinion polls and surveys on consumer attitudes. Media often use these professional research services and publish the results (e.g. people's answers to that evergreen question 'Which party would you vote for if there was a general election today?').

Research Methods in Real Life
How to buy the Pope's car

For centuries auctions have been a well-known institution to match a seller and a buyer. However, the types of product that were auctioned rather than exchanged through the usual retail channels were mostly limited to expensive and rare goods, such as antiques. The main disadvantage of auctions was that the seller and the interested buyer had to meet each other at a specified time. Thus, sellers would only auction their goods if they could be certain that sufficient potential buyers would be willing to attend the auction at the specified time.

The Internet has changed the market for auctions as it has enabled access to virtual auctions. Now sellers and buyers are virtually matched. Internet auctions typically end at a specified time, but buyers do not need to be present at the specified time and can place their initial bids beforehand and even increase their bids as long as the auction has not finished. Probably the most well-known online auction platform is eBay. On eBay nearly everything is auctioned, even products that you cannot obtain in a shop. For example:

- A second-hand Volkswagen Golf is a popular car that is often auctioned on eBay but is also available at second-hand car dealers. But one Golf auction was particularly special as this Golf was formerly owned by Pope Benedict XVI. It was sold for €189,000 to the Golden Palace Casino in Austin, Texas. In March 2013 after Benedict XVI resigned, the Golden Palace auctioned the Golf again and the bidding stopped at €16,750.
- On 25 October 2007, the inaugural flight of the Airbus A380 left Singapore and arrived in Sydney. Singapore Airlines auctioned all tickets for this flight and the return leg on eBay. Everyone could have been part of this historical event in aviation history, at least if they had been willing to spend €402 for an economy seat or €72,172 for a first-class suite. In total, the auction of the flight tickets raised close to €1,000,000, which was donated to charity.

What makes online auctions appealing for researchers is that they can follow thousands of real bidding processes, as eBay records them automatically. Everybody with an eBay account can see the following information during and at the end of the auction: number of buyers who inspected the product, number of bids, time and height of each bid and the final price. Moreover, it is revealed how experienced the sellers and bidders are (indicated by the number of auctions completed successfully) and the reputation of sellers and bidders (indicated by the percentage of previous well-proceeded auctions).

Therefore, it is not surprising that recently many scientific articles investigating auction theory used eBay as a source for secondary data. For example, one study discussed how the reputation of a seller affects the final price achieved at an auction. Daniel Houser and John Wooders followed different offers of an identical product, a Pentium III 500 processor, to see whether sellers with a higher reputation achieved a higher price. As this and other studies show, eBay is a fruitful source for secondary data.

But what are the limits of these secondary data? What cannot be investigated?

References and further reading

Houser, Daniel and Wooders, John (2006) 'Reputation in auctions: theory, and evidence from eBay', *Journal of Economics and Management Strategy* 15(2), pp. 353–68.

www.ebay.de

news.bbc.co.uk/2/hi/europe/4518939.stm

vonality.com/singapore-airlines-a380-case-study.html

Financial data and stock market information make up another area that is well covered by commercial sources. Standard & Poor's and Moody are well-known research firms that provide all kinds of financial data and studies. Both firms have a reputation for the high-quality financial assessment of firms, as reflected in the breadth of acknowledgement of their credit ratings for government and company bonds. Other research firms, such as GfK and ACNielsen, specialize in marketing research, collecting information on consumer attitudes and behaviour, market shares, and so on. From a researcher's perspective the main problem with commercial sources is that accessing them is either not possible or often very costly. Commercial research companies earn their money by providing and collecting information. Many business firms commission studies from them as they have a wealth of expertise in the area of conducting research; however, these firms will usually insist on exclusive rights to any information collected.

The Internet has had a tremendous effect also on research methods. In Chapter 7 we already discussed web surveys, and web auctions, as a research subject as described above, is another example how the Internet impacts what and how we study phenomena. The Internet provides us every day with a million pages of new information. Not surprisingly researchers have started to develop instruments to extract information from it for research purposes.

Web data extraction goes beyond using the Internet to download information and data files provided by statistical offices, international organizations, etc. It refers to automated tools that search on multiple web pages for information. These tools are web crawlers or wrappers. A wrapper identifies certain information on target web sites, extracts the information and saves the information obtained. In social network research, researchers have used those techniques to crawl the public profile pages of people on social media sites, such as Twitter or LinkedIn, and thereby obtained information about who is connected to whom. Others have used those techniques to collect data on product prices and price changes in online shops. In fact wrappers are reverse web-page builders. While web-page builders combine information to templates, wrappers de-construct a web page into its information pieces, identify the relevant pieces and store them in a database.

9.3 How to use secondary data efficiently

We have looked at the advantages and disadvantages, as well as sources of secondary data, and illustrated numerous problems using them. Those occasions when you can identify and ensure full access to secondary data that enable you to answer your initial research problem fully are quite rare. However, if budget constraints do not allow you to collect primary information, you will have to rely on secondary data and put up with the imperfections. The following three considerations can ease the burden of living with these imperfections:

- merging of multiple secondary data sources
- adjusting your research problem to the available data
- investigating which research problems can be investigated with the available data.

A common problem when using secondary data sources is that they do not contain the information required. In some cases, the information required *is* available but not stored in one source. As we have already seen, this is when the merging of different sources is a solution. For example, a firm's internal sources might provide sufficient information on how the firm's operations perform in different countries, but contain no information concerning the external environment. Combining the internal data with external data on economic, social and political country factors will create a much richer dataset, which will permit the investigation of how different external conditions affect the firm's performance or internal procedures. It should be noted that using information from external sources is also a good strategy for enriching any primary data collected. You are often likely to record nominal information, such as country or industrial sector, in a primary survey. Such information becomes much more meaningful if you combine it with externally available information on countries or sectors.

Merging information from different sources into one database requires you to have some information that is available in all sources. If such 'matching' information is missing, you cannot merge the information, but you can still use different sources of secondary data to investigate your research problem. In Chapter 11, we discuss case studies and mention the method of triangulation (i.e. looking for evidence not just in one source but in multiple sources). Finding supporting evidence in multiple sources increases the validity of your results as, for example, it becomes less likely that the outcome is the result of a method or sample bias.

Adjusting your research problem to the available data is a very delicate strategy, as it carries the risk that the data and not the management problem drive your research. When cutting the research problem down to 'fit' the data, the most important question is always, 'Does it still make sense to embark on a research venture with such a "cleaned-up" research problem?' Generally speaking, the larger the deficiencies of the secondary data with regard to the original research problem, the less helpful it will be to adjust the research problem. Secondary data deficiencies can exist in terms of what information is available and how detailed that information is. An initial research question may refer to subjects in the secondary data. If the sampled subjects in the secondary data do not correspond with the population you are interested in, you need to ask yourself whether you can still learn something if you investigate the sub-optimal non-corresponding sample. For example, if you want to investigate the economic position of immigrants in your country, but the secondary data only contain information on immigrants from Mediterranean countries such as Italy, Turkey, Egypt and Morocco, it might be reasonable to use this data only if immigrants from Mediterranean countries form a large proportion of the immigrants in your country. Thus, secondary data on Mediterranean immigrants are reasonably useful in studying the economic position of immigrants in a western European country, but much less useful for a study in the USA.

Exhibit 9.3 Secondary data sources (selected examples).

Publishers of books and periodicals (see also Exhibit 3.11)		
McGraw-Hill Education	Publisher of scientific books and academic textbooks	www.mcgraw-hill.co.uk
Pearson	Publisher of scientific books and academic textbooks, and the *Financial Times*	home.pearsonhighered.com
Oxford University Press	Publisher of scientific books and academic textbooks	www.oup.co.uk
Data archives		
Social science data archives	Links to data archives in many countries	www.sociosite.net/databases.php
DANS	Data archive site of the Royal Dutch Academy of Science (KNAW)	www.dans.knaw.nl/en
UK Data Archive	Offers access to many research databases especially from the social sciences.	www.data-archive.ac.uk/
Government and supranational institutions		
Office for National Statistics	UK national statistics	www.ons.gov.uk
Statline	Dutch national statistics	www.cbs.nl/statline
OECD Statistics	Economic statistics at an international level	www.oecd.org
European Social Survey	Information on the values and social background of people in more than 20 European countries	www.europeansocialsurvey.org
Eurostat	Statistical agency of the European Union	ec.europa.eu/eurostat
Federal Reserve Bank	Economic data on federal reserve system and government time series	www.stls.frb.org
National Trade Data Bank of the US Department of Commerce	Offers access to various databases covering topics such as price indices, export opportunities per industry, country and product, political and socio-economic conditions and so on	Available on CD-ROM

Professional and trade associations		
British Furniture Manufacturers	Membership directories, industry information	www.bfm.org.uk
CBI (Confederation of British Industry)	Business surveys (not free), studies on British industry	www.cbi.org.uk
European Express Service Providers	Industry information, studies on the sector	www.euroexpress.org
Media sources		
FT Info	Company information	www.ft.com/companies
BusinessWeek	Company information, special reports on selected issues, news	www.businessweek.com
Commercial sources		
TNS-NIPO	Market and opinion research, offers some of the results of its studies free of charge	tns-nipo.com
Social media platforms		
Facebook LinkedIn Twitter	Social media platforms that allow to access a lot of information of their users	www.facebook.com www.linkedin.com www.twitter.com

If secondary data miss information or are less detailed, you again need to assess how severe the data problem is. For example, in an explanatory or predictive study it is very serious if you miss information on the dependent variable, but less serious if information on an independent or control variable is unavailable. Sometimes, it is even possible to use other available information as a proxy or indicator for missing information. For example, in a study investigating why people choose to become self-employed, the authors wanted to know whether their respondents came from wealthy families or not. Unfortunately, the secondary data did not contain information on the wealth of their families, but it did offer information on the educational level of respondents' fathers. As educational level is highly correlated with income, the authors decided to use 'father's educational level' as a proxy for the wealth of the family.[4]

The third consideration suggests data availability as the point of departure for any research venture. Rather than starting from a specific management dilemma, which is then reformulated to a researchable question, you start by looking at the available data and thinking about what interesting question it could be used to answer. Such a strategy does not aim to provide answers and solutions to a specific management problem, rather it intends to use existing information more efficiently. With the spread of information and communication technology, the amount of information collected and recorded has become infinite. However, this information is still underutilized. Data-mining, which will be discussed in the following sections, improves the utilization of existing information bases by applying advanced techniques. One should, however, note that many academic scholars are sceptical towards such a data-driven approach. Exploring data and taking the results as proven reality does not follow the scientific method, as theory is missing. The two routes to bring in theory are: first, one understands such explorations as an inductive venture to generate and develop new theory and second, before analysing the data one selects an existing theory that is testable with the information contained in the secondary data.

Student Research

Football and diversity

Fatima Büruk loves football. She is rather well informed about what is going on in European football and especially about the Turkish and German competition. Fatima is the daughter of Turkish migrants and grew up in Cologne. Given her background, it is not surprising that team diversity was a topic catching her attention early on, as she herself strongly believed that diverse teams outperform less diverse teams as they bundle a wider range of experiences, take different perspectives on a problem, and so on.

For her research project, she combined her love for football and her interest in team diversity and studied the diversity and performance of German football teams. Football teams seemed to be ideal for such a study, as national diversity in professional football teams varies considerably but it is also rather high; success of the teams depends crucially on how well the team plays together and team performance is rather easily measured. Moreover, for each professional player, it is quite easy to obtain information.

For her research, Fatima consulted several information sources. Information on the diversity of the teams was obtained from a leading football magazine in Germany, *Kicker*, that publishes a special edition at the start of each season portraying the clubs and their players. In addition, she consulted the website www.fussballdaten.de, which provides a rich source for all kind of information regarding football. As Fatima was also interested in characteristics of the coach and management of the clubs, she also consulted the websites of the clubs, the national football association DFB and others to fill in gaps.

In the end, she had collected information on 29 clubs, who all played at least four seasons in the last 11 years in the Bundesliga. To measure performance, she employed a relative indicator, namely the ratio between points gained against the maximum points possible (102 points = 34 matches × 3 points for a win) in a specific season. For the diversity measures, she relied on the players' information, namely tenure (years a player remained with the club), age, skill (players' year average grade in the magazine *Kicker*) and nationality. Moreover, she included the tenure of the coach and manager in her analysis.

Fatima used the assessments of the football magazine to measure the skills of the players. Would you trust such assessments or might they be biased? Is the nationality information used sufficient to measure the cultural diversity in a team? For the curious, Fatima's study shows that culturally more diverse German football teams perform better. Does that mean that managers should invest in team diversity or is it that better performing teams are more active on the international player market resulting in more diverse teams?

9.4 Secondary data in qualitative research

Secondary data have a prominent role in qualitative research: for example, case studies usually rely on multiple data sources, such as personal interviews with key people in an organization and also internal documents or, say, newspaper clippings connected with the organization being investigated in the case. Moreover, official statistics provide useful information for determining general context, such as general or sector-specific economic conditions, and so on. Qualitative researchers often make use of secondary data, which were originally produced without any intention of analysing them. Secondary data from official statistics, but also from internal databases, are usually collected in order to conduct only a descriptive analysis of a current situation. Many other secondary data, such as letters, memos, autobiographies, newspapers and journals, are produced with a completely different intention. However, researchers can still use the information contained in these sources in their qualitative analysis. Information from such sources becomes extremely valuable if the problem statement addresses developments that may have started or occurred a long time ago. The growing field of business history is a typical example of research relying heavily on such secondary data sources.

In business research, organizational documents are another important source of secondary data. Many organizational documents are freely accessible, such as annual reports, information supplied to shareholders, press releases, public relations material and advertisements, either in printed or electronic form. Other documents, such as newsletters, memos, internal and external letters, manuals, company procedures and the like, are not public and the researcher needs to ask permission from the organization to access them (e.g. through company archives).

As with any secondary data the researcher needs to assess the quality of the data, and their relevance and usefulness for the research problem addressed. An obvious problem with organizational documents is that they are mostly written for a specific purpose and may present information strategically. This is obviously the case with advertisements and public relations material, which is produced to present a company and its products or activities in the most favourable light. However, even accounts of internal communication (e.g. emails exchanged within a department) are often written with a hidden agenda in mind, of which you as a researcher may be unaware.

9.5 Data-mining

Every day, organizations at all levels collect a tremendous amount of information and record it in databases. Such information is not gathered to investigate specific research problems; rather, it is part of an advanced control and monitoring process. Although the objective of collecting and recording the information is not related to business research, such information can be very useful in investigating research problems.

The term **data-mining** describes the process of uncovering knowledge from databases stored in data warehouses. The purpose of data-mining is to identify valid, novel, useful and ultimately understandable patterns in data.[5] Similar to traditional mining, where miners search beneath the surface for valuable ore, data-mining searches large databases for information that is indispensable to managing an organization. Both types of mining call for a large amount of material to be sifted before a profitable vein is discovered. Data-mining is a useful tool; it is an approach that combines exploration and discovery with confirmatory analysis. Data-mining can be seen as a very sophisticated tool for inductive discovery processes, since it departs from real observations, the stored data. It applies complex techniques (see Deeper Insight below) to restructure given data such that new insights can be gained.

An organization's own internal historical data is often an underutilized source of information in the exploratory phase. While digging through data archives can be as simplistic as sorting through a file containing past shipping manifests or rereading company reports that have grown dusty with age, we will concentrate the remainder of our discussion on more sophisticated structures and techniques.

A **data warehouse** is an electronic repository for databases that organizes large volumes of data into categories to facilitate retrieval, interpretation and sorting by end-users. The data warehouse provides an accessible archive to support dynamic organizational intelligence applications. The key phrase here is 'dynamically accessible'. Data warehouses that offer archaic methods of data retrieval are seldom used. Data in a data warehouse must be updated continuously to ensure that managers have access to data appropriate for real-time decisions. In a data warehouse, the contents of departmental computers are duplicated in a central repository where standard architecture and consistent data definitions are applied. These data are available to departments or cross-functional teams for direct analysis, or through intermediate storage facilities or **data marts** that compile locally required information. The entire system must be constructed for integration and compatibility among the different data marts.

The more accessible the databases that comprise the data warehouse, the more likely it is that a researcher will use such databases to reveal patterns. Thus, researchers are more likely to mine electronic databases than paper ones. It is useful to remember that data in a data warehouse were once primary data, collected for a specific purpose. When researchers data-mine a company's data warehouse, all the data contained within that database become secondary data. The patterns revealed will be used for purposes other than those originally intended. For example, in an archive of sales invoices, we have a wealth of data about what was sold, how much of each item or service, at what price level, to whom, and where, when and how the products were shipped. Initially, the company generated the sales invoice to facilitate the process of getting paid for the items shipped. When a researcher mines that sales invoice archive, the search is for patterns of sales, by product, category, region of the country or world, price level, shipping method, and so on.

Traditional database queries are unidimensional and historical – for example, 'How many chocolate bars were sold during December 2010 in the Netherlands?' In contrast, data-mining attempts to discover patterns and trends in the data, and to infer rules from these patterns. For example, an analysis of retail sales by the Dutch supermarket chain Edah identified products that are often purchased together – like candy bars and soft drinks – although they may appear to be unrelated. With the rules discovered from the data-mining, a manager is able to support, review and/or examine alternative courses of action for solving a management dilemma, alternatives that may later be studied further in the collection of new primary data.

The evolution of data-mining

The complex algorithms used in data-mining have existed for more than two decades. Customized data-mining software using neural networks, fuzzy logic and pattern recognition has been employed to spot tax fraud, eavesdrop on foreign communications and process satellite imagery.[6] Until recently these tools have been available only to very large corporations or agencies due to their high costs. However, this is changing rapidly. In the evolution from business data to information, each new step has built on previous ones. For example, large database storage is crucial to the success of data-mining. The four stages listed in Exhibit 9.4 were revolutionary because each allowed new management questions to be answered accurately and quickly.[7]

Exhibit 9.4 *The evolution of data-mining.*

Evolutionary step	Investigative question	Enabling technology	Characteristics
Data collection (1960s)	What was my average total revenue over the last five years?	Computer, tapes, disks	Retrospective static data delivery
Data access (1980s)	What were the unit sales in Sweden last December?	Relational databases, structured query language	Retrospective, dynamic data delivery at record level
Data navigation (1990s)	What were the unit sales in Sweden last December? Drill down to Uppsala.	Online analytical processing, multidimensional databases, data warehouses	Retrospective, dynamic data delivery at multiple levels
Data-mining (2000s)	What is likely to happen with Uppsala sales next month? Why?	Advanced algorithms, multiprocessor computers, massive databases	Prospective, proactive information delivery
Big data (2010s)	Should we make a special offer to a customer who just entered the shop?	Automatic storage and combination of data traces people leave when using the web, customer cards and mobile phone applications.	Lifetime data analyses, proactive and predictive delivery

The process of extracting information from data has been present in some industries for years. Insurance companies often compete by finding small market segments where the premiums paid greatly outweigh the risks. They then issue specially priced policies to a particular segment with profitable results. However, two problems have limited the effectiveness of this process: getting the data has been both difficult and expensive; and processing it into information has taken time – making it historical rather than predictive. Now, instead of incurring high data-collection costs in order to resolve management questions, secondary data are available to assist the manager's decision-making.

Data-mining tools

An understanding of statistics is essential to the data-mining process. Data-mining tools perform exploratory and confirmatory statistical analysis to discover and validate relationships. Data-mining tools even extend confirmatory statistical approaches by allowing the automated examination of large numbers of hypotheses. Suppose that there are 12 variables in a survey and we have a process, the outcome of which can be predicted when three variables are in a particular range. However, we are unfamiliar with the process and do not know which variables are relevant. With this small problem there are $12 \times 11 \times 10 = 1{,}320$ combinations. If you spent a minute examining a plot of each pair of variables, you could easily spend 22 hours on the problem.

Data-mining tools can be programmed to sweep regularly through databases and identify previously hidden patterns. An example of **pattern recognition** is the detection of stolen credit cards based on the analysis of credit card transaction records. MasterCard processes 12 million transactions daily and uses data-mining to detect fraud.[8] Other uses include finding retail purchase patterns (used for inventory management), identifying call centre volume fluctuations (used for staffing), and locating anomalous data that could represent data-entry errors (used to evaluate the need for training, employee evaluation or security).

Predictions are another example for data-mining that is for example often used in targeted marketing. Using data from past promotional mailings to identify the targets most likely to maximize return on investment, future mailings can be made more effective. The Bank of America uses data-mining software to pinpoint marketing programmes that attract high-margin, low-risk customers.[9] Other predictive problems include forecasting bankruptcy and loan default, and finding population segments with similar responses to a given stimulus. Data-mining tools can also be used to build risk models for a specific market, such as discovering the top 10 most significant buying trends each week.

Deeper Insight into Research Methods

Data-mining techniques

Numerous techniques are used in data-mining; often they are used together. The type of data available and the nature of information sought determine the technique used. Here we explore the following six tools:

- data visualization
- clustering
- neural networks
- tree models
- classification

Data visualization

By viewing aggregated data on multiple dimensions (e.g. product, brand, date of sale and region), both the analyst and the end-user gain a deeper, more intuitive understanding of the data in picture form. This is known as **data visualization**. A multidimensional database typically contains three axes: (i) dimensions, like the fields in a table; (ii) measurements, aggregate computations to be viewed; and (iii) hierarchies, which impose structure on the dimensions. For example, a set consisting of months, quarters, years is a time-based hierarchy.[10] Using this approach the researcher views the data at various levels ('drill down/drill up'). Starting with a total of sales of breakfast cereal by region, say, the researcher observes that one region is more profitable than others. Next, she drills down to sales by store and discovers that one store is outperforming all others. Looking deeper yet reveals that this store spends the most on training warehousing personnel.

Clustering

Clustering enables the researcher to segment a population. This approach assigns each data record to a group or segment. The assignment process is performed automatically by clustering algorithms that identify the similar characteristics in the dataset and then partition them into groups often referred to as the 'nearest neighbours'. Clustering is often used as the first step in data-mining. For example, it may be used to segment a customer database for further analysis of customers' buying habits to decide which segments to target for a new sales campaign.

Neural networks

Neural networks are collections of simple processing nodes that are connected. Each node operates only on its local data and on the inputs it receives via the connections. The result is a non-linear predictive model that resembles biological neural networks and learns through training. The neural model has to train its

▶

network on a training dataset. One drawback is that no explanation of the results is available. Neural networks are best used where a predictive model is more useful than an explanatory model. For database marketing, a neural network can be constructed that predicts whether a specific person is likely to purchase a particular product. This enables the marketing organization to be very specific in its target marketing, reducing costs and dramatically improving sales 'hits'.

Decision tree models

This technique segregates data by using a hierarchy of if-then statements based on the values of the variables, and creates a tree-shaped structure that represents the segregation decisions. **Decision tree models** are faster and easier to understand than neural networks, but the data must be interval or categorical. Specific decision tree methods include classification and regression trees (CART) and chi-square automatic interaction detection (CHAID), a type of automatic interaction detection model.

Classification

Classification uses a set of pre-classified examples to develop a model that can classify the population of records at large. Fraud detection and risk assessments of credit applications are particularly well suited to this type of analysis. Classification frequently employs decision trees or neural network-based classification algorithms (see the descriptions below). Classification begins with training the software with a set of pre-classified sample transactions. For a fraud-detection application, this would include complete records of both fraudulent and valid activities. The algorithm uses these cases as criteria to set the parameters for proper discrimination. Once developed, the model can correctly classify new records into the same pre-defined classes. For example, a model capable of classifying loan applicants may generate a rule stating: 'If applicant earns €45,000, is between 35 and 45 years old, and lives in a specific area, then the applicant is a good credit risk.' Estimation is a variation of classification. Instead of using a binary classifier (e.g. a loan applicant is a good risk or a bad risk), estimation generates a score (e.g. of creditworthiness) based on a prescored training set.

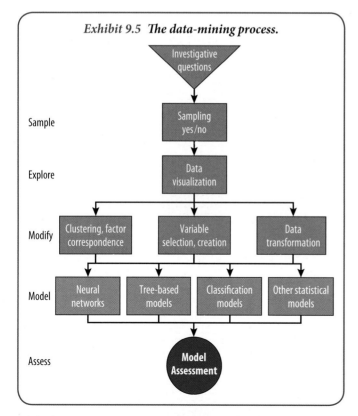

Exhibit 9.5 The data-mining process.

The data-mining process

Data-mining, as illustrated in Exhibit 9.5, involves a five-step process.[11]

1 Sample: decide between census and sample data.
2 Explore: identify relationships within the data.
3 Modify: modify or transform data.
4 Model: develop a model that explains the data relationships.
5 Assess: test the model's accuracy.

To better visualize the connections between the techniques just described and the process steps listed in this section, you may want to download a demonstration version of data-mining software from the Internet, such as the SAS Enterprise Miner (www.sas.com/service/consult/usconsult/miningcompaq.html), Compaq Advanced Data Mining Center (www.compaq.com, keyword search: data mining) or the SPSS demo (www.spss.com/lementine/newshow/sld003.htm).

Sample

Exhibit 9.5 suggests that the researcher must decide whether to use the entire dataset or a sample of the data.[12] If the dataset in question is not large, if the processing power is high or if it is important to understand patterns for every record in the database, sampling should not be done. However, if the data warehouse is very large (terabytes of data), the processing power is limited or speed is more important than complete analysis, it is wise to draw a sample (see Chapter 6 on sampling). In some instances, researchers may use a data mart for their sample – with local data that are appropriate for their geography. Alternatively, the researcher may select an appropriate sampling technique. Since fast turnaround for decisions is often more important than absolute accuracy, sampling is appropriate. If general patterns exist in the data as a whole, these patterns will be found in the sample. If a niche is so tiny that it is not represented in a sample yet is so important that it influences the big picture, it will be found using exploratory data analysis (EDA).

Explore

After the data are sampled, the next step is to explore them visually or numerically for trends or groups. Both visual and statistical exploration (data visualization) can be used to identify trends. The researcher also looks for outliers to see if the data need to be cleaned, cases need to be dropped or a larger sample needs to be drawn.

Research Methods in Real Life

Do you have more friends than your grandparents?

Yes, of course you have, as on average young people have more friends than older people. But the more interesting question is whether you are better connected to friends than your grandparents were when they were in their twenties? In 1967, Stanley Milgram conducted a social-psychological experiment. Milgram gave a postcard to 300 participants and requested them to hand this postcard to a target person in a distant city. They could only hand over the postcard via a person that they knew well. Thus, if I asked you to deliver such a card to Francesco Campi, an electrician living in Firenze, you would probably not know that person directly, but to deliver the card you would scan your network for an Italian friend, preferable one from Firenze. Assume you have an Italian friend but she lives in Milano. She receives the card and as her network contains more people in Italy, chances are pretty good that she knows somebody in Firenze. Firenze is a big city and it is unlikely that our Firenzian contact knows Francesco directly, but he might know an electrician in Firenze and chances are pretty good that electricians know each other. Thus, although you don't know Francesco Campi, it took you just four steps to give the postcard. When Milgram conducted his experiment in 1967, just a quarter of the postcards got delivered, but those that got delivered needed six steps on average. This is called the 'small-world phenomena', i.e. we can reach the whole world through a very limited number of contacts.

In 2013, researchers from University degli Studi di Milano joined forces with Facebook and analysed the 721 million Facebook users and their 69 billion friendship links, which suggests that people have on average close to 200 Facebook friends. The average distance between Facebook users is 4.74 and if you restrict the Facebook sample to the US, like Milgram did, the average distance becomes 4.32. For those interested, the average Facebook distance within Italy is 3.89, within Sweden 3.9, and combining Sweden and Italy it is 4.16.

What can we learn from the Facebook big data? Are people really better connected today than 50 years ago? Can you compare the average distances within the US between the Milgram experiment (5.7) and Facebook's big data (4.32)? Has the world become smaller?

References and further reading

Travers, Jeffrey and Milgram, Stanley, 'An experimental study of the small world problem', *Sociometry* 32(4), 1969, pp. 425–443.

http://people.cam.cornell.edu/~jugander/papers/websci12-fourdegrees.pdf

Modify

Based on the discoveries in the exploration phase, the data may require modification. Clustering, fractal-based transformation and the application of fuzzy logic are completed during this phase as appropriate. A data-reduction program, such as factor analysis, correspondence analysis, or clustering, may be used (see Chapter 20). If important constructs are discovered, new factors may be introduced to categorize the data into these groups. In addition, variables based on combinations of existing variables may be added, recoded, transformed or dropped. At times, descriptive segmentation of the data is all that is required to answer the investigative question. However, if a complex predictive model is needed, the researcher will move to the next stage of the process.

Model

Once the data are prepared, construction of a model begins. Modelling techniques in data-mining include neural networks as well as decision tree, sequence-based, classification and estimation, and genetic-based models.

Assess

The final step in data-mining is to assess the model to estimate how well it performs. A common method of assessment involves applying a portion of data that was not used during the sampling stage. If the model is valid, it will work for this 'holdout' sample. Another way to test a model is to run the model against known data. For example, if you know which customers in a file have high loyalty and your model predicts loyalty, you can check to see whether the model has selected these customers accurately.

The validity of the data mining information can be based on the following criteria:

- accuracy
- reliability
- reality check.

Accuracy. Accuracy is gained when the data gathered are complete and match with the kind of information you were looking for. This means we need to avoid assumptions about what the data measure, unless we have prior proof that the assumption is true. Accuracy refers to the fact that we often interpret existing information broader than what is actually stated. For example, if we observe a sharp increase in web searches for pregnancy can we conclude that more people are thinking about having a baby and can we predict that in the next year we will experience a boom in newborn babies?

Reliability. The reliability of information is based on the idea to what extent the information obtained is independent from different settings. Reliability is linked to accuracy, as it is only high when assumptions made hold in different circumstances.

Reality check. A potential pitfall of data-mining is that one uses advanced analysis techniques provided by different software packages without fully understanding the involved mathematics. Three problems do easily emerge: over-identification of models; capitalization on chance; and the difference between statistically significant and practically relevant. Over-identification occurs if the model is fitted more and more to the data by making certain assumptions. In the end the data fit the model perfectly, but the model does not offer any more generalizable results. Capitalization on chance occurs when researchers are seduced to fit thousands of models and then select the model that offers the best results. Finally, especially with large datasets, even tiny differences between groups become significant, but that does not mean that they are practically relevant. For example, based on a very large dataset you might find that people who make international calls at least once a week spend on average €0.50 more on their weekly groceries. Even if this difference is significant, it might not justify a targeted marketing campaign.

Big data

Big data is a more recent discussion that engages many people in business and academia. Big data refers to the tremendous amount of data traces each of us leaves, when we use the web, our mobile (smart)phones as well as customer, credit and debit cards. For some companies hosting sites on the web or offering free apps for smartphones, collecting these individual data is a central element for their business model. They offer us a useful survey for free and get detailed information about us in exchange, which they can re-sell to interested parties. If we allow access to all the information stored in our smartphones, we tell others who are our friends (contact list), how often we speak to them, for how long (call list), where we have been and where we stayed. Such information is valuable for businesses, but also for researchers in the social and businesses sciences.

Big data offer tremendous opportunities and a recent report by McKinsey reveals that companies' capability to utilize big data will become one of the major competitive advantages. In the last US presidential elections, it is said that Obama's victory was largely explained by his campaign team's ability to analyse all kinds of existing voter information at the detailed level and translate that to personalized approaches towards potential voters.

Although there are opportunities available through big data, there are also concerns. A major concern is to what extent big data collection infringes privacy, security and intellectual property rights. Currently these discussions are rather high on the political agenda and the EU seems to favour more stringent privacy protection policies than the USA. Next to these legal and political issues, another issue is, of course, how valid and how reliable the information is. Take the example above on the friendship network within Facebook. What is a Facebook friend – usually someone you know, but is it really a friend? Does somebody with more than 1,000 Facebook friends have a more fulfilled social life than somebody with just 20 Facebook friends? There is no clear answer to this question, as all the data traces we leave behind on the web are just indicators of our motives and behaviours, but not direct measures. Up to now the traces we leave are also fragmented. That means your purchases with your credit card are not connected to your comments on Facebook or to web-surfing behaviour on your tablet. Thus, currently despite the enormous amount of data, one does not know how complete the information is.

Running Case Study 9
Other sources?

One evening, Rebecca browsed the Internet to broaden her view on ethics. While surfing the web she came across a paper on the ethics of managers and entrepreneurs with an empirical analysis based on the European Social Survey. To her surprise the data used were freely accessible (www.europeansocialsurvey.com). Looking at that website, she discovered that the European Social Survey is a very large survey held every two years in almost all European countries among representative country samples. The number of respondents is astonishingly large; the sample size is about 40,000 for the whole sample and at least around 1,000 for the samples of each country. In 2004, the survey contained an additional questionnaire about economic morality. In total, each respondent answered 30 questions on economic morality (see below). Rebecca was fascinated by this rich source of data. So she downloaded them and played around with them.

Thirty additional questions on economic morality in the European Social Survey 2004

I now want to ask you about how citizens and members of society should behave. Please rate the statement below on a scale from 1 (completely agree) to 5 (completely disagree).

1 Citizens should spend at least some of their free time helping others.
2 Society would be better off if everyone just looked after themselves.
3 Citizens should not cheat on their taxes.

How much would you trust the following groups to deal honestly with people like you? Please rate the groups from 1 (distrust a lot) to 5 (trust a lot).

4 Plumbers, builders, car mechanics and other repair people.
5 Financial companies such as banks or insurers.
6 Public officials.

How often, if ever, have each of these things happened to you in the last five years? (Answers from never to more than twice).

7 A plumber, builder, car mechanic or other repair person overcharged you or did unnecessary work.
8 You were sold food that was packed to conceal the worse bits.
9 A bank or insurance company failed to offer you the best deal you were entitled to.

10 You were sold something second-hand that quickly proved to be faulty.

11 A public official asked you for a favour or a bribe in return for a service.

12 **We have just asked you about experiences of being treated dishonestly over the past five years. Using this card, how worried are you that things like this will happen to you (not all worried is 1 and very worried is 4)?**

How wrong, if at all, do you consider the following ways of behaving to be? Please rate between 1 (not wrong at all) and 4 (seriously wrong)

13 . . . someone paying cash with no receipt so as to avoid paying VAT or other taxes?

14 . . . someone selling something second-hand and concealing some or all of its faults?

15 . . . someone making an exaggerated or false insurance claim?

16 . . . a public official asking someone for a favour or bribe in return for their services?

How much do you agree (1) or disagree (5) with these statements about how people see rules and laws?

17 If you want to make money, you can't always act honestly.

18 You should always strictly obey the law even if it means missing good opportunities.

19 Occasionally, it is alright to ignore the law and do what you want to.

How much do you agree or disagree with each of these statements about the way the economy works these days?

20 Nowadays businesses are only interested in making profits and not in improving service or quality for customers.

21 Nowadays large firms work together in order to keep their prices unnecessarily high.

22 Nowadays customers and consumers are in a better position to protect their interests.

23 **Suppose you planned to get benefits or services you were not entitled to. How many of your friends or relatives do you think you could ask for support?** (Answers from none to almost all)

How often, if ever, have you done each of these things in the last five years? How often, if ever, have you . . . (Answers from never, once, twice, or more than twice).

24 . . . kept the change from a shop assistant or waiter knowing they had given you too much?

25 . . . paid cash with no receipt so as to avoid paying VAT or other taxes?

26 . . . sold something second-hand and concealed some or all of its faults?

27 . . . misused or altered a card or document to pretend you were eligible for something you were not?

28 . . . made an exaggerated or false insurance claim?

29 . . . offered a favour or bribe to a public official in return for their services?

30 . . . over-claimed or falsely claimed government benefits such as social security or other benefits?

Yesterday Mehmet had an interview with Gerrit Pans, the director of the starter centre of the local Chamber of Commerce. One outcome of the interview was that Gerrit Pans offered Mehmet access to the databases of the Chamber of Commerce. These databases contain basic descriptive information of all businesses in the city, such as legal form, date of foundation, sector, address, names of the owners. Moreover all businesses are required to deposit their balance sheet and larger businesses are also required to provide some information on their profits. However, the database is far from perfect. It contains many firms that are still registered at the Chamber of Commerce but do not operate anymore. Moreover, many firms do not keep their records up to date. The financial information seemed especially rather messy.

Somehow Mehmet had the feeling that Mr Pans was mainly looking for a student to work on their data. He would even do it for free, if the data would really add something to his thesis. But currently he had the feeling it would take days if not weeks to understand the database and to get some useful information out of it.

1 How could Rebecca combine her primary data collection with the secondary data of the European social survey?

2 Should Mehmet use the secondary data at the municipality level as suggested by the Chamber of Commerce manager? What are the disadvantages of incorporating those secondary data in his case study research?

3 Which sources could be useful for Rebecca and Mehmet? Start with those mentioned in Appendix A.

Summary

1   Secondary data are an important information source in all research phases. In the exploratory phase of the research process, secondary data allow you to expand your understanding of the research dilemma. Secondary data can also be used to test theories or arguments. Moreover, secondary data often deliver fruitful information on the context of the study.

2   The main advantages of using secondary data rest in time and money savings as well as the high quality of secondary data if they originate from reputable sources, such as government statistics. The use of secondary data is problematic if the information therein does not fit the research problem well.

3   One of the harder tasks associated with using secondary sources is evaluating the quality of the information. Five factors to consider when evaluating the quality of the source are purpose, scope, authority, audience and format.

4   Secondary data play an important role in qualitative research, as they are frequently based on multiple sources. Moreover, secondary data can provide useful information on the context of the phenomena investigated and therefore add more to the total perspective.

5   Managers faced with current decisions requiring immediate attention often overlook internal data in a company's data warehouse. Data-mining refers to the process of discovering knowledge from databases. Data-mining technology provides two unique capabilities to the researcher or manager: pattern discovery, and the prediction of trends and behaviours. Data-mining tools perform exploratory and confirmatory statistical analyses to discover and validate relationships. These tools even extend confirmatory statistical approaches by allowing the automated examination of large numbers of hypotheses. The type of data available and the nature of information sought determine which of the numerous data-mining techniques to select. Data-mining involves a five-step process: sample, explore, modify, model and assess.

Discussion questions

Terms in review

1   Explain how each of the five evaluation factors for a secondary source influences its management decision-making value:
   a   purpose
   b   scope
   c   authority
   d   audience
   e   format.

2   Define the distinctions between primary and secondary data.

3   What are potential sources of secondary data?

4   How can you evaluate the quality of a secondary data source?

5   What role does secondary data play in qualitative research?

6   What is data-mining?

7   Explain how internal data-mining techniques differ from a literature search.

Making research decisions

8 Some researchers find that their sole sources are secondary data. Why might this be? Name some management questions for which secondary data sources are probably the only feasible ones.

9 Assume you are asked to investigate the use of mathematical programming in accounting applications. You decide to depend on secondary data sources. What search tools might you use? Which do you think would be the most fruitful? Sketch a flow diagram of your search sequence.

10 Below are a number of requests that a staff-assistant might receive. What specific tools or services would you expect to use to find the requisite information? (Hint: use Appendix A and the CD that accompanies this text.)

   a Has the EU published any recent statements (within the last year) concerning its position on monetary stabilization?

   b I need a list of the major companies located in Bergen, Norway.

   c Does the ownership structure of a public firm influence its financial and stock market performance?

   d Should an ethnic marketing campaign (i.e. a campaign directed towards ethnic minorities) be controlled on a national or regional level?

Classroom discussion

11 Discuss the trustworthiness and reliability of secondary data. Should you trust the data if you trust the source (e.g. official statistics)?

12 Discuss the statement that data collected by national offices of statistics should be made accessible to the public. For example, students should be allowed to make use of databases maintained by the state for their Master's research project.

13 Discuss how you as a researcher should deal with conflicting information from different trustworthy information sources. For example, how would you deal with the following contradiction? According to secondary data from official statistics, consumer prices did not rise exceptionally after the introduction of the euro in January 2002. Newspaper clippings and street interviews with consumers provide a completely different picture, however, and most consumers complain that everything has become far more expensive since the introduction of the euro.

Recommended further reading

Atkinson, Anthony B. and Brandolini, Andrea, 'Promises and pitfalls in the use of "secondary" data-sets: income inequality in OECD countries as a case study', *Journal of Economic Literature* **39(3), 2001, pp. 771–99.** This article highlights the problems and opportunities of using secondary data, particularly for cross-country studies.

Berry, Michael J.A. and Linoff, Gordon, *Mastering Data-mining: The Art and Science of Customer Relationship Management.* **New York: John Wiley & Sons, 2000.**

Cowton, Christopher J., 'The use of secondary data in business ethics research', *Journal of Business Ethics* **17(4), 1998, pp. 423–34.** This article demonstrates the many forms of secondary data that can be used in research.

Fayyad, U.M. and Piatesky-Shapiro, G., *Advances in Knowledge Discovery and Data-mining.* **Cambridge, MA: AAAI Press–MIT Press, 1996.** An excellent text that provides an overview of knowledge discovery and data-mining using statistical methods.

Katz, William A. (ed.), *Introduction to Reference Work Volume I and II* **(8th edn). New York: McGraw-Hill, 2001.** The two volumes explain the basis of the reference process and all kinds of information sources.

Levitas, Ruth and Guy, Will (eds), *Interpreting Official Statistics.* **London: Routledge, 1996.** This book provides information about official statistics in the UK since 1979, and many methodological issues associated with statistics, such as the Labour Force Survey.

Woy, James (ed.), *Encyclopedia of Business Information Sources* **(14th edn). Farmington Hills: Gale Group, 2000.** A bibliographic guide to more than 20,000 citations covering more than 1,000 interest areas in business.

Get started with understanding statistical techniques!

When you have read this chapter, log on to the Online Learning Centre website at *www.mcgraw-hill.co.uk/textbooks/blumberg* to explore chapter-by-chapter test questions, additional case studies, a glossary and more online study tools for *Business Research Methods*.

Notes

1 Statistics Netherlands (CBS), the official statistical bureau of the Dutch government, offers free online access to information at www.cbs.nl/statline.

2 Advertisement in *BusinessWeek*, 28 June 1999, p. 3.

3 'Lots of online brokers say they are number one. Here's what some of the industry sources have to say', Schwab.com, 1 January 2001 (www.schwab.com/SchwabNOW/SNLibrary/SNLib132/SN132mainAwardsAndRatingsHome/).

4 R. Srikant and R. Agrawal, 'Mining sequential patterns: generalizations and performance improvements', Proceedings of the 5th International Conference on Extending Database Technology, Paris, France, March 1996.

5 B. DePompe, *There's Gold in Databases*, CMP Publications, 8 January 1996 (website: www.techweb.cmp.com/iwk).

6 Table adapted from DIG White Paper 95/01, 'An overview of data mining at Dun & Bradstreet', Data Intelligence Group, Pilot Software, Cambridge, MA, September 1995.

7 DePompe, CMP Publications (website: www.techweb.cmp.com/iwk).

8 'Data mining: plumbing the depths of corporate databases', *Computer World Customer Publication*, insert in *Computer World*, 12 April 1997, pp. 6, 18.

9 The section on data-mining techniques was adapted from Bruce Moxon, 'Defining data mining', *DBMS Data Warehouse Supplement*, DBMS Online (August 1996), www.dbmsmag.com; Mark Kantrowitz, Erik Horstkotte and Cliff Joslyn, 'Fuzzy logic FAQ', www.comp.ai.fuzzy newsgroup; DIG White Paper 95/01 and FAQ on data-mining (website: www.rdnuggets.com/faq/).

10 Information Discovery Inc. (website: www.idi.com).

11 SAS Institute Inc., 'Data mining' (website: www.sas.com).

12 Exhibit 9.5 was adapted from SAS Institute Inc., 'Data mining' (website: www.sas.com).

CHAPTER 10

Content analysis and other qualitative approaches

Chapter contents

Learning objectives

When you have read this chapter, you should understand:

1 the essentials of content analysis and how you can conduct it

2 what narrative analysis is

3 the basics of action research

4 the basics of grounded theory.

In the two previous chapters, we discussed qualitative interviews and observations, methods widely used in qualitative research. From a methodological viewpoint, a central advantage of qualitative research is the opportunity to easily combine various methods. In fact, triangulation of evidence across various methods makes a sound qualitative study. In the first part of this chapter, we discuss other methods available that are ideally combined with interviews and observations, namely content analysis and narrative analysis. In the second part, we address ethnography, action research and grounded theory. These three approaches describe research strategies emphasizing the understanding and explanation of specific phenomena, and represent more general frameworks for qualitative research.

10.1 Content analysis

Content analysis is a technique based on the manual or automated coding of transcripts, documents, (newspaper) articles or even audio and video material. Therefore, it is useful for all research approaches working with textual data. It can be used to analyse the transcripts of qualitative interviews, but it can also be used to analyse documents and other forms of textual secondary data. The primary objective of content analysis is to reduce the often copious information to a manageable amount. Often the textual information is even transformed into numerical data that can be used in further statistical analysis. The two main measures to reduce the amount of information are meaning condensation and categorization.

In applied business research, content analysis is often used to measure the success of public relations efforts. For example, on 29 June 2007, Apple Inc. started selling the iPhone® through its stores in the USA. But long before the first iPhone® was sold it had received tremendous media coverage. Content analysis is a method that allows you to systematically investigate the media coverage. In a first step you might simply count how often the word 'iPhone' occurs in articles of major national newspapers and magazines. A simple content analysis would count the word iPhone by analysing how often the product name is mentioned in different media. Advanced forms of content analysis also investigate in which context the word 'iPhone' appears. The information could be used to answer the following types of question:

1 What are the antecedents of media coverage? For example, why does the media coverage vary over time? Is there a relation with press announcements by Apple?
2 What are the characteristics of the media coverage? For example, why do some newspapers report positively about the iPhone and others negatively? Is there a relation with the political orientation of the newspaper?
3 What are the effects of the media coverage? For example, why do some newspapers report about the iPhone later than others? How can we explain the diffusion of certain information through the media?

The general forms of the three questions above describe the basic categories of content analysis, namely the analysis of antecedents, the analysis of characteristics and the analysis of effects. You should note that content analysis is more than a tool for descriptive analysis; it also enables us to investigate explorative and explanative questions.

Advantages and disadvantages

The main advantage of following a strict procedure in content analysis is that it adds to the transparency; that is, it is clear to readers of the study what you as a researcher did. Based on your information regarding the categorization, others can take your textual information and replicate your research. Some scholars have also argued that content analysis is unobtrusive and non-reactive (see section 10.4). This holds certainly for the analysis of documentary resources that have not been produced to be used in a content analysis, but to a lesser extent to transcripts of qualitative interviewing, as the interview itself could be subject to reactivity biases.

Content analysis is, however, not without limitations. First, its quality depends crucially on the input. Especially if you rely on sources produced for another purpose, the appropriateness of the sources for your specific research needs to be carefully assessed (see also Chapter 9 on 'secondary sources'). Second, the coding procedures developed to condense and categorize the information are of course subject to interpretation biases. A glass of water described as half full or half empty refers to the same factual glass but each description gives a different meaning to the fact.

The process of content analysis

The process of content analysis is similar to the process of any research and is depicted in Exhibit 10.1.

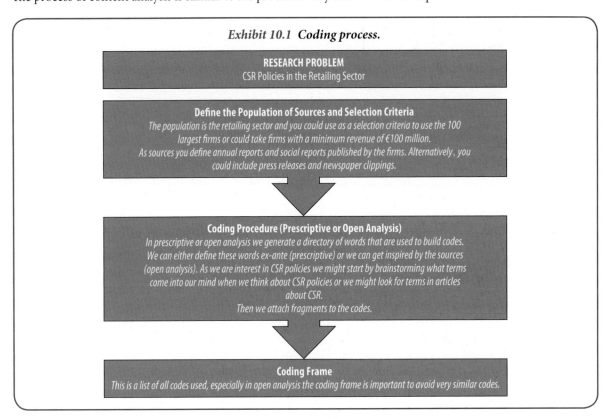

Exhibit 10.1 Coding process.

RESEARCH PROBLEM
CSR Policies in the Retailing Sector

Define the Population of Sources and Selection Criteria
The population is the retailing sector and you could use as a selection criteria to use the 100 largest firms or could take firms with a minimum revenue of €100 million.
As sources you define annual reports and social reports published by the firms. Alternatively, you could include press releases and newspaper clippings.

Coding Procedure (Prescriptive or Open Analysis)
In prescriptive or open analysis we generate a directory of words that are used to build codes. We can either define these words ex-ante (prescriptive) or we can get inspired by the sources (open analysis). As we are interest in CSR policies we might start by brainstorming what terms come into our mind when we think about CSR policies or we might look for terms in articles about CSR.
Then we attach fragments to the codes.

Coding Frame
This is a list of all codes used, especially in open analysis the coding frame is important to avoid very similar codes.

Define the population of sources and selection procedure

What are the sources used for the content analysis? The sources include archival material, recordings of current conversations and, specifically for research purposes, obtained material, e.g. responses in an unstructured interview. Each of the sources has different advantages. Archival material also covers past events and is often non-reactive, as when it was produced it was not apparent that it would be used for research purposes. Recordings of current conversations are more likely to include unintended and spontaneous expressions and are therefore less filtered than archival sources, but collection of those conversations is time-consuming. If researchers themselves collect the material for a content analysis, they can exercise control regarding the sources and the content and gain a better focus in their research project; but the larger control comes at the cost of larger reactivity. The following example illustrates the difference. Assume you are interested in CSR (corporate social responsibility) policies of firms. If you make use of archival material, e.g. annual reports of EUROSTOXX companies, you will be able to track developments since 2000 or even further back. Compare this to recordings of management team meetings discussing the corporate social responsibility strategy. Obtaining such recordings from many EUROSTOXX companies is time-consuming if at all feasible. However, those recordings will include statements made during the discussion that you will never find in an annual report, but they will reflect the managements position regarding CSR much better. And finally compare both to an analysis of unstructured interviews a researcher had with managers on corporate social responsibility. As a researcher you might be interested in a broad definition of CSR that includes not only environmental issues but social issues, such as fair wages and child labour as well. In an interview, you can easily address these issues, while annual reports or recorded discussion in the management team might not address those social issues.

Once you know the source, you need to decide how to select the sources. In the example above, you might ask yourself whether you only include annual reports of companies or you also include other publications of the company or even reports about the company and interviews with company officials that appeared in newspapers and magazines. Similarly, if we are interested in media coverage, we would have to define the set of media of interest, for example, all newspapers or only weekly women's magazines, and so on. In other studies, our population could be press releases of a company. Depending on the size of the population, we might either use all sources, for example all Barclays Bank press releases in 2010, or sample sources out of the entire population.

When applying content analysis the information investigated might stem from different actors. First, content analysis can be applied to different sources; for example, we analyse the transcripts of various qualitative interviews or we analyse the letter to the shareholders in various annual reports. Then we need to decide whether we want to compare the outcomes across different sources; for example, compare the letter to the shareholders across companies or whether we use different sources to account for one phenomenon. We could, for example, look at several qualitative interviews to get a better understanding of the organizational culture. Second, if we just look at one source alone, the source might reflect just the perspective of one actor or multiple actors. Transcripts of qualitative interviews usually reflect one actor, but a newspaper article might contain statements of different actors. In the latter case, it becomes important to first identify the different actors and to collect information on characteristics. In a second step, one links statements to the respective actors.

Coding procedure

The cornerstone of qualitative data analysis is the coding of the interview transcripts or any other documents. Coding is the process of categorizing and combing the data for themes and ideas and categories and then marking similar passages of text (fragments) with a code label. All fragments that have the same code are about the same theme or idea. It is possible to start coding with themes identified from a priori ideas such as pre-existing theories or just to let new codes emerge from your data set as you read it, as grounded theory suggests.

In a prescriptive analysis, we need to define words and phrases that we search for in the text a priori. In an open analysis, we attempt to distil the general message of the text. In **prescriptive analyses**, we either create a dictionary of key words or we might even use standard dictionaries, that is, we count, for example, the frequency of words listed in any common dictionary. If you set up a list of codes yourself, possible themes can come from previous theories, your research questions, your interview questions or even your gut feeling.

Even if we start with a predefined set of words and phrases to code, we will often discover new words and phrases that are synonyms. Once we detect such a synonym we need to include it in our coding scheme and, unfortunately, we also need to screen all our sources again for the occurrence of the synonym. In our CSR example, you could, for example, look for key words such as 'balancing economic and environmental demands', 'reducing CO_2 emissions', 'becoming carbon neutral', which could be classified as environmental aspects in the CSR policy. If you read words such as 'developing the skills of workers', 'offering additional training', 'sending children to school rather than to work' you would label these fragments as labour-oriented CSR or if you prefer to be more specific, you would label the first two as 'developing skills' and the last one has 'opposing child labour'.

Open analysis does not rely on dictionaries, but requires the researcher to identify themes and topics in the source material alongside the analysis. In an open analysis, the researcher is less interested in turning textual into numerical information. The objective is rather to read between the lines and to discover the full meaning of the source in its context. Naturally, such an approach goes beyond the dull counting of words and phrases and it requires that you set aside any prejudices and prior knowledge to focus on the finding of new ideas. The following questions help you to code openly:

- What is going on?
- What are the involved actors doing?
- What are the actors saying?
- What is taken for granted?
- What is the structure of actors, statements and actions?

A general problem all coders will face is how to avoid the material you go through for coding in the beginning influencing your perspective on your later material. More specifically, how can you ensure that the coding of interview 1 does not interfere with the coding of interview 2. Constant comparison is the technique to avoid that problem and to ensure consistency in your coding. Constant comparison requires that every time you code a fragment you compare it with all previous fragments with the same code and check whether the two fragments are similar. Some scholars even suggest comparing fragments not only with those bearing the same code, but also with fragments bearing related codes and with fragments from cases that are very different. For example, assume you have interviews with trade union representatives and managers. In that case you would compare fragments of the interviews with the trade union representative with the fragments from the interviews with the managers.

Coding frame. During the coding process you usually mark the transcript of field notes to assign fragments to codes. Next to this you should also create a separate list of the codes you have constructed and their definition. Whenever you find a fragment that could be coded in an existing code you can check if it exists on your list, and next time you find a passage that you think can be coded with an existing code, you can see if it exists in your frame or list; if it does, check with the definition to be sure that it does fit there. If you cannot find an appropriate code, then you can create a new one. An important point has to be made regarding the creation of new codes: every time you create a new code, you need to read through the already coded material to see whether it contains fragments that could also be assigned to that new code.

At some point during coding, the number of codes will have become rather large. Then you will find it necessary to sort them into families (groups). You may find several codes group together as types or kinds of something. In that case move them together and put them either in a list of their own, or make them sub-codes of a major code representing all. Two things may emerge from this reorganization: (i) you will be able to categorize codes, and (ii) you will be able to form dimensions along codes. For example, in your research you might have observed that people react differently to the breakdown of the computer system. Some use it to take a coffee break, some become aggressive and hit the computer, some panic and hit arbitrarily on the keyboard. These are all dimensions of 'responding to a computer system breakdown'. This dimensioning has two consequences: (i) you can think of dimensions that you do not yet have a code for, and (ii) categorization and dimensionalizing will raise questions about the relationship between codes or between cases.

Exhibit 10.2 clarifies the coding procedure with a small example on the vision and mission statements of the textile retailer Zara. In particular we looked which subjects the statement mentioned and identified three subject categories, namely customers, employees and systems/processes. How to obtain those categories is a difficult question. In the example, the categories chosen are inspired by stakeholder theory and that is appropriate if the research builds upon stakeholder theory. In case the vision and mission statement is, however, analyzed for a different purpose – for example, an investigation about companies' objectives – other categories will emerge, such as market leadership and quality. There are a few general principles that category systems should adhere to: categories should be unidimensional, exhaustive, mutually exclusive and independent. Thus, coding units should only fit in one category and entry in one category does not influence entries in other categories.

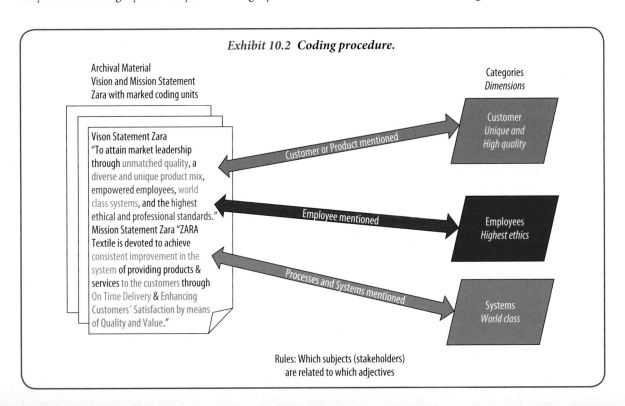

Exhibit 10.2 Coding procedure.

The coding dimensions turn the categories into variables that take values, i.e. range from low to high. In the example below we have looked for close-by adjectives describing the category. This approach always involves researchers' judgement. An alternative often-used approach is to use frequency of occurrence as measurement. In the example, we would see that the word 'customer' is mentioned twice, while the word 'employee' is just mentioned once. Measuring categories through occurrence also has the advantage that it is possible to measure what is not mentioned. In the Zara case, we see for example that customers and employees are addressed, while other stakeholders such as the shareholders, suppliers or society at large are not mentioned.

Rules determine how the coding system is applied to the source, i.e. how coding units are identified. In the example, it was decided to associate coding units that mention the words 'customer' or 'product' with the category customer. Another rule was to use close-by adjectives to assess the category dimension.

It is of utmost importance that you document the coding process in detail in a coding manual. You need to keep written notes that are meaningful to you even three months later during your coding process. Typically, information you could document includes: why did you create that specific code; a detailed description of the code; have you renamed the codes and if so, why did you rename them; and any thoughts and questions that came up while you coded.

Research Methods in Real Life

Swine flu and Google

In late April 2009, the World Health Organization (WHO) declared a public health emergency with global dimensions when the first H1N1 virus, commonly named 'swine flu' was confirmed in the USA and hundreds of infections were reported in Mexico. Facing the threat of an influenza pandemic, pharmaceutical companies strengthened their efforts to develop an effective vaccine and governments ordered millions of vaccine doses. Two hundred and nine countries had confirmed swine flu cases and the virus caused almost 15,000 deaths by January 2009. Early apprehensions that swine flu could reach or even exceed the magnitude of the 1918 Spanish flu, which killed 50–100 million people, proved, however, to be wrong. In December 2009, German and Spanish public health officials even announced the intention to return excess supplies of swine flu vaccine to the manufacturers or to countries still in need of them. Financial analysts estimated that the excess vaccine in those two countries resulted in a 15 per cent downside risk for the vaccine revenues. The 2009 swine flu outbreak shows how important it is to have reliable estimates of how quickly a virus can spread and how many people could be affected, to ensure that on the one hand sufficient vaccines are available, but on the other hand that public health spending does not suffer from excess orders.

Every day millions turn to Google to start a search query to find websites satisfying their need for information. While the frequency of some search queries, such as 'hotels London', is relatively constant, other search queries fluctuate over time. For example, before the 2010 UK elections, more people Googled 'Gordon Brown' and 'David Cameron' than on any given day in 2009.

Google researchers also discovered that search queries for 'swine flu' inform us about flu activity. Comparing how often people searched for flu on Google with figures from traditional flu surveillance systems revealed a close relationship and that a content analysis of the search inquiries at Google produced good estimates for the flu activity in specific countries. The important question remaining is, however, does a content analysis of Google search inquiries help us to detect future trends or is it merely a description of the current state?

References and further reading

www.google.org/flutrends/

www.who.int/csr/don/2010_01_29

Ginsberg, Jeremy, Matthew H. Mohebbi, Rajan S. Patel, Lynnette Brammer, Mark S. Smolinski and Larry Brilliant, 'Detecting influenza epidemics using search engine query data', *Nature* 457, 19 February 2009, pp. 1012–14.

Software packages for content analysis

Currently, many software packages are available to automate coding. Exhibit 10.3 provides examples of common software packages and their main properties. The main features distinguishing the packages are whether they can handle only text as input or also other formats, such as multimedia sources. All packages count words and phrases, but some packages are also able to detect more complex patterns or investigate the context key words are occurring in. A last important difference between the packages is whether they have a built-in dictionary or whether the researcher has to create one. Clearly, a built-in dictionary saves time in creating your own, but limits the researcher to the analysis of words contained in the dictionary. For example, you could analyse financial newspapers from 2007 when the Dutch bank ABN Amro was the target of a takeover battle between Barclays Bank on the one hand and a consortium led by Royal Bank of Scotland on the other hand. You could analyse the public statement made by ABN Amro CEO, Rijkman Groenink, and check how often and in what context he mentions Barclays and the Royal Bank of Scotland. For such an analysis you would need a package that allows you to create your own dictionary in which you could list the names of the involved firms, and also the names of key players associated with the two British banks.

Exhibit 10.3 An (incomplete) overview of software packages for content analysis.

Package	Input data	Counting, pattern recognition	Others	More information available at
ATLAS.ti	Text, audio and video	Counts words and phrases, connects segments, semantic editor		www.atlasti.com
NVivo	Text, audio, video	Counts words, phrases connects segments, interfaces to other software packages	Multi-lingual	www.qsrinternational.com/products_nvivo.aspx
General Inquirer	Text	Word counts	Combined with a dictionary	www.wjh.harvard.edu/~inquirer/
Intext	Text	Word counts	Public domain software	www.intext.de
Qualrus	Text and multimedia	Word counts and language scripting	Provides support for coding	www.ideaworks.com/qualrus
SPSS text analytic for surveys	Text	Word counts	SPSS module	ibm.com/software/products/gb/en/spss-text-analytics-surveys
Textpack	Text	Word counts and keywords in contexts		www.gesis.org/en/services/data-analysis/software/textpack

Narrative analysis

Narrative analysis is a qualitative research method allowing for in-depth investigations. Labov defined narratives as one method of recapitulating past experience by matching verbal sequences of clauses to the sequences of events which actually occurred.[1] Thus, narrative analysis examines stories focusing on how its elements are sequenced and how they are evaluated. It is important that the respondents are part of the stories they tell and that they are more than a mere observer of events.

Of course, narrative accounts are subjective, but they tap rich anecdotal information that allows the researcher to get an insight into the perspective of the respondents. Narrative analysis is usually based on in-depth interviews, but one can also base it on secondary data, such as biographies. As narrative analysis misses elements such as representative sampling, operationalization of variables, and so on, it is unsuitable for explanatory research, but a very powerful approach for explorative research.

Procedures in narrative analysis

While content analysis often emphasizes smaller elements of a text or story, narrative analysis has a strong emphasis on understanding the narrative as a whole, preserving the perspective and its context. A narrative's perspective describes the view of what happened while the context accounts for the historical time and the social setting in which the narrative is told. By and large, the procedure in narrative analysis is similar to that in content analysis. You need to start with a clear objective for the study that guides you through the selection of the sources and the narrative material.

There are different approaches to narrative analysis. One typology[2] distinguishes between structural, thematic and interactional analysis.

Structural analysis and key functions of a narrative

Structural analysis emphasizes how stories are told and involves language and linguistic analyses. Consequently, the researcher needs to have a good understanding of language and linguistics, like quantitative researchers need to have a good background in statistics.

The following *key functions* of any narrative build the structural categories:[3]

1 *Abstract* statement.
2 *Orientation segments* inform us about when (time) and where (place) the story took place, which situation is described and who is involved (participants).
3 *Complicating action* builds up the sequence of events as actions have events as antecedents and cause new events.
4 *Evaluation* describes how storytellers assess the actions and informs the researcher about their attitude. The evaluation segment provides the researcher with the meaning of the actions from the teller's perspective.
5 *Resolution* describes what finally happened or what the conclusion of the story is.
6 *Coda* offers insights into the importance of the story; thus, they indicate which current phenomena or actions relate to the story told.

Although other categories for structuring a narrative are possible the one above is a widely used one in narrative analysis.

Thematic analysis

The thematic analysis focuses on the content of the narrative, on what has been said and is less concerned with how something was told. The main objective of thematic analyses is identifying common seams in a bundle of stories. Thus, while the structural analysis is the detailed investigation of a single story, the thematic analyses compares multiple stories from different tellers. A potential weakness of the thematic analysis is that through the comparison of different stories the context of each story gets neglected.

A technique of narrative analysis is to examine the *temporal organization* of the story. Thus, the researcher cuts the story into smaller pieces (events) and orders these pieces sequentially, deciding which events occurred simultaneously and which sequentially. Analyzing the temporal organization in narrative analysis also points at an important difference from content analysis discussed above. From a content analysis perspective, the following two sentences would not yield different results, but from a narrative perspective the difference in sequence is important. 'Company A did not deliver the goods to company B as promised, then company B did not pay.' And, 'Company B did not pay company A for the ordered goods, then company A did not deliver the goods to company B.'

Interactional analysis

Finally, the interactional perspective applies to dialogues between storyteller and listener and accounts for the collaborative processes between the two in constructing a story. An example here is the narrative discourse analysis conducted in a study of a cross border merger between Scandinavian financial institutions.[4] In this study the researcher opposes the merger stories told by involved Swedish, Finnish and Danish executives and how those stories created different perspectives on the merged organization and reflected the power struggles between the different sub-units and the organizational politics played.

Considering context

Given that narrative analysis is a qualitative method, it should incorporate the specific context in its analysis. Narratives vary within contexts; how a respondent tells others about an accident will differ depending on whether the story is told at work, at home or to team mates at a sporting club. Likewise, how a story is told might differ across different times. How do you tell a story about a conflict with a high-school teacher that will change over time? When you tell the story as a pupil, directly after the conflict, it will differ from how you tell it as a student and from how you will tell the story to your grandchildren. The differences in the stories told in different contexts particularly yield insights into the evaluation segments, and by considering the context we are better able to understand the process as a whole. A recent review[5] of the use of the narrative analysis in business studies revealed that typical phenomena investigated by narrative analysis include politics and power, sense-making, communication, learning and change and identity and structuration. All of those are phenomena where the context in which they occur is of importance and often the boundary between the two is blurred.

Ethnographic studies

Ethnographic studies are usually associated with other social sciences, especially anthropology and sociology, and most people hearing the term ethnography think of studies on isolated tribes at the Amazon or in the African bush. But ethnography is used to study business phenomena more often than one might imagine – however, not usually by scholars in economics and business, and more often by business journalists. Books describing the history, or certain period in the history, of a company often share many characteristics with ethnographic study, especially concerning the gathering of information and presentation of the facts. What distinguishes a popular book describing the history of a corporation from an ethnographic study is that the former omits any problem statement and, consequently, the analysis and interpretation of the information gathered in the light of the problem statement. Examples of ethnographic studies in business contexts are accounts of how a product development company use brainstorming groups to remain innovative[6] and how neighbouring farmers settle conflicts outside the juridical system.[7]

A main characteristic of ethnographic studies is its richness in the description of the world it studies. Rather than describing, for example, a firm with a couple of key figures, such as sales, profit, growth, number of employees, sector, and so on, as you would in a survey study, an ethnographic study considers many more aspects. Exhibit 10.4 shows how an ethnographic study of an organization, such as a business firm, would achieve this richness and 'thickness' of information.

Exhibit 10.4 Elements of an ethnographic study.

Element	Examples
Multiple information sources	Combine interviews with observations, informal talks and archive studies
Employing different perspectives	Obtain information from different types of information provider, such as management, employees, labour unions, industry experts, economic media
Record and present different types of information	Simple quantitative information (frequencies), qualitative verbal information (citations from interviews or documents), qualitative behavioural information (anecdotes on specific behaviours or descriptions of habits), qualitative non-behavioural information (visualizations of the company in logos and brochures, the architecture of the company buildings or the office furniture)

Classical ethnographic studies in anthropology examined social phenomena in just one or a few social settings, often small tribes. Researchers had to take part in the daily life of the tribe for long periods to unravel routine behaviour, habits, and so on. Therefore, participant observation and qualitative interviews (see Chapter 8) are the main methods of data collection in ethnographic studies. Usually an ethnographic study gets more and more focused over time. It starts with a broad theme, often culture, and in the course of the research more specific analytical constructs emerge. You should note that identifying relevant analytical constructs as the study unfolds requires substantial experience in the field. As students usually lack this experience and their research projects have a rather limited time frame, ethnographic studies are rarely done by students.

An important part of ethnographic research is taking field notes, as the material collected in an ethnographic study does not only consist of recorded interviews, but also of observations by the researcher. An alternative to writing the notes on a notepad is voice recording, which might, however, be perceived as obtrusive, although usually participants get used to recording machines after some time. Moreover with the increased occurrence of tablets, carrying one with you has become common, especially in organizational environments. The quality and usefulness of field notes increases with the following guidelines:

1 As with all efforts to collect information, the quality of the information increases the better you have been able to define the objective of your study.
2 Take the notes as soon as possible, at least at the end of every day.
3 Include information on the people involved, the place and the time to each note.
4 Make a clear distinction between notes that reflect your own interpretation, assessment of an observed situation, notes that reflect other's interpretations and assessments and notes that merely describe what has happened.
5 Ensure that you will still understand the note when you read later.

Action research

Action research has its origins in the social sciences, and Kurt Lewin introduced the term in 1943 when US authorities commissioned a study on the use of tripe as part of the regular diet of American families.[8] The objective of the research was to find out how housewives could be encouraged to include tripe rather than beef, which was scarce during wartime, in their cooking. Lewin's set-up for the study was to start by training a number of housewives in how to use tripe in their cooking and, later, look at how this training affected their cooking behaviour. While the main objectives of the research methods discussed so far emphasize the acquisition of knowledge – what the researcher mainly wants to explain – action research focuses on another objective, namely social change or the production of socially desirable outcomes. In the case of Lewin's study, the main objective was to change the diet of Americans by substituting beef with tripe.

After the Second World War, action research also became prominent in management science, especially in Europe. The Tavistock Institute in the UK and the Norwegian Industrial Democracy Project employed this methodology to encourage social change on the shop floor. Researchers from the Tavistock Institute wanted to find out why the introduction of new technologies in British coalmines did not result in the expected productivity gains. Based on action research, they came up with the finding that the work organization, which still followed the Tayloristic idea of dividing labour into small sub-activities, was no longer suited to new technologies, which required greater coordination and communication between work groups.[9] The gap between business science and practice is a major catalyst for the re-emergence of action research and in 2003 the new scientific journal *Action Research* was published by Sage. Not surprisingly, many action research projects are carried out by part-time students with regular jobs or organizational consultants, who investigate problems at their companies or clients by applying the knowledge gained at university.

Exhibit 10.5 summarizes the core characteristics of action research and mirrors them against the more traditional research methods discussed in previous chapters. One main difference between action research and other more traditional research approaches is that the latter attempt to identify general principles, which are useful in explaining phenomena in different contexts. Action research cares less about general principles, although those can be the outcome of a project, as in the case of the coalmining study mentioned above, but places a strong emphasis on the interplay between action and research to achieve desired changes. In action research, research and implications are a united iterated process and good action research consists of a successful implantation of the conclusion and solution of the problem. Another distinctive feature is that action research overcomes the division between researchers and participants. While other research approaches often emphasize that these two roles need to be clearly separated to avoid conflicts of interest, action research actually builds upon the close cooperation.

Exhibit 10.5 Characteristics of action research compared with those of other research methods.

Action research	Other research methods
Addresses real-life problems and is bounded by the context	Address real-life as well as scientific problems, and attempt to identify general principles and their contingencies
Continuous reflecting process of research and action	Usually clear division between the research process and implementation processes
Credibility – the validity of action research is measured on whether the actions solve the problems and realize the desired change	Credibility – the validity of research is established by statistical core figures and successful replications
Collaborative venture of researchers, participants and practitioners	Clear division of roles between researchers, participants and practitioners

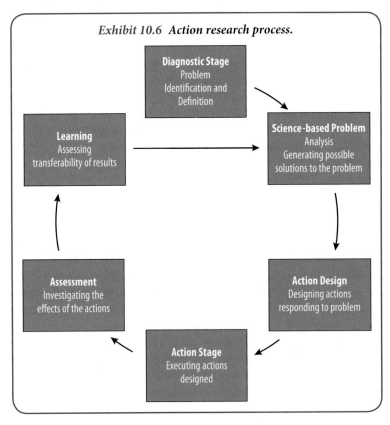

Exhibit 10.6 Action research process.

Exhibit 10.6 depicts action research as having a cyclical process that is jointly governed by the researcher and practitioners. Although the similarities with the standard research process are visible, important differences need to be noted. First, both researcher and practitioner participate in the process, but their involvement will differ in the respective stages. For example, the researcher is likely to have a larger role in the science based problem analysis, while the practitioner will be more engaged in the action stage. Again a good research project starts with a well-identified and well-defined problem. Once the problem is formulated, researchers look to see if existing knowledge provides ideas for possible solutions and courses of action for the problem. The possible solutions constitute the design stage, which is typically the phase where science and practice need to come together. The action stage is the implementation of the designed actions, which (hopefully) result in the solution of the problem. At the end the whole action research project needs to be evaluated in terms of the effectiveness of the chosen actions in solving the problem. The whole process is finally concluded with answering the question whether the insights gained in that specific action project are transferable to other situations and to what extent the outcomes of the current project can function as an input to future problem analyses.

The main criticism of action research is that the findings produced are just anecdotal evidence, and transferring the knowledge acquired in one research project to another context is difficult and sometimes even impossible.[10] As action research is often very context-dependent, the research approach becomes problematic if, say, one wishes to investigate problems within a larger context, such as rising unemployment rates in the European Union (EU). Another substantial criticism concerns the problems associated with the direct participation of the researcher and attempts to integrate research with organizational goals, which neglects the critical distance of a researcher essential for conducting good academic research.[11] Further, although action research is designed to change the environment, the researchers rarely have full control over the environment. As one author pointed out: 'Rarely will an organization cede ultimate authority to an external researcher. This guarded commitment is reasonable since the researcher's motives are divided between research goals and organizational problem-solving goals.'[12] Still one needs to acknowledge that action research is a legitimate scientific approach that is like other approaches in this chapter not assessable by criteria rooted in the positivistic perspective and it offers a great potential for understanding and managing issues prevalent in business.

10.5 Grounded theory

Barney Glaser and Anselm Strauss are the founding fathers of grounded theory, an approach in qualitative research they introduced in 1967. Grounded theory builds on the theoretical perspective of symbolic interactionism, which assumes that the social world is created through an interactive process of sense-making and interpretation between humans and the world. Later on Glaser and Strauss disagreed about the 'right' grounded theory and split. The main differences between the two are that Glaser sees grounded theory as a general approach, which is also applicable for survey and statistical data, while Strauss limits it to qualitative analysis. In addition, Glaser emphasizes theory-building through induction, while Strauss stresses the importance of a systematic approach and sound validation of codings and constructs.

A main characteristic of the grounded theory approach is that it starts with the data and not with a theory or even predefined research projects. In its purest form, the researcher should neither read the existing previous literature on the topic, nor should he or she transcribe interviews nor talk with others about the emerging theory during the research process. This is in order to eliminate any influence of preconceptions that distract the researcher from the data collected. This does not, however, mean that you could ignore the literature entirely.

Following Strauss, research in grounded theory is an iterative three-stage process (see Exhibit 10.7). It starts with **open coding**, a conceptualization process of the original raw data. Each piece of information (a word, a sentence or a paragraph) is disaggregated into conceptual units receiving a label. This results in a collection of labels that are compared with each other to find related ones that can be placed in categories. The open coding occurs during the fieldwork and while it continues, new conceptual units will emerge, triggering new comparisons often requiring recategorizations. In the end, the emerged categories represent themes worthy of being researched more deeply. The second step is **axial coding** referring to the process of linking categories of data and thereby developing theoretical explanations. Once relationships between the categories have been recognized, the researcher checks whether the relationship also holds for newly collected data. The final step is called **selective coding**. It takes place at the end of the research process, that is, after several rounds of open and axial coding. In the selective coding process, the researcher focuses on a few principal categories and its relations and attempts to develop a new grounded theory.

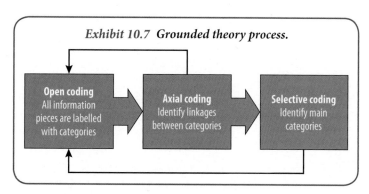

Exhibit 10.7 Grounded theory process.

Student Research

Competitive recruitment: coding of a new phenomenon

Maria Majewski was interested in a more recent phenomenon on the labour market, namely competitive recruitment, that is, attracting employees from competitors. More specifically, she was interested in why companies poach people with certain skills, what makes those employees so attractive and how companies deploy skills acquired from a competitor. Maria decided to use a general inductive approach to qualitative data analysis to explore the phenomenon of competitive recruitment. Maria's inductive analysis was based on 15 interviews with managing partners of executive search firms, which took between 45 and 120 minutes. These interviews resulted in more than 200 pages of transcription that needed to be coded.

Her coding process encompassed five steps. First, she and a friend read independently through the interviews and assigned free codes derived from the original research questions to text fragments. During this first coding step the coders also noted down all other thoughts they had while reading through the interview. In a second step, the two coders compared their coding of three interviews to achieve consensual validation. Then they discussed which of the coded fragments related to different topics, for example to issues of deployment, to form code families. These code families formed the base of a first coding scheme. The 12 remaining interviews were then coded according to this first scheme. In the third step, Maria tried to structure all codes and discussed her results with the second coder to create a final coding scheme (see Exhibit 10.8 for an excerpt of the coding scheme).

In a fourth step, the coders coded the interviews according to the final coding scheme and discussed the results of their coding to increase consensual validation. Based on these discussions the coding scheme was adjusted again in the fifth step. The final coding scheme consisted of 18 general codes; five of them are depicted in Exhibit 10.8.

Exhibit 10.8 *Excerpt of coding scheme.*

What is the role of the hiring firm when skills of competitor recruit (CR) are deployed?

CODES	COMMENTS THAT PROVIDED FACTORS INFLUENCING THE DEGREE OF DEPLOYMENT, FIT AND PERFORMANCE LEVEL OF THE RECRUIT		
Accordance with promises	Any statement about the impact of firm promises on CR recruit (e.g. managerial responsibility)	Any promises impacting CR recruit	No department level or national culture
Integration	Any statements concerning how the hiring firm supports the CR recruit to integrate workwise and socially (e.g. structural orientation programmes)	Any unilateral actions initiated by the hiring firm	No informal unilateral initiatives
Training and development	Any statements about the impact of training and development	Any direct financial performance effects	No soft performance criteria
Internal communication	Any statement about the impact of firm's reputation on recruit productivity (e.g. through employee satisfaction, identification, turnover rate)	Any direct firm's reputation effects	No hard performance criteria
Compensation	Any statement about the impact of the CR recruit's salary on his or her deployment (e.g. pecuniary motivation)	Any direct and visible retention effort effects	Only explicit retention efforts and no pure deployment initiatives

The whole research process above is facilitated by two principles, namely theoretical sampling and theoretical saturation. **Theoretical sampling** follows a completely different objective than probability sampling (see Chapter 6). The main objective of probability sampling is to collect observations that are representative of the population. In theoretical sampling, we are not concerned with representativeness; rather we are concerned about which additional cases would be most useful to build and develop our theory. Grounded theory is an iterative process and this raises the question of when you should stop. **Theoretical saturation** provides the stopping rule for identifying new categories as well as for investigating new cases. The principal idea is that you stop if new categories or cases do not improve our understanding of the phenomena. This is similar to the question, 'When should I stop searching for literature?' You should stop when the information you find does not add relevant knowledge to your problem.

While other research strategy refers to reliability and validity to assess how well a research has been conducted and how sound its results are, grounded theory uses four different criteria:

1 *Fit* describes how well the categories represent the real incidents.
2 *Relevance* describes how useful a theory is for practice. Research endeavours that are mainly or even solely interesting for the academic community score low on relevance.
3 *Workability* refers to the quality of the explanation offered and is an assessment of the question, 'Does the theory work?'
4 *Modifiability* refers to whether the theory can be adapted if new data is compared to it. You should note here that proponents of grounded theory are not positivists who see theory as general laws applicable at all times and places. Scholars engaging in grounded theory assume at least to some extent that the world is a social construct and how humans see the world will change over time and differ between places. Therefore, it is important that a grounded theory is flexible enough to accommodate such changes and differences.

Grounded theory is a widely used general strategy in qualitative research. Its clear advantage is that it provides a convincing framework for a systematic inquiry into qualitative data involving theory development. Thus grounded theory provides all the elements necessary for scientific research. Nevertheless, the approach also has critics. Part of this criticism can be summarized in the category of feasibility problems, such as the problem that it is impossible for researchers to be free of pre-categorizations or theoretical thoughts. Another practical problem, at least for students, is that grounded theory research is very time-consuming because of its iterative character. Six months, the typical time for writing a full Master's research project, is much too short for a grounded theory approach. Next to the more practical motivated criticism, grounded theory is also criticized for not generating theories but just categorization systems, and that researchers miss the context of a phenomenon as the coding procedures come along with data fragmentation.

Running Case Study 10
What helps to become an entrepreneur: Business plans, role models or action?

In his interviews with entrepreneurs, Mehmet has always asked them about their preparations before they started a business. Especially, he asked them whether they had written a business plan before they started, as the scientific as well as the practitioner literature suggests. He asked those who had written a business plan whether he could have a copy. Those who had started their business recently were reluctant to hand him the plan, as it contained sensitive information regarding financial and strategic issues. Mehmet promised to treat any information as confidential and even offered them the option of taking out that sensitive information. Two entrepreneurs removed the financial chapter from their business plan before handing it to Mehmet and three were still not willing to share it. Overall, Mehmet has managed to collect 19 business plans and is now wondering how to research them. He has heard about content analysis and thought that this could be an appropriate tool to investigate the 19 business plans. Mehmet used a book on how to write a business plan to determine what needs to be covered in a business plan. He has come up with the following list: executive summary; company description; description of product or service; market analysis; ▶

strategy and implementation; management team; and financial analysis. Only after this did he start reading the business plans. First, he just scored whether a business plan contained each of the seven elements, but later on he decided to give school marks from 1 (pretty bad) to 10 (excellent) for each of the seven items. He had a good feeling with this approach as he really could differentiate between good business plans and more moderate ones. However, his supervisor Flowermountain seemed to be less enthusiastic, as he demanded a more systematic approach.

Another question running through Mehmet's head was how to present all the information he had obtained from the interviews with the entrepreneurs. Recently, he had read a biography about Stelios Haji-Ioannou, the founder of easyJet. Of course, Mehmet does not have sufficient information to write a whole book on each of the entrepreneurs he has interviewed. Moreover, he wants to finish within the next month. Nevertheless, Mehmet thought that writing some short biographies could be very helpful – maybe not for all, but for some exemplary entrepreneurs he had interviewed. For example, he liked the life story of Dr Saito and he also admired Mr Simsek, who started with a small snack bar selling kebabs at the time when more and more kebab shops were popping up in different neighbourhoods. But Simsek did not run small kebab shops anymore. Years ago he started to supply other kebab shops with the large meat skewers and this business turned into a Turkish butchery supplying Turkish supermarkets with halal meat products, i.e. meat produced according to Islamic law. As Mr Simsek was one of the first, he made a fortune. Just recently he invested this money in hotels on the Turkish Black Sea as he was confident that this region would develop into a tourist hot spot. Mehmet had the feeling that Mr Simsek was a Turkish Stelios Haji-Ioannou; maybe a size smaller, but still a person that turned everything he touched into gold.

His supervisor Flowermountain was not really enthusiastic about the biographic idea, claiming that it would be too descriptive and would hardly offer explanations. Mehmet was a bit frustrated. He did not want to write a dull academic dissertation according to the criteria set by his supervisor. For him it was important that others would read his thesis and that he learnt something that he could use in his own career as a self-employed entrepreneur. A friend told him that he should read about action research. After reading a bit, Mehmet started to like this idea as it would allow him to turn his research project into the starting point for a consulting business. Now he needed to convince his supervisor about this approach.

1 Some of the entrepreneurs Mehmet interviewed showed him their initial business plans. Are those business plans useful for a content analysis?

2 Mehmet has read the Lois Jones book on easyJet founded by Stelios Haji-Ioannou. Would it make sense to use this book as a base for a narrative analysis?

3 Mehmet really wants to help migrant entrepreneurs and is thinking about designing training for those that participate in his research. Does this qualify as action research?

Summary

1 Content analysis is a qualitative or quantitative approach to systematically analyse texts. The latter approach is based on counting the occurrence of words and phrases as well as detecting how far specific words stand apart in a text. The former approach puts more emphasis on detecting the general meaning of a text to categorize it.

2 Narrative analysis is based on stories. It is a qualitative explorative approach that allows a researcher to understand phenomena from the respondent's perspective.

3 Action research is a research approach that, unlike more traditional research approaches, places an emphasis on the objective of inducing social change in the research process. Further, it relies heavily on continuous interaction between researchers, participants and practitioners.

4 Grounded theory provides a general framework for conducting qualitative research. It starts from data collected and uses this data in an iterative process of coding, categorizing and comparing to formulate a new grounded theory.

Discussion questions

Terms in review

1 Distinguish between content and narrative analysis.

2 Describe what action research is about.

3 Describe the central elements of grounded theory.

4 Describe the differences in coding in content analysis and in grounded theory.

5 Explain the term 'theoretical sampling'.

From concept to practice

6 Obtain a current copy of a popular management magazine and a copy of the same management magazine from 10 years ago. Use content analysis to establish the hot management phrases at both times.

7 Develop a sketch for an action research plan to investigate a management problem. Pay particular attention to the issue of how the desired change can be induced by the research project itself.

8 Develop a coding scheme for a qualitative study interested in the classroom attendance and participation of students.

Classroom discussion

9 Discuss why some researchers are rather critical towards qualitative research and how their criticism is related to their research philosophy.

10 Discuss the merits and problems of a researcher actively involved in the phenomenon investigated.

Recommended further reading

Bailey, Kenneth D., *Methods of Social Research* **(4th edn). New York: Free Press, 1995.** Includes a thorough discussion of observational strategies.

Denzin, Norman K. and Lincoln, Yvonna S., *Handbook of Qualitative Research* **(2nd edn). Thousand Oaks, CA: Sage, 2000.** Of particular interest is Part 3 on strategies of inquiry, and Part 4 on methods of collecting and analysing empirical materials.

DeWalt, Katherine M. and DeWalt, Billie R., *Participant Observation.* **Walnut Creek, CA: Alta Mira, 2002.** An introductory text on ethnographic research, emphasizing the technique of participant observation.

Glaser, B. and Strauss, A., *The Discovery of Grounded Theory.* **Chicago, Il: Aldine, 1967.** The classic text on grounded theory, one of the most cited books in the social sciences.

Greenwood, Davydd J. and Levin, Morten, *Introduction to Action Research: Social Research for Social Change.* **Thousand Oaks, CA: Sage, 1998.** One of the good introductions and standard reference texts on action research.

Hodson, Randy, *Analyzing Documentary Accounts.* **Thousand Oaks, CA: Sage, 1998.** Good account on how to develop coding procedures within content analysis.

Huxham, Chris and Vangen, Siv, 'Researching organizational practice through action research: case studies and design choices', *Organizational Research Methods* **6(3), 2003, pp. 383–403.** The article presents several case studies on how action research can be used in management and business research.

Strauss, A. and Corbin, J., *Basics of Qualitative Research* **(2nd edn). Newbury Park, CA: Sage, 1998.** A good introduction to the grounded theory approach in the perspective of Strauss.

Weber, Robert P., *Basic Content Analysis* **(2nd edn). Newbury Park, CA: Sage, 1990.** A standard introductory overview.

Whyte, W.F. (ed.), *Participatory Action Research.* **London: Sage, 1991.** Good overview of action research.

Get started with understanding statistical techniques!

When you have read this chapter, log on to the Online Learning Centre website at *www.mcgraw-hill.co.uk/textbooks/blumberg* to explore chapter-by-chapter test questions, additional case studies, a glossary and more online study tools for *Business Research Methods*.

Notes

1 W. Labov, *Language in the Inner City*. Philadelphia, PA: University of Pennsylvania Press, 1972.

2 Catherine Kohler Rlessmann, 'Narrative analysis' in M.S. Lewis-Beck, A. Bryman and T. Futing Liao (eds.) *The Sage Encyclopedia of Social Science Research Methods, Vol 3*. Thousand Oaks: Sage, 2003.

3 Labov, *Language in the Inner City*.

4 A-M. Søderberg, 'Narrative interviewing and narrative analysis in a study of a cross-border merger', *Management International Review* 46 (2006), pp. 397–416.

5 C. Rhodes and A.D. Brown, 'Narratives, Organizations and Research', *International Journal of Management* 7 (2005), pp. 167–88.

6 R.I. Sutton and A. Hargadon, 'Brainstorming Groups in Context: Effectiveness in a Product Design Firm', *Administrative Science Quarterly* 41(4) (1996), pp. 685–718.

7 R.C. Ellickson, *Order without Law: How Neighbors Settle Disputes*. Cambridge, MA: Harvard University Press, 2009.

8 Kurt Lewin, 'Forces behind food habits and methods of change', *Bulletin of the National Research Council* 108 (1943), pp. 35–65. Interestingly, tripe is considered a very fine food in certain European regions, for example France and southern Germany.

9 E. Trist and K.W. Bamforth, 'Some social and psychological consequences of the long-wall method of coal getting', *Human Relations* 4 (1951), pp. 3–38.

10 P. Reason, 'Sitting between appreciation and disappointment: a critique of the special edition of human relations on action research', *Human Relations* 14 (1993), pp. 1253–70.

11 Matthew David, 'Problems of participation: the limits of action research', *International Journal of Social Research Methodology* 5 (2002), pp. 11–17.

12 D. Avison, R. Baskerville and M.D. Myers, 'Controlling action research projects', *Information Technology and People* 14 (2001), pp. 28–47.

CHAPTER 11

Case studies

Chapter contents

Learning objectives

When you have read this chapter, you should understand:

1 what a case study is and how it differs from the methods discussed so far

2 why case studies are a very useful research approach

3 what makes a good case study.

Case study objectives

In the following sections, you will learn more about what case study research is about and how it differs from the other methods of conducting research discussed so far. We have decided to discuss case studies here very extensively, as case study research is widely used and very effective in business and management research. Furthermore, it is a very popular approach among students preparing their final research projects, as it combines business practice with science and also allows them to supplement their studies (i.e. writing a research project) with gaining practical experience (e.g. by following an internship).

Case study research is suitable for explanatory, descriptive and exploratory research, like the other approaches. The suggestion that case study research is especially, or even only, appropriate for exploratory research is a prejudiced view held by people who have little experience with case studies. You should, however, note that an explanatory case study will test propositions differently from a quantitative study and that an exploratory case study builds up theory differently from an exploratory study based on quantitative secondary data.

Yin defines a case study as 'an empirical inquiry that investigates a contemporary phenomenon within its real-life context; when the boundaries between phenomenon and context are not clearly evident; and in which **multiple sources of evidence** are used'.[1] This definition shows clearly how case study research differs from other research approaches in terms of scope and methods used.

The main difference between case study research and the methods discussed so far is that case study research is much more an approach to investigate a phenomena rather than a specific method to collect information. Case study researchers, in fact, combine many of the methods discussed. Typically case study research is built upon interviews (structured and unstructured) and participant observations, but next to those methods often small surveys are conducted or the researcher relies on secondary data sources.

As you will see throughout the chapter, case studies are a very flexible methodological approach. This flexibility is also caused by an unclear definition of what a case study is. In Exhibit 11.1 we compare ideas regarding case study research from four scholars to whom case study researchers often refer.

Exhibit 11.1 Comparison of different perspectives on case studies.

	Eisenhardt (1989)	Yin (2009)	Stake (1995)	Burawoy (1991)
Underlying research philosophy	Positivistic	Positivistic	Interpretivistic	Critical, reflective
Purpose	Development of hypotheses/propositions	Confirming, extending and challenging theories	Social construction of meaning	Reconstruction of theory
Starting point	Starts from a phenomenon to develop new theory	Starts from existing theories	Starts with a number of questions, experience and scientific knowledge	Starts from a case that is unusual according to theory
Sampling logic	Theoretical sampling	Single versus multiple case study	Case is already selected or purposeful selection	Theoretical sampling
Data analysis	Pattern matching	Pattern matching	Category aggregation	Category aggregation, structuration

The comparison in Exhibit 11.1 documents clearly that there are considerable differences between the perspectives. You should, however, note that most of the differences can be explained by the different research philosophies the authors adhere too. Eisenhardt and Yin who are positivist acknowledge the case study as an important element in theory generation and theory development and advocate a systematic analysis through pattern matching. Stake and Buraway adhere more to a reflective or interpretivistic research philosophy. Consequently, the case itself is in the centre of the focus and interpretive, reflective and critical analysis methods are emphasized. Despite these differences, which you should have in mind while reading the chapter, all of the four agree with each other on the methodological properties of case study research. All support the notion that case studies need to be based on multiple sources of evidence, and that triangulation is important to check the validity of the results.

Case study objectives

While survey research and even more experiments typically address a well-defined and focused problem, case studies take a broader view on a problem. Experiments usually deliberately divide the phenomenon from the context and often isolate the phenomenon from the natural context that is replaced by a laboratory setting, while case study research emphasizes the embeddedness of a phenomenon in its real-life context. Although survey researchers can account for the context, their ability to do so is limited as the number of variables they can investigate is limited and predefined by the researcher. Historical studies also broadly acknowledge the context, but contrary to historic studies, case studies focus on contemporary phenomena. Case studies allow you better to shed light on a phenomenon from multiple perspectives defined by its context than other approaches. Moreover, the broader scope of case studies allows you to detect patterns and potential explanations that you initially neither expected nor looked for, which makes them a good approach to build theory. Taking a broader scope comes along with a broader use of research methods. In experiments and surveys, researchers take utmost care to ensure that participants and respondents follow the same procedures and are subject to identical measurement instruments. Case studies take a different approach and rely on multiple sources of evidence, that is, researchers use different approaches, such as observations, unstructured, semi-structured and structured interviews along with available secondary data simultaneously. You should note that using multiple sources allows you to compensate weaknesses of one approach with the strength of another approach.

The role and function of case study research within scientific research is often disputed; the most common prejudices to be heard concerning case studies are that they do not contribute to building and testing theories and that their results are not generalizable. Case studies, however, offer a useful approach for use in theory development as they are especially appropriate for answering 'Why?' and 'How?' questions. A good case study starts with a problem that is not well understood, that is, with a problem that we cannot explain or a problem that is explained by various often contradicting explanations. The objective of a case study is to understand a real problem and to use the gained insights for developing new explanations and theoretical dispositions. Although case study results are not generalizable to a population, they are generalizable to a theoretical disposition. Thus, from a case study looking at the decision behaviour of a British manager in the construction industry, we cannot learn anything about British managers in general, not even about British managers in the construction business. We can, however, learn how managers decide and develop theoretical arguments that help us to explain the decision behaviour of managers.

With a case study, theories are developed and tested in a sequential, step-by-step, manner. Starting with a previously developed theory the researcher compares the results of the case study with the theory, just as an experimenter designs experiments with the objective of testing one or a few specific theoretical predicted relations. Just as an experiment is not sufficient to support or reject a theory, one case study cannot test a theory – however, a series of experiments or case studies permits the assessment of a theory.

The choice of whether to use either case study research or survey research to investigate a specific problem depends very much on the personal preferences of the researchers, which are likely to be rooted in the traditions of the academic schools at which they were trained and in the approaches that they have used in previous studies. This is why similar problem statements may be investigated using different approaches. Although many problems can be investigated using case studies or surveys, case study research is usually more appropriate if the number of variables that needs to be considered is quite large, that is, if the context is very important. With the survey approach, a large number of relevant variables calls for a similarly large number of observations.

Single versus multiple case studies

Within case study research it is possible to distinguish between single and multiple case studies (**single case study** versus **multiple case studies**). The former rely on one single case (as the name suggests), while the latter call for the investigation of several cases. Of course, investigating an issue in more than one context (i.e. case) is usually better than basing results on just one case. There are, however, occasions when a single case study is quite sufficient. If the intended case study research provides the closing critical study to a longer series of case studies written by others, a single case is adequate. Such a critical case study requires, of course, and as well as previous studies, a well-developed theory, and the case should be an acceptable real-life example of the circumstances in which the theoretical propositions need to be investigated. Single case studies are also appropriate for investigating extreme or unique cases. Extreme cases (i.e. extreme combinations of circumstances) occur, according to the rules of probability, very rarely; hence, there is often no more than one or just a few cases available. An example could be rogue traders, like Nick Leeson, who sent the UK bank Barings into bankruptcy in 1995, or Jérôme Kerviel, who accumulated losses up to € 4.9 billion for his employee, the French bank Société Générale.

Moreover, a single case study may be justified for pragmatic reasons (which do not include the researcher's laziness!). For example, if a researcher is able to access information that is rarely accessible to researchers, a single case study is sufficient as it will offer as yet unknown insights. Suppose, for example, you had been allowed to carry the briefcase of George Osborne, British Chancellor of the Exchequer at the time (a position akin to the Minister of Finance in other nations) and observe all his actions while he is discussing the budget of the European Union. The opportunity to follow one of the key players in the political struggle would be a unique case, for which pragmatic reasons advocate a single case study.

As mentioned above, multiple case studies are more appealing, though, as their results are considered more robust. Conducting multiple case studies requires considerable thought as to which cases to select, however. Contrary to survey research the selection of cases – or, if you will, observational units – is not based on sampling logic but on **replication logic**. The main idea behind replication logic is that according to a theory, one would expect that the same phenomenon occurs under the same or similar conditions or that the phenomenon differs if the circumstances change.

Suppose you shadow some information technology (IT) consultants who are implementing new customer relationship management (CRM) systems in several pharmaceutical firms. In a series of case studies, you wish to investigate how employees in different jobs respond to the new system, why resistance occurs and how employees utilize the new system. In each of the pharmaceutical firms, the consultants use, on the whole, the same step-by-step implementation approach (i.e. each implementation case is a literal replication of the previous cases). If your study of these implementation projects reveals that the processes and outcomes are about the same in each case, the generalization of the case results to the theoretical propositions becomes more robust – that is, you are more convinced that your theoretical idea provides a helpful explanation of real-world phenomena.

A literal replication of case studies aims to select very similar case studies, and predicts that the processes and outcomes discovered in each study are also similar. Another kind of replication logic does not select similar cases but explicitly selects cases that differ from each other on theoretically important dimensions. Again, take the example of the implementation of CRM projects mentioned above, and suppose that you have the idea that organizational culture influences the course of the processes and the outcomes. Rather than selecting firms with a similar culture, you would select firms with different cultures.

The richness of multiple evidence sources

The main advantage of case studies compared to other approaches is that they permit the combination of different sources of evidence. It is possible to distinguish roughly three sources of evidence:

1 interviews
2 documents and archives
3 observation.

Interviews

Interviews are the most widely used source for collecting information for evidence. Unlike interviews carried out with respondents to a survey, case study interviews are often unstructured, or even in the form of quite informal discussions with a key informant for the case. Informal discussions, or open-ended interviews with key informants, are a crucial part of many case studies, as the key informants provide valuable insights into the case's issues and can also point the case researcher towards other sources of evidence, such as relevant documents, archival surveys, or an existing internal survey or study.

The importance of discussions with key informants can also, however, give rise to the threat of the researcher becoming too dependent on them. Relying too much on just a few key informants can jeopardize the validity of a study if the informants present a biased picture of the case issue. For example, a case study based on following George Osborne, which heavily focuses on the British Chancellor of the Exchequer, is likely to present a picture of the situation biased towards the position held by the British government.

Semi-structured, or focused, interviews are another type of interview that is often used in case study research. In such cases, the researcher schedules interviews with people who possess relevant information on the case issues, and follows a particular structure (i.e. a set of open questions) in order to collect information. Semi-structured interviews have two main objectives: on the one hand, the researcher wants to know the informant's perspective on the issue but, on the other, they also want to know whether the informant can confirm insights and information the researcher already holds. This latter aspect, in particular, calls for a knowledgeable and socially competent interviewer. It is easy to ask people for their view on certain events and issues – confronting them with other views and asking them to reflect on their own view is more difficult. It requires a socially competent interviewer, who is able to dig deeper into the mind of the interviewee without starting an argument and ruining the cooperative atmosphere of the interview.

Finally, an interview within a case study can take the form of a structured interview as it is used in survey research, where the respondent is asked to respond to a fixed set of (mostly) closed questions. In Research Methods in Real Life on 'Bossnappings in France' overleaf, a case study on the occurrence of this form of workers' protest could be supplemented with a survey among the workers in the respective plants on their satisfaction with their jobs and colleagues. Sometimes case study researchers get lucky and can gain access to secondary survey data.

Documents and archives

Documents including archival sources form a rich source of evidence, which is rarely exploited in other research approaches and plays a crucial role in case study research. Documents can take many forms, including letters, internal memos and reports, newspaper articles, agendas, and so on. Documents and interviews supplement each other. On the one hand, documents – such as reports and newspaper articles – are very useful in preparing the outline of any interview and in discovering and identifying issues relevant to the case. On the other hand, interviewees can lead the researcher to documents that will corroborate information obtained in an interview. Getting hold of documents for a case study requires a systematic search approach, and the researcher should use interviews to locate them and ask for permission to access them.

Although documents are an essential source of evidence, you should also be aware of their shortcomings. As most documents are in written form, they appear to be objective and truthful; however, most documents are written with a specific purpose in mind, and addressed to a specific audience. For example, the views expressed in an internal memo from the head of the procurement department on the performance of a specific supplier could differ markedly from an assessment of the same supplier by the production department.

Archival records, which are often available in digital form rather than in print, are another important source. Examples of archival sources are survey data (e.g. surveys on customer satisfaction), internal records (e.g. production statistics, personnel files, databases of customer complaints), charts and maps (e.g. charts relating to the organization) and personal records (e.g. diaries, notes of telephone conversations). With respect to such archival records, you should also consider the purpose of their creation and explore their usefulness for your case study. However, if you can obtain access to relevant archives containing reliable information, you will have an extremely valuable source.

Observation

Observation is a research approach in itself (see Chapters 7 and 8). As with information obtained from documents, information from observations augments other sources and is especially useful in providing tacit information.

Suppose you are interested in the culture of an organization. Documents and interviews give the impression of a dynamic and innovative company. Just examining the architecture and furniture of the office will tell you whether this image is reflected in the appearance of the company. You look around and observe that the last redecoration of the offices took place about 20 years ago, the office furniture reminds you of the sort of chairs and desks you would see in a 1960s movie, and when you ask an interviewee for an email address, he or she gives you a private Hotmail address, as the company does not have employee-specific email addresses. This discrepancy (or 'lack of fit') between your own observations and what you have read in documents and heard in interviews is extremely valuable to your analysis of the firm's culture.

Two general types of observation can be distinguished: direct observation and participant observation. The latter describes the situation in which you as a researcher are a member of the organization under investigation. Examples of participant observations are:

- A student writes a research project on bossnappings and travels to the plant as soon as the news of a manager held hostage by workers is aired.
- A student writes a research project on student associations and is also the president of one.

The major advantage of participant observation is that it often offers access to information that is not available to other researchers. This deep involvement in the organization, however, also carries with it a risk: the researcher may lose their neutral, objective view.

For both types of observation, either a systematic or a more casual approach may be used. 'More casual' means that your collection of observational information is a by-product of being involved in the organization, or a by-product of your visits to the organization to hold interviews and sift through documents and archives. How to collect observational information systematically is explained in Chapters 7 and 8.

Research Methods in Real Life
Bossnappings in France

As a reaction to announcements of plant closure and workforce lay-offs, French workers have remembered a 1968 strategy to revive talks between management and unions. On 12 March 2009, Sony France chief executive officer (CEO) Serge Foucher visited the Pontox sur l'Adour plant, to announce its closure in April resulting in the sacking of 311 employees. Workers locked Foucher and the head of human resources in a meeting room and provided food, drinks and access to a bathroom but both executives spent the night on the floor in their suits. After 18 hours, they were only released when local officials negotiated that talks between management and staff would continue at the council's building.

Twelve days later, on 24 March, militant trade unionists captured 3M director Luc Rousselet when he was leaving a plant in Pithiviers, 60 km south of Paris, where about 50 per cent of the workforce were going to be laid off. The workers kept Rousselet for two days in an office while talks between workers and management resumed.

A week later, on 31 March, another bossnapping occurred in Grenoble, a town in the French Alps. Four Caterpillar managers were locked in their offices in a truck plant. Although the managers claimed that they were not authorized to renegotiate the sacking of 700 out of 2,500 employees, they were only released when French President Nicolas Sarkozy said that Caterpillar would not abandon the site.

- Why is the phenomenon of bossnapping suited for case study research?
- Would you focus on one case or study all three cases?
- Can you develop an idea on which elements of the context should be considered?

References and further reading

www.guardian.co.uk/world/2009/mar/13/sony-france-boss-hostage

www.guardian.co.uk/world/2009/apr/01/boss-hostage-france-caterpillar

www.independent.co.uk/news/world/europe/french-boss-barricaded-in-office-by-employees-1654292.html

How to conduct good case study research

One often hears the suspicion voiced that case studies produce biased evidence. Without doubt there are many case studies that follow highly questionable procedures in collecting information, apply dubious methods in analyzing the information and finish with questionable conclusions. Unfortunately, however, this is also true of studies based on experiments, surveys or any other approach. It is not the approach that determines the quality of a study, but how the study is conducted. The quality of a case study depends very much on the skilful exploitation of its advantages and the rigour of its conducting.

Chapter 1 looked at the criteria for good research; Exhibit 11.2 applies these criteria to case study research. We now look at each of the points addressed in Exhibit 11.2 in more detail.

Exhibit 11.2 *Producing good-quality case study research.*

Criteria for good research	How may these be achieved in case studies?
Purpose clearly defined	• Be explicit in the formulation of the research objectives and research problem. In particular, formulate unambiguously the theoretical propositions you want to generalize to
Research process detailed	• Provide all information pertaining to the research process, including information on who you interviewed, what documents you obtained, what archives you looked through, which secondary data you used • Plan which sources of evidence you will employ next to interviews
Research design thoroughly planned	• Explain clearly the thinking behind your selection of the case(s) • Plan carefully how you are going to obtain information from different sources of evidence. Who do you want to interview? How long will those interviews take? In what kind of documents and archives are you interested? Who can you ask for help in finding and accessing them? • Design a case study information base that clearly distinguishes the information obtained from the case study report
High ethical standards applied	• Protect the rights of other actors involved in the study, such as sponsors and respondents or interviewees • Ensure that your research fulfils the quality standards of good research by (i) giving an accurate account of the observation you have obtained, (ii) mentioning any information that does not fit with your theoretical proposition(s), and (iii) basing your conclusions and recommendations on the findings of the case study, and resisting the desire to exceed the scope of your study
Limitations frankly revealed	• Discuss to what extent the picture your case study reveals can be considered a complete one • Mention when you deviated from the planned procedures in order to collect information
Adequate analysis of decision-maker's needs	• Explain, in detail, how you assessed the information obtained through observations • Explain, in detail, how you combined and weighted evidence from different sources • Do not get bogged down in details – keep the line of your argument(s) in mind at all times
Findings presented unambiguously	• Use a clear structure that allows you to include all relevant details, and that prevents the reader from getting lost • Use tables and graphs to support the presentation of your findings
Conclusion justified	• Ensure that the conclusions you make are always supported by your findings and do not go beyond what you have researched

---

Purpose clearly defined

A clear definition of purpose requires an explicit formulation of the study's objectives and the problem under investigation. Try to be as specific as possible in defining the purpose. In the case study on CRM systems mentioned above, the purpose should be more than just an attempt to investigate the implementation of a CRM system. The researcher should also define what aspects of this implementation process he or she wants to investigate. Are they interested in responses including the resistance of employees affected by the new system? Are they interested in how the employees utilize the new system? Are they interested in the interactions between the IT consultants and the firm's management in the implementation process?

It is also of utmost importance that you as a researcher clearly disclose any theoretical expectation you have, because any pre-considerations you have about the piece of research will largely determine the design of your study (i.e. to whom you will talk, which questions you will ask, which documents you will look at). It does not matter if the theoretical expectation you had at the start of the research does not match the study's outcome. In fact, good case studies often start with a well-reasoned theoretical proposition, which is sequentially broken down in the course of the study by presenting findings that point to other explanations.

Research process detailed

A detailed description of the research process increases the accountability of the research, as readers are thus better able to assess it. As survey studies should inform the reader of the population used, the sampling method and the communication approach used with respondents, a case study researcher also has to describe in detail how he or she obtained the information presented. This means that you should provide information on your interview partners: who are they, what role they have in the issue investigated, how you approached them, how often and how long you talked with them, and so on. Similarly, you should describe in detail the documents and archives you have consulted, by showing what kind of information they contained, how you accessed them, why they were written and kept, and so on.

Research design thoroughly planned

Case study research involves careful planning of its design. For example, if you visit a firm rather wet behind the ears, and do not know exactly what you want to investigate, your own opinion on the relevant issues or the kind of information that you are looking for, the chances of you obtaining valuable information for your study will be close to zero. You are the researcher, and you have to find and impart the relevant information. This task cannot be done even by people within the firm. So, before you approach a firm or person for an interview, define clearly what you want to get out of the interview.

Do not forget that case studies thrive on the multiple sources of evidence used, and that you have to find out what sources exist and how you can arrange access to them. The rationale behind using multiple sources of evidence is that you develop converging lines of inquiry, and can apply a process of **triangulation** (i.e. the different sorts of evidence provide different measurements of the same phenomenon and increase the construct validity). The principle of triangulation increases the power of your evidence only if the sources are independent from each other.

The independence of two separate sources of evidence becomes doubtful if both can be traced back to the same origin. For example, if you obtain certain information about employee resistance during an interview with a member of the workers' union and this information is also supported by information found in a report, these two sources of evidence are not independent if the report was compiled by the same member of the union that you interviewed.

Sound case study research should delineate clearly a line between the information obtained and the report. In survey research the information obtained in the course of the survey is stored in data files, which do not usually form part of the study report. Likewise, as a case study researcher you should build up a database in which is stored all the information you obtained electronically, written or in any other form. Be aware that any notes you make during interviews or after visiting an organization are not part of the report, but part of your database. Building up a database with all the information obtained helps you to organize the information and ensure that nothing is lost. Moreover, your research becomes transparent to others as you document what you did and others could replicate it and check whether they come to the same conclusions.

Student Research

Joint venture failure

Last summer, Carina worked as an intern in the analytical laboratory of a large chemical company. For a few years, the lab had not only worked for departments of its parent company, but also worked on external projects. Most of those external projects were for another chemical company that originally belonged to the lab's parent, but that part was acquired recently by another company. Carina's task was to develop a system how to assess external and internal projects. At the end of the internship, Carina asked whether she could write her Master's thesis together with the company, and as everybody appreciated Carina's work, she and the management thought about a suitable project.

One of the most strategic issues was that their biggest external customer, the one who was previously part of the parent company, had suggested transforming the analytical lab into a joint venture. It was now decided that Carina should investigate what would be necessary to form such a joint venture. Carina spent hours and nights in the library reading a lot about contracting, joint ventures, opportunism and transaction cost theory. Backed up with this knowledge, she scheduled interviews with people from the analytical lab, the two joint venture companies and even other external customers of the lab. These interviews allowed Carina to sketch a quite precise picture of the different stakeholders' interests and she kept on investigating which measures could be taken to balance the different interests and to mitigate the worries of some.

Then on a Monday morning, she came into the office and her mentor called her in and said to her that the board had decided on Friday to call the joint venture plans off. Both parties do not believe in the joint venture anymore. Carina was shocked. What would happen to her thesis; were three months of hard work for nothing? She couldn't believe that the joint venture in which everybody at the lab believed had been called off.

Sitting down at her desk looking at her material, she became desperate and her mood hardly improved over the following days. She kept on talking with people about what had happened to the plans, but she still did not know how she could finish her thesis. Then on the Thursday afternoon she had that Eureka moment. She read quickly through the transcripts of her interviews and realised her mistake: for months, she had worked with the wrong assumption in her mind. She assumed that a good joint venture can be achieved when both parties engage in giving and taking to find a viable compromise. But finding a compromise between the two partners was not the real problem: the real problem was that within both companies there were supporters and opponents of the joint venture. In her own company, top management and the people working in the analytical lab were mostly proponents, but the general managers of the business units were opponents because they were afraid that knowledge would leak out through the joint venture.

In the next days, Carina recoded the material and did not distinguish anymore between company A and B, but between joint venture supporters and opponents. In the end she did not write a thesis about how to form a successful joint venture, but how internal opposition can torpedo a project.

What kind of case study did Carina conduct?

High ethical standards applied

As with any other research a researcher has to meet certain ethical standards when conducting a case study. In Chapter 4, we discussed which ethical standards a researcher needs to comply with. Briefly, these ethical standards can be summarized in terms of two main guidelines. First, the researcher needs to ensure that the rights of other people involved are not infringed by his or her action, or the research itself. Privacy issues can be critical in case study research, as case studies usually reveal a great deal of information. If you promised confidentiality to the sponsor, you will need to ensure that well-informed third parties, such as competitors, cannot identify the sponsor, especially if your report is made publicly available. For the same reason, the right to confidentiality of informants can be at stake in case studies. In the Running Case Study example of free-riding behaviour at university, you would have to promise confidentiality to your informants (e.g. to the student who confesses to having been a free-rider or cheated during an exam) and not provide sufficient information on them to enable people within the company to identify them.

Second, researchers need to be honest in their assessment and interpretation of the information obtained. A researcher should always raise the question of whether every other researcher would come to the same conclusions and interpretations of the information arrived at. If the answer to this question is yes, you will know that your assessment and interpretation of the information is a reasonable and justifiable account of the issue under investigation.

Limitations frankly revealed

Any study, case study or not, should frankly reveal its limitations. This revelation refers first of all to whether procedures desired from a methodological viewpoint could really be followed during the research. Were the researchers able to fully obtain all information they required, i.e. did they have access to all written documents, could they interview all persons they were interested in? For example, assume you study the effects of a firm's reorganization. Certainly, interviewing people who had been laid off in that reorganization would be important. However, it might be difficult to trace such people, as they may have moved to another city or may be less than willing to share their experiences and opinions with researchers. Furthermore, you should report and discuss any doubts you have concerning the reliability and quality of your information – for example, if you suspect that certain information has been strategically distorted or an important piece of information is unavailable for any reason.

Limitations also refer to the general applicability of the study. Although case studies do not attempt to give a representative picture of an issue, they still attempt to reveal certain effects or mechanisms that are likely to occur in other similar settings. For this reason a case researcher needs to make sure that findings in a case study are not based just on the idiosyncrasies of a specific case.

Please note that revealing and discussing limitations is not the same thing as undermining the results of a study; rather, it should serve to reinforce the reader's confidence in the study.

Adequate case study analysis

Survey researchers can use quantitative analysis methods – a rich, standardized and advanced toolkit – to analyse their information. Case study researchers are still bereft of such finely honed equipment; however, their toolkit is far from empty. They have tools that will enable them to analyse adequately any information obtained – via, for example, pattern matching and time-series analysis. Still one often observes that case study researchers do not fully utilize the potential of their rich data, as they remain unclear about their analysis strategy.

Adequate analysis: general strategies

Before you think about specific techniques allowing the analysis of the collected data, it is important to develop a general strategy. As mentioned above, case study research can be explorative as well as explanatory. Thus, the first question you should ask yourself is what is my objective: am I more interested in new theory building through rich descriptions or am I more interested in finding and documenting evidence for theoretical propositions?

If new theory building is your objective, your case study should emphasize the rich content of your material. This requires the identification of main themes along which you structure your research. Taking the example of bossnapping above, you could structure your case along the actors involved (workers of the plant, the local managers, the trade unions, the top management, etc.) or you could use the main themes of the phenomenon, such as the economic rationale of the plant closing, the consequences of the closing for the workers and the community, the communication and negotiation patterns between the management and workers and their representatives. Up front there is no optimal structure, but you need to think carefully which structure allows you best to help the reader to capture the full complexity of the phenomenon and follow your line of data-based reasoning towards your conclusions.

If theoretical dispositions are central to your case study, you have developed a theoretical idea prior to your data collection. In that case a common structure for your case study is to start with the research question and the proposition followed by a description of the case context. Then you present the information collected and link it to the propositions before you interpret the findings and conclude.

Adequate analysis: analytical techniques

The rationale behind pattern matching is to form a general picture of the case by detecting patterns in the information. There are several approaches to this. One is to split the theoretical dependent variables into different non-equivalent variables. In our example of the implementation of a CRM system mentioned above, we might expect a certain pattern between organizational structure and resistance, and could, for example, arrive at the following propositions:

1 Employees affected by the new CRM system will approach the workers' union representative and rely on him to discuss the implications of the new system for the shop floor rather than discussing the new system directly with management.
2 Departments affected by the new CRM system will experience an increase in sickness leave days and resignations, and a reduced willingness to work extra hours.
3 The atmosphere in meetings becomes more controversial and formal, and informal communication becomes less open.

Each of these three propositions refers to an aspect of resistance in the company. If the information provided by the case study supports each of these propositions, the researcher can argue more convincingly that resistance in the investigated case is high.

The second approach is closely related to the theoretical replication of a case study, by looking for patterns with rival explanations. Thus, in the CRM implementation example, the researchers formulate rival explanations for the occurrence of resistance by defining for each explanation an exclusive set of independent variables. Then they check either within a single case study or across multiple case studies whether the case points to one of the rival explanations, as the case, in reality, matches with this explanation's set of independent variables.

Time-series analysis is often conducted in experiments and quasi-experiments (see also Chapter 12). Time-series analysis can be very simple – for example, following the trend of a certain variable over time. This trend is then compared to a theoretical explanation and a rival explanation, and other trends. Suppose you wish to study on-the-job training in a plaster factory and you have the proposition, among others, that it takes between one and three months for on-the-job training to result in productivity gains. If you built up a time-series analysis of on-the-job training and productivity changes, the line representing the training must precede changes in the productivity line, and the lag between the two should be between one and three months. So, for example, if your interviews and documents reveal that the firm had on-the-job training programmes in place in the Wolshire plant in February 2002 and in the Moerdijk plant in September 2002, you should observe an increase in productivity in the Wolshire plant around April 2002 and in the Moerdijk plant around November 2002. To exclude alternative explanations you need, however, to ensure that alternative explanations do not explain the findings, such as installing better equipment or better communication between managers and employees.

More complex time-series analysis involves looking at the trend over time of multiple variables, and investigating whether changes in one variable are followed by changes in others. More complex time-series analyses are suitable bases for theoretical propositions on causes and effects between variables and especially for investigating chain reactions in which one thing leads to the next.

Findings presented unambiguously

In a good case study the findings are presented unambiguously. As mentioned already in the section on ethical standards above, this includes disclosing all insights that you have arrived at, including those that contradict your proposition. Furthermore, it is important that the reader of the study can easily identify the main points you wish to make. This requires that you attempt to state your outcomes unconditionally, and if the outcome is conditional this is made explicit. In case study research in particular the researcher often presents so much information that the reader can get easily lost in it. For this reason, you need to distinguish clearly between your main findings and any additional findings and information. Graphs, tables and figures are useful devices in helping to summarize findings and facilitate a quick understanding of them. You could, for example, provide a table in which the columns represent different sources of evidence and each row a different theoretical proposition. In the cells of the table you can then indicate the information obtained through a source and whether it supports or rejects your proposition.

Conclusion justified

You need to be careful that your conclusion is justified and does not expand the scope of your study. In particular you should not generalize the case study conclusion to much broader theoretical propositions. So, if your case study supports the proposition that less hierarchical organizations experience lower resistance during the implementation of a new CRM system, you must reveal that your study is on the relationship between organizational structure and resistance to new IT systems, but not on the relationship between organizational structure and resistance to change in general.

As mentioned above, case studies permit generalization to theoretical propositions but not to populations. Therefore, it is important that you resist the temptation to generalize results from your case study to others. Take the method issues in the real-life example of workers taking executives hostage at French factories of 3M, Sony and Caterpillar. Suppose a researcher investigated this issue with a case study on the incident at the Sony plant. In the final chapter of the study, the conclusions for Sony are applied to the incident at Caterpillar. The report suggests that Caterpillar could solve the issue if it followed the suggestions made for Sony. Such a final chapter would be unreasonable. Instead, the researcher should have made it clear that the study is limited to Sony and that any suggestions arising from the study cannot be applied to other companies unless one shows that the specific situation analyzed at the Sony plant also applies to the other company.

Case study research offers a very valuable approach to investigating scientific and business problems, and the results of case studies will provide essential insights into how and why certain processes work as they do, and what is required to get things moving in the intended direction. However, case studies will only provide useful insights if they are conducted well. The poor quality of case studies is a major facet in the many prejudices surrounding this method.

Business students often prefer to take the case study approach in their own research projects (e.g. in a Master's research project), as they believe that conducting case study research is easier than setting up an experiment or designing a survey. The opposite is in fact true. Good case studies call for immense effort. Just interviewing three or four people in a company does not make a case study. It is necessary to collect information from a range of other sources, such as documents and archives, or by observation, as noted above. Analysis of the information that has been collected is also more difficult than may be supposed. Although the outcome of a quantitative survey can be summarized and correlated fairly easily with widely available statistics software packages, such as SPSS or STATA, for case studies such standard techniques – which can summarize, categorize and present information – do not exist. Furthermore, there are no generally accepted rules that determine whether a detected pattern is really a 'deliberate' one (i.e. as opposed to merely random). Neither do case study researchers have the benefit of levels of significance. With each study they do, they have to convince others that the observations they have made do or do not fit with theoretical explanations. Case study research might appear easy to do and the soft option, but the reality is that, because its structure is so flexible and its points of reference are vague, conducting a good piece of case study research is in fact the hard road to take, especially for the inexperienced researcher.

Particularly, data-minded positivist scholars often criticize case studies for their missing generalizability and missing standards to define whether a difference is there or not, like the significance level. In our view this criticism is neither valid nor fruitful. First, the social sciences including business science are based on probabilities. Thus, even if we find that people with a higher income are more likely to drink champagne, we will always find rich people who prefer a good bitter to champagne and poorer people who save money just to have this one bottle of champagne on New Year's Eve. Focusing on the average effect within a population, even if correctly calculated, does not acknowledge the full variety observed in reality. Case study research is especially suited to deal with those cases that do not fit with our theoretical predictions and those 'faulty' cases will teach us more about reality than all the confirmed cases. Second, case study researchers never claim that their findings are universal laws. Accusing them of missing generalizability is accusing case study of a claim never made. Third, we acknowledge that we have seen many badly conducted case studies, but we have seen as many badly conducted empirical studies. Whether a study is sound or not is not a matter of the chosen matter but a matter of the researcher's rigour.

Running Case Study 11
Multiple sources of evidence

In the course of his research project, Mehmet has become more and more interested in the outcomes of migrant entrepreneurship; not just on an individual level, but also on a more aggregated level, the macro level of a neighbourhood. In the previous weeks, Mehmet had been an active networker and made contact with many entrepreneurs, but also with people running projects to stimulate the economic development in cities and neighbourhoods. Just yesterday, he had talked to Hans Visser, the deputy head of the police station Oosterpark, who told him how closer cooperation between the municipality, the police and local businessmen has helped to reduce vandalism and other civil crimes like shoplifting. Mr Visser explained that such initiatives also have a positive effect on the economic climate, as people would think twice before starting a business in a neighbourhood that is known for above-average crime rates. Mr Visser did not need to convince Mehmet about the importance of the external environment for new companies. For a business student, the environment is always a strategic factor to be considered. But Mehmet had become curious whether business also had a direct effect on the neighbourhood.

Suddenly, Mehmet had the design of his case studies before his eyes. His cases would not be different migrant businesses – he would investigate just one case, a typical migrant neighbourhood in Amsterdam. Mehmet chose the Oosterpark neighbourhood. In his eyes it was an ideal neighbourhood to study migrant entrepreneurship. Oosterpark is a residential neighbourhood close to the centre of Amsterdam. It was developed between 1880 and 1920; most houses are built from brick and mostly between three to five floors high. Between World War I and World War II, the neighbourhood attracted predominantly middle-income workers. But in the 1950s and 1960s, the area experienced a rapid decline, as people moved to the suburbs, preferring terraced houses with a small garden patch to flats in the city. In the 1980s that decline was reversed as migrants from Turkey, Morocco, but also the former Dutch colonies, settled in the neighbourhood. Today, the neighbourhood is multi-cultural with many small businesses owned by Dutch natives and migrants. Mehmet's real reason to choose Oosterpark was, however, that he wanted to live in Amsterdam. Studying in Maastricht, a small provincial capital in the south, was nice for a start, but now he wanted to live on his own in a real city. It had taken some time to convince his father that moving to Amsterdam would not jeopardize his work on his Master's project; with modern communication technologies, location does not matter anymore. But once he convinced him, his father offered him a small studio apartment on the 4th floor in one of the houses he owned in Amsterdam's Oosterpark. Actually, the first travel agency his father opened in Amsterdam was still located in that house.

Although Mehmet had already spoken to a couple of migrant entrepreneurs, up to now his investigations were not very systematic. Now he wanted to change this and for the next two weeks he had two objectives: (1) developing an interview guide and (2) writing a chapter describing the Oosterpark neighbourhood, as this would be the main context of his research.

He had already collected information brochures and policy reports from the town hall of Amsterdam East, the city district Oosterpark belonged to. Then he consulted the online service *Statline* of Statistics Netherlands to get some basic quantitative information on the neighbourhood. Today, Oosterpark is one of those multicultural neighbourhoods characterized by above-average crime rates and a relatively large share of people with a low income – average income is about €12,000 – on the one hand. On the other hand, the neighbourhood has a young age structure: more than two-thirds of the population is 45 or younger.

A couple of weeks ago, Mehmet had moved to his new apartment in Oosterpark. Now he was living right in the middle of the neighbourhood he wanted to investigate. Although he had to work hard on his research paper and, in addition, worked a couple of hours each week in his father's travel agency, he also had time to stroll through the neighbourhood. He usually took lunch outside and when he walked down the streets he observed the street life. He recognized that some migrant shopkeepers mainly sold to migrant customers, while other shopkeepers had much more diversified customers. But it was not only the differences in customers that caught his eyes, there was also something different about the shops themselves. In the following weeks, he studied the different shops in more detail and even bought something in each. He

►

recognized that the shops selling to more diverse customers were bigger, they employed not only family members, but also other people; some even employed people that did not belong to their ethnic group. One of the larger shops even mirrored the melting-pot Amsterdam had become; Mehmet had the impression that the shop had at least one employee from each United Nations member country. During a Skype talk, his advisor told him to structure his observations better. Up to then, Mehmet had usually simply written down some notes after each walk through the neighbourhood, but now he prepared a table (see example below) summarizing the information of the 32 shops he had observed so far.

Shop	Owner characteristics	Customer characteristics	Appearance of shop	Other
Chefchaouen	Moroccan, above 60, only family members are working there, owner speaks Dutch badly, son speaks Dutch well	Mainly Moroccan and other Arab nationalities	Small, sells mainly vegetables and fruit, small butcher shop, clean but house is a bit run down. Neighbouring shops, left side empty (to rent), right side phone shop, above shop three families, rented	When the sun is shining owner puts chairs on the pavement and sits there with other older Moroccans
Medeterraneo	Moroccan, owner is 32, friend of mine who took over the business from his father, 12 Moroccans working there and two Turks. Father the only other family member working there (sometimes his sisters help out), speak Dutch well	Mixed customers, many native Dutch shop there	Butcher shop, large fish counter, exotic vegetables and fruit. Large corner shop which is combined with shops of the right side house and back house. Delivery car can be parked in back yard. Houses owned by owner. Owner lives above shop and 5 other flats are rented	Delivers also to some restaurants in the neighbourhood
Guiyang	Chinese owner	Mixed	Sells only pre-packaged food from Asia and household ware, very small shop, rented shop, two families live above	

The table became larger and larger and did not fit a page anymore. He glued the pages together and the table was covering half of his desks. Looking at his desk Mehmet saw the table produced from his observations, the printouts from the secondary data, transcripts from his interviews and the notebooks in which he had documented all the informal talks he had with local politicians, business advisors and so on. It looked to him that he had material for five research projects, but how should he put all this information together?

1 How does Mehmet ensure the richness of evidence in this research project?
2 Mehmet has prepared a table to record his observations. Does this table structure his interviews too much?
3 Is triangulation a solution to combine the different sources and how would you proceed?

Summary

Case study research is an important, and in business science also widely used, research approach. Unlike survey research it does not follow the sampling logic but the replication logic, and case study results are therefore not generalizable to a population but to a theoretical proposition. The main advantages of the case study approach compared to other approaches is that it relies on multiple sources of evidence, such as interviews, observations and documents, and allows the consideration of the specific context. Especially in qualitative research, unstructured or semi-structured interviews are very appropriate as it allows researchers to obtain a good understanding of a situation or phenomena and to gain a better insight in what respondents really think. Focus group interviews are similar to unstructured interviews, but in addition they allow the researcher to observe interaction patterns between respondents. Unstructured as well as focus group interviews have high demands regarding the social and communication skills of the interviewer/moderator.

Discussion questions

Terms in review

1 What distinguishes the case study research approach from other research approaches?

2 Describe the sources of evidence that should be used in case study research, and how to collect and analyse the information.

Making research decisions

3 The company relations office at your university offers an internship at IKEA. The intern will work for the project team assigned to prepare IKEA's expansion to China. You are lucky and get this job, and you are even luckier because one of your professors is willing to supervise your research project on entry strategies for China.
  a How would you design case study research combining your internship at IKEA and your research project on entry strategies?
  b To whom would you like to talk?
  c What documents would be valuable to you?
  d How could you ensure that you are not biased?

Classroom discussion

4 Discuss in the classroom or in sub-groups what would be needed to write a good case study on the following topics. Discuss explorative and explanatory research questions for each topic potential, what information you would need and which sources you could approach.
  a The emergence of standards and their consequences in the telecommunications industry.
  b The effects of developments in information and communication technologies on the music recording industry.
  c The basis of Ryanair's success as a low-cost airline.

5 Discuss the following statement:

Only case study research will produce meaningful insights as it is the only approach considering the specific context.

Recommended further reading

Eisenhardt, Kathleen M., 'Building theory from case study research', *Academy of Management Review* **14(4), 1989, pp. 532–50.** This article describes the process of inducting theory, from case studies to writing conclusions, and discusses when case study is particularly useful.

Yin, Robert K., *Case Study Research: Design and Methods* **(4th edn). Newbury Park, CA: Sage, 2008.** An excellent guide and one of the standard references for case study research. Designing and conducting a case study along the lines suggested in this text almost guarantees a good case study.

Get started with understanding statistical techniques!

When you have read this chapter, log on to the Online Learning Centre website at *www.mcgraw-hill.co.uk/textbooks/blumberg* to explore chapter-by-chapter test questions, additional case studies, a glossary and more online study tools for *Business Research Methods*.

Note

1   Robert K. Yin, *Case Study Research: Design and Methods.* London: Sage, 1989, p. 23.

CHAPTER 12

Experimentation

Chapter contents

Learning objectives

When you have read this chapter, you should understand:

1 the uses for experimentation

2 the advantages and disadvantages of the experimental method

3 the seven steps of a well-planned experiment

4 internal and external validity with experimental research designs

5 the three types of experimental design, and the variations of each.

What is experimentation?

Why do events occur under some conditions and not under others? Research methods that answer such questions are called **causal methods** (recall the discussion of causality in Chapter 5). *Ex-post facto* research designs – where a researcher interviews respondents or observes what is or what has been – also have the potential for discovering causality. The distinction between these methods and experimentation is that the researcher is required to accept the world as it is found, whereas an experiment allows the researcher to alter systematically the variables of interest and observe what changes follow.

In this chapter we define experimentation, and discuss its advantages and disadvantages. Next to the classical laboratory experiment, we also discuss field and quasi-experiments. An outline for the conduct of an experiment is presented as a vehicle to introduce important concepts. The questions of internal and external validity are also examined:

- Does the experimental treatment determine the observed difference or was some extraneous variable responsible?
- How can one generalize the results of the study across times, settings and persons?

Experiments are studies involving intervention by the researcher beyond that required for measurement.[1] The usual intervention is to manipulate a variable in a setting and observe how it affects the subjects being studied (e.g. people or physical entities). The researcher manipulates the independent or explanatory variable and then observes whether the hypothesized dependent variable is affected by the intervention. (You may wish to revisit the discussion of causality in Chapter 5.)

An example of such an intervention is the study of bystanders and thieves.[2] In this experiment, students were asked to go to an office where they had an opportunity to see a fellow student steal some money from a receptionist's desk. A confederate of the experimenter, of course, did the stealing. The major **hypothesis** concerned whether people observing a theft would be more likely to report it (i) if they observed the crime alone or (ii) if they were in the company of someone else.

There is at least one **independent variable (IV)** and one **dependent variable (DV)** in a causal relationship. We hypothesize that in some way the IV 'causes' the DV to occur. The independent or explanatory variable in our example was the state of either being alone when observing the theft or being in the company of another person. The dependent variable was whether the subjects reported observing the crime. The results suggested that bystanders were more likely to report the theft if they observed it alone rather than in another person's company.

On what grounds did the researchers conclude that people who were alone were more likely to report crimes observed than people in the company of others? Three types of evidence form the basis for this conclusion:

- Independent and dependent variable are correlated, i.e. lone observers (IV_1) report theft more often (DV) than paired observers (IV_2).
- Time order, the dependent variable should not precede the independent variable, but they may occur almost simultaneously. In the example the reporting clearly comes after the theft.
- No other extraneous variable influenced the dependent variable. In the example, there was a laboratory set up as an office. The receptionist and the thief were instructed to speak and act in the same way and with each trial the same process was repeated. Thus, it is highly unlikely that another variable has influenced the outcome.

While such controls are important, further precautions are needed so that the results achieved reflect only the influence of the independent variable on the dependent variable.

An evaluation of experiments

Advantages

When we elaborated on the concept of cause in Chapter 5, we said causality could not be proved with certainty but the probability of one variable being linked to another could be established convincingly. The experiment comes closer than any other method in accomplishing this goal. The foremost advantage is the researcher's ability to manipulate the independent variable. Consequently, the probability that changes in the dependent variable are a function of that manipulation increases. Further, a **control group** serves as a comparison to assess the existence and potency of the manipulation and **pre-** and **post-test** measurements allow checking that the manipulation occurred before the outcome.

The second advantage of the experiment is that contamination from extraneous variables can be controlled more effectively than in other designs. This helps the researcher isolate experimental variables and evaluate their impact over time.

Third, the convenience and cost of experimentation are often superior to other methods. These benefits allow the experimenter opportunistic scheduling of data collection and the flexibility to adjust variables and conditions that evoke extremes not observed under routine circumstances. In addition, the experimenter can assemble combinations of variables for testing rather than having to search for their fortuitous appearance in the study environment.

Fourth, **replication** (repeating an experiment with different subject groups and conditions) leads to the discovery of an average effect of the independent variable across people, situations and times.

Finally, researchers can use naturally occurring events and, to some extent, **field experiments** to reduce subjects' perceptions of the researcher as a source of intervention or deviation in their everyday lives.

Disadvantages

The artificiality of the laboratory is arguably the primary disadvantage of the experimental method. However, many subjects' perceptions of a contrived environment can be improved by investment in the facility.

Second, generalization from non-probability samples can pose problems: the extent to which a study can be generalized, say, from college students to managers or executives is open to question; and when an experiment is disguised unsuccessfully, volunteer subjects are often those with the most interest in the topic.

Third, the number of variables one can include in an experiment is much more limited than, for example, in survey research. Experiments are not appropriate in research problems that involve many influential factors.

Fourth, despite the low costs of experimentation, many applications of experimentation far outrun the budgets for other primary data-collection methods.

Fifth, experimentation is most effectively targeted at problems of the present or immediate future. Experimental studies of the past are not feasible, and studies about intentions or predictions are difficult. Furthermore, the factors included in the investigation should be easy to manipulate. This requirement is hard to meet if the factors considered are characteristics of the respondent, such as education, social competence, and so on.

Sixth, designing an experiment involves creating an intervention, but how effective is that intervention? In the example above the distinction between being alone and in a pair seems to be very effective. But assume somebody is interested whether people with similar personalities work better as a team than people with different personalities. The researcher measures the personality through a validated questionnaire before the experiment and then forms teams with similar personality and different personality. But would participants recognize whether other group members have a different or similar personality, or would they rather assess their group members' surface characteristics, like age, ethnicity and gender.

Finally, management research is often concerned with the study of people. There are limits to the types of manipulation and control that are ethical.

12.3 Conducting an experiment[3]

In a well-executed experiment, researchers must complete a series of activities to carry out their craft successfully. Although the experiment is the premier scientific methodology for establishing causation, the resourcefulness and creativeness of the researcher are needed to make the experiment live up to its potential. In this section, we discuss seven activities the researcher must accomplish in order to make the endeavour successful:

1 selecting relevant variables
2 specifying the level(s) of treatment
3 controlling the experimental environment
4 choosing the experimental design
5 selecting and assigning subjects
6 pilot testing, revising and testing.

We now look at each of these in turn.

Selecting relevant variables

Throughout this book we have discussed the idea that a research problem can be conceptualized as a hierarchy of questions starting with a management problem. The researcher's task is to translate an amorphous problem into the question or hypothesis that best states the objectives of the research. Depending on the complexity of the problem, investigative questions and additional hypotheses can be created to address specific facets of the study or data that need to be gathered. Further, we have mentioned that a hypothesis is a relational statement because it describes a relationship between two or more variables. It must also be **operationalized**, a term we used earlier in discussing how concepts are transformed into variables to make them measurable and subject to testing.

Consider the following research question as we work through the six points listed above: Do homogeneous teams, that is groups of people with the same nationality, perform better in a management game?

Research Methods in Real Life

Experiments on the web?

We all know that the Internet is useful for data collection. But what about using it to conduct experiments? Actually conducting experiments through the web has many advantages over the traditional experiments in a lab. First, experimental studies often suffer from a rather low number of participants resulting in a low statistical power and as a consequence, it is often impossible to consider more than just a few variables. Internet-based experiments can easily get a couple of hundred participants, which solves the statistical power issue. Second, most experiments in the social sciences are based on students and often on students from one university. This raises questions regarding the generalizability of the results. Although Internet users are also not representative of the world population, they are more heterogeneous than students and can be recruited easily from all over the world. Third, Internet-based experiments require less time and financial effort. Once programmed, you do not need to schedule lab hours, you are not restricted to the opening hours of the university and participants are volunteers who are not paid.

No doubt Internet-based experiments also raise new problems, but most of them can be solved with advanced techniques. One main problem is that people will cheat and participate in an experiment more than once: storing IP addresses in combination with an email address solves this problem to a large extent. There is also the problem of self-selection. Who are those people who spend time behind the computer to do experiments? How did they find the experiment? But this holds for traditional experiments as well. Another issue is that Internet-based experiments can be less controlled. Of course, the experiment remains the same for every participant, but the environment in which the experiment is done differs. Is the participant alone behind the computer or with somebody else? Is the participant engaging in the experiment during a lunch break from their office or late at night from their sofa after having a couple of drinks? Given that people get randomly assigned to the conditions, the larger number of participants will compensate for random errors in the environment (see also Chapters 6 and 18). Researchers conducting an Internet-based experiment can always conduct the same experiment in the traditional manner and compare the two to see whether the delivery mode of the experiment has mattered. Finally, of course there are experiments that cannot be translated into an Internet-based experiment, e.g. the theft experiment we described above. But the examples on the websites mentioned below document that in the field of economics and business, there are many opportunities for Internet-based experiments.

References and further reading

Reips, U.D. (2002), 'Standards for Internet-based experimenting', *Experimental Psychology* 49(4), pp. 243–56.

The websites below provide examples for Internet-based experiments:

www.wexlist.net/

www.philosophyexperiments.com

http://eeps.caltech.edu/

www.aton.com.au/

This website provides access to software to help create Internet-based experiments:

http://wextor.org/wextor/en/

Since a hypothesis is a tentative statement – a speculation – about the outcome of the study, it might take this form:

Homogeneous teams, that is, groups of people with the same nationality, perform better than mixed teams, that is, groups of people with different nationalities, in a management game. The researchers' challenges at this step are as follows:

1 Select variables that are the best operational representations of the original concepts.
2 Determine how many variables to test.
3 Select or design appropriate measures for them.

The researchers would need to select variables that best operationalize the concepts 'team homogeneity' and 'performance'. The product's classification and the nature of the intended audience should also be defined. In addition, the term 'better' could be operationalized statistically by means of a significance test.

The number of variables in an experiment is constrained by the project budget, the time allocated, the availability of appropriate controls and the number of subjects being tested. For statistical reasons, the number of subjects (participants) needs to be larger than the number of variables.[4] How many subjects you need depends on the variance in the variables and the desired precision of your estimates (see also Chapters 6 and 17 (significance chapter)). A rule of thumb, however, is to have included about 10–30 subjects for each treatment level.

The selection of measures for testing requires a thorough review of the available literature and instruments. In addition, measures must be adapted to the unique needs of the research situation without compromising their intended purpose or original meaning.

Specifying the level(s) of treatment

The treatment levels of the independent variable are the distinctions that the researcher makes between different aspects of the treatment condition. For example, if salary is hypothesized to have an effect on employees exercising stock purchase options, it might be divided into high, middle and low ranges to represent three levels of the independent variable.

The levels assigned to an independent variable should be based on simplicity and common sense. In the management game example, the experimenter should not define homogeneous teams as groups of people with the same nationality and mixed teams as a group, in which all members but one share the same nationality. Thus, in the first trial, the researcher is likely to form teams in which all people have the same nationality and teams in which each team member has a different nationality.

Under an entirely different hypothesis, several levels of the independent variable may be needed to test order-of-presentation effects. Here we use only two. Alternatively, a control group could provide a base level for comparison. The control group is composed of subjects who are not exposed to the independent variable(s), in contrast to those who receive the **experimental treatment** (manipulation of the independent variable(s)).

Controlling the experimental environment

Chapter 1 discussed the nature of extraneous variables and the need for their control. In our management game experiment, extraneous variables can appear as differences in age, gender, business experience, communications competence and many other characteristics of the game or the situation. These have the potential for distorting the effect of the treatment on the dependent variable and must be controlled or eliminated. However, at this stage we are principally concerned with **environmental control**, holding constant the physical environment of the experiment. All participants in the experiment would get the same written instruction and play exactly the same management game. The arrangement of the room, the time of administration, the experimenter's contact with the subjects, and so on, must all be consistent across each administration of the experiment.

Other forms of control involve subjects and experimenters. When subjects do not know if they are receiving the experimental treatment, they are said to be **blind**. When the experimenters do not know if they are giving the treatment to the experimental group or to the control group, the experiment is said to be **double blind**. Both approaches control unwanted complications such as subjects' reactions to expected conditions, or experimenter influence.

Choosing the experimental design

Many of the experimental designs are diagrammed and described later in section 12.5 of this chapter. Unlike the general descriptors of research design that were discussed in Chapter 5, experimental designs are unique to the experimental method. They serve as positional and statistical plans to designate relationships between experimental treatments and the experimenter's observations or measurement points in the temporal scheme of the study. In the conduct of the experiment, the researchers apply their knowledge to select one design that is best suited to the goals of the research. Judicious selection of the design improves the probability that the observed change in the dependent variable was caused by the manipulation of the independent variable and not by another factor. It simultaneously strengthens the generalizability of results beyond the experimental setting.

Selecting and assigning subjects

The subjects selected for the experiment should be representative of the population to which the researcher wishes to generalize the study's results. This may seem self-evident, but the authors of this book have witnessed several decades of experimentation with second-year college students that contradict that assumption. In the management game example, managers in a decision-making capacity, or at least management trainees, would provide better generalizing power than undergraduate college students.

The procedure for random sampling of experimental subjects is similar in principle to the selection of respondents for a survey. The researcher first prepares a sampling frame and then assigns the subjects for the experiment to groups using a randomization technique. Systematic sampling may be used if the sampling frame is free from any form of periodicity that parallels the sampling ratio. Since the sampling frame is often small, experimental subjects are recruited; thus, they are a self-selecting sample. However, if randomization is used, those assigned to the experimental group are likely to be similar to those assigned to the control group. Random assignment to the groups is required to make the groups as comparable as possible with regard to the dependent variable. Randomization does not guarantee that if a pre-test of the groups was conducted before the treatment condition, the groups would be pronounced identical, but it is an assurance that those differences remaining are randomly distributed. In our example, we would need two randomly assigned groups. (Random sampling is discussed in Chapter 6.)

When it is not possible to randomly assign subjects to groups, **matching** may be used. Technically, matching employs a non-probability quota sampling approach. The objective of matching is to have subjects in the control and experimental group that are similar to each other – that match. Thus, if a 25-year-old Scottish female junior manager is in the experimental group, you would look for another person with these characteristics and assign her to the control group. This becomes more cumbersome as the number of variables and groups in the study increases. Since the characteristics of concern are only those that are correlated with the treatment condition or the dependent variable, they are easier to identify, control and match.[5] In the management game experiment, if a large part of the sample was composed of female financial managers who recently completed training in strategic financial management, we would not want the characteristics of gender, function and training to be disproportionately assigned to one group.

Some authorities suggest a **quota matrix** as the most efficient means of visualizing the matching process.[6] In Exhibit 12.1, one-third of the subjects from each cell of the matrix would be assigned to each of the three groups. If matching does not alleviate the assignment problem, a combination of matching, randomization and increasing the sample size would be used.

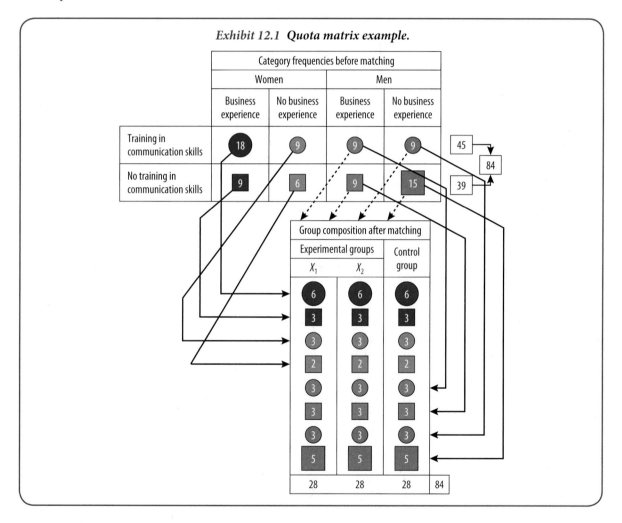

Exhibit 12.1 Quota matrix example.

Pilot testing, revising and testing

The procedures for this stage are similar to those for other forms of primary data collection. Pilot testing is intended to reveal errors in the design, and improper control of extraneous or environmental conditions. Pretesting the instruments permits refinement before the final test. This is the researcher's best opportunity to revise scripts, look for control problems with laboratory conditions and scan the environment for factors that might confound the results. In field experiments, researchers are sometimes caught off guard by events that have a dramatic effect on subjects: the test marketing of a competitor's product announced before an experiment or a reduction in force, reorganization or merger before a crucial organizational intervention. The experiment should be timed so that subjects are not sensitized to the independent variable by factors in the environment.

12.4 Validity in experimentation

Even when an experiment is the ideal research design, it is not without problems. There is always a question about whether the results are true. We defined validity earlier as whether a measure accomplishes its claims. While there are several different types of validity, here only the two major varieties are considered: **internal validity** – do the conclusions we draw about a demonstrated experimental relationship truly imply cause? – and **external validity** – does an observed causal relationship generalize across people, settings and times?[7] Each type of validity has specific threats that must be guarded against.

Internal validity

Among the many threats to internal validity, we now consider the following seven:

1 history
2 maturation
3 testing
4 instrumentation
5 selection
6 statistical regression
7 experiment mortality.

History

During the time that an experiment is taking place, some events may occur that confuse the relationship being studied. In many experiment designs, we take a control measurement (O_1) of the dependent variable before introducing the manipulation (X). After the manipulation, we take an after-measurement (O_2) of the dependent variable. The difference between O_1 and O_2 is the change that the manipulation has caused.

A company's management may wish to find the best way to educate its workers about the financial condition of the company before the annual pay negotiations. To assess the value of such an effort, managers give employees a test on their knowledge of the company's finances (O_1). Then they present the educational campaign (X) to these employees, after which they again measure their knowledge level (O_2).

Between O_1 and O_2, however, many events could occur to confound the effects of the treatment, the educational campaign. A critical newspaper article might appear about the company's financial situation, a union meeting might be held at which this topic is discussed or another occurrence could distort the effects of the company's education test.

Maturation

Changes also may occur within the subject that are a function of the passage of time and are not specific to any particular event. These are of special concern when the study covers a long period, but they may also be factors in tests that are as short as an hour or two. A subject can become hungry, bored or tired in a short time, and this condition can affect response results. In our management game example, teams that performed poorly in the first rounds of the game may become less enthusiastic about the game than those who performed well.

Testing

The process of taking a test can affect the scores of a second test. The mere experience of taking the first test can have a learning effect that influences the results of the second test. In the example of taking additional efforts to inform the employees about the company's financial position, that campaign might motivate employees to follow economic news more thoroughly and discuss more intensively which position employees should take in the up-coming wage negotiations.

Instrumentation

This threat to internal validity results from changes between observations in either the measuring instrument or the observer. Using different questions at each measurement is an obvious source of potential trouble, but using different observers or interviewers also threatens validity. There can even be an instrumentation problem if the same observer is used for all measurements. Observer experience, boredom, fatigue and anticipation of results can all distort the results of separate observations.

Selection

An important threat to internal validity is the differential selection of subjects for experimental and control groups. Validity considerations require that the groups should be equivalent in every respect. If subjects are randomly assigned to experimental and control groups, this selection problem can largely be overcome. Additionally, matching the members of the groups on key factors can enhance the equivalence of the groups.

Statistical regression

Statistical regression is also called regression to the mean and describes the idea that many phenomena suffer from some random fluctuation over time. Even if you are generally a good-humoured person, there will be days when you are for no obvious reason less receptive to others and other days when you are very good-humoured. In experimental designs, such random fluctuations become problematic if groups are selected based on extreme values.

Suppose we measure the output of all workers in a department for a few days before an experiment and then conduct the experiment with only those workers whose productivity scores are in the top 25 per cent and bottom 25 per cent. No matter what is done between O_1 and O_2, there is a strong tendency for the average of the high scores at O_1 to decline at O_2 and for the low scores at O_1 to increase. This tendency results from imperfect measurement that, in effect, records some people abnormally high and abnormally low at O_1. In the second measurement, members of both groups score more closely to their long-run mean scores.

Experiment mortality

This occurs when the composition of the study groups changes during the test. Attrition is especially likely in the experimental group and with each drop-out, the group changes. Because members of the control group are not affected by the testing situation, they are less likely to withdraw. Suppose a campaign informing employees about the current state of the company is only offered to a randomly selected group of employees and they are regularly invited to join information meetings. Over time employees in that group may withdraw from the test group, that is, they do not show up at the information meetings any more. This action could distort the comparison with the control group that has continued working without being informed, perhaps without knowing a test is under way.

Further threats

All the threats mentioned to this point are generally, but not always, dealt with adequately in experiments by random assignment. However, five additional threats to internal validity are independent of whether or not one randomizes[8] (the first three have the effect of equalizing experimental and control groups):

1 Diffusion or imitation of treatment: if people in the experimental and control groups talk, then those in the control group may learn of the treatment, eliminating the difference between the groups.
2 Compensatory equalization: where the experimental treatment is much more desirable, there may be an administrative reluctance to deprive the control group members. Compensatory actions for the control groups may confound the experiment.
3 Compensatory rivalry: this may occur when members of the control group know they are in the control group. This may generate competitive pressures, causing the control group members to try harder.
4 Resentful demoralization of the disadvantaged: when the treatment is desirable and the experiment is obtrusive, control group members may become resentful of their deprivation and lower their cooperation and output.

5 Local history: the regular history effect already mentioned impacts both experimental and control groups alike. However, when one assigns all experimental persons to one group session and all control people to another, there is a chance for some idiosyncratic event to confound results. This problem can be handled by administering treatments to individuals or small groups that are randomly assigned to experimental or control sessions.

External validity

Internal validity factors cause confusion about whether the experimental treatment (X) or extraneous factors are the source of observation differences. In contrast, external validity is concerned with the interaction of the experimental treatment with other factors and the resulting impact on the ability to generalize to (and across) times, settings or persons. Among the major threats to external validity are the following interactive possibilities.

The reactivity of testing on X

The reactive effect refers to sensitizing subjects via a pre-test so that they respond to the experimental stimulus (X) in a different way. A before-measurement of a subject's knowledge about, say, a company's financial situation will often sensitize the subject to various experimental communication efforts that might be made about the company. This before-measurement effect can be particularly significant in experiments where the IV is a change in attitude.

Interaction of selection and X

The process by which test subjects are selected for an experiment may be a threat to external validity. The population from which one selects subjects may not be the same as the population to which one wishes to generalize results. Suppose you use a selected group of workers in one department for a test of the piece-work incentive system. The question may remain as to whether you can extrapolate those results to all production workers. Or consider a study in which you ask a cross-section of a population to participate in an experiment, but a substantial number refuses. If you conduct the experiment only with those who agree to participate (self-selection), can the results be generalized to the total population?

Other reactive factors

The experimental settings themselves may have a biasing effect on a subject's response to X. An artificial setting can obviously produce results that are not representative of larger populations. Suppose the workers who are given the incentive pay are moved to a different work area to separate them from the control group. These new conditions alone could create a strong reactive condition.

If subjects know that they are participating in an experiment, there may be a tendency to role-play in a way that distorts the effects of X. Another reactive effect is the possible interaction between X and subject characteristics. An incentive pay proposal may be more effective with persons in one type of job, with a certain skill level or with a certain personality trait. Problems of internal validity can be solved by the careful design of experiments, but this is less true for problems of external validity. External validity is largely a matter of generalization, which, in a logical sense, is an inductive process of extrapolating beyond the data collected. In generalizing, we estimate the factors that can be ignored and that will interact with the experimental variable. Assume that the closer two events are in time, space and measurement, the more likely they are to follow the same laws. As a rule of thumb, first seek internal validity. Try to secure as much external validity as is compatible with the internal validity requirements by making experimental conditions as similar as possible to conditions under which the results will apply.

12.5 Experimental research designs

Experimental designs vary widely in their power to control contamination of the relationship between independent and dependent variables. In this section, we start with the true experimental design and then discuss deviations from this design, often called pre-experimental design. Finally, we discuss field and quasi-experiments. A Deeper Insight box (on p. 330) introduces you to more complex experimental designs.

True experimental designs

The cornerstones of true experimental designs are:

1 They consist of an experimental group (also called treatment group) and a control group.
2 The researcher ensures that the experimental and control group are equal either through randomly assigning subjects to both groups or through matching.

Exhibit 12.2 shows the symbols but not the different designs. We explain in this exhibit the symbols used to illustrate the different experimental designs in this chapter.

Exhibit 12.2 Key to design symbols used in this chapter.

X	represents the introduction of an experimental stimulus to a group. The effects of this independent variable(s) are of major interest
O	identifies a measurement or observation activity
R	indicates that the group members have been randomly assigned to a group

The *X*s and *O*s in the diagram are read from left to right in temporal order

*X*s and *O*s vertical to each other indicate that the stimulus and/or observation take place simultaneously

An *R* in the first column indicates that the comparison groups have been equalized by the randomization process

R	X	O
R		O

Pre- and post-test design (within subject design)

This design is the standard within design; it does not meet the requirements of a true experiment. The first measurement is taken before the treatment and the next one after it.

$$O_1 \quad X \quad O_2$$

For example, one measures the skills of an employee before and after training to assess whether the training is effective. The main weakness of this design is that between the first and second measurement, other things than the treatment can happen, i.e. the internal validity is threatened by history, maturation, testing and instrumentation effects (see section 12.4). One could, for example, suspect that between the two measurements, the employee gains not only more experience through the training but also because he gets more on-the-job experience simultaneously. Being selected for training could also motivate the employee and therefore the performance increases in measurement moment 2. This design has, however, also an advantage compared to the next design. As we measure the skills of the same person or group of persons, we do not need to worry about differences between persons or groups of persons.

Post-test-only control group design (between subject design)

In this design, the pre-test measurement is omitted, but a control group is added. Pre-tests are well established in classical research design but are not really necessary when it is possible to randomize. The design is:

$$R \quad X \quad O_1$$
$$R \qquad O_2$$

The experimental effect is measured by the difference between O_1 and O_2, $E = O_1 - O_2$. Internal validity threats from history, maturation, selection and statistical regression are not present as each participant is measured just once. However, in this design internal validity is threatened by selection effects, which occur when the experimental group differs from the control group on any characteristics, such as age, gender composition etc. Through random assignment of participants into one of the groups the selection effect can be reduced substantially if both groups are large enough. You should, however, note that just a few people randomly assigned to each group will not equalize the groups. Different mortality rates between experimental and control groups continue to be a potential problem. Furthermore, in case the treatment is desirable and the control group knows that they are the control group this knowledge can bias the results. Our earlier management game example comes close to this design.

Pre-test–post-test control group design

This design consists of an experimental and a control group and random assignment to the two groups (indicated by the R below). The diagram is:

$$R \quad O_1 \quad X \quad O_2$$
$$R \quad O_3 \qquad O_4$$

The effect of the experimental variable is:

$$E = (O_2 - O_1) - (O_4 - O_3)$$

If randomization was very effective, that is, the experimental and control groups are rather large and we applied true random assignment, one would expect that O_1 and O_3 are equal. If not, this points to problems in the random assignment process.

In this design, the seven major internal validity problems are dealt with fairly well, although there are still some difficulties. Local history may occur in one group and not the other. Also, if communication exists between people in test and control groups, there can be rivalry and other internal validity problems.

Maturation, testing and regression are handled well because one would expect them to be felt equally in experimental and control groups. Mortality, however, can be a problem if there are different drop-out rates in the study groups. Selection is adequately dealt with by random assignment.

The record of this design is not as good on external validity, however. There is a chance for a reactive effect from testing. This might be a substantial influence in attitude change studies where pre-tests introduce unusual topics and content. Nor does this design ensure against reaction between selection and the experimental variable. Even random selection may be defeated by a high decline rate by subjects. This would result in using a disproportionate share of people who are essentially volunteers and who may not be typical of the population. If this occurs, we will need to replicate the experiment several times with other groups under other conditions before we can be confident of external validity.

Deeper Insight into Research Methods
Extensions of true experimental designs

True experimental designs have been discussed in their classical forms, but researchers normally use an operational extension of the basic designs discussed. These extensions differ from the classical design forms in (i) the number of different experimental stimuli that are considered simultaneously by the experimenter, and (ii) the extent to which assignment procedures are used to increase precision.

Before we consider the types of extension, some terms that are commonly used in the literature of applied experimentation must be introduced. **Factor** is widely used to denote an independent variable. Factors are divided into levels, which represent various sub-groups. A factor may have two or more levels, such as (i) male and female or (ii) no training, brief training and extended training. These levels should be operationally defined.

Factors may also be classified by whether the experimenter can manipulate the levels associated with the subject. **Active factors** are those the experimenter can manipulate by causing a subject to receive one level or another. **Treatment level** is used to denote the different levels of active factors. With the second type, the **blocking factor**, the experimenter can only identify and classify the subject on an existing level. Gender, age group, customer status and organizational rank are examples of blocking factors, because the subject comes to the experiment with a pre-existing level of each.

Completely randomized design

The basic form of the true experiment is a completely randomized design. To illustrate its use, and that of more complex designs, consider a decision now facing the pricing manager at Top Cannery. He would like to know what the ideal difference in price is between Top's private brand of canned tomato soup and national brands such as Unox and Lacroix.

It is possible to set up an experiment on price differentials for canned tomato soup. Eighteen company stores and three price spreads (treatment levels) of 7 cents, 12 cents and 17 cents between the company brand and national brands are used for the study. Six of the stores are assigned randomly to each of the treatment groups. The price differentials are maintained for a period, and then a tally is made of the sales volumes and gross profits of the canned tomato soup for each group of stores.

This design can be diagrammed as follows:

$$R \quad O_1 \quad X_a \quad O_2$$
$$R \quad O_3 \quad X_b \quad O_4$$
$$R \quad O_5 \quad X_c \quad O_6$$

Here, O_1, O_3 and O_5 represent the total gross profits for canned tomato soup in the treatment stores for the month before the test. X_a, X_b and X_c represent 7-, 12- and 17-cent treatments, while O_2, O_4 and O_6 are the gross profits for the month after the test started.

It is assumed that the randomization of stores to the three treatment groups was sufficient to make the three store groups equivalent. Whether there is reason to believe this is not so, we must use a more complex design.

Randomized block design

When there is a single major extraneous variable, the randomized block design is used. Random assignment is still the basic way to produce equivalence among treatment groups, but something more may be needed for two reasons. The more critical of these is that the sample being studied may be so small that it is risky to depend on random assignment alone to guarantee equivalence. Small samples, such as the 18 company stores, are typical in field experiments because of high costs or because few test units are available. Another reason for blocking is to learn whether treatments bring different results among various groups of subjects.

Consider again the canned tomato soup pricing experiment. Assume that there is reason to believe that lower-income families are more sensitive to price differentials than are higher-income families. This factor could seriously distort our results unless we stratify the stores by customer income. Therefore, each of the 18 stores is assigned to one of three income blocks and randomly assigned, within blocks, to the price difference treatments. The design is shown in Exhibit 12.3.

Exhibit 12.3 An example of randomized block design.

Active factor – price difference		Blocking factor – customer income		
		High	Medium	Low
7 cents	R	X_1	X_1	X_1
12 cents	R	X_2	X_2	X_2
17 cents	R	X_3	X_3	X_3

Note: The Os have been omitted. The horizontal rows no longer indicate a time sequence, but various levels of blocking factor. However, before and after measurements are associated with each treatment.

In this design, one can measure both **main effects** and interaction effects. The main effect is the average direct influence that a particular factor has. Thus in this case we could see how price differences and customer income affect the sale of tomato soup. Moreover, we could check whether different customer income groups react differently to the price differences; for example, one might expect that low-income customers are more price-sensitive than high-income customers. In that case the differences between the outcomes for the three price difference levels would be larger for the low-income group than for the high-income group.

Whether the randomized block design improves the precision of the experimental measurement depends on how successfully the design minimizes the variance within blocks and maximizes the variance between blocks. If the response patterns are about the same in each block, there is little value to the more complex design. Blocking may be counterproductive.

Latin square design

The Latin square design may be used when there are two major extraneous factors. To continue with the pricing example, assume we decide to block on the size of store and on customer income. It is convenient to consider these two blocking factors as forming the rows and columns of a table. Each factor is divided into three levels to provide nine groups of stores, each representing a unique combination of the two blocking variables. Treatments are then randomly assigned to these cells so that a given treatment appears only once in each row and column. Because of this restriction, a Latin square must have the same number of rows, columns and treatments. The design looks like the example shown in Exhibit 12.4.

Exhibit 12.4 An example of Latin square design.

Store size	Customer income		
	High	Medium	Low
Large	X_3	X_1	X_2
Medium	X_2	X_3	X_1
Small	X_1	X_2	X_3

Treatments can be assigned by using a table of random numbers to set the order of treatment in the first row. For example, the pattern may be 3, 1, 2, as shown above. Following this, the other two cells of the first column are filled similarly, and the remaining treatments are assigned to meet the restriction that there can be no more than one treatment type in each row and column.

The experiment is carried out, sales results are gathered and the average treatment effect is calculated. From this, we can determine the main effect of the various price spreads, the shop size and the customers' income on the sales of tomato soup. With cost information, we can discover which price differential produces the greatest margin.

A limitation of the Latin square is that we must assume that there is no interaction between treatments and blocking factors. Thus, we cannot investigate whether low-income customers respond more strongly to the price spreads than high-income customers or whether the effects of the price spreads differ with the size of the store. This limitation exists because there is not an exposure of all combinations of treatments, store sizes and customer income groups. To do so would take a table of 27 cells, while this one has only 9. This can be accomplished by repeating the experiment twice to furnish the number needed to provide for every combination of store size, customer income and treatment. If one is not especially interested in interaction, the Latin square is much more economical.

Factorial design

One commonly held misconception about experiments is that the researcher can manipulate only one variable at a time. This is not true: with factorial designs, you can deal with more than one treatment simultaneously. Consider again the pricing experiment. The managing director of the chain might also be interested in finding the effect of posting unit prices on the shelf to aid shopper decision-making. Exhibit 12.5 can be used to design an experiment that includes both the price differentials and the unit pricing.

Exhibit 12.5 Example of factorial design.

Unit price information	Price spread		
	7 cents	12 cents	17 cents
Yes	X_1Y_1	X_1Y_2	X_1Y_3
No	X_2Y_1	X_2Y_2	X_2Y_3

This is known as a 2×3 factorial design in which we use two factors: one with two levels and one with three levels of intensity. The version shown here is completely randomized, with the stores being randomly assigned to one of six treatment combinations. With such a design, it is possible to estimate the main effects of each of the two independent variables and the interactions between them. The results can help to answer the following questions:

1 What are the sales effects of the different price spreads between company and national brands?
2 What are the sales effects of using unit-price marking on the shelves?
3 What are the sales-effect interrelations between price spread and the presence of unit-price information?

The experimental approach can also be combined with the survey approach. An example of implementing experimental designs into surveys is the **factorial survey**, also known as **vignette research**.[9] In factorial surveys, the researcher presents the respondent with a brief and explicit description of a situation and then asks him or her to assess the situation or to make a decision. The description of the situation contains the independent variables, while the respondent's answer is the dependent variable. In a study investigating how banks decided on which loan applications to approve, researchers create hypothetical loan applications and then ask bankers whether they would approve such an application or not (see Student Research overleaf). Factorial surveys have also been used to investigate which incomes people perceive as justified for certain professions or to investigate discrimination of ethnic minorities when applying for a job.

Student Research

House banks' role in the succession of family businesses

An important issue in the succession of family businesses is the transfer of the bank relations from the former owner to the new owner. Floor Schuiling heard that this process is often complicated, as the existing bank relations often use the succession to change the loan conditions in their favour. Often other banks offer even better conditions than the current house bank. As it is hard to find sufficient businesses that are currently in a succession phase and even harder to convince them to reveal their financing details to a student researcher, Floor opted for a factorial survey. In that survey she presented bankers with hypothetical situations describing a succession. An example of such a hypothetical description is shown in the following example (Exhibit 12.6). The factors mentioned are highlighted; in the original questionnaire they were of course not highlighted.

Exhibit 12.6 Example of a vignette (hypothetical situation).

Mr and Mrs Lee founded ROMANUS 27 years ago, a company specializing in the redecoration of shops and restaurants. They started with redecorating restaurants, but currently they mainly redecorate fashion shops and gas stations. Their main customers are large national chains, who hire ROMANUS to organize the decoration of new outlets they have rented or bought or to change the decoration of existing outlets. The financial position of the company is solid and it has always met its financial obligations. Currently the company employs 14 people.

Currently, the house bank of ROMANUS is *XY-Bank*.

Mr and Mrs Lee want to transfer their company ROMANUS to their youngest *daughter* Claire. Claire has *not worked in the business before*. She has worked for a couple of years in an *operational function* at another company, which is active in the *same sector* as ROMANUS. To facilitate the succession process, the Lees have *hired a business consultant* specialized in the succession of small and medium-sized businesses. The business consultant visits the Lees once a month to discuss the current state of affairs and to moderate between the parties if problems arise. The Lees and their daughter have *prepared a plan* that lays down when certain responsibilities will be shifted from the parents to the daughter. *The accountant* also involved in the succession has been working for the company for years.

Mr and Mrs Lee will *remain financially involved* in the company and they will support their daughter *in the operation*, but will not formally be involved in the management of the company. The Lees' private finances will be done *through the bank* financing the succession.

Claire needs some additional financing to take over the company from her parents. She has applied for credit at your bank. You have received a business plan that describes the current situation of the firm, the short- and long-term planning, financial projections for the coming year and the credit application.

How great is the chance that you would approve such a credit application?

As you can see, the hypothetical situation contains a lot of variables that Floor believed to be important in the financing decision. The first paragraph of the description is the same for all vignettes as Floor was mainly interested in how factors describing the succession affect the financing. Therefore, she held other factors like financial situation, size and sector of the company constant. In particular she looked at the following variables (see Exhibit 12.7).

Given the factors above, you can design 6,144 unique vignettes ($6,144 = 2 \times 2 \times 2 \times 2 \times 2 \times 2 \times 2 \times 2 \times 2 \times 2 \times 3 \times 2$), but often this number is reduced as certain combinations are theoretically impossible – for example, having worked in the company and no sector experience – or highly unlikely – for example, situations in which many factors score no. After removing impossible or unlikely vignettes, still 2,108 unique vignettes remained. These formed the vignette population.

A nice feature of factorial survey is that the unit of analysis is the vignette and if you present a larger set of vignettes to one respondent, you quickly reach sample sizes with sufficient statistical power.

(*Note*: Of course you should be aware that vignettes filled in by the same respondent are not independent from each other and you will need to take that into account in later analyses.) Floor approached 28 bank

Exhibit 12.7 Factors and their levels in the vignette.

Variable	Possible levels	Level in Exhibit 12.6
House bank	Your bank (yes) or XY Bank (no)?	No (XY bank)
Family member?	Yes or no?	Yes (daughter)
Works in company	Yes or no?	No (works at other company)
Work experience	Operational or Management	Operational
Branch experience	Yes or no?	Yes (same industry)
Business plan exists	Yes or no?	Yes
External adviser involved	Yes or no?	Yes
Accountant involved	Yes or no?	Yes
Plan for succession	Yes or no?	Yes
Current owner remains financially involved	Yes or no?	Yes
Current owner remains involved in company	No, at operational or at management level?	Operational level
Current owner will do private banking at the bank financing the succession	Yes or no?	Yes?

employees and each employee had a look at a set of seven different vignettes resulting in a sample size $n = 196$. To ensure that each respondent had vignettes for which financing was very likely, questionable and not very likely, the population was stratified into three groups: good, medium and bad financing prospects. For each respondent two vignettes were drawn from the good prospect pool, three from the medium prospect pool and two from the bad prospect tool.

A common critique to experiments is that they do not reflect reality. For example, it could be that the bankers decide on a vignette differently than on a real company requesting credit. Moreover, Floor did not vary the general characteristic of the business and presented a healthy business. This raises the question of whether her vignettes are a good reflection of reality.

Field and quasi-experiments[10]

Most people imagine a scientist mixing chemical substances or a rat running through a maze when they hear about research experiments. Even when they know that humans are the test units, they still think of a laboratory. The advantages of laboratory experiments are unmistakable: the researcher's ability to fully control the research setting and to exclude any unwanted external influences. However, this control comes at the cost of an artificial setting. Even if researchers attempt to simulate reality as far as possible in the laboratory (e.g. by building a 'normal' office as in the theft/bystander example), participants are at least sensitized to the fact that they are participating in an experiment, and the behaviour that they exhibit might differ from their behaviour in the 'real' world. Field experiments are conducted in a natural setting and, often, participants do not know that their behaviour is being monitored.

A modern version of the bystander-and-thief field experiment mentioned at the beginning of this chapter involves the use of electronic article surveillance to prevent shrinkage due to shoplifting. In a proprietary study, a shopper came to the optical counter of an upmarket store and asked the salesperson if they could look at some special designer frames. The salesperson, a confederate of the experimenter, replied that she would get them from a case in the adjoining department, and disappeared. The 'thief' selected two pairs of sunglasses from an open display, deactivated the security tags at the counter, and walked out of the store; 35 per cent of the subjects (store customers) reported the theft on the return of the salesperson; 63 per cent reported it when the salesperson asked about the shopper. Unlike previous studies, the presence of a second customer did not reduce the willingness to report a theft.

Research Methods in Real Life
Science-fiction shopping on the Rhine

Metro, the fifth largest retailer in the world, has cooperated with SAP, Intel and IBM, as well as other partner companies from the information technology (IT) and consumer goods industries, to develop the store of the future. The initiative is a platform for technical and process-related developments and innovations in retailing. These technologies enrich the service to consumers and improve processes in retailing. Technologies to aid the customer include a personal shopping assistant, intelligent scales, mobile payment, self-checkout and information terminals. Radio-frequency identifiers (RFIDs) are the basis of smarter inventory management.

These technologies have already been realized and, in April 2003, Metro opened a 'future store' in Rheinberg, Germany, which it moved to Tönisvorst in 2008. In the future store, METRO tests new technologies and about 2,500 customers visit this shopping laboratory each day.

When those customers holding a personal loyalty card enter the store, they pick up a mobile computer – the personal shopping assistant (PSA) – which can be fixed to their shopping trolley. The PSA recalls the customer's last shopping list, guides the customer through the shopping aisles if they cannot find a certain product, allows the customer to self-scan their purchases and, finally, offers customized information on its display (details of special offers, etc.). When the customer has finished shopping, he or she proceeds to the checkout, the PSA transmits details of the purchases to the cash register and the customer can then pay without having to unload their purchases onto the conveyor belt and then back into their trolley again.

In the future store, Metro also develops new shopping concepts. For example in Tönisvorst, they developed a new fresh fish counter in a Mediterranean style with sea sounds from the ceiling and an interactive game on the floor which customers could control by moving their feet. This new counter won several awards as best and most innovative fresh fish counter.

Is the future store a sophisticated laboratory experiment or a field experiment? What are the potential problems when conducting experiments in the future store?

References and further reading

www.future-store.org

www.future-store.org/fsi-internet/get/documents/FSI/multimedia/pdfs/broschueren/WISSB_Publikationen_Broschueren_Welcome-to-realFutureStore.pdf

Compare the bystander/thief experiment conducted in a laboratory that has been made to resemble an office and that conducted in a shop in an upmarket shopping centre. First, the participants in the laboratory experiment are very likely to be students or employees of the university. In the field experiment, the participants are people who usually visit shops in a shopping centre at a given day and time, which the researcher can vary. By and large, in the field experiment the participants form a much more heterogeneous group, which reflects the population better than the laboratory experiment. Second, as people in the field experiment are not aware of their participation, they are less likely to conceal or adjust their behaviour. People who know that they are participating in a laboratory experiment might, for example, observe their environment more carefully. Third, in laboratory experiments, the experimenter effect is more problematic, as experimenter and participants interact more – for example, when the experimenter introduces the procedures of the experiment.

Given these advantages of field experiments, we now turn to the disadvantages. The researcher's ability to manipulate the independent variables is the most interesting and distinguished feature of experiments. In field experiments, this advantage is partly lost, as the researcher has fewer opportunities to control the research setting. In the bystander/thief experiment conducted in the shop, the researcher has hardly any influence on who approaches the instructed salesperson in the shop and becomes a participant. Further, the number of bystanders in the shop might even vary during the experiment as people leave or enter the shop. Another problem of field experiments is that they raise ethical questions. Participants have usually not given their prior consent to participate in the research.

Quasi-experiment

As we have discussed previously, the most important and distinguished characteristics of an experiment are (i) the researcher's ability to control the experimental setting and to manipulate the independent variables, and (ii) the random assignment of subjects (test units) to the experimental and control groups. However, there are many occasions when the researcher cannot meet these prerequisites of true experiments, as it is not feasible to assign subjects at random or to fully control the research setting. In a quasi-experiment, we often cannot know when or to whom to expose the experimental treatment. Usually, however, we can decide when and who to measure. A **quasi-experiment** is inferior to a true experimental design, but is usually superior to pre-experimental designs if it is conducted with caution. Quasi-experimental designs are especially useful in studying the effects of well-defined events, such as the introduction of a new law, the succession of a chief executive officer (CEO), a natural disaster, and the like. The occurrence of such events is beyond the influence of the researcher and it is often unfeasible to assign subjects randomly. Two groups of quasi-experimental designs may be distinguished:

1 non-equivalent control group designs
2 time-series design.

We look at each of these now.

Non-equivalent control group design

This is a strong and widely used quasi-experimental design. It differs from the pre-test–post-test control group design because the test and control groups are not randomly assigned. The design is diagrammed as follows:

$$\frac{O_1 \quad X \quad O_2}{O_3 \qquad O_4}$$

Note that the members of the two groups are not assigned randomly, but that the researcher either investigates two natural groups, for example different classes in a school or two different plants of a company, or asks volunteers to apply for the experimental group experiencing a treatment and compares them with non-volunteers; for example, employees applying for a certain training programme. The more the experimental and the control group are alike the better and comparison of pre-test results $(O_1 - O_3)$ is one indicator of the degree of equivalence between test and control groups. If the pre-test results are significantly different, there is a real question about the groups' comparability. On the other hand, if pre-test observations are similar between groups, there is more reason to believe that the internal validity of the experiment is good.

Time series and comparison groups

A time-series design introduces repeated observations before and after the treatment, and allows subjects to act as their own controls. The single treatment group design has before-and-after measurements as the only controls. There is also a multiple design with two or more comparison groups, as well as the repeated measurements in each treatment group. The time-series format is especially useful where regularly kept records are a natural part of the environment and are unlikely to be reactive. The time-series approach is also a good way to study unplanned events in an *ex-post facto* manner. If the federal government suddenly begins price controls, for example, we could still study the effects of this action later if we had collected records regularly for the period before and after the advent of price control.

The different charts in Exhibit 12.8 show the hypothetical share price development of different firms in the oil and gas sector between April 2002 and November 2003.[11] In September 2002 UK Oil announced that Jody Jolly, 49 years old, had been appointed as the new CEO to commence in December 2002. Jody Jolly is believed to be one of, if not *the*, best managers in the world, a fact that is supported by several Manager of the Year awards from business magazines. Our research question here is whether Jody is indeed such an exceptional manager.

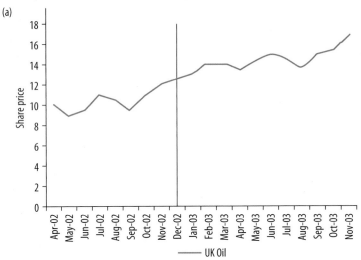

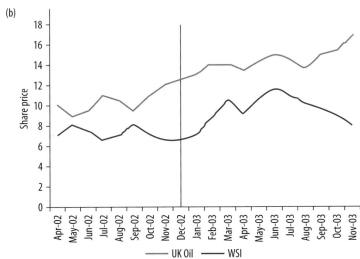

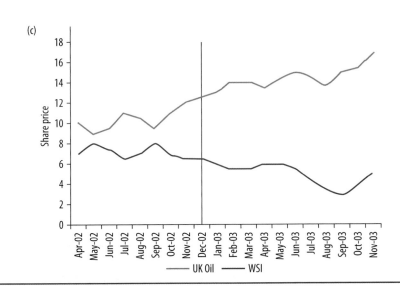

Exhibit 12.8 Different hypothetical scenarios of UK Oil's share price development compared to some indices.

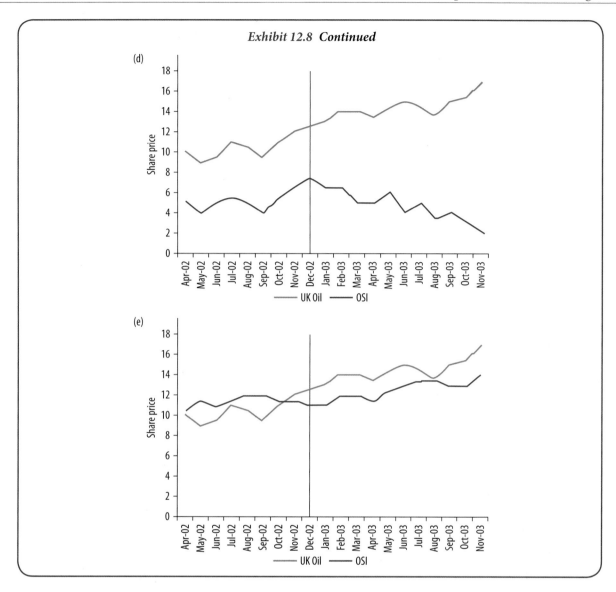

Exhibit 12.8 Continued

Exhibit 12.8a is a chart such as you might see accompanying a portrait of Jody Jolly in a popular business magazine. It shows the share price of UK Oil, and the vertical line marks the month during which Jody became the new CEO of the company. It shows that the share price of UK Oil increased from September 2002 (when Jody's appointment was announced) and has continued to rise since then. Can you deduce from this chart that Jody really made a difference? From an experimental viewpoint Exhibit 12.8a is a single interrupted time series, comparable to the pre-test–post-test design. As there is no control group with which we can compare the share price development of UK Oil, it is hard to conclude that the share price increase can be ascribed to Jody Jolly. We would have to rule out alternative explanations. But can we? A possible alternative explanation could, for example, be that the stock markets as a whole performed better in 2003. A better quasi-experimental design would include a control group, such as a stock index.

Exhibits 12.8b and 12.8c compare the development of UK Oil's share price with the World Stock Index (WSI). Suppose the WSI has moved as displayed in Exhibit 12.8b. In this case we speak of a non-effect outcome, that is, the appointment of Jody had no effect, as the price of other stocks increased as well. However, how would we answer the research question if the WSI developed as shown in Exhibit 12.8c? Since the appointment of Jody Jolly, the share price of UK Oil has increased, while the performance of the WSI is roughly a horizontal line. Can we conclude from Exhibit 12.8c, then, that Jody Jolly made a difference? An alternative explanation could be that oil companies in general outperformed the WSI in 2003. The fact that the ups and downs of the share price and the index are not parallel suggests that factors other than the appointment of a new CEO affect the share price. For instance, favourable conditions in the oil business and not the appointment of Jody Jolly might be the cause of UK Oil's rising share price.

Exhibits 12.8d and 12.8e compare the share price of UK Oil with an index averaging the share price of other major oil companies (OSI). In Exhibit 12.8d the average share price of other oil companies is substantially lower than that of UK Oil, and from 2003 onwards, UK Oil's share price increases while the average share price of other oil companies does not increase as much. In the hypothetical case of Exhibit 12.8d, the conclusion that Jody made a difference is much stronger than if we base this conclusion on Exhibit 12.8c, as by choosing a more similar control group we have excluded some alternative explanations, such as industry effects. However, the initial difference in the share prices might point to the fact that UK Oil as a company has competitive advantages above other oil companies. Thus, the better stock market performance of UK Oil is caused by firm characteristics and not Jody Jolly.

Suppose Exhibit 12.8e offered a comparison between UK Oil and other oil companies. In this case, the share prices move parallel until December 2002, but after that UK Oil has performed better. Thus, from the moment Jody Jolly was appointed, UK Oil's share price took a different path from that of the other oil companies.

A quasi-experimental outcome as in Exhibit 12.8e gives strong support to the hypothesis that Jody Jolly is an exceptional manager. Any alternative explanation would have to explain why UK Oil's share price took off at the moment of Jody Jolly's appointment.

Compared to true experiments, a major deficiency of the quasi-experiment is that the test units are not assigned at random to the treatment. Often, the treatment – such as the appointment of a new CEO, as in the example above, or the introduction of a new law – is a response to developments in the past: companies appoint a new CEO because the old one performed poorly; a government tightens immigration laws as a response to an increase in the number of (economic) refugees seeking entry to a country. Interventions (treatments) as a response to previous developments – that is, no random assignments – impede the interpretation of the outcomes of time series with comparison groups.

Referring again to the example of Jody Jolly, Exhibit 12.9 displays the share price development of UK Oil and Petrol US, its main competitor. The vertical line in the exhibit indicates once again the appointment of Jody Jolly. Before Jody Jolly was appointed, UK Oil's share price was much more volatile than that of Petrol US, and Jody Jolly might have been appointed as a reaction to this unstable and poor performance. Indeed, we see that after Jody Jolly's appointment, UK Oil's share price rose from a three-year low and even exceeded that of Petrol US. Is Jody Jolly's appointment the explanation for the share price rise in 2003? This is hard to conclude from Exhibit 12.9, because we have to deal with 'reversion to the trend', which is similar to reversion of the mean.

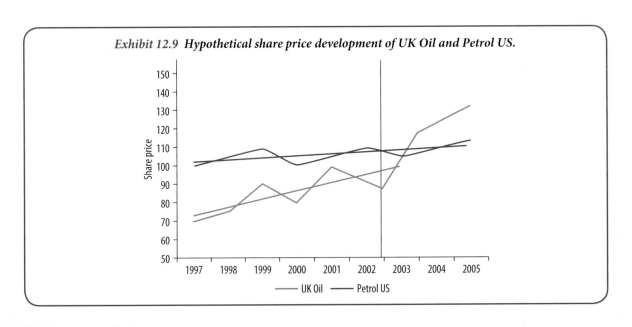

Exhibit 12.9 Hypothetical share price development of UK Oil and Petrol US.

Whenever a time series reaches extreme points, it is very probable that in the following period the series moves again towards the trend, that is after reaching an extreme high (or low) the time series falls (or rises). While this regression artefact can explain the better performance of UK Oil in 2003, it cannot explain the better performance in 2004 and 2005. Hence, we can conclude that the appointment of Jody Jolly is a reasonable explanation for the better performance of UK Oil since 2003.

Research Methods in Real Life

Airports take off

With the following exhibits, we show how some descriptive information on the development of passenger airports in Germany can be used to understand better what happened in that sector in the last decades. Taking a quasi-experimental approach makes the figures talk.

Exhibit 12.10 shows annual passenger numbers for the seven main German airports: Frankfurt, Munich, Düsseldorf, Hamburg, Cologne, Stuttgart and the combined Berlin Airports. In 1992 Munich Airport moved from its old location, Riem, to a newly constructed airport at Erdinger Moos, about 30 km north-east of Munich. One of the major objectives for building a new airport at a new location was to establish Munich as the second largest airport (after Frankfurt) in Germany. Similarly, currently a new airport is built in Berlin. Could you conclude from Exhibit 12.10 that the construction of an airport at a new location is essential for further airport growth? Does the growth in passenger numbers justify the construction of a new airport in Berlin? Is the overall growth in passenger numbers similar across all airports or do we see that some airports fall behind?

Exhibit 12.10 ***Passenger volumes at large German airports.***

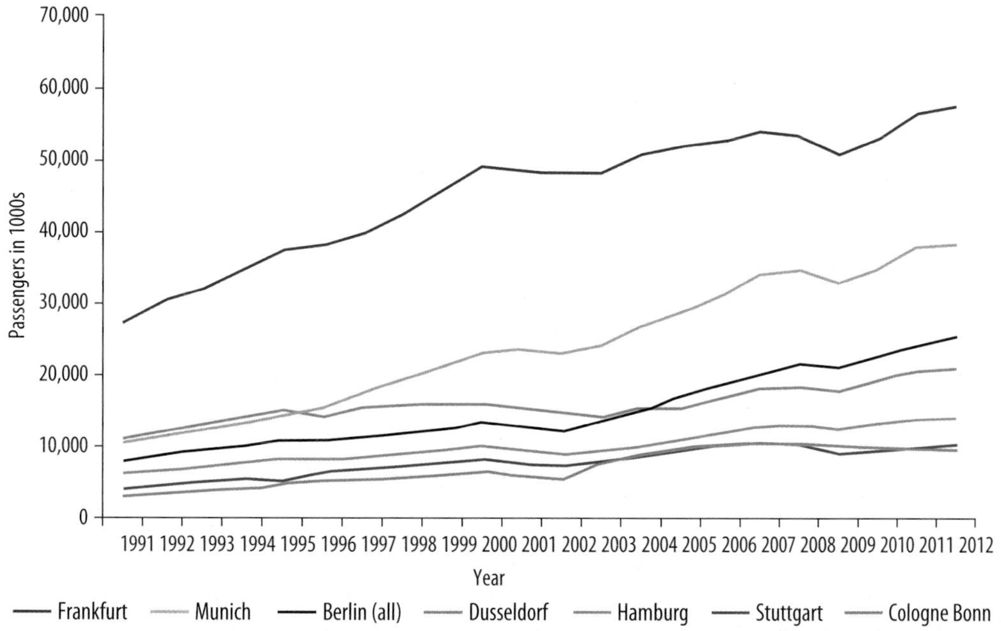

Our attitudes to and methods of flying have changed dramatically in the last decade. A number of European airlines, such as Ryanair, AirBerlin and easyJet, have copied the successful business concept of SouthWest Airlines in the USA. The basic idea behind these airlines is to offer low fares by following a cost leadership approach and removing costly added services. The price differences are substantial, but the classical airlines are also offering competitive prices especially if booked well in advance.

The emergence of these so-called no-frills airlines has also affected the airports. Exhibit 12.11 shows again annual passenger numbers for a number of German airports. Some of these airports are mainly served by no-frills and charter airlines: Munster (Air Berlin), Lübeck (Ryanair), Hahn (Ryanair) and Paderborn (Air Berlin); some are mainly served by national flag carriers (Hannover, Nurnberg). Comparing Exhibits 12.10 and 12.11 reveals that compared to major airports, the passenger numbers are much more volatile for these medium-sized regional airports. Hahn, one of the German hubs of RyanAir experienced a tremendous growth between 2001 and 2007 but has declined since then. Unlike the larger airports, on average the passenger numbers of these regional airports has not increased since 2008. What can we conclude from this?

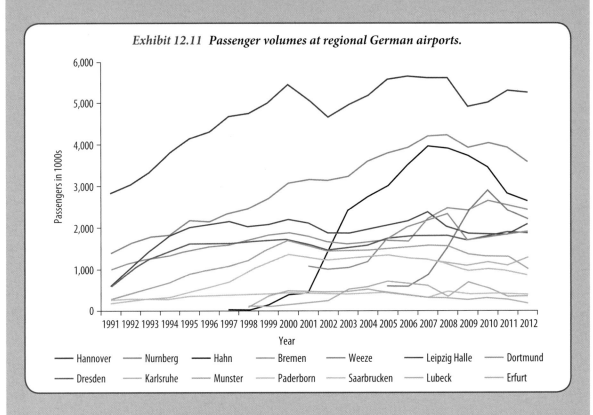

Exhibit 12.11 Passenger volumes at regional German airports.

Looking at this figure, how would you assess the following statements?

1 Attracting a no-frills airline to one's airport guarantees a substantial rise in the number of passengers.
2 Newly established airports, such as Hahn and Lübeck, draw passengers away from already existing airports.
3 The figure shows convincingly that the market airports operate in has changed from public governance to dynamic competition.

References and further reading

www.adv.aero/verkehrszahlen/verkehrsentwicklung-2013/

www.flughafen-luebeck.de/en/facts-a-figures/statistics.html

www.flughafen-paderborn-lippstadt.de/index.php?__lang=en&catalog=/flughafen/ueber_uns/statistiken

Running Case Study 12

Experimentation

Surfing the web, Rebecca discovered a widely used moral experiment, the trolley experiment, and wondered whether playing this experimental game with her respondents would allow her to assess their morality. The thought experiment is designed as follows:

Trolley Experiment

Please, answer for each of the scenarios below the question asked.

Scenario 1

A trolley runs out of control down a track. In its path are 5 people, tied to the track. They cannot be untied in time and if the trolley hits them, all die. You can flip a switch, which will lead the trolley to a different track to which just one person is tied, who dies if you flip the switch.

Do you flip the switch?   ☐ Yes   ☐ No

Scenario 2

A trolley runs out of control down a track. In its path are 5 people, tied to the track. They cannot be untied in time and if the trolley hits them, all die. You stand on a bridge over the track; if you throw something very heavy on the track it will stop the trolley. It happens that next to you stands a very fat person. If you hustle this very fat person down the bridge on the track, the person will stop the trolley, but die.

Do you hustle the person?   ☐ Yes   ☐ No

Scenario 3

A trolley runs out of control down a track. In its path are 5 people, tied to the track. They cannot be untied in time and if the trolley hits them, all die. You stand on a bridge over the track; if you throw something very heavy on the track it will stop the trolley. If you hustle your mother down the bridge on the track, she will stop the trolley, but die. (You cannot jump on the track yourself.)

Do you hustle your mother?   ☐ Yes   ☐ No

But Rebecca also thought about another experiment that she developed based on a game she used to play at high school. She wanted to see whether people are honest. The game is played with two dice and called 'piglet'. The highest score possible is a 1 and a 2, followed by each of the six doubles in order, and then the sum of the two dice. Two players play the game. The first player throws the dice with a dice cup and looks secretly at the result. Then they announce the result to the other player, who can either believe it or not. If the following player believes it, they have to throw a higher result and announce that to the next player who again can either believe or not. If a player does not believe an announcement, they lift the dice cup. If the announcement is right, the announcer gets a point and the play continues. If the announcement is wrong, the person disbelieving the announcement gets a point and a new round starts. Rebecca designed the following scenarios and a friend of hers programmed it as a small computer game. Based on all three scenarios, Rebecca wanted to construct an honesty score.

▶

Rebecca thought about playing this game on a computer with the following scenarios.

Scenario 1

The computer announces that it has thrown a 6 and 3. The announcement is correct. Now the respondent throws the dice and gets a 4 and a 2. Respondents have to write in their announcement.

Note: If they are honest, the respondents automatically lose a point. Thus, most people will not be honest and say, for example, double 1.

Scenario 2

The computer announces that it has thrown a 1 and 3 (the lowest score possible). Now the respondent throws the dice and gets a 4 and a 2, a pretty low score. Respondents have to write in their announcement.

Note: Respondents can be honest, but they can also announce a higher result that is more difficult to beat in the next round.

Scenario 3

The computer announces that it has thrown a 1 and 3 (the lowest score possible). Now the respondent throws the dice and gets a double 1, a pretty good score. Respondents have to write in their announcement.

Note: Respondents can be honest, but they can also announce a higher result that is more difficult to beat in the next round.

1 Do you think that participants in the ethical game designed by Rebecca behave differently in real life? Why? And if you think they behave differently, do they behave more, or less, ethically?
2 What is the experimental design Rebecca's ethical game follows?
3 Is the idea of looking at the ethical behaviour of business students at two different universities a kind of quasi-experiment?

Summary

1 Experiments are studies involving intervention by the researcher beyond that required for measurement. The usual intervention is to manipulate a variable (the independent variable) and observe how it affects the subjects being studied (the dependent variable).

   An evaluation of the experimental method reveals several advantages: (i) the ability to uncover causal relationships, (ii) provisions for controlling extraneous and environmental variables, (iii) the convenience and low cost of creating test situations rather than searching for their appearance in business situations, (iv) the ability to replicate findings and thus rule out idiosyncratic or isolated results, and (v) the ability to exploit naturally occurring events.

2 Some advantages of other methods that are liabilities for the experiment include: (i) the artificial setting of the laboratory, (ii) generalizability from non-probability samples, (iii) disproportionate costs in select business situations, (iv) a focus restricted to the present and immediate future, and (v) ethical issues related to the manipulation and control of human subjects.

3 Consideration of the following activities is essential for the execution of a well-planned experiment:
   a select relevant variables for testing
   b specify the levels of treatment
   c control the environmental and extraneous factors
   d choose an experimental design suited to the hypothesis
   e select and assign subjects to groups
   f pilot-test, revise and conduct the final test
   g analyse the data.

4 We judge various types of experimental research design by how well they meet the tests of internal and external validity. An experiment has high internal validity if one has confidence that the experimental treatment has been the source of change in the dependent variable. More specifically, a design's internal validity is judged by how well it meets seven threats. These are history, maturation, testing, instrumentation, selection, statistical regression and experiment mortality.

External validity is high when the results of an experiment are judged to apply to some larger population. Such an experiment is said to have high external validity regarding that population. Three potential threats to external validity are testing reactivity, selection interaction, and other reactive factors.

5 Experimental research designs include (i) pre-experiments, (ii) true experiments and (iii) quasi-experiments. The main distinction among these types is the degree of control that the researcher can exercise over validity problems.

Three pre-experimental designs are presented in this chapter. These designs represent the crudest form of experimentation and are undertaken only when nothing stronger is possible. Their weakness is the lack of an equivalent comparison group; as a result, they fail to meet many internal validity criteria. They are (i) the one-shot control study, (ii) the one-group pre-test–post-test design and (iii) the static group comparison.

Two forms of the true experiment were also presented. Their central characteristic is that they provide a means by which we can assure equivalence between experimental and control groups through random assignment to the groups. These designs are (i) pre-test–post-test control group and (ii) post-test-only control group.

The classical two-group experiment can be extended to multi-group designs in which different levels of the test variable are used as controls rather than the classical non-test control. In addition, the true experimental design is extended into more sophisticated forms that use blocking. Two such forms – the randomized block and the Latin square – were discussed. Finally, the factorial design was discussed in which two or more independent variables can be accommodated.

Between the extremes of pre-experiments, with little or no control, and true experiments, with random assignment, there is a grey area in which we find quasi-experiments. These are useful designs when some variables can be controlled, but equivalent experimental and control groups cannot usually be established by random assignment. There are many quasi-experimental designs, but only three are covered in this chapter: (i) non-equivalent control group design, (ii) separate sample pretest –post-test design; and (iii) group time-series design.

Discussion questions

Terms in review

1 Distinguish between the following:
   a   internal validity and external validity
   b   pre-experimental design and quasi-experimental design
   c   history and maturation
   d   random sampling, randomization and matching
   e   active factors and blocking factors
   f   environmental variables and extraneous variables.

2 Compare the advantages of experiments with the advantages of survey and observational methods.

3 Why would a noted business researcher say, 'It is essential that we always keep in mind the model of the controlled experiment, even if in practice we have to deviate from an ideal model'?

4 What ethical problems do you see in conducting experiments with human subjects?

5 What essential characteristics distinguish a true experiment from other experimental research designs?

Making research decisions

6 A lighting company seeks to study the percentage of defective glass shells being manufactured. Theoretically, the percentage of defectives is dependent on temperature, humidity and the level of artisan expertise. Complete historical data are available for the following variables on a daily basis for a year:
   a   temperature (high, normal, low)
   b   humidity (high, normal, low)
   c   artisan expertise level (expert, average, mediocre).

Some experts feel that defectives also depend on production supervisors. However, data on supervisors in charge are available for only 242 of the 365 days. How should this study be conducted?

7 Suppose you want to investigate whether groups are more effective in generating ideas than the same number of people working independently. Thus, is it in terms of idea generation more effective to ask six people to brainstorm for 45 minutes or to ask six people to take 45 minutes to generate ideas individually? Describe how you would operationalize variables for an experiment investigating this research question.

8 You are asked to develop an experiment for a study of the effect that compensation has on the response rates secured from personal interview subjects. This study will involve 300 people, who will be assigned to one of the following conditions: (i) no compensation, (ii) €1 compensation and (iii) €3 compensation. A number of sensitive issues will be explored concerning various social problems, and the 300 people will be drawn from the adult population. Describe how your design would be set up if it were (a) a completely randomized design, (b) a randomized block design, (c) a Latin square and (d) a factorial design (suggest another active variable to use). Which would you use? Why?

9 What type of experimental design would you recommend in each of the following cases? Suggest in some detail how you would design each study.
   a   A test of three methods of compensation of factory workers. The methods are hourly wage, incentive pay and weekly salary. The dependent variable is direct labour cost per unit of output.
   b   A study of the effects of various levels of advertising effort and price reduction on the sale of branded grocery products by a retail grocery chain.
   c   A study to determine whether it is true that the use of fast-paced music played over a store's public address system will speed up the shopping rate of customers without an adverse effect on the amount spent per customer.
   d   A study investigating to what extent the terrorist attacks in New York and Washington on 12 September 2001 and Madrid on 11 March 2004 have affected the stock market.

From concept to practice

10 Using Exhibit 12.2, diagram an experiment described in one of the Research Methods in Real Life featured in this chapter using research design symbols.

11 For experiments and surveys on the web, visit www.psych.upenn.edu/links. html#webexpts and participate in an online experiment. Prepare a short paper describing your experience and make suggestions for improving the experimental design.

Classroom discussion

12 Discuss the practice relevance of results obtained from experimental studies. How large is the trade-off between controlled conditions and a good representation of real-life situations?

Recommended further reading

Campbell, Donald T. and Russo, M. Jean, *Social Experimentation*. Thousand Oaks, CA: Sage, 1998. The evolution of the late Professor Campbell's thinking on validity control in experimental design.

Campbell, Donald T. and Stanley, Julian C., *Experimental and Quasi-experimental Designs for Research*. Chicago, IL: Rand McNally, 1963. A universally quoted discussion of experimental designs in the social sciences.

Cook, Thomas D. and Campbell, Donald T., 'The design and conduct of quasi-experiments and true experiments in field settings', in Marvin D. Dunnette and Leaetta M. Hough (eds), *Handbook of Industrial and Organizational Psychology* (2nd edn). Palo Alto, CA: Consulting Psychologists Press, 1990; and *Quasi-Experimentation: Design and Analysis Issues for Field Settings*. Chicago: Rand McNally, 1979. Major authoritative works on both true and quasi-experiments and their design. Already classic references.

Green, Paul E., Tull, Donald S. and Albaum, Gerald, *Research for Marketing Decisions* (6th edn). Englewood Cliffs, NJ: Prentice-Hall, 1991. A definitive text with sections on the application of experimentation to marketing research.

Greenberg, Jerald and Tomlinson, Edward C., 'Situated experiments in organizations: transplanting the lab to the field', *Journal of Management* 30(5), 2004, pp. 702–24. The article discusses the strengths and weaknesses of laboratory and field experiments, and explains a mixed form combining the strengths of the laboratory with those of the field.

Kagel, John and Roth, Alvin (eds), *Handbook of Experimental Economics*. Princeton, NJ: Princeton University Press, 1998. A collection of essays reflecting all areas where experimental research plays a prominent role in economic research.

Kirk, Roger E., *Experimental Design: Procedures for the Behavioral Sciences* (3rd edn). Belmont, CA: Brooks/Cole, 1994. An advanced text on the statistical aspects of experimental design.

Shadish, William R., Cook, Thomas D. and Campbell, Donald T., *Experimental and Quasi-experimental Designs for Generalised Causal Inference*. Willmington, MA: Houghton Mifflin, 2001. A completely rewritten version of the best-selling 1979 edition, with more emphasis on design issues than on data analysis and statistics.

Shaughnessy, John J., Zechmeister, Eugene B. and Zechmeister, Jeanne S., *Research Methods in Psychology* (6th edn). New York: McGraw-Hill, 2003. Parts III and IV of the book offer a broad coverage of issues related to experimental designs, conducting experiments as well as quasi-experiments.

Get started with understanding statistical techniques!

When you have read this chapter, log on to the Online Learning Centre website at *www.mcgraw-hill.co.uk/textbooks/blumberg* to explore chapter-by-chapter test questions, additional case studies, a glossary and more online study tools for *Business Research Methods*.

Notes

1 As we will see later, in quasi-experiments it is often not the researcher who intervenes, rather he or she frames an existing situation as an experiment and defines the occurrence of an event as intervention.

2 Bibb Latane and J.M. Darley, *The Unresponsive Bystander: Why Doesn't He Help?* New York: Appleton-Century-Croft s, 1970, pp. 69–77. Research into the responses of bystanders who witness crimes was stimulated by an incident in New York City where Kitty Genovese was attacked and killed in the presence of 38 witnesses who refused to come to her aid or summon the authorities.

3 This section is largely adapted from Julian L. Simon and Paul Burstein, *Basic Research Methods in Social Science* (3rd edn). New York: Random House, 1985, pp. 128–33.

4 For a thorough explanation of this topic, see Helena C. Kraemer and Sue Thiemann, *How Many Subjects? Statistical Power Analysis in Research.* Beverly Hills, CA: Sage, 1987.

5 Kenneth D. Bailey, *Methods of Social Research* (2nd edn). New York: Free Press, 1982, pp. 230–33.

6 The concept of a quota matrix and the tabular form for Exhibit 12.1 were adapted from Earl R. Babbie, *The Practice of Social Research* (5th edn). Belmont, CA: Wadsworth, 1989, pp. 218–19.

7 Donald T. Campbell and Julian C. Stanley, *Experimental and Quasi-experimental Designs for Research.* Chicago, IL: Rand McNally, 1963, p. 5.

8 Thomas D. Cook and Donald T. Campbell, 'The design and conduct of quasi-experiments and true experiments in field settings', in Marvin D. Dunnette (ed.), *Handbook of Industrial and Organizational Psychology.* Chicago, IL: Rand McNally, 1976, p. 223.

9 For more information on factorial surveys, see P.H. Rossi and S.L. Nock (eds), *Measuring Social Judgments: The Factorial Survey Approach.* Beverly Hills, CA: Sage, 1982.

10 For an in-depth discussion of many quasi-experiment designs and their internal validity, see ibid., pp. 246–98.

11 The hypothetical example used here is based on an idea presented in Campbell and Stanley, Chapter 7. For more detailed information, students interested in quasi-experimental designs are referred to this source and other publications by Campbell and Stanley.

PART Research instruments 3

Part contents

CHAPTER 13

Fieldwork: questionnaires and responses

Chapter contents

Learning objectives

When you have read this chapter, you should understand:

1 the link forged by the management research question hierarchy between the management dilemma and questionnaire

2 the influence of communication method on instrument design

3 how to construct good questions

4 how question design issues influence instrument quality, reliability and validity

5 sources of measurement questions

6 the importance of pre-testing questions and instruments.

In Chapter 7 we intensively discussed different survey approaches, namely surveys taken face to face in a personal interview, phone surveys, paper and pencil surveys and web-based surveys. In survey research, the questionnaire is the most important instrument. Therefore, we devote this whole chapter to developing a questionnaire. We start with the question we should ask and address this in sections 13.1 and 13.2. In section 13.3, we address what depth of answer we expect from our respondents. Section 13.4 deals with how we should formulate questions that they are well understood by the respondents. In section 13.5, we address how we can pre-formulate possible answer possibilities for the respondents. Section 13.6 provides many sources of well-formulated questions and in section 13.7, we discuss which principles one should adhere to when arranging and organizing in a questionnaire.

13.1 Developing the instrument design strategy

New researchers often want to draft questions immediately. They are reluctant to go through the preliminaries that make for successful surveys. Exhibit 13.1 is a suggested flowchart for instrument design. The procedures followed in developing an instrument vary from study to study, but the flowchart suggests three phases. Each phase is discussed in this chapter, starting with a review of the management research question hierarchy and its application to the study presented in the case study. The chapter concludes with a discussion of procedures for pre-testing the completed instrument.

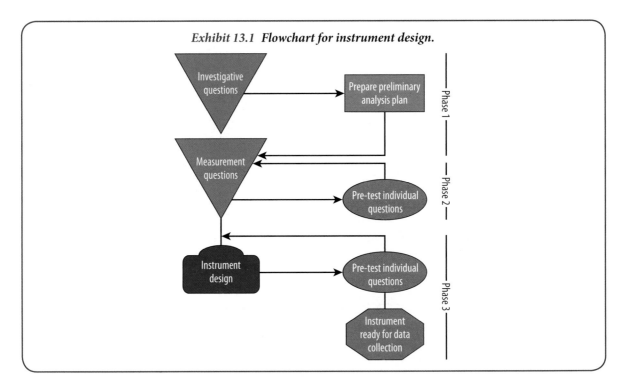

Exhibit 13.1 Flowchart for instrument design.

13.2 The management research question hierarchy revisited: phase 1

The management research question hierarchy is the foundation of successful instrument development (see Exhibit 13.2). The process of moving from the general management or research dilemma to specific measurement questions goes through four question levels:

1 Dilemma question – the dilemma, stated in question form, that the manager or researcher wants to solve.
2 Research question(s) – the fact-based translation of the question the researcher must answer to contribute to the solution of the management question.

3 Investigative questions – specific questions the researcher must answer to provide sufficient detail and coverage of the research question; within this level, there may be several questions as the researcher moves from the general to the specific.

4 Measurement questions – questions participants must answer if the researcher is to gather the required information and resolve the management question.

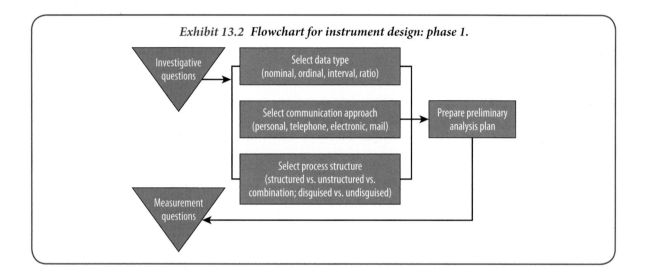

Exhibit 13.2 Flowchart for instrument design: phase 1.

Addressing the dilemma research question hierarchy is the first step in planning for the collection of data. Investigative questions are the core of the researcher's information needs. In many studies, an exploratory investigation helps the researcher understand all dimensions of the subject.

The case in this section reveals the thinking that leads to the final questionnaire; it also illustrates the direction of this chapter. Normally, once the researcher understands the connection between the investigative questions and the potential measurement questions, the next logical step is to plan a strategy for the survey. This requires the researcher to get down to the nitty-gritty of instrument design. The following are prominent among the strategic concerns.

- What type of data is needed to answer the management question?
- What communication approach will be used?
- Should the questions be structured, unstructured or a combination of the two?
- Should the questioning be undisguised or disguised? If the latter, to what degree?

Type of data

Data type determines the analytical procedures that are possible during data analysis. Chapters 5 and 14 discuss nominal, ordinal, interval and ratio data, and how the characteristics of each type influence the analysis (statistical choices and research project testing). We now demonstrate how to code and extract the data from the instrument, and select appropriate descriptive measures or tests; the results will be analysed in Chapters 16–21.

Communication approach

As discussed in Chapter 7, communication-based research may be conducted by personal interview, telephone, mail, computer or some combination of these. Decisions regarding which method to use, as well as where to interact with the participant (at home, at a neutral site, at the sponsor's place of business, etc.), will affect the design of the instrument. In personal interviewing and computer questioning, it is possible to use graphics and other questioning tools more easily than when questioning is done by mail or telephone. The differing delivery mechanisms result in different introductions, instructions, instrument layout and conclusions.

Question structure

The degree of question and response structure must also be decided upon. Response strategy decisions (the type of question used) depend on the content and objectives of specific questions. Question wording is affected largely by the communication mode chosen and attempts to control bias. Questionnaires and interview schedules (**interview schedule** is an alternative term for the questionnaire used in an interview) can range from those that have a great deal of structure to those that are essentially unstructured. Both questionnaires and interview schedules contain three types of measurement question:

1 administrative questions
2 classification questions
3 target questions (structured or unstructured).

Administrative questions identify the participant, interviewer, interview location and conditions. These questions are rarely asked of the participant but are necessary if the researcher wishes to study patterns within the data and identify possible error sources. **Classification questions** are usually demographic variables that allow participants' answers to be grouped so that patterns are revealed and can be studied. **Target questions** address the investigative questions of a specific study. Target questions may be **structured questions** (they present the participants with a fixed set of choices, often called closed questions) or **unstructured questions** (they do not limit responses but do provide a frame of reference for participants' answers, sometimes referred to as open-ended questions).

The type of interview also affects question structure. In extremely unstructured interviews, the interviewer's task is to encourage the participant to talk in depth about a set of topics. The **in-depth interview** encourages participants to share as much information as possible in an unconstrained environment. The interviewer uses a minimum of prompts and guiding questions.

With more focused in-depth interviews, the researcher provides additional guidance by using a set of questions to promote discussion and elaboration by the participant. In these interviews, the researcher guides the topical direction and coverage. Whether the interview is focused or more in depth, the aim is to provide a relaxed environment in which the participant will be open to fully discuss topics. This kind of questioning is often used in exploratory research or where the investigator is dealing with complex topics that do not lend themselves to structured interviewing. If we were doing case research among various participants at a major event, a substantial portion of the questioning would be unique to each participant and would benefit from an unstructured approach.

Interviews with participants in **focus groups** are widely used in exploratory research. As noted in Chapter 8, the interviewer-moderator generally has a list of specific points he or she would like to see discussed, and these are used to prompt the group members. When the discussion stays within these bounds, the interviewer lets group members continue their interaction.

Disguising objectives and sponsors

Another consideration in communication instrument design is whether the purpose of the study should be disguised. Some degree of disguise is often present in survey questions. A **disguised question** is designed to conceal the question's true purpose. The researcher will disguise the sponsor and the objective of a study if he or she believes that participants will respond differently than they would if both or either were known.

The accepted wisdom is that, often, we must disguise the study's objective or abandon the research. The decision about when to use disguised questioning may be made easier by identifying four situations where disguising the study objective is or is not an issue:

1 willingly shared, conscious-level information
2 reluctantly shared, conscious-level information
3 knowable, limitedly conscious-level information
4 subconscious-level information.

Willingly shared, conscious-level information

When requesting this type of information, either disguised or undisguised questions may be used, but the situation rarely requires disguised techniques. For example: 'Have you attended the showing of a foreign-language film in the last six months?'

Reluctantly shared, conscious-level information

When we ask for an opinion on some topic on which participants may hold a socially unacceptable view, we often use **projective techniques** (a disguised questioning method) because participants may not wish to reveal their true feelings or may give stereotypical answers. The researcher can encourage more accurate answers by phrasing the questions in a hypothetical way or by asking how 'people around here feel about this topic'. The assumption is that responses to these questions will indirectly reveal the participant's opinions.

Knowable, limitedly conscious-level information

In some situations individuals know that they have a certain attitude but it is not clear to them why they hold that attitude. A classic example is a study of government bond-buying during the Second World War.[1] A survey sought reasons why, among people with equal ability to buy, some bought more war bonds than others. Frequent buyers had been personally solicited to buy bonds while most infrequent buyers had not received personal solicitation. No direct 'why' question to participants could have provided the answer to this question because participants did not know that they were receiving differing solicitation approaches.

Subconscious-level information

Seeking insight into the basic motivations, underlying attitudes or consumption practices may or may not require disguised techniques. Projective techniques (such as sentence-completion tests, cartoon or balloon tests, and word-association tests) thoroughly disguise the study objective, but they are often difficult to interpret. For example: interview probes – 'Would you say, then, that the attitude you just expressed indicates you oppose or favour requiring adult drivers to declare their position on being an organ donor at the time of licence renewal?'

Another form of disguising refers to not revealing the sponsor of a research to participants. First, sponsors might not want others to know their identity for strategic reasons. For example, companies commissioning research to test a market often disguise their name and remain anonymous to ensure that their strategic plans are kept confidential. Second, researchers will disguise the name of sponsors if they believe the name would influence the answer behaviour of the participants. This holds especially for sponsors that provoke strong associations with at least a proportion of the respondents, such as political parties or a company that has recently been the subject of a public scandal. In both cases the decision not to reveal the identity of the sponsor contains an ethical dimension, as knowledge of who is going to use the responses is part of the principal rights of the participant (see also Chapter 4 on research ethics).

Preliminary analysis plan

Researchers are concerned with adequate coverage of the topic and with securing the information in its most usable form. A good way to test how well a study plan meets these needs is to develop 'dummy' tables that display the data one expects to secure. This serves as a check on whether the planned measurement questions meet the data needs of the research question. It also helps the researcher determine the type of data needed for each question – a preliminary step to developing measurement questions for investigative questions.

13.3 Constructing and refining the measurement questions: phase 2

Drafting the questions begins once you develop a complete list of investigative questions and decide on the collection processes to be used. In phase 2 (see Exhibit 13.3) you draft specific measurement questions considering subject content, the wording of each question (influenced by the degree of disguise and the need to provide operational definitions for constructs and concepts), and response strategy (each producing a different level of data as necessary for your preliminary analysis plan). In phase 3 you must address topic and question sequencing. We will discuss these topics sequentially, although in practice the process is not orderly. For this discussion, we will assume that the questions are structured. The order, type and wording of the measurement questions, the introduction, the instructions, the transitions and the closure in a quality communication instrument should accomplish the following tasks.

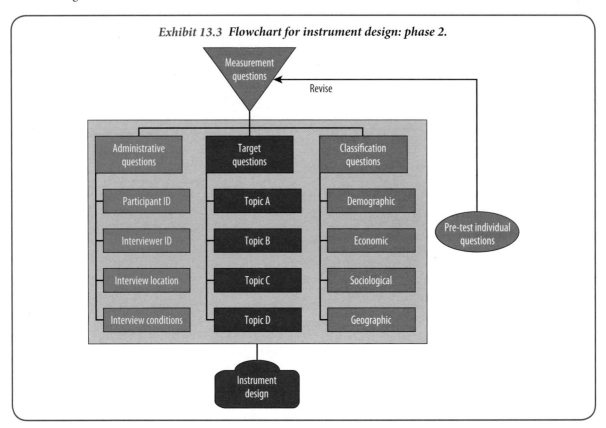

Exhibit 13.3 Flowchart for instrument design: phase 2.

Encourage each participant to provide accurate responses

The proverb 'children and drunkards speak the truth' points at the danger that extensive cognitive processes intended to deliver more accurate answers might in fact disguise the 'truth'. A quick answer is often closer to what a respondent 'really' thinks and feels, than a well-elaborated one. For example, quick answers to the rating question, 'How much do you like your boss?' will provide better responses than a thoroughly thought-through answer considering how your response to this question will affect the picture you give of your boss. Likewise, you have to know a priori what level of accuracy is sufficient for your study. For example, scholars at INSEAD were able to obtain a dataset from an investment bank. This dataset contains information on how each investment banker rated the support that they received from their fellow investment bankers, along with demographic information on the respondents. The bank, however, was reluctant to give accurate figures on the salary and bonuses each investment banker received; instead of precise figures, it 'only' provided a ranking of the investment banker's income on a 20-point scale without attaching real euro values to each scale. The researchers were very happy with this level of accuracy, because this ranking was sufficient for their purposes. Knowing the real values of income might even have depressed them, as investment bankers count their income in millions (salary levels beyond the reach and imagination of academics!).

Encourage each participant to provide an adequate amount of information

This is a particular problem in unstructured interviews. While some respondents are very talkative, others are very limited in their answers. The skills of the interviewer are crucial in ensuring that participants deliver comparable information. Probing (i.e. repeating the answer to provoke additional responses) is one strategy used to encourage 'lazy' respondents to provide more information as well as to encourage talkative respondents to focus their extensive response accounts on the crucial points.

Discourage each participant from refusing to answer specific questions

The chance of response refusal increases with the sensitivity of the question. Emphasizing that the answer of the respondent to a particular question is essential for the study, and that the answer is confidential, can increase the response to such questions. Acknowledging the sensitivity of the question in its introduction encourages participants to answer. For example, assume that you ask employees in a firm whether they have ever engaged in an affectionate relationship with colleagues. An introduction to the question, stating that we know from previous studies that in every organization where people work together closely, professional relationships sometimes turn into affectionate relationships, signals to the participant that these relationships are not unusual. Consequently, the respondent is more likely to provide an 'honest' account as the researcher has changed the frame of what is socially desirable.

Discourage each participant from early discontinuation of participation

This applies mainly to mail questionnaires, because in telephone and personal interviews you have the chance to convince the participant to continue. The main point here is that participants enjoy answering your questions, that is, they have the feeling that the questions relate to what they experience. Here follows a bad example. Recently one of the authors of this book received an online questionnaire investigating why academics choose to publish in certain journals:

> "I started filling in my demographic details, an easy task. Then I was asked to select three journals in which I had published recently. Having answered this question I was confronted with a battery of questions investigating my reasons for choosing the particular journals for publishing, along with a general assessment of each journal. However, many questions asked did not even touch on the criteria I had used to assess or choose a journal (such as 'Please rate the scientific appearance of the journal's cover page on a 5-point scale'). Furthermore, answers to other questions required such complex comparative elaborations, that thinking about the answer simply took too long for an online mail questionnaire. After running through two-thirds of the questions for the first journal, and imagining that I would get the same questions for the other two journals I had mentioned, I soon decided to abandon the questionnaire, which resulted in the appearance of a popup window with the statement: 'Unfortunately, you did not complete our questionnaire. Please click the button below, as we are interested very much in YOUR motives.' I just hit Alt-F4 to exit."

Leave the participant with a positive attitude about survey participation

Introducing a survey with an emphasis on the importance of the participant's responses to the project, and closing it with an appreciation of the participant's willingness to cooperate, are simple and easy ways to create a general positive attitude to the survey. In addition, it is often wise to include questions that are crucial to the investigation of the topic from the participant's perspective, even if they are not of any particular interest to you as a researcher. With this in mind, you could also include an open question at the end of the survey asking whether respondents want to add anything that they consider to be important.

13.4 Question content

How you should formulate the questions is another challenge in designing a questionnaire. Four questions, covering numerous issues, guide the instrument designer in selecting appropriate question content:

1 Should this question be asked?
2 Is the question of proper scope and coverage?

3 Can the participant adequately answer this question, as asked?

4 Will the participant willingly answer this question, as asked?

Should this question be asked?

Issue 1: Purposeful versus interesting

Questions that merely produce 'interesting information' cannot be justified on either economic or research grounds. Challenge each question's function. Does it contribute significant information towards answering the research question? Will its omission limit or prevent the thorough analysis of other data? Can we infer the answer from another question? Is the information asked for available from other easily accessible and equally, or even more, reliable sources? A good question designer knows the value of learning more from fewer questions.

Research Methods in Real Life

Earn a penny for taking surveys

Are you annoyed by telephone calls from marketing research agencies just as you sit down to dinner or to watch your favourite TV show? Telephone interviews have been an extremely popular way of conducting opinion polls and consumer research. Conducting a telephone survey is quite cheap and data collection can be done in a very short time. Have you ever responded to a request for a telephone interview with asking for a small reward, say €4 for a 20-minute interview? Why not? By answering similar questionnaires online, you can earn these amounts.

Ciao! has been one of Europe's largest consumer opinion websites, with about nine million customers from five European core markets as users. Once you have registered as a user you can earn a penny either by writing product reviews or by answering online questionnaires. The information collected by *Ciao!* was so valuable that Microsoft bought the portal for $500 million and integrated it in its search portal *Bing*. Websites such as www.apennyearned.co.uk/surveys.html provide even more links to the sites of research agencies that will either pay you directly or enrol you in prize lotteries in return for answering questionnaires. In the UK, Lightspeed is one such online panel that rewards its members for filling in surveys. Time is money. Why waste time doing a telephone interview when you can do a similar job and earn money?

What do you think of such online surveys from a researcher's point of view? Do you think that in the future people will still be willing to participate in non-paying telephone interviews and, if so, what kind of people?

References and further reading

Lightspeed: www.uk.mysurvey.com

www.apennyearned.co.uk/

www.ciao.co.uk/

Is the question of proper scope and coverage?

Issue 2: Incomplete or unfocused

We can test this content issue by asking, 'Will this question reveal all we need to know?' We sometimes ask participants to reveal their motivations for particular behaviours or attitudes by asking them, 'Why?' This simple question is inadequate for probing the range of most causal relationships. When studying product-use behaviour, for example, direct two or three questions on product use to the heavy-use consumer and only one question to the light user.

Questions are also inadequate if they do not provide the information you need to interpret responses fully. If you ask about, say, the Prince Corporation's image as an employer (see Chapter 14), have you recognized that different groups of employees may have different reactions? Do you need to ask the same question about other companies so that you can evaluate relative attitudes?

Issue 3: Multiple questions

Does the question request so much content that it should be broken into two or more questions (**multiple questions**)? While reducing the overall number of questions in a study is highly desirable, do not try to ask **double-barrelled questions** (two or more questions in one that the participant might need to answer differently in order to preserve the accuracy of the data). Here is a common example posed to menswear retailers: 'Are this year's shoe sales and gross profits higher than last year's?' Couldn't sales be higher with stagnant profits, or profits higher with level or lower sales? A less obvious multiple question is the question that we ask to identify a family's TV station preference. A better question would ask the station preference of each family member separately or, alternatively, screen for the member who most often controls channel selection on Monday evenings during prime time. Also, it is highly probable that no one station would serve as an individual's preferred station when we cover a wide range of times (8–11 p.m.). This reveals another problem: the imprecise question.

Issue 4: Precision

To test a question for precision ask, 'Does the question ask precisely what we want and need to know?' We sometimes ask for a participant's income when we really want to know the family's total annual income before taxes in the past calendar year. We ask what a participant purchased 'last week' when we really want to know what he or she purchased in a 'typical seven-day period during the past 90 days'. In particular, if you ask about recurring events, it is wise either to keep the time period asked for short or to extend the answer possibilities from yes/no to a frequency estimate. For example, more precise alternatives to the question 'Did you visit a pub last year?' (which is very likely to be answered with a yes by the vast majority of the respondents) include: (i) 'Did you visit a pub in the last week?' and (ii) 'How often did you visit a pub in the last month?'

A second precision issue deals with common vocabulary between researcher and participant. To test your question for this problem ask, 'Do I need to offer operational definitions of concepts and constructs used in the question?' For example, in a survey among micro-businesses, the researchers also asked for some information regarding the financial structure of the business. Terms like 'equity capital' are comprehensible to business students, managers, and so on, but many owners of a micro-business do not really have any idea what equity capital is. This points to the need for operational definitions as part of question wording.

Can the participant answer adequately?

Issue 5: Time for thought

Although the question may address the topic, is it asked in such a way that the participant will be able to frame an answer, or is it reasonable to assume that the participant can determine the answer? This is also a question that drives sample design, but once the ideal sample unit is determined, researchers often assume that participants who fit the sample profile have all the answers, preferably on the tips of their tongues. To frame a response to some questions takes time and thought; such questions are best left to self-administered questionnaires. Another approach especially useful for personal interviews is, when you make the appointment for the interview, to inform the participant of the kind of detailed information you will be asking about.

Issue 6: Participation at the expense of accuracy

Participants typically want to cooperate in interviews; thus they assume giving any answer is more helpful than denying knowledge of a topic. Their desire to impress the interviewer may encourage them to give answers based on no information. A classic illustration of this problem occurred with the following question:[2] 'Which of the following statements most closely coincides with your opinion of the Metallic Metals Act?' The response pattern shows that 70 per cent of those interviewed had a fairly clear opinion of the Metallic Metals Act; however, there is no such Act. Similarly, research has shown that on a question asking for a subjective assessment of the performance of individual cabinet members, a fantasy name (i.e. the name of a person who does not belong to the cabinet) usually receives quite moderate performance ratings. The participants apparently assume that if a question is asked they should provide an answer. Given reasonable-sounding choices, they will select one even though they know nothing about the topic.

In telephone interviews such questions are called screening questions, because they determine whether the person on the other end of the line is a qualified sample unit.

Issue 7: Presumed knowledge

The question designer should consider the participants' information level when determining the content and appropriateness of a question. In some studies, the degree of participant expertise can be substantial, and simplified explanations are inappropriate and discourage participation. In asking the public about gross margins in menswear stores, we would want to be sure that the 'general public' participant understands the nature of 'gross margin'. If our sample unit were a merchant, explanations might not be needed. A high level of knowledge among our sample units, however, may not eliminate the need for operational definitions. Among merchants, gross margin per unit in dollars is commonly accepted as the difference between cost and selling price; but when offered as a percentage rather than a dollar figure, it can be calculated as a percentage of unit selling price or as a percentage of unit cost. A participant answering from the 'cost' frame of reference would calculate gross margin at 100 per cent; another participant, using the same dollars and the 'selling price' frame of reference, would calculate gross margin at 50 per cent. If a construct is involved and differing interpretations of a concept are feasible, operational definitions may still be needed.

Issue 8: Recall and memory decay

The adequacy problem also occurs when you ask questions that overtax participants' recall ability. People cannot recall much that has happened in their past, unless it was dramatic. If the events surveyed are of incidental interest to participants, they will probably be unable to recall them correctly even a short time later. An unaided recall question, such as, 'What radio programmes did you listen to last night?' might identify as few as 10 per cent of those individuals who actually listened to a programme.[3] Retrospectiveness is another precision problem, and becomes more severe the longer the period between the occurrence of the behaviour and the time of the interview because participants find it harder to remember events the longer the time since their occurrence. For example, if you ask a representative sample of the population whether they have been unemployed in the last year or whether they are currently unemployed, this will yield higher unemployment rates for the latter question, as respondents tend to forget short periods of unemployment once they are employed again.

Issue 9: Balance (general versus specific)

Answering adequacy also depends on the proper balance between generality and specificity. We often ask questions in terms too general and detached from participants' experiences. Asking for average annual consumption of a product may make an unrealistic demand for generalization on people who do not think in these terms. Why not ask how often the product was used last week or last month? Too often, participants are asked to recall individual use experiences over an extended time and to average them for us. This is asking participants to do the researcher's work and encourages substantial response errors. It may also contribute to a higher refusal rate and higher discontinuation rate.

There is a danger in being too narrow in the time frame applied to behaviour questions. We may ask about cinema attendance for the last seven days, although this is too short a time span on which to base attendance estimates. It may be better to ask about attendance, say, for the last 30 days. There are no firm rules about this generality–specificity problem. Developing the right level of generality depends on the subject, industry, setting and experience of the question designer.

Issue 10: Objectivity

The ability of participants to answer adequately is also often distorted by questions whose content is biased by what is included or omitted. The question may explicitly mention only the positive or negative aspects of the topic or make unwarranted assumptions about the participant's position. Consider an experiment in which two different forms of a question were asked: 57 randomly chosen graduate business students answered version A, and 56 answered version B. Their responses are shown in Exhibit 13.4.

Exhibit 13.4 Response effects depending on question format.

Response	Version A	Version B
	What is your favourite brand of ice-cream?	Some people have a favourite brand of ice cream, while others do not have a favourite brand. In which group are you? (please tick) ☐ I have a favourite ice-cream brand. ☐ I do not have a favourite ice-cream brand. What is your favourite (if you have a favourite)?
Named a favourite brand	77%	39%
Named a favourite flavour rather than a brand	19%	18%
Had no favourite brand	4%	43%
Total	100%	100%
	n = 57	*n* = 56

The probable cause of the difference in brand preference is that A is a **leading question**. It assumes and suggests that everyone has a favourite brand of ice-cream and will report it. Version B indicates that the participant need not have a favourite.

A deficiency of both versions is that about one participant in five misinterpreted the meaning of the term brand. This misinterpretation cannot be attributed to low education, low intelligence, lack of exposure to the topic, or quick or lazy reading of the question. The subjects were students who had taken at least one course in marketing in which branding was treated prominently. (Word-confusion difficulties are discussed in greater detail later in this chapter.)

Will the participants answer willingly?

Issue 11: Sensitive information

Even if participants have the information, they may be unwilling to give it. Some topics are considered too sensitive to discuss with strangers. These vary from person to person, but one study suggests that the most sensitive topics concern money matters and family life.[4] More than a quarter of those interviewed mentioned these as the topics about which they would be 'least willing to answer questions'. Participants of lower socioeconomic status also included political matters in this 'least willing' list.

Participants may also be unwilling to give correct answers for ego reasons. Many exaggerate their incomes, the number of times they visit a museum, their social status and the amount of high-prestige literature they read. They also minimize their ages and the amount of low-prestige literature they read. Many participants are reluctant to try to give an adequate response. Often this will occur when they see the topic as irrelevant to their own interests or to their perception of the survey's purpose. They participate half-heartedly, often answer with 'don't know', give negative replies, refuse to be interviewed, or give stereotypical responses.

Question wording

It is frustrating when people misunderstand a question that has been written painstakingly. This problem is partially due to the lack of a shared vocabulary. The difficulty of understanding long and complex sentences or involved phraseology aggravates the problem further. Our dilemma arises from the requirements of question design (the need to be explicit, to present alternatives and to explain meanings). All contribute to longer and more involved sentences.[5]

The difficulties caused by question wording exceed most other sources of distortion in surveys. They have led one social scientist to conclude:

> "To many who worked in the Research Branch it soon became evident that error or bias attributable to sampling and to methods of questionnaire administration were relatively small as compared with other types of variations – especially variation attributable to different ways of wording questions."[6]

While it is impossible to say which wording of a question is best, we can point out several areas that cause participant confusion and measurement error. The diligent question designer will put a given question through many revisions before it satisfies the following criteria:[7]

- Is the question stated in terms of a shared vocabulary?
- Does the question contain vocabulary with a single meaning?
- Does the question contain unsupported or misleading assumptions?
- Does the question contain biased wording?
- Does the question contain double negations?
- Is the question personalized correctly?
- Are adequate alternatives presented within the question?

Issue 12: Shared vocabulary

Because surveying is an exchange of ideas between interviewer and participant, each must understand what the other says, and this is possible only if the vocabulary used is common to both parties.[8] Two problems arise. First, the words must be simple enough to allow adequate communication with persons of limited education. This is dealt with by reducing the level of word difficulty to simple English words and phrases (more is said about this in Issue 4 on precision).

Technical language is the second issue. Even highly educated participants cannot answer questions stated in unfamiliar technical terms. Technical language also poses difficulties for interviewers. In one study of how corporation executives handled various financial problems, interviewers had to be conversant with technical financial terms. This necessity presented the researcher with two alternatives – hiring people knowledgeable in finance and teaching them interviewing skills or teaching financial concepts to experienced interviewers.[9]

This vocabulary problem also exists where similar or identical studies are conducted in different countries and multiple languages. In surveys conducted in multiple languages the problem of shared vocabulary becomes even more severe, as, for example, the connotation of the word 'friend' can be rather different. In some cultures people refer only to close friends as friends, while in other cultures even loose acquaintances are called 'friend'. In some African countries, you are even likely to be called a 'brother' or 'sister', meaning that you are considered a 'good friend'. At the other extreme, studies on relationships among colleagues show that Germans hardly ever have 'friends' at work, because they would call them 'good colleagues'. One widely used method in cross-country studies to mitigate translation problems is to define a research master language, for example English, and then ask a translator to translate the English questionnaires into the other language. The translated questionnaire is then handed to another translator with the request to translate it back into English. Comparing the master questionnaire with the back-translated questionnaire will reveal the questions and words that are difficult to translate.

A great obstacle to effective question wording is choice of words. Questions to be asked of the public should be restricted to the 2,000 most common words in the language used.[10] Even the use of simple words is not enough. Many words have vague references or meanings that must be gleaned from their context. In a repair study, technicians were asked, 'How many radio sets did you repair last month?' This question may seem unambiguous, but participants interpreted it in two ways. Some viewed it as a question of them alone; others interpreted 'you' more inclusively, as referring to the total output of the shop. There is also the possibility of misinterpreting 'last month', depending on the timing of the questioning. Using 'during the last 30 days' would be much more precise and unambiguous. Typical of the many problem words are: any, could, would, should, fair, near, often, average and regular. One author recommends that after stating a question as precisely as possible, we should test each word against the following checklist:

- Does the chosen word mean what we intend?
- Does the word have multiple meanings? If so, does the context make the intended meaning clear?
- Does the chosen word have more than one pronunciation? Is there any word with similar pronunciation with which the chosen word might be confused?
- Is a simpler word or phrase suggested or possible?[11]

What percentage of the population would understand the terms conglomerate or multinational company? We cause other problems when we use abstract concepts that have many overtones or emotional qualifications.[12] Without concrete referents, meanings are too vague for the researcher's needs. Examples of such words are business, government and society. Suppose we asked the question, 'How involved is business in the affairs of our society?' What is meant by 'involved'? What parts of 'society'? Is there such a thing as 'business' per se?

Shared vocabulary issues are addressed by using the following:

- simple rather than complex words
- interviewers with content knowledge
- commonly known, unambiguous words
- precise words.

Issue 13: Unsupported assumptions

Unwarranted assumptions contribute to many problems of question wording. One national newspaper, the *National Chronicle*, conducted a study in an attempt to discover what readers would like to see in its redesigned lifestyle section. One notable question asked readers: 'Who selects your clothes? You or the man in your life?' In this age of educated, working, independent women, the question managed to offend a significant portion of the female readership. In addition, the *National Chronicle* discovered that many of its female readers were younger than researchers had originally assumed and the only man in their lives was their father, not the spousal or romantic relationship alluded to by the questions that followed. Once men reached this question, they assumed that the paper was interested in serving only the needs of its female readers. The unwarranted assumptions built into the questionnaire caused a significantly smaller response rate than expected and caused several of the answers to be uninterpretable.

Issue 14: Frame of reference

Inherent in word-meaning problems is also the matter of a frame of reference. Each of us understands concepts, words and expressions in light of our own experience. How many people are self-employed, for instance, differs considerably depending on the question one asks. If you ask the simple question, 'Are you currently self-employed?' you are likely to miss all self-employed people who are part-time self-employed alongside the paid job they hold. You would have erroneously assumed that there would be a common frame of reference between you and the participants on the meaning of self-employed. Unfortunately, many persons viewed themselves primarily or foremost as wage earners or students. They failed to report that they also earned some money from self-employed work. This difference in frame of reference results in a consistent underestimation of the number of people who are self-employed in a country.

Alternatively, you could replace this question with two questions, the first of which seeks a statement on the participant's major activity during the week. If the participant gives a non-self-employment classification, a second question is asked to determine if he or she has done any self-employed work for pay besides this major activity.

The frame of reference can be controlled in two ways. First, the interviewer may seek to learn the frame of reference used by the participant. When asking participants to evaluate their reasons for judging a labour contract offer, the interviewer must learn the frames of reference that they use. Is the contract offer being evaluated in terms of the specific offer, the failure of management to respond to other demands, the personalities involved or the personal economic pressures that have resulted from a long strike?

Second, it is useful to specify the frame of reference for the participant. In asking for an opinion about the new labour contract offer, the interviewer might specify that the question should be answered based on the participant's opinion of the size of the offer, the sincerity of management, or another frame of reference of interest.

Issue 15: Biased wording

Bias is the distortion of responses in one direction. It can result from many of the problems already discussed, but word choice is often the major source. Obviously, words or phrases such as politically correct or fundamentalist must be used with great care. Strong adjectives can be particularly distorting. One alleged opinion survey concerned with the subject of preparation for death included the following question: 'Do you think that decent, low-cost funerals are sensible?' Who could be against anything that is decent or sensible? There is a question about whether this was a legitimate survey or a burial service sales campaign, but it shows how suggestive an adjective can be.

Members of parliament have been known to use surveys as a means of communicating with their constituencies. Questions are often worded, however, to imply the issue stance that the representative favours. In opinion surveys, in particular, questions are often phrased in a way that makes the outcome very predictable. A cruel example would be the following two-question sequences on the issue of whether a general speed limit should be introduced on German highways:

Sequence A: Every year, thousands of people are killed in traffic accidents, which are often caused by driving too fast. Do you think that less speedy driving would reduce the number of fatal accidents on our streets? Would you support a parliament initiative to introduce a general speed limit on highways?

Sequence B: German car manufacturers have earned a worldwide reputation for the quality and technological advances of their cars, including many safety devices that have reduced the occurrence and severity of accidents. Do you think that the faster cars of today are safer than those of 10 years ago? Would you support a parliament initiative to introduce a general speed limit on highways?

A more subtle form of bias is that we know that respondents are more likely to agree with a question and answer it with a yes, especially if they do not have a strong opinion on the issue asked. For example, a recurring discussion in pubs and bars is whether the number of football teams in the national premier leagues, such as the Premier League in England, Serie A in Italy or the Bundesliga in Germany, should be decreased in order to reduce the number of matches. If you are in favour of such a reduction you should ask, 'Would you prefer a reduction of the number of teams in the premier league?' If you are against such a reduction you should ask, 'Do you think that the current number of teams in the premier league is the optimal amount?'

We can also strongly bias the participant by using prestigious names in a question. In a historic survey on whether the US war and navy departments should be combined into a single defence department, one survey said, 'General Eisenhower says the army and navy should be combined', while the other version omitted his name. Given the first version (name included), 49 per cent of the participants approved of having one department; given the second version, only 29 per cent favoured one department.[13]

We also can bias response through the use of superlatives, slang expressions and fad words. These are best excluded unless they are critical to the objective of the question. Ethnic references should also be stated with care.

Issue 16: Personalization

How personalized should a question be? Should we ask, 'What would you do about . . . ?' or should we ask, 'What would people with whom you work do about . . . ?' The effect of personalization is shown in a classic example reported by Cantril.[14] A split test was made of a question concerning attitudes about the expansion of US armed forces in 1940:

Should the United States do any of the following at this time?

A   Increase our armed forces further, even if it means more taxes.

B   Increase our armed forces further, even if you have to pay a special tax.

Eighty-eight per cent of those answering question A thought that the armed forces should be increased, while only 79 per cent of those answering question B favoured increasing the armed forces.

These and other examples show that personalizing questions changes responses, but it is not clear whether this change is for the better or the worse. We often cannot tell which method is superior. Perhaps the best that can be said is that when either form is acceptable, we should choose that which appears to present the issues more realistically. If there are doubts, then split survey versions should be used.

Issue 17: Adequate alternatives

Have we adequately expressed the alternatives with regard to the point of the question? It is usually wise to express each alternative explicitly to avoid bias. This is illustrated well with a pair of questions that were asked of matched samples of participants (see Exhibit 13.5).[15]

Exhibit 13.5 Response effects depending on adequate alternatives.

	Do you think most manufacturing companies that lay off workers during slack periods could arrange things to avoid layoffs and give steady work throughout the year?	Do you think most manufacturing companies that lay off workers in slack periods could avoid layoffs and provide steady work right through the year, or do you think layoffs are unavoidable?
Company could avoid layoffs	63%	35%
Company could not avoid layoffs	22%	41%
No opinion	15%	24%

Often the above issues are present simultaneously in a single question. Exhibit 13.6 reveals several questions drawn from actual mail surveys. We have identified the problem issues and suggest one solution for improvement. While the suggested improvement might not be the only possible solution, it does correct the issues identified. What other solutions could be applied to correct the problems identified?

Exhibit 13.6 Reconstructing questions.

	Poor measurement question	Improved measurement question
Problems: Checklist appears to offer options that are neither exhaustive nor mutually exclusive. Also, it doesn't fully address the content needs of understanding why people choose a hotel when they travel for personal reasons versus business reasons. **Solution:** Organize the alternatives. Create sub-sets within choices; use colour or shading to highlight sub-sets. For coding ease, expand the alternatives so the participant does not frequently choose 'Other'.	If your purpose for THIS hotel stay included personal pleasure for what ONE purpose specifically? ☐ Visit friend/relative ☐ Sightseeing ☐ Weekend escape ☐ Family event ☐ Sporting event ☐ Vacation ☐ Other:	Which reason BEST explains your purpose for THIS personal pleasure hotel stay? ☐ Dining ☐ Visit friend/relative . . . was this for a . . . ☐ Sport-related event ☐ Theatre, musical or other performance ☐ Museum or exhibit ☐ Shopping ☐ Entertainment ☐ Vacation . . . was this primarily for . . . ☐ Sightseeing ☐ Weekend break ☐ Other:

Exhibit 13.6 Continued

	Poor measurement question	Improved measurement question

Problems: Double-barrelled question: no time frame for the behaviour; 'frequently' is an undefined construct for eating behaviour; depending on the study's purpose, 'order' is not as powerful a concept for measurement as others (e.g. purchase, consume or eat).
 Solution: Split the questions; expand the response alternatives; clearly define the construct you want to measure.
	When you eat out, do you frequently order appetizers and dessert?
	 ☐ Yes
	 ☐ No
		Considering your personal eating experiences away from home in the last 30 days, did you purchase an appetizer or dessert more than half the time?
		
		          More than Less than
		          half the time half the time
		 Purchased an appetizer ☐ ☐
		 Purchased a dessert ☐ ☐
		 ☐ Purchased neither appetizers nor desserts

Problems: Non-specific time frame; likely to experience memory decay; non-specific screen (not asking what you really need to know to qualify a participant). **Solution:** Replace 'ever' with a more appropriate time frame; screen for the desired behaviour	Have you ever attended a college basketball game? ☐ Yes ☐ No	In the last six months, have you been a spectator at a basketball game played by college teams on a college campus? ☐ Yes ☐ No
Problems: Question faces serious memory decay as a coat may not be purchased each year; not asking if the coat was a personal purchase or for someone else; nor do you know the type of coat purchased; nor do you know whether the coat was purchased for full price or at a discount.	How much did you pay for the last coat you purchased? _____	Did you purchase a dress coat for your personal use in the last 60 days? ☐ Yes ☐ No Thinking of this dress coat, how much did you pay? (to the nearest euro) € ___ .00 Was this coat purchase made at a discounted price? ☐ Yes ☐ No

13.5   Response strategy

A third major decision area in question design is the degree and form of structure imposed on the participant. The various response strategies offer options that include **unstructured response** (open-ended response, the free choice of words) and **structured response** (closed response, specified alternatives provided). Free responses, in turn, range from those in which the participants express themselves extensively to those in which participants' latitude is restricted by space, layout or instructions to choose one word or phrase, as in a 'fill-in' question. Closed responses are typically categorized as dichotomous, multiple-choice, checklist, rating or ranking response strategies.

Situational determinants of response strategy choice

Several situational factors affect the decision of whether to use open-ended or closed questions.[16] The decision is also affected by the degree to which the following factors are known to the interviewer:

- objectives of the study
- participant's level of information about the topic
- degree to which participant has thought through the topic
- ease with which participant communicates
- participant's motivation level to share information.

Issue 18: Objective of the study

If the objective of the question is only to classify the participant on some stated point of view, then the closed question will serve well. Assume you are interested only in whether a participant approves of or disapproves of a certain corporate policy. A closed question will provide this answer. This response strategy ignores the full scope of the participant's opinion and its antecedents. If the objective is to explore a wider territory, then an open-ended question (free-response strategy) is preferable.

Open-ended questions are appropriate when the objective is to discover opinions and degrees of knowledge. They are also appropriate when the interviewer seeks sources of information, dates of events and suggestions, or when probes are used to secure more information. When the topic of a question is outside the participant's experience, the open-ended question may offer the better way to learn his or her level of information. Open-ended questions also help to uncover certainty of feelings and expressions of intensity, although well-designed closed questions can do the same.

Finally, it may be better to use open-ended questions when the interviewer does not have a clear idea of the participant's frame of reference or level of information. Such conditions are likely to occur in exploratory research or in pilot testing. Closed questions are better when there is a clear frame of reference, the participant's level of information is predictable, and the researcher believes that the participant understands the topic.

Issue 19: Thoroughness of prior thought

If a participant has developed a clear opinion on the topic, a closed question will serve well. If an answer has not been thought out, an open-ended question may give the participant a chance to ponder a reply, then elaborate on and revise it.

Issue 20: Communication skill

Open-ended questions require a stronger grasp of vocabulary and a greater ability to frame responses than do closed questions.

Issue 21: Participant motivation

Experience has shown that closed questions typically require less motivation, and answering them is less threatening to participants. But the response alternatives sometimes suggest which answer is appropriate; for this reason, closed questions may be biased. Moreover, respondents might feel that the offered answer options do not reflect what they would like to answer, as either an option is missing or respondents feel that they are in between two options.

While the open-ended question offers many advantages, closed questions are generally preferable in large surveys. They reduce the variability of response, make fewer demands on interviewer skills, are less costly to administer, and are much easier to code and analyse. After adequate exploration and testing, we can often develop closed questions that will perform as effectively as open-ended questions in many situations. Experimental studies suggest that closed questions are equal or superior to open-ended questions in many more applications than is commonly believed.[17]

Response strategies illustrated

The characteristics of participants, the nature of the topic(s) being studied, the type of data needed, and your analysis plan dictate the response strategy. Examples of the strategies described in this section are given in Exhibit 13.7.

Exhibit 13.7 Alternative response strategies.

Free response
What factors influenced your enrolment at Lake University?

Dichotomous selection
Did you attend either of the 'A Day at College' programmes at Lake University?
☐ YES   ☐ NO

(Paired-comparison dichotomous selection)
In your decision to attend Lake University, which was more influential: the semester calendar or the many friends attending from your home town?
☐ Semester calendar
☐ Many friends attending from home town

Multiple choice
Which one of the following factors was most influential in your decision to attend Lake University?
☐ Good academic reputation
☐ Specific programme of study desired
☐ Enjoyable campus life
☐ Many friends from home attend
☐ High quality of the faculty

Checklist
Which of the following factors encouraged you to apply to Lake University? (Check all that apply)
☐ Tuition cost
☐ Specific programme of study desired
☐ Parents' preferences
☐ Opinion of brother or sister
☐ Many friends from home attend
☐ High school counsellors
☐ High quality of the faculty
☐ Good academic reputation
☐ Enjoyable campus life
☐ Closeness to home

Rating
Each of the following factors has been shown to have some influence on a student's choice in applying to Lake University. Using your own experience for each factor please tell us whether the factor was 'strongly influential', 'somewhat influential', or 'not at all influential'.

	Strongly influential	Somewhat influential	Not at all influential
Good academic reputation	☐	☐	☐
Enjoyable campus life	☐	☐	☐
Many friends from home attend	☐	☐	☐
High quality of the faculty	☐	☐	☐
Semester calendar	☐	☐	☐

Ranking
Please rank-order your top three factors from the following list based on their influence in encouraging you to apply to Lake University. Use 1 to indicate the most encouraging factor, 2 the next most encouraging factor, and so on.

_____ Closeness to home
_____ Enjoyable campus life
_____ Good academic reputation
_____ High quality of the faculty
_____ High school counsellors
_____ Many friends from home attend
_____ Opinion of brother or sister
_____ Parents
_____ Specific programme of study desired
_____ Tuition cost

Free-response strategy

Free-response questions, also known as open-ended questions, ask the participant a question while the interviewer pauses for the answer (which is unaided), or the participant records his or her ideas in his or her own words in the space provided on a questionnaire.

Dichotomous response strategy

A topic may present clearly dichotomous choices: something is a fact or it is not; a participant can either recall or not recall information; a participant attended or did not attend an event. **Dichotomous questions** suggest opposing responses, but this is not always the case. One response may be so unlikely that it would be better to adopt the middle-ground alternative as one of the two choices. For example, if we ask participants whether they are underpaid or overpaid, we are not likely to get many selections of the latter choice. The better alternatives to present to the participant might be 'underpaid' and 'fairly paid'.

In many two-way questions, there are potential alternatives beyond the stated two alternatives. If the participant cannot accept either alternative in a dichotomous question, he or she may convert the question to a multiple-choice or rating question by writing in his or her desired alternative. For example, the participant may prefer an alternative such as 'don't know' to a yes/no question, or 'no opinion' when faced with a favour/oppose option. In other cases, when there are two opposing or complementary choices, the participant may prefer a qualified choice ('yes, if X doesn't occur', or 'sometimes yes and sometimes no', or 'about the same'). Thus, two-way questions may become multiple-choice or rating questions, and these additional responses should be reflected in your revised analysis plan.

Multiple-choice response strategy

Multiple-choice questions are appropriate where there are more than two alternatives or where we seek gradations of preference, interest or agreement; the latter situation also calls for **rating questions**. While such questions offer more than one alternative answer, they request the participant to make a single choice. Multiple-choice questions can be efficient, but they also present unique design problems.

Assume we ask whether work safety rules should be determined by (i) companies, (ii) employees, (iii) state government, or (iv) the European Commission. One type of problem occurs when one or more responses have not been anticipated. For example, the union has not been mentioned in the alternatives on work safety rules. Many participants might combine this alternative with 'employees', but others will view 'unions' as a distinct alternative. Exploration prior to drafting the measurement question attempts to identify the most likely choices.

A second problem occurs when the list of choices is not exhaustive. Participants may want to give an answer that is not offered as an alternative. This may occur when the desired response is one that combines two or more of the listed individual alternatives. Many people may believe that the state government and the employees acting jointly should set work safety rules, but the question does not include this response. When the researcher tries to provide for all possible options, the list of alternatives can become exhausting. We guard against this by discovering the major choices through exploration and pre-testing (discussed in detail below). We may also add the category 'other (please specify)' as a safeguard to provide the participant with an acceptable alternative for all other options. In our analysis of a self-administered questionnaire we may create a combination alternative.

Yet another problem occurs when the participant divides the question of work safety into several questions, each with different alternatives. Some participants may believe rules dealing with air quality should be set by a state agency, while those dealing with length of the working day should be set by company and union representatives. Still others want local management–worker committees to make rules. To address this problem, the instrument designer would need to divide the question. Pre-testing should reveal whether a multiple-choice question is really a multiple question.

Another challenge in alternative selection occurs when the choices are not mutually exclusive (the participant thinks two or more responses overlap). In a multiple-choice question that asks students, 'Which one of the following factors was most influential in your decision to attend Lake University?' these response alternatives might be listed:

1 good academic reputation
2 specific programme of study desired
3 enjoyable campus life
4 many friends from home attend
5 high quality of the faculty.

Some participants might view items 1 and 5 as overlapping, and some may see items 3 and 4 in the same way.

It is also important to seek a fair balance in choices. One study showed that an off-balance presentation of alternatives biases the results in favour of the more heavily offered side.[18] If four gradations of alternatives are on one side of an issue and two are offered reflecting the other side, responses will tend to be biased toward the better-represented side.

It is necessary in multiple-choice questions to present reasonable alternatives – particularly when the choices are numbers or identifications. If we ask, 'Which of the following numbers is closest to the number of students enrolled in UK colleges and universities today?' the following choices might be presented:

1 75,000
2 750,000
3 2,500,000
4 7,500,000
5 25,000,000.

It should be obvious to most participants that at least three of these choices are not reasonable, given general knowledge about the population of the UK.

The order in which choices are given can also be a problem. Numbers are normally presented in order of magnitude. This practice introduces bias. The participant assumes that if there is a list of five numbers, the correct answer will lie somewhere in the middle of the group. Researchers are assumed to add a couple of incorrect numbers on each side of the correct one. To counteract this tendency to choose the central position, put the correct number at an extreme position more often when you design a multiple-choice question.

Order bias with non-numeric alternatives often leads the participant to choose the first alternative (primacy effect) or the last alternative (recency effect) over the middle ones. The explanation for this response behaviour lies in the short- and long-term memory of our brains. The first answer choices can easily access our long-term memory, as it is not occupied then and the last answer choices are still present in the short-term memory. In personal face-to-face interviews you can partly control these effects by presenting cards with all answer choices supporting the respondents' memory. Nevertheless, research has shown that even using cards or written questionnaires suffers from these memory problems. Using the split-ballot technique allows you to identify this bias. To implement this strategy in face-to-face interviews, list the alternatives on a card to be handed to the participant when the question is asked. Cards with different choice orders can be alternated to ensure positional balance. You need, however, to understand that this technique does not solve the problem, because a random ordering of answer choices does not remove the bias but ensures that the bias is randomly distributed across the sample. Moreover, you can check whether respondents' answers depend on the position of the answer, giving you an idea about the magnitude of the problem. A further good practice in designing such answer cards is leaving the choices unnumbered on the card so participants reply by giving the choice itself rather than its identifying number. It is recommended to use cards like this any time there are four or more choice alternatives. This saves the interviewer's reading time and ensures a more valid answer by keeping the full range of choices in front of the participant.

In most multiple-choice questions, there is also a problem of ensuring that the choices represent a unidimensional scale – that is, the alternatives to a given question should represent different aspects of the same conceptual dimension. In the college selection example, the list included features associated with a college that might be attractive to a student. This list, while not exhaustive, illustrated aspects of the concept 'college attractiveness factors within the control of the college'. The list did not mention other factors that might affect a school attendance decision. Parents and peer advice, local alumni efforts and one's high school adviser may influence the decision, but these represent a different conceptual dimension of 'college attractiveness factors' – those not within the control of the college.

Multiple-choice questions usually generate nominal data. When the choices are numbers, this response structure will produce at least interval and sometimes ratio data. When the choices represent ordered numerical ranges (e.g. a question on family income) or a verbal rating scale (e.g. a question on how you prefer your steak prepared: well-done, medium-well, medium-rare or rare), the multiple-choice question generates ordinal data.

Checklist response strategy

When you want a participant to give multiple responses to a single question, you will ask the question in one of three ways. If relative order is not important, the **checklist** is the logical choice. Questions like, 'Which of the following factors encouraged you to apply to Lake University? (Check all that apply)' force the participant to exercise a dichotomous response (yes, encouraged; no, didn't encourage) to each factor presented. Of course you could have asked for the same information as a series of dichotomous selection questions, one for each individual factor, but that would have been time- and space-consuming. Checklists are more efficient. Checklists generate nominal data.

Rating response strategy

Rating questions ask the participant to position each factor on a companion scale, either verbal, numeric or graphic. For example: 'Each of the following factors has been shown to have some influence on a student's choice to apply to Lake University. Using your own experience, for each factor please tell us whether the factor was "strongly influential", "somewhat influential" or "not at all influential".' Generally, rating-scale structures generate ordinal data; some carefully crafted scales generate interval data.

Ranking response strategy

When the relative order of alternatives is important, the **ranking question** is ideal. For example:

> Please rank-order your top three factors from the following list based on their influence in encouraging you to apply to Lake University. Use 1 to indicate the most encouraging factor, 2 the next most encouraging factor, and so on.

The checklist strategy would provide the three factors of influence, but we would have no way of knowing the importance that the participant places on each factor. Even in a personal interview, the order in which the factors are mentioned is not a guarantee of influence. Ranking as a response strategy solves this problem.

One concern surfaces with ranking activities. How many presented factors should be ranked? If you listed the 15 brands of potato chips sold in a given market, would you have the participant rank all 15 in order of preference? In most instances it is helpful to remind yourself that while participants may have been selected for a given study due to their experience or the likelihood that they can provide the desired information, this does not mean that they have knowledge of all conceivable aspects of an issue. It is always better to have participants rank only those elements with which they are familiar. If you want motivation to remain strong, avoid asking a participant to rank more than seven items, even if your list is longer. Ranking generates ordinal data.

All types of response strategy have their advantages and disadvantages. Several different strategies are often found in the same questionnaire, and the situational factors mentioned earlier are the major guides in this matter. There is a tendency, however, to use closed questions instead of the more flexible open-ended type. Exhibit 13.8 summarizes some important considerations in choosing between the various response strategies.

Exhibit 13.8 Characteristics of response strategies.

Characteristics	Dichotomous	Multiple choice	Checklist	Rating	Rank ordering	Free response
Type of data	Nominal	Nominal, ordinal or ratio	Nominal	Ordinal or interval	Ordinal	Nominal or ratio
Usual number of answer alternatives provided	2	3 to 10	10 or fewer	3 to 7	10 or fewer	None
Desired number of participant answers	1	1	10 or fewer	7 or fewer	10 or fewer	1
Used to provide . . .	Classification	Classification, order or specific numerical estimate	Classification	Order or distance	Order	Classification (of idea), order or specific numerical estimate

13.6 Sources of existing questions

The tools of data collection should be adapted to the problem, not the reverse. Thus, the focus of this chapter has been on crafting an instrument to answer specific investigative questions. But inventing and refining questions demands considerable time and effort. For some topics, a careful review of the related literature and an examination of existing instrument sourcebooks can shorten this process.

A review of literature will reveal instruments used in similar studies that may be obtained by writing to the researchers or, if copyrighted, purchased through a clearing house. Many instruments are available through compilations and sourcebooks. While these tend to be oriented towards social science applications, they are a rich source of ideas for tailoring questions to meet a manager's needs. Several compilations are recommended and these are noted in Exhibit 13.9.[19]

Exhibit 13.9 Sources of questions.

Author(s)	Title	Source
Philip E. Converse, Jean D. Dotson, Wendy J. Hoag and William H. McGee III (eds)	American Social Attitudes Data Sourcebook, 1947–1978	Cambridge, MA: Harvard University Press, 1980
Alec Gallup and George H. Gallup (eds)	The Gallup Poll Cumulative Index: Public Opinion, 1935–1997	Wilmington, DE: Scholarly Resources Inc., 1999
George H. Gallup Jr. (ed.)	The Gallup Poll: Public Opinion 1998	Wilmington, DE: 1999
Elizabeth H. Hastings and Philip K. Hastings (eds)	Index to International Public Opinion 1986–1987	Westport, CT: Greenwood Press, 1988
Philip K. Hastings and Jessie C. Southwick (eds)	Survey Data for Trend Analysis: An Index to Repeated Questions in the US National Surveys Held by the Roper Public Opinion Research Center	Storrs, CT: Roper Center for Public Opinion Research, Inc., 1974
Elizabeth Martin, Diana McDuffee and Stanley Presser	Sourcebook of Harris National Surveys: Repeated Questions 1963–1976	Chapel Hill: Institute for Research in Social Science, University of North Carolina Press, 1981
National Opinion Research Center	General Social Surveys 1972–1985: Cumulative Code Book	Chicago: NORC, 1985
John P. Robinson, Robert Athanasiou and Kendra B. Head	Measures of Occupational Attitudes and Occupational Characteristics	Ann Arbor: Institute for Social Research, University of Michigan, 1968
John P. Robinson, Philip R. Shaver and Lawrence S. Wrightsman	Measures of Personality and Social-psychological Attitudes	San Diego, CA: Academic Press, 1991

Student Research

Ecopreneurs – what makes them special?

Ben Nicolay always had a keen interest in the relationship between ecological and economic issues. Do you really make less profit if you care for the environment? Is a company's claim to be environmental-friendly deeply rooted in a 'green' belief or is it just a way to enter new customer segments? These were questions Ben was interested in and consequently he wrote his research project on ecopreneurship. His first struggle was to find an appropriate industry, which included 'green' companies as well as 'non-green' companies. First, Ben thought about the usual suspects if one talks about 'green businesses', such as the regenerative energy sector. But unfortunately there are hardly any 'non-green' businesses in these sectors, inhibiting a sound comparison between greens and non-greens.

As Ben was not only a Walloon, but also a wallower, the wine industry came to his mind. In recent years, he had observed that more and more wine growers started to produce organic wine, but the majority of the wine growers still employed traditional methods including the use of pesticides. Specifically Ben was interested in whether green wineries differ from traditional ones regarding their characteristics on the one hand and the strategy followed on the other hand. An additional question was, however, whether a winery's motivation to produce organic wine was mainly a concern for the environment or mainly the opportunity to get a piece of the growing market for organic products.

Distinguishing green from non-green wineries was easy, as Ben could verify whether a wine grower was a member of a 'green' winery association, such as Terra Vitis or Tyflo. But how could he identify idealistic green wineries from opportunity-based green wineries? Ben asked the wineries about their motivation to become green and he used the answers to classify them either as idealistic or opportunity-based.

What was your motivation to engage in organic wine production? Please rate the two statements below.

	Not important	A little bit important	Neutral	Important	Very important
Values and personal beliefs	☐	☐	☐	☐	☐
Identification of a market opportunity	☐	☐	☐	☐	☐

Can you see the problems of this measurement? What happens if a respondent rates both motivations as very important? Does this indicate an idealistic green winery or an opportunity-based winery? And indeed, later on Ben found that he could not clearly classify all the green wineries as idealistic or opportunity-seeking and he had to introduce a third category 'undecided'.

Using established scales and questions is, as we discussed above, usually advantageous, but sometimes it is better to adapt questions to the specific population you have in mind. In his wine ecopreneur study, Ben was interested in the strategies of the wineries – for example, their innovation strategy. A review of the literature showed Ben that there are almost as many measurements for innovation as there are studies. Ben also had a strong feeling that an innovation measure should be industry-specific and therefore he adapted and combined a couple of questions found in other studies:

1 How many years ago did you introduce a new wine to your product range?
2 Please rate the three statements below:

	Disagree	Partly disagree	Neutral	Partly agree	Agree
Our winery adopts new agricultural processes easily	☐	☐	☐	☐	☐
Our winery adopts new processes in wine making easily	☐	☐	☐	☐	☐
Our winery adopts new commercial activities easily	☐	☐	☐	☐	☐

Then, he reversed the first question, as low values indicated a higher degree of innovation and combined all four questions to one variable innovation, as Cronbach's alpha, a measure for reliability, was sufficiently high ($\alpha = .744$) to justify taking the four items together.

Do you think it is a good idea to adapt items to the industry or company you are investigating? What do you gain and what do you lose?

Borrowing items from existing sources is not without risk. It is quite difficult to generalize the reliability and validity of selected items or portions of a questionnaire that have been taken out of the original context. Pre-testing is also warranted if it is necessary to report the reliability and validity of the instrument being constructed. Time and situation-specific fluctuations should be scrutinized. Remember that the original estimates are only as good as the sampling and testing procedures, and many researchers you borrow from may not have reported that information.

Language, phrasing and idiom can also pose problems. Questions tend to age and may not appear (or sound) as relevant to the participant as freshly worded ones would. Integrating existing and newly constructed questions is problematic. When adjacent questions are relied on to carry context in one questionnaire and then are not selected for the customized application, the newly selected question is left without necessary meaning.[20] Whether an instrument is constructed from scratch or adapted from the ideas of others, pre-testing is recommended.

13.7 Drafting and refining the instrument: phase 3

As depicted in Exhibit 13.10, phase 3 of instrument design – drafting and refinement – is a multistep process, as outlined below:

1   Develop the participant-screening process (personal or telephone interview), along with the introduction.
2   Arrange the measurement question sequence:

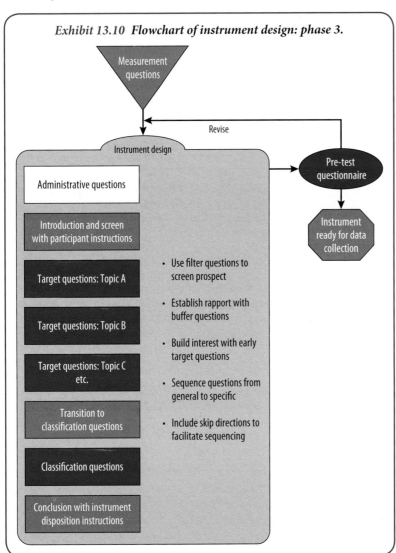

Exhibit 13.10 Flowchart of instrument design: phase 3.

a identify topic groups
b establish a logical sequence for the question groups and questions within groups
c develop transitions between these groups.
3 Prepare and insert instructions – for the interviewer or participant – including termination, skip directions and probes.
4 Create and insert a conclusion, including a survey return statement.
5 Pre-test specific questions and the instrument as a whole.

Introduction and participant screening

The introduction must supply the sample unit with the motivation to participate in the study. It must reveal enough about the forthcoming questions, usually by revealing some or all of the topics to be covered, for participants to judge their interest level and their ability to provide the desired information. In any communication study, the introduction also reveals the amount of time participation is likely to take. In a personal or telephone interview, the introduction usually contains a filter or **screen question** to determine if the potential participant has the knowledge or experience necessary to participate in the study. The introduction also reveals the identity of the research organization and/or sponsor (unless the study is disguised) and possibly the objective of the study. At a minimum, a telephone or personal interviewer will introduce him or herself to help establish critical rapport with the potential participant. Exhibit 13.11 provides an example introduction and other components of a telephone study of non-participants to a self-administered mail survey.

Exhibit 13.11 *Example of components in communication instruments.*

Introduction	Good evening. May I speak with (name of participant)? Mr/Ms (last name of participant), I'm (your name) calling on behalf of the Alumni Network of Hull University. You have recently requested information concerning the Alumni Network. Could you take 10 minutes to tell us what you think about the activities employed by the Alumni Network?
Transition	The next set of questions asks about your career since you left university.
Instructions for . . . (a) terminating (following a filter or screen question informing you that the participant never attended Hull University)	I am sorry; today we are only talking with individuals who attended Hull University, but thank you for speaking with me (pause for reply). Goodbye.
(b) participant discontinue	Would there be a time I could call back to complete the interview, which is more convenient for you? (pause: record time) (repeat day and time). Thank you for talking with me this evening. Goodbye.
(c) skip directions (between questions or group of questions)	3. Did you ever participate in an activity organized by the Alumni Network or visit the annual Alumni Day at Hull University? Yes, both (go to next question). Yes, visited Alumni Day (go to next question). Yes, visited other Alumni Activity (go to question 8). No (go to question 12).
(d) Return instructions	A postage-paid envelope was included with your survey. Please refold your completed survey and mail it to us in the postage-paid envelope.
Conclusion (a) phone or personal interview	That's my last question. Your insights and the ideas of other valuable alumni will help us to improve the service and activities of the Alumni Network. Thank you for talking with us this evening (pause for participant reply). Good evening.
(b) Self-administered questionnaire (usually precedes the return instructions)	Thank you for sharing your ideas about the Alumni Network and its activities. Your insights will help us to serve you and other alumni better.

Measurement question sequencing

Often the content of one question (called a **branched question**) assumes other questions have been asked and answered. The psychological order of the questions is also important; question sequence can encourage or discourage commitment and promote or hinder the development of researcher–participant rapport.

The design of survey questions is influenced by the need to relate each question to the others in the instrument. The basic principle used to guide sequence decisions is: the nature and needs of the participant must determine the sequence of questions and the organization of the interview schedule. Four guidelines are suggested to implement this principle:

1 The question process must quickly awaken interest and motivate the participant to participate in the interview. Place the more interesting topical target questions early on.
2 The participant should not be confronted by early requests for information that might be considered personal or ego threatening. Place questions that might influence the participant to discontinue or terminate the questioning process near the end.
3 The questioning process should begin with simple items and move to the more complex, and also from general items to the more specific. Place taxing and challenging questions later in the questioning process.
4 Changes in the frame of reference should be small and should be clearly pointed out. Use transition statements between the different topics of the target question set.

Awaken interest and motivation

We awaken interest and stimulate motivation to participate by choosing or designing questions that are attention-getting and not controversial. If the questions have human-interest value, so much the better. It is possible that the early questions will contribute hard data to the major study objective, but their major task is to overcome the motivational barrier.

Sensitive and ego-involving information

Regarding the introduction of sensitive information too early in the process, two forms of this error are common. Most studies need to ask for personal classification information about participants. Participants will normally provide these data, but the request should be made towards the end of the process. If made immediately, it often causes participants to feel threatened, dampening their interest and motivation to continue. It is also dangerous to ask any question at the start that is too personal. For example, participants in one survey were asked whether they suffered from insomnia. When the question was asked immediately after the interviewer's introductory remarks, about 12 per cent of those interviewed admitted to having insomnia. When a matched sample was asked the same question after two **buffer questions** (neutral questions designed chiefly to establish rapport with the participant), 23 per cent admitted suffering from insomnia.[21]

Complex to simplistic

Deferring complex questions or simple questions that require much thought can help reduce the number of 'don't know' responses that are so prevalent early in interviews.

General to specific

The procedure of moving from general to more specific questions is sometimes called the **funnel approach**. The objectives of this procedure are to learn the participant's frame of reference and to extract the full range of desired information while limiting the distortion effect of earlier questions on later ones. This process may be illustrated with the following series of questions:

1 How do you think this country is getting along in its relationship with other countries?
2 How do you think we are doing in our relationship with Israel?
3 Do you think we ought to be dealing with Israel differently than we are now?
4 (If yes) What should we be doing differently?
5 Some people say we should get tougher with Israel and others think that we are too tough as it is; how do you feel about it?[22]

The first question introduces the general subject and provides some insight into the participant's frame of reference. The second narrows the concern to a single country, while the third and fourth seek views on how the home country should deal with Israel. The fifth question illustrates a specific opinion area and would be asked only if this point of toughness had not been covered in earlier responses. Question 4 is an example of a branched question; the response to the previous question determines whether or not question 4 is asked of the participant.

There is also a risk of interaction whenever two or more questions are related. Question-order influence is especially problematic with self-administered questionnaires, because the participant is at liberty to refer back to questions previously answered. In an attempt to 'correctly align' two responses, accurate opinions and attitudes may be sacrificed. Exhibit 13.12 illustrates this problem by showing the percentages of respondents agreeing to two related questions depending on the question order.

Exhibit 13.12 shows that, apparently, some participants who first endorsed a salary reduction for the management board felt obliged to extend this consequence to all employees of the firm. Where the decision was first made against reducing employees' salaries, a percentage of participants felt constrained in agreeing to reduce management salaries.

Exhibit 13.12 An example of the effect of question-order influence.

Questions	Percentage answering yes	
	A asked first	B asked first
A. Should the fixed salary of the management board be reduced if the firm's performance has been poor in the previous year?	55%	48%
B. Should the wages and salaries of employees be reduced if the firm's performance has been poor in the previous year?	28%	17%

Question groups and transitions

The last question-sequencing guideline suggests arranging questions to minimize shifting in subject matter and frame of reference. Participants often interpret questions in the light of earlier questions and miss shifts of perspective or subject unless they are clearly stated. Participants fail to listen carefully and frequently jump to conclusions about the import of a given question before it is completely stated. Their answers are strongly influenced by their frame of reference. Any change in subject by the interviewer may not register with them unless it is made strong and obvious. Most questionnaires that cover a range of topics are divided into sections with clearly defined transitions between sections to alert the participant to the change in frame of reference. Exhibit 13.11 provides a sample of a transition in a study of Hull University Alumni Network when measurement questions changed from personal questions to questions asking for an assessment of the Alumni Network.

Instructions

Instructions to the interviewer or participant attempt to ensure that all participants are treated equally, thus avoiding building error into the results. Two principles form the foundation for good instructions: clarity and courtesy. Instruction language needs to be unfailingly simple and polite.

Instruction topics include the following:

- Termination of an unqualified participant – how to terminate an interview when the participant does not correctly answer the screen or filter questions.
- Termination of a discontinued interview – how to conclude an interview when the participant decides to discontinue.
- Skip directions – instructions for moving between topic sections of an instrument when movement is dependent on the answer to specific questions or when branched questions are used.
- Return instructions – telling the respondent to a self-administered instrument how to return the completed questionnaire.

In a self-administered questionnaire, instructions must be contained within the survey instrument. Personal interviewer instructions are sometimes in a document that is separate from the questionnaire (a document thoroughly discussed during interviewer training) or are distinctly and clearly marked (highlighted, printed in coloured ink, or boxed on the computer screen) on the data-collection instrument itself. Sample instructions are presented in Exhibit 13.11.

Conclusion

The role of the conclusion is to leave the participant with the impression that his or her involvement has been valuable. Subsequent researchers may need this individual to participate in new studies. If every interviewer or instrument expresses appreciation for participation, cooperation in subsequent studies is more likely. A sample conclusion is shown in Exhibit 13.11.

Overcoming instrument problems

There is no substitute for a thorough understanding of question wording, question content and sequencing issues. However, the researcher can do several things to help improve survey results, among them:

- build rapport with the participant
- redesign the questioning process
- explore alternative response strategies
- use methods other than surveying to secure the data
- pre-test all the survey elements.

Build rapport with the participant

Most information can be secured by direct undisguised questioning if rapport has been developed. Rapport is particularly useful in building participant interest in the project, and the more interest participants have, the more cooperation they will give. One can also overcome participant unwillingness by providing some material compensation for cooperation. This approach has been especially successful in mail surveys. Using an experimental design, Statistics Netherlands investigated the effects of different incentives on the response rate. The three modes were (i) no incentive, (ii) a prepaid telephone card (value: €5) was sent along with the questionnaire, and (iii) a prepaid telephone card (value: €5) was promised once the respondent had returned the questionnaire. The overall response rate was highest in mode 2 and, in particular, increased the response rate among younger men, who are notorious for being lazy respondents.

The assurance of confidentiality can also increase participants' motivation. One approach is to give discreet assurances, both by question wording and interviewer comments and actions, that all types of behaviour, attitudes and positions on controversial or sensitive subjects are acceptable and normal. Where you can say so truthfully, guarantee that participants' answers will be used only in combined statistical totals. If participants are convinced that their replies contribute to some important purpose, they are more likely to be candid, even about taboo topics.

Redesign the questioning process

You can redesign the questioning process to improve the quality of answers by modifying the administrative process and the response strategy. We might show that confidentiality is indispensable to the administration of the survey by using a group administration of questionnaires, accompanied by a ballot-box collection procedure. Even in face-to-face interviews, the participant may fill in the part of the questionnaire containing sensitive information and then seal the entire instrument in an envelope. While this does not guarantee confidentiality, it does suggest it.

We can also develop appropriate questioning sequences that will gradually lead a participant from 'safe' questions to those that are more sensitive. As already noted in our discussion of disguised questions, indirect questioning (using projective techniques) is a widely used approach for securing opinions on sensitive topics. The participants are asked how 'other people' or 'people around here' feel about a topic. It is assumed that the participants will reply in terms of their own attitudes and experiences, but this outcome is hardly certain. Indirect questioning may give a good measure of the majority opinion on a topic but fail to reflect the views either of the participant or minority segments.

With certain topics, it is possible to secure answers by using a proxy code. When we seek family income classes, we can hand the participant a card with income brackets like these:

A Under €25,000 per year
B €25,000 to €49,999 per year
C €50,000 to €74,999 per year
D €75,000 and over per year

The participant is then asked to report the appropriate bracket as either A, B, C or D. For some reason, participants are more willing to provide such an obvious proxy measure than to verbalize actual monetary values.

Explore alternative response strategies

At the original question drafting, try developing positive, negative and neutral versions of each type of question. This practice dramatizes the problems of bias, helping you to select question wording that minimizes such problems. Sometimes use an extreme version of a question rather than the expected one.

Minimize non-responses to particular questions by recognizing the sensitivity of certain topics. In a self-administered instrument, for example, asking a multiple-choice question about income or age, where incomes and ages are offered in ranges, is usually more successful than using a free-response question such as 'What is your age, please? _____'.

Use methods other than surveying

Sometimes surveying will not secure the information needed. A classic example concerns a survey conducted to discover magazines read by participants. An unusually high rate was reported for prestigious magazines, and an unusually low rate was reported for tabloid magazines. The study was revised so that the subjects, instead of being interviewed, were asked to contribute their old magazines to a charity drive. The collection gave a more realistic estimate of readership of both types of magazine.[23] Another study on the use of similar unobtrusive measures cites many other types of research situation where unique techniques have been used to secure more valid information than was possible from a survey.[24]

The value of pre-testing

The final step towards improving survey results is **pre-testing** (see Exhibits 13.4 and 13.12). There are abundant reasons for pre-testing individual questions, questionnaires and interview schedules. In this section we discuss several of these and raise questions to help you plan an effective test of your instrument. Most of what we know about pre-testing is prescriptive. According to contemporary authors:

> "There are no general principles of good pre-testing, no systematization of practice, no consensus about expectations, and we rarely leave records for each other. How a pre-test was conducted, what investigators learned from it, how they redesigned their questionnaire on the basis of it – these matters are reported only sketchily in research reports, if at all."[25]

Nevertheless, conventional wisdom suggests that pre-testing is not only an established practice for discovering errors but is also useful for training the research team. Ironically, professionals who have participated in scores of studies are more likely to pre-test an instrument than a newly qualified researcher who is hurrying to complete a project. Revising questions five or more times is not unusual. Yet inexperienced researchers often underestimate the need to follow the design–test–revise process.

Participant interest

An important purpose of pre-testing is to discover participants' reactions to the questions. If participants do not find the experience stimulating when an interviewer is physically present, how will they react on the telephone or in the self-administered mode? Pre-testing should help to discover where repetitiveness or redundancy is bothersome or what topics were not covered that the participant expected. An alert interviewer will look for questions or even sections that the participant perceives to be sensitive or threatening, or topics about which the participant knows nothing. Another valuable approach to testing questionnaires is to discuss them within focus groups (see Chapter 8 for a more detailed discussion on focus groups). A typical set-up for such a focus group would be to send out the questionnaire to the participants of the focus group discussion a week before the meeting, with the request to have a look at the questionnaire. Then in the focus group discussion you would start by asking for the general impression the questionnaire made, and continue by running through each question and asking for comments from the focus group members. The participants in a focus group discussion need not be restricted to those who would fit the population for which the questionnaire is intended. For example, one of the authors discussed a CAPI questionnaire intended for people who recently started a business not only with new business starters, but also in focus groups consisting of other field experts, such as representatives from banks, the chamber of commerce and fellow researchers from other universities.

Meaning

Questions that we borrow or adapt from the work of others carry an authoritativeness that may prompt us to avoid pre-testing them, but they are often most in need of examination. Are they still timely? Is the language relevant? Do they need context from adjacent questions? Newly constructed questions should similarly be checked for meaningfulness to the participant. Does the question evoke the same meaning as that intended by the researcher? How different is the researcher's frame of reference from that of the average participant? Words and phrases that trigger a 'What do you mean?' response from the participant need to be singled out for further refinement.

Question transformation

Participants do not necessarily process every word in the question and they may not share the same definitions of the terms they hear. When this happens, participants modify the question to make it fit their own frame of reference or simply change it so it makes sense to them. Probing is necessary to discover how participants have transformed a question when this is suspected.[26]

Continuity and flow

In self-administered questionnaires, questions should read effortlessly and flow from one to another, and from one section to another. In personal and telephone interviews, the sound of the question and its transition must be fluid as well. A long set of questions with nine-point scales that worked well in a mail instrument would not be effective on the telephone unless you were to ask participants to visualize the scale as the touch keys on their telephone. Moreover, transitions that may appear redundant in a self-administered questionnaire may be exactly what needs to be heard in personal or telephone interviewing.

Question sequence

Question arrangement can play a significant role in the success of the instrument. Many authorities recommend starting with stimulating questions and placing sensitive questions last. Since questions concerning income and family life are most likely to be refused, this is often good advice for building trust before getting into a refusal situation. However, interest-building questions need to be tested first to be sure that they are stimulating. And when background questions are asked earlier in the interview, some demographic information will be salvaged if the interview stops unexpectedly. Pre-testing with a large enough group permits some experimentation with question sequence.

Skip instructions

In interviews and questionnaires, **skip patterns** and their contingency sequences may not work as envisioned on paper. Skip patterns are designed to route or sequence the response to another question contingent on the answer to the previous question (branched questions). Pre-testing in the field helps to identify problems with box-and-arrow schematics that the designers may not have thought of. By correcting them at the revision stage, we also avoid problems with flow and continuity. In general, you should minimize skip patterns in self-administered questionnaires, while telephone and personal interviews can contain more complex skip patterns if the interviewers are trained accordingly. Any form of computer-assisted interview also allows the use of more complex skipping. You need, however, to consider that the more complex the skip pattern, the more difficult it is even for the researcher to oversee the whole structure of the questionnaire, which may result in skipping certain questions that were not intended to be skipped. Thus, the more complex the skip patterns you use, the more pretesting is needed to ensure that the computer or the interviewer carries out the skipping instructions correctly.

Variability

With a small group of participants, pre-testing cannot provide definitive quantitative conclusions but will deliver an early warning about items that may not discriminate among participants or places where meaningful sub-grouping may occur in the final sample. With 25–100 participants in the pre-test group, statistical data on the proportion of participants answering yes or no or marking 'strongly agree' to 'strongly disagree' can supplement the qualitative information noted by the interviewers. This information is useful for sample size calculations and for getting preliminary indications of reliability problems with scaled questions.

Length and timing

Most draft questionnaires or interview schedules suffer from lengthiness. By timing each question and section, the researcher is in a better position to make decisions about modifying or cutting material. In personal and telephone interviews, labour is a project expense. Thus, if the budget influences the final length of the questionnaire, an accurate estimate of elapsed time is essential. Videotaped or audiotaped pre-tests may also be used for this purpose. Their function in reducing errors in data recording is widely accepted.

Pre-testing options

There are various ways that pre-testing can be used to refine an instrument. They range from informal reviews by colleagues to creating conditions similar to those of the final study.

Researcher pre-testing

Designers typically test informally in the initial stages and build more structure into the tests along the way. Fellow instrument designers can do the first-level pre-test. Their many differences of opinion are likely to create numerous suggestions for improvement. Usually at least two or three drafts can be effectively developed by bringing research colleagues into the process.

Participant pre-testing

Participant pre-tests require that the questionnaire be field-tested by sample participants or participant surrogates (individuals with characteristics and backgrounds similar to the desired participants).

Field pre-tests also involve distributing the test instrument exactly as the actual instrument will be distributed. Most studies use two or more pre-tests. National projects may use one trial to examine local reaction and another to check for regional differences. Although many researchers try to keep pre-test conditions and times close to what they expect for the actual study, personal interview and telephone limitations make it desirable to test in the evenings or at weekends in order to interview people who are not available for contact at other times.

Test mailings are useful, but it is often quicker to use a substitute procedure, in which you ask people you already know to test the questionnaire. For example, the survey we looked at elsewhere, among self-employed people, was pre-tested by young entrepreneurs, who were contacted at a local trade fair for young entrepreneurial talent. After these entrepreneurs had filled in the questionnaire, they were also invited to participate in a focus-group discussion to reflect on the questionnaire.

Collaborative pre-tests

Different approaches taken by interviewers and the participants' awareness of those approaches affect the pre-test. If the researcher alerts participants to their involvement in a preliminary test of the questionnaire, the participants are essentially being enlisted as collaborators in the refinement process. Under these conditions, detailed probing of the parts of the question, including phrases and words, is appropriate. Because of the time required for probing and discussion, it is likely that only the most critical questions will be reviewed. The participant group may therefore need to be conscripted from colleagues and friends to secure the additional time and motivation needed to cover an entire questionnaire. If friends or associates are used, experience suggests that they introduce more bias than strangers, argue more about wording, and generally make it more difficult to accomplish other goals of pre-testing such as timing the length of questions or sections.[27]

Occasionally, a highly experienced researcher may improvise questions during a pre-test. When this occurs, it is essential to record the interview or take detailed notes so that the questionnaire may be reconstructed later. Ultimately, a team of interviewers would be required to follow the interview schedule's prearranged sequence of questions. Only experienced investigators should be free to depart from the interview schedule during a pre-test and explore participants' answers by adding probes.

Non-collaborative pre-tests

When the researcher does not inform the participant that the activity is a pre-test, it is still possible to probe for reactions but without the cooperation and commitment of time provided by collaborators. The comprehensiveness of the effort also suffers because of flagging cooperation. The virtue of this approach is that the questionnaire can be tested under conditions approaching those of the final study. This realism is similarly useful for training interviewers.

Running Case Study 13

Fieldwork: questionnaire and responses

Rebecca designed an online questionnaire and sent out emails with links to the questionnaire. An online questionnaire is built up in separate screens; below you can see the 12 screens of Rebecca's questionnaire.

SCREEN 1

Dear participant!

Thank you very much for participating in this research. It represents an essential part of my Master's Thesis. The study is concerned with investigating unethical behaviour among students. The questionnaire will take about 15 minutes. The collected data will be used for academic purposes only and will be treated strictly confidentially.

Thank you for your support and your time invested.

Rebecca

If you have any questions and comments do not hesitate to contact me:

r.nash@student.maastrichtuniversity.nl

SCREEN 2

In the following you will be provided with five case scenarios. Please read them carefully and answer the questions. In order to provide you with a better understanding of the questions to be answered please read through a short description of relevant variables:

Plagiarism: Refers to taking and using another person's ideas, writing or inventions as one's own; it also includes copying answers from other students during exams

Free-riding: Refers to a situation in which one or more members of a group do not do their fair share of the work project and rely on others to compensate their behaviour

Information sharing: Refers to individuals' unwillingness to share relevant information such as learning materials, expertise, knowledge or job vacancies

But before we start, let me ask you one simple question:

Have you ever cheated in an exam during the last 12 months?

☐ never   ☐ once   ☐ twice   ☐ three or more times

SCREEN 3

Scenario 1

Rules and regulations at your faculty state that if you do not pass an exam and/or fail a project or participation, you will have the chance to do a retake. Unethical practices are common at your faculty and tend to be accepted by your social surrounding. Tutors assign project groups to be worked in so that you don't know other group members beforehand. You neither feel a strong commitment to fellow students nor do you feel a strong commitment to your teachers.

Given this situation, on a percentage scale from 0–100 (0 = definitely not;

100 = definitely), how likely are you to:

Plagiarism: _____

Free-riding: _____

Unwillingness to share information: _____

SCREEN 4

Scenario 2

Rules and regulations at your faculty state that if you do not pass an exam and/or fail a project or participation, you will have the chance to do a retake. Unethical practices are uncommon at your faculty and tend to be disrespected by your social surrounding. Tutors assign project groups to be worked in so that you don't know other group members beforehand. You neither feel a strong commitment to fellow students nor do you feel a strong commitment to your teachers.

Given this situation, on a percentage scale from 0–100 (0 = definitely not;

100 = definitely), how likely are you to:

Plagiarism: _____

Free-riding: _____

Unwillingness to share information: _____

SCREEN 5

Scenario 3

Rules and regulations at your faculty state that if you do not pass an exam and/or fail a project or participation, you run the risk of being expelled from university. Unethical practices are common at your faculty and tend to be accepted by your social surrounding. Tutors assign project groups to be worked in so that you don't know other group members beforehand. You neither feel a strong commitment to fellow students nor do you feel a strong commitment to your teachers.

Given this situation, on a percentage scale from 0–100 (0 = definitely not;

100 = definitely), how likely are you to:

Plagiarism: _____

Free-riding: _____

Unwillingness to share information: _____

SCREEN 6

Scenario 4

Rules and regulations at your faculty state that if you do not pass an exam and/or fail a project or participation, you run the risk of being expelled from university. Unethical practices are uncommon at your faculty and tend to be disrespected by your social surrounding. Tutors assign project groups to be worked in so that you don't know other group members beforehand. You neither feel a strong commitment to fellow students nor do you feel a strong commitment to your teachers.

Given this situation, on a percentage scale from 0–100 (0 = definitely not; 100 = definitely), how likely are you to:

Plagiarism: _____

Free-riding: _____

Unwillingness to share information: _____

SCREEN 7

Scenario 5

Rules and regulations at your faculty state that if you do not pass an exam and/or fail a project or participation, you will have the chance to do a retake. Unethical practices are uncommon at your faculty and tend to be disrespected by your social surrounding. You select project groups to be worked in yourself so that you know other group members beforehand. You neither feel a strong commitment to fellow students nor do you feel a strong commitment to your teachers.

Given this situation, on a scale from 0–100% how likely would:

Plagiarism: _____

Free-riding: _____

Unwillingness to share information: _____

SCREEN 8

How old are you?

_____ years

What is your nationality?

☐ Dutch

☐ Other, please specify _____

What is your gender?

☐ Female

☐ Male

At which University are you currently studying?

☐ Universiteit van Amsterdam (UVA)

☐ Vrije Universiteit Amsterdam (VU)

☐ Universiteit Maastricht (UM)

☐ Erasmus Universiteit Rotterdam (EUR)

☐ Other _____

What is your realistic final average grade?

☐ 8,0 and better

☐ Above 7,0 but below 8,0

☐ 7,0 and worse

How important is a career to you?

☐ Very unimportant

☐ Unimportant

☐ Indifferent

☐ Important

☐ Very important

SCREEN 9

The following questions do not ask about a hypothetical situation as the ones above, but they ask you about your real behaviour and thoughts. Please, be honest and be assured that your answers are confidential.

Have you cheated in an exam during the last 12 months?

☐ never   ☐ once   ☐ twice   ☐ three or more times

Cheating in exams is unfair with respect to fellow students.

☐ fully disagree   ☐ partly disagree   ☐ neutral   ☐ partly agree   ☐ fully agree

Cheating in exams is acceptable if study pressure is very high.

☐ fully disagree   ☐ partly disagree   ☐ neutral   ☐ partly agree   ☐ fully agree

Cheating in exams is acceptable if the exam is very difficult.

☐ fully disagree   ☐ partly disagree   ☐ neutral   ☐ partly agree   ☐ fully agree

Cheating in exams is acceptable if the lecturer has been bad.

☐ fully disagree   ☐ partly disagree   ☐ neutral   ☐ partly agree   ☐ fully agree

The university should introduce and enforce tougher sanctions if cheating in an exam is discovered.

☐ fully disagree   ☐ partly disagree   ☐ neutral   ☐ partly agree   ☐ fully agree

SCREEN 10

Below you find several methods to cheat in exams, please indicate their severity.

	No cheating	A little bit cheating	A bit cheating	Cheating	Strong cheating
Copying from your neighbour					
Whispering with your neighbour					
Preparing and using a crib sheet					
Asking a friend who has good marks to take the exam in your place					
Secretly sending an SMS to a friend who looks up answer and replies					
Other (please describe)					

SCREEN 11

Have you ever cheated in an exam?

☐ yes   ☐ no

If you answered yes, can you please describe the situation and why you cheated?

_____

_____

_____

_____

_____

_____

_____

▶

Summary

1 The instrument design process starts with a comprehensive list of investigative questions drawn from the management research question hierarchy. Instrument design is a three-phase process with numerous issues within each phase: (phase 1) developing the instrument design strategy, (phase 2) constructing and refining the measurement questions, and (phase 3) drafting and refining the instrument.

2 Several choices must be made in designing a communication study instrument. Surveying can be a face-to-face interview, or it can be much less personal, using indirect media and self-administered questionnaires. The questioning process can be unstructured, as in in-depth interviewing, or the questions can be clearly structured. Responses may be unstructured and open-ended, or structured with the participant choosing from a list of possibilities. The degree to which the objectives and intent of the questions should be disguised must also be decided.

3 Instruments obtain three general classes of information. Target questions address the investigative questions and are the most important. Classification questions concern participant characteristics and allow participants' answers to be grouped for analysis. Administrative questions identify the participant, interviewer, and interview location and conditions.

4 Question construction involves three critical decision areas. These are (i) question content, (ii) question wording and (iii) response strategy. Question content should pass the following tests:
- Should the question be asked?
- Is it of proper scope?
- Can and will the participant answer adequately?

Question wording difficulties exceed most other sources of distortion in surveys. Retention of a question should be confirmed by answering the following questions:
- Is the question stated in terms of a shared vocabulary?
- Does the vocabulary have a single meaning?
- Does the question contain misleading assumptions?
- Is the wording biased?
- Is it correctly personalized?
- Are adequate alternatives presented?

The study's objective and participant factors affect the decision as to whether to use open-ended or closed questions. Each response strategy generates a specific level of data, with available statistical procedures for each data type influencing the desired response strategy. Participant factors include level of information about the topic, degree to which the topic has been thought through, ease of communication, and motivation to share information. The decision is also affected by the interviewer's perception of participant factors.

Both dichotomous response and multiple-choice questions are valuable but, on balance, the latter are preferred if only because few questions have just two possible answers. Checklist, rating and ranking strategies are also common.

5 Question sequence can drastically affect participant willingness to cooperate and the quality of responses. Generally, the sequence should begin with efforts to awaken the participant's interest in continuing the interview. Early questions should be simple rather than complex, easy rather than difficult, non-threatening and, obviously, germane to the announced objective of the study. Frame-of-reference changes should be minimal, and questions should be sequenced so that early questions do not distort replies to later ones.

6 Sources of questions for the construction of questionnaires include the literature on related research, and sourcebooks of scales and questionnaires. Borrowing items has attendant risks, such as time- and situation-specific problems, or reliability and validity. The incompatibility of language and idiom also needs to be considered.

7 Pre-testing the instrument is recommended to identify problems before the actual collection of data begins. Insights and ideas for refining instruments result from thoroughness in pre-testing. Effective revision is the result of determining participant interest, discovering if the questions have meaning for the participant, checking for participant modification of a question's intent, examining question continuity and flow, experimenting with question-sequencing patterns, evaluating skip instructions for the interviewers, collecting early warning data on item variability, and fixing the length and timing of the instrument.

Discussion questions

Terms in review

1 Distinguish between:
   a   direct and indirect questions
   b   open-ended and closed questions
   c   research, investigative and measurement questions
   d   alternative response strategies.

2 Why is the survey technique so popular? When is it not appropriate?

3 What special problems do open-ended questions have? How can these be minimized? In what situations are open-ended questions most useful?

4 Why might a researcher wish to disguise the objective of a study?

5 One of the major reasons why survey research may not be effective is that the survey instruments are less useful than they should be. What would you say are the four possible major faults of the survey instrument design?

6 Why is it desirable to pre-test survey instruments? What information can you secure from such a pre-test? How can you find the best wording for a question on a questionnaire?

7 One design problem in the development of survey instruments concerns the sequence of questions. What suggestions would you give to researchers designing their first questionnaire?

8 One of the major problems facing the designer of a survey instrument concerns the assumptions made. What are the major 'problem assumptions'?

Making research decisions

9 Below are six questions that might be found on questionnaires. Comment on each as to whether or not it is a good question. If it is not, explain why. (Assume that no lead-in or screening questions are required. Judge each question on its own merits.)
   a   Do you read *National Geographic* magazine regularly?
   b   What percentage of your time is spent asking for information from others in your organization?
   c   When did you first start chewing gum?
   d   How much discretionary buying power do you have each year?
   e   Why did you decide to attend Hull University?
   f   Do you think that the prime minister is doing a good job now?

10 In a class project, students developed a brief self-administered questionnaire by which they might quickly evaluate a professor. One student submitted the following instrument. Evaluate the questions asked and the format of the instrument.

Professor Evaluation Form

1 Overall, how would you rate this professor? _____ Good _____ Fair _____ Poor
2 Does this professor:
   a   have good class delivery? _____
   b   know the subject? _____
   c   have a positive attitude towards the subject? _____
   d   grade fairly? _____
   e   have a sense of humour? _____
   f   use audio-visuals, case examples or other classroom aids? _____
   g   return exams promptly? _____
3 What is the professor's strongest point? _____
4 What is the professor's weakest point? _____
5 What kind of class does the professor teach? _____
6 Is this course required? _____
7 Would you take another course from this professor? _____

11 Below is a copy of a covering letter and mail questionnaire received by a professor who is also a member of the national professional trainer association (NPTA). Please evaluate the usefulness and tone of the letter and the questions and format of the instrument.

Dear NPTA member,

In partial fulfilment of Master's degree work, I have chosen to do a descriptive study of the professional trainer in our country. Using the roster of the NPTA as a mailing list, your name came to me. I am enclosing a short questionnaire and a return envelope. I hope you will take a few minutes and fill out the questionnaire as soon as possible, as the sooner the information is returned to me, the better.

Sincerely,

Professor XYZ

Questionnaire

Directions: please answer as briefly as possible

1 With what company did you enter the field of professional training?

   _____

2 How long have you been in the field of professional training?

   _____

3 How long have you been in the training department of the company where you are presently employed?

   _____

4 How long has the training department in your company been in existence?

   _____

5 Is the training department a subsidiary of another department? If so, what department?

   _____

6 For what functions (other than training) is your department responsible?

   _____

7 How many people, including yourself, are in the training department of your company (local plant or establishment)?

   _____

8 What degrees do you hold and from what institutions?

_____

Major _____

Minor _____

9 Why were you chosen for training? What special qualifications prompted your entry into training?

_____

10 What experience would you consider necessary for an individual to enter into the field of training with your company? Include both educational requirements and actual experience.

From concept to practice

12 Develop a flowchart for instrument design for your Master's research project.

13 Develop a flowchart for instrument design for a study assessing the quality of lectures at your university.

Classroom discussion

14 Take some questionnaires, which were conducted either for scientific or commercial purposes, to your next class session and discuss how they could be improved.

15 Discuss the problems of translating questionnaires to be used in cross-national studies.

Recommended further reading

Converse, Jean M. and Presser, Stanley, _Survey Questions: Handcrafting the Standardized Questionnaire._ **Beverly Hills, CA: Sage, 1986.** A worthy successor to Stanley Payne's classic (see below). Advice on how to write survey questions based on professional experience and the experimental literature.

Deutskens, Elisabeth, de Ruyter, Ko, Wetzels, Martin and Oosterveld, Paul, 'Response rates and response quality of internet-based surveys: an experimental study', _Marketing Letters_ 15(1), 2004, pp. 21–36. This article reports the results of a study on design effects on the response behaviour of people in Internet surveys.

Dillman, Don A., Smyth, Jolene D. and Christian, Leah Melani, _Internet, Mail and Mixed-Mode Surveys: The Tailored Design Method_ **(3rd edn). New York: Wiley, 2008.** A contemporary treatment of Dillman's classic work.

Fink, Arlene, _How to Conduct Surveys: A Step-by-Step Guide_ **(4th edn). Thousand Oaks, CA: Sage, 2008.** Emphasis on computer-assisted and interactive surveys, and a good section on creating questions.

Foddy, William, _Constructing Questions for Interviews and Questionnaires: Theory and Practice in Social Research._ **Cambridge: Cambridge University Press, 1994.** This book provides clear theory-based guidelines on how questions should be formulated.

Payne, Stephen L., _The Art of Asking Questions._ **Princeton, NJ: Princeton University Press, 1992.** An enjoyable book on the many problems encountered in developing useful survey questions. A classic resource.

Sudman, Seymour, Bradburn, Norman N. and Schwarz, Norbert, _Thinking about Answers: Application of Cognitive Processes to Survey Methodology._ **San Francisco, CA: Jossey-Bass, 1995.** This book provides a sound theoretical foundation for surveys.

Get started with understanding statistical techniques!

When you have read this chapter, log on to the Online Learning Centre website at _www.mcgraw-hill.co.uk/textbooks/blumberg_ to explore chapter-by-chapter test questions, additional case studies, a glossary and more online study tools for _Business Research Methods_.

Notes

1 Dorwin Cartwright, 'Some principles of mass persuasion', *Human Relations* 2, 1948, p. 266.

2 Sam Gill, 'How do you stand on sin?' *Tide* (14 March 1947), p. 72.

3 Unaided recall gives respondents no clues as to possible answers. Aided recall gives them a list of radio programmes that were played last night and then asks them which ones they heard. See Harper W. Boyd Jr. and Ralph Westfall, *Marketing Research* (3rd edn). Homewood, IL: Irwin, 1972, p. 293.

4 Gideon Sjoberg, 'A questionnaire on questionnaires', *Public Opinion Quarterly* 18 (Winter 1954), p. 425.

5 More will be said on the problems of readability in Chapter 15.

6 S.A. Stouffer et al., *Measurement and Prediction: Studies in Social Psychology in World War II*, Vol. 4. Princeton, NJ: Princeton University Press, 1950, p. 709.

7 An excellent example of the question revision process is presented in Payne, *The Art of Asking Questions*. Princeton, NJ: Princeton University Press, 1951, pp. 214–25. This example illustrates that a relatively simple question can go through as many as 41 different versions before being judged satisfactory.

8 Robert L. Kahn and Charles F. Cannell, *The Dynamics of Interviewing*. New York: Wiley, 1957, p. 108.

9 Ibid., p. 110.

10 Payne, *The Art of Asking Questions*, p. 140.

11 Ibid., p. 141.

12 Ibid., p. 149.

13 National Opinion Research Center, Proceedings of the Central City Conference on Public Opinion Research. Denver, CO: University of Denver, 1946, p. 73.

14 Hadley Cantril (ed.), *Gauging Public Opinion*. Princeton, NJ: Princeton University Press, 1944, p. 48.

15 Payne, *The Art of Asking Questions*, pp. 7–8.

16 Kahn and Cannell, *The Dynamics of Interviewing*, p. 132.

17 Barbara Snell Dohrenwend, 'Some effects of open and closed questions on respondents' answers', *Human Organization* 24 (Summer 1965), pp. 175–84.

18 Cantril, *Gauging Public Opinion*, p. 31.

19 Jean M. Converse and Stanley Presser, *Survey Questions: Handcrafting the Standardized Questionnaire*. Beverly Hills, CA: Sage, 1986, pp. 50–1.

20 Ibid., p. 51.

21 Frederick J. Thumin, 'Watch for these unseen variables', *Journal of Marketing* 26 (July 1962), pp. 58–60.

22 F. Cannell and Robert L. Kahn, 'The collection of data by interviewing', in *Research Methods in the Behavioral Sciences*, (eds) Leon Festinger and Daniel Katz. New York: Holt, Rinehart & Winston, 1953, p. 349.

23 Percival White, *Market Analysis*. New York: McGraw-Hill, 1921.

24 Eugene J. Webb, Donald T. Campbell, Richard D. Schwartz and Lee Sechrest, *Unobtrusive Measures: Nonreactive Research in the Social Sciences*. Chicago: Rand McNally, 1966.

25 Converse and Presser, *Survey Questions*, p. 52.

26 W.R. Belson, *The Design and Understanding of Survey Questions*. Aldershot, England: Gower, 1981, pp. 76–86.

27 The sections in this chapter on the methods and purposes of pre-testing have largely been adapted from Converse and Presser, *Survey Questions*, pp. 51–64; and Survey Research Center, *Interviewer's Manual* (rev. edn). Ann Arbor, MI: Institute for Social Research, University of Michigan, 1976, pp. 133–4. For an extended discussion of the phases of pre-testing, see Converse and Presser, *Survey Questions*, pp. 65–75.

CHAPTER 14

Measurement and scales

Chapter contents

Learning objectives

When you have read this chapter, you should understand:

1 the distinction between measuring objects, properties and indicants of properties

2 the similarities and differences between the four scale types used in measurement, and when each is used

3 the four major sources of measurement error

4 the criteria for evaluating the soundness of a measurement approach

5 the six critical decisions involved in selecting an appropriate measurement scale

6 the various scale formats for measurement, and how to construct each.

The nature of measurement

In everyday usage, **measurement** occurs when an established yardstick verifies the height, weight or another feature of a physical object. How well you like a song, a painting or the personality of a friend is also a measurement. In a dictionary-definition sense, to measure is to discover the extent, dimensions, quantity or capacity of something, especially by comparison with a standard. We measure casually in daily life, but in research the requirements for measurement are rigorous. Measurement in research consists of assigning numbers to empirical events in compliance with a set of rules. This definition implies that measurement is a three-part process:

1 selecting observable empirical events
2 developing a set of mapping rules – a scheme for assigning numbers or symbols to represent aspects of the event being measured
3 applying the mapping rule(s) to each observation of that event.[1]

Assume you are studying people who attend a car show where all of the year's new models are on display. You are interested in learning the male-to-female ratio among attendees. You observe those who enter the show area. If a person is female, you record an F; if male, an M. Any other symbols, such as 0 and 1 or # and %, may also be used if you know what group the symbol identifies. Exhibit 14.1 uses this example to illustrate the above components.

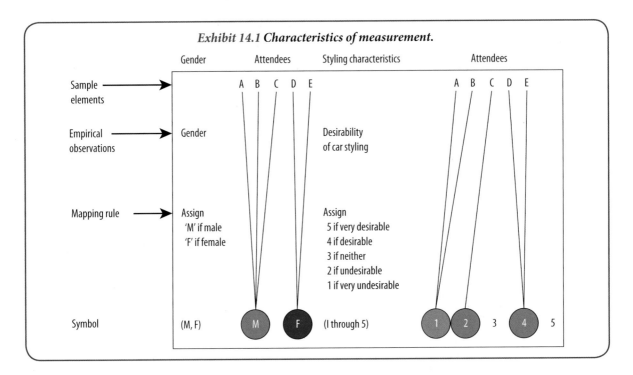

Exhibit 14.1 Characteristics of measurement.

Researchers may also wish to measure, say, the desirability of the styling of the new BMW 3 series. With this in mind, they interview a sample of visitors and assign, with a different mapping rule, their opinions to the following scale.

What is your opinion of the styling of the BMW 3 series?

Very desirable   Very undesirable

          5   4   3   2   1

Numbers as symbols within a mapping rule can reflect both qualitative and quantitative concepts. The goal of measurement – indeed, the goal of 'assigning numbers to empirical events in compliance with a set of rules' – is to provide the highest-quality, lowest-error data for testing hypotheses. Researchers deduce from a hypothesis that certain conditions should exist. Then they measure these conditions in the real world. If found, the data lend support to the hypothesis; if not found, researchers conclude the hypothesis is faulty. An important question at this point is, 'Just what does one measure?'

What is measured?

Variables being studied in research may be classified as objects or as properties. **Objects** include the things of ordinary experience, such as tables, people, books and cars. Objects also include things that are not as concrete as these, such as attitudes, opinions and peer-group pressures. **Properties** are the characteristics of the objects. A person's physical properties may be stated in terms of weight, height and posture. Psychological properties include attitudes and intelligence. Social properties include class affiliation, status, number or kind of friends. These and many other properties of an individual can be measured in a research study.

In a literal sense, researchers do not measure either objects or properties. They measure indicants of the properties or indicants of the properties of objects. It is easy to observe that A is taller than B and that C participates more than D in a group process. Or suppose you are analysing members of a sales force of several hundred people to learn what personal properties contribute to sales success. The properties are age, years of experience and number of calls made per week. The indicants in these cases are so accepted that one considers the properties to be observed directly.

In contrast, it is not easy to measure properties like 'motivation to succeed', 'ability to withstand stress', 'problem-solving ability' and 'persuasiveness'. Since each property cannot be measured directly, one must infer its presence or absence by observing some indicant or pointer measurement. When you begin to make these inferences, there is often disagreement about how to operationalize the indicants.

Not only is it a challenge to measure such constructs, but a study's quality depends on what measures are selected or developed, and how they fit the circumstances. The nature of measurement scales, sources of error and characteristics of sound measurement are considered next.

Data types

In measuring, one devises a mapping rule and then translates the observation of property indicants using this rule. For each concept or construct, several types of data are possible; the appropriate choice depends on what you assume about the mapping rules. Each data type has its own set of underlying assumptions about how the numerical symbols correspond to real-world observations.

Mapping rules have four characteristics:

1 Classification: numbers are used to group or sort responses. No order exists.
2 Order: numbers are ordered and transitivity applies. A is greater than (>), less than (<) or equal to (=) B and if A > B > C, then A is also greater than (>) C.
3 Distance: differences between numbers are ordered. The difference between any pair of numbers is greater than, less than or equal to the difference between any other pair of numbers.
4 Origin: the number series has a unique origin indicated by the number zero.

Combinations of these characteristics of classification, order, distance and origin provide four widely used classification of measurement scales:

1 nominal
2 ordinal
3 interval
4 ratio.

The characteristics of these measurement scales are summarized in Exhibit 14.2. As shown, ratio variables contain the most information and nominal variables the least information. Moreover, you can easily transform a ratio variable into an interval, ordinal or nominal variable, but not the other way around, that is, in Exhibit 14.2 you can move upwards, but not downwards. Age is clearly a ratio variable if you would have asked for the number of years; if you would have asked for age categories (e.g., 15 years and younger; 16–25 years; 26–35 years; 36–45 years; 46–55 years; and 56 years and older), you would have an ordinal scale; and if you would have asked 'Are you an adult, i.e. 18 years or older?' you would get a nominal variable. If you know the age in years (ratio level), you could classify each respondent into the different age categories (ordinal level) or determine whether a respondent is adult or not (nominal) level. Consequences of the data type for statistical analyses are discussed in the online chapters.

Exhibit 14.2 Types of data and their measurement characteristics.

Type of data	Data characteristics				Basic empirical operation	Example
	Classification	Order	Distance	Origin		
Nominal	+				Determination of equality	Gender (male vs. female)
Ordinal	+	+			Determination of greater or lesser value	Doneness of meat (well, medium, rare) School marks
Interval	+	+	+		Determination of equality of intervals or differences	Temperature in Celsius
Ratio	+	+	+	+	Determination of equality of ratios	Age in years Profits in €

Nominal data

In business and social science research, **nominal data** are probably quite often collected. With nominal data, you are collecting information on a variable that naturally or by design can be grouped into two or more categories that are mutually exclusive and collectively exhaustive.

Exhibit 14.3 Mapping rules.

Mapping Rule A	Mapping Rule B
1 = agriculture and fishing	1 = manufacturing
2 = utility	2 = wholesale and retail
3 = food	3 = service
4 = manufacturing	4 = other
5 = hotels and restaurants	
6 = transport	
7 = business services	

The counting of members in each group is the only possible arithmetic operation when a nominal scale is employed. If we use numerical symbols within our mapping rule to identify categories, these numbers are recognized as labels only and have no quantitative value. Nominal classifications may consist of any number of separate groups if the groups are mutually exclusive and collectively exhaustive. Thus, one might classify the businesses in a city according to their industry. Mapping Rule A, given in Exhibit 14.3, is not a sound nominal scale because it is not collectively exhaustive, that is, there will be businesses that do not fit any of the categories such as a grocery shop. Mapping Rule B meets the minimum requirements, although this classification may be more useful for some research purposes than others. The category 'others' is often used as a final category to ensure exhaustiveness of a mapping rule.

Nominal scales are the least powerful of the four data types. They suggest no order or distance relationship, and have no arithmetic origin. The scale wastes any information a sample element might share about varying degrees of the property being measured.

Since the only quantification is the number count of cases in each category (the frequency distribution), the researcher is restricted to the use of the mode as the measure of central tendency.[2] You can conclude which category has the most members, but that is all. There is no generally used measure of dispersion for nominal scales. Several tests for statistical significance may be utilized; the most common is the chi-square test. For measures of association, phi, lambda or other measures may be appropriate.

While nominal data are weak, they are still useful. If no other scale can be used, one can almost always classify one set of properties into a set of equivalent classes. Moreover, nominal measures are often sufficient if you are less interested in securing precise measurements, but in more explorative work and uncovering relationships. For example, you might argue that the benefits of networking activities depend on the technological dynamics in the industry. Rather than securing a precise measurement for technological dynamics, you could take a low- and a high-technology industry and investigate whether networking activities differ between the two industries. This data type is also widely used in survey and other *ex-post facto* research when data are classified by major sub-groups of the population. Classifications such as participants' marital status, gender, political persuasion or exposure to a certain experience abound. Cross-tabulations of these and other variables provide insight into important data patterns. Researchers often classify their objects into nominal categories and (implicitly) assume that a category reflects certain characteristics that can at least be interpreted as ordinal. An example will serve to illustrate this.

Suppose you investigate customer loyalty to a specific bank and you discover that customers living in a rural area are less likely to switch to another bank than customers living in cities. Interpretations of this result are that competition between banks in rural areas is lower and, consequently, customers have fewer banks to choose from, or that people living in rural areas have a stronger attitude to maintaining existing relationships and are more reluctant to make any changes. Both interpretations seem reasonable and additional research may indeed reveal that competition among banks is lower in rural areas and that the attitudes of rural people differ from those of city people. Strictly speaking, though, both interpretations are not backed up by data and it would be necessary to measure the competition in the specific regions, for example the number of banks operating there, or a direct measurement of the respondent's openness to change using a psychological scale. Interpreting the nominal scale 'rural and city' as an ordered scale is questionable, because not every rural area is characterized by low competition between banks and because not every rural resident has a high resistance to change.

Sometimes, however, interpreting a nominal scale as an ordinal scale can be reasonable. Suppose you divide a group of employees into those with a university degree and those without. The statement that the former group has gained a higher education is very reasonable, because the nominal categorization is basically derived from the construct 'educational level' or 'years of schooling'.

Ordinal data

Ordinal data include the characteristics of the nominal scale plus an indicator of order. Ordinal data are possible if the transitivity postulate is fulfilled. This postulate states that 'if a is greater than b and b is greater than c, then a is greater than c'.[3] The use of an ordinal scale implies a statement of 'greater than' or 'less than' (an equality statement is also acceptable) without stating *how much* greater or less. While ordinal measurement speaks of 'greater than' and 'less than' measurements, other descriptors may be used – 'superior to', 'happier than', 'poorer than' or 'above'. Like a rubber yardstick, this can stretch varying amounts at different places along its length. Thus, the difference between ranks 1 and 2 on a happiness scale may be larger or smaller than the difference between ranks 2 and 3.

An ordinal concept can be generalized beyond the three cases used in the simple illustration of a > b > c. Any number of cases can be ranked.

A third extension of the ordinal concept occurs when more than one property is of interest. We may, for example, ask a taster to rank varieties of wine in terms of acid, flavour, colour and a combination of these characteristics. We can secure the combined ranking either by asking the participant to base his or her ranking on the combination of properties or by constructing a combination ranking of the individual rankings on each property. To develop this overall index, the researcher typically adds and averages ranks for each of the three properties. This procedure is technically incorrect for ordinal data and, especially for a given participant, may yield misleading results. When the number of participants is large, however, these errors average out. A more sophisticated way of combining a number of dimensions into a total index is to use a multidimensional scale (see Chapter 19).

The researcher faces another difficulty when combining the rankings of several participants. Here again, it is not uncommon to use weighted sums of rank values for a combined index. If there are many observations, this approach will probably give adequate results, though it is not theoretically correct. A better way is to convert ordinal data into **interval data**, the values of which can then be added and averaged. One well-known example is Thurstone's Law of Comparative Judgement.[4] In its simplest form, Thurstone's procedure says that the distance between scale positions of two objects, A and B, depends on the percentage of judgements in which A is preferred to B.

Examples of ordinal data include opinion and preference scales. Because the numbers of such scales have only a rank meaning, the appropriate measure of central tendency is the median. A percentile or quartile measure reveals the dispersion. Correlation is restricted to various rank-order methods. Measures of statistical significance are technically confined to that body of methods known as non-parametric methods.[5]

Researchers in the behavioural sciences differ about whether more powerful parametric significance tests are appropriate with ordinal measures. One position is that this use of parametric tests is incorrect on both theoretical and practical grounds:

> "If the measurement is weaker than that of an interval scale, by using parametric methods tests the researcher would 'add information' and thereby create distortions."[6]

At the other extreme, some behavioural scientists argue that parametric tests are usually acceptable for ordinal data:

> "The differences between parametric and rank-order tests were not great insofar as significance level and power were concerned."[7]

A view between these extremes recognizes that there are risks in using parametric procedures on ordinal data, but these risks are usually not great:

> "The best procedure would seem to be to treat ordinal measurements as though they were interval measurements but to be constantly alert to the possibility of gross inequality of intervals."[8]

Because non-parametric tests are abundant, simple to calculate, have good power efficiencies and do not force the researcher to accept the assumptions of parametric testing, we advise their use with nominal and ordinal data. It is understandable, however, that because parametric tests (such as the t-test or analysis of variance) are so versatile, accepted and understood, they will continue to be used with ordinal data when those data approach interval data characteristics.

Interval data

Interval data have the power of nominal and ordinal data plus one additional strength: they incorporate the concept of equality of interval (the distance between 1 and 2 equals the distance between 2 and 3). Calendar time is one such scale. For example, the elapsed time between 3 and 6 a.m. equals the time between 4 and 7 a.m. One cannot say, however, that 6 a.m. is twice as late as 3 a.m., because 'zero time' is an arbitrary origin. Centigrade and Fahrenheit temperature scales are other examples of classical interval scales. Both have an arbitrarily determined zero point. Many attitude scales are presumed to be interval. Thurstone's differential scale was an early effort to develop such a scale.[9] Users also treat intelligence scores, semantic differential scales and many other multipoint graphical scales as interval.

When a scale is interval, you use the arithmetic mean as the measure of central tendency. You can compute the average time of first arrival of trucks at a warehouse or the average attitude value on an election for union workers versus non-union workers. The standard deviation is the measure of dispersion for arrival times or worker opinions. Product moment correlation, t-tests, F-tests and other parametric tests are the statistical procedures of choice.[10]

When the distribution of scores computed from interval data lean in one direction or the other (skewed right or left), we use the median as the measure of central tendency and the interquartile range as the measure of dispersion. The reasons for this are discussed in Chapter 16.

Ratio data

Ratio data incorporate all the powers of the previous data types plus the provision for absolute zero or origin. Ratio data represent the actual amounts of a variable. Measures of physical dimensions such as weight, height, distance and area are examples. In the behavioural sciences, few situations satisfy the requirements of the ratio scale – the area of psychophysics offering some exceptions. In business research, we find ratio scales in many areas. There are money values, population counts, distances, return rates, productivity rates and amounts of time in a time-period sense.

All statistical techniques mentioned up to this point are usable with ratio scales. Other manipulations carried out with real numbers may be done with ratio-scale values. Thus, multiplication and division can be used with this scale but not with the others mentioned. Geometric and harmonic means are measures of central tendency, and coefficients of variation may also be calculated.

Researchers often encounter the problem of evaluating variables that have been measured at different data levels. The gender of an accountant is a nominal, dichotomous variable, and salary is a ratio variable. Certain statistical techniques require the measurement levels to be the same.

Since the nominal variable does not have the characteristics of order, distance or point of origin, we cannot create them artificially after the fact. The ratio-based salary variable, on the other hand, can be reduced. Rescaling salary downwards into high-low, high-medium-low or another set of categories simplifies the comparison of nominal data. This example may be generalized to other measurement situations – that is, converting or rescaling a variable involves reducing the measure from the more powerful and robust level to a lesser one.[11] The loss of measurement power accompanying this decision is sometimes costly in that only non-parametric statistics can then be used in data analysis. Thus, the design of the measurement questions should anticipate such problems and avoid them where possible.

14.3 Sources of measurement differences

The ideal study should be designed and controlled for precise and unambiguous measurement of the variables. Since 100 per cent control is unattainable, error does occur. Much potential error is **systematic error** (results from a bias) while the remainder is **random error** (occurs erratically). One authority has pointed out several sources from which measured differences can come.[12]

Assume you are conducting an *ex-post facto* study of the residents of a major city. The study concerns the Prince Corporation, a large retailer with its headquarters and several shops located in the city. The objective of the study is to discover the public's opinions about the company and the origin of any generally held adverse opinions.

Error sources

Ideally, any variation of scores among the participants would reflect true differences in their opinions about the company. Attitudes towards the firm as an employer, as an ecologically sensitive organization or as a progressive corporate citizen would be expressed accurately. However, four major error sources may contaminate the results:

1 participant
2 situational factors
3 measurer
4 data-collection instrument.

We now look at each of these in turn.

Participant

Opinion differences that affect measurement come from relatively stable characteristics of the participant. Typical of these are employee status, ethnic group membership, social class and nearness to plants. The skilled researcher will anticipate many of these dimensions, adjusting the design to eliminate, neutralize or otherwise deal with them. However, even the skilled researcher may not be as aware of less obvious dimensions. The latter variety might be a traumatic experience a given respondent had with a former employer about whom he is questioned. Participants may be reluctant to express strong negative (or positive) feelings or opinions that they perceive as being different from those of others, or they may have little knowledge about Prince but be reluctant to admit this ignorance. This reluctance can lead to an interview of 'guesses'.

Participants may also suffer from temporary factors like fatigue, boredom, anxiety or other distractions; these limit the ability to respond accurately and fully. Hunger, impatience or general variations in mood may also have an impact.

Situational factors

These potential problem areas are legion. Any condition that places a strain on the interview or measurement session can have a serious effect on the interviewer–participant rapport. If another person is present, that person can distort responses by joining in, by distracting or merely by their very presence. If the participants believe anonymity is not guaranteed, they may be reluctant to express certain feelings. Curbside or intercept interviews are unlikely to elicit elaborate responses, while in-home interviews do so more often.

Measurer

The interviewer can distort responses by rewording, paraphrasing or reordering questions. Stereotypes in appearance and action introduce bias. Inflections of voice and conscious or unconscious prompting with smiles, nods, and so on, may encourage or discourage certain replies. Careless mechanical processing – checking the wrong response or failure to record full replies – will obviously distort findings. In the data analysis stage, incorrect coding, careless tabulation and faulty statistical calculation may introduce further errors.

Data-collection instrument

A defective instrument can cause distortion in two major ways. First, it can be too confusing and ambiguous. The use of complex words and syntax beyond participant comprehension is typical. Leading questions, ambiguous meanings, mechanical defects (inadequate space for replies, response choice omissions, poor printing, etc.), and multiple questions suggest the range of problems.

A more elusive type of instrument deficiency is poor selection from the universe of content items. Seldom does the instrument explore all the potentially important issues. The Prince Corporation study might treat company image in areas of employment and ecology but omit the company management's civic leadership, its support of local education programmes or its position on minority issues. Even if the general issues are studied, the questions may not cover enough aspects of each area of concern. While we might study the Prince Corporation's image as an employer in terms of salary and wage scales, promotion opportunities and work stability, perhaps such topics as working conditions, company management relations with organized labour, and retirement and other benefit programmes should also be included.

Characteristics of sound measurement

What are the characteristics of a good measurement tool? An intuitive answer to this question is that the tool should be an accurate counter or indicator of what we are interested in measuring. In addition, it should be easy and efficient to use. There are three major criteria for evaluating a measurement tool:

- Validity refers to the extent to which a test measures what we actually wish to measure.
- Reliability has to do with the accuracy and precision of a measurement procedure.
- Practicality is concerned with a wide range of factors of economy, convenience and interpretability.[13]

In the following sections, we discuss the nature of these qualities and how researchers can achieve them in their measurement procedures.

Validity

Many forms of **validity** are mentioned in the research literature, and the number grows as we expand the concern for more scientific measurement. This text features two major forms: external and internal validity.[14] The external validity of research findings refers to the data's ability to be generalized across persons, settings and times; we discussed this in reference to sampling in Chapter 6, and in reference to experiments in Chapter 12.[15] In this chapter, we discuss only the internal validity of measurements. Hence, internal validity is further limited in this discussion to the ability of a research instrument to measure what it is purported to measure. Does the instrument really measure what its designer claims it does?

Research Methods in Real Life
Measuring attitudes to copyright infringement

In the midst of the Napster file-swapping controversy, and in connection with an issue centring on privacy issues, the editors of *American Demographics* hired TNS Intersearch to conduct a study of adults regarding their behaviour and attitudes relating to copyright infringement. The survey instrument for the telephone study asked 1,051 adult respondents several questions about activities that might or might not be considered copyright infringement. The lead question asked about specific copyright-related activities.

Do you know someone who has done or tried to do any of the following?

1 Copying software not licensed for personal use.
2 Copying a prerecorded videocassette such as a rental or purchased video.
3 Copying a prerecorded audiocassette or compact disc.
4 Downloading music free of charge from the Internet.
5 Photocopying pages from a book or magazine.

A subsequent question asked respondents: 'In the future, do you think that the amount of (ACTIVITY) will increase, decrease or stay the same?' Each respondent was also asked to select a phrase from a list of four 'that best describes how you feel about (ACTIVITY)', and to select a phrase from a list of four phrases that 'best describes what you think may happen as a result of (ACTIVITY)'. The last content question asked the degree to which respondents would feel favourably towards a company that provided 'some type of media content for free': more favourable, less favourable or 'it wouldn't impact your impression of the company'.

As you might expect, younger adults had different behaviours and attitudes compared to older adults on some indicants.

What measurement issues were involved in this study?

References and further reading

Data tabulation generated by TaylorNelson Sofres Intersearch.

John Fetto, 'Americans voice their opinions on intellectual property rights violations', *American Demographics*, September 2000, p. 8.

Measurement instrument prepared by TaylorNelson Sofres Intersearch.

www.americandemographics.com

www.tnsglobal.com

Validity in this context is the extent to which differences found with a measuring tool reflect true differences among participants being tested. We want the measurement tool to be sensitive to all the nuances of meaning in the variable and to changes in nuances of meaning over time. The difficulty in meeting the test of validity is that usually one does not know what the true differences are. Without direct knowledge of the dimension being studied, you must face the question, 'How can one discover validity without directly confirming knowledge?' A quick answer is to seek other relevant evidence that confirms the answers found with the measurement device, but this leads to a second question: 'What constitutes relevant evidence?' There is no short answer this time. What is relevant depends on the nature of the research problem and the researcher's judgement. One way to approach this question is to organize the answer according to measure-relevant types. One widely accepted classification consists of three major forms of validity (see Exhibit 14.4):

1 content validity
2 criterion-related validity
3 construct validity.[16]

We now look at each of these in turn.

Exhibit 14.4 Summary of validity estimates.

Type	What is measured	Methods
Content	Degree to which the content of the items adequately represents the universe of all relevant items under study	Judgemental or panel evaluation with content validity ratio
Criterion-related	Degree to which the predictor is adequate in capturing the relevant aspects of the criterion	Correlation
Concurrent	Description of the present; criterion data are available at the same time as predictor scores	
Predictive	Prediction of the future; criterion data are measured after the passage of time	
Construct	Answers the question, 'What accounts for the variance in the measure?' Attempts to identify the underlying construct(s) being measured and determine how well the test represents it (them)	Judgemental correlation of proposed test with established measures (scales) Convergent-discriminant techniques

---

Content validity

The **content validity** of a measuring instrument (the composite of measurement scales) is the extent to which it provides adequate coverage of the investigative questions guiding the study. If the instrument contains a representative sample of the universe of subject matter of interest, then content validity is good. To evaluate the content validity of an instrument, one must first agree on what elements constitute adequate coverage. Let us use an example: suppose you are interested in the question, 'How ethical are managers?' We must decide what behaviours, attitudes and opinions are relevant to the measurement of ethics, that is, which topics cover managers' ethics. One could limit the topics to issues corresponding to legal offences, such as falsifying documents or using insider information. One could also include actions that are not legal offences but considered 'wrong', such as intentionally gossiping or taking advantage of legal loopholes. If the data-collection instrument adequately covers the topics that have been defined as the relevant dimensions, we conclude that the instrument has good content validity.

Determination of content validity is judgemental and can be approached in several ways. First, the designer may determine it through a careful definition of the topic of concern, the items to be scaled and the scales to be used. This logical process is often intuitive and unique to each research designer.

A second way to determine content validity is to use a panel of people to judge how well the instrument meets the standards. A panel independently assesses the test items for a performance test. It judges each item to be essential, useful but not essential, or not necessary, in assessing performance of a relevant behaviour. The 'essential' responses on each item from each panel list are evaluated by a content validity ratio, and those meeting a statistical significance value are retained. In both informal judgements and in this systematic process, 'content validity is primarily concerned with inferences about test construction rather than inferences about test scores'.[17] It is important not to define content too narrowly. If you were to secure only superficial expressions of opinion in the study of managers' ethics, it would probably not have adequate content coverage.

Criterion-related validity

Criterion-related validity reflects the success of measures used for prediction or estimation. You may want to predict an outcome or estimate the existence of a current behaviour or condition. These are predictive and concurrent validity, respectively. They differ only in a time perspective. An opinion questionnaire that correctly forecasts the outcome of a union election has predictive validity. An observational method that correctly categorizes families by current income class has concurrent validity. While these examples appear to have simple and unambiguous validity criteria, there are difficulties in estimating validity. Consider the problem of estimating family income. There clearly is a knowable true income for every family. However, we may find it difficult to secure this figure, because next to wage incomes the family income can also consist of income from capital or other irregular income streams, such as profits from incidental sales on eBay, for instance. Respondents are more likely to forget reporting such smaller and less frequent parts of their income. Thus, while the criterion is conceptually clear, it may be unavailable.

In other cases, there may be several criteria, none of which are completely satisfactory. Consider again the problem of judging success among the sales force at SalePro (which we looked at in Chapter 2). A researcher may want to develop a pre-employment test that will predict sales success. There may be several possible criteria, none of which individually tells the full story. Total sales per salesperson may not adequately reflect territory market potential, competitive conditions or the different profitability rates of various products. One might rely on the sales manager's overall evaluation, but how unbiased and accurate are those impressions? The researcher must ensure that the validity criterion used is itself 'valid'. One source suggests that any criterion measure must be judged in terms of four qualities:

1 relevance
2 freedom from bias
3 reliability
4 availability.[18]

A criterion is relevant if it is defined and scored in the terms we judge to be the proper measures of salesperson success. If you believe sales success is adequately measured by monetary sales volume achieved per year, then it is the relevant criterion. If you believe success should include a high level of penetration of large accounts, then sales volume alone is not fully relevant. In making this decision, you must rely on your judgement in deciding what partial criteria are appropriate indicants of salesperson success.

Freedom from bias is attained when the criterion gives each salesperson an equal opportunity to score well. The sales criterion would be biased if it did not show adjustments for differences in territory potential and competitive conditions.

A reliable criterion is stable or reproducible. An erratic criterion (using monthly sales, which are highly variable from month to month) can hardly be considered a reliable standard by which to judge performance on a sales employment test. Yet if an unreliable criterion is the only one available, it is often chosen for the study's purpose. In such a case, it is possible to use a 'correction for attenuation' formula that lets you see what the correlation between the test and the criterion would be if they were made perfectly reliable.[19]

Finally, the information specified by the criterion must be available. If it is not available, how much will it cost to access it and how difficult will it be to secure? The amount of money and effort that should be spent on development of a criterion depends on the importance of the problem for which the test is used.

Once there are test and criterion scores, they must be compared in some way. The usual approach is to correlate them. For example, you might correlate test scores of 40 new salespeople with first-year sales achievements adjusted to reflect differences in territorial selling conditions.

Construct validity

One may also wish to measure or infer the presence of abstract characteristics for which no empirical validation seems possible. Attitude scales, and aptitude and personality tests generally, concern concepts that fall into this category. Although this situation is much more difficult, some assurance is still needed that the measurement has an acceptable degree of validity.

In attempting to evaluate **construct validity**, we consider both the theory and the measuring instrument being used. If we were interested in measuring the effect of ceremony on organizational culture, the way in which 'ceremony' was operationally defined would have to correspond to an empirically grounded theory. Once assured that the construct was meaningful in a theoretical sense, we would next investigate the adequacy of the instrument. If a known measure of ceremony in organizational culture was available, we might correlate the results obtained using this measure with those derived from our new instrument. Such an approach would provide us with preliminary indications of convergent validity.

Returning to our example above, another method of validating the ceremony construct would be to separate it from other constructs in the theory or related theories. To the extent that ceremony could be separated from stories or symbols, we would have completed the first steps towards discriminant validity. Established statistical tools such as factor analysis and multitrait–multimethod analysis help determine the construct adequacy of a measuring device.[20]

In the Prince Corporation study, you may be interested in securing a judgement of 'how good a citizen' the firm is. Variations in participant ratings may be drastically affected if substantial differences exist among the participants regarding what constitutes proper corporate citizenship. One participant may believe that any company is an economic organization designed to make profits for its stockholders. She sees a relatively little role for corporations in the wide-ranging social issues of the day. At the other end of the continuum, another participant views the corporation as a leader in solving social problems, even at the expense of profits.

Both of these participants might understand Prince's role in the community but judge it quite differently in light of their differing views about what its role should be. If these different views were held, you would theorize that other information about these participants would be logically compatible with their judgements. You might expect the first participant to oppose high corporate taxes, to be critical of increased involvement of government in family affairs, and to believe that a corporation's major responsibility is to its stockholders. The second participant would be more likely to favour high corporate income taxes, to opt for more governmental involvement in daily life, and to believe that a corporation's major responsibility is a social one.

Participants may not be consistent on all questions because the measurements may be crude and the 'theory' may be deficient. When hypothesized tests do not confirm the measurement scale, you are faced with a two-sided question: 'Is your measurement instrument invalid or is your theory invalid?' These answers require more information or the exercise of judgement.

We discuss the three forms of validity separately, but they are interrelated, both theoretically and operationally. Predictive validity is important for a test designed to predict employee success. In developing such a test, you would probably first postulate the factors (constructs) that provide the basis for useful prediction. For example, you would advance a theory about the variable in employee success – an area for construct validity. Finally, in developing the specific items for inclusion in the success prediction test, you would be concerned with how well the specific items sample the full range of each construct (a matter of content validity).

In the corporate image study for the Prince Corporation, both content and construct validity considerations have been discussed, but what about criterion-related validity? The criteria are less obvious than in the employee success prediction, but judgements will be made of the quality of evidence about the company's image. The criteria used may be both subjective – 'Does the evidence agree with what we believe?' – and objective – 'Does the evidence agree with other research findings?'

Looking at Exhibit 14.5, we can approach the concepts of validity and reliability by using an archer's bow and target as an analogy. High reliability means that repeated arrows shot from the same bow would hit the target in essentially the same place – although not necessarily the intended place (upper row of the graphic). If we had a bow with high validity as well, then every arrow would hit the bull's-eye (upper-left panel). If reliability is low or decreases for some reason, arrows would be more scattered (lacking similarity or closeness, like those shown in the lower row).

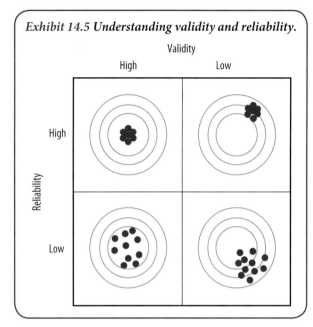

Exhibit 14.5 Understanding validity and reliability.

High validity means that the bow would shoot true every time. It would not pull to the right or send an arrow careening into the woods. Arrows shot from a high-validity bow will be clustered around a central point (the bull's-eye), even when they are dispersed by reduced reliability (left column of the graphic). We would not hit the bull's-eye we were aiming at because the low-validity bow – like the flawed data-collection instrument – would not perform as planned. When low validity is compounded by low reliability, the pattern of arrows is not only off bull's-eye but is also dispersed (lower-right panel).

Research Methods in Real Life
Footprint prices

That carbon dioxide is one of the main causes for global warming is now a fact rather than a suspicion. Most scientists agree that carbon dioxide is causing global warming. Carbon dioxide is always emitted if we use fossil-based fuel, such as oil and gas, to generate energy for heating, cooling or moving. Every time we use fossil-based fuel we leave a footprint, a carbon footprint, symbolizing the damage to our planet.

How can we measure the size of our footprints and the removal costs? Although air travel accounts for less than 5 per cent of the total carbon dioxide emissions, it has become a primary target for non-profit organizations to increase our awareness that consuming energy has external effects. A possible reason is certainly that kerosene, the fuel aircraft need, is less taxed, if at all, than fuel for cars. For example, many German petrol stations inform their customers that the tax share of each litre of petrol is 86 per cent, more than for any other goods that individuals purchase. The common rationale for taxing petrol is that driving a car creates external effects (costs) that need to be covered.

Aircraft fuel has not been taxed yet and this raises the question of how to measure the external costs of air travel. Recently, a couple of organizations offered certificates to individuals for emitting carbon dioxide. Thus, everybody can voluntarily buy certificates that cover the environmental costs of emitting carbon dioxide. Suppose you live in London and plan a weekend trip to Berlin. You buy a return ticket from

London Heathrow (LHR) to Berlin Tegel (TXL) and you want to pay off your carbon footprint. Exhibit 14.6 shows you how different organizations assess the size of your footprint (in kg of emitted carbon dioxide) and the price they charge to remove that footprint.

Exhibit 14.6 *Prices of footprints.*

Organization (website)	Footprint of airtravel LHR-TXL-LHR (kg CO_2)	Costs of footprint removal in (€)	Cost per ton (€)
terrapass.com	235	4.59	19.53
climatecare.org	230	2.00	8.70
Southpolecarbon.com	857	14.57	17.00
lufthansa.com	294	6.00	20.41
carbonfund.org*	1,130	8.54	7.56

Note: calculations based on accessing the websites on 14 May 2013.

*carbonfund.org allows you to calculate your precise carbon footprint which is 270 kg according to their calculator, but to offset your footprint they offer a standard package for two flights up to 6,000 miles assumed to produce 1,130 kg CO_2.

What do we see? First, we see that the emission caused by the trip differs for each organization. While climatecare.org calculates 202 kg of carbon dioxide emissions, Southpolecarbon.org estimates the footprint at 857 kg and carbonfund.org categorizes all flights below 6,000 miles to produce 1,130 kg. What explains these large differences? First, among others the carbon footprint will depend on the fuel efficiency of the used aircraft and on the assumed load factor, i.e. the share of seats sold. Second, it will depend on whether you only consider the CO_2 emissions of burning the fuel or you include the CO_2 emissions of producing and transporting the fuel.

The next step, transforming emissions to a price, even increases the differences between the certificates' prices. It seems that Lufthansa's carbon-offsetting projects cost almost three times as much as those of carbonfund.org. Does this suggest the latter have found a more efficient way to remove the footprint? Or more to the point, which organization should you purchase a certificate from to ensure that the footprint of your trip to Berlin has really been removed?

Given these uncertainties in calculating the amount of emissions and pricing them, it might not be surprising that British Airways stopped their carbon footprint offsetting program by September 2011. They replaced it with a new program called 'one destination', in which passengers can donate to sustainability projects that do not just care about the environment, but take a broader perspective and care for local communities, diversity and inclusion as well. What is the right response to measuring difficulties? Taking a broader approach or trying hard although you know it will never be perfect?

References and further reading

www.onedestination.co.uk/about-one-destination/

https://shop.southpolecarbon.com/en/category/flight

www.climatecare.org

www.carbonfund.org/individuals

www.lufthansa.com/uk/en/Carbon-Offsetting

www.terrapass.com

Reliability

Reliability means many things to many people, but in most contexts the notion of consistency emerges. A measure is reliable to the degree that it supplies consistent results. Reliability is a necessary contributor to validity but is not a sufficient condition for validity. The relationship between reliability and validity can be simply illustrated with the use of bathroom scales. If the scales measure your weight correctly (using a concurrent criterion such as scales known to be accurate), then they are both reliable and valid. If they consistently overweigh you by six pounds, then they are reliable but not valid. If the scales measure erratically from time to time, then they are not reliable and therefore cannot be valid. So if a measurement is not valid, it hardly matters if it is reliable – because it does not measure what the designer needs to measure in order to solve the research problem. In this context, reliability is not as valuable as validity, but it is much easier to assess.

Reliability is concerned with estimates of the degree to which a measurement is free of random or unstable error. Reliable instruments can be used with confidence that transient and situational factors are not interfering. Reliable instruments are robust; they work well at different times under different conditions. This distinction of time and condition is the basis for frequently used perspectives on reliability: stability, equivalence and internal consistency (see Exhibit 14.7).

Exhibit 14.7 Summary of reliability estimates.

Type	Coefficient	What is measured	Methods
Test-retest	Stability	Reliability of a test or instrument inferred from examinee scores. Same test is administered twice to same subjects over an interval of less than six months	Correlation
Parallel forms	Equivalence	Degree to which alternative forms of the same measure produce same or similar results. Administered simultaneously or with a delay inter-rater estimates of the similarity of observations or scores	Correlation
Split-half, KR20 and Cronbach's alpha	Internal consistency	Degree to which instrument items are homogeneous and reflect the same underlying construct(s)	Specialized correlational formulas

Deeper Insight into Research Methods
Measuring job satisfaction

Measuring the job satisfaction and motivation of employees is a recurring activity in many firms. Within the scientific literature you will find it easy to locate studies reporting such findings, as well as details of how exactly the researchers measured job satisfaction and motivation.

An early account of such a study is a piece of research conducted at five geographically separate units of the Tennessee Valley Authority (TVA), three divisions of an electronics company, and five departments of an appliance manufacturing company. The procedure for developing the measures was first to hold a number of informal interviews with supervisory and non-supervisory employees. From the knowledge acquired, the researchers constructed the questions. These were then pre-tested and revised twice using separate groups of TVA employees. Out of this process came the six-item questionnaire 'Interest in Work Innovation', shown in Exhibit 14.8. This instrument and the others were completed by employees of the three companies.

The reliability of the Interest in Work Innovation Index was measured by a test-retest of individual questions. The retest was done one month after the first test. Correlating the test-retest scores question by ▶

question gave the following results (see the Pearson correlation coefficient in Chapter 19 for more information on how these correlation coefficients were computed).

Question	r
Q1	.72
Q2	.72
Q3	.64
Q4	.67
Q5	.54
Q6	.85

Exhibit 14.8 Interest in work innovation index.

1 In your kind of work, if a person tries to change his or her usual way of doing things, how does it generally turn out?

  (1) _____ Usually turns out worse; the tried and true methods work best in my work.

  (3) _____ Usually doesn't.

  (5) _____ Usually turns out better; our methods need improvement.

2 Some people prefer doing a job in pretty much the same way because this way they can count on always doing a good job. Others like to go out of their way in order to think up new ways of doing things. How is it with you on your job?

  (1) _____ I always prefer doing things pretty much in the same way.

  (2) _____ I mostly prefer doing things pretty much in the same way.

  (4) _____ I mostly prefer doing things in new and different ways.

  (5) _____ I always prefer doing things in new and different ways.

3 How often do you try out, on your own, a better or faster way of doing something on the job?

  (5) _____ Once a week or more often.

  (4) _____ Two or three times a month.

  (3) _____ About once a month.

  (2) _____ Every few months.

  (1) _____ Rarely or never.

4 How often do you get chances to try out your own ideas on the job, either before or after checking with your supervisor?

  (5) _____ Several times a week or more.

  (4) _____ About once a week.

  (3) _____ Several times a month.

  (2) _____ About once a month.

  (1) _____ Less than once a month.

5 In my kind of job, it's usually better to let my supervisor worry about new or better ways of doing things.

  (1) _____ Strongly agree.

  (2) _____ Mostly agree.

  (4) _____ Mostly disagree.

  (5) _____ Strongly disagree.

6 How many times in the past year have you suggested to your supervisor a different or better way of doing something on the job?

  (1) _____ Never had occasion to do this during the past year.

  (2) _____ Once or twice.

  (3) _____ About three times.

  (4) _____ About five times.

  (5) _____ Six to ten times.

  (6) _____ More than ten times had occasion to do this during the past year.

Source: Martin Patchen, *Some Questionnaire Measures of Employee Motivation and Morale*, Monograph No. 41. Ann Arbor, MI: University of Michigan, 1965, pp. 15–16.

Note: Numbers in parentheses preceding each response category indicate the score assigned to each response.

The researchers measured criterion-based validity by comparing worker scores on the six questions to ratings of the same workers by their supervisors. Supervisors were asked to 'think of specific instances where employees in their units had suggested new or better ways of doing the job'. They then ranked employees they personally knew on 'looking out for new ideas'.[21] The median correlation between the index scores and the supervisor ratings was about .35. At TVA, where there was an active suggestion system in operation, they also found that the index scores of those making suggestions were significantly higher than those not making suggestions.

Construct validity was evaluated by comparing scores on the Interest in Work Innovation Index to other job-related variables. Mean scores on the index were computed for 90 work groups at TVA. These means were then correlated with group scores on other variables that were hypothesized to relate to interest in innovation. The results are shown in Exhibit 14.9.

The researchers concluded, 'The Index of Interest in Work Innovation, while a rough one, shows adequate reliability and sufficient evidence of validity to warrant its use in making rough distinctions among groups of people (or among units).'[22] In addition, they tested a short version of the index (items 1, 5 and 6) and found its validity to be almost equal to that of the longer form.

Suppose you were asked to conduct a survey on job satisfaction and motivation for your firm's human resources department. One option would be to use questions from an earlier study. However, the head of the human resources department believes she needs a device tailored to the unique situation of the firm (a belief that is common among many managers and researchers). Such a belief can be costly and time-consuming. Reliability testing may be ignored and validity assessments may be confined to impressions about content. Typically, there is no comparable evidence from other studies by which to calibrate the findings but, currently, so many measures for job satisfaction exist that you should be able to find one that is suitable for your firm and you can even obtain those that are copyrighted from commercial sources.

Exhibit 14.9 Relation of scores on interest in work innovation index* to scores on other job-related variables† for 90 work groups at TVA (Pearson product-moment correlation coefficient, r).

Correlation	Variable name
.44‡	Job difficulty
.39‡	Identification with own occupation
.29‡	Control over work methods
.28‡	Perceived opportunity for achievement
.19	Feedback on performance
.13	Control over goals in work
.06	Need for achievement§
−.05	Pressure from peers to do a good job
.36‡	General job motivation
.36‡	Willingness to disagree with supervisors
.12	Acceptance of changes in work situation
.00	Identification with TVA
.21‖	Overall satisfaction (with pay, promotion, supervisors and peers)

Source: Martin Patcher, *Some Questionnaire Measures of Employee Motivation and Morale*, Monograph No. 41. Ann Arbor: Institute for Social Research, University of Michigan, 1965, p. 24.

Notes:
* The shorter three-item Index B was used for these correlations.
† Variables listed are all indexes; each index is composed of several specific questions.
‡ $p < .01$, two-tailed t-test.
§ This is the Achievement Risk Preference Scale developed by P. O'Connor and J.W. Atkinson (1960).
‖ $p < .05$, two-tailed t-test.

Stability

A measure is said to possess **stability** if you can secure consistent results with repeated measurements of the same person with the same instrument. An observational procedure is stable if it gives the same reading on a particular person when repeated one or more times. It is often possible to repeat observations on a subject and to compare them for consistency. When there is much time between measurements, there is a chance for situational factors to change, thereby affecting the observations. The change would appear incorrectly as a drop in the reliability of the measurement process.

Stability measurement in survey situations is more difficult and less easily executed than in observational studies. While you can observe a certain action repeatedly, you usually can resurvey only once. This leads to a test-retest arrangement – with comparisons between the two tests to learn how reliable they are. Some of the difficulties that can occur in the test-retest methodology and cause a downward bias in stability include:

- time delays between measurements – leads to situational factor changes (also a problem in observation studies)
- insufficient time between measurements – permits the participant to remember previous answers and repeat them, resulting in biased reliability indicators
- participant's discernment of a disguised purpose – may introduce bias if the respondent holds opinions related to the purpose but not assessed with current measurement questions
- topic sensitivity – occurs when the participant seeks to learn more about the topic, or to form new and different opinions, before the retest
- introduction of extraneous moderating variables between measurements – may result in a change in the participant's opinions from factors unrelated to the research.

A suggested remedy is to extend the interval between test and retest (from two weeks to a month). While this may help, the researcher must be alert to the chance that an outside factor will contaminate the measurement and distort the stability score. Consequently, stability measurement through the test-retest approach has limited applications. More interest has centred on equivalence.

Equivalence

A second perspective on reliability considers how much error may be introduced by different investigators (in observation) or different samples of items being studied (in questioning or scales). Thus, while stability is concerned with personal and situational fluctuations from one time to another, **equivalence** is concerned with variations at one point in time among observers and samples of items. A good way to test for the equivalence of measurements by different observers is to compare their scoring of the same event. An example of this is the scoring of Olympic figure skaters by a panel of judges.

In studies where a consensus among experts or observers is required, the similarity of the judges' perceptions is sometimes questioned. How does a panel of supervisors render a judgement on image improvements, a new product's packaging or future business trends? Inter-rater reliability may be used in these cases to correlate the observations or scores of the judges and render an index of how consistent their ratings are.

The major interest with equivalence is typically not how participants differ from item to item but how well a given set of items will categorize individuals. There may be many differences in response between two samples of items, but if a person is classified the same way by each test, then the tests have good equivalence. One tests for item sample equivalence by using alternative or parallel forms of the same test administered to the same persons simultaneously.

Research Methods in Real Life

Figure skating: a sport on thin ice

Figure skating is among the best-loved events at any Winter Olympics. The (gold) medal winners in the women's single, men's single, mixed pairs and ice dance often become the superstars of the games. In addition, an Olympic medal in figure skating really pays off. Medal winners can easily switch from amateur status to professional, presenting their skills and talents on ice at commercial ice shows, such as *Holiday on Ice*. Such professional ice show contracts pay very well.

Such a background makes figure skating an ideal setting for drama. But to complicate matters further, figure skating lacks by its very nature an objective instrument to measure the athletes' performance. Nine judges determine who wins the competition by casting scores simultaneously (from 0 to 6) on technical performance (weight: one-third) and on presentation (weight: two-thirds). Doubts on the system's justice had already arisen during the Winter Olympics 1998 in Nagano. Jean Senf, a Canadian judge, produced audiotaped evidence to prove that he had been approached by Yuri Balkov, a Ukrainian judge, to agree on a vote-swapping arrangement.

In 2002, at the Winter Olympics in Salt Lake City, USA, another drama was added to the history of figure skating. The Russian pair, Elena Berezhnaya and Anton Sikharulidze, emerged on to the ice and skated to the classical music piece 'Thais' by Jules Massenet. Although their performance contained several surprising and innovative elements, it also contained six technical errors. Next, Jamie Sale and David Pelletier came on to the ice and skated to the theme from *Love Story*, presenting a programme that was similar to those showcased in two previous international competitions. The judges from Canada, Germany, Japan and the USA usually prefer more 'traditional' presentations and marked the Canadian pair in first place. The judges from China, Poland, Russia and Ukraine ranked the Russian pair first. The French judge, Marie-Reine La Gougne, had the decisive position and voted for Berezhnaya and Sikharulidze, who were awarded the gold medal. The spectators in the ice hall were outraged and responded to the decision of the judges with whistles and boos.

A few hours later, it was reported that La Gougne had been pressured to vote for the Russian pair by Didier Gailhaguet, president of the French Skating Federation, as part of a 'contra-deal' to secure votes for the French couple, Marina Anissina and Gwendal Peizarat, who were to appear in the ice dance competition. Although La Gougne later recast her vote, a scandal was unavoidable. The International Skating Federation took action and immediately suspended La Gougne as a judge and Gailhaguet as a member of the French Skating Federation, and decided that the Salt Lake City gold medal in pairs' figure skating would be awarded jointly to Berezhnaya/Sikharulidze and Sale/Pelletier.

The current system of assessing athletes' performances obviously does not work well at all.

How could the International Skating Federation improve the system?

References and further reading

'Figure skating: a sport on thin ice' (www.time.com/time/arts/article/0,8599, 203477–2,00.html).

The results of the two tests are then correlated. Under this condition, the length of the testing process is likely to affect the subjects' responses through fatigue, and the inferred reliability of the parallel form will be reduced accordingly. Some measurement theorists recommend an interval between the two tests to compensate for this problem. This approach, known as delayed equivalent forms, is a composite of test-retest and the equivalence method. As in test-retest, one would administer form X followed by form Y to half the examinees and form Y followed by form X to the other half to prevent 'order-of-presentation' effects.[23]

The researcher can include only a limited number of measurement questions in an instrument. This limitation implies that a sample of measurement questions from a content domain has been chosen and another sample producing a similar number will need to be drawn for the second instrument. It is frequently difficult to create this second set. Yet if the pool is initially large enough, the items may be randomly selected for each instrument. Even with the more sophisticated procedures used by publishers of standardized tests, it is rare to find fully equivalent and interchangeable questions.[24]

Internal consistency

A third approach to reliability uses only one administration of an instrument or test to assess the **internal consistency** or homogeneity among the items. The split-half technique can be used when the measuring tool has many similar questions or statements to which the subject can respond. The instrument is administered and the results are separated by item into even and odd numbers, or into randomly selected halves. When the two halves are correlated, if the results of the correlation are high the instrument is said to have high reliability in an internal consistency sense. The high correlation tells us that there is similarity (or homogeneity) among the items. The potential for incorrect inferences about high internal consistency exists when the test contains many items, which inflates the correlation index.

The Spearman–Brown correction formula is used to adjust for the effect of test length and to estimate the reliability of the whole test. A problem with this approach is that the way the test is split may influence the internal consistency coefficient. To remedy this, other indexes are used to secure reliability estimates without splitting the test's items. The Kuder–Richardson Formula 20 (KR20) and Cronbach's coefficient alpha are two frequently used examples. Cronbach's alpha has the most utility for multi-item scales at the interval level of measurement. The KR20 is the method from which alpha was generalized and is used to estimate reliability for dichotomous items (see Exhibit 14.7).

Improving reliability

The researcher can improve reliability by choosing among the following options:

- Minimize external sources of variation.
- Standardize conditions under which measurement occurs.
- Improve investigator consistency by using only well-trained, supervised and motivated persons to conduct the research.
- Broaden the sample of measurement questions used by adding similar questions to the data-collection instrument, or adding more observers or occasions to an observational study.
- Improve internal consistency of an instrument by excluding data from analysis drawn from measurement questions eliciting extreme responses. This approach requires the assumption that a high total score reflects high performance and a low total score, low performance. One selects the extreme scorers – say, the top 20 per cent and bottom 20 per cent – for individual analysis. By this process, you can distinguish those items that differentiate high and low scorers. Items that have little discriminatory power can then be dropped from the test.

Practicality

The scientific requirements of a project call for the measurement process to be reliable and valid, while the operational requirements call for it to be practical. **Practicality** has been defined as economy, convenience and interpretability.[25] While this definition refers to the development of educational and psychological tests, it is meaningful for business measurements too.

Economy

Some trade-off usually occurs between the ideal research project and the budget. Instrument length is one area where economic pressures dominate. More items give more reliability, but in the interests of limiting the interview or observation time (and therefore costs), we hold down the number of measurement questions. The choice of data-collection method is also often dictated by economic factors. The rising cost of personal interviewing first led to an increased use of long-distance telephone surveys and, subsequently, to the current rise in online surveys. In standardized tests, the cost of test materials alone can be such a significant expense that it encourages multiple re-use. Add to this the need for fast and economical scoring, and you can see why computer scoring and scanning are attractive.

Convenience

A measuring device passes the convenience test if it is easy to administer. A questionnaire with a set of detailed but clear instructions, with examples, is easier to complete correctly than one that lacks these features. In a well-prepared study, it is not uncommon for the interviewer instructions to be several times longer than the interview questions. Naturally, the more complex the concepts, the greater the need for clear and complete instructions. We can also make the instrument easier to administer by paying close attention to its design and layout. Crowding of material, poor reproduction of illustrations, and the carry-over of items from one page to the next make completion of the instrument more difficult.

Interpretability

This aspect of practicality is relevant when persons other than the test designers must interpret the results. It is usually, but not exclusively, an issue with standardized tests. In such cases, the designer of the data-collection instrument provides several key pieces of information to make interpretation possible:

- a statement of the functions the test was designed to measure and the procedures by which it was developed
- detailed instructions for administration
- scoring keys and instructions
- norms for appropriate reference groups
- evidence about reliability
- evidence regarding the inter-correlations of sub-scores
- evidence regarding the relationship of the test to other measures
- guides for test use.

The nature of measurement scales

When you develop measurement questions for your research study, you will often be called upon to choose between standardized scales and custom-designed ones. When what you measure is concrete (e.g. the length of an assembly line), you will usually choose a standardized measure (like measuring the assembly line with an electronic range-finder or tape-measure). When what you want to measure is a more abstract and complex construct (like customer attitudes about a product service programme), standardized measures may neither exist nor provide a close enough fit to a particular manager's scenario. In these situations, developing a customized scale to measure the construct is the only option. Otherwise, you are left to measure a construct with a tool designed for something else. This would be like measuring the length of the assembly line with your forearm instead of visible laser-beam technology.

The remainder of this chapter covers procedures that will help you to understand measurement scales, so that you can select or construct measures that are appropriate to your research. We will concentrate on the problems of measuring more complex constructs, like attitudes and opinions.

Scaling defined

Scaling is a 'procedure for the assignment of numbers (or other symbols) to a property of objects in order to impart some of the characteristics of numbers to the properties in questions'.[26]

What is scaled?

Procedurally, we assign numbers to indicants of the properties of objects. Thus one assigns a number scale to the various levels of heat and cold, and calls it a thermometer. If you want to measure the temperature of the air, you know that a property of temperature is that its variation leads to an expansion or contraction of mercury. A glass tube with mercury provides an indicant of temperature change by the rise or fall of the mercury in the tube.

In another context, you might devise a scale to measure the durability (property) of paint. You secure a machine with an attached scrub brush that applies a predetermined amount of pressure as it scrubs. You then count the number of brush strokes that it takes to wear through a 1 mm thickness of paint. The scrub count is the indicant of the paint's durability. Or you may judge a person's supervisory capacity (property) by asking a peer group to rate that person on various questions (indicants) that you create.

Scale selection

Scaling may be reviewed in several ways, but here we cover those approaches that are of greatest value for management research.[27] Selection or construction of a measurement scale requires decisions in six key areas:

1 study objective
2 response form
3 degree of preference
4 data properties
5 number of dimensions
6 scale construction.

We now look at each of these in turn.

Study objective

Researchers face two general study objectives:

1 to measure certain characteristics of the participants who complete the study
2 to use participants as judges of the objects or indicants presented to them.

Assume you've been contracted by the city of Amager Beach to conduct a study supposedly of visitors' approval or disapproval of one or more regulatory programmes. In the first type of study, your scale would measure the visitors' political orientation as conservative or liberal. You might combine each person's answers to form an indicator of that person's political orientation. The emphasis in this first study objective is on measuring attitudinal differences among people. With the second study objective, you might use the same data but in this case you are really interested in how satisfied people are with different governmental programmes. In this study objective, your real interest is in the differences in the acceptance level of one or more regulatory programmes.

Response form

Measurement scales are of three types: rating, ranking and categorization. A rating scale is used when participants score an object or indicant without making a direct comparison to another object or attitude. For example, they may be asked to evaluate the styling of a new car on a five-point rating scale. Ranking scales constrain the study participant to make comparisons among two or more indicants or objects. Participants may be asked to choose which one of a pair of cars has the more attractive styling. They could also be asked to order the importance of comfort, ergonomics, performance and price for the target vehicle. **Categorization** asks participants to put themselves or property indicants in groups or categories. Asking car show participants to identify their gender or ethnic background, or to indicate whether a particular prototype car design would attract a youthful or mature clientele, would require a categorization response strategy.

Degree of preference

Measurement scales may involve preference measurement or non-preference evaluation. In the former, each participant is asked to choose the object he or she favours or the solution he or she would prefer. In the latter, participants are asked to judge which object has more of some characteristic or which solution takes the most resources, without reflecting any personal preference towards objects or solutions.

Data properties

Measurement scales may also be viewed in terms of the data properties generated by each scale. Earlier, we saw that data are classified as nominal, ordinal, interval or ratio. The assumptions underlying each data type determine how a particular measurement scale's data can be handled statistically.

Number of dimensions

Measurement scales are either unidimensional or multidimensional. With a **unidimensional scale**, one seeks to measure only one attribute of the participant or object. One measure of employee potential is promotability. It is a single dimension. Several items may be used to measure this dimension and, by combining them into a single measure, a manager may place employees along a linear continuum of promotability. Multidimensional scaling recognizes that an object might be better described in an attribute space of n-dimensions rather than on a unidimensional continuum. The employee promotability variable might be better expressed by three distinct dimensions: managerial performance, technical performance and teamwork.

Scale construction

We can classify measurement scales by the methods used to build them. Five construction approaches are used in research practice:

1 *Arbitrary*: a scale is custom-designed to measure a property or indicant. Arbitrary scales may measure the concepts for which they have been designed, but the researcher has no advance evidence of a particular scale's validity and reliability. Nevertheless, researchers commonly choose this construction approach.
2 *Consensus*: developed by a panel of judges, who evaluate the items to be included based on topical relevance and lack of ambiguity.
3 *Item analysis*: measurement scales are tested with a sample of participants. In item analysis, after administering the test, a total score is calculated for each scale. Individual items (a scale or part of a scale) are then analysed to determine which best discriminate between persons or objects with high total scores and low total scores.
4 *Cumulative*: scales are chosen for their conformity to a ranking of items with ascending and descending discriminating power. In the cumulative approach, the endorsement of an item that represents an extreme position results in the endorsement of all items of less extreme positions.
5 *Factoring*: scales are constructed from inter-correlations of items from other studies. Finally, in factoring, common factors account for the relationships. The relationships are measured statistically through factor analysis or cluster analysis.[28]

The business researcher studies both the type of measurement scale and the scale's construction when selecting an appropriate scale. These topics form the basis for the remainder of the chapter.

Student Research
Entrepreneurial intentions

At the 2003 Lisbon summit, European leaders took the first steps for a turn in the EU enterprise and innovation policy with the objective that the EU should be the most competitive and knowledge-driven economy by 2010. One of the major issues for that process has been the removal of red tape to encourage entrepreneurship throughout Europe, as lacking entrepreneurship is one of the major reasons for the missing economic dynamics in Europe. But who are the future entrepreneurs? In the USA, many knowledge-intensive companies are founded by graduate students and people with a university background, but just 10 per cent of European students ever consider becoming an entrepreneur. These figures triggered Anthony Jackson to write a research project on the entrepreneurial intentions of students at Bath University.

More specifically, he wanted to investigate to what extent on the one hand personality traits, such as proactive personality and risk-taking propensity, and on the other hand participation in entrepreneurship courses affect entrepreneurial intentions. In other words, Anthony wanted to shed some light on the question of whether entrepreneurship could be in part taught or whether it only depends on the people themselves.

The research question involves concepts that are deeply rooted in psychology, such as intentions, personality and risk-taking propensities; concepts that are not easily measured, as they are not directly observable. Thus, questionnaires in which respondents report their thoughts, feelings and intuition, were the only viable option to conduct the study. But which questions should Anthony ask? Would it be sufficient to ask: Do you intend to become an entrepreneur? Do you consider yourself as a proactive person? Do you like to take risks?

Certainly such questions would not be a good measurement. Rather than thinking about appropriate questions himself, Anthony looked through the literature to see what other researchers had done before him. He then collected all questions found in previous studies and categorized them along his research variables. Exhibit 14.10 gives you an overview of Anthony's categorization process.

Exhibit 14.10 Measurement questions assigned to theoretical variables.

Entrepreneurial intentions

- Are you currently self-employed?[1]
- Do you plan to become self-employed in the foreseeable future after your graduation?[1]
- Estimate the probability (0–100%) that you start your own business within the next five years?[2]
- Estimate the probability (0–100%) that you start your own business within the next year?[6]

Participation in entrepreneurship education

- Have you ever participated in any form of entrepreneurship education?[6]
- Have you ever participated in entrepreneurship education at Bath University in courses such as 'Advanced Business Innovation' or 'Small Business Management and Accounting'?[6]
- Have you ever participated in entrepreneurship courses from 'Highstarters Bath', such as 'Masterclass Entrepreneurship and Business-planning'?[6]

Proactive personality

- I enjoy facing obstacles and overcoming obstacles to my ideas.[3]
- Nothing is more exciting than seeing my ideas turn into reality.[3]
- I excel at identifying opportunities.[3]
- I love to challenge the status quo.[3]
- I can spot a good opportunity long before others can.[3]

Risk-taking propensity

- I can take risks with my money, such as investing in stocks.[4]
- When I travel I tend to take new routes.[4]
- I like to try new food, new places and totally new experiences.[4]
- Among 10 people, £100 is disposed of by a lottery. What is the most that you would be willing to pay for a ticket in this lottery?[5]
- I will take a serious risk within the next six months.[6]

Sources of questions:

1 Lüthje, C. and N. Franke (2003), 'The making of an entrepreneur: testing a model of entrepreneurial intent among engineering students at MIT', *R&D Management* 33, 135–47.
2 Krueger, N.F., M.D. Reilly and A.L. Carsrud (2000), 'Competing models for entrepreneurial intentions', *Journal of Business Venturing* 15, 411–32.
3 Kickul, J. and L.K. Gundry (2002), 'Prospecting for strategic advantage. The proactive entrepreneurial personality and small firm innovation', *Journal of Small Business Management* 40, 85–97.
4 Hisrich, R.D. and M.P. Peters (2002), *Entrepreneurship* (5th edn). New York: McGraw-Hill.
5 Hartog, J., A. Ferrer-i-Carbonell and N. Jonker (2000), *On a simple measure of individual risk aversion*. Tinbergen Institute Discussion Paper No. 74.
6 Own thoughts.

Reading through the paper, you will see that Anthony sometimes used a scale developed by other researchers; sometimes he combined questions from different sources and sometimes he even added his own questions. For a proactive personality he relied fully on Kickul and Gundry, while for risk-taking propensity he used Hisrich and Peters, Hartog et al. and a question of his own. Regarding participation in entrepreneurship education, Anthony used a couple of very specific items, which were fine-tuned for the respondents he questioned

What do you think about Anthony's measurement strategy? Is it a good idea to combine questions from different sources? Should one ask questions that are applicable to many people or should one ask specific questions for the sample investigated? Is it necessary to develop additional items?

 # Response methods

We said that questioning is a widely used stimulus for measuring concepts and constructs. A manager, for example, may be asked his or her views concerning an employee. The response could be 'a good machinist', 'a troublemaker', 'a union activist', 'reliable' or 'a fast worker with a poor record of attendance'. These answers, because they represent such different frames of reference for evaluating the worker, and thus lack comparability, would be of limited value to the researcher.

Two approaches improve the usefulness of such replies. First, various properties may be separated and the participant asked to judge each specific facet. Here, the researcher would substitute several distinct questions for a single one. Second, the researcher can replace the free-response reply with structuring devices. To quantify dimensions that are essentially qualitative, rating or ranking scales are used.

Rating scales

You can use **rating scales** to judge properties of objects without reference to other similar objects. These ratings may be in such forms as 'like–dislike', approve–indifferent–disapprove' or other classifications using even more categories.

Number of scale points

There is little conclusive support for choosing a three-point scale over scales with five or more points. Some researchers think that the greater the number of points on a rating scale, the greater the sensitivity of measurement and extraction of variance. The most widely used scales range from three to seven points, but it does not seem to make much difference which number is used – with two exceptions.[29] First, a larger number of scale points are needed to produce accuracy when using single-dimension versus multiple-dimension scales. Second, in cross-cultural measurement, the culture may condition participants to a standard metric. In Italy and the Netherlands, school marks are given on a ten-point scale (scores of five and lower are insufficient), while Germans use a six-point scale (scores of five and higher are considered insufficient) and the UK even uses letters from A* (highest grade) to G (lowest grade). Hence, if you used the same six-point scale for a survey conducted in both the UK and Germany, the Germans would interpret the values of the scale in a different way to the British.

Alternative scales

Examples of rating scales are shown in Exhibit 14.11. This exhibit amplifies the overview presented in this section.[30] Later in the chapter, construction techniques for some commonly used rating scales are presented.

Exhibit 14.11 Sample rating scales.

Simple category scale
[dichotomous]
data: nominal

Have you ever been self-employed?
☐ Yes
☐ No

Multiple choice single-response scale
data: nominal

For which department are you working?
☐ Production
☐ Service
☐ Marketing and sales
☐ Research and development
☐ Other (specify: _____)

Multiple-choice multiple-response scale
[checklist]
data: nominal

Check any of the sources where you collect information on new technologies
☐ Visit to suppliers
☐ Visit from suppliers
☐ Trade fairs
☐ Magazines
☐ Informal talk with others
☐ Consulting service firms
☐ Other (specify: _____)

Likert scale summated rating
data: interval

The Internet is superior to traditional libraries for comprehensive searches

STRONGLY AGREE	AGREE	NEITHER AGREE OR DISAGREE	DISAGREE	STRONGLY DISAGREE
(5)	(4)	(3)	(2)	(1)

Semantic differential scale
data: interval

Heathrow Airport

FAST _____ : _____ : _____ : _____ : _____ : SLOW

HIGH QUALITY _____ : _____ : _____ : _____ : _____ : LOW QUALITY

Numerical scale
data: ordinal or* interval

EXTREMELY FAVOURABLE   5   4   3   2   1   EXTREMELY UNFAVOURABLE

Employee's cooperation _____

Employee's knowledge _____

Employee's planning _____

Multiple rating list scale	Please indicate how important or unimportant each service characteristic is						
		IMPORTANT				UNIMPORTANT	
data: interval	Fast reliable repair	7	6	5	4	3	2	1
	Service at my location	7	6	5	4	3	2	1
	Maintenance by manufacturer	7	6	5	4	3	2	1
	Knowledgeable technicians	7	6	5	4	3	2	1
	Notification of upgrades	7	6	5	4	3	2	1
	Service contract after warranty	7	6	5	4	3	2	1

Fixed sum scale
data: ratio

Taking all the supplier characteristics we've just discussed and now considering *cost*, what is their relative importance to you (dividing 100 units)

Being one of the lowest-cost suppliers

All other aspects of supplier performance

Sum   100

Stapel scale
data: ordinal or*
interval

(Company name)

+5	+5	+5
+4	+4	+4
+3	+3	+3
+2	+2	+2
+1	+1	+1
Technology leader	Exciting products	World-class reputation
+1	+1	+1
+2	+2	+2
+3	+3	+3
+4	+4	+4
+5	+5	+5

Graphic rating scale
data: ordinal
or* interval or ratio

How likely are you to recommend British Airways to others?
(Place an X at the position along the line that best reflects your judgement)

VERY LIKELY |————————————————| VERY UNLIKELY

|————————————————|

(Alternative with graphic)

Note: *Earlier in the chapter we noted that researchers differ in the ways that they treat data from certain scales. If you are unable to establish the linearity of the measured variables or you cannot be confident that you have equal intervals, it is proper to treat data from these scales as ordinal.

The **simple category scale** (also called a dichotomous scale) offers two mutually exclusive response choices. In Exhibit 14.11 they are 'yes' and 'no', but they could just as easily be 'important' and 'unimportant', 'male and female' or another set of discrete categories had the question been different. This response strategy is particularly useful for demographic questions or where a dichotomous response is adequate.

When there are multiple options for the rater but only one answer is sought, the **multiple-choice–single-response scale** is appropriate. Our example has five options. The primary alternatives should encompass 90 per cent of the range with the 'other' category completing the participant's list. When there is no possibility for 'other', or exhaustiveness of categories is not critical, the 'other' response may be omitted. Both the multiple-choice, single-response and the simple category scale produce nominal data.

A variation, the **multiple-choice–multiple-response scale** (also called a checklist) allows the rater to select one or several alternatives. In the example in Exhibit 14.11 we are measuring seven items with one question, and it is possible that all seven sources were consulted. The cumulative feature of this scale can be beneficial when a complete picture of the participant's choices is desired. This scale generates nominal data. Answers to a multiple-response scale can be transformed into one single numeric score by assigning unique values to each answer category following the numeric series 2n with n representing the number of categories (i.e. 1, 2, 4, 8, 16, . . .) and then adding the values of all ticked answer categories.

The **Likert scale** is the most frequently used variation of the summated rating scale. Summated scales consist of statements that express either a favourable or unfavourable attitude towards the object of interest. The participant is asked to agree or disagree with each statement. Each response is given a numerical score to reflect its degree of attitudinal favourableness, and the scores may be totalled to measure the participant's attitude. In our example, the participant chooses one of five levels of agreement. The numbers indicate the value to be assigned to each possible answer with 1 the least favourable impression of Internet superiority and 5 the most favourable. These values are not normally printed on the instrument but are shown in Exhibit 14.11 to indicate the scoring system. Between 20 and 25 properly constructed questions about an attitude object would be required for a reliable Likert scale.

Likert scales help us to compare one person's score with a distribution of scores from a well-defined sample group. This measurement scale is useful for a manager when, say, an organization plans to conduct an experiment or undertake a programme of change or improvement. The researcher can measure attitudes before and after the experiment or change, or judge whether the organization's efforts have had the desired effect. This scale produces quasi-interval data. The **semantic differential scale** measures the psychological meanings of an attitude object. Managers use this scale for brand image and other marketing studies of institutional images, political issues and personalities, and organizational studies. It is based on the proposition that an object can have several dimensions of connotative meaning. The meanings are located in multidimensional property space, called semantic space. The method consists of a set of bipolar rating scales, usually with seven points, by which one or more participants rate one or more concepts on each scale item. In the example in Exhibit 14.11, two sets of bipolar pairs are shown, one from the traditional source and one adapted to the research purpose. Based on the construction requirements discussed later, we might choose 10 scale items to score Heathrow Airport.

The semantic differential has several advantages. It produces interval data, and offers an efficient and easy way to secure attitudes from a large sample. These attitudes may be measured in both direction and intensity. The total set of responses provides a comprehensive picture of the meaning of an object and a measure of the subject doing the rating. It is a standardized technique that is easily repeated, but escapes many problems of response distortion found with more direct methods.

Numerical scales have equal intervals that separate their numeric scale points. The verbal anchors serve as the labels for the extreme points. Numerical scales are often five-point scales, as shown in Exhibit 14.11, but may have seven or ten points. The participant writes a number from the scale next to each item. If numerous questions about employee performance were included in the example, the scale would provide both an absolute measure of importance and a relative measure (ranking) of the various items rated. The scale's linearity, simplicity and production of ordinal or interval data make it popular with managers and researchers.

The **multiple rating list scale** is similar to the numerical scale but differs in two ways:

1 It accepts a circled response from the rater.
2 The layout permits the visualization of the results.

The advantage is that a mental map of the participant's evaluations is evident to both the rater and the researcher. This scale produces interval data.

A scale that helps the researcher discover proportions is the **fixed-sum scale**. In the example, two categories are presented that must sum to 100. Up to 10 categories may be used, but both participant precision and patience suffer when too many stimuli are proportioned and summed. A participant's ability to add up is also taxed in some situations; thus this is not a response strategy that can be used effectively with children or the uneducated. The advantage of the scale is its compatibility with per cent (100 per cent) and the fact that continuous data (versus discrete categories) can be compared for the alternatives. The scale is used to record attitudes, behaviour and behavioural intent. It produces interval data.

The **stapel scale** is used as an alternative to the semantic differential, especially when it is difficult to find bipolar adjectives that match the investigative question. In the example in Exhibit 14.11 there are three attributes of corporate image. The scale is composed of the word (or phrase) identifying the image dimension and a set of 10 response categories for each of the three attributes. Fewer response categories are sometimes used. Participants select a plus number for the characteristic that describes the named company. The more accurate the description, the larger is the positive number. Similarly, the less accurate the description, the larger is the negative number chosen. Ratings range from + 5 to − 5, very accurate to very inaccurate. Like the semantic differential, stapel scales usually produce interval data.

The **graphic rating scale** was created to enable researchers to discern fine differences. Theoretically, an infinite number of ratings is possible if the participant is sophisticated enough to differentiate and record them. The participant checks his or her response at any point along a continuum. Usually, the score is a measure of length (e.g. millimetres) from either end point. The results are usually treated as interval data. The difficulty is in coding and analysis. This response strategy requires more time than scales with predetermined categories. Other graphic rating scales use pictures, icons or other visuals to communicate with the rater, and represent a variety of data types. Graphic scales are often used with children, whose more limited vocabulary prevents the use of scales anchored with words.

Deeper Insight into Research Methods
Scaling customer satisfaction

Recently a manufacturer of PADs has experienced increasing customer complaints about the functioning of the PADs. Usually such complaints were taken by the customer service desk and then channelled to the service, repair or customer communication department. Due to the sharp increase in customer complaints Jason, the head of the customer service department, suspects that the complaints are not being handled properly and he would like to investigate the matter. In the process of designing a questionnaire to do this, he encounters the issue of which scales he should choose.

He had narrowed the choice to three scales: a Likert scale, a conventional rating scale with two verbal anchors, and their hybrid expectation scale. All were five-point scales that were presumed to measure at the interval level.

They needed a statement that could accompany the scale for preliminary evaluation. Returning to their list of investigative questions, they found a question that seemed to capture the essence of the repair process: 'Are customers' problems resolved?' Translated into an assertion for the scale, the statement became 'Resolution of problems that prompted service/repair'. It was important for the distance between the numbers to resemble the psychological distance implied by the words. Appropriate versions of the investigative question were constructed and then the scales were added.

After consulting colleagues within the marketing department, Jason discussed the advantages of the scale with Tosca, who works for a marketing research firm. Tosca suggested it was unlikely that the complaint handling would meet none of the customers' expectations. And, with errors of positive leniency, 'none' should be replaced by the term 'few' so the low end of the scale would be more relevant. Jason had read a *Marketing News* article that said Likert scales frequently produced a heavy concentration of 4s and 5s – a common problem in customer satisfaction research.

They also considered a seven-point scale to remedy this but in the end thought that the term exceeded on the expectation scale could compensate for scores that clustered on the positive end, making the end point ▶

less susceptible to leniency. They were ready for a pilot test. They decided to compare their hybrid expectation scale with a conventional Likert rating scale. The Likert scale required that they create more potential items than they had room for on the postcard. Using the Customer Complaint database, names, addresses and phone numbers were selected, and 30 customers were selected at random from those who had had recent service. They chose the delayed equivalent forms method for reliability testing. Tosca administered the expectation scale followed by the satisfaction scale to half of the participants and the satisfaction scale followed by the expectation scale to the other half. Each half of the sample experienced a time delay. No 'order of presentation' effects were found. Subsequently, they correlated the satisfaction scores with the expectation scores and plotted the results, which are shown in Exhibit 14.12.

Exhibit 14.12 Plot of scale evaluation.

Likert scale

The problem that prompted service/repair was resolved

Strongly disagree	Disagree	Neither agree nor disagree	Agree	Strongly agree
1	2	3	4	5

Conventional Likert scale rating

To what extent are you satisfied that the problem that prompted service/repair was resolved?

Very dissatisfied				Very satisfied
1	2	3	4	5

Hybrid expectation scale

Resolution of the problem that prompted service/repair

Met few expectations	Met some expectations	Met most expectations	Met all expectations	Exceeded expectations
1	2	3	4	5

Plot of scale evaluation

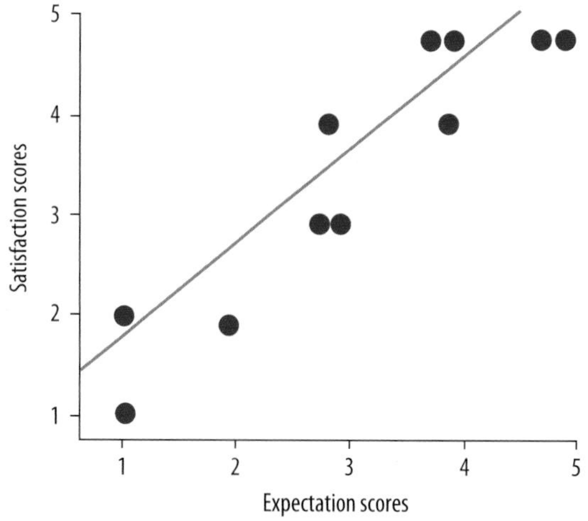

Errors to avoid with rating scales

The value of rating scales for measurement purposes depends on the assumption that a person can and will make good judgements. Before accepting participants' ratings, we should consider their tendencies to make errors of three types:[31]

1 leniency
2 central tendency
3 halo effect.

Leniency

The error of **leniency** occurs when a participant is either an 'easy rater' or a 'hard rater'. The latter is an error of negative leniency. Raters are inclined to score higher people they know well and with whom they are 'ego involved'. The opposite case also applies: where acquaintances are rated lower because one is aware of the tendency towards positive leniency and attempts to counteract it. One way to deal with positive leniency is to design the rating scale to anticipate it. An example might be an asymmetrical scale that has only one unfavourable descriptive term and four favourable terms (poor – fair – good – very good – excellent). The scale designer expects that the mean ratings will be near 'good' and that there will be a symmetrical distribution about that point.

Central tendency

Raters are reluctant to give extreme judgements, and this fact accounts for the error of **central tendency**. This is most often seen when the rater does not know the object or property being rated. To counteract this type of error try taking the following steps:

- Adjust the strength of descriptive adjectives.
- Space the intermediate descriptive phrases further apart.
- Provide smaller differences in meaning between the steps near the ends of the scale than between the steps near the centre.
- Use more points in the scale.

Halo effect

The **halo effect** is the systematic bias that the rater introduces by carrying over a generalized impression of the subject from one rating to another. You may expect the student who does well on the first question of an examination to do well on the second, for instance. You conclude a report is good because you like its form or you believe someone is intelligent because you agree with him or her. Halo is a pervasive error. It is especially difficult to avoid when the property being studied is not clearly defined, not easily observed, not frequently discussed, involves reactions with others or is a trait of high moral importance.[32] One way to counteract the halo effect is to rate one trait at a time for all subjects or to have one trait per page.

Rating scales are widely used in management research and generally deserve their popularity. The results obtained with careful use compare favourably with other methods.

Ranking scales

In **ranking scales**, the subject directly compares two or more objects and makes choices among them. Frequently, the participant is asked to select one as the 'best' or the 'most preferred'. When there are only two choices, this approach is satisfactory, but it often results in 'ties' when more than two choices are found. For example, assume participants are asked to select the most preferred among three or more models of a product. In response, 40 per cent choose model A, 30 per cent choose model B, and 30 per cent choose model C. Which is the preferred model? The analyst would be taking a risk to suggest that A is most preferred. Perhaps that interpretation is correct, but 60 per cent of the participants chose some model other than A. Perhaps all B and C voters would place A last, preferring either B or C to it. This ambiguity can be avoided by using some of the techniques described in this section.

Research Methods in Real Life
Comparing apples and oranges: the PISA report

The Organization for Economic Co-operation and Development (OECD) investigates the educational performance in their member countries every three years in the PISA studies. The last PISA report appeared in 2009, covers 74 countries and is based on test results of 520,000 pupils.

The results of the reports always attract a great deal of attention and have an enormous impact on education policy debates. Especially in countries whose performance was significantly below the average, politicians of all hues called for immediate action. The suggested actions, however, differ considerably. To back their view proponents of certain actions usually refer to the educational systems of top PISA countries. For example, experts suggesting that schools should once again place more emphasis on the learning of facts referred to Korea. Others highlighting full boarding schools and a late selection of children in different school types used Finland as a model example.

Exhibit 14.13 Rating of selected countries in 2009 PISA study.

	Reading literacy (country score in parenthesis)	Mathematical literacy (country score in parenthesis)	Scientific literacy (country score in parenthesis)
OECD Average	493	496	501
Countries scoring significantly above the average score	China Shanghai (556)	China Shanghai (600)	China Shanghai (575)
	Korea (539)	Korea (546)	Finland (554)
	Finland (536)	Chinese Taipei (543)	Japan (539)
	Canada (524)	Finland (541)	Korea (538)
	New Zealand (521)	Switzerland (534)	New Zealand (532)
	Japan (520)	Japan (529)	Canada (529)
	Australia (513)	Canada (527)	Australia (527)
	Netherlands (508)	Netherlands (526)	Netherlands (522)
	Belgium (506)	New Zealand (519)	Germany (520)
	Norway (503)	Belgium (515)	Chinese Taipei (520)
	Estonia (501)	Australia (514)	Switzerland (517)
	Switzerland (501)	Germany (513)	UK (514)
	Poland (500)	Estonia (512)	Slovenia (512)
		Denmark (503)	Poland (508)
		Slovenia (501)	Ireland (508)
			Belgium (507)
Countries with a score not significantly different from the average	USA (500)	Norway (498)	Hungary (503)
	Sweden (497)	France (497)	USA (502)
	Germany (497)	Slovak Republic (497)	Czech Republic (500)
	Ireland (496)	Austria (496)	Norway (500)
	France (496)	Poland (495)	Denmark (499)
	Chinese Taipei (495)	Sweden (494)	France (498)
	Denmark (495)	Czech Republic (493)	
	UK (494)	UK (492)	
	Hungary (494)	Hungary (490)	
	Portugal (489)		

Exhibit 14.13 Continued

	Reading literacy (country score in parenthesis)	Mathematical literacy (country score in parenthesis)	Scientific literacy (country score in parenthesis)
Countries scoring significantly below the average score	Italy (486)	Ireland (487)	Sweden (495)
	Slovenia (483)	USA (487)	Austria (494)
	Greece (483)	Portugal (487)	Portugal (493)
	Spain (481)	Italy (483)	Slovak Republic (490)
	Czech Republic (478)	Spain (483)	Italy (489)
	Slovak Republic (477)	Russia (468)	Spain (488)
	Croatia (476)	Greece (466)	Croatia (486)
	Israel (474)	Croatia (460)	Russia (478)
	Austria (470)	Israel (447)	Greece (470)
	Russia (459)	Argentina (388)	Israel (455)
	Argentina (398)		Argentina (401)

Source: Executive summary PISA 2009 (available online at www.oecd.org/pisa/pisaproducts/46619703.pdf).

Overall, it seems that most educational experts did not try to learn from the PISA report, but handpicked the results that supported the view they held before the report was published. Given its major impact on the political agenda, it seems fair to ask how valid and reliable the results are.

The PISA study is a cross-country measurement of students' performance by asking students (respondents) to answer open and closed test questions. One of the important questions in any cross-country study is whether you measured the same in each country. Two measurement issues arise. First, as the tests were taken in countries with a different mother language, the original questions had to be translated. Half of the original test questions were formulated in French and half in English. To ensure the quality of the translation, the researchers used three independent translators. For example, the first translated the original English question into German, the second would get the German translation and was asked to translate it back into English without knowing anything about the original text and the third would assess the differences between the two previous translations. However, critics point to the fact that countries with French or English as mother tongue score better, on average, than countries with another mother tongue. Does this support the claim that it is purely the language of the test that influences the results?

In addition, students had to answer the questions with a time constraint: the whole test should not exceed two hours. However, German instructions are on average about one-third longer than the same instructions in English. Hence, students taking the test in German needed more time to read the questions and had as a consequence less time to think about the answers. Are differences in country scores caused by using different languages in the measurement?

Some of the test questions are open questions, and markers had to assess the quality of the answers. Of course, these people were instructed as to how to mark answers. A cross-country comparison of markings reveals that in 92 per cent of cases an international verifier agreed with the assessment of the national markers. This result implies that 8 per cent of the markings are somehow ambiguous.

How does this measurement error translate into the significant differences in the performance scores as shown in Exhibit 14.13? You should note a difference of 100 points translates roughly into a difference of two years in schooling.

References

www.oecd.org/pisa/pisaproducts/pisa2009/pisa2009keyfindings.htm

Using the **paired-comparison scale**, the participant can express attitudes unambiguously by choosing between two objects. Typical of paired comparisons would be the bottled water preference example (see Exhibit 14.14). The number of judgements required in a paired comparison is $[(n)(n-1)/2]$, where n is the number of stimuli or objects to be judged. When four bottled waters are evaluated, the participant evaluates six paired comparisons $[(4)(3)/2 = 6]$.

Exhibit 14.14 *Examples of ranking scales.*

Paired-comparison scale

data: ordinal

For each pair of bottled waters listed, place a tick beside the one you would most prefer if you had to choose between them:

—— Perrier & San Pellegrino

—— Highland Spring & Spa

—— Perrier & Highland Spring

—— Spa & San Pellegrino

—— Spa & Perrier

—— San Pellegrino & Highland Spring

Forced ranking scale

data: ordinal

Rank bottled waters in your order of preference.
Place the number 1 next to the most preferred, 2 by the second choice, and so on:

—— Highland Spring

—— Perrier

—— San Pellegrino

—— Spa

Comparative scale

data: ordinal

Compared to the previous bottled water, the taste of this is:

SUPERIOR		ABOUT THE SAME		INFERIOR
——	——	——	——	——
1	2	3	4	5

In another example we might compare two bargaining proposals available to union negotiators (see Exhibit 14.15). Generally, there are more than two stimuli to judge, resulting in a potentially tedious task for participants. If 15 suggestions for bargaining proposals are available, 105 paired comparisons would be made.

Reducing the number of comparisons per participant without reducing the number of objects can lighten this burden. You can present each participant with only a sample of the stimuli. In this way, each pair of objects must be compared an equal number of times. Another procedure is to choose a few objects that are believed to cover the range of attractiveness at equal intervals. All other stimuli are then compared to these few standard objects. If 36 bottled waters are to be judged, four may be selected as standards and the others divided into four groups of eight each. Within each group, the eight are compared to each other. Then the 32 are individually compared to each of the four standard bottled waters. This reduces the number of comparisons from 630 to 240.

Paired comparisons run the risk that participants will tire to the point that they give ill-considered answers or refuse to continue. Opinions differ about the upper limit, but five or six stimuli are not unreasonable when the participant has other questions to answer. If the data collection consists only of paired comparisons, as many as 10 stimuli are reasonable.

While a paired comparison provides ordinal data, there are methods for converting it to interval data. The Law of Comparative Judgement involves converting the frequencies of preferences (such as in Exhibit 14.15) into a table

---

Exhibit 14.15 Response patterns of 200 union members' paired comparisons on five suggestions for bargaining proposal priorities.

Paired-comparison data may be treated in several ways. If there is substantial consistency, we will find that if A is preferred to B, and B to C, then A will be consistently preferred to C. This condition of transitivity need not always be true but should occur most of the time. When it does, take the total number of preferences among the comparisons as the score for that stimulus.

Assume a union-bargaining committee is considering five major demand proposals. The committee would like to know how the union membership ranks these proposals. One option would be to ask a sample of the members to pair-compare the personnel suggestions. With a rough comparison of the total preferences for each option, it is apparent that B is the most popular.

	Suggestion				
	A	B	C	D	E
A	–	164*	138	50	70
B	36	–	54	14	30
C	62	146	–	32	50
D	150	186	168	–	118
E	130	170	150	82	–
Total	378	666	510	178	268
Rank order	3	1	2	5	4
Mp	0.478	0.766	0.610	0.278	0.368
Zj	−0.060	0.730	0.280	−0.590	−0.340
Rj	0.530	1.320	0.870	0.000	0.250

Note: *Interpret this cell, 164 members preferred suggestion B (column) to suggestion A (row).

---

of proportions, which are then transformed into a Z matrix by referring to the table of areas under the normal curve.[33] Guilford's composite-standard method is another alternative.[34]

The **forced ranking scale** shown in Exhibit 14.14 lists attributes that are ranked relative to each other. This method is faster than paired comparisons and is usually easier and more motivating to the participant. With five items, it takes 10 paired comparisons to complete the task, and the simple forced ranking of five is easier. Also, ranking has no transitivity problem where A is preferred to B, and B to C, but C is preferred to A.

A drawback to forced ranking is the number of stimuli that can be handled by this method. Five objects can be ranked easily, but participants may grow careless in ranking 10 or more items. In addition, rank ordering produces ordinal data since the distance between preferences is unknown.

Often the manager or researcher is interested in benchmarking. This calls for a standard by which other programmes, processes, brands, points of sale or people can be compared. The **comparative scale** is ideal for such comparisons if the participants are familiar with the standard. In the Exhibit 14.14 example, the standard is the participant's previous bottled water. The new bottled water is being assessed relative to it. The provision to compare yet other bottled waters to the standard is not shown in the example but is nonetheless available to the researcher.

Some researchers treat the data produced by comparative scales as interval data since the scoring reflects an interval between the standard and what is being compared. We would treat the rank or position of the item as ordinal data unless the linearity of the variables in question could be supported.

None of the ranking methods covered is particularly useful when there are many items. The method of **successive intervals** is sometimes used to sort the items (usually one per card) into piles or groups representing a succession of values. From the sort, an interval scale can then be developed.[35] This procedure is not used frequently and then only in unique studies.

 ## Measurement scale construction

Earlier we discussed scales in terms of the techniques used to construct them. Of the five techniques examined, three are used frequently: the arbitrary approach, item analysis and factoring. These are highlighted in this section along with a preview of multivariate scales (which is described in more detail in Chapter 20). Consensus and cumulative methods receive less attention because they are time-consuming to construct or have fewer management applications. They are mentioned briefly because of their influence on current methods.

Arbitrary scaling

We design **arbitrary scales** by collecting several items that we believe are unambiguous and appropriate to a given topic. Some are chosen for inclusion in the instrument. To illustrate, consider a company image study.

We choose a sample of items that we believe are the components of company image. We might score each of these from 1 to 5, depending on the degree of favourableness reported. The results may be studied in several ways. Totals may be made by individual items, by company, by companies as places to work, for ecological concern, and so on. Totals for each company or for individuals may be calculated to determine how they compare to others. Based on a total for these four items, each company would receive from 4 to 20 points from each participant. These data may also be analysed from a participant-centred point of view. Thus, we might use the attitude scores of each individual to study differences among individuals.

Arbitrary scales are easy to develop, inexpensive, and can be designed to be highly specific. They provide useful information and are adequate if developed skilfully. There are also weaknesses, though. The design approach is subjective. The researcher's insight and ability offer the only assurance that the items chosen are a representative sample of the universe of content (the totality of what constitutes 'company image'). We have no evidence that participants will view all items with the same frame of reference. While arbitrary scales are often used, there has been a great effort to develop construction techniques that overcome some of their deficiencies. An early attempt was consensus scaling.

Consensus scaling

Consensus scaling requires items to be selected by a panel of judges and then evaluated on:

- their relevance to the topic area
- their potential for ambiguity
- the level of attitude they represent.

A widely known form of this approach is the Thurstone **equal-appearing interval scale**. Also known as the Thurstone scale, this approach resulted in an interval rating scale for attitude measurement. Often, 50 or more judges evaluate a large number of statements expressing different degrees of favourableness towards an object. There is one statement per card. The judges sort each card into one of 11 piles representing their evaluation of the degree of favourableness that the statement expresses. The judge's agreement or disagreement with the statement is not involved. Of the 11 piles, three are identified to the judges by labels of 'favourable' and 'unfavourable' at the extremes, and 'neutral' at the midpoint. The eight intermediate piles are left unlabelled to create the impression of equal-appearing intervals between the three labelled positions. This method of scale construction is rarely used in applied management research these days. Its cost, time and staff requirements make it impractical. The importance of this historic method, however, is its influence on the Likert and semantic differential scales.

Research Methods in Real Life
International leagues: the pitfalls of rankings

Rankings are becoming more and more popular; one on the educational performance of pupils based on the PISA study we presented earlier in this chapter. Newspapers regularly publish rankings such as *Business Week*'s ranking of business schools and *The Times*' ranking of the top 100 employers for graduates. And likewise international organizations and research institutes, such as the World Bank, Transparency International or the Penn World Table, publish country rankings with respect to human development, corruption, governance and so on. What is common to all those rankings is that they are usually not based on a single criterion but are a composite of different criteria. Sometimes the detailed background of the composite is known, sometimes just a rough idea is provided.

What are the pitfalls of such composite indices?

1 The underlying figures are often rough estimates, especially figures about developing countries are critical. The Penn World Table estimates the error margin for GDP growth to be up to 40% for sub-Saharan countries. Given that official statistics of those countries are highly unreliable, researchers have tried other methods. One group compares satellite images of night-time lights to assess the differences in economic activities. For some countries the differences are remarkable. The annual average GDP growth between 1992/1993 and 2004/2005 for Myanmar is estimated at 10.02%, while the light data suggest just 3.25%; for Burundi the estimated rate was −0.71% and light data suggested a positive annual growth of 3.04%.

2 The items that an index is based on are narrower than what they suppose to reflect, i.e. the content validity is questionable. Does the number of patents filed really reflect the technological power of a country? First, we know that the majority of patents never turn into sellable products or services. Second, many countries hardly file any or just a few patents. In 2011, China took the first position with more than 530,000 filed patents, the USA followed second with 503,000 and this might reflect the rising technological power of China. But how should one interpret the 71 patents filed by Estonia or the 77 patents filed by Iceland compared to more than 1,000 patents filed by Peru, Morocco and Egypt. Are these three countries much more technologically advanced than Iceland and Estonia?

3 The composition of the index is unclear, i.e. the weights given to different items are unknown. Mercer Consulting publishes quality of living measures for major cities in the world, which is often translated into the best cities to live in. In 2012, Vienna scored the top position. The index is based among others on the following subcategories: consumer goods, natural environment, political and social environment, recreation, schools and socio-cultural environment. What is more important to you, consumer goods or a natural environment and do these preferences hold for everybody? Weighting is problematic as preferences differ.

4 Some rankings are based on surveys and perceptions. Transparency International, an international NGO, publishes the corruption perception index. In its 2012 version, Finland, Denmark and New Zealand share the first place, while Afghanistan. North Korea and Somalia close the list. But whose perceptions are considered, those of people in the respective countries, those of experts on corruption? No matter whose perception we trust, we need to acknowledge that perceptions are always biased.

5 Although the publishers and developers of most serious indices are very cautious in drawing conclusions from their rankings, others using the rankings are less cautious. Small adjustments to the data often change the ranking completely and differences in ranks are often not statistically significant. Take the PISA table earlier in this chapter. The mathematical literacy in Denmark is significantly higher than the OECD mean, while the Norwegian score does not differ from the mean. But from that we cannot conclude that the Danish pupils are better in maths than Norwegians, as the difference between these two countries is not significant. Thus ranking suggest large difference which are often minuscule in reality.

▶

References

Alan Heston, Robert Summers and Bettina Aten, Penn World Table Version 7.1, Center for International Comparisons of Production, Income and Prices at the University of Pennsylvania, July 2012

www.top100graduateemployers.com

www.businessweek.com/bschools/rankings/

https://pwt.sas.upenn.edu/php_site/pwt_index.php

www.wipo.int/export/sites/www/ipstats/en/wipi/pdf/941_2012_stat_tables.pdf

www.mercer.com/qualityofliving

http://transparency.org/whatwedo/publications

J. Vernon Henderson, Adam Storeygard and David N. Weil (2012), 'Measuring Economic Growth from Outer Space', *American Economic Review* 102(2), pp. 994–1028.

Item analysis scaling

Item analysis scaling is a procedure for evaluating an item based on how well it discriminates between those persons whose total score is high and those whose total score is low. The most popular scale using this approach is the summated or Likert scale.

Item analysis involves calculating the mean scores for each scale item among the low scorers and high scorers. The item means between the high-score group and the low-score group are then tested for significance by calculating t values. Finally, the 20 to 25 items that have the greatest t values (significant differences between means) are selected for inclusion in the final scale.[36]

Likert-type scales are relatively easy to construct compared to the equal-appearing interval scale.[37] The first step is to collect a large number of statements that meet two criteria:

1 Each statement is believed to be relevant to the attitude being studied.
2 Each is believed to reflect a favourable or unfavourable position on that attitude.

People similar to those who are going to be studied are asked to read each statement and to state the level of their agreement with it, using a five-point scale. A scale value of 1 might indicate a strongly unfavourable attitude; 5, a strongly favourable attitude (see Exhibit 14.12).

Each person's responses are then added to secure a total score. The next step is to array these total scores and select some portion representing the highest and lowest total scores: say, the top 25 per cent and the bottom 25 per cent. These two extreme groups represent people with the most favourable and least favourable attitudes towards the topic being studied. The extremes are the two criterion groups by which we evaluate individual statements. Through a comparative analysis of response patterns to each statement by members of these two groups, we learn which statements consistently correlate with low favourability and which correlate with high favourability attitudes.

This procedure is illustrated in Exhibit 14.16. In evaluating response patterns of the high and low groups to the statement 'I consider my job exciting', we secure the results shown. After finding the t values for each statement, we rank-order them and select those statements with the highest t values. As an approximate indicator of a statement's discrimination power, Edwards suggests using only those statements whose t value is 1.75 or greater, provided there are 25 or more subjects in each group.[38] To safeguard against response-set bias, we should word approximately one-half of the statements to be favourable and the other half to be unfavourable.

Exhibit 14.16 Evaluating a scale statement by item analysis.

Response categories	Low total score group				High total score group			
	X	f	fX	fX²	X	f	fX	fX²
Strongly agree	5	3	15	75	5	22	110	550
Agree	4	4	16	64	4	30	120	480
Undecided	3	29	87	261	3	15	45	135
Disagree	2	22	44	88	2	4	8	16
Strongly disagree	1	15	15	15	1	2	2	2
Total		73	177	503		73	285	1183
		n_L	ΣX_L	ΣX_L^2	n_H	ΣX_H	ΣX_H^2	

Steps

1 For the statement 'I consider my job exciting', we select the data from the bottom 25 per cent of the distribution (low total score group) and the top 25 per cent (high total score group). There are 73 people in each group. The remaining 50 per cent in the middle of the distribution are not considered for this analysis. For each of the response categories, the scale's value X is multiplied by the frequency or number of respondents (f) who chose that value. These values produce the product (fX). This number is then multiplied by X (fX^2). For example, there are three respondents in the low-score group who scored a 5 (strongly agreed with the statement): (fX) = 5×3 = 15; (fX^2) = 15×5 = 75.
2 The frequencies, products and squares are summed.
3 A mean score for each group is computed.
4 Deviation scores are computed, squared and summed as required for the formula.
5 The data are tested in a modified t-test that compares the high- and low-scoring groups for the item. Notice the mean scores in the numerator of the formula.
6 The calculated value is compared with a criterion, 1.75. If the calculated value (in this case 8.92) is equal to or exceeds the criterion, the statement is said to be a good discriminator of the measured attitude. (If it is less than the criterion, we would consider it a poor discriminator of the target attitude and delete it from the measuring instrument.) We then select the next item and repeat the process.

The Likert scale has many advantages that account for its popularity. It is easy and quick to construct. Each item that is included has met an empirical test for discriminating ability. Since participants answer each item, it is probably more reliable and it provides a greater volume of data than many other scales.

A widely used indicator to test how well different items form one scale is **Cronbach's alpha**. Formally, Cronbach's α is the average correlation between all items corrected for the number of items. It can take values between −1 and +1 and a general rule of thumb is that $\alpha \geq 0.7$ provides a good scale. Nevertheless, you should not use Cronbach's α without thought about the content of the items and the construct they should measure. A good scale for a construct is based on items covering the construct's full breadth. If the items cover just one aspect of the construct, that is, items are only superficially dissimilar, you will usually get a high Cronbach's α, as the items are very similar and therefore highly correlated. But despite the high Cronbach's α, the scale is poor, as it neglects import aspects of the construct.

Cumulative scaling

Total scores on **cumulative scales** have the same meaning. Given a person's total score, it is possible to estimate which items were answered positively and which negatively. A pioneering scale of this type was the **scalogram**. Scalogram analysis is a procedure for determining whether a set of items forms a unidimensional scale.[39] A scale is unidimensional if the responses fall into a pattern in which endorsement of the item reflecting the extreme position also results in endorsing all items that are less extreme.

Assume we are surveying opinions regarding a bottled water called 'Pure Source'. We have developed a preference scale of four items as follows:

1 'Pure Source' tastes good.
2 I will insist on 'Pure Source' next time because it tastes great.
3 The flavour of 'Pure Source' is acceptable to me.
4 I prefer the taste of 'Pure Source' to other tastes.

Participants indicate whether they agree or disagree with each item. If these items form a unidimensional scale, the response patterns will approach the ideal configuration as shown in Exhibit 14.17.

Exhibit 14.17 *Ideal scalogram response pattern.*

Item				Respondent Score
I will insist on 'Pure Source' next time because it tastes great	I prefer the 'Pure Source' taste to other tastes	'Pure Source' tastes good	The flavour of 'Pure Source' acceptable to me	
2	4	1	3	
X	X	X	X	4
–	X	X	X	3
–	–	X	X	2
–	–	–	X	1
–	–	–	–	0
X = Agree		– = Disagree		

A score of 4 indicates that all statements are agreed upon and represents the most favourable attitude. Persons with a score of 3 should disagree with item 2 but agree with all others, and so on. According to scalogram theory, this pattern confirms that the universe of content (attitude towards the appearance of this running shoe) is scalable.

The scalogram and similar procedures for discovering underlying structure are useful for assessing behaviours that are highly structured, such as social distance, organizational hierarchies and evolutionary product stages.[40] Although used less often today, the scalogram retains potential for managerial applications.

Factor scaling

Factor scales include a variety of techniques that have been developed to address two problems:

1 how to deal with a universe of content that is multidimensional
2 how to uncover underlying (latent) dimensions that have not been identified by exploratory research.

These techniques are designed to inter-correlate items so that their degree of interdependence may be detected. There are many approaches that the advanced student will want to explore, such as latent structure analysis (of which the scalogram is a special case), factor analysis, cluster analysis, and metric and non-metric multidimensional scaling. We limit the discussion in this section to the semantic differential (SD), which is based on factor analysis.[41]

Osgood and his associates developed the semantic differential method to measure the psychological meanings of an object to an individual.[42] They produced a long list of adjective pairs useful for attitude research. Searching *Roget's Thesaurus* for such adjectives, they located 289 pairs. These were reduced to 76 pairs that were formed into rating scales. They chose 20 concepts that evoked the psychological meanings they wished to probe. The concepts from this historical study illustrate the wide applicability of the technique to persons, abstract concepts (such as leadership), events, institutions and physical objects.[43]

By factor-analysing the data, they concluded that semantic space is multidimensional rather than unidimensional. Three factors contributed most to meaningful judgements by participants:

1 evaluation
2 potency
3 activity.

The evaluation dimension usually accounts for one-half to three-quarters of the extractable variance. (The evaluation dimension is the only dimension possessed by Likert scales.) Potency and activity are about equal, and together account for a little over one-quarter of the extractable variance. Occasionally, the potency and activity dimensions combine to form 'dynamism'. The results of the thesaurus study are shown in Exhibit 14.18.

Exhibit 14.18 Results of the thesaurus study based on Osgood et al.

Evaluation (E)		Potency (P)	Activity (A)
Good–bad		Hard–soft	Active–passive
Positive–negative		Strong–weak	Fast–slow
Optimistic–pessimistic		Heavy–light	Hot–cold
Complete–incomplete		Masculine–feminine	Excitable–calm
Timely–untimely		Severe–lenient	Tenacious–yielding

Sub-categories of evaluation

Meek goodness	*Dynamic goodness*	*Dependable goodness*	*Hedonistic goodness*
Clean–dirty	Successful–unsuccessful	True–false	Pleasurable–painful
Kind–cruel	High–low	Reputable–disreputable	Beautiful–ugly
Sociable–unsociable	Meaningful–meaningless	Believing–sceptical	Sociable–unsociable
Light–dark	Important–unimportant	Wise–foolish	
Meaningful–meaningless			
Altruistic–egotistical	Progressive–regressive	Healthy–sick	
Grateful–ungrateful		Clean–dirty	
Beautiful–ugly			
Harmonious–dissonant			

Source: adapted from Charles E. Osgood, G.J. Suci and P.H. Tannenbaum, *The Measurement of Meaning*. Urbana, IL: University of Illinois Press, 1957, Table 5, pp. 52–61.

The SD scale should be adapted to each research problem. SD construction involves the following steps:

1 Select the concepts. The concepts are nouns, noun phrases or non-verbal stimuli such as visual sketches. Concepts are chosen by judgement and reflect the nature of the investigative question. Or in a study to evaluate multiple candidates for an executive position in an industry association, the concept might be a candidate, for example 'Darnell Williams'.

2 Select the original bipolar word pairs or pairs you adapt to your needs. If the traditional Osgood items are used, several criteria guide your selection. The first is the factor(s) composition.

   a You need at least three bipolar pairs for each factor to use evaluation, potency and activity. Scores on these individual items should be averaged, by factor, to improve their test reliability.

   b The scale must be relevant to the concepts being judged. Choose adjectives that allow connotative perceptions to be expressed. Irrelevant concept-scale pairings yield neutral midpoint values that convey little information.

   c Scales should be stable across subjects and concepts. A pair such as 'large–small' may be interpreted by some to be denotative when judging a physical object such as a 'car' but may be used connotatively in judging abstract concepts such as 'quality management'.

   d Scales should be linear between polar opposites and pass through the origin. A pair that fails this test is 'rugged–delicate', which is non-linear on the evaluation dimension. When used separately, both adjectives have favourable meanings.[44]

Exhibit 14.19 shows the scale being used by a panel of corporate leaders to rate candidates for an industry leadership position. The selection of concepts in this case is simple: there are three candidates, plus a fourth – the ideal candidate.

Exhibit 14.19 SD scale for analysing candidates for an industry leadership position.

Analyse (candidate) for current position:

(E)	Sociable	(7):	:____	:____	:____	:____	:____	:____	:____	: (1) Unsociable
(P)	Weak	(1):	:____	:____	:____	:____	:____	:____	:____	: (7) Strong
(A)	Active	(7):	:____	:____	:____	:____	:____	:____	:____	: (1) Passive
(E)	Progressive	(7):	:____	:____	:____	:____	:____	:____	:____	: (1) Regressive
(P)	Yielding	(1):	:____	:____	:____	:____	:____	:____	:____	: (7) Tenacious
(A)	Slow	(1):	:____	:____	:____	:____	:____	:____	:____	: (7) Fast
(E)	True	(7):	:____	:____	:____	:____	:____	:____	:____	: (1) False
(P)	Heavy	(7):	:____	:____	:____	:____	:____	:____	:____	: (1) Light
(A)	Hot	(7):	:____	:____	:____	:____	:____	:____	:____	: (1) Cold
(E)	Unsuccessful	(1):	:____	:____	:____	:____	:____	:____	:____	: (7) Successful

The nature of the problem determines the selection of dimensions and bipolar pairs. Since the person who wins this position must influence business leaders, we decide to use all three factors. The candidate must deal with many people, often in a social setting; must have high integrity; and must take a leadership role in encouraging more progressive policies in the industry. The position will also involve a high degree of personal activity. Based on these requirements, we choose 10 scales to score the candidates from 7 to 1. The negative signs in the original scoring procedure (−3, −2, −1, 0, +1, +2, +3) were found to produce coding errors.

Exhibit 14.19 illustrates the scale used for the research. The letters along the left side, which show the relevant factor, would be omitted from the actual scale, as would the numerical values shown. Note also that the evaluation, potency and activity scales are mixed, and about half are reversed to minimize the halo effect. To analyse the results, the set of evaluation (E) values is averaged, as are those for the potency (P) and activity (A) dimensions.

The data are plotted in Exhibit 14.20. Here the adjective pairs are reordered so evaluation, potency and activity descriptors are grouped together with the ideal factor reflected by the left side of the scale. Profiles of the three candidates may be compared to each other and to the ideal.

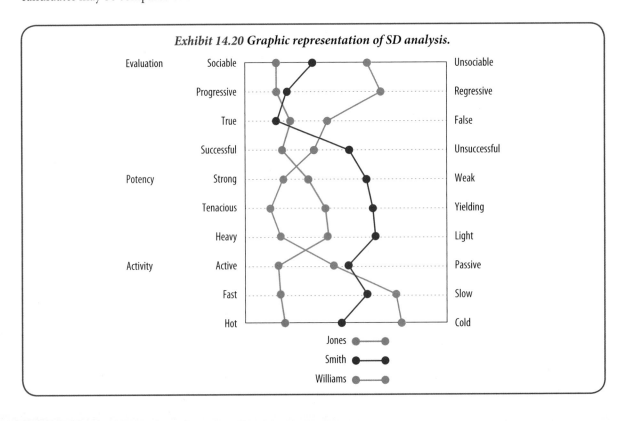

Exhibit 14.20 Graphic representation of SD analysis.

Adapting SD scales to the management question

One study explored a retail store image using 35 pairs of words or phrases classified into eight groups. These word pairs were especially created for the study. Excerpts from this scale are presented in Exhibit 14.21. Other categories of scale items were 'general characteristics of the company', 'physical characteristics of the store', 'prices charged by the store', 'store personnel', 'advertising by the store' and 'your friends and the store'. Since the scale pairs are associated closely with the characteristics of the store and its use, one could develop image profiles of various stores.

Exhibit 14.21 Adapting SD scales for retail store image study 1.

Convenience of reaching the store from your location

	: ___	: ___	: ___	: ___	: ___	: ___	: ___	: ___ :	
Nearby	: ___	: ___	: ___	: ___	: ___	: ___	: ___	: ___ :	Distant
Short time required to reach store	: ___	: ___	: ___	: ___	: ___	: ___	: ___	: ___ :	Long time required to reach store
Difficult drive	: ___	: ___	: ___	: ___	: ___	: ___	: ___	: ___ :	Easy drive
Difficult to find parking place	: ___	: ___	: ___	: ___	: ___	: ___	: ___	: ___ :	Easy to find parking place
Convenient to other stores I shop at	: ___	: ___	: ___	: ___	: ___	: ___	: ___	: ___ :	Inconvenient to other stores I shop at

Products offered

Wide selection of different kinds of product	: ___	: ___	: ___	: ___	: ___	: ___	: ___	: ___ :	Limited selection of different kinds of product
Fully stocked	: ___	: ___	: ___	: ___	: ___	: ___	: ___	: ___ :	Understocked
Undependable products	: ___	: ___	: ___	: ___	: ___	: ___	: ___	: ___ :	Dependable products
High quality	: ___	: ___	: ___	: ___	: ___	: ___	: ___	: ___ :	Low quality
Numerous brands	: ___	: ___	: ___	: ___	: ___	: ___	: ___	: ___ :	Few brands
Unknown brands	: ___	: ___	: ___	: ___	: ___	: ___	: ___	: ___ :	Well-known brands

Source: Robert F. Kelly and Ronald Stephenson, 'The semantic differential: an information source for designing retail patronage appeals', *Journal of Marketing* 31, October 1967, p. 45.

Advanced scaling techniques

New construction approaches have removed many of the deficiencies of traditional scales. Some have evolved to handle specific management research applications. Most techniques mentioned in this section rely on complex computer algorithms and require an understanding of multivariate statistics. Students interested in further information on these topics should refer to the statistical examples in Chapter 19 and the references.

Multidimensional scaling (MDS) describes a collection of techniques that deal with property space in a more general manner than the semantic differential. With MDS, one can scale objects, people or both, in ways that provide a visual impression of the relationships among variables. The data-handling characteristics of MDS provide several options: ordinal input (with interval output), and fully metric (interval) and non-metric modes. The various techniques use proximities as input data. A **proximity** is an index of perceived similarity or dissimilarity between objects. The objects might be 20 nations (or 10 primary exports) that participants are asked to judge in pairs of possible combinations as to their similarity. By means of a computer program, the ranked or rated relationships are then represented as points on a map in multidimensional space.[45]

We may think of three types of attribute space, each representing a multidimensional map. First, in objective space a product can be positioned in terms of, say, its price, taste and brand image. Second, a person's perceptions may also be positioned in subjective space using similar dimensions. These maps do not always coincide, but they do provide information about perceptual disparities. Since the subjective maps vary over time, they also provide important trend data. Third, we can describe our preferences for the object's ideal attributes. All objects close to the ideal are more preferred than those further away. These various configurations are said to reflect the 'hidden structure' of the data and make complicated problems much easier to understand.

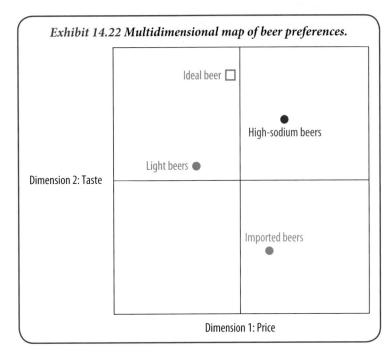

Exhibit 14.22 Multidimensional map of beer preferences.

In Exhibit 14.22 two dimensions are plotted: price and taste. The high-sodium beers are closest to the ideal beer on the price dimension while the imported beers are farthest away.

Another approach, representing a collection of techniques, is conjoint analysis. **Conjoint analysis** is used to measure complex decision-making that requires multi-attribute judgements. Its primary focus has been the explanation of consumer behaviour, with numerous applications in product development and marketing.[46]

When discovering and learning about products, consumers define a set of attributes or characteristics they use to compare competing brands or models in a product class. Using these attributes, they evaluate the product range and eliminate some brands. Then a final set of alternatives (including a non-purchase or delayed purchase decision) is developed. These evaluations can change if there is new information about additional competitors, corrections to attribute knowledge or further thoughts about the attribute. Algebraic theory can be used to model these cognitive processes and develop statistical approximations that reveal the rules the consumer follows in decision-making.[47]

For example, a consumer might be considering the purchase of a personal computer. Brand A has a fast processing speed and a high price. Brand B has a low price and a slower processor. The consumer's choice will be evidence of the utility of the processing-speed attribute. Simultaneously, other attributes are being evaluated – such as memory, portability, graphics support and user-friendliness.

Conjoint analysis can produce a scaled value for each attribute as well as a utility value for attributes that have levels (e.g. memory may have a range of 7 to more than 16 gigabytes). Both ranking and rating inputs may be used to evaluate product attributes. Conjoint analysis is not restricted to marketing applications, nor should it be considered a single generalized technique (see Chapter 20).

Finally, advanced students who are interested in the above techniques may also wish to investigate magnitude estimation scaling.[48] Magnitude scales provide access to ratio measurement and open new alternatives to management problems previously addressed through ordinal scales alone. Adaptive testing models also offer alternative approaches to a range of traditional measures, from dichotomous responses to Likert-type response formats.[49]

Running Case Study 14

Measurement and scales

Rebecca has looked at various studies and how they measure cheating in exams. So far she has collected the following measurement instruments:

Questions she found from a dissertation at Lake University

1 Have you cheated in an exam during the last 12 months?
   ☐ never ☐ once ☐ twice ☐ three or more times

2 Cheating in exams is unfair with respect to fellow students.
   ☐ fully disagree ☐ partly disagree ☐ neutral ☐ partly agree ☐ fully agree

3 Cheating in exams is acceptable if study pressure is very high.
   ☐ fully disagree ☐ partly disagree ☐ neutral ☐ partly agree ☐ fully agree

4 Cheating in exams is acceptable if the exam is very difficult.
   ☐ fully disagree ☐ partly disagree ☐ neutral ☐ partly agree ☐ fully agree

5 Cheating in exams is acceptable if the lecturer has been bad.
   ☐ fully disagree ☐ partly disagree ☐ neutral ☐ partly agree ☐ fully agree

6 The university should introduce and enforce tougher sanctions if cheating in an exam is discovered.
   ☐ fully disagree ☐ partly disagree ☐ neutral ☐ partly agree ☐ fully agree

Rebecca also discovered a site on the Internet where students discussed different methods to cheat on an exam. She used questions from this Internet site and developed the following set of questions.

1 How could one cheat on an exam? Please describe the best method that you know.

   _____

   _____

   _____

   _____

2 Have you used this method in the last 12 months?
   ☐ yes   ☐ no

3 Have you used other methods to cheat in the last two months?
   ☐ yes   ☐ no

4 Below you find several methods of cheating on exams; please indicate their severity.

	No cheating	A little bit cheating	A bit cheating	Cheating	Strong cheating
Copying from your neighbour					
Whispering with your neighbour					
Preparing and using a crib sheet					
Asking a friend who has good marks to take the exam in your place					
Secretly sending an SMS to a friend who looks up answer and replies					
Other (please describe)					

▶

Rebecca also read that projective techniques could be very useful if the questions are likely to provoke socially desirable answers. That gave her the idea to ask the following questions.

1   Many students at this university cheat in their exams.
    ☐ fully disagree ☐ partly disagree ☐ neutral ☐ partly agree ☐ fully agree

2   I have heard from others that they cheated during an exam.
    ☐ never ☐ once ☐ incidental ☐ sometimes ☐ often

3   Many students think that cheating in exams is acceptable.
    ☐ fully disagree ☐ partly disagree ☐ neutral ☐ partly agree ☐ fully agree

4   I can understand that students cheat if the exam is unfair.
    ☐ fully disagree ☐ partly disagree ☐ neutral ☐ partly agree ☐ fully agree

At the end of the questionnaire, Rebecca wanted to ask the following question:

Have you ever cheated in an exam?

☐ yes   ☐ no

If you answered yes, can you please describe the situation and why you cheated?

_____

_____

_____

_____

_____

_____

_____

_____

_____

_____

_____

1   Discuss the different options to measure cheating in exams in terms of reliability and validity.

2   What do you think about Rebecca's scale to measure students' ethics?

3   Is the proposed open question at the end useful?

Summary

1   While people measure things casually in daily life, research measurement is more precise and controlled. In measurement, one settles for measuring properties of the objects rather than the objects themselves. An event is measured in terms of its duration. What happened during it, who was involved, where it occurred, and so on, are all properties of the event. To be more precise, what are measured are indicants of the properties. Thus, for duration, one measures the number of hours and minutes recorded. For what happened, one uses some system to classify the types of activity that occurred. Measurement typically uses some sort of scale to classify or quantify the data collected.

2   There are four scale types. In increasing order of power, these are nominal, ordinal, interval and ratio. Nominal scales classify without indicating order, distance or unique origin. Ordinal data show magnitude relationships of more than and less than but have no distance or unique origin. Interval scales have both order and distance but no unique origin. Ratio scales possess all these features.

3   Instruments may yield incorrect readings of an indicant for many reasons. These may be classified according to error sources: (i) the participant or subject, (ii) situational factors, (iii) the measurer, and (iv) the instrument.

4   Sound measurement must meet the tests of validity, reliability and practicality. Validity reveals the degree to which an instrument measures what it is supposed to measure to assist the researcher in solving the research problem. Three forms of validity are used to evaluate measurement scales. Content validity exists to the degree that a measure provides an adequate reflection of the topic under study. Its determination is primarily judgemental and intuitive. Criterion-related validity relates to our ability to predict some outcome or estimate the existence of some current condition. Construct validity is the most complex and abstract. A measure has construct validity to the degree that it conforms to predicted correlations of other theoretical propositions.

A measure is reliable if it provides consistent results. Reliability is a partial contributor to validity, but a measurement tool may be reliable without being valid. Three forms of reliability are stability, equivalence and internal consistency. A measure has practical value for the research if it is economical, convenient and interpretable.

5   Scaling describes the procedures by which we assign numbers to measurements of opinions, attitudes and other concepts. Selection of a measurement scale to best meet our needs involves six decisions:

a   Study objective: do we measure the characteristics of the participant or the stimulus object?
b   Response form: do we measure with a rating scale or a ranking scale?
c   Degree of preference: do we measure our preferences or make non-preference judgements?
d   Data properties: do we measure with nominal, ordinal, interval or ratio data?
e   Number of dimensions: do we measure using a unidimensional or multidimensional scale?
f   Scale construction: do we develop scales by arbitrary decision, consensus, item analysis, cumulative scaling or factor analysis?

In this chapter, two classifications – the response form and scale construction techniques – were emphasized.

6   When using rating scales, one judges an object in absolute terms against certain specified criteria. Several scales were proposed: simple category; multiple-choice, single-response; multiple-choice, multiple-response; Likert scales; semantic differential; numerical scales; multiple rating lists; fixed sum scales; stapel scales; and graphic rating scales. When you use ranking methods, you make relative comparisons against other similar objects. Three well-known methods are the paired-comparison, forced ranking and the comparative scale.

7   Scaled measurement strategies are classified by the techniques used to construct them. Of the five techniques, three are used frequently: the arbitrary approach, item analysis and factoring. Consensus and cumulative methods receive less attention because they are time-consuming or have fewer business applications. Arbitrary scales are designed by the researcher's own subjective selection of items. These scales are simple to construct and have content validity only.

In the consensus method, a panel is used to judge the relevance, ambiguity and attitude level of scale items. Those items that are judged best are then included in the final instrument. The Thurstone method of equal-appearing intervals is a historic consensus method that has given impetus for many current scales.

With the item analysis approach, one develops many items believed to express either a favourable or an unfavourable attitude towards some general object. These items are then pre-tested to decide which ones discriminate between persons with high total scores and those with low total scores on the test. Those items that meet this discrimination test are included in the final instrument. The most successful Likert scales are developed using this approach.

With the cumulative approach scales, it is possible to estimate how a participant has answered individual items by knowing the total score. The items are related to each other on a particular attitude dimension, so that if one agrees with a more extreme item, one will also agree with items representing less extreme views. The scalogram is the classic example.

Factoring develops measurement questions through factor analysis or similar correlation techniques. It is particularly useful in uncovering latent attitude dimensions, and it approaches scaling through the concept of multidimensional attribute space. The semantic differential scale is an example.

Other developments in scaling include multidimensional scaling and conjoint analysis. Each represents a family of related techniques with a variety of applications for handling complex judgements. Magnitude estimation and Rasch models provide an avenue for reconceptualizing traditional scaling techniques for greater efficiency and freedom from error.

Discussion questions

Terms in review

1 What can we measure about the four objects listed below? Be as specific as possible.
   a   laundry detergent
   b   employees
   c   factory output
   d   job satisfaction

2 What are the essential differences among nominal, ordinal, interval and ratio scales? How do these differences affect the statistical analysis techniques we can use?

3 What are the four major sources of measurement error? Illustrate by example how each of these might affect measurement results in a face-to-face interview situation.

4 Do you agree or disagree with the following statements? Explain.
   a   Validity is more critical to measurement than reliability.
   b   Content validity is the most difficult type of validity to determine.
   c   A valid measurement is reliable, but a reliable measurement may not be valid.
   d   Stability and equivalence are essentially the same thing.

5 Discuss the relative merits of and problems with:

   a   rating and ranking scales

   b   Likert and differential scales

   c   unidimensional and multidimensional scales.

Making research decisions

6 You have data from a corporation on the annual salary of each of its 200 employees.

   a   Illustrate how the data can be presented as ratio, interval, ordinal and nominal data.

   b   Describe the successive loss of information as the presentation changes from ratio to nominal.

7 Below are listed some objects of varying degrees of abstraction. Suggest properties of each of these objects that can be measured by ranking or rating scales:

   a   store customers

   b   voter attitudes

   c   hardness of steel alloys

   d   preference for a particular common stock

   e   profitability of various divisions in a company.

8 You have been asked by the head of marketing to design an instrument by which your private, for-profit school can evaluate the quality and value of its various curricula and courses. How might you try to ensure that your instrument has:

   a   stability

   b   equivalence

   c   internal consistency

   d   content validity

   e   predictive validity

   f   construct validity?

9 A new employee at Michelin, you are asked to assume the management of the *Red Michelin Restaurant Guide*. Each restaurant striving to be included in the guide needs to be evaluated. Only a select few restaurants may earn three-star status. What dimensions would you choose to measure to apply one to three stars in the *Red Michelin Restaurant Guide*?

10 You have been asked to develop an index of student morale at your school.

   a   What constructs or concepts might you employ?

   b   Choose several of the major concepts and specify their dimensions.

   c   Select observable indicators you might use to measure these dimensions.

   d   How would you compile these various dimensions into a single index?

   e   How would you judge the reliability and/or validity of these measurements?

11 Suppose your firm had planned a major research study. Two months before the study, the government resigned. It is the third government resignation in less than three years. This government, and all previous governments, were unable to obtain a majority of votes in the parliament for law initiatives reducing state expenditure on social welfare. In the meantime, the state's budget deficit is rising and exceeds 3 per cent of gross national product (GNP), a criterion set by the members of the Eurozone. Given these recent developments, your superior decides to add a question to the study. The question must measure consumers' confidence that the economic system will be able to rebound in the next 12 months, and the subsequent effects (increased lay-offs, higher unemployment, numerous firms failing to meet their sales and profit projections, lower holiday retail sales, war on terrorism). Draft a scale of each of the following types to measure that confidence level:

   a   fixed sum scale

   b   Likert-type summated scale

   c   semantic differential scale

   d   stapel scale

   e   forced ranking scale.

12 An investigative question in your employee satisfaction study seeks to assess employee 'job involvement'. Create a measurement question that uses the following scales:
   a   a graphic rating scale
   b   a multiple rating list.
   c   Which do you recommend and why?

13 You receive the results of a paired-comparison preference test of four soft drinks from a sample of 200 people. The results are as shown in the table below:

	Koak	Zip	Pabze	Mr Peepers
Koak	–	50*	115	35
Zip	150	–	160	70
Pabze	85	40	–	45
Mr Peepers	165	130	155	–
*reads as 50 people preferred Zip to Koak.				

   a   How do these brands rank in overall preference in this sample?
   b   Develop an interval scale for these four brands.

14 One of the problems in developing rating scales is the choice of response terms to use. Below are samples of some widely used scaling codes. Do you see any problems with them?
   a   Yes __ Depends __ No __
   b   Excellent __ Good __ Fair __ Poor __
   c   Excellent __ Good __ Average __ Fair __ Poor __
   d   Strongly Approve __ Approve __ Uncertain __ Disapprove __Strongly Disapprove __

15 You are working on a consumer perception study of four brands of bicycle. You will need to develop measurement questions and scales to accomplish the following tasks. Also be sure to explain which data levels (nominal, ordinal, interval, ratio) are appropriate and which quantitative techniques you will use.
   a   Prepare an overall assessment of all the brands.
   b   Provide a comparison of the brands for each of the following dimensions:
       i   styling
       ii   durability
       iii gear quality
       iv   brand image.

16 Below is a Likert-type scale that might be used to evaluate your opinion of the educational programme you are in. There are five response categories: 'Strongly agree' (SA) via 'Neither agree nor disagree' (AND) to 'Strongly disagree' (SD). If 5 represents the most positive attitude, how would the different items be valued?
   a   This programme is not very challenging.
       SA AND SD
   b   The general level of teaching is good.
       SA AND SD
   c   I really think I am learning a lot from this programme.
       SA AND SD
   d   Students' suggestions are given little attention here.
       SA AND SD
   e   This programme does a good job of preparing one for a career.
       SA AND SD
   f   This programme is below my expectations.
       SA AND SD

   Record your answers to the above items. In what two different ways could such responses be used? What would be the purpose of each?

From concept to practice

17 Using Exhibits 14.11 and 14.14, match each question to its appropriate data type. For each data type not represented, develop a measurement question that would obtain that type of data.

18 Using the response strategies within Exhibit 14.11 or 14.14, which would be appropriate to, and add insight to, understanding the various indicants of student demand for the academic programme in which they are enrolled?

Classroom discussion

19 The story of how business studies has attempted to explain organizational performance is a disappointing one. Although thousands of quantitative as well as qualitative studies have looked at the question of why certain firms perform better than others, we still know next to nothing about the reasons. Studies revealing that certain success factors, such as firm size, market share, research and development (R&D) expenditure, and so on, enhance organizational performance are contradicted by other studies that find no evidence for this, or even a negative correlation between these factors and performance. The problem starts with the question, 'What do we mean when we talk about organizational performance?' Brainstorm in the class about the meanings of the term 'organizational performance' and then discuss how the relationship between certain success factors and performance is affected by the different meanings attached to the term.

20 In psychology, in particular, the development and validation of scales has become a commercial business. For example, several research institutes offer validated scales to measure emotional intelligence (EQ) but you are only allowed to use them if you strictly follow their procedures and provide them with the data you collected. Discuss the consequences of such commercial practice in terms of the advancement of knowledge, cross-checking of the quality of research studies, and so on.

Recommended further reading

Edwards, Allen L., *Techniques of Attitude Scale Construction*. New York: Irvington, 1979. Thorough discussion of basic unidimensional scaling techniques.

Embretson, Susan E. and Hershberger, Scott L., The *New Rules of Measurement*. Mahwah, NJ: Lawrence Erlbaum Associates, 1999. Bridges the gap between theoretical and practical measurement.

Kelley, D. Lynn, *Measurement Made Accessible: A Research Approach Using Qualitative, Quantitative, and TQM Methods*. Thousand Oaks, CA: Sage Publications, 1999. Sections on bias, reliability and validity are appropriate for this chapter.

Miller, Delbert C. and Salkind, Neil J., *Handbook of Research Design and Social Measurement* (6th edn). Thousand Oaks, CA: Sage, 2002. Presents a large number of existing sociometric scales and indexes as well as information on their characteristics, validity and sources.

Nunnally, J.C. and Bernstein, Ira, *Psychometric Theory* (3rd edn). New York: McGraw-Hill, 1993. The classic text on psychometric theory.

Osgood, Charles E., Suci, George J. and Tannenbaum, Percy H., *The Measurement of Meaning*. Urbana, IL: University of Illinois Press, 1957. The basic reference on SD scaling.

Singh, Jagdip, 'Tackling measurement problems with item response theory: principles, characteristics and assessment, with an illustrative example', *Journal of Business Research* 57(2), 2004, pp. 184–208. This article introduces several new measurement models developed by psychometricians and discusses how these can be applied in a business research context.

Get started with understanding statistical techniques!
When you have read this chapter, log on to the Online Learning Centre website at *www.mcgraw-hill.co.uk/textbooks/blumberg* to explore chapter-by-chapter test questions, additional case studies, a glossary and more online study tools for *Business Research Methods*.

Notes

1 Fred N. Kerlinger, *Foundations of Behavioral Research* (3rd edn). New York: Holt, Rinehart & Winston, 1986, p. 396; S. Stevens, 'Measurement, statistics, and the schemapiric view', *Science* (August 1968), p. 384.

2 We assume the reader has had an introductory statistics course in which measures of central tendency such as arithmetic mean, median and mode have been treated. Similarly, we assume familiarity with measures of dispersion such as the standard deviation, range and interquartile range. For a brief review of these concepts, refer to the 'Descriptive statistics' section in Chapter 16 online or see an introductory statistics text.

3 While this might intuitively seem to be the case, consider that one might prefer a over b, b over c, yet c over a. These results cannot be scaled as ordinal data because there is apparently more than one dimension involved.

4 L.L. Thurstone, *The Measurement of Values*. Chicago, IL: University of Chicago Press, 1959.

5 Parametric tests are appropriate when the measurement is interval or ratio, and when we can accept certain assumptions about the underlying distributions of the data with which we are working. Non-parametric tests usually involve much weaker assumptions about measurement scales (nominal and ordinal), and the assumptions about the underlying distribution of the population are fewer and less restrictive. More on these tests is found in Chapters 17–19 and Appendix D.

6 Sidney Siegel, *Nonparametric Statistics for the Behavioral Sciences*. New York: McGraw-Hill, 1956, p. 32.

7 Norman A. Anderson, 'Scales and statistics: parametric and nonparametric', *Psychological Bulletin* 58(4), pp. 315–16.

8 Kerlinger, *Foundations*, p. 403.

9 See later in this chapter for a discussion of the differential scale.

10 See Chapters 18 and 19 for a discussion of these procedures.

11 The exception involves the creation of a dummy variable for use in a regression or discriminant equation. A non-metric variable is transformed into a metric variable through the assignment of a 0 or 1, and used in a predictive equation.

12 Claire Selltiz, Lawrence S. Wrightsman and Stuart W. Cook, *Research Methods in Social Relations* (3rd edn). New York: Holt, Rinehart & Winston, 1976, pp. 164–9.

13 Robert L. Thorndike and Elizabeth Hagen, *Measurement and Evaluation in Psychology and Education* (3rd edn). New York: Wiley, 1969, p. 5.

14 Examples of other conceptualizations of validity are factorial validity, job-analytic validity, synthetic validity, rational validity and statistical conclusion validity.

15 Thomas D. Cook and Donald T. Campbell, 'The design and conduct of quasi experiments and true experiments in field settings', in Marvin D. Dunnette (ed.), *Handbook of Industrial and Organizational Psychology*. Chicago, IL: Rand McNally, 1976, p. 223.

16 *Standards for Educational and Psychological Tests and Manuals*. Washington, DC: American Psychological Association, 1974, p. 26.

17 Wayne F. Cascio, *Applied Psychology in Personnel Management*. Reston, VA: Reston Publishing, 1982, p. 149.

18 Thorndike and Hagen, *Measurement and Evaluation*, p. 168.

19 See, for example, Cascio, *Applied Psychology*, pp. 146–7; Edward G. Carmines and Richard A. Zeller, *Reliability and Validity Assessment*. Beverly Hills, CA: Sage, 1979, pp. 48–50.

20 Emanuel J. Mason and William J. Bramble, *Understanding and Conducting Research*. New York: McGraw-Hill, 1989, pp. 260–3.

21 See, for example, Milton Lodge, *Magnitude Scaling: Quantitative Measurement of Opinions*. Beverly Hills, CA: Sage, 1981; Donald R. Cooper and Donald A. Clare, 'A magnitude estimation scale for human values', *Psychological Reports* 49 (1981).

22 David Andrich, *Rasch Models for Measurement*. Beverly Hills, CA: Sage, 1988.

23 Cascio, *Applied Psychology*, pp. 135–6.

24 Mason and Bramble, *Understanding and Conducting Research*, p. 268.

25 Thorndike and Hagen, *Measurement and Evaluation*, p. 199.

26 Bernard S. Phillips, *Social Research Strategy and Tactics* (2nd edn). New York: Macmillan, 1971, p. 205.

27 For a discussion of various scale classifications, see W.S. Torgerson, *Theory and Methods of Scaling*. New York: Wiley, 1958, Chapter 3.

28 E.A. Suchman and R.G. Francis, 'Scaling techniques in social research', in J.T. Doby (ed.), *An Introduction to Social Research*. Harrisburg, PA: Stackpole, 1954, pp. 126–9.

29 A study of the historic research literature found that more than three-quarters of the attitude scales used were of the five-point type. An examination of more recent literature suggests that the five-point scale is still common but that there is a growing use of longer scales. For the historic study, see Daniel D. Day, 'Methods in attitude research', *American Sociological Review* 5 (1940), pp. 395–410. Single versus multiple-item scaling requirements are discussed in Jum C. Nunnally, *Psychometric Theory*. New York: McGraw-Hill, 1967, Chapter 14.

30 This section is adapted from Pamela L. Alreck and Robert B. Settle, *The Survey Research Handbook*. Burr Ridge, IL: Irwin, 1995, Chapter 5.

31 J.P. Guilford, *Psychometric Methods*. New York: McGraw-Hill, 1954, pp. 278–79.

32 P.M. Synonds, 'Notes on rating', *Journal of Applied Psychology* 9 (1925), pp. 188–95.

33 See L.L. Thurstone, 'A law of comparative judgment', *Psychological Review* 34 (1927), pp. 273–86.

34 Guilford, *Psychometric Methods*.

35 See Milton A. Saffir, 'A comparative study of scales constructed by three psychophysical methods', *Psychometrica* 11(3) (September 1937), pp. 179–98.

36 Allen L. Edwards, *Techniques of Attitude Scale Construction*. New York: Appleton-Century-Crofts, 1957, pp. 152–4.

37 One study reported that the construction of a Likert scale took only half the time required to construct a Thurstone scale. See L.L. Thurstone and K.K. Kenney, 'A comparison of the Thurstone and Likert techniques of attitude scale construction', *Journal of Applied Psychology* 30 (1946), pp. 72–83.

38 Edwards, *Techniques*, p. 153.

39 Louis Guttman, 'A basis for scaling qualitative data', *American Sociological Review* 9 (1944), pp. 139–50.

40 John P. Robinson, 'Toward a more appropriate use of Guttman scaling', *Public Opinion Quarterly* 37 (Summer 1973), pp. 260–7.

41 For more on the process of factor analysis, see Chapter 20.

42 Charles E. Osgood, G.J. Suci and P.H. Tannenbaum, *The Measurement of Meaning*. Urbana, IL: University of Illinois Press, 1957.

43 Ibid., p. 49. See also James G. Snider and Charles E. Osgood (eds), *Semantic Differential Technique*. Chicago, IL: Aldine, 1969.

44 Ibid., p. 79.

45 See, for example, Joseph B. Kruskal and Myron Wish, *Multidimensional Scaling*. Beverly Hills, CA: Sage, 1978; Paul Green and V.R. Rao, *Applied Multidimensional Scaling: A Comparison of Approaches and Algorithms*. New York: Holt, Rinehart & Winston, 1972; Paul E. Green and F.J. Carmone, *Multidimensional Scaling in Marketing Analysis*. Boston: Allyn & Bacon, 1970.

46 See P. Cattin and D.R. Wittink, 'Commercial use of conjoint analysis: a survey', *Journal of Marketing* 46 (1982), pp. 44–53; Cattin and Wittink, 'Commercial use of conjoint analysis: an update', paper presented at the ORSA/TIMS Marketing Science Meetings, Richardson, TX, 12–15 March 1986.

47 Jordan J. Louviere, *Analyzing Decision Making: Metric Conjoint Analysis*. Beverly Hills, CA: Sage, 1988, pp. 9–11.

CHAPTER 15

Writing up and presenting research outcomes

Chapter contents

Learning objectives

When you have read this chapter, you should understand:

1 the link between presentation quality and perceived study quality

2 that writing a research report requires you to consider its purpose, readership, circumstances/limitations and use

3 that most statistical data are best presented in tables, charts or graphs.

The written research report

It may seem unscientific and even unfair, but a poor final report or presentation can destroy a study. Research technicians may appreciate the brilliance of badly reported content, but most readers will be influenced by the quality of the reporting. A main reason for this is that an argument that is presented well is more easily understood. If you want to transmit information, either orally or in writing, it is mainly your responsibility to ensure that the transmission between the sender (you) and the receiver (the people you want to address) does not suffer from disturbing 'noise'. This fact should prompt researchers to make a special effort to communicate clearly and fully.

The research report contains findings, analyses of findings, interpretations, conclusions and, sometimes, recommendations. The researcher is the expert on the topic and knows the specifics in a way no one else can. Because a research report is an authoritative one-way communication, it imposes a special obligation for maintaining objectivity. Even if your findings seem to point to an action, you should exercise restraint and caution when proposing that course.

Reports may be defined by their degree of formality/design and the audience. The formal report follows a well-delineated and relatively long format. This is in contrast to the informal or short report. Further, writing a report on the outcomes of a study for an academic audience, such as a research project, a working paper or an article for an academic journal, requires additional considerations.

Short reports

Short reports are appropriate when a problem is well defined, is of limited scope, and has a simple and straightforward methodology. Most informational, progress and interim reports are of this kind: a report on cost-of-living changes for upcoming labour negotiations or a report on the general socio-economic conditions of a country to which a firm is considering exporting.

Short reports are about five pages long. At the beginning, there should be a brief statement about the authorization for the study, the problem examined, and its breadth and depth. Next come the conclusions and recommendations, followed by the findings that support them. Section headings should be used.

A **letter of transmittal** is a vehicle to convey short reports. A five-page report may be produced to track sales on a quarterly basis. The report should be direct, make ample use of graphics to show trends, and refer the reader to the research department for further information. Detailed information on the research method would be omitted, although an overview could appear in an appendix. The purpose of this type of report is to distribute information quickly in an easy-to-use format. Short reports are also produced for clients with small, relatively inexpensive research projects.

The letter is a form of a short report. Its tone should be informal. The format follows that of any good business letter and should not exceed a few pages. A letter report is often written in personal style (using the words 'we', 'you', etc.), although this depends on the situation. Memorandum reports are another variety and follow the 'To, From, Subject' format.

The following suggestions may be helpful in writing short reports:

- Tell the reader why you are writing (it may be in response to a request).
- If the memo is in response to a request for information, remind the reader of the exact point raised, answer it and follow with any necessary details.
- Write in an expository style with brevity and directness.
- If time permits, write the report today and leave it for review tomorrow before sending it.
- Attach detailed materials as appendices when needed. Be selective with those appendices and refer to them in the main text.

Long reports

Long reports are of two types: the technical or base report, and the management report. The choice of which approach to take depends on the audience and the researcher's objectives.

Many projects will require both types of report: a technical report, written for an audience of researchers, and a management report, written for the non-technically oriented manager or client. While some researchers try to write a single report that satisfies both needs, this complicates the task and is seldom satisfactory. The two types of audience have different technical training, interests and goals.

The management report

Sometimes the client has no research background and is interested in results rather than in methodology. The major communication medium in this case is the **management report**. It is still helpful to have a technical report if the client later wishes to have a technical appraisal of the study.

Because the management report is designed for a non-technical audience, the researcher faces some special problems. Readers are less concerned with methodological details but more interested in learning quickly the major findings and conclusions. They want help in making decisions. Often the report is developed for a single person and needs to be written with that person's characteristics and needs in mind.

The style of the report should encourage rapid reading and quick comprehension of major findings, and it should prompt understanding of the implications and conclusions. The report tone is journalistic and must be accurate. Headlines and underlining for emphasis are helpful; pictures and graphs often replace tables. Sentences and paragraphs should be short and direct. Consider liberal use of white space and wide margins. It may be desirable to put a single finding on each page. It also helps to have a theme running through the report, and even graphic or animated characters designed to vary the presentation.

The technical report

The **technical report** should include full documentation and detail. It will normally survive all working papers and original data files, so will become the major source document. It is the report that other researchers will want to see because it has the full story of what was done and how it was done.

While completeness is a goal, you must guard against including non-essential material. A good guide is that sufficient procedural information should be included to enable others to replicate the study. This includes sources of data, research procedures, sampling design, data-gathering instruments, index construction and data analysis methods. Most information should be attached in an appendix. A technical report should also include a full presentation and analysis of relevant data. Conclusions and recommendations should be clearly related to specific findings.

Research Methods in Real Life
Not all Chinese people can have a car!

Global warming is a widely acknowledged threat to the future of our planet and mainly caused by the burning of fossil fuels and the associated CO_2 emissions. Almost all scientists agree that we need to reduce our energy consumption to fight global warming. China, the country with the largest population in the world, has experienced a tremendous economic growth in the last two decades, which went along with a dramatic increase in energy consumption, so that nowadays China is responsible for the largest share of emissions (23.5 per cent of world emissions in 2008). Estimates even for 2011 show, however, that US citizens still consume twice as much energy per capita as Chinese. In the USA, every 1,000 people own almost 800 cars, in the UK it is 520, in China 85 and in India just 18. Thus, what would happen if car ownership in China and India became as common as in the UK or even the US?[1] Facing global warming, many people in the developed world quickly draw the conclusion: 'Not all Chinese people can have a car!'

Hans Rosling, a Swedish statistician does not share this conclusion, but no matter which statistical figures he presented to his students, he could not convince them that the solution to the problem would not be to restrict Chinese citizens from buying cars. Hans Rosling then thought about how to present facts convincingly to a broader audience. Using storytelling and dynamic data visualization, he developed methods to present statistical facts in a manner that makes the data easier to understand and therefore his arguments more compelling. Meanwhile he has held many inspiring talks at TED conferences (see www.ted.com/speakers/hans_rosling.html).

References and further reading

www.gapminder.org

www.pbl.nl/en

[1] Figures taken from the World Bank (www.worldbank.org).

The academic report

If your study also has a scientific objective, the technical report comes close to offering what is needed in the writing of a working paper or even a contribution to a scientific journal. What distinguishes a technical report from a research project, working paper or article in an academic journal is that the latter will have a substantial theoretical section. Usually, such a section will contain a review of the current academic literature on the issue (see also Chapter 3) and elaborated argumentation regarding the development of a new theory or the extension/adjustment of an existing theory. With respect to the section reporting the findings of a study, an academic report discusses the study's outcomes in light of the particular theory followed. Similarly, the conclusions also discuss the outcome in terms of its impact on theory development. Finally, writers of academic reports are more inclined to refer to the work of others and to acknowledge their contribution to the field, which results in much longer lists of references.

With regard to style, academic reports have their own language, and may tend to use particular words. For example, in academic writing the word 'significant(ly)' is used with the statistical definition of significance in mind, while in a management report the word might be used to denote importance, although no one has checked any test statistics. If you are writing a paper for publication in an academic journal, it is important to bear in mind that you will need to comply with the rules of the specific journal, which will either be available at the journal's website or from the editor. Such rules lay out how you must refer to the literature, whether you should use footnotes or endnotes, how tables and figures should be labelled and presented, and what writing style is preferred.

Research report components

Research reports, long and short, have a set of identifiable components. Usually headings and sub-headings divide the sections. Each report is individual: sections may be dropped or added, condensed or expanded to meet the needs of the audience. Exhibit 15.1 lists five types of report, the sections that are typically included, and the general order of presentation. Each of these formats can be modified to meet the needs of the audience.

The technical report and the academic report follow the flow of the research. The prefatory materials, such as a letter of authorization and a table of contents, are first in the technical report, but not contained in the academic one. An introduction covers the purpose of the study. An academic report continues with an elaborated theoretical section, while the technical report moves straight to a section on methodology. The findings are presented next, including tables and other graphics. The conclusions section includes recommendations. Finally, the appendices contain technical information, instruments, glossaries and references.

In contrast to the technical report, the management report is for the non-technical client. The reader has little time to absorb details and requires prompt exposure to the most critical findings; thus the report's sections are in an inverted order. After the prefatory and introductory sections, the conclusions are presented, along with

Exhibit 15.1 *Research report sections and their order of inclusion.*

Report modules	Short report		Long report		Academic report
	Memo or letter	Short technical	Management	Technical	
Prefatory information		1	1	1	1
Letter of transmittal			✓	✓	✓
Title page		✓	✓	✓	✓
Authorization statement		✓	✓	✓	
Executive summary or abstract		✓	✓	✓	✓ (suitable for researchers)
Table of contents			✓	✓	
Introduction	1	2	2	2	2
Problem statement	✓	✓	✓	✓	✓
Research objectives	✓	✓	✓	✓	✓
Background	✓	✓	✓	✓	✓
Theoretical section			✓ (briefly)	✓ (briefly)	3
Literature review					✓
Theory development (deriving of hypotheses)					✓
Methodology		✓ (briefly)	✓ (briefly)	3	4
Sampling design				✓	✓
Research design				✓	✓
Data collection				✓	✓
Data analysis				✓	✓
Limitations		✓	✓	✓	✓
Findings		3	4	4	5
Conclusions	2	4	3	5	6
Appendices		5	5	6	7
Bibliography				7	8

accompanying recommendations. Individual findings are presented next, supporting the conclusions already made. The appendices present any necessary methodological details. The order of the management report allows clients to grasp the conclusions and recommendations quickly, without much reading. Then, if they wish to go further, they may read on into the findings. The management report should make liberal use of visual display.

The short technical report covers the same items as the long technical report but in an abbreviated form. The methodology is included as part of the introduction and takes no more than a few paragraphs. Most of the emphasis is placed on the findings and conclusions. A memo or letter format covers only the minimum: what the problem is and what the research conclusions are.

The modules in detail

In the following, we describe the modules in detail with a special emphasis on writing a research project or academic report.

Prefatory items

Prefatory materials do not have a direct bearing on the research itself. Instead, they assist the reader in using the research report. Examples of such items in a research project are a CD-ROM containing the data, transcripts, screenshots of used websites, and so on.

Letter of transmittal

When the relationship between the researcher and the client is formal, a letter of transmittal should be included. This is appropriate when a report is for a specific client (e.g. the company president) and when it is generated for an outside organization. The letter should refer to the authorization for the project, and any specific instructions or limitations placed on the study. It should also state the purpose and scope of the study. For many internal projects and academic reports, it is not necessary to include a letter of transmittal.

Title page

The title page should include four items: the title of the report, the date, and for whom and by whom it was prepared. The title should be brief but include the following three elements:

1 the variables included in the study
2 the type of relationship among the variables
3 the population to which the results may be applied.[1]

If including these three elements results in a very long title, a possible solution is to work with a sub-title, which is divided by a full stop or colon from the main title and often printed in a smaller font. This applies particularly if in the final design of your report, the title reappears in the page heading; in such a case it is advisable to work with sub-titles. Superfluous phrases such as 'A report on . . .' and 'A discussion of . . .' add length to a title but little else. Single-word titles are also of little value. Exhibit 15.2 shows three acceptable ways to word report titles. It should be noted that most universities have formal requirements of what needs to be included in a research project on the title page, and these should be checked with your university.

Exhibit 15.2 Sample report titles.

Descriptive study	The five-year demand outlook for plastic pipes in France
	Five-year demand outlook for plastic pipes. A study of the French market
Correlation study	The relationship between the value of the dollar in world markets and the national inflation rates in emerging markets
	Value of the dollar in world markets and national inflation rates. A correlational study in emerging markets
Causal study	The effect of various motivation methods on worker attitudes among British workers in the chemical industry
	The effect of various motivation methods on worker attitudes. An investigation among British workers in the chemical industry

---

Authorization letter

When the report is sent to a public organization, it is common to include a letter of authorization showing the authority for undertaking the research. This is especially true for reports conducted for federal and state governments and non-profit organizations. The letter not only shows who sponsored the research but also delineates the original request.

Executive summary

An **executive summary** can serve two purposes. It may be a report in miniature – covering all the aspects in the body of the report, but in abbreviated form – or it may be a concise summary of the major findings and conclusions, including recommendations. Two pages are generally sufficient for executive summaries. Write this section once the rest of the report is finished. It should not include new information but may require graphics to present a particular conclusion. Expect the summary to contain a high density of significant terms since it is repeating the highlights of the report. Academic reports are also accompanied by a summary, often called an **abstract**, which briefly reflects the problem statement, the theoretical approach used, the research design and the main finding. A summary of an academic report is usually very short (i.e. less than half a page). Executive summaries are especially useful for a research project that has been written with the support of any organization.

Table of contents

As a rough guide, any report of several sections that totals more than 10 pages should have a table of contents. If there are many tables, charts or other exhibits, these should also be listed after the table of contents in a separate table of illustrations/figures.

Introduction

The introduction prepares the reader for the report by describing the parts of the project: the problem statement, research objectives and background material.[2] In most projects, the introduction can be taken from the research proposal with minor editing. A research project introduction needs to provide a rationale for the research project, that is, you need to tell the reader what the added value of your research project is, and why it is worth reading. The introduction serves the following functions:

- introduce and develop the problem statement
- show the relevance of the problem statement
- provide an outline for the paper.

There are a couple of standard answers why a research project is important. Suppose you write a research project on telecommunication markets in some African countries. Here are a few rationales you might use:

- *We do not know a lot about the topic.* Here, you need to show in the introduction that the main literature hardly covers the topic; there might be a lot of literature on telecommunication markets but not in Africa or there might be a lot of literature on markets in developing countries, but not telecommunication markets or other markets characterized by intensive technology and network effects. There is, however, one potential caveat to this answer, namely that others could argue the reason that we do not know a lot about the topic is that the topic is not interesting.
- *Other people think that the problem is important.* Start with quoting a scholar, preferably a well-known one, claiming that more research on markets in developing nations is needed. Using the quote of a well-known scholar shows that you are not the only one who thinks that the problem is interesting, but the question is why should you research what other people believe and not what you like?
- *My research problem affects a lot of people and can save money.* This rationale is convincing to most. For example, you could argue that telecommunication markets in all industrialized countries are saturated, but that developing countries still show remarkable growth rates, or you could argue that building up mobile telecommunication structures in developing countries is an important infrastructure investment that enables much larger parts of the population to engage in worldwide communication and thereby become part of a globalized world. However, the academic world views research studies that only focus on providing benefits in terms of money with some scepticism. If (consulting) firms or governments conduct such studies that is fine, but the scientific community expects something more than just a pecuniary motive; it expects that the study contributes to our understanding of the world, that is, contributes to our theoretical knowledge.
- *The research is theoretically important.* This rationale is the most respected in academics and although the chances that your research project will be the founding stone of a new theory are small, a research project should contribute to the knowledge. From a theoretical perspective, even the replication of an existing study can be a valuable contribution if you conduct the study in a different country, industry, and so on. Thus, in our example case, you might argue that we are well aware of how the innovation of mobile telephones penetrated Western markets, but we are not aware how this happens in developing nations. In other cases you might take an idea from a theoretical paper and explore it through a case study, that is, you are the first to present some empirical evidence for the theory.

There are, of course, many other arguments to build up a rationale for your research project, but the above are very often used and you should check whether you can use some of them eventually together with any other arguments you have in mind to build a rationale for your research project.

Problem statement and research objective

The problem statement contains the need for the research project and is usually represented in question form. Note that from a scientific perspective why-like questions are much more interesting than what-like questions, as the former really attempt to find an explanation for a mechanism, while answers to the latter are sufficient if they purely provide a descriptive account of the phenomena or situation. If you start with a why question, you can either attempt to check the validity of certain explanations (explanatory study) or you can attempt to find possible explanations (explorative study). Which type of study is more appropriate mainly depends on what is already known about a phenomenon and how complex the explanation is.

In quantitative studies, the research problem is often followed by some indication of the main hypotheses you want to test, that is, when you start specifying the problem statement, you state what kind of explanation you are advancing. Whether you state them as real hypotheses or additional sub-questions does not matter; what matters is that you inform the reader in which direction you are heading, that is, what kind of theories and explanations you will test. In qualitative studies, you often do not have main hypotheses, as you are still exploring and searching for suitable explanations. Nevertheless, even when you start a qualitative study you have some kind of expectations, which might turn out right or wrong, and it is important to inform the reader about these expectations.

If the problem you investigate is rather complex, that is, it takes into account multiple possible explanations and/or multiple phenomena that are interrelated, it might be advisable to use a figure sketching the relations you are testing or exploring. Boiling a problem statement down to a simple figure also helps you to clearly state which variables or phenomena are of concern and how they are defined, how they are distinct from other variables or phenomena, and how they relate with other variables.

Finally, you briefly state your target group in this section. Thus, if you conduct a qualitative study, you could state that the study will be based on mobile telephone users in Ethiopia or you could state that it would be a comparison of the telecommunication markets in 25 African countries. In the case of a quantitative study, you could state that the exploration is based on a case study of how mobile telecommunication was introduced to a small village in the north of Ghana. Thus, you give the reader a first idea in which context you will examine the research question later on.

Theoretical section

As mentioned earlier, this section distinguishes academic reports from all other types of report; it forms a substantial part of any scientific paper. The two typical elements of a theoretical section are the review of the current academic literature on the issue investigated and a substantial part covering the theory development presented in the report. The style of a theoretical section depends largely on what kind of study is presented. In theoretical studies, this section will provide a detailed description and argument for the theoretical model developed. In quantitative empirical studies, you will use this section either to introduce the formal mathematical model or to provide convincing arguments for the hypotheses you derive. In qualitative empirical studies, this section usually contains a very critical and extensive review of the literature, closing with convincing arguments concerning the points you will make later on.

There are three ways to look at the literature you collected:

1 You can read through it *to identify problems*. If a book or article makes a claim that seems inaccurate or too simplistic to you, you have detected a research problem, as you can now investigate whether a more complex or differentiated explanation would describe the phenomena better. For example, at the beginning of transaction cost theory, most studies argued that firms can choose to make or buy, that is, they could either produce an input they needed themselves (hierarchy) or buy it on the market. However, this claim was inaccurate to the extent that firms also used other structures to govern the exchange, such as long-term contracting or alliances. A new branch of research investigating contracting and alliances was the response to the oversimplified view that inter-firm transactions occur either via markets or with a hierarchy (the firm).
2 You can read through *to find arguments*. Suppose your research problem starts with the observation that the market leaders in the mobile telephone market have changed rather quickly in the last 20 years, while in other markets the number 1 firm remained stable for long periods. Microsoft has been the number 1 software company for more than two decades and General Motors the number 1 in cars for even more than two decades.

But in mobile telecommunication, we observed that Motorola lost its number 1 position to Nokia, which, in turn, lost it to Samsung. What would explain that some markets are more dynamic than others? Reading through articles you will find several explanations for the dynamic within markets. Likely arguments mentioned in the literature are technology shocks that restructure the industry, or changes in consumer preferences, such as fashion waves that favour certain brands until the brand is so widely accepted that it gets 'uncool'.

3 You can read *to find evidence.* Previous literature is often used to support the claims that you made yourself. If you look through the literature to find such evidence it is important to distinguish whether previous literature just also claims what you claim or whether it provides evidence for the claim, that is, they have qualitative or quantitative data that supports the claim. If previous studies present evidence supporting your claim, that is a start. It shows that at least one other person has similar thoughts but, of course, just one other person is not sufficient evidence to claim that your argument is valid.

Next to reviewing the literature, the development of your own theory is an important part of this section. Developing a theory is essentially based on good arguments. To check whether an argument you use is good and sound, you should ask the following five questions. You can also use these questions to check the quality of the arguments made by others.

1 *What is the claim exactly?* You need to be very precise on what your claim is. For example, the following two claims differ substantially: (i) large firms are more innovative than small firms; and (ii) large firms are more innovative than small firms in industries with a high research and development (R&D) intensity. The first claim applies in general, while the second is restricted to specific industries.

2 *What reasons support the claim?* A viable reason for the second restricted claim would be that in an industry with high R&D expenditure it is costly to innovate, that is, you need to invest large sums of money up front before you introduce a new product. Only large firms with sufficient resources are able to finance such large up-front investments.

3 *What is the evidence pointing to the reasons mentioned?* Here you need to find studies that show a positive correlation between firm size and the number of new products or patents in R&D-intensive industries.

4 *Are there alternative explanations for the evidence?* With regard to the first question, we ask whether differences in financial resources really explain the relationship between firms' size and innovativeness. Alternative explanations could be that large firms are better able to attract good people and are more innovative even if you control for financial resources. Or large firms are more innovative, not because they have more resources, but because they have different resources that encourage them to combine different types of resource resulting in innovations. Especially in a world in which we too easily rely on facts, it is important to think about what the possible reasons are behind the facts and often we come to the conclusion that there are multiple reasons for the observation of a phenomenon.

5 *Is there different evidence?* The second question asks how valid the evidence is. Are there R&D-intensive industries where small firms are more innovative than large firms? Is the biotechnology sector a counter-example, that is an R&D-intensive sector in which small firms are more innovative? Although the provision of a counter-example does not allow us to conclude that the opposite argument is true, each counter-example points at the limited range of an argument and it is up to you to show these range restrictions.

The better your argument withstands these five questions, the sounder it is. Sound arguments lead either to strong hypotheses or strong potential explanations in explorative studies and are the cornerstones of any good research study.

Methodology

Management and short academic reports usually do not have a separate section on the methodology. However, for technical and academic reports, that is also for research projects, the section on methodology is important. One important reason for being explicit on methodology is that this section is the only part in a research project where you can show how much effort you have put into the collection and analysis of the information. Approaching respondents, collecting information and editing the collected information often takes a substantial slice of the total time devoted to a research project. The methodological section or chapter is the place where you can show how thorough you have been on these issues.

1 *Sampling design or research participants:* The researcher explicitly defines the target population being studied and the sampling methods used. In quantitative studies this will include answers to the questions: What was the intended population? What did the population look like from the sample that was drawn? Was this a probability or non-probability sample? If probability, was it simple random or complex random? How were the elements selected? How was the size determined? How much confidence do we have, and how much error was allowed? If you report on a qualitative study, typical elements covered would be a thicker and more detailed description of where the research was conducted and would include answers to the questions: Which firm(s) or department(s) does the study address? Who provided the information? Thus, to summarize, you start a methodological section by describing who you researched and how you approached the research participants. In a second step, it is wise to justify that the sample population or the case chosen is based on a sensible selection. As it is impossible to research all people or all firms in the world, you usually address a particular country, industry or even firm. Give some arguments why it makes sense to investigate this particular country, industry or firm. What do they have in particular that makes them an interesting case or sample for your research problem? The reasons given here often link to the rationale of the whole research. For example, a specific country can be interesting to research if it has not yet been covered by previous research, or an industry is interesting to examine because you expect that the phenomena that interest you are particularly strong in this industry.

2 *Research design:* The coverage of the design must be adapted to the purpose. In an experimental study, the materials, tests, equipment, control conditions and other devices should be described. In descriptive or *ex-post facto* designs, it may be sufficient to cover the rationale for using one design instead of competing alternatives. Even with a sophisticated design, the strengths and weaknesses should be identified, and the instrumentation and materials discussed. Copies of materials, such as the questionnaire used, are placed in an appendix.

3 *Data collection:* This part of the report describes the specifics of gathering the data. Its contents depend on the design selected. Survey work generally uses a team with field and central supervision. How many were involved? What was their training? How were they managed? When were the data collected? How much time did it take? What were the conditions in the field? How were irregularities handled? In an experiment, we would want to know about subject assignment to groups, the use of standardized procedures and protocols, the administration of tests or observational forms, manipulation of the variables, and so on. For a qualitative case study, you would extensively describe from which sources you obtained the information and by what means (e.g. interviews, observations, etc.). What kind of observation, if any, did you conduct? What kind of archival sources and documents did you look at? How long did it take to collect the information and who else was involved in collecting it?

4 *Measurements:* There is always a gap between the information you gathered and the concepts or variables that you used in the theoretical section; identity between these two is extremely rare. In the measurement sections, you describe how you transformed the information collected to the theoretical concepts and variables. For example, in a research project based on a quantitative survey you describe which question you combined to generate a new variable reflecting the theoretical concept you are interested in and you also report any results from reliability and scaling tests. Studies employing a more qualitative methodology also need a measurement section that clarifies how you decided that the qualitative information obtained really indicates that a certain situation occurred or a certain behaviour happened. Has it been sufficient if a certain issue was mentioned just by one interviewee or had it to be mentioned by more than one, or has any information that was obtained from the interview been cross-checked with the information obtained from archival sources? Explaining how you assessed the information obtained, either quantitative or qualitative, is an important element in building up readers' confidence in the validity of your study.

Data analysis

This section summarizes the methods used to analyse the data. It describes data handling, preliminary analysis, statistical tests, computer programs and other technical information. The rationale for the choice of analysis approaches should be clear. A brief commentary on assumptions and appropriateness of use should be presented.

Limitations

This topic is often handled with ambivalence. Some people wish to ignore the matter, feeling that mentioning limitations detracts from the impact of their study. This attitude is unprofessional and possibly unethical. Others seem to adopt a masochistic approach of detailing everything. The section should be a thoughtful presentation of significant methodology or implementation problems and the consequences these limitations might have for the validity of the outcomes. An even-handed approach is one of the hallmarks of an honest and competent investigator.

Some people put this section at the end of the report, but a good reason to put it before the conclusions is that you do not want to finish the report with a section pointing at the weaknesses of the research, rather you want to close your research project or report with a statement on what the research project or report contributes.

The main concern of any limitation is that it might bias your results, that is, it might lead to the wrong results. Common limitations refer to the used sample, the used measurements and the used analysis techniques:

- *Sample*: If you use a specific sample, for example employees in information technology (IT) firms, your results might be biased because employees in IT firms earn above-average salaries, work in less hierarchical firms, and so on.
- *Measurement*: Your measurement might be flawed, because you only used a limited set of questions; it has not been validated in previous studies; you are unsure whether respondents from different countries understood the question in the same way; and you had to impute data, and so on.
- *Analysis*: You could not use more advanced analysis techniques because your sample size was not large enough to employ them.

A good way to discuss the limitations is to assess how much they could bias your results. You should note that not all biases work in your favour, that is, the bias makes it more likely that you support a hypothesis. For example, if you use a specific sample, this usually means that the variance in the sample is smaller than in the larger population and smaller variance means that it is harder to obtain significant effects. Thus, such a bias does not make your results better, but the consequences of the bias are less severe, because the estimates you obtain are more likely to be an underestimation than an overestimation.

Findings

This is generally the longest section of the report. The objective is to explain the data rather than draw interpretations or conclusions. When quantitative data can be presented, this should be done as simply as possible with charts, graphics and tables.

The data need not include everything you have collected. The criterion for inclusion is, 'Is this material important to the reader's understanding of the problem and the findings?' However, make sure that you include findings unfavourable to your hypotheses as well as those that support them.

Conclusions

Summary and conclusions

The summary is a brief statement of the essential findings. Sectional summaries may be used if there are many specific findings. These may be combined into an overall summary. In simple descriptive research, a summary may complete the report, because conclusions and recommendations may not be required.

Findings state facts; conclusions represent inferences drawn from the findings. A writer is sometimes reluctant to make conclusions and thus leaves the task to the reader. Avoid this temptation when possible. As the researcher, you are the one best informed on the factors that critically influence the findings and conclusions.

There are several goals of a conclusion. First, you should assess your research project regarding whether you reached your objectives. Remind the reader of the project's goal, write about the steps you took in the process and discuss the issues that affected the process. Then present the main findings and place them in a greater context. Second, the conclusion should relate the results to the real world by making recommendations based on what one has learned from your research project. Third, you can use the conclusion to discuss what needs to be done in the future, i.e. present suggestions for future research.

Student Research

What makes an excellent research project?

In most study programmes, the research project marks the end of the programme and most students are willing to put considerable effort into their project. After having worked so hard, read so many books and articles, analysed so much information and written so many pages, most of them expect a good grade for their effort. But some are disappointed once they read or hear the verdict and discover that their hard work earned a mark below the average. In the last few years, I have supervised dozens of research projects and have been a second reader for many more. Just a few months ago, one of my research project students won the university award and a €500 cheque, but another student almost failed. What does it take to write an excellent – emphasis on excellent – research project?

The answer is easy: an excellent research project surprises me. Based on the many projects I have read, I have compiled a list of the surprising elements in those that belong to the top 10 per cent. All those projects showed solid craftsmanship, they provided a thorough literature review, their argumentation was clear and convincing, the design was sound and well executed, they used the appropriate analysis tools and they provided a conclusion with some recommendations for science and practice. These were preconditions for an excellent research project, but the excellence came with something more:

- In a time when the average Master's research project was about 100 pages at our university, Floor Schuilings wrote a project with just 40 pages. In these 40 pages nothing was missing and not one sentence was superfluous. That really made an impression.
- Mathieu Brummer wrote a research project on social capital and regional entrepreneurship rates, a rather conceptual paper with some secondary data analysis. A solid project, what made it excellent was that he managed to take a broad perspective on the topic. He referred to theoretical arguments from sociology, business, economics, psychology, political science and even geography, compared them, and intertwined them to build his own reasoning. Thus, the project excelled by taking a broad perspective on a well-defined narrow topic.
- Till Prinz was interested in social loafing among students, especially whether personality traits could explain social loafing. Such an approach if well executed would have made a good research project, but Till went further. First, he integrated considerations from impression management into his theoretical reasoning, something that seems obvious, but no one has done that before. Second, he collected data over time, which allowed him to show the dynamics in social loafing behaviour.
- Eline Artz did a research project about isomorphism, which describes the process that members of a population, for example an industry, start to resemble other members that face the same environmental conditions. The topic itself was already unusual for a research project, at least at our university, and it is certainly one of the tougher topics to write about. But what really impressed us was how Eline investigated it: she took the MBA market as a case and analysed the curricula and admission requirements for 67 programmes.

The four examples above should show you that excellence requires more than solid work; it requires something noteworthy, something that supervisors rarely encounter. It is hard to plan excellence ahead, as you never know when the bright idea on how to give your research project the decisive twist comes up. But a bright idea is not sufficient. All these four students were not only bright, but they also worked harder than average. They really loved their research topic and could not stop talking about it; probably they even dreamt about it. Without such a deep devotion you cannot achieve excellence.

Appendices

The appendices are the place for complex tables, statistical tests, supporting documents, copies of forms and questionnaires, detailed descriptions of methodology, instructions to fieldworkers, and other evidence important for later support. The reader who wishes to learn about the technical aspects of the study and to look at statistical breakdowns will want a complete appendix.

Bibliography

The use of secondary data requires a bibliography. Proper citation styles and formats are unique to the purpose of the report. The instructor, programme, institution or client often specifies style requirements. The uniqueness of varying requirements makes detailed examples in this chapter impractical although the endnotes and references in this book provide one example. As cited in Chapter 2, on the research proposal, we recommend the *Publication Manual of the American Psychological Association*; Kate L. Turabian, *A Manual for Writers of Term Papers, Research Projects, and Dissertations*; and Joseph Gibaldi and Walter S. Achtert, *MLA Handbook for Writers of Research Papers*.

Writing the report

Students often pay inadequate attention to reporting their findings and conclusions. This is unfortunate. A well-presented study will often impress the reader more than a study with greater scientific quality but a weaker presentation. Report-writing skills are especially valuable to academic researchers and the junior executive or management trainee.

Pre-writing concerns

Before writing, one should ask again, 'What is the purpose of this report?' Responding to this question is one way to crystallize the problem.

The second pre-writing question is, 'Who will read the report?' Thought should be given to the needs, temperament and biases of the audience. You should not distort facts to meet these needs and biases, but should consider them while developing the presentation. Knowing who will read the report may suggest its appropriate length. For management reports, the higher the report goes in an organization, the shorter it should be.

Another consideration is technical background – the gap in subject knowledge between the reader and the writer. The greater the gap, the more difficult it is to convey the full findings meaningfully and concisely. In academic writing, it is safe to assume that the reader's knowledge is very similar to the author's knowledge.

The third pre-writing question is, 'What are the circumstances and limitations under which you are writing?' Is the nature of the subject highly technical? Do you need statistics? Charts? What is the importance of the topic? A crucial subject justifies more effort than a minor one. What should be the scope of the report? How much time is available? Deadlines often impose limitations on the report.

Finally, 'How will the report be used?' Try to visualize the reader using the report. How can the information be made more convenient? How much effort must be given to getting the attention and interest of the reader? Will the report be read by more than one person? If so, how many copies should be made? What will be the distribution of the report?

The outline

Once the researcher has made the first analysis of the data, drawn tentative conclusions and completed statistical significance tests, it is time to develop an outline. A useful system employs the following organization structure, using Roman numbers for the major headings, and letters and Arabic numbers for the different sub-levels. Others also use small Roman numbers (i, ii, iii, iv . . .) or even Greek letters (α, β, γ, δ . . .) to add structure.

I. Major topic heading
    A. Major sub-topic heading
        1. Sub-topic
           a. Minor sub-topic
              (1) Further detail
                  (a) Even further detail

The structure depth of your outline depends very much on the total length of the report. Short reports should not be structured deeper than the second level. In addition, you might choose not to use letter or number 'numbering' at the lower levels, but just different printing formats, such as bold, underlined or italic text. When choosing the depth of your outline structure, you should try to keep some balance in the depth. Thus, structuring your second section B deep down to the sixth level, while all other sections are structured much less deeply creates an unbalanced structure. Further, you should be aware that introducing a new lower level requires that you have at least two distinct aspects at this level. Thus, if you introduce a minor sub-topic – (a) – to your sub-topic – 1. – you also need a minor sub-topic (b).

Software for developing outlines and visually connecting ideas simplifies this once-onerous task. Two styles of outlining are widely used: the topic outline and the sentence outline. In the **topic outline**, a key word/phrase is used. The assumption is that the writer knows its significance and will later remember the nature of the argument represented by that word or phrase or, alternatively, the outliner knows that a point should be made but is not yet sure how to make it.

The **sentence outline** expresses the essential thoughts associated with the specific topic. This approach leaves less development work for later writing, other than elaboration and explanation to improve readability. It has the obvious advantages of pushing the writer to make decisions on what to include and how to say it. It is probably the best outlining style for the inexperienced researcher because it divides the writing job into its two major components: what to say and how to say it.

Exhibit 15.3 gives an example of the type of detail found with each of these outlining formats.

Exhibit 15.3 *Example of a structure.*

Topic outline	Sentence outline
I. Demand	I. Demand for refrigerators
A. How measured?	A. Measured in terms of factory shipments as reported by the EU trade commission
1. Voluntary error	1. Error is introduced into year-to-year comparisons because reporting is voluntary
2. Shipping error	2. A second factor is variations from month to month because of shipping and invoicing patterns
(a) Monthly variances	(a) Variations up to 30 per cent this year depend on whether shipments were measured by actual shipping date or invoice date

---

The bibliography

Long reports, particularly technical ones, require a bibliography. A bibliography documents the sources used by the writer. Although bibliographies may contain work used as a background or for further study, it is preferable to include only those sources used in preparing the report.

Bibliographic retrieval software allows researchers to locate and save references from online services and translate them into database records. Entries can be further searched, sorted, indexed and formatted into bibliographies of any style. Many retrieval programs are network compatible and connect to popular word processors. (Chapter 10 also mentions a recording system for converting source notes to footnotes and bibliographies.)

Style manuals provide guidelines on form, section and alphabetical arrangement, and annotation. Projects using many electronic sources may benefit from the comparison of APA and MLA citations in Exhibit 15.4.

Exhibit 15.4 Citing electronic sources.

Type	APA	MLA
Full-text sources from library resources (online and CD-ROM)	Last name of author, first initial. (Year, month, day.) Title. Journal [type of medium], volume (issue), paging if given or other indicator of length. Available: supplier/database name and number/identifier number, item or accession number [access date].	Last name of author, first initial. Title. *Journal* [type of medium] volume (issue) (year): paging if given or other indicator of length. Available: supplier/database name and number/identifier number, item or accession number [access date].*
	Crow, P. (1994). GATT shows progress in Congress. *The Oil and Gas Journal* [Online], 92(49), 32 (1p.). Available: Information Access/Expanded Academic Index ASAP/ A15955498 [1996, 13 March].	Crow, P. 'GATT shows progress in Congress' in *The Oil and Gas Journal* [Online] 92(49) (1994): 32–3. Online. Available: Information Access Company. *Expanded Academic Index ASAP*. 13 March 1996.
Websites: individual works with print equivalent	Last name of author/editor, first initial. (Year, month, day.) Title (Edition). [Type of medium]. Producer. Available: address or source/path/file [access date].	Last name of author/editor, first name. Title of print version of work. Edition statement. Place of publication: publisher, date. Title of electronic work. Medium [Online]. Information supplier. Available protocol: www.address. goes. here. Access date [dy mo yr].
	Bartlett, J. (1995, March). *Familiar quotations: Passages, phrases and proverbs traced to their sources* (9th edn). [Online]. Columbia University. Available: www.columbia. edu/acis/bartleby/bartlett/ [1996, 19 March].	Bartlett, J. *Familiar Quotations: Passages, Phrases & Proverbs Traced to Their Sources in Ancient & Modern Literature*. 9th edn. Boston: Little, Brown & Co., 1995. Online. Columbia University. Available: www.columbia. edu/acis/bartleby/bartlett. 19 March 1996.
Websites: parts of works	Last name of author/editor, first initial. (Year, month, day.) Title of article or document. In Title of Source (edition), [Online], volume (issue), paging or indicator of length. Available: address or source/path/file [access date].	Last name of author, first name. 'Title of Article or Document'. Newsletter, or Conference volume (issue number) (year) or date of publication: number of pages or pars. Medium [online]. Available protocol: www.address. goes. here. Access date [dy mo yr].
	Steinfield, C., Kraut, R. & Plummer, A. (1995). The impact of inter-organizational networks on buyer–seller relationships. *Journal of Computer-mediated Communication* [Online], 1(3), 56 paragraphs. *Available:* www.shum.juji.ac.il/jcmc/vol1/issue3/ steinfld.html [1996, April 22].	Steinfield, C., Kraut, R. & Plummer, A. 'The Impact of Interorganizational Networks on Buyer-Seller Relationships'. *Journal of Computer-mediated Communication* 1(3) (1995): 56 pars Online. Available HTTP: www.shum.juji.ac.il/jcmc/vol1/ issue3/steinfld. html. 22 April 1996.
Websites: email, listserv and discussion list messages	Last name of author, first initial (if known). 'Subject line from posting.' Message. Discussion list [online]. Available email: LISTSERV@email address [Access date]. Wagner, K. (1996, 6 February). Re: Citing/evaluating web resources. NETLIBS [Online]. Available email netlibs@qut.edu.au [1996, 7 February].	Last name of author, first name (if known). 'Subject line from posting.' Discussion list email: LISTSERV@email address. Access date. Wagner, Kurt W. 'Re: Citing/ evaluating web resources'. Available email: netlibs@qut. edu.au 7 February 1996.
Websites: homepages	Last name of author/editor, first initial (if known). (Last update or copyright date). Home Page Title [Home page of . . .]. Available: www.address.goes.here [Access date].	
	House, P. (1997, 26 March – last update). The Smithsonian: America's treasure house for learning [Home Page of the Smithsonian Institution] [Online]. Available: www.si.edu/ newstart.htm[1997 27 March].	

Source: adapted from *APA Guides for Citing Electronic Sources and Guidelines for Citing Electronic Sources*. MLA, Cedarville College Centennial Library, Cedarville, OH, 45315.
Note: *access date not needed if CD-ROM.

Writing the draft

Once the outline is complete, decisions can be made on the placement of graphics, tables and charts. Each should be matched to a particular section in the outline. It is helpful to make these decisions before your first draft. While graphics might be added later or tables changed into charts, it is helpful to make a first approximation of the graphics before beginning to write. Choices for reporting statistics will be reviewed later in this chapter.

Each writer uses different mechanisms for getting thoughts into written form. Some will write in longhand, relying on someone else to transcribe their prose into word-processed format. Others are happiest in front of a word processor, able to add, delete and move sections at will. Use whatever is the best approach for you.

Computer software packages check for spelling errors and provide a thesaurus for looking up alternative ways of expressing a thought. A CD-ROM can call up the 20-volume *Oxford English Dictionary*, believed to be the greatest dictionary in any language. Currently, even some common word confusion ('there' for 'their', 'to' for 'too' or 'effect' for 'affect') will be found by standard spellcheckers, but there are some mistakes that they are unable to detect. Advanced programs will scrutinize your report for grammar, punctuation, capitalization, repeated words, transposed letters, homonyms, style problems and readability level. The style checker will reveal misused words and indicate awkward phrasing.

Readability

Sensitive writers will consider the reading ability of their audience in order to achieve high readership levels. You can obtain high readership more easily if the topic interests the readers and is in their field of expertise. In addition, you can demonstrate the usefulness of your report by pointing out how it will help the readers. Finally, you can write at a level that is appropriate to the readers' reading abilities. To test writing for difficulty level, there are standard **readability indexes**. The Flesch Reading Ease Score gives a score between 0 and 100. The lower the score, the harder the material is to read. The Flesch–Kincaid Grade Level and Gunning's Fog Index both provide a score that corresponds with the grade level needed to easily read and understand a document. Although it is possible to calculate these indexes by hand, some software packages will do it automatically. The most sophisticated packages allow you to specify the preferred reading level. Words that are above that level are highlighted to allow you to choose an alternative.

Advocates of readability measurement do not claim that all written material should be at the simplest level possible. They argue only that the level should be appropriate for the audience. They point out that comic books score about 6 on the Gunning scale (that is, a person with a sixth-grade education should be able to read that material), while *Time* magazine usually scores about 10. Material that scores much above 12 becomes difficult for the public to read comfortably. Such measures obviously give only a rough idea of the true readability of a report, and good writing calls for a variety of other skills to enhance reading comprehension.

Comprehensibility

Good writing varies with the writing objective. Research writing is designed to convey information of a precise nature. Avoid ambiguity, multiple meanings and allusions. Take care to choose the right words – words that convey thoughts accurately, clearly and efficiently. When concepts and constructs are used, they must be defined, either operationally or descriptively.

Words and sentences should be organized and edited carefully. Misplaced modifiers run rampant in carelessly written reports. Subordinate ideas mixed with major ideas make the report confusing to readers, forcing them to sort out what is important and what is secondary when this should have been done for them.

Finally, there is the matter of pace. Pace is defined as:

> "The rate at which the printed page presents information to the reader . . . The proper pace in technical writing is one that enables the reader to keep his mind working just a fraction of a second behind his eye as he reads along. It logically would be slow when the information is complex or difficult to understand; fast when the information is straightforward and familiar. If the reader's mind lags behind his eye, the pace is too rapid; if his mind wanders ahead of his eye (or wants to) the pace is too slow."[3]

If the text is overcrowded with concepts, there is too much information per sentence. By contrast, sparse writing has too few significant ideas per sentence. Writers use a variety of methods to adjust the **pace** of their writing, as outlined below:

- Use ample white space and wide margins to create a positive psychological effect on the reader.
- Break large units of text into smaller units with headings and sub-headings to show organization of the topics.
- Relieve difficult text with visual aids when possible.
- Emphasize important material and de-emphasize secondary material through sentence construction and judicious use of italicizing, underlining, capitalization and parentheses.
- Choose words carefully, opting for the known and short rather than the unknown and long. Graduate students, in particular, seem to revel in using jargon, pompous constructions, and long or arcane words. Naturally, technical terms are appropriate, when they belong to the common jargon of the audience.
- Repeat and summarize critical and difficult ideas so readers have time to absorb them.
- Make strategic use of service words. These are words that 'do not represent objects or ideas, but show relationship. Transitional words, such as the conjunctions, are service words. So are phrases such as "on the other hand," "in summary," and "in contrast."'[4]

Tone

Review the writing to ensure that the tone is appropriate. The reader can, and should, be referred to, but researchers should avoid referring to themselves. One author notes that the 'application of the "you" attitude . . . makes the message sound like it is written to the reader, not sent by the author. A message prepared for the reader conveys sincerity, personalization, warmth, and involvement on the part of the author.'[5] To accomplish this, remove negative phrasing and rewrite the thought positively. Do not change your recommendations or your findings to make them positive. Instead, review the phrasing. Which of the following sounds better?

1 End-users do not want the Information Systems Department telling them what software to buy.
2 End-users want more autonomy over their computer software choices.

The messages convey the same information, but the positive tone of the second message will not put readers from the Information Systems Department on the defensive.

Final proof

It is helpful to put the draft away for a day before doing the final editing. Go to the beach, ride a bicycle in the park or go to the cinema – do anything that is unrelated to the research project. Then return to the report and read it with a critical eye. Does the writing flow smoothly? Are there transitions where they are needed? Is the organization apparent to the reader? Do the findings and conclusions adequately meet the problem statement and the research objectives? Are the tables and graphics displaying the proper information in an easy-to-read format? After assuring yourself that the draft is complete, write the executive summary.

Presentation considerations

The final consideration in the report-writing process is production. Reports can be printed on an ink-jet, laser, colour or other printer; or sent out for typesetting. Most student and small research reports are produced on a computer printer. The presentation of the report conveys to the readers the professional approach used throughout the project. Care should be taken to use compatible fonts throughout the entire report. The printer should produce consistent, easy-to-read letters on quality paper. When reports are photocopied for more than one reader, make sure that the copies are clean and have no black streaks or grey areas.

Overcrowding of text creates an appearance problem. Readers need the visual relief provided by ample white space. We define 'ample' as 2.5 cm of white space at the top, bottom and right-hand margins. On the left side, the margin should be at least 3 cm to provide room for binding or punched holes. Even greater margins will often improve report appearance and help to highlight key points or sections. Overcrowding also occurs when the report contains page after page of large blocks of unbroken text. This produces an unpleasant psychological effect on readers because of its formidable appearance. Overcrowded text, however, may be avoided in the following ways:

- Use shorter paragraphs. As a rough guide, any paragraph longer than half a page is suspect. Remember that each paragraph should represent a distinct thought. But also be aware that a paragraph should be longer than one sentence.
- Indent parts of text that represent listings, long quotations or examples.
- Use headings and sub-headings to divide the report and its major sections into homogeneous topical parts.
- Use vertical listings of points (such as this list).

Inadequate labelling creates another physical problem. Each graph or table should contain enough information to be self-explanatory. Text headings and sub-headings also help with labelling. They function as signs for the audience, describing the organization of the report and indicating the progress of discussion. They also help readers to skim the material and to return easily to particular sections of the report.

Presentation of statistics[6]

The presentation of statistics in research reports is a special challenge for writers. Four basic ways to present such data are in:

1 a text paragraph
2 semi-tabular form
3 tables
4 graphics.

Text presentation

This is probably the most common method of presentation when there are only a few statistics. The writer can direct the reader's attention to certain numbers or comparisons and emphasize specific points. The drawback is that the statistics are submerged in the text, requiring the reader to scan the entire paragraph to extract the meaning. For example, the material in the paragraph below has a few simple comparisons but becomes more complicated when text and statistics are combined.

> "A comparison of the three largest PC sellers in Europe shows that the position of the market leader, Compaq, was threatened in 1999. Its growth was just 4.0 per cent – although its market share remains 50 per cent larger than that of the second largest competitor, Fujitsu-Siemens, which sold 3.5 million units. This compares to sales growth for Fujitsu-Siemens of 19.5 per cent, and Dell with a sales increase of 16.3 per cent. In 1999 Fujitsu-Siemens reached a market share of 10.8 per cent, Compaq sold 5 million units for a market share of 15.6 per cent and Dell reached a market share of 9.2 per cent, selling 2.5 million units."

Semi-tabular presentation

When there are just a few figures, they may be taken from the text and listed. Lists of quantitative comparisons are much easier to read and understand than embedded statistics. Exhibit 15.5 offers an example of semi-tabular presentation.

Exhibit 15.5 Semi-tabular presentation.

	PC units sold 1999 (thousands)	Growth 1998–9 (%)	Market share 1999 (%)
Compaq	5,000	+4.0	15.6
Fujitsu-Siemens	3,500	+19.5	10.8
Dell	3,500	+16.3	9.2

Note: A comparison of the top three sellers in Europe in 1999 shows that Compaq still holds the largest market share, but that Fujitsu-Siemens and Dell are growing faster.

Tabular presentation

Tables are generally superior to text for presenting statistics, although they should be accompanied by comments directing the reader's attention to important figures in the table. Tables facilitate quantitative comparisons and provide a concise, efficient way to present numerical data.

Tables are either general or summary in nature. General tables tend to be large, complex and detailed. They serve as the repository for the statistical findings of the study and are usually presented in the appendix of a research report. Summary tables contain only a few key pieces of data, closely related to a specific finding. To make them inviting to the reader (who might otherwise skip over them), the table designer should omit unimportant details and collapse multiple classifications into composite measures that may be substituted for the original data.

Any table should contain sufficient information to enable the reader to understand its contents. Thus, tables need to be customized and should not be a copy and paste operation from the output of a statistical analysis package. The title should explain the subject of the table, how the data are classified, the time period, or other related matters. A sub-title is sometimes included under the main title to explain something about the table; most often this is a statement of the measurement units in which the data are expressed. The contents of the columns should be clearly identified by the column heads, and what is written in the row labels should do the same for the rows. The body of the table contains the data, while the footnotes contain any necessary explanations. Footnotes should be identified by letters, or symbols such as asterisks (*), rather than by numbers, to avoid confusion with data values. Finally, there should be a source note if the data do not come from your original research. Exhibit 15.6 illustrates the various parts of a table.

Exhibit 15.6 Sample tabular findings.

CO_2 – emission in Europe[a]			
Country	Million tons 1990	Million tons 1996[b]	Change in %
Germany[c]	1,015	910	−10.3
UK[d]	615	593	−3.6
Italy	442	448	+1.4
France[e]	392	399	+1.8
Spain	226	248	+9.7
Netherlands	161	185	+15.9
Belgium	116	129	+11.2
Greece	85	92	+9.3
Finland[f]	59	66	+11.9
Sweden[f]	55	63	+15.5
EU total	3,372	3,348	−0.7

Source: WUA, www.eea.eu.int.
Notes:
(a) Including CO_2 emissions from uses other than fossil energy.
(b) Latest available figures for all countries; due to the climate, the total CO_2 emission in the EU was larger in 1996 than in 1995, 1997 and 1998.
(c) Decrease mainly in Eastern Germany.
(d) Decrease due to switching from coal to gas for energy generation.
(e) Relatively low due to the large share of nuclear energy.
(f) Relatively low due to the large share of energy from water power.

Graphics

Compared with tables, graphs show less information and often only approximate values. However, they are more often read and remembered than tables. Their great advantage is that they convey quantitative values and comparisons more readily than tables. With PC charting programs, you can easily turn a set of numbers into a chart or graph.

There are many different graphic forms. Exhibit 15.7 shows the most common ones and how they should be used. Statistical explanation charts such as boxplots, stem-and-leaf displays and histograms are discussed in Chapter 16. Line graphs, area, pie and bar charts, and pictographs and 3-D graphics receive additional attention here.

Exhibit 15.7 Guide to graphs.

Column Compares sizes and amounts of categories usually for the same time. Places categories on *X* axis and values on *Y* axis.

Bar Same as the column but positions categories on *Y* axis and values on *X* axis. Deviations, when used, distinguish positive from negative values.

Stacked bar In either bar or column shows how components contribute to the total of the category.

Pie Shows relationship of parts to the whole. Wedges are raw values of data.

Stacked pie Same as pie but diplays two or more data series.

Multiple pie Uses same data as stacked pie but plots separate pies for each column of data without stacking.

Line Compares values over time to show changes in trends.

Filled line Similar to line chart, but uses fill to highlight series.

Area (surface) Like line chart, compares changing values but emphasizes relative value of each series.

Step Compares discrete points on the value axis with vertical lines showing difference between points. Not for showing a trend.

Scatter Shows if relationship between variables follows a pattern. May be used with one variable at different times.

Bubble Used to introduce third variable (dots of different sizes). Axes could be sales, profits: bubbles are assets.

Spider [and radar] Radiating lines are categories; values are distances from centre (shows multiple variables, e.g. performance, ratings, progress).

Polar Shows relationship between a variable and angle measured in degrees (cyclical trends, pollution source vs. wind direction, etc.)

Open-high-low-close Shows fluctuating values in a given period (hour, day); often used for investments.

Boxplot Displays distribution(s) and compares characteristics of shape.

Pictographic Special chart that uses pictures or graphic elements in lieu of bars.

Line graphs

Line graphs are used chiefly for time series and frequency distribution. There are several guidelines for designing a line graph:

- Put the time units or the independent variable on the horizontal axis.
- When showing more than one line, use different line types (solid, dashed, dotted, dash-dot) to enable the reader to distinguish between them easily.
- Try not to put more than four lines on one chart.
- Use a solid line for the primary data.

It is important to be aware of perceptual problems with line diagrams. The first is the use of a zero baseline. Since the length of the bar or distance above the baseline indicates the statistic, it is important that graphs give accurate visual impressions of values. A good way to achieve this is to include a zero baseline on the scale on which the curves are plotted. To set the base at some other value is to introduce a visual bias. This can be seen by comparing the visual impressions in Parts A and B of Exhibit 15.8. Both are accurate plots of the oil price in US$ per barrel between April 2003 and April 2004. In Part A, however, using the baseline of zero places the curve well up on the chart and gives a better perception of the relation between the absolute level of the oil price and the changes between two months. The graph in Part B, with a baseline at US$20, can easily give the impression that the increase was at a more rapid rate. When space or other reasons dictate using shortened scales, the zero base point should still be used but with a break in the scale as shown in Part C of Exhibit 15.8. This will warn the reader that the scale has been reduced.

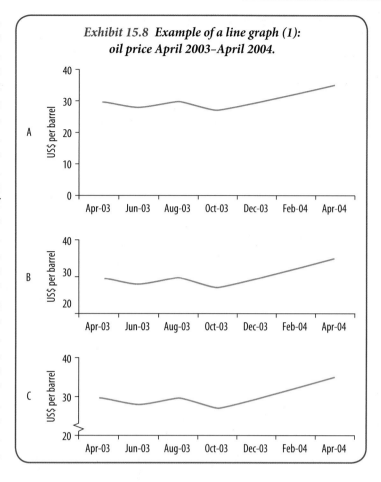

Exhibit 15.8 Example of a line graph (1): oil price April 2003–April 2004.

The balance of size between vertical and horizontal scales also affects the reader's impression of the data. There is no single solution to this problem, but the results can be seen by comparing Parts B and C of Exhibit 15.8.

In Part C, the horizontal scale is twice that in Part B. This changes the slope of the curve, creating a different perception of growth rate.

A third distortion with line diagrams occurs when relative and absolute changes among two or more sets of data are shown. In most charts, we use arithmetic scales where each space unit has identical value. This shows the absolute differences between variables, as in Part A of Exhibit 15.9, which presents the total wind energy production between 1986 and 1998 in the USA, Germany, Denmark and India. This is an arithmetically correct way to present these data; but if we are interested in rates of growth, the visual impressions from a semi-logarithmic scale are more accurate. A comparison of the line diagrams in Parts A and B of Exhibit 15.9 shows how much difference a semi-logarithmic scale makes. Each is valuable and each can be misleading. In Part A, notice that all countries have growing wind energy production and that in the 1980s wind energy production in Germany, Denmark and India was only a small portion of US wind energy production. One can even estimate what this proportion is. Part B gives an insight into growth rates that are not clear from the arithmetic scale. Part B shows that the growth in wind energy production in the USA is very moderate, Danish production increased substantially in the late 1980s, while German and Indian wind energy production grew mainly in the 1990s.

Area (stratum or surface) charts

An **area chart** is also used for a time series. Consisting of a line that has been divided into component parts, it is best used to show changes in patterns over time. The same rules apply to stratum charts as to line charts (see Exhibit 15.7).

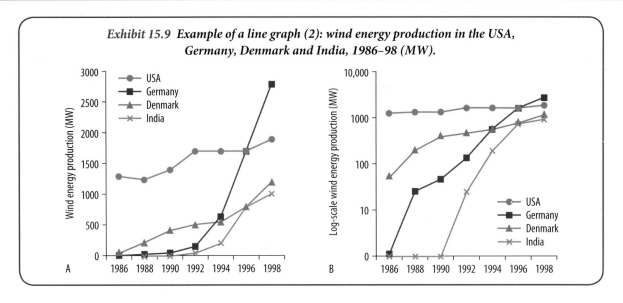

Exhibit 15.9 Example of a line graph (2): wind energy production in the USA, Germany, Denmark and India, 1986–98 (MW).

Pie charts

Pie charts are another form of area chart. They are often used with business data. However, they can easily mislead the reader or be improperly prepared. Research shows that readers' perceptions of the percentages represented by the pie slices are consistently inaccurate.[7] Consider the following suggestions when designing pie charts:

- Show 100 per cent of the subject being graphed.
- Always label the slices with 'call-outs' and with the percentage or amount that is represented. This allows you to dispense with a legend.
- Put the largest slice at 12 o'clock and move clockwise in descending order.
- Use light colours for large slices, darker colours for smaller slices.
- In a pie chart of black and white slices, a single red one will command the most attention and be memorable. Use it to communicate your most important message.[8]
- Do not show evolution over time with pie charts as the only medium. Since pie charts always represent 100 per cent, growth of the overall whole will not be recognized. If you must use a series of pie charts, complement them with an area chart.

As shown in Exhibit 15.10, pie charts portray frequency data in interesting ways. In addition, they can be stacked to show relationships between two sets of data.

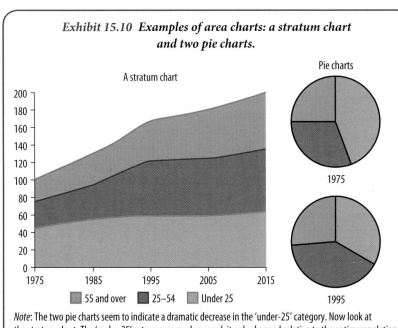

Exhibit 15.10 Examples of area charts: a stratum chart and two pie charts.

Note: The two pie charts seem to indicate a dramatic decrease in the 'under-25' category. Now look at the stratum chart. The 'under-25' category never decreased; it only changed relative to the entire population. It is important not to use pie charts alone in a time series, to avoid giving erroneous impressions.

Bar charts

Bar charts can be very effective if constructed properly. Use the horizontal axis to represent time, and the vertical axis to represent units or growth-related variables. Vertical bars are generally used for time series and for quantitative classifications. Horizontal bars are rarely used for time series, but mainly for nominal categories (e.g. European Union (EU) member countries). If neither variable is time related, either format can be used. A computer-charting program will generate charts quickly and easily. If you are preparing a bar chart by hand, leave space between the bars equal to at least half the width of a bar. An exception to this is the specialized chart – the histogram – where continuous data are grouped into intervals for a frequency distribution. A second exception is the multiple-variable chart, where more than one bar is located at a particular time segment. In this case, the space between the groups of bars is at least half the width of the group. Bar charts come in a variety of patterns as illustrated in Exhibit 15.7.

Pictographs and geographics

Pictographs (geographics) are used in popular magazines and newspapers because they are eye-catching and imaginative. Broad audience magazines and newspapers, such as *BusinessWeek* and the *Daily Mirror*, are often guilty of taking this to the extreme, creating graphs that are incomprehensible. A pictograph uses pictorial symbols (an oil drum for barrels of oil, a wrench figure for numbers of workers, or a pine tree for amount of wood). The symbols represent data volume and are used instead of a bar in a bar-type chart. It is proper to stack same-size images to express more of a quantity and to show fractions of an image to show less. But altering the scale of the symbol produces problems. Since the pictures represent actual objects, doubling the size will increase the area of the symbol by four (and the volume by more). This misleads the reader into believing that the increase is larger than it really is. The exception is a graphic that is easily substituted for a bar, such as the pencils in Exhibit 15.7.

Geographic charts use (a portion of) the world's map, in pictorial form, to show differences in regions. They can be used for product production, per capita rates, demographics or any of a number of other geographically specific variables. The geographic chart in Exhibit 15.11 shows a map of Europe and the Russian Federation. Countries are shaded in different colours, representing the number of physicians per 100,000 inhabitants.

Stacked data sets produce variables of interest that can be aligned on a common geographical referent. The resulting pictorial display allows the user to drill through the layers and visualize the relationships. With better

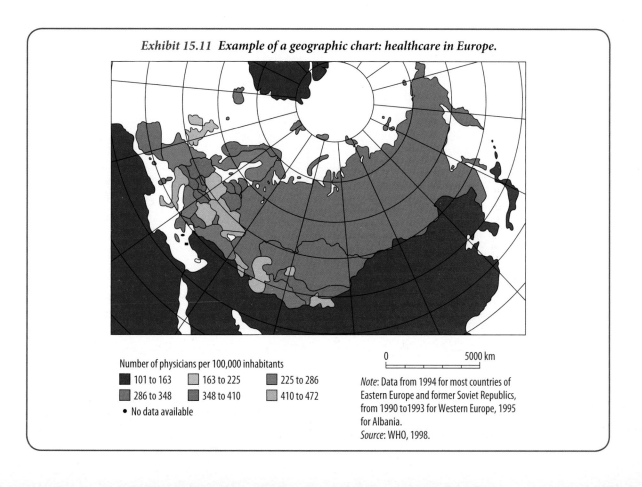

Exhibit 15.11 Example of a geographic chart: healthcare in Europe.

Number of physicians per 100,000 inhabitants

- 101 to 163
- 163 to 225
- 225 to 286
- 286 to 348
- 348 to 410
- 410 to 472
- • No data available

0   5000 km

Note: Data from 1994 for most countries of Eastern Europe and former Soviet Republics, from 1990 to 1993 for Western Europe, 1995 for Albania.
Source: WHO, 1998.

Windows-based software, and government agencies providing geocodes and reference points, geographic spatial displays like the image in Exhibit 15.11 are becoming a more common form of graphic.

3-D graphics

With current charting techniques, virtually all charts can now be made three-dimensional. Although **3-D graphics** add interest, they can also obscure data. Care must be used in selecting 3-D chart candidates (see Exhibit 15.12). Pie and bar charts achieve dimensionality simply by adding depth to the graphics; this is not 3-D. A 3-D column chart allows you to compare three or more variables from the sample in one bar chart-type graph. If you want to display several quarters of sales results for the Hertz, Avis, Budget and National car-rental chains, you have 3-D data. But be careful about converting line charts to ribbon charts, and area charts to 3-D area charts.

Exhibit 15.12 Examples of 3D charts.

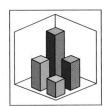
3-D Column
A variation on column charts, they compare variables to each other or over time.
Axes: X = categories
Y = series, Z = values.
Other variations include 3-D area charts and connect-the-dots scatter charts.

3-D Ribbon
This example is a one-wall plot showing columns of data (series) as ribbons. One or more columns are used.
Axes: X = categories, Y = series, Z = values.

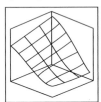
3-D Wireframe
A variation of a contour or response surface; suitable for changes in time and multivariate data.
Axes: X = categories, Y = series, Z = values.

3-D Surface line
Handles three columns of data and plots XYZ coordinates to show a response surface. Helpful for multivariate applications.

Surface charts and 3-D scatter charts are helpful for displaying complex data patterns if the underlying distributions are multivariate. Otherwise, do not enter the third dimension unless your data are there.

15.5 Oral presentations

Researchers often present their findings orally. These presentations have some unique characteristics that distinguish them from most other kinds of public speaking: only a small group of people is involved; statistics normally constitute an important portion of the topic; the audience members are, in a business context, managers or, in an academic context, fellow researchers. Both usually have an interest in the topic, but they want to hear only the critical elements; speaking time will often be as short as 20 minutes but may run longer than an hour; and the presentation is normally followed by questions and discussion.

Preparation

A successful presentation typically calls for a lengthy and complex body of information to be condensed. Since speaking rates should not exceed 100–150 words per minute, a 20-minute presentation limits you to about 2,000 to 3,000 words. If you are to communicate effectively under such conditions, you must plan carefully. Begin by asking two questions. First, how long should you plan to talk? Usually, there is an indication of the acceptable presentation length. If the time is severely limited, then the need for topical priorities is obvious. This leads to the second question: What is the purpose of the presentation? Is it to raise concern about problems that have been uncovered? Is it to add to the knowledge of audience members? Is it to give them conclusions and recommendations for their decision-making? Questions such as these illustrate the general objectives of the report. Having answered these questions, you should develop a detailed outline of what you are going to say. Such an outline should contain the following major parts.

Opening

A brief statement, probably not more than 10 per cent of the allotted time, sets the stage for the body of the report. The opening should be direct, grab attention and introduce the nature of the discussion that follows. It should explain the nature of the project, how it came about and what it attempted to do.

Findings and conclusions

The conclusions may be stated immediately after the opening remarks, with each conclusion followed by the findings that support it.

Recommendations

Where appropriate, these are stated in the third stage; each recommendation may be followed by references to the conclusions leading to it. Presented in this manner, they provide a natural climax to the report. At the end of the presentation, it may be appropriate to call for questions from the audience.

Two further important planning decisions

Early in the planning stage you need to make two further decisions. The first concerns the type of audio-visuals (AVs) that will be used and the role they will play in the presentation. AV decisions are so important that they are often made before the briefing outline and text are developed.

Presenting your research findings using PowerPoint® or other presentation software requires preparation similar to presenting with non-electronic **visual aids**. The researcher must still determine his or her style of presentation, the order of findings, and which findings will be presented graphically, in tabular format or verbally. As most visual aids are prepared using computer software, the key hyperlink files are already available. It might seem as though the presenter could bypass the costly printing of visual aids, which can be a time-consuming task. However, the electronic presenter must have a contingency plan for a malfunctioning computer. Colour transparencies are the low-technology back-up, but clearly do not allow the full range of possibilities that electronic hyperlinks afford. A second laptop and projection system, as well as multi-prong power cords and spare computer connection cords, make up the usual high-technology insurance plan. The same general rule applied to all presentations is critical for electronic ones – practise, practise, practise – but a caveat is added: practise with your equipment so that movement between files and between hyperlinks and your PowerPoint control presentation seems effortless.

The second decision you must make as you plan for your presentation is what type it will be. Will it be memorized, read from your manuscript or given extemporaneously? Your reputation and the research effort should not be jeopardized by 'winging it'.

Memorization is a risky and time-consuming course to follow. Any memory slip during the presentation can be a catastrophe, and the delivery will sound stilted and distant. Memorization virtually precludes establishing rapport with the audience and adapting to their reactions while you speak. It produces a self- or speaker-centred approach and is not recommended.

Reading a manuscript is not advisable either, even though many professors seem to reward students who do so (perhaps because they themselves get away with it at professional meetings). The delivery sounds dull and lifeless because most people are not trained to read aloud and therefore do it badly. They become focused on the manuscript to the exclusion of the audience. This head-down preoccupation with the text is clearly inappropriate for management presentations.

The **extemporaneous presentation** is audience-centred and made from minimal notes or an outline. This mode permits the speaker to be natural, conversational and flexible. Clearly, it is the best choice for an organizational setting. Preparation consists of writing a draft along with a complete sentence outline and converting the main points to notes. In this way, you can try lines of argument, experiment with various ways of expressing thoughts, and develop phraseology. Along the way, the main points are fixed sequentially in your mind, and supporting connections are made.

Audiences accept notes, and their presence does wonders in allaying speaker fears. Even if you never use them, they are there for psychological support. Many speakers prefer to use A6 cards for their briefing notes because they hold more information and so require less shuffling than the smaller A7 size. Card contents vary widely, but here are some general guidelines for their design:

- Place title and preliminary remarks on the first card.
- Use each of the remaining cards to carry a major section of the presentation. The amount of detail depends on the need for precision and the speaker's desire for supporting information.
- Include key phrases, illustrations, statistics, dates and pronunciation guides for difficult words. Also include quotations and ideas that bear repeating.
- Along the margin, place instructions and cues, such as 'SLOW', 'FAST', 'EMPHASIZE', 'TRANSPARENCY A', 'TURN CHART' and 'GO BACK TO CHART 3'.

After the outline and the AV aids comes the final stage of preparation: the rehearsal. Rehearsal, a prerequisite to effective briefing, is too often overlooked, especially by inexperienced speakers. Giving a presentation is an artistic performance, and nothing improves it more than for the speaker to demonstrate mastery of the art. First rehearsal efforts should concentrate on those parts of the presentation that are awkward or poorly developed. After the problem areas have been worked out, there should be at least a few full-scale practice sessions under simulated presentation conditions. All parts should be timed and edited until the target time is met. A videotape recorder is an excellent diagnostic tool.

Delivery

While the content of a report is the chief concern, the speaker's delivery is also important. A polished presentation adds to the receptiveness of the audience, but there is some danger that the presentation may overpower the message. Fortunately, the typical research audience knows why it is assembled, has a high level of interest and does not need to be entertained. Even so, the speaker faces a real challenge in communicating effectively. The delivery should be restrained. Demeanour, posture, dress and overall appearance should be appropriate for the occasion. Speed of speech, clarity of enunciation, pauses and gestures all play their part. Voice pitch, tone quality and inflections are proper subjects for concern. There is little time for anecdotes and other rapport-developing techniques, yet the speaker must grab and hold audience attention.

Speaker problems

Inexperienced speakers have many difficulties in making presentations. They are often nervous at the start of a presentation and may even find breathing difficult. This is natural and should not be of undue concern.

It may help to take a deep breath or two, holding each for a brief period before exhaling as fully as possible. This can be done inconspicuously on the way to the podium.

Several characteristics of inexperienced speakers may be summarized as questions. Even if you are an accomplished speaker, it is still helpful to review them as you watch a videotape of your presentation.

Vocal characteristics

a Do you speak so softly that people cannot hear you well? It is helpful to have someone at the back of the room who can signal if your voice is not carrying far enough. Another trick for people who tend to speak softly is to do some sound exercises before the presentation, like those that theatre actors do – for example, make a 'mmm' (humming) sound as hard as you can (i.e. so hard that your lips tremble).

b Do you speak too rapidly? Remind yourself to slow down. Make deliberate pauses before sentences. Speak words with precision without exaggerating. At the opposite end of the spectrum, some people talk too slowly, and this can make the audience restive.

c Do you vary volume, tone quality and rate of speaking? Any of these can be used successfully to add interest to the message and engage audience attention. Speakers should not let their words tail off as they complete a sentence.

d Do you use overworked pet phrases, repeated 'uhs', 'you know' and 'in other words'? It is hard to get rid of such phrases, because you use them unconsciously. Being aware of using pet phrases is an important first step in controlling them.

Physical characteristics

a Do you rock back and forth, or roll or twist from side to side or lean too much on the lectern?

b Do you hitch or tug on your clothing, scratch, or fiddle with your loose change, keys, pencils or other devices?

c Do you stare into space? Lack of eye contact is particularly bothersome to listeners and is a common failing of inexperienced speakers. Many seem to choose a spot above the heads of the audience and continue to stare at this except when looking at their notes. Eye contact is important. Audience members need to feel that you are looking at them. It may be helpful to pick out three people in the audience (left, right and centre) and practise looking at them successively as you talk.

d Do you misuse visuals by fumbling, putting them on in the incorrect order or upside-down?

e Do you turn your back to the audience to read from visuals? Be aware that an overhead projector offers the opportunity to read directly from the transparency and you can be sure that there is no difference between the transparency and what is projected on the screen. If you use computer equipment to show a presentation on a screen, make sure that you have a good view of the computer screen from the point where you speak.

Audio-visuals

Researchers can use a variety of AV media with good results. While there is a need for computer-assisted media in many business applications, they will be mentioned only briefly. Our emphasis is on visual aids that are relatively simple and inexpensive to make.

Chalkboards and whiteboards

Chalkboards are flexible, inexpensive, and require little specific preparation. On the other hand, they are not novel and do not project a polished appearance. If you use a chalkboard, make sure that it is wiped clean before your presentation and does not appear dusty. Whiteboards, both portable and fixed, provide visual relief, particularly when coloured markers are used. Both varieties reduce speaking time while the speaker is writing. If you use either, write legibly or print, leave space between lines and do not talk to the board with your back to the audience. If you are in an unfamiliar room, it is best to arrive prepared with erasable markers (or chalk) and erasure materials. You should, however, note that chalkboards and whiteboards can be extremely helpful in a post-presentation discussion, when you are responding to questions.

Research Methods in Real Life

Overcoming the jitters

The fear of public speaking ranks up there with the fear of heights or public nudity. Whether you are a seasoned pro or a first-time speaker, stage fright – the illogical fear of facing an audience – can be a paralysing emotion. How do you handle those times when your mind starts going blank and your stomach is turning? Patricia Fripp, an award-winning keynote speaker and speech coach, provides some answers. She suggests that you 'need to anticipate your speech mentally, physically and logistically'. Mental preparation is key and should be on a six-to-one ratio: invest three hours of preparation for a 30-minute speech. There is no substitute for rehearsal. Spend some time memorizing your opening and closing remarks – three or four sentences each. Although you may speak from notes, knowing your opening and closing remarks helps your fluency, allowing you to make the vital connection in rapport with your audience when you are likely to be most nervous.

Logistically, know the room. Go there as early as possible to get comfortable in the environment. Practise using the microphone and check the equipment. A quick review of your visual aids is also helpful. Then, during the presentation, you can focus on your audience and not be concerned with the environment.

The physical part of overcoming nervousness is varied and may be constrained by your setting. In a small-group setting, shake hands, exchange greetings and make eye contact with everybody beforehand. In a larger

▶

meeting, at least connect with the people in the front row. Do so sincerely and they will be cheering for your success. They are not waiting for you to fail – they are far too worried about themselves – and they are there to listen to you. If possible, avoid sitting while you are waiting to speak. Find a position in the room where you can stand occasionally. The rear of the room gives you access to the bathroom and drinking fountain.

If your anxiety level is still high, then you need an outlet for your energy. Comedians and actors find that doing light exercises in their dressing rooms or in another private area can release excess energy. Fripp adds, 'Find a private spot, and wave your hands in the air. Relax your jaw, and shake your head from side to side. Then shake your legs one at a time. Physically shake the tension out of your body.' The object is to release enough nervous energy to calm your anxieties – without becoming so stress-free that you forget your purpose and audience.

References and further reading

Patricia Fripp CSP CPAE, award-winning keynote speaker and speech coach, author of *Get What You Want!* and past president of the National Speakers Association. E-mail: PFripp@fripp.com, Tel: +1–800–634–3035, Website: www.fripp.com.

Handout materials

These are inexpensive but can have a professional appearance if prepared carefully. Handouts can include pictures and graphic materials that might otherwise be difficult to display. The disadvantages include the time needed to produce them and their distracting impact if not used properly. You may distribute them when the audience leaves, but a better use is to refer to them during your presentation. If you use them this way, do not hand them out until you are ready to refer to them.

Flipcharts

You can show colour, pictures and large letters with these. They are easy and inexpensive to make; they can focus listener attention on a specific idea. If not well made, however, they can be distracting. Unless they are large, they should be restricted to small groups and to types of material that can be summarized in a few words.

Computer-drawn visuals

For transparencies and slides, the draw-and-paint programs available for personal computers provide the presenter with limitless options for illustrating his or her message. Stored visuals can be teamed with a device for projecting the computer output to a screen, or the briefer can use the software to create the image at the moment a question is asked or a demonstration is appropriate. Be careful that the technology does not distract from the purpose of the message.

LCD projectors

In recent years, LCD projectors have become more and more popular and are widely available. The LCD projector is linked to a computer and projects what you see on the computer monitor on a large screen. The big advantage of LCD projectors is their ability to use multimedia. You can easily integrate photographs, audio and video clips, you can access any website on the Internet 'live', you can project classical PowerPoint® slides, but you could also show how you run any other software package. There are two cautions in using LCD projectors. First, if you connect your own laptop to a LCD projector, the general settings of the two may not be entirely compatible and you might see only a part of what you see on your computer on the screen. Of course fixing the problem is often possible, but the occurrence of such a problem just minutes before the start of your presentation makes even experienced computer users nervous. Instead of getting focused on your presentation, you focus on fixing the computer problem. Presentations with LCD projectors often use colours, but especially older LCD projectors sometimes distort colours, for example what appears orange on your laptop monitor appears yellow on the screen. This becomes a problem if you refer to an orange box, but the audience does not see it because it appears yellow.

The choice of visual aids is determined by your intended purpose, the size of the audience, meeting room conditions, time and budget constraints, and available equipment.

Choosing visual aids

Visual aids serve the presenter of a research presentation in several ways. They make it possible to present materials that cannot otherwise be communicated effectively. Statistical relationships are difficult to describe verbally, but a picture or graph communicates well. How better to describe some object or material than to show or picture it?

Visual aids help the speaker to clarify major points. With visual reinforcement of a verbal statement, the speaker can stress the importance of points. In addition, the use of two channels of communication (hearing and sight) enhances the probability that the listener will understand and remember the message.

The continuity and memorability of the speaker's message are also improved with visual aids. Verbal information is so transient that any slight lapse of listener attention results in losing the information thread. The failure to fully comprehend a given point cannot be remedied by going back to hear it again, for the speaker has gone on. With a visual aid, however, there is more opportunity to review this point, relate it to earlier comments by the speaker and improve retention.

Running Case Study 15
Writing up

What a journey. After five months, Rebecca had finally typed the last word of her conclusion into her laptop. She was done – almost done. She emailed the thesis to her mother, who as a teacher had an eye for detecting any grammar and spelling mistakes. A few weeks earlier, her mother offered to proofread her project. Rebecca knew that her mother was incredibly good at detecting typos, but she was concerned that her mother would also comment on her thesis in general. A few months earlier, when she discussed her thesis topic with her parents at a weekend at home, her mother had given her a stack of books on ethics. According to her, these books would serve well to build a fundamental base for her thesis. Later Rebecca had a look at these books, but somehow these books were so different from the articles she had. In the end, she did not even use her mother's books, and she was afraid her mother would be disappointed to find no references to the books in the final draft. Just three days later, Rebecca's phone rang – her mother. Her mother told her that she had finished proofreading her thesis and that she would email it to her straight away. Then, she continued and said that she was very surprised reading the text, as its style and structure was so different from what she expected. The writing seemed to her very technical and straightforward. Although she did not understand it, she was impressed by the statistical analyses with all the Greek letters and formulas. Her mother concluded that for her the thesis was too technical and even a bit dry, but she supposed that this was the way scientific papers are written in the business field. Therefore, she corrected obvious language mistakes but also some style issues. For example, she was surprised that Rebecca had put so many sentences in the passive voice. Rebecca replied the passive voice is scientific, but her mother replied it is just bad style. Rebecca was not sure, as she once had heard that in scientific writing you never use the words 'I' and 'we'. She would need to check with her supervisor.

Her mother had really done a terrific job. Despite the fact that Rebecca had looked for typos in her thesis by reading it on screen and as a print out, her mother still had detected 15 more. In the meantime, she also started to improve the layout of the figures and tables. Her friend Joseph had shown her the deeper secrets of word processing and she applied them. It had already taken her two days to give her thesis a nice

▶

layout and still she was not finished. What a waste of time she thought. But Joseph insisted that a text can never become better than its layout. Rebecca felt that, in the end, the content should matter and not the font type or how many colours you used.

Mehmet had almost finished his thesis as well. But before he handed in the printed version, the chairman of a local business round table invited him to give a presentation about his thesis at one of their regular meetings (which took place in the Hotel Ambassador, a nice four star hotel in the city centre). Mehmet was really looking forward to this meeting, as he knew that it was attended by very important business people – very important at least at the local level. Therefore, he invested a lot of time in this presentation, as it needed to be perfect to make an impression.

1 Rebecca asked her friend Joseph to help her with the layout of her thesis. How much work should you put in the layout of the thesis, given it is the content that should matter?
2 Looking at Rebecca's and Mehmet's final result as described in the cases, what made their research project special, i.e. what are the innovative or surprising parts?
3 In his presentation to local business people, Mehmet focuses on his most 'interesting' results. Would you also advise such prioritizing for presentation to business scholars?

Summary

1 A good-quality presentation of research findings can have an inordinate effect on a reader's or listener's perceptions of a study's quality. Recognition of this fact should prompt a researcher to make a special effort to communicate skilfully and clearly.

2 Research reports contain findings, analysis, interpretations, conclusions and sometimes recommendations. They may follow the short, informal format typical of memoranda and letters, or they may be longer and more complex. Long reports are of either an academic, technical or management type. In the former two, the problem is presented and followed by the findings, conclusions and recommendations. In the management report, the conclusions and recommendations precede the findings. The academic report addresses fellow researchers; the technical report is targeted at the technically trained reader; the management report is intended for the manager–client.

3 The writer of research reports should be guided by four questions:
    a What is the purpose of this report?
    b Who will read it?
    c What are the circumstances and limitations under which it is written?
    d How will the report be used?

Reports should be clearly organized, physically inviting and easy to read. Writers can achieve these goals if they are careful with mechanical details, writing style and comprehensibility.

4 There is a special challenge in presenting statistical data. While some of this data may be incorporated in the text, most statistics should be placed in tables, charts or graphs. The choice of a table, chart or graph depends on the specific data and presentation purpose.

5 Oral presentations of research findings are common and should be developed with concern for the communication problems that are unique to such settings. Presentations are usually conducted under time constraints; good briefings require careful organization and preparation. Visual aids are a particularly important aspect of briefings but are too often ignored or treated inadequately.

Whether written or oral, poor presentations do a grave injustice to what might otherwise be excellent research. Good presentations, on the other hand, add lustre to both the research and the reputation of the researcher.

Discussion questions

Terms in review

1 Distinguish between the following:
   a speaker-centred presentation and extemporaneous presentation
   b academic report, technical report and management report
   c topic outline and sentence outline.

Making research decisions

2 What should you do about each of the following?
   a Putting information in a research report concerning the study's limitations.
   b The size and complexity of tables in a research report.
   c The physical presentation of a report.
   d Pace in your writing.

3 What type of report would you suggest be written in each of the following cases?
   a The president of the company has asked for a study of the company's pension plan and its comparison to the plans of other firms in the industry.
   b You have been asked to write up a survey on the relationship between pay and satisfaction among paid employees of voluntary organizations, which you recently completed, for submission to the organization Studies Research.
   c Your division manager has asked you to prepare a forecast of cash requirements for the division for the next three months.
   d The European Commission has given you a grant to study the relationship between industrial accidents and departmental employee morale.

4 There are a number of graphic presentation forms. Which would you recommend to show each of the following? Why?
   a A comparison of changes in average annual per capita income for the UK, Germany and France from 1990 to 2000.
   b The percentage composition of average family expenditure patterns, by the major types of expenditures, for families whose heads of household are under age 35, compared with families whose heads of household are 55-plus.
   c A comparison of the change between 31 December 2001 and 31 December 2000 in the value of the common stock of the six largest European banks. How would you design a graphic representing not 6 firms, but all 50 firms of the EUROSTOXX index?

From concept to practice

5 Outline a set of visual aids that you might use in an oral briefing on these topics:
   a How to write a research report.
   b The outlook for the economy over the next year.
   c The major analytical article in the latest issue of *BusinessWeek*.

6 Conduct a search of websites that provide Internet presentations. Select one and critique its content, visuals and the presenter's skills.

7 Research reports often contain statistical materials of great importance that are presented poorly. Find examples of research reports, annual reports or government reports that illustrate this point and devise ways to improve their presentation.

Classroom discussion

8 Discuss whether the proverb 'There is no accounting for taste' also holds for presentations. Would you enjoy multimedia elements, such as photographs, short video segments, music, or moving and blinking objects, in a research report presentation?

9 Discuss whether there is a trade-off between a research report that is understandable to a broad audience and the accuracy of the findings presented.

Recommended further reading

Booth, Wayne C., Colomb, Gregory G. and Williams, Joseph M., *The Craft of Research* (2nd edn). Chicago: University of Chicago Press, 2003. A thorough guide on how to do research.

Campbell, Steve, *Statistics You Can't Trust*. Parker, CO: Think Twice Publishing, 2000. An enjoyable and entertaining approach to interpreting statistical charts and arguments.

Kosslyn, Stephen M., *Elements of Graph Design*. San Francisco, CA: W.H. Freeman, 1993. Fundamentals of graph and chart construction.

Lesikar, Raymond V. and Flatley, Marie E., *Basic Business Communication* (10th edn). New York: McGraw-Hill, 2004. Practical guidance for writing and presenting reports.

Levin, Peter, *Write Great Essays*. London: Open University Press, 2009. The second updated edition of this book, essential for anyone who needs to write.

Murray, Neil and Hughes, Geraldine, *Writing up your University Assignments and Research Projects*. London: Open University Press, 2008. An accessible book covering what is needed to write a good report.

Strunk, William Jr. and White, E.B., *The Elements of Style*. New York: Macmillan, 1959. A classic on the problems of writing style.

Tufte, Edward R., *The Visual Display of Quantitative Information*. New Haven, CT: Graphics Press, 1992. The book that started the revolution against gaudy infographics.

Tufte, Edward R., *Visual Explanations: Images and Quantities, Evidence and Narrative*. New Haven, CT: Graphics Press, 1997. Uses the principle of 'the smallest effective difference' to display distinctions in data. Beautifully illustrated.

Get started with understanding statistical techniques!

When you have read this chapter, log on to the Online Learning Centre website at *www.mcgraw-hill.co.uk/textbooks/blumberg* to explore chapter-by-chapter test questions, additional case studies, a glossary and more online study tools for *Business Research Methods*.

Notes

1 Paul E. Resta, *The Research Report*. New York: American Book Company, 1972, p. 5.

2 John M. Penrose Jr., Robert W. Rasberry and Robert J. Myers, *Advanced Business Communication*. Boston: PWS–Kent Publishing, 1989, p. 185.

3 Robert R. Rathbone, *Communicating Technical Information*. Reading, MA: Addison-Wesley, 1966, p. 64 (reprinted with permission).

4 Ibid., p. 72.

5 Penrose, Rasberry and Myers, *Advanced Business Communication*, p. 89.

6 The material in this section draws on Stephen M. Kosslyn, *Elements of Graph Design*. San Francisco: W.H. Freeman, 1993; DeltaPoint, Inc., *DeltaGraph User's Guide* 4.0. Monterey, CA: Delta-Point, Inc., 1996; Gene Zelazny, *Say it with Charts*. Homewood, IL: Business One Irwin, 1991; Jim Heid, 'Graphs that work', MacWorld (February 1994), pp. 155–6; and Penrose, Rasberry and Myers, *Advanced Business Communication*, Chapter 3.

7 Marilyn Stoll, 'Charts other than pie are appealing to the eye', *PC Week*, 25 March 1986, pp. 138–9.

8 Stephen M. Kosslyn and Christopher Chabris, 'The mind is not a camera, the brain is not a VCR', *Aldus Magazine* (September/October) 1993, p. 34.

Glossary

3-D graphics A statistical presentation technique that adds interest to obscure data and permits you to compare three or more variables from the sample in one chart; types: column, ribbon, wire frame, and surface line.

A

A priori contrasts A special class of tests used after the null hypothesis was rejected with the F test to compare measurements of specific populations.

Abstract A summary of an academic report or articles. In most scientific journals each article is preceded by an abstract.

Action research A research approach that emphasizes that interplay between research and specific actions to achieve desired changes.

Active factors Those independent variables (IV) the researcher can manipulate by causing the subject to receive one treatment level or another.

Administrative questions A type of measurement question that identifies the respondent, interviewer, interview location, and conditions (usually nominal data).

Alternative hypothesis That a difference exists between the sample parameter and the population statistic to which it is compared; the logical opposite of the null hypothesis used in significance testing (notation: H_A).

Analysis of variance (ANOVA) A statistical test for testing the null hypothesis that the means of several populations are equal; test statistic is the F ratio; used when you need k independent samples tests.

Applied research Uses theories to investigate real phenomena that are of relevance for practitioners. Applied research often builds upon basic research. It has an emphasis on solving practical problems.

Arbitrary scales Universal practice of ad hoc scale development used by instrument designers to create scales that is highly specific to the practice or object being studied.

Area charts A statistical presentation technique used for time series and frequency distributions over time; a.k.a. stratum or surface charts.

Area sampling A type of cluster sampling usually applied to a population in a specific spatial area with well-defined political or natural boundaries but without a detailed sample frame; population is divided into homogeneous clusters from which a single-stage or multistage sample is drawn.

Artefact correlations Where distinct groups combine to give the impression of one.

Asymmetrical relationship A relationship in which we postulate that change in one variable (independent variable) is responsible for change in another variable (dependent variable).

Audience The intended reader of the secondary source; one of the five factors used to evaluate the value of a secondary source.

Authority The credibility of a secondary source as indicated by the credentials of the author and publisher; one of five factors used to evaluate the value of a secondary source.

Axial coding In grounded theory, this step refers to relating categories formed through open coding with each other.

B

Backward elimination In modelling and regression, one of the methods for sequentially adding or removing variables; begins with a model containing all independent variables and removes the variable that changes R^2 the least; see also backward elimination and stepwise selection.

Bar charts A statistical presentation technique that represents frequency data as horizontal or vertical bars; vertical bars are most often used for time series and quantitative classifications (histograms, stacked bar, and multiple variable charts are specialized bar charts).

Bar code Technology used to simplify the researcher's role as a data recorder, involving a label reading device that scans electronically codes (stripes) on product labels and service documents.

Basic research Attempts to understand processes and their outcomes, which form the fundaments for explaining levels of and changes in characteristics, attitudes and behaviour. Furthermore, theory development is mostly part of basic research. It is mostly conducted within university and research institutes. In business research, basic research often provides the theoretical framework used in applied research. Basic research is also called pure research.

Bayesian statistics An approach that goes beyond sampling data for making decisions by including all available data – specifically subjective probability estimates based on general experience rather than on specific data collected (see Appendix B).

Beta weights Another term for standardized regression coefficients, where the size of the number reflects the level of influence on Y that an individual X exerts.

Bibliographic database An electronic database containing the bibliographic information plus abstract and increasingly full texts. EBSCO is an example of such a database. A researcher often sets up their databases with all the articles and books they have read or referred to.

Bibliography A list of the bibliographic details (usually author's name, date of publication, title of book or article, title of journal, pages, publisher, editors) of the sources used, including those not referred to in the text. Most scientific journals but also thesis guidelines ask for a list of references, which contains only the sources referred to in the text.

Big Data With the increased usage of the Internet and mobile telecommunication, users leave trillions of data traces when they visit websites, make phone calls, send and receive emails, post messages on social media sites etc. All this data is called Big Data and companies use these data to understand consumers better and to make targeted offerings.

Bivariate correlation analysis Measures of correlation that use non-contiguous variables and that distinguish between independent and dependent variables.

Bivariate normal distribution An assumption of correlation analysis that data are from a random sample of a population where the two variables are normally distributed in a joint manner.

Blind A condition that exists when subjects do not know if they are being exposed to the experimental treatment. See also double blind.

Blocking factors A variable on which the researcher can only identify and classify a subject – not manipulate (e.g. gender, age, customer status, etc.); these are often the classification variables within a questionnaire.

Box plot An EDA technique that reduces the detail of the stem-and-leaf display but provides a visual image of the variable's distribution location, spread, shape, tail length, and outliers; a.k.a. box-and-whisker plot.

Branched questions A type of measurement question that determines the respondent's path (question sequencing) in a study; the answer to one question assumes other questions have been asked or answered, and directs the respondent to answer specific questions that follow and skip other questions.

Buffer question A type of neutral measurement question designed chiefly to establish rapport with the respondent (usually nominal data or qualitative data).

Business research Refers to studies dealing with phenomena in the business world including nonprofit and (semi) governmental organizations to guide their decisions.

C

Call-backs Procedure involving repeated attempts to make contact with a targeted respondent to ensure that the targeted respondent is reached and motivated to participate in the study. They are important to reduce the non-response error.

CAQDAS Stands for computer assisted qualitative data analysis software.

Case study Emphasizes the full and detailed contextual analysis of a single or fewer events or conditions and their interrelations for a single subject or respondent. It often relies on multiple sources to crosscheck the obtained information.

Case study research A research approach that investigates the phenomenon in question in its context. It is the most suitable research if the number of variables that needs to be considered is very large and if the phenomena and its antecedents can not yet be clearly distinguished.

Categorization A type of scale in which the respondents put themselves or property indicants in groups or categories.

Causal hypothesis See Explanatory hypothesis.

Causal method See Causal study.

Causal study Attempts to reveal the relationship between variables (A produces B or causes B to occur).

Causation The essential element of causation is that A produces B or forces B to occur. Causation is always based on an inductive (see Induction) conclusion and is therefore a probabilistic statement, as we can not account for all possible, imaginable and unimaginable processes that may drive the relation between A and B.

Cells In a cross-tabulation, a subgroup of the data created by the value intersection of two (or more) variables, where each cell contains the count of cases as well as the percentage of the joint classification.

Census A sample that contains all element of the population. For example for the UK census all people (~59 millions) living in the UK are interviewed.

Central limit theorem For sufficiently large samples ($n > 30$), the sample means of repeatedly drawn samples will be distributed around the population mean approximately in a normal distribution.

Central tendency A measure of location, most commonly the mean, median, and mode.

Central tendency (error) An error that results because the respondent is reluctant to give extreme judgments, usually due to lack of knowledge.

Centroid A multi-variate mean.

Checklist A measurement question that poses numerous alternatives and encourages multiple responses, but where relative order of those responses is not important (nominal data).

Chi-square (χ^2) test A non-parametric test of significance used for nominal measurements.

Chi-square-based measures Tests to detect the strength of the relationship between the variables tested with a chi-square test: phi, Cramer's V, and contingency coefficient C.

Classical statistics An objective view of probability in which the decision-making rests totally on an analysis of available sampling data where a hypothesis is rejected or accepted based on the sample data collected.

Classification In data mining, using a set of reclassified examples to develop a model that can group or classify the population of records at large.

Classification question A type of measurement question that provides sociological-demographic variables for use in grouping respondent's answers nominal, ordinal, interval or ratio data).

Closed question/response A type of measurement question that presents the respondent with a fixed set of choices (nominal, ordinal or interval data).

Cluster analysis A technique that identifies homogeneous subgroups or clusters of study objects or people, then displays the relevant clusters in a diagram (endogamy); viewing the data by segments or groups of data cases.

Cluster sampling A sampling plan that involves dividing the population into clusters or subgroups, and then drawing a sample from each subgroup in a single-stage or multi-stage design.

Clustering A data-mining technique that assigns each data record to a group or segment automatically by clustering algorithms that identify the similar characteristics in the data set and then partition them into groups.

Code of ethics A comprehensive source that contains the firm's policies with respect to ethical conduct [ethics]; effective codes are regulative, protect the public interest, are behaviour specific, and are enforceable.

Codebook Contains the coding rules for assigning numbers or other symbols to each variable; a.k.a. coding scheme.

Coding (process) Assigning numbers or other symbols to answers to responses that can be tallied and grouped into a limited number of classes or categories.

Coding frame A list with all the codes that had been assigned to fragments of qualitative data.

Coefficient of determination R^2 = the amount of common variance in X and Y, two variables in association; is the ratio of the line of best fit's error over that incurred by using mean value of Y.

Cohort In statistics a cohort describes a group of similar people. Often it is used to describe people with the same age. The baby boomers or generation Y are examples of age cohorts. First-year, second-year and third-year students is another example of a cohort.

Collinearity The situation when two or more of the independent variables are highly correlated; causes estimated regression coefficients to fluctuate widely, making interpretation difficult; a.k.a. multicollinearity.

Communalities In factor analysis, the estimate of the variance in each variable that is explained by the factors being studied.

Communication approach A study approach involving questioning or surveying people (by personal interview, telephone, mail, computer or some combination of these) and recording their responses for analysis.

Comparative scale A scale where the respondent evaluates an object against a standard using a numeric, graphical, or verbal scale.

Computer-administered telephone survey A study conducted wholly by computer contact between respondent and interviewer, where questions are either appear on the computer or are voice-synthesized and data are tallied continuously.

Computer-assisted interviewing The interviewer types the answer of a respondent directly into a computer.

Computer-assisted personal interviewing (CAPI) A personal, face-to-face interview where the researcher may be guided by computer-sequenced questions, where data may be entered as responses are given, or where visualization techniques may be provided digitally to each participant.

Computer-assisted telephone interviewing (CATI) A study conducted wholly by telephone contact between respondent and interviewer where interview is software-driven, usually in a central location with interviewers in acoustically isolated interviewing carrels; data are tallied, as they are collected.

Concealment A technique in an observation study where the observer is shielded from the subject to avoid behaviour modification by the subject caused by observer presence; this is accomplished by one-way mirrors, hidden cameras, hidden microphones, etc.

Concept A generally accepted bundle of meanings or characteristics associated with certain events, objects, conditions, or situations.

Conceptual scheme The interrelationships between concepts and constructs.

Concordant When a subject that ranks higher on one ordinal variable also ranks higher on another variable, the pairs of variables are concordant.

Confidence interval The combination of interval range and the degree of confidence. We are confident (to the stated degree) that the true value of mean lies within the interval.

Confidentiality A privacy guarantee to retain validity of the research, as well as to protect respondents. It can refer to the sponsor, i.e. the sponsor of the study remains unknown to the respondents, and to the respondents, i.e. the information provided by the respondents will only be revealed in a form that guarantees that an individual respondent cannot be identified and linked to the information provided.

Confirmatory data analysis An analytical process guided by classical statistical inference in its use of significance and confidence.

Confirmatory factor analysis (CFA) A statistical procedure, which differs from exploratory factor analysis in that common factors are assumed to be uncorrelated, observed variables are affected by only some of the common factors, and the variables, which define the construct, are researcher defined.

Confounding variable An extraneous variable that influences the relation between independent (see Independent variable) and dependent variable, similar to a moderating variable.

Conjoint analysis A technique that uses input from non-numeric independent variables to secure part-worth's that represent the importance of each aspect in the subject's overall assessment; used to measure complex decision making (e.g. consumer purchase behaviour) that requires multi-attribute judgements; produces a scale value for each attribute or property. See also Factorial survey.

Consensus scaling Scale development by a panel of experts evaluating instrument items based on topical relevance and lack of ambiguity.

Construct A definition specifically invented for an image or idea for a given research project.

Construct validity The degree to which a research instrument is able to measure or infer the presence of an abstract property. See also Validity.

Content analysis A technique used to analyse qualitative data, such as texts, by counting the occurrence of certain key words, the length of sentences and the text etc.

Content validity The degree to which a research instrument provides adequate coverage of the topic under study. See also Validity.

Contingency coefficient C A measure of association between two variables.

Contingency tables A cross-tabulation table constructed for statistical testing, with the test determining whether the classification variables are independent.

Continuous variable A variable that can take any value in a given range. Income, temperature and age are examples of a continuous variable.

Control The ability to replicate a scenario and dictate a particular outcome; the ability to exclude, isolate or manipulate the influence of a variable in a study; a critical factor in inference from an experiment, implies that all factors, with the exception of the independent variable (IV), must be held constant and not confounded with another variable that is not part of the study.

Control dimension In quota sampling, a descriptor used to define the sample's characteristics (e.g. age, education, religion, etc.).

Control group A group of subjects (respondents) that is not exposed to the independent variable IV being studied but still generates a measure for the dependent variable DV. Comparing the outcomes of the DV for the control and experimental group allows an assessment of the IV-DV relationship.

Control variable A variable that is assumed or discounted in a study; in data analysis, a variable introduced to help interpret the statistically significant (see Significance) relationship between variables.

Convenience samples A low-cost but less reliable non-probability sample where element selection is unrestricted or left to those elements easily accessible by the researcher. For example, if you want to investigate bookshops and select those you know.

Correlation hypothesis Variables occur together in some specified manner without implying that one causes the other (see also Hypothesis).

Correlation matrix A table used to display coefficients for more than two variables.

Cramer's V (used with chi-square) A measure of association for nominal, non-parametric variables; ranges from zero to +1.0 and used for larger than 2×2 chi-square tables; does not provide direction of the association or reflect causation.

Criterion variable Alternative term for dependent variable.

Criterion-related validity The success of measures used for prediction or estimation; types are predictive and concurrent. See also Validity.

Critical review While a literature review is usually one section in a published study, the critical review is a piece of writing on its own. It is a critical assessment of an article or book. It is either part of the peer-review process established for many scientific journals to check and improve the quality of submitted papers or it is a published assessment to judge recently published books.

Critical path method (CPM) A scheduling tool for complex or large research proposals that cites milestones and time involved between milestones.

Critical value The dividing point(s) between the region of acceptance and the region of rejection; these values can be computed in terms of the standardized random variable due to the normal distribution of sample means.

Critique A detailed and well-founded assessment of a theory or a text based on a thorough analysis.

Cronbach's alpha A coefficient measuring internal consistency. It indicates how reliable a measurement based on multiple items is, and varies between 0 and 1. Measurements with a Cronbach alpha above 0.7 are considered good measurements.

Cross-sectional study The study is conducted only once and reveals a snapshot of one point in time.

Cross-tabulation A technique for comparing two classification variables (usually nominal data variables).

Cumulative scaling A scale development technique in which scale items are tested based on a scoring system, where agreement with one extreme scale item results also in endorsement of all other items that take a less extreme position.

D

Data Facts (attitudes, behaviour, motivations, etc.) collected from respondents or observations (mechanical or direct) plus published information; categorized as primary and secondary.

Data analysis Editing and reducing accumulated data to a manageable size, developing summaries, looking for patterns, and applying statistical techniques.

Data entry The process of converting information gathered by secondary or primary methods to a medium for viewing and manipulation; usually done by keyboarding or optical scanning.

Data fields A single element of data (e.g. a single answer to a question).

Data files Sets of data records or sets of data cases.

Data mart Intermediate storage facilities that compile locally required information.

Data mining Data mining is a technique to detect relationships and patterns in very large databases, often organized in data warehouses (see Data warehouse). It is a tool combining exploration and discovery with confirmatory analysis.

Data visualization The process of viewing aggregate data on multiple dimensions to gain a deeper, intuitive understanding of the data.

Data warehouse An electronic repository for databases that organizes very large amounts of data into categories to facilitate retrieval, sorting and interpretation. It is an accessible archive of information to support dynamic organizational intelligence applications.

Database A collection of data organized for computerized retrieval that defines data fields, data records and data files.

Debriefing Explains the truth to participants and describes the major goals of the research study and the reasons after deception has been used.

Deception When respondents are told only part of the truth or the truth is fully compromised to prevent biasing respondents or to protect sponsor confidentiality. Balancing deception and informed consent is an important ethical issue.

Decision tree models A data-mining technique that segregates data by using a hierarchy of if-then statements based on the values of variables and creates a tree-shaped structure that represents the segregation decisions; used with interval or categorical data.

Deduction A form of inference in which the conclusion must necessarily follow from the reasons given. If the reasons (premises) are true and the conclusion follows necessarily from the reasons, the deduction is valid (see also Induction).

Dependency techniques Those techniques where criterion or dependent variables and predictor or independent variables are present (e.g. multiple regression, MANOVA, discriminate analysis, etc.).

Dependent variable (DV) The variable measured, predicted (see Predictive study), or otherwise monitored by the researcher, expected to be affected by a manipulation of the independent variable. Notation usually DV.

Descriptive hypothesis States the existence, size, form or distribution of some variable (see also Hypothesis).

Descriptive statistics Display characteristics of the location, spread and shape of an array of data.

Descriptive studies Descriptive studies sketch the current state of a phenomenon. Attempts to describe or define a subject, often by creating a profile of a group of problems, people or events, through the collection of data and the tabulation of the frequencies on research variables or their interaction; the study reveals who, what, when, where, or how much; the study concerns a univariate question or hypothesis in which the research asks about or states something about the size, form, distribution, or existence of a variable. They are distinct from reporting studies by providing interpretations of the information found.

Dichotomous question A measurement question that poses two opposing responses (nominal or ordinal data).

Dichotomous variable A variable that only can take two values. Examples are gender (female or male) or yes – no variables, such as having children, being a foreign company. It generates nominal or ordinal data.

Dictionary Dictionaries are books explaining the meaning of a word in other words. Next to general dictionaries, many specialized dictionaries exists, such as dictionaries for acronyms or specialized dictionaries for financial terms, business terms etc. Dictionaries are especially useful if you want to know a good definition of a term.

Direct observation When the observer is physically present and personally monitors and records the behaviour of the subject.

Direct questions Questions that ask the respondent to provide their own view on a matter.

Directory Directories are books containing names, addresses and often further data. The phone directory is very simple, but could still be used to sample people in a certain city. Specialized directories include for example all companies in a specific sector and might provide next to contact address details further basic information on the firm.

Discordant When a subject that ranks higher on one ordinal variable ranks lower on another variable, the pairs of variables are discordant; as discordant pairs increase over concordant pairs, the association becomes negative.

Discourse analysis A qualitative analysis approach to look at the flow of communication and especially its relational aspects.

Discriminate analysis The joining of a nominal dependent variable with one or more independent internal or ratio variables into an equation that is used to predict the classification of a new observation.

Disguised question A measurement question designed to conceal the question's and study's true purpose.

Disproportionate stratified sampling The sample has different proportions of the stratification criteria than the population. If 10 per cent of all top managers are women, the proportion of women in the sample would be higher, e.g., 30 per cent to increase statistical efficiency.

Distribution (of data) The array of value counts from lowest to highest value, resulting from the tabulation of incidence for each variable by value.

Domain analysis A higher-ordered category that includes other categories and formalizes relationships between categories.

'Don't know' (DK) responses A response provided by respondents: when they have insufficient knowledge to answer the question; when the instrument fails to provide an understandable operational definition for a construct; when the respondents have not formed a judgment on an issue, are reluctant to provide an answer, or feel the issue is too unimportant to formulate an answer.

Double blind (study) A condition that exists when neither the researchers nor the subjects know when a subject is being exposed to the experimental treatment (IV). See also Blind.

Double movement of reflective thought The sequential use of induction and deduction in research reasoning to develop a plausible hypothesis.

Double sampling A procedure for selecting a sub-sample from a sample for further study; a.k.a. sequential sampling or multiphase sampling. Such a sampling design is especially useful if you are only interested in a specific subgroup of the total population, but do not know which subject of the population belongs to the specific subgroup.

Double-barrelled question A type of multiple questions that includes two or more questions in one that the respondent might need to answer differently to preserve the accuracy of the data.

Dummy variable Nominal variable used in multiple regressions and coded 0, 1 as all other variables must be interval or ratio measures.

E

Editing A customary first step in analysis for detecting errors and data omissions, correcting them when possible, and certifying that minimum data quality standards are achieved.

Effect size statistics It is used in meta analysis and describes the statistics which transform effect statistics of different empirical studies into one single effect.

Emerging coding A coding technique to develop codes and categories while reading through the data, i.e. the data themselves are an inspiration source to develop codes.

Encyclopaedia Encyclopaedias can be used to find some background information on a topic. For example, if you conduct an international study, you might use them to find the basic background information on the countries involved in your study. Encyclopaedias exist in printed form but also in electronic form. The former look nicer and more prestigious on the shelf, the latter are more convenient as they include advanced search options and a lot of cross-references.

Environmental control Holding constant the (physical) environment of the experiment.

Equal-appearing interval scale An expensive, time-consuming type of consensus scaling which results in an interval rating scale for attitude measurement, a.k.a. Thurston scale.

Equivalence In measurement theory equivalence describes the condition that measures of the same object taken by different people are the same or at least very similar and the condition that the measures of different items designed to measure one construct are also very similar.

Error term The deviations of the actual values of Y from the regression line representing the mean value of Y for a particular value of X.

Ethics Norms or standards of behaviour that guide moral choices about research behaviour.

Ethnographic studies Research approach that emphasizes the description and interpretation of the social world by primary qualitative (see Qualitative research) information collection, such as direct observation.

Event sampling The process of selecting some elements or behavioural acts or conditions from a population of observable behaviour or conditions to represent the population as a whole.

Ex post facto design Researchers have no ability to manipulate the variables, but can report what has happened or is happening to the variables. This design is very common in business research.

Ex post facto evaluation Ex post facto evaluation refers to an assessment of the benefits and outcomes of a research project after the research has been conducted.

Executive summary (final report) This document is written as the last element of a research report and is either a concise summary of the major findings, conclusions and recommendations or can be a report-in-miniature covering all aspects in abbreviated form.

Executive summary (proposal) An informative abstract providing the essentials of the proposal without the details.

Experience survey An exploratory technique where knowledgeable experts share their ideas about important issues or aspects of the subject and relate what is important across the subject's range of experience; usually involves a personal or phone interview.

Experiment Studies involving intervention (manipulation of one or more variables) by the researcher beyond that required for measurement to determine the effect on another variable.

Experimental treatment The manipulated independent variable.

Explanatory hypothesis Statement that describes a relationship between two variables with respect to some case, one variable leads to an effect on the other variable (a.k.a. causal hypothesis).

Explanatory studies Explanatory studies go beyond descriptive studies. They attempt to explain the reasons for phenomena by using theories or at least derived hypotheses (see Hypothesis) and provide answers to questions starting with why or how?

Exploration See Exploratory study.

Exploratory data analysis (EDA) A process whereby the actual data patterns guide the data analysis or suggest revisions to the preliminary data analysis plan.

Exploratory study The process of collecting information to formulate or refine management, research, investigative, or measurement questions; loosely structured studies that discover future research tasks, including developing concepts, establishing priorities, developing operational definitions, and improving research design; a phase of a research project where the researcher expands understanding of the research dilemma, looks for ways others have addressed and/or solved problems similar to the research dilemma or research question, and gathers background information on the topic to refine the research question.

Extemporaneous presentation An oral presentation technique made from minimal notes or an outline, with a more conversational style.

External validity When an observed causal relationship can be generalized across persons, settings and times.

Extra linguistic behaviour The recording of vocal, temporal, interaction and verbal stylistic behaviours of human subjects.

F

F ratio The result of an F test, done to compare measurements of k independent samples.

Factor In experiments it denotes an independent variable (IV); these are divided into treatment levels for the experiment.

Factor analysis Techniques for discovering patterns among the variables to determine if an underlying combination of the original variables (a factor) can summarize the original set.

Factor scales Types of scales that deal with multidimensional content and underlying dimensions, such as scalogram, factor, and cluster analyses, and metric and non-metric multidimensional scaling.

Factorial survey A survey technique in which subjects are asked to assess pre-described situations, which are made up from different combinations of vignettes. A.k.a. vignette studies (see also Conjoint analysis).

Factual What is measured is exactly what is observed. If we measure the time it takes to unload a truck using a clock, we have factually measured the time.

Falsification Refers to the intentional change or fabrication of data and results. It is a serious ethical offence.

Field condition The actual environmental conditions where the research study occurs.

Field experiment A study that occurs under the actual environmental conditions where the dependent variable occurs and is measured.

Filter question A question used to qualify the respondent's knowledge about the target questions of interest.

Findings non-disclosure A type of confidentiality, when the sponsor restricts the researcher from revealing the findings of the research project to third parties and does not allow publishing of the results (see also Non-disclosure).

Five-number summary The median, upper and lower quartiles, and the largest and smallest observations of a variable's distribution.

Fixed-sum scale A scale where the respondent assigns mostly 100 points to different continuous or discrete categories, e.g. how much time he spends on average per day on specified activities, such as paid working, commuting, child care, household work, leisure. It generates interval data.

Focus group An information collection approach widely used in exploratory studies involving a panel of subjects led by a trained moderator that meets for 90 minutes to two hours; the moderator uses group dynamics to explore ideas, feelings and experiences on a specific topic.

Follow-up questions Questions that are asked to motivate the respondents to elaborate deeper on an answer given.

Forced ranking scale A scale where the respondent orders several objects or properties of objects; faster than paired comparison to obtain a rank order.

Formal study Begins with a hypothesis or research question and involves precise procedures and data source specifications; tests the hypothesis or answers the research questions posed.

Format How the information is presented and how easy it is to find a specific piece of information within a secondary source; one of five factors used to evaluate the value of a secondary source.

Forward selection In modelling and regression, one of the methods for sequentially adding or removing variables; starts with the constant and adds variables that result in the largest R^2 increase; see also Backward elimination and Stepwise selection.

Fractal-based transformation A technique that can work on gigabytes of data and offers the possibility of identifying tiny subsets of data that have common characteristics.

Free-response question A type of measurement question to which the respondent provides the answer without the aid of an interviewer (either in phone, personal interview or self-administered surveys); a.k.a. open-ended question (generates all kind of data).

Frequency table A device for arraying data from lowest value to highest value, with columns for per cent, per cent adjusted for missing values, and cumulative per cent.

Funnel approach A type of question sequencing that moves the respondent from general to more specific questions and is designed to learn the respondent's frame of reference while extracting full disclosure of information on the topic (nominal, ordinal, interval or ratio data).

Fuzzy logic An extension of conventional (Boolean) logic that handles the concept of partial truth – with truth values between 'completely true' and 'completely false'; used in more complex data mining.

G

Gamma Uses a preponderance of evidence of concordant pairs vs. discordant pairs to predict association; the gamma value is the proportional reduction of error when prediction is done using preponderance of evidence (values from −1.0 to +1.0).

Genetic algorithms Optimization techniques for search and identification of meaningful relationships.

Glossary A glossary provides a short description of specific terms used in a text. You are just reading a glossary entry for this book.

Goodness of fit A measure of how well the regression model is able to predict Y.

Graphic rating scale A scale where the rater places their response along a line or continuum; the score or measurement is its distance in millimetres from either end point.

H

Halo effect (error) A systematic bias that the rater introduces by carrying over a generalized impression of the subject from one rating to another.

Handbook A handbook is a collection of articles or facts around a topic. Those containing articles usually provide a good overview over the current state of the field and are useful to identify the most prominent articles and debates in the field.

Hermeneutical analysis The theory of interpretations that addresses in a systematic way challenges faced in interpretation.

Heuristic research A qualitative analysis approach that starts with a personal question that is answered in a process of self-enquiry and dialogue.

Histogram A bar chart data display technique that groups data values into equal intervals; especially useful for revealing skewness, kurtosis and modal pattern.

Holdout sample A portion of the sample – usually 1/3 or 1/4 – is set aside and the remainder is used to compute the estimating equation. The equation is then used on the holdout data to calculate R^2 for comparison.

Hypothesis A statement formulated for empirical testing; a tentative or conjectural declarative belief or statement that describes the relationship between two or more variables. One distinguishes descriptive (see Descriptive hypothesis), u, explanatory (see Explanatory hypothesis) and relational hypotheses (see Relational hypothesis).

I

Independent variable (IV) The variable manipulated by the researcher, which causes an effect or change on the dependent variable. Notation is IV.

In-depth interview A type of interview, usually unstructured and in an unconstrained environment, which encourages the respondent to talk extensively, sharing as much information as possible.

Index You find the index at the end of a book, it tells you on which page a specific term or name is mentioned. Index is also used for the word bibliography.

Indirect observation When the recording of data is done by mechanical, photographic or electronic means. For example, if you study videotapes showing how children interact in a group.

Indirect questions Questions that do not ask for what the respondent thinks, but what is generally thought by them.

Induction To draw a conclusion from one or more particular facts or pieces of evidence; the conclusion explains the facts.

Inferential What is measured is not what we actually observe, but deducted from the observation. We measure the quality of an airline by looking at the percentage of delayed and cancelled flights. What we measure are delayed and cancelled flights, but not directly the quality.

Inferential statistics Includes the estimation of population values and the testing of statistical hypotheses.

Informed consent Respondent gives full consent to participation after receiving full disclosure of the procedures of the proposed survey. (See also Deception.)

Interaction effect The influence that one moderating factor has on the relationship between an independent and a dependent variable.

Interactional analysis One approach in narrative analysis focuses on the dialogues between teller and listener.

Intercept One of two regression coefficients, β_0, is the value for the linear function when it crosses the Y-axis or the estimate of Y when X is zero.

Intercept interview A face-to-face communication that approaches passers-by to participate in an interview in a centralized location, such as a shopping centre.

Interdependency techniques Those techniques where criterion or dependent variables and predictor or independent variables are not present (e.g. factor analysis, cluster analysis, multidimensional scaling, etc.).

Internal consistency A characteristic of measurement in which an instrument measures consistency among responses of a single respondent. See also Reliability.

Internal database Internal databases are archives of information that are kept within an organization and that are usually not freely accessible to everyone. Sometimes they are organized in data warehouses (see Data warehouse).

Internal validity The ability of a research instrument to measure what it is purported to measure; when the conclusion(s) drawn about a demonstrated experimental relationship truly implies cause.

Interpreting questions In such questions the interviewer repeats the answers of the respondents and asks whether the interviewer's interpretation of the answer is correct.

Interpretivism A research philosophy built upon the principles that the social world is constructed and given subjective meanings by humans, and that the researcher is driven by interests and part of what is observed. It assumes that social phenomena can only be understood if one looks at the totality and how people give meaning and interpret the social world. (See also Positivism.)

Interquartile range (IQR) A calculated statistic using the largest and smallest values in a variable's distribution that measures the distance between the first and third quartiles of the distribution; a.k.a. midspread; the distance between the hinges in a box plot.

Interrogation/communication study The researcher questions the subjects and collects their responses by personal or impersonal means.

Interval data Data with order and distance but no unique origin; data which incorporate equality of interval (the distance between one measure and the next measure); e.g. temperature scale.

Intervening variable A factor that affects the observed phenomenon but cannot be seen, measured, or manipulated, thus its effect must be inferred from the effects of the independent (see Independent variable) and moderating variables on the dependent variable; notation is IVV.

Interview guide A guide that states which topics should be covered in the interview and which information is sought.

Interview schedule An alternative rarely used term for the questionnaire used in an interview (phone or in-person communication approaches to collecting data).

Interviewer error Error that results from interviewer influence of the respondent; includes problems with motivation, instructions, voice inflections, body language, question or response order, or cheating via falsification of one or more responses.

Introductory questions General questions that are asked to collect basic information on the respondent and that are usually easy to answer.

Investigative question Questions the researcher must answer to obtain the information necessary to answer the research question. (See also Management research question hierarchy.)

Item analysis scaling Scale development where instrument designers develop instrument items and test them with a group of respondents; individual items are analysed to determine those which highly discriminate between persons or objects; e.g. Likert scale and summated scale.

J

Judgement sampling A type of purposive sampling in which the researcher arbitrarily selects elements to conform to some criterion.

K

***k* independent samples test** The parametric test used when interval or ratio measurements are taken from three or more samples (ANOVA), and the non-parametric test used when nominal (chi-square) or interval (Kruskal-Wallis) measurements are taken from three or more samples.

k related samples test The parametric (ANOVA) and non-parametric tests (Cochran Q for nominal measurements and Friedman for ordinal measurements) used when comparing measurements from more than two groups from the same sample or more than two measures from the same subject or respondent.

Kurtosis A statistic that measures a distribution's peakedness or flatness (ku); a neutral distribution has a ku of 0, a flat distribution is negative and a peaked distribution is positive.

L

Laboratory conditions Studies that occur under conditions that do not simulate actual environmental conditions.

Lambda A measure of how well the frequencies of one nominal variable offer predictive evidence about the frequencies of another variable; values (vary between zero to 1.0) show the direction of the association.

Leading question A measurement question that assumes and suggests to the respondent the desired answer (nominal, ordinal, interval or ratio data).

Leniency (error) An error that results when the respondent is consistently an easy or reluctant rater; for example, the rater is very optimistic in their judgement, or very pessimistic.

Letter of transmittal An element of the final report, this letter refers to the authorization for the project and any specific instructions or limitations placed on the study and states the purpose and scope of the study; not necessary for internal projects.

Level of significance The probability of rejecting a true null hypothesis. See also Significance.

Likert scale A variation of the summated rating scale; this scale asks a rater to agree or disagree with statements that express either favourable or unfavourable attitudes toward the object. The strength of attitude is reflected in the assigned score and individual scores may be totalled for an overall attitude measure.

Line graphs A statistical presentation technique used for time series and frequency distributions over time.

Linearity An assumption of correlation analysis, that a straight line passing through the data cloud can describe the collection of data.

Linguistic behaviour The observation of human verbal behaviour during conversation, presentation, or interaction; may also include content analysis.

LISREL A technique (linear structural relationships) useful in explaining causality among constructs that cannot be directly measured, by analysing covariance structures.

Literature review Summarizes and interprets recent or historically relevant research studies, company data or industry reports that act as the basis for the proposed study.

Literature search The process of collecting information (facts, articles, books, etc.) relevant to the research problem. Literature search is an important phase at the start of your research to get acquainted with the field.

Loadings In principal components analysis, the correlation coefficients between the factor and the variables.

Longitudinal study The study is repeated over an extended period of time, tracking changes in variables over time; includes panels or cohort groups.

M

Mail survey A relatively low cost self-administered (see Self-administered questionnaire) study, where the respondent receives a questionnaire by mail and also returns it by mail. Email is also increasingly used to distribute mail surveys.

Main effects The average direct influence that a particular treatment has on the DV independent of other factors.

Management dilemma A symptom of a management problem or an early indication of a management opportunity; a problem or opportunity that requires a management decision.

Management question The management dilemma restated in question format; categorized as 'choice of objectives', 'generation and evaluation of solutions', or 'trouble-shooting or control of a situation'. (See also Management research question hierarchy.)

Management report A report written for the non-technically oriented manager or client.

Management research question hierarchy Process of sequential question formulation that leads a researcher from management dilemma to investigative questions.

Manager-researcher relationship Describes the responsibilities of and conflicts between the manager contracting for the research and the firm providing or conducting the research process.

Mapping rule Developing and applying a set of rules for assigning numbers to empirical events.

Marginal(s) A term for the column and row totals in a cross tabulation.

Market-basket analysis The most common form of association, which studies patterns of products purchased together; used to change store layout, adjust inventories or target promotional campaigns.

Matching A process analogous to quota sampling for assigning subjects to experimental and control groups by having subjects match every descriptive characteristic used in the research; used when random assignment is not possible; an attempt to eliminate the effect of confounding variables that groups subjects so the confounding variable is present proportionally in each group.

Matrix and logical analysis A qualitative analysis approach that uses graphics to structure information.

Mean The arithmetic average.

Measurement Assigning numbers to empirical events in compliance with a mapping rule.

Measurement question The questions asked to the respondents or the observations that must be recorded. (See also Management research question hierarchy.)

Measures of location Another term for measure of central tendency in a dispersion of data (mean, mode, median).

Measures of shape Statistics that describe departures from the symmetry of a distribution; a.k.a. moments, skewness, and kurtosis.

Measures of spread Statistics that describe how scores cluster or scatter in a distribution; a.k.a. dispersion or variability (variance, standard deviation, range, interquartile range and quartile deviation).

Median The midpoint of a distribution of data, where half the cases fall above and half the cases fall below.

Mediating variable Intervening variable is another word for it. It is a variable positioned between the independent and dependent variable and describes the theoretical mechanism through which the independent variable influences the dependent variable.

Meta analysis A technique to quantitatively analyse and summarize different empirical studies on the same research problem.

Method of least squares A procedure for finding a regression line that keeps errors (deviations from actual value to the line value) to a minimum.

Method reactivity biases Research participants or respondents behave or answer differently, because they know that they are subject to a research. People will behave more politely if they know they are observed. People might also be less inclined to not confess that they have shoplifted something in a personal interview compared to an anonymous web survey. These differences in (answer) behaviour create a bias induced by the method.

Metric/non-metric measures Refers to statistical techniques using interval and ratio measures (metric) and ordinal and nominal measures (non-metric).

Missing data Information that is missing about a respondent or data record; should be discovered and rectified during data preparation phase of analysis; e.g. miscoded data, out-of-range data, or extreme values.

Mode The most frequently occurring value in an array of data; data may have more than one mode.

Model A representation of a system that is constructed to study some aspect of that system or the system as a whole.

Moderating variable A second independent variable, believed to have a significant contributory or contingent effect on the originally stated relationship between independent and dependent variable. The moderating variable is also called interacting variable. Notation is MV.

Monitoring See Observation study.

Multicollinearity The situation where some or all of the independent variables are highly correlated; a.k.a. collinearity.

Multidimensional scaling (MDS) A scaling technique for objects or people where the instrument scale seeks to measure more than one attribute of the respondents or object; results are usually mapped; develops a geometric picture or map of the locations of some objects relative to others on various dimensions or properties; especially useful for difficult-to-measure constructs.

Multi-phase sampling See Double sampling.

Multiple case study A case study research that relies on more than one case, i.e. the phenomenon in question is investigated in different settings; each setting is a single case.

Multiple choice question A question that asks the respondent to select from a predefined one answer alternative (see Multiple choice–single response scale) or all appropriate answer alternatives (see Multiple choice–multiple response scale).

Multiple choice–multiple response scale A scale that offers respondents multiple options and solicits one or more answers (nominal or ordinal data); a.k.a. checklist.

Multiple choice–single response scale A measurement question that poses more than two responses but seeks a single answer, or one that seeks a single rating from a gradation of preference, interest or agreement (nominal or ordinal data); a.k.a. multiple choice question.

Multiple comparison (post hoc) procedures Tests of significance on comparison measures done after the results are compared; tests use group means and incorporate the MS_{error} term of the F ratio.

Multiple question A question that requests so much content that it would be better if separate questions were asked. See also Double-barrelled question.

Multiple rating list scale A numerical scale where raters circle their responses and the layout allows visualization of the results (generates interval data).

Multiple regression A descriptive tool used to (1) develop a self-weighting estimating equation by which to predict values for a dependent variable from the values of independent variables, (2) control confounding variables to better evaluate the contribution of other variables, or (3) test and explain a causal theory.

Multiple sources of evidence One base principle in case study research that refers to the fact that any observation should be backed by different sources of evidence, such as mentioned by more than one interview partner and being in line with written documents.

Multivariate analysis Those statistical techniques that focus upon and bring out in bold relief the structure of simultaneous relationships among three or more phenomena.

Multivariate analysis of variance (MANOVA) A technique that assesses the relationship between two or more dependent variables and classificatory variables or factors; frequently used to test differences among related samples.

N

Narrative analysis A qualitative research method that emphasizes that stories should be interpreted as a whole to preserve also contextual factors.

Negative leniency (error) An error that results when the respondent is consistently a hard or critical rater.

Neural networks Collections of sample processing nodes plus their connections, resulting in a non-linear predictive model that resembles biological neural networks.

Nominal data Data without the properties of order, distance, or origin but capable of being partitioned into mutually exclusive and collectively exhaustive categories.

Non-contact rate Ratio of potential non-contacts (no answer, busy, answering machine, and disconnects) to all potential contacts.

Non-disclosure Various types of confidentiality involving research projects, including sponsor, findings and purpose nondisclosures.

Non-parametric tests One of the two general classes of significance tests, these tests use data derived from nominal and ordinal measurements and must meet three other assumptions: independence of observations, normally distributed populations, and equal variances.

Non-probability sampling A non-random and subjective procedure where each population element does not have a known non-zero chance of being included, as the probability of selecting population elements is unknown.

Non-resistant statistics A statistical measure that is susceptible to the effects of extreme values and does not represent typical values well under condition of asymmetry; e.g. mean, standard deviation.

Non-response error Error that develops when an interviewer cannot locate the person with whom the study requires communication or when the targeted respondent refuses to participate; especially troublesome in studies using probability sampling.

Non-verbal behaviour Observation of human behaviour without the use of conversation between observers and subjects (e.g. body movement, facial expressions, exchanged glances, eye blinks).

Normal probability plot A diagnostics tool that compares the observed values with those expected from a normal distribution.

Null hypothesis That no difference exists between the sample parameter and the population statistic to which it is compared; notation: H_0.

Numerical scales A scale where equal intervals separate the numeric scale points, while verbal anchors serve as labels for the extreme points.

O

Objects Concepts of ordinary experience, like people, books, autos, genes, or peer-group pressures.

Observation The full range of monitoring behavioural and non-behavioural activities and conditions (including record analysis, physical condition analysis, physical process analysis, nonverbal analysis, linguistic analysis, extra linguistic analysis and spatial analysis).

Observational checklist A measurement instrument where observed data are recorded; analogous to a questionnaire in a communication study.

Observational study A monitoring approach to collecting data where the researcher inspects the activities of a subject or the nature of some material without attempting to elicit responses from anyone.

Observer drift A source of error in an observation study caused by decay in reliability or validity of recorded observations over time that affects the coding of categories.

One-sample tests Tests that involve measures taken from a single sample.

One-tailed test A directional test of a null hypothesis that considers only one possibility: that the sample parameter is not the same as the population statistic.

Online focus group Unlike the traditional focus group, online focus groups only meet virtually. They can be organized synchronically (all participants are virtually present at the same time) or asynchronically (participants do not contribute at the same time, but can read what others have posted previously, as in a web discussion board).

Open analysis A coding technique where the codes to assign to fragments of qualitative data are developed while you go through the data.

Open coding Open coding describes the process of labelling pieces of qualitative information.

Open-ended question A type of measurement question in which the respondent provides the answer without the aid of an interviewer (either by phone, personal interview, or self-administered [see Self-administered questionnaire] surveys); a.k.a. unstructured or free response question (nominal, ordinal or ratio data).

Operational definition A definition for a variable stated in terms of specific testing criteria or operations, specifying what must be counted, measured or gathered through our senses.

Operationalized The process of transforming concepts and constructs into measurable variables suitable for testing.

Optical character recognition (OCR) Software programs that transfer printed text into a computer file in order to edit and use the information without re-keying the data.

Optical mark recognition (OMR) Software that uses a spreadsheet style interface to read and process data from user-created forms.

Optical scanning A data-entry process whereby respondent answers are recorded on computer-readable forms then scanned to form a dataset; reduces data handling and the errors that accompany such data handling.

Ordinal data Data with order, but no distance or unique origin; data capable of determining greater than, equal to, or less than status of a property or an object.

Ordinal measures Measures of association between variables generating ordinal data. See also gamma, Somer's d, Spearman's rho, tau b, tau c.

Outliers Data points that exceed +1.5 the interquartile range (IQR).

P

Pace A measure of comprehensibility, the rate at which the printed page presents information to the reader; it should be slower when the material is complex, faster when the material is straightforward.

Paired-comparison scale The respondent chooses a preferred object between several pairs of objects on some property; results in a rank ordering of objects.

Panels A technique for longitudinal survey work using the same respondents repeatedly over time, using personal, phone, and computer interviewing as well as self-administered (see Self-administered questionnaire) survey techniques; the use of mail-delivered diaries is common.

Parametric tests One of the two general classes of significance tests, these tests use data derived from interval and ratio measurements.

Pareto diagram A statistical presentation technique that includes a bar chart of frequency statistics in bar chart form, ordered from most to least, plus the cumulative percentage at each variable level indicted as a line chart.

Participant initiated error They occur if participants do not fully answer the questions or even lie either on purpose or because they do not have the knowledge.

Participant observation When the observer acts as both observer and participant with the subjects; the observer can be known or concealed.

Path analysis The use of regression to describe an entire structure of linkages that have been advanced by a causal theory.

Path diagram A diagram that presents predictive and associative relationships among constructs and indicators in a structural model.

Pattern recognition A technique used in data mining to structure vast amount of information.

Pearson correlation coefficient The r represents the estimate of linear association based on sampling data and varies over a range of $+1$ to -1; the prefix $(+, -)$ indicates the direction of the relationship (positive or inverse), while the number represents the strength of relationship (closer to 1, the stronger the relationship; $0 =$ no relationship); and the p represents the population correlation.

Peer-reviewed This term refers to the process how articles are selected for a journal. Peer-reviewed means that peers (other notable scientists) evaluate the quality of the article, suggest improvements and give their opinion on whether the article should be published in the journal. The process of peer reviewing ensures the quality of research published.

Personal interview A face-to-face, two-way communication initiated by an interviewer to obtain information from a respondent.

Phenomenology Qualitative analysis technique where the understanding of reported experiences is central.

Phi (used with chi-square) A measure of association for nominal, non-parametric variables; ranges from zero to $+1.0$ and is used best with 2×2 Chi-square tables; does not provide direction of the association or reflect causation.

Physical condition analysis The collection of data from the observation of current conditions, including inventory, signs, obstacles or hazards, cleanliness, etc.

Physical trace A type of observation that collects measures of wear data (erosion) and accretion data (measures of deposit) rather than direct observation (e.g. a study of trash).

Pictographs (geographics) A statistical presentation technique that uses pictorial symbols to represent frequency data rather than a bar in a bar-type chart; the symbol has an association with the subject of the statistical presentation and one symbol represents a specific count of that variable.

Pie charts A statistical presentation technique that uses sections of a circle (slices of a pie) to represent 100% of a frequency distribution of the subject being graphed; not appropriate for changes over time.

Pilot testing A trial collection of data to detect weaknesses in design and instrumentation and provide proxy data for selection of a probability sample. See also Pre-testing.

Plagiarism Means one uses the (parts of the) work of others and claim that it is one's own work. It is a serious violation of copyright.

Population The total collection of elements (people, firms, decisions etc.) about which we wish to make some inferences.

Population element The individual subject on which the measurement is taken; a.k.a. the population unit, case, subject or record.

Population parameters Summary descriptors of variables (e.g. incidence, mean, variance) of interest in the population.

Population proportion of incidence The number of elements in the population belonging to the category of interest, divided by the total number of elements in the population.

Portal Websites providing a gateway to a wide array of information or offering you access to further information, such as search engines, directories etc.

Positivism A research philosophy that builds on the principles that the social world can be viewed objectively, research is value free and the researcher is independent. It assumes that the social world can be observed by collecting objective facts and consists of simple elements to which it can be reduced. See also Interpretivism.

Post hoc fallacy Describes unwarranted conclusions, as causation is difficult to establish with an ex post facto research that does not allow manipulating the independent variable and isolating multiple causes.

Power of the test One minus the probability of committing a Type II error, or one minus the probability that we will correctly reject the false null hypothesis.

Practical significance When a statistically significant difference has real importance to the decision maker.

Practicality A characteristic of sound measurement concerned with a wide range of factors of economy, convenience and interpretability.

Pre- and post-test The pre-test refers to measuring a variable before the experiment is conducted and the post-test refers to measuring the same variable after the experiment has been conducted. If the two measurements differ the experiment has an effect.

Pre-coding Assigning codebook codes to variables in a study and recording them on the questionnaire, thus eliminating a separate coding sheet.

Prediction and confidence bands Bow-tie shaped confidence interval around a predictor; predictors farther from the mean have larger band widths.

Predictive studies Builds on theory and attempts to provide answers to the question what (is likely to) happen in the future. It is distinct from pure speculation as the prediction on 'proofed' theoretical explanations, often derived from basic research.

Pre-testing An established practice for discovering errors in questions, question sequencing, instructions, skip directions, etc. See also Pilot test.

Prescriptive analysis (or coding) A technique used in coding qualitative data. Before you start coding you develop a list of words and phrases you are looking for.

Primary data Original research where the data being collected are designed specifically to answer the research question.

Primary source These are full text publications of theoretical or empirical studies. Original works of research or raw data without interpretation or pronouncements. Do not confuse it with primary data. See also Secondary sources.

Principal components analysis The most frequently used method of factor analysis, which transforms a set of variables into a new set of composite variables that are linear and not correlated with each other; see also Factor analysis.

Prior or interim evaluations Prior or interim evaluations refer to assessments of research projects before (prior) or during (interim) the research process. Prior evaluations usually try to assess the cost and benefits based on a research proposal, while interim evaluations will also assess the quality of first results and the timeliness.

Probability sampling A controlled, randomized procedure that assures that each population element is given a known non-zero chance of selection.

Probing Techniques for stimulating respondents to answer more fully and relevantly to posed questions.

Probing questions Similar to follow-up questions, but they address a part of the answer more specifically by asking for additional broader information.

Process (activity) analysis The observation and monitoring of processes and activities, such as traffic flows at a road crossing or how often a piece of luggage is handled from the check-in counter until it is loaded into the aircraft.

Project management A master plan revealing how all phases of the research will be brought together and how the research is organized.

Projective techniques Various techniques (e.g. sentence completion tests, cartoon or balloon tests, word association tests, etc.) used as part of an interview to disguise the study objective and allow the respondent to transfer or project attitudes and behaviour on sensitive subjects to third parties; the data collected via these techniques are often difficult to interpret (nominal, ordinal or ratio data).

Properties Characteristics of objects; a person's properties are their weight, height, posture, hair colour, etc.

Proportional reduction in error (PRE) A type of statistical analysis used with contingency tables (a.k.a. cross-tabulations), including lambda, gamma, tau, Somer's d, and Spearman's rho.

Proportionate stratified sampling The stratification of the sample is equal to the proportions of the population. If guests of a hotel group are 40 per cent English, 15 per cent German, 10 per cent Dutch, 10 per cent Irish and 25 per cent other nationalities the stratified sample would have the same proportions.

Proposal A work plan, prospectus, outline, statement of intent, or draft plan for a research project that incorporates all decisions made in the early planning phases of the study including proposed budget. A proposal is usually in a written form, if the researcher needs a sponsor for the research, such as a funding institution or a supervisor for a thesis.

Proposition A statement about concepts that may be judged as true or false if it refers to observable phenomena. Researchers often call a statement derived purely from reasoning a proposition and distinguish it from a hypothesis, which is a statement asking for empirical testing.

Proximity An index of perceived similarity or dissimilarity between objects.

Pure research See Basic research.

Purpose What the author (or in the case of many Internet sites, the collective authors in an institution) is trying to accomplish with the secondary source; one of five factors in secondary source evaluation.

Purpose non-disclosure A type of confidentiality; when the sponsor camouflages the true research objective of the research project, often to mitigate biased answer behaviour of the respondent. See also Non-disclosure.

Q

Qualitative interviews Another term for unstructured interviews, as those interviews usually result in qualitative information.

Qualitative techniques A fundamental approach of exploration and analysis, including in-depth interviews, participant observation, videotaping of subjects, projective techniques and psychological testing, case studies, street ethnography, elite interviewing and document and content analysis.

Quartile deviation In a normal distribution, the median plus one quartile deviation on either side encompasses 50 per cent of the observations, eight covers the full range of data; symbol = Q; always used with the median for ordinal data.

Quasi-experiment A research strategy in which the researcher frames a real situation as an experiment without having the possibility of random assignment and manipulation.

Quota matrix A means of visualizing and organizing the matching process.

Quota sampling A type of purposive sampling in which relevant characteristics are used to stratify the sample in an attempt to improve the representativeness of the sample. Another motive for using quota sampling is to ensure that elements with a certain rarely occurring characteristic, which is important to the research, are included in the sample.

R

Random assignment A process that uses a randomized sample frame for assigning subjects to experimental (see Experimental group) and control groups in an attempt to assure that the groups are as comparable as possible with respect to the dependent variables; each subject must have an equal chance for exposure to each level of the independent variable. A.k.a. randomization.

Random dialling A procedure for bypassing out-of-date phone directories that requires choosing phone exchanges or exchange blocks and then generating random numbers within these blocks for calling. In certain countries, law restricts the use of random dialling.

Random error Error that occurs erratically, without pattern; see also Sampling error.

Randomization See Random assignment.

Range The difference between the largest and smallest score in the distribution; a very rough measure of spread of a dispersion.

Ranking question A measurement question that asks the respondent to compare and order two or more objects or properties using a numeric scale. See also Ranking scale.

Ranking scale A measurement approach that asks the respondent to make comparisons among two or more objects or properties in relation to each other using a numeric scale, thus providing a relative order of those factors (ordinal or interval data). See also Ranking question.

Rating question A measurement question that asks the respondent to position each property or object on a companion verbal, numeric or graphic scale. See also Rating scale.

Rating scale A measurement approach that asks the respondent to score an object or property without making a direct comparison to another object and thus position each factor on a companion scale, either verbal, numeric or graphic (ordinal or interval data). See also Rating question.

Ratio data Data with order, distance, equal intervals (distance) and unique origin; numbers used as measurements have numerical value; e.g. weight of an object.

Reactivity response The phenomenon where subjects alter their behaviour due to the presence of the observer.

Readability indexes Indexes that measure the difficulty level of written material; e.g. Flesch Reading Ease Score, Flesch Kincaid Grade Level, Gunning's Fog Index; most word-processing programs calculate one or several of the indexes.

Realism A research philosophy that shares principles of positivism and interpretivism. It accepts the existence of a reality independent of human beliefs, but still concedes that understanding requires acknowledgement of human subjectivity.

Reciprocal relationship Two variables mutually influence or reinforce each other.

Record A set of data fields that are related, usually by subject or respondent; represented by rows in a spreadsheet or statistical data base; a.k.a. data case, data record.

Record analysis The extraction of data from current or historical records, either private or in the public domain; a technique of data mining.

Refusal rate Ratio of respondents who decline the interview to all potential/eligible contacts.

Regions of acceptance Area between the two regions of rejection based on a chosen level of significance (two-tailed test) or the area above/below the region of acceptance on a one-tailed test.

Regions of rejection Area beyond the region of acceptance set by the level of significance.

Regression analysis Uses simple and multiple predictions to predict Y from X values.

Regression coefficients The two association measures between X and Y variables, intercept and slope.

Relational hypothesis Describes the relationship between two variables with respect to some case; relationships are co-relational or explanatory.

Reliability A characteristic of measurement concerned with accuracy, precision and consistency; a necessary but not sufficient condition for validity (if the measure is not reliable, it cannot be valid, but reliable measures are not necessarily valid).

Reliability-equivalence A characteristic of measurement in which an instrument can secure consistent results with repeated measures by the same investigator or by different samples.

Reliability-stability A characteristic of measurement in which an instrument can secure consistent results with repeated measurements of the same person.

Replication The process of repeating an experiment with different subject groups and conditions to determine the average effect of the IV across people, situations and times.

Replication logic The rationale of case study research. If a case study offers support for a specific theoretical proposition, replicating the research in a slightly different setting through a new case study reinforces the theoretical proposition.

Reporting study Provides an account or summation of some data, perhaps the generation of some statistics, but requires little inference or conclusion drawing.

Request for proposal (RFP) Bid request for research to be done by an outside supplier of research services.

Research design The blueprint for fulfilling research objectives and answering the research questions.

Research dilemma A symptom of a problem or an early indication of an opportunity. A problem or opportunity that requires a decision based on a systematic inquiry. While a management dilemma refers to a problem or opportunity managers face, research dilemma can include issues beyond the interest of managers, e.g. societal issues or academic puzzles.

Research process Various decision stages involved in a research project, and the relationship between those stages.

Research question The choice hypothesis that best states the objective of the research; the answer to this question provides the desired information necessary to make a decision with respect to the research dilemma.

Research variable See variable.

Residual What remains after the regression line is fitted (the difference between the regression line value of Y and the real Y value).

Resistant statistics A statistical measure that is relatively unaffected by outliers within a dataset; e.g. median and quartiles.

Respondent Another term for a participant in a communication study.

Response error Error created when the data reported differs from the actual data.

Right to privacy The respondent's right to refuse to be interviewed or to refuse to answer any questions in an interview. Furthermore, it is closely related to confidentiality. A researcher, who has obtained information from others, is not allowed to use this information in a way that might harm the provider of the information.

Right to quality The client's right to a research design appropriate for the research question, maximum value for the resources expended, and data handling and reporting techniques appropriate for the data collected.

Right to safety The right of interviewers, surveyors, experimenters, observers and subjects to be protected from any threat of physical or psychological harm.

Rotation In principal components analysis, a technique used to secure less ambiguous relationships between factors and variables by performing a matrix analysis and thus aid in interpretation of the analysis.

S

Sample A group of cases, respondents, or records comprised of part of the target population, carefully selected to represent that population. See also Pilot testing, Data mining.

Sample statistics Descriptors of the relevant variables computed from sample data.

Sampling The process of selecting some elements from a population to represent the population as a whole.

Sampling error A reflection of the influences of chance in drawing the sample from the population; the error not accounted for by systematic variance.

Sampling frame A list of elements in the population from which the sample is actually drawn, such as a directory.

Scaling The assignment of numbers or symbols to an indicant of a property of objects to impart some of the characteristics of the numbers to the property.

Scalogram A procedure for determining whether a set of items forms a unidimensional scale and is therefore appropriate for scaling.

Scatterplots A visual technique for depicting both the direction and the shape of a relationship between variables.

Scientific method Disciplined procedures for generating quality research including direct observation of phenomena; clearly defined variables, methods, and procedures; empirically testable hypotheses; the ability to rule out rival hypotheses; and statistical rather than linguistic justification of conclusions.

Scope The degree of comprehensiveness of coverage of a secondary source (by time frame, topics, geography, etc.); one of the five factors for evaluating the quality of secondary sources.

Screen question The question(s) asked during a phone interview, to determine whether the person answering the phone is a qualified sample unit (nominal data). See also Filter question.

Search query A statement combining different terms with logical operators, such as 'and', 'or', 'not', 'smaller than' etc. to search a database. It is advisable to generate a list of alternative key terms and combine those to various search queries.

Secondary data Studies done by others and for different purposes than for which the data are being reviewed and reused.

Secondary source Compilations of information in printed or electronic form and subsequent forms of publications of primary sources. Including interpretations of primary sources. Do not confuse it with secondary data.

Selective coding Specific term used in grounded theory to describe the final step in which major categories are formed to generate a new grounded theory.

Self-administered questionnaire A survey delivered to the respondent via personal (intercept) or non-personal (computer-delivered, mail delivered) means that is completed by the respondent without additional contact with an interviewer. See also Mail survey.

Self-select survey Respondents choose to participate and the researcher has only very limited control on who participates. They are usually used as web-based questionnaires. Pop-up windows on websites asking you to assess the website are a widely used example.

Semantic differential scale A scale that measures the psychological meanings of an attitude object and produces interval data; uses bipolar nouns, noun phrases, adjectives or non-verbal stimuli such as visual sketches.

Semi-structured interviews The researcher formulates the questions before the interview, but usually does not offer the respondent a choice among answer alternatives, i.e. the questions are open. Moreover, it is possible to deepen an answer to a specific question by asking additional questions.

Semiotic analysis A qualitative analysis approach that looks for patterns and structures between visual, linguistic and aural signs.

Sentence outline One of two types of outlines normally used in the pre-writing phase of report development uses complete sentences rather than key words or phrases to draft each report section.

Sequence-based analysis A variant of traditional market-basket analysis, used to tie together a series of activities or purchases, taking into account not only the association of items but their order.

Sequential sampling See Double sampling.

Simple category scale A scale with two response choices; a.k.a. dichotomous scale.

Simple cluster sampling A cluster sampling procedure with only one phase, thus we sample clusters and take all elements within the cluster. If all clusters have the same size, this is analogous to simple random sampling.

Simple observation Another term for data collection during the exploratory phase of a study. See also Observation.

Simple random sample A probability sample in which each element has a known and equal chance of selection.

Simulations A study in which the conditions of a system or process are replicated.

Single case study A research using one case study, e.g., one particular firm or event to investigate a phenomenon.

Skewness A measure of a distribution's deviation from symmetry; if fully symmetrical the mean, median and mode are in the same location.

Skip pattern Instructions designed to route or sequence the respondent to another question based on the answer to a branched question.

Slope One of two regression coefficients, β1, is the change in Y for a one-unit change in X.

Snowball sampling A non-probability sampling procedure in which initial sample elements, which may or may not have been chosen by probability techniques, refer to additional sample elements based on similar characteristics. For example you start interviewing people interested in starting a business selected from an address list of a seminar on entrepreneurship and ask them if they know other people who intend to start a business.

Social-media-based surveys Surveys that use social media sites, such as Facebook or LinkedIn to find respondents. Researcher post an invitation to participate in a survey on a social media site and ask their friends to spread that posting. See also Snowball sampling.

Solicited proposal Proposal developed in response to an RFP.

Somer's d A measure of association for ordinal data that compensates for 'tied' ranks and adjusts for direction of the independent variable. See also Ordinal measures.

Source evaluation The five-factor process for evaluating the quality and value secondary sources and also secondary data (see Purpose, Scope, Authority, Audience and Format).

Sources of evidence Refers to the sources where you get the information from to describe phenomena or measure variables. They include formal and informal interviews, documents, databases, etc.

Spatial relationships The recording of human behaviour and how humans physically relate to each other, including proxemics (the study of how people organize the territory around them and the discrete distances they maintain between themselves and others).

Spearman's rho One of the most popular ordinal measures of association; correlates ranks between two ordered variables.

Specification error A bias that overestimates the importance of the variables included in a structural model.

Specifying questions Questions that ask the respondent to explain an answer more deeply.

Sponsor non-disclosure A type of confidentiality; when the sponsor of the research disassociates itself from the sponsorship of the research project. See also Non-disclosure.

Spreadsheet Data-entry software that arranges data cases or records as rows, with a separate column for each variable in the study.

Stability A characteristic of measurement in which an instrument can secure consistent results with repeated measurements of the same person. See also Reliability.

Standard deviation The positive square root of the variance, it is the most frequently used measure of the spread or variability of a data dispersion; symbol = s, or σ, or std. dev.; affected by extreme scores.

Standard error of the mean A measure of the standard deviation of the distribution of sample means.

Standard normal distribution The most significant theoretical distribution in statistics, which is the standard comparison for describing distributions of sample data and is used with inferential statistics that assume normally distributed variables.

Standard scores (Z scores) A calculation that conveys distance in standard deviation units; a mean of 0 and a standard deviation of 1; designed to improve compatibility among variables that come from different scales yet require comparison; includes both linear manipulations and non-linear transformations.

Standardized coefficients The X values re-stated in terms of their standard deviations (a measure of the amount that Y varies with each unit change of the associated X variable).

Stapel scale A numerical scale with up to 10 categories (5 positive, 5 negative) where the central position is an attribute. The higher the positive number, the more accurately the attribute describes the object or its indicant.

Statistical process control A statistical tool to analyse, monitor and improve process (a business system that transforms inputs to outputs) performance.

Statistical significance The quality of the difference between a sample value and its population value; the difference is statistical significance if it is unlikely to have occurred by chance (represent random sampling fluctuations).

Statistical study A study that attempts to capture a population's characteristics by making inferences from a sample's characteristics; involves hypothesis testing and is more comprehensive than a case study.

Stem-and-leaf display An EDA technique closely related to a histogram that reveals frequency distribution for each data value, without equal interval grouping.

Stepwise selection In modelling and regression, the most popular method for sequentially adding or removing variables; combines forward and backward sequential methods.

Stratified random sampling A probability sampling technique where the sample is constrained to include elements from each of the mutually exclusive segments or strata within a population.

Stratified random sampling-disproportionate A probability sampling technique in which each stratum's size is not proportionate to the stratum's share of the population; allocation is usually based on variability of measures expected from the stratum, cost of sampling from a given stratum and size of the various strata.

Stratified random sampling-proportionate A probability sampling technique in which each stratum is properly represented so the sample drawn from it is proportionate to the stratum's share of the population; higher statistical efficiency than a simple random sample.

Stress index An index used in multidimensional scaling that ranges from 1 (worst fit) to 0 (perfect fit).

Structural analysis One approach used in narrative analysis that is based on language and linguistic analysis.

Structured interviews In a structured interview the questions and the possible answers are defined *ex ante*. Self-administered questionnaires are a typical example of structured interviews.

Structured observation The observation follows a pre-defined scheme. For example, at a road crossing one counts how many cars approach it at which hour from which direction.

Structured question A type of measurement question that presents the respondent with a fixed set of choices (nominal, ordinal or interval data). See also Structured response, Closed question.

Structured response A response that is based on a fixed, predefined set of alternative answer options. See also Structured question.

Structuring questions Questions that are asked to allow a smooth transition to a new topic.

Subjects' perceptions The subtle or major changes that occur in subjects' responses when they perceive that a research study is being conducted.

Successive intervals Infrequently used process for ordering many objects where the respondent groups objects by property; cards are allocated to piles or groups representing a succession of values or importance of properties.

Survey A means of questioning a respondent via a collection of questions and instructions for both the respondent and the interviewer; a.k.a. questionnaire or instrument.

Symmetrical relationship A relationship where two variables fluctuate with each other but do not cause each other. For example, we will observe that the share price of Lloyds Bank and Royal Bank of Scotland fluctuate with each other but they do not cause each other; rather developments in the financial sector and the general economic conditions move both share prices.

Systematic error Error that results from a bias; see also Systematic variance.

Systematic observation Data collection through observation that employs standardized procedures, trained observers, schedules for recording and other devices for the observer that mirror the scientific procedures of other primary data methods.

Systematic review A specific form of a literature review in which the subjectivity bias is reduced. In a systematic review the researcher clarifies and documents the criteria used to include a study in the review as well as the criteria to assess the quality of each included study and how results were synthesized.

Systematic sampling A complex probability sampling technique in which the population (N) is divided by the desired sample (n) to obtain a skip pattern (k). Using a random start between $1 - k$, each kth element is chosen from the sample frame; usually treated as a simple random sample but statistically more efficient.

Systematic variance The variation in measures due to some known or unknown influences that cause the scores or measurements to skew in one direction or another; see also Systematic error.

T

t **distribution** A normal distribution with more tail area than in a Z normal distribution.

Target question A type of measurement question that addresses the investigative questions (core information questions) of a specific study.

Target web survey The researcher use the web as a data-collection tool, but only a target group approached by the researcher can access the survey. The researcher remains in control of who can answer the questionnaire.

tau Uses table marginals to reduce prediction errors, with measures from 0 to 1.0 reflecting percentage of error estimates for prediction of one variable based on another variable.

tau *b* (used with Spearman's rho) A refinement of gamma for ordinal data that considers 'tied' pairs, rather than only discordant and concordant pairings (values from −1.0 to +1.0); used best on square tables (one of the most widely used measures for ordinal data).

tau *c* (used with Spearman's rho) A refinement of gamma for ordinal data that considers 'tied' pairs, rather than only discordant and concordant pairings (values from −1.0 to +1.0); useful for any sized table (one of the most widely used measures for ordinal data).

Taxonomy Describes a system in which similar things are grouped together under one new broader term.

Technical report A report written for an audience of researchers.

Telephone interview A study conducted wholly by telephone contact between respondent and interviewer.

Test unit An alternative term for a subject within an experiment; it can be a person, an animal, a machine, a geographic entity, etc.

Thematic analysis One approach in narrative analysis that focuses strongly on what has been said and less on how it has been said.

Theoretical sampling While traditional sampling starts with the objective to obtain a sample representative of the population under investigation, theoretical sampling is an approach to sample new cases on the basis of what is required to develop a theory further.

Theoretical saturation Provides the stopping rule when one should stop selecting new cases or developing new codes, namely when further cases or codes do not add to our understanding anymore.

Theory A set of systematically interrelated concepts, definitions and propositions that are advanced to explain or predict phenomena (facts); the generalizations we make about variables and the relationships among variables.

Time sampling The process of selecting some time points or intervals to observe elements, acts, or conditions from a population of observable behaviour or conditions to represent the population as a whole;

three types include time-point samples, time-interval samples or continuous real-time samples.

Topic outline One of two types of outlines normally used in the pre-writing phase of report development uses key words or phrases rather than complete sentences to draft each report section.

Transcribing The process to transform recordings of interviews into a written account. Very labour intensive.

Transformation The re-expression of data on a new scale using a single mathematical function for each data point; designed to improve interpretation when the researcher finds alternate ways to understand the data and discover patterns or relationships not revealed by original scales (for interval data; possible for nominal and ordinal data).

Treatment (factor) The experimental factor to which subjects are exposed.

Treatment level The arbitrary or natural groupings within the independent variable of an experiment.

Trials (repeated measures) Repeated measures taken from the same subject.

Triangulation A process of verifying information through multiple sources to increase the validity of the description of what is observed. Triangulation is especially important in case study research.

***t*-test** A parametric test to determine the statistical significance between a sample distribution mean and a population parameter, when the population standard deviation is unknown and the sample standard deviation is used as a proxy.

Two independent samples tests Parametric and non-parametric tests used when the measurements are taken from two samples that are unrelated (*Z* test, *t*-test, chi-square, etc.).

Two related samples tests Parametric and non-parametric tests used when the measurements are taken from closely matched samples or the phenomena are measured twice from the same sample (*t*-test, McNemar test, etc).

Two-tailed test A non-directional test of a null hypothesis that considers two possibilities: that the sample parameter is either greater than the population statistic or less than the population statistic.

Type I error A type of hypothesis testing error when a true null hypothesis (there is no difference) is rejected; the alpha (α) value called the level of significance is the probability of rejecting the true null hypothesis.

Type II error A type of hypothesis testing error when a false null hypothesis (there is no difference) is rejected; the beta (β) value is the probability of incorrectly rejecting the false null hypothesis; the power of the test $= 1 - \beta$, and is the probability that we will correctly reject the false null hypothesis.

Typology Describes a structure that organizes things (concepts or codes) into distinct categories.

U

Unidimensional scale Instrument scale that seeks to measure only one attribute of the respondents or object.

Unit of analysis It refers to the level at which the phenomenon occurs and at which the research needs to be conducted. For example if you want to investigate internationalization strategies, you might select firms as unit of analysis, but depending on the explanations you are looking for it might be better to investigate a firm's decision to enter a foreign market.

Unobtrusive measures A set of observational approaches that encourage creative and imaginative forms of indirect observation, archival searches, and variations on simple and contrived observation, including physical traces observation (erosion and accretion).

Unsolicited proposal A suggestion by a contract researcher for research that might be done.

Unstructured interviews In an unstructured interview, the researcher rather defines topic areas that will be addressed in the interview and is flexible to change the course of the interview depending on the answers given.

Unstructured question A type of measurement question in which the respondent provides the answer without the aid of an interviewer (either by phone, personal interview or self-administered surveys); see also Open-ended question, Unstructured response or Free response question.

Unstructured response A response strategy where participant's opinions are limited only by space, layout, instructions or time; usually free-response or 'fill-in' response strategies. See also Unstructured question.

Utility scores (part-worths) Used in conjoint analysis and computed from a subject's rankings or ratings of a set of cards, with each card describing one possible configuration of combined concepts and constructs.

V

Validity A characteristic of measurement concerned that a test measures what the researcher actually wishes to measure; that differences found with a measurement tool reflect true differences among respondents drawn from a population. See also Construct validity, Content validity, Criterion-related validity.

Variability Another term for measures of spread or dispersion within a dataset.

Variable A characteristic, trait or attribute that is measured; a synonym for a construct or the property being studied; a symbol to which values are assigned; includes several different types: continuous, control, decision, dependent, dichotomous, discrete, dummy, extraneous, independent, intervening and moderating variables.

Variance Calculated as the squared deviation scores from the data distribution's mean, it is a measure of score dispersion about the mean; the greater the dispersion of scores, the greater the variance in the dataset.

Vector A quantity that has direction and magnitude commonly represented by a directed line segment whose orientation in space represents the direction and length represents the magnitude.

Vignette research See Factorial survey.

Visual aids Presentation tools used to facilitate understanding of content (e.g. chalkboards, whiteboards, handouts, flip charts, overhead transparencies, slides, computer-drawn visuals, computer animation).

Voice recognition Computer systems programmed to record verbal answers to questions.

W

Web-based questionnaire Special surveys designed to be delivered via the Internet with data capture and processing a potential part of the process. Two options currently exist: proprietary solutions offered through research firms and off-the-shelf software for researchers who possess the necessary knowledge and skills.

Web-based surveys A survey that is not presented on paper, but on a web page.

Web crawlers Small programs that copy information from other websites and work as automated collectors of website data.

Wrapper Small program that extracts information from websites and transforms it from HTML format into an accessible format.

Z

Z distribution The normal distribution of measurements assumed for comparison.

Z test The parametric test to determine the statistical significance between a sample distribution mean and a population parameter employs the Z distribution.

Index